SHAKESPEARE SURVEY

ADVISORY BOARD

Aspects of *Macbeth*
Aspects of *Othello*
Aspects of *Hamlet*
Aspects of *King Lear*
Aspects of Shakespeare's 'Problem Plays'

SHAKESPEARE SURVEY

AN ANNUAL SURVEY OF

SHAKESPEARE STUDIES AND PRODUCTION

54

Shakespeare and Religions

EDITED BY

PETER HOLLAND

CAMBRIDGE
UNIVERSITY PRESS

PUBLISHED BY THE PRESS SYNDICATE OF THE UNIVERSITY OF CAMBRIDGE
The Pitt Building, Trumpington Street, Cambridge, United Kingdom

CAMBRIDGE UNIVERSITY PRESS
The Edinburgh Building, Cambridge CB2 2RU, UK
40 West 20th Street, New York NY 10011–4211, USA
10 Stamford Road, Oakleigh, VIC 3166, Australia
Ruiz de Alarcón 13, 28014 Madrid, Spain
Dock House, The Waterfront, Cape Town 8001, South Africa

http://www.cambridge.org

First published 2001

Printed in Great Britain at the University Press, Cambridge

Typeset in Bembo 10/12pt [CE] System [3b2]

A catalogue record for this book is available from the British Library

ISBN 0 521 80341 1 hardback

Shakespeare Survey was first published in 1948. Its first
eighteen volumes were edited by Allardyce Nicoll.
Kenneth Muir edited volumes 19 to 33.
Stanley Wells edited volumes 34 to 52.

EDITOR'S NOTE

Volume 55, on 'King Lear and its Afterlife' will be at press by the time this volume appears. The theme of Volume 56, which will include papers from the 2002 International Shakespeare Conference, will be 'Shakespeare and Comedy'. The theme of Volume 57 will be 'Macbeth and its Afterlife'.

Submissions should be addressed to the Editor at The Shakespeare Institute, Church Street, Stratford-upon-Avon, Warwickshire CV37 6HP, to arrive at the latest by 1 September 2002 for Volume 56. Pressures on space are heavy; priority is given to articles related to the theme of a particular volume. Please either enclose postage (overseas, in International Reply Coupons) or send a copy you do not wish to be returned. Submissions may also be made via email attachment to p.d.holland@bham.ac.uk. All articles submitted are read by the Editor and at least one member of the Advisory Board, whose indispensable assistance the Editor gratefully acknowledges.

Unless otherwise indicated, Shakespeare quotations and references are keyed to the modern-spelling Complete Oxford Shakespeare (1986).

Review copies should be addressed to the Editor, as above. In attempting to survey the ever-increasing bulk of Shakespeare publications our reviewers inevitably have to exercise some selection. We are pleased to receive offprints of articles which help to draw our reviewers' attention to relevant material.

P. D. H.

CONTRIBUTORS

DAVID DANIELL, *King's College, London*
PÉTER DÁVIDHÁZI, *Hungarian Academy of Sciences*
JANETTE DILLON, *University of Nottingham*
MICHAEL DOBSON, *Roehampton Institute, University of Surrey*
RICHARD FOULKES, *University of Leicester*
PAUL FRANSSEN, *University of Utrecht*
DONNA B. HAMILTON, *University of Maryland*
JANE KINGSLEY-SMITH, *University of Hull*
TETSUO KISHI, *Kyoto University*
JEFFREY KNAPP, *University of California*
PETER LAKE, *Princeton University*
LAURENCE LERNER, *Vanderbilt University, Tennessee*
TOM McALINDON, *University of Hull*
RICHARD C. McCOY, *The City University of New York*
THOMAS MERRIAM, *King's College, University of London*
FR PETER MILWARD, SJ, *Sophia University, Tokyo*
ROBERT S. MIOLA, *Loyola College, Maryland*
ALFREDO MICHEL MODENESSI, *Universidad Nacional Autónoma de Mexico*
EDWARD PECHTER, *Concordia University*
WILLIAM POOLE, *Linacre College, Oxford*
ERIC RASMUSSEN, *University of Nevada*
NIKY RATHBONE, *Birmingham Shakespeare Library*
HANNA SCOLNICOV, *Tel-Aviv University*
BOIKA SOKOLOVA, *Royal Holloway, University of London and St Kliment Ohridski, University of Sofia*
GARY TAYLOR, *University of Alabama*
LESLIE THOMSON, *University of Toronto*

CONTENTS

vii

CONTENTS

ILLUSTRATIONS

LIST OF ILLUSTRATIONS

SHAKESPEARE AND THE PROTESTANT MIND

DAVID DANIELL

Recently the orthodoxies of Reformation study have changed, several times. Electronics are disseminating access. Records of sixteenth-century Eastern Europe are showing experiences more important and flexible than had been thought:[1] central Europe was more of a cultural unity than our post-Second World War notion of East and West has implied – Wittenberg is far nearer to Prague than to London. Extraordinary things happened all over Europe, some of them only now being approached. Radical changes were either repulsed, as in Italy or Spain, or quite quickly accepted, as in Germany. The Reformation's 'second wind' of Calvinism became central in Switzerland, France, the Netherlands, England and Scotland. No longer does anyone think of the Reformation in England as being from 1529 to 1559: it now has a long pre-history, and an even longer reach forward, even to 1800.[2] Moreover, England's Reformation emerges as something of an anomaly: in Patrick Collinson's question, how did 'one of the most Catholic countries become one of the least?'[3] To this 'how?' has been added the question whether the Reformation in England was ever more than 'a succession of legislative enactments'.[4]

Students of British history have for some years been encouraged to conclude that 'the English Reformation was a failure'. They have been directed to two books: Christopher Haigh's *English Reformations* of 1995, which carries forward his earlier work on local records, to show, according to him, a sixteenth-century

nation of bewildered people, baffled by the sudden changes made to their religion by their political masters, quite unable to follow what was going on or what they ought to think or do. Though the people were given the Bible in English, unofficially from 1526, officially from 1537, it was taken away again in 1543. There was no popular Reformation at all. Parishes with reforming ministers were the sixteenth-century minority (Haigh's insistent word). The strategies of the court failed. Protestantism proved ineffective. The word is 'failure'.

Students will then have been moved by the other key book on their reading-list, Eamon Duffy's massive – and massively bought – 1992 *The Stripping of the Altars*, telling the story of the total destruction, by strict government edict, under Henry VlII, and Edward Vl (especially), all across England, of all that so many of the people loved in their old religion, the objects and observances, leaving them grieving and even more bewildered. Protests and rebellions meant that the old religion still flourished in England. For this is the point of the new revisionism: the sixteenth-century 'continuity of Catholicism', hidden until now.

These revisionist readings have broken up the

---

[1] Andrew Pettegree, Introduction to *The Reformation World*, ed. Pettegree (London and New York, 2000), pp. 1–2, and *passim*.
[2] See *England's Long Reformation: 1500–1800*, ed. Nicholas Tyacke (London, 1988), *passim*.
[3] Quoted in Tyacke, *England's Long Reformation*, p. 75.
[4] Ibid.

old comfortable agreement, whereby in three decades England became God's Protestant nation. Yet, three things need to be pointed out. First, such revisionism is far from new, being laid down long ago in both historical method and dogma in books of Catholic polemic. Secondly, Haigh omits large areas of English life: the universities and intellectual life generally, and the true effect of the print culture. He does not note that under Henry's late Act forbidding bible reading there were no prosecutions. Thirdly, in Duffy's book the Reformation, rather than having its observable long pre-history, is made to arrive like an incomprehensible bolt from the blue by government edict. Evidence from some parishes is extrapolated as a national effect. Duffy, too, ignores the universities, the learned bishops, and all the intellectual life of the time.

Shakespeare's poems and plays provide no evidence about whether he was Protestant or Catholic. In the Folger Library there is, however, an interesting 1632 Folio which between 1641 and 1651 was censored for the Inquisition by an English Jesuit living in Spain: he found much to delete. Some of it was on the level of removing from Cranmer the epithet 'good', but much is doctrinal. His total excision, oddly, was not *King John*, but *Measure for Measure*, which he cut cleanly out of the volume. R. M. Frye noted, in 1963, that these expurgations 'should put us on our guard . . . against the overly eager identification of Shakespeare's plays with Christian teachings in general and with the Catholic tradition in particular'.[5]

In his fifty-two years, Shakespeare lived in a nation that was officially, aggressively and massively Protestant. It is true that after Pope Gregory XIII excommunicated and deposed Queen Elizabeth in 1570, there were the smuggled-in Seminarians, Jesuit priests hiding, and well-attended masses in barns and some great houses in the north-west and elsewhere. But the Protestant Books of Common Prayer had been in daily use in every parish in England and Wales, including Stratford-upon-Avon, for half a century by 1600; the 39 Articles of the English Church, printed in each copy, were out-and-out Protestant, even Calvinist; and the Books of Homilies to be preached in every pulpit, mixed as they were in origin, were solidly Protestant.

Peter Lake writes:

While [some Catholics] met in barns and private households, the godly inherited the public space of the parish church. And where the altars had been effectively stripped, that was now a public space that proclaimed, at a number of levels, the alteration of religion. The prominently displayed royal coat of arms aside, wall paintings had been whitewashed over, the Ten Commandments and the odd scriptural verses replacing them. The altar was now a communion table; the rood loft with its doom images as well as the images of saints had been removed. The liturgy was in English, not Latin; the mass had been replaced with a communion service. No trace of the cult of the saints or the notion of Purgatory – such central features of the religious system described by Eamon Duffy – was left in either the service book or the outward ceremonial face of the Church. Again, whatever else this was, it was not continuity.[6]

The English war of religion, we might add, the seventeenth-century Civil War, was fought between Protestant and Protestant. Even Christopher Haigh, in three pages at the close of his *English Reformations*, gives the evidence for, and announces, a popular Reformation ('the ministers were creating a Protestant nation'). We need to remember that Protestantism is not some sort of watered-down version of 'the real thing', Catholicism gone wrong. In the sixteenth century the spectrum of belief was wide: some Protestants remained closer to Catholicism: some Catholics admired Protestant beliefs. Protestantism as it emerges in that century,

---

[5] R. M. Frye, *Shakespeare and Christian Doctrine* (Princeton, 1963), p. 293.

[6] Peter Lake, 'Religious Identities in Shakespeare's England' in *A Companion to Shakespeare*, ed. David Scott Kastan (Oxford, 1999), p.76.

however, is radically, 180 degrees, different from Catholicism. The attacks on Purgatory, the cults of the saints, confession in the ear, a celibate priesthood and so on were not some sort of nibbling at the edges of Church practice. The denial of those traditions, and many more, came out of a burning core of radical – and newly available – New Testament belief. Protestantism claimed, passionately, itself to be 'the real' – that is, New Testament – 'thing' from which, from even before the supremacy of the Popes in the sixth century, the Catholic Church had departed. (We may take it as understood that sixteenth-century Protestantism throughout Europe was in the stream of lament for what were seen as the usurping powers of the Pope, an ancient water-course that had became a torrent of protest at the Pope's most recent demands for money.) Since the Papal hierarchy did not acknowledge the supreme authority of Scripture in the Church (which, with the supreme authority of the King in the State, was the central political tenet of English Protestantism), almost the only thing in common between the two systems was some belief in 'the redemption of the world by Our Lord Jesus Christ'. Even there, William Tyndale, grieving for all the believing Christians in the land, noted in his *Obedience of a Christian Man* in 1528 that the Pope's Church was selling for money what Christ promised freely.[7]

So to the English Protestant mind. The very first thing is to remind us that in these islands the Protestant mind thought, wrote and spoke in English. Overwhelmingly, printed matter was in English. Latin remained, and there were Latin plays – 150 of them between 1550 and 1650 performed in Oxford and Cambridge – and Latin poems and prose works, and continued printing of the Latin Bible: but the early and later reformers powerfully cultivated skills with the mother tongue for Scripture and for the greatly developed preaching. England quite suddenly had an English literature, full, bursting at the seams, overflowing. It needn't have been like that. Erasmus, in five visits to England

between 1499 and 1517, two of them long, and one a two-year stint teaching in Cambridge, neither spoke nor wrote a word of English. Thomas More would not have his *Utopia*, printed in Louvain in 1516, published in English, lest it be mauled by the common people. John Skelton, a poet who knew things, mocked English in the early 1500s. Yet long before the end of the century, instead of a few wills and churchwardens' accounts being in English, as in Skelton's time, almost everything in national life was in English, a vigorous, flexible language, more powerful than any other in Europe, and we have Sidney, Spenser, and so on – and Shakespeare. Of course, to put it too briefly, this is a Renaissance effect, particularly for the elite, for Sidney, Spenser and so on. But I shall argue that the scale and suddenness of this remarkable literature in English, and especially its spread far beyond an elite, do all owe a good deal to Protestantism.

Secondly, and again briefly, that new English Protestantism was an intellectual movement. It was powered by university men, dependent on free discussion, and, at all levels of education, on being able to read *or hear books read* (a still very under-noticed factor). It was not humanism, though distantly related to it; and the new enquiring was a release from an Aristotelian world of scholastic speculation. Enormous and demanding books in English were increasingly bought in many thousands, and read and heard and thought about. Translations from the classical and modern worlds into English poured off the presses. There was a strong element of belonging to a European movement of reform; but people freshly studied national history, aware of a new and alert English Protestant nationalism. This begins early: as a reformer, Tyndale in the late 1520s and 1530s is alert to the force of a new English history, told in English. From the middle of the century, these were large volumes of history, Protestant large

---

[7] William Tyndale, *The Obedience of a Christian Man* (London, 2000), pp. 125 and 170.

volumes. Holinshed absorbed Hall, a Protestant account of England's recent upheavals, clearly based on Bible typology. Foxe's *Acts and Monuments* gave the British a new Protestant history from long before the Reformation. In its final editions 'Foxe's Book of Martyrs' was a huge folio of over 2,000 double-column pages, and very expensive to buy: yet it has been estimated that there were sold, between the first English edition of 1563 and Shakespeare's death in 1616, 28,000 copies unabridged, and thousands more abridged. A significant number were publicly available, chained in churches: many more were read aloud in lectures and sermons. Off the coast of Mexico, we are told, Drake read it to his Spanish prisoners. A modern Foxe scholar reports that these great volumes were greatly treasured by households, and 'rather uniquely, among early modern English books, this was a book which women were encouraged to read, which did seem to be popular with them'.[8] Foxe had two effects: he printed a large number of documents of all kinds, an invaluable resource: and the martyrologies expressed a national grief. One of the sorrows of reading Early Modern English history is watching the culling of the best minds: John Frith, Robert Barnes, William Tyndale, Thomas Cranmer, Nicholas Ridley, Hugh Latimer, and dozens more. Laments for Jesuits executed bloodily in Shakespeare's lifetime, and claims that Shakespeare was expressing secret sympathy, have to be set in the context of the many hundreds of Lollards and Protestants burned alive not long before. In the popularity of Foxe, they were always fresh in Elizabethan and Jacobean minds.

Most Early Modern historians today, in 2001, tell us that England was a Protestant nation by 1580 (if not quite a nation of Protestants), and that the cutting edge of that Protestantism, among intellectuals and writers, was Calvinism. For centuries it has been unpopular to say so. 'Calvinist' has been a dirty word: serious modern writings on Spenser set out to 'rescue' him from Calvinism.[9] Yet the Church of England was largely Calvinist in Shakespeare's lifetime: five of its 39 Articles are explicitly so.

My first two points have been the new dominance of the English language in religion and national life, and intellectual enquiry expressed in it. My third is equally clear to see: the sense of liberty, the release of being able to say things without the danger of a charge of heresy. This, as we shall see, went with a new inventiveness, a release of imagination into words. There were disagreements, but Protestants did not burn Protestants alive. Too much, in any case, has been made of the factionalism. Sixteenth-century Protestants disagreed with each other, and American historians have been alert to these conflicts, for understandable reasons: the American eastern seaboard in the seventeenth century is a monument to them. Yet in most concerns, and for most of them, Protestants in these islands were facing the same way, and enjoying the very new freedom to say what they understood the Bible to tell them.

Fourthly, there is powerful energy abroad. The liberated mind and spirit ventured largely. The Latin plays were performed in a few Oxbridge halls and Inns of Court before the dons and sometimes a bored and reluctant monarch. The English plays were in state-of-the-art theatres afternoon after afternoon, performed for thousands of ordinary people right across all classifications of rank or class or education.

One of the revisionist historians' reasons for announcing failure is that the leading edge in the parishes in the Reformation, the preaching, was either all about admissions of failure, or boring, or both. Historians feel that they can make this judgement, having read the printed sermons. A Protestant trope in Reformation England was the 'Hosead' or 'Jeremiad', attacks on the lumpen people, for not waking up and

---

[8] T. S. Freeman, in *Journal of British Studies* (2000), 31–2.
[9] See Anthea Hume, *Edmund Spenser: Protestant Poet* (Cambridge, 1984), p. 4 and notes.

embracing their religion, like those made by the prophets Hosea or Jeremiah. Such hyperbolic Protestant 'complaint' writing has always been common. There is plenty of evidence of preachers finding dullness in the parishes, or attacking the people for preferring football to church (substitute circuses, and that goes back to the fifth century).

Care must be taken to stay in the historical context. There is vivid English writing by preachers about the people's indifference to their preaching, 'like the smith's dog, who can lie under the hammer's noise, and the sparks flying, and yet fast asleep'.[10] Yet the very vividness of that phrase opens a chink of light. What can be seen is that attending a sermon in Shakespeare's time could be a dramatic experience. The mass performed in Latin had been distant drama, with its gestures, processions and tableaux. Church attendance was all now changed. Moreover, because some modern historians are bored readers, it does not at all mean that the original occasions were boring. It could have been dramatic for people of all kinds to go as a body to a church service in English, where everything was close at hand; particularly to take communion together (in both kinds, the New Testament tradition still relatively new again in Europe), with English words; to hear a long sermon, a speech of carefully crafted plain English delivered from only a few feet away. This view of English parish life has obvious relation to the – albeit much heightened – experience of the London theatres.

A learned ministry, which was one of the first aims of the reformers everywhere, meant ensuring instruction in preaching. Thomas Wilson's *The Art of Rhetorique* is surprisingly early, in 1553 at the end of Edward's reign. In this volume, his first book (out of two) about the civilising effect of rhetoric, has two threads among others, one of biblical references and one of the use of rhetoric for plain preaching – with a strong appeal to *moving* the hearers. Protestant English sermons were very popular, as the massive holdings of a library like the Bodleian

show. Large numbers indicate a market. People do not buy to be bored. We are aware of the presence of that religious English Plain Style, so cultivated by Cranmer, Latimer, Crowley and the earlier reformers, so visible in the Prayer Books, the Homilies (especially Cranmer's) and above all the English Bible. The effect of that preaching was intellectual, emotional and spiritual energy. The aim was to be effective, to convert.

Which brings me to what has been missing in what I have said so far: the English Bible. I want to pause on this, before I come fully to Shakespeare. Reading widely in recent Early Modern history is to be struck by something odd. Writers can express themselves puzzled by how the British people became Protestant at all. They find a mystery. Offshoots of Keith Thomas's work are made to suggest the importance of folklore. Yet hardly any of them puts into the picture the impact on the nation of the Bible newly in English. A few mention a few Bibles: use the name Tyndale, have a footnote about the 1560 Geneva Bible or the King James Version of 1611, or declare that the Geneva margins were unacceptably Calvinist, which is not true. They write as though the Bible as a force did not exist at all. As in those doctored Stalinist photographs from Moscow, its one-time presence has simply been air-brushed out.

The writing of the New Testament has nothing whatever to do with that myth of the 'Seventy' who 'miraculously' produced identical Greek translations of the Hebrew Scriptures. The New Testament was written by its Christian authors in Greek. It is the best attested ancient Greek text, with about five thousand manuscripts surviving. This Greek New Testament was, in the course of the first

---

[10] J. Rogers, *The Doctrine of Faith* (1634), pp. 97–9; quoted by Eamon Duffy, 'The Long Reformation: Catholicism, Protestantism and the multitude' in Tyacke, *England's Long Reformation*, p. 41.

centuries, translated into Latin, several times. In the late fourth century, a secretary to the Pope, Jerome, was commissioned to produce a standard Latin version. Though even he acknowledged faults in the result, his work became the Bible text of the Church, and remained so as the 'Vulgate' or common text. The original Greek was forgotten.

In 1516, as the Greek text was again sought out, the greatest scholar in Europe, Erasmus, produced his own Latin translation to begin to correct what were increasingly seen as the many errors in the Vulgate. This caused scandal in the Church: but for confirmation of his accuracy he printed alongside his Latin the New Testament in its original Greek. This printed Greek New Testament, it can be argued, was the single most important text in the sixteenth century. It was the basis of the new printed vernacular versions throughout Europe, so denounced by the Church. Protestants were astounded that accurate translations of God's word from the original Greek should be declared blasphemous.

The first complete printed New Testaments in English, freshly translated from Erasmus's Greek text by William Tyndale, were smuggled into Britain in 1526 (one copy of an unfinished attempt in 1525 survives). The first royally licensed complete English Bible was in 1537. The only version ever authorized, the Great Bible of 1539, was placed, open, in every one of the 9,500 parishes in England and Wales. People went to the church, out of service hours, to hear the Bible read aloud. Even under Mary, when there were no Bible printings, large assemblies to hear the Bible read in cities (London, Bristol) were left untouched. Under Elizabeth the printings of Bibles were very large. Including Tyndale's first New Testament of 1526, and the 1611 King James version, there was a majestic line of eleven new translations or heavy revisions, of the New Testament or whole Bible. This did not happen to Ovid or Plutarch. Why that happened partly concerns improving textual scholarship and knowledge of Greek and Hebrew, of course; but it also has to

do with demand. (The numbers given here are taken from the standard catalogue of printed editions of the English Bible, 1525–1961, by T. H. Darlow, H. F. Moule and A. S. Herbert (1968)). To consider only Shakespeare's lifetime: there were in those years three different editions of the Rheims New Testament, the Roman Catholic version, first printed in 1582. The Bishops' Bible had first appeared in 1568: before Shakespeare died there were forty different editions of it. After 1611, and the first edition of the King James Bible, even in the five years before Shakespeare died there were twenty-six different editions of it. But in Shakespeare's lifetime alone, April 1564 to April 1616, there were printed of the Geneva Bible one hundred and forty-two different editions – editions, not reprintings, in three parallel basic states, well beyond the original 1560 to which Shakespeare scholars refer. That makes a total of two hundred and eleven Bibles or New Testaments, in English, freshly edited and produced while Shakespeare was alive. We cannot calculate print-runs, but even an over-modest estimate of 3,000 each makes 633,000 English Bibles bought, well over half a million, while Shakespeare was alive, in a population of six million. How can that fact have been airbrushed out? Further, a little recent work has been done on the publication of (Protestant) catechisms as separate books, not just as automatically printed in Prayer Books. Both total figures, for catechisms and for Prayer Books, in the sixteenth century alone, are colossal. All this is not to include the hearing of the Bible in church, as set out in the Books of Common Prayer: from 1549, the New Testament was to be read right through three times a year (later, as now, twice), most of the Old Testament once, and all the Psalms every month, as ever since. The modern airbrushing out of the Bible from English national life of the time becomes even more astonishing.

The Protestant mind was, above all things, biblical. Not everyone agreed with William Chillingworth's aphorism, 'The Bible, the Bible only I say, is the religion of Protestants.'[11] There was room in God's plan for other works as well. But the Reformation in England *was* a popular movement, as well as intellectual, driven in both cases by knowledge of the very widely circulated Bible in English. At the court of Edward VI, the Book of Deuteronomy was vital. Edward was the young King Josiah, who led his nation to religious reform through the discovery of the lost book.[12]

Shakespeare knew his English Bible well. Work done on his biblical references for a century and a half, culminating in the devoted recent labour of Naseeb Shaheen, to which all modern editors must be indebted, makes that clear. That suggests that he was a good Protestant. He also knew his Ovid and his Plutarch very well. That suggests that he was a good pagan. Shakespeare's use of Bible references implies that he expected his audiences and readers to take them on the spot, because they knew their English Bibles. The references were not intended to wait for explication by clever scholars. For what came in so freshly, and was available so widely, was the whole Bible, well printed, relatively cheap, and in any case open for reading in every parish church (with, also in every parish church, Erasmus's *Paraphrases of the New Testament* in English, alongside for guidance, something rarely mentioned today). Protestants believed, as the third *sola* (after *sola gratia* and *sola fides*) in *sola scriptura*. Given the whole Bible, it would be found to interpret itself, without help from Church traditions, not to mention those secret and influential 'unwritten verities' on which the Church depended. The Protestants' point was a true one. The Christian Bible does intensely cross-refer. Take the Hebrew Scriptures out of the New Testament, and it shrivels. To lift out one or two Latin words from the Apocrypha of the Old Testament on which to base a central doctrine of the Church (as with Purgatory, Protestants remarked, from a few words at the end of chapter 12 of 2 Maccabees, a book of late Jewish military history and priestly controversy) was to make the Bible a means of superstition, not faith in Christ.

What is also not now recognized in sufficient detail is a stylistic fact of our earliest English Bibles. We know that Luther, from his first 'September [New] Testament' of 1522 united the states of Germany with a common language. Yet far more significant for the whole English-speaking world has been the gift, largely from Tyndale from 1526, of our Bibles, uniquely in Europe, in a direct clear language of great simplicity and power. Tyndale's register is just a little above common English speech, with a close relation to proverbs. He can use a Latinate word when he wants, but usually he goes for short sentences in which the verb (as in Greek) is the power, not the noun (as in Latin), so that in English Plain Style someone might fear to die rather than be trepidatory of mortality. Tyndale's syntax – subject–verb–object, with frequent use of 'and', avoiding subordinations – is Saxon: not 'And when they found the stone rolled away from the sepulchre, and as they went in', nor 'Finding the stone rolled away . . . and going in', but 'And they found . . . and went in.' Tyndale's vocabulary is Saxon, even to 'one of the wenches', to eighteenth-century and Victorian derision. Parallel to this, and I believe coming directly from it, is the conscious, and rhetorically controlled, Plain Style cultivated so brilliantly by Cranmer and the rest in prayers and homilies. Tyndale was alone in spreading this in 1526, and within a few years he was demonstrating a range of English styles quite astonishing for the time, particularly in translating the Hebrew Scriptures, which he was the first to do and print in English. He

---

11 Quoted by Patrick Collinson, *The Religion of Protestants* (Oxford, 1982), p. viii.

12 See Diarmaid MacCulloch, *Tudor Church Militant: Edward VI and the Protestant Reformation* (London, 1999), pp. 14–15 and *passim*: and Christopher Bradshaw, 'David or Josiah? Old Testament Kings as Exemplars in Edwardian Religious Polemic' in Bruce Gordon, ed. *Protestant History and Identity in Sixteenth-Century Europe* (Aldershot, 1996), pp. 77–90.

believed with passion and good reason that Hebrew went well into English, and that Latin makes a mess of it.

In Tyndale's translation, the Sunamite woman in 2 Kings 4 does not say to Elisha in her grief at the death of her promised son 'did I desire a son of my lord? did I not say that thou shouldst not deceive me?' All other translations that I have seen say that. But the Hebrew doesn't quite say 'deceive': she is expressing an element of having been led into a different, and false, world. So Tyndale has 'did I not say, that thou shouldst not bring me in a fool's paradise?'

Here again is Tyndale's Plain Style, from Luke 16.

And it fortuned that the beggar died, and was carried by the angels into Abraham's bosom. The rich man also died, and was buried. And being in hell in torments, he lift up his eyes and saw Abraham afar off, and Lazarus in his bosom, and he cried and said: Father Abraham, have mercy on me, and send Lazarus that he may dip the tip of his finger in water, and cool my tongue: for I am tormented in this flame.

How easy it sounds: until you begin to notice effects like the three small high 'i' sounds, 'dip . . . tip . . . finger', and how they help a good deal with the contrast of scale in the request, leading to the extended and lower 'tormented'. Tyndale can be 'modern': he says men 'sleep with' women. Hundreds of such examples can be found. We know that the King James New Testament is 83% pure Tyndale: generally where it differs, it goes back to Latin-based words.

It is good to see some long-hidden Catholic books of Shakespeare's time, some in English, now getting back into print. But they are few. Shakespeare inherited a vast, vigorous and open Protestant English literature of many kinds. A good deal of this was in the relatively new Plain English, the basic language of all the English Bibles except the Catholic Rheims New Testament, translated from the Latin (and even that has many moments of silent dependence on the 'heretic' Tyndale). English in Skelton's time

deserved his scorn: it was a shapeless mixture of Norman-French, Latin and Anglo-Saxon. It had been different in Chaucer's time. It was unthinkable in the 1520s and 1530s that it might be able to carry any large and serious freight. Yet Tyndale in those years made the Bible not only in English but in a remarkable language of great range.

The English rhetoricians hold up the English Bible as a model. Thomas Wilson is full of the English Bible, giving stories as big examples of how to do it, knowing that his readers will follow and learn, from the way the English Bible does it. There has just come into print for the first time Thomas Swynnerton's manuscript *The tropes and figures of Scripture*, dedicated to Thomas Cromwell probably in 1537–8, but clearly intended for a larger audience. Here is the first book of rhetoric in English, and it is all about Tyndale's bible translations as models. Swynnerton tells the reader to look further into the writing of 'Master William Tyndale'. Swynnerton's sixth chapter ends, 'Every man hathe a Testament in his hande, wolde to God in his harte.'[13] That can only have been Tyndale's.

When Shakespeare wants to turn our hearts over, he is generally plain and Saxon: 'Pray you undo this button', 'I am dying, Egypt, dying'. Falstaff, before Shrewsbury, does not say, as befits a Latin-educated knight, 'the advent of the imminent hostilities elevates my apprehensions', but 'I would 'twere bed-time, Hal, and all well.' Shakespeare's ability to use such near-proverbial directness is wonderful. It is not, I believe, coincidence that the Gospels had been in such an English for seventy years, and 'every man hathe a [New] Testament in his hande'. Nor is it coincidence that our late Tudor poets were at liberty to be so inventive with words. Tyndale, needing a word, made it up, from Saxon roots: he invented words like 'scapegoat'

---

[13] *A Reformation Rhetoric: Thomas Swynnerton's 'The tropes and figures of Scripture'*, ed. Richard Rex (Cambridge, 1999), p. 171.

and 'Passover'. That freedom, and others, were sources of anger to Thomas More. Shakespeare, needing words, makes them up by the bucketful. He can do anything. Erasmus taught Tudor schoolboys how to invent – in Latin. A switch was thrown to send the current into inventiveness in English. There were many hands on the switch, no doubt, but the neglected one has been the Protestant Bible in English.

I want to come properly to Shakespeare through what I see as a Protestant inheritance, simply as an inheritance, without making any statement about his personal beliefs. I shall do the Protestant thing, and take the whole book.

In his comedies, Shakespeare, I am not alone in seeing, was unusual in that he moves his beautiful young people into love and marriage. Love comes before money and business intrigue. Perhaps they find each other in somewhere 'other', a King's park, a wood, Belmont, a forest and so on: but love means marriage and real life, as Rosalind makes starkly clear. The lovers are to join, in love, and reproduce – Rosalind longs for her child's father. My own private definition of the Reformation is 'people reading Paul', and the marriages making one flesh in Shakespeare's comedies are Pauline in doctrine. The maker and re-maker of marriages at the end of *The Winter's Tale* is called Paulina. This matter of Paul, and of Shakespearian comedy, make a large subject, ludicrously sketched here. On tragedies I shall be even more ludicrous. There are many biblical references, to English Bibles, to be taken. Judges 11 is expected to be understood in *Hamlet* 2.2 (Jephthah's daughter). On the widest canvas, the individual, as his creator is free from the threat of a heresy-hunt, is able to make his own tragic destiny in relation to whatever god he serves.

David Norbrook notes the strategies of many of the poets of Shakespeare's time to preserve, politically and religiously, a degree of independence.[14] This is vital. Shakespeare does his unique things for his own poetic and dramatic reasons. Yet in choosing to write, and to rewrite, English history, he cannot help being in a Protestant stream of Providential national historiography. Hall, Grafton, Holinshed and Foxe, to name but four, Protestant re-writers all, were doing that, and they were only the higher end of the culture. In the second half of the century, a strong tradition of anonymous chronicle-writing, often in doggerel, used the voice of the people to give historical examples, much as Tyndale does at a more dignified level in *The Practice of Prelates*: most of it was apocalyptic in direction, following John Bale.[15]

In her book, *Shakespeare's Theory of Drama* (1996), Pauline Kiernan discovers a sort of Shakespearian *Defence of Drama* by finding that Shakespeare rejected the mimetic aesthetic of Sidney and his late Renaissance humanist peers. Shakespeare, Pauline Kiernan finds, did something quite different, valuing instead what she notes as 'presence', the living human body on stage, with its necessarily intensely subjective set of responses.[16] Also in 1996, Deborah Shuger, remarking how Shakespeare's religion has been wrongly seen as defending a conservative social order, notes that in fact he gives dramatic life to 'poor and common speech', the self, as she puts it, as suffering subject. In a memorable illustration, Professor Shuger remarks that 'Lear's pedigree does not fundamentally alter the fact that he is a powerless and hurt old man tormented by rage, guilt and thankless children . . . the displacement of social discourses of suffering and poverty on to psychological representations', as she says, is a discourse of Protestant subjectivity.[17]

---

[14] David Norbrook, *Poetry and Politics in the English Renaissance* (London, 1984), p. 6.

[15] See Thomas Betteridge, *Histories of the English Reformations, 1530–83* (Aldershot, 1999), pp. 10, 51–79.

[16] Pauline Kiernan, *Shakespeare's Theory of Drama* (Cambridge, 1996), p. 9 and *passim*.

[17] Deborah K. Shuger, 'Subversive Faiths and Suffering Subjects – Shakespeare and Christianity' in *Religion, Literature and Politics in post-Reformation England, 1540–1688*, ed. Donna B. Hamilton and Richard Strier (Cambridge, 1996), pp. 56, 58, 59, 61.

William Tyndale is relevant here. First, always subjective in responses to the work of the gospel, in all his writing that is not biblical translation (particularly his *Wicked Mammon* and his *Obedience of a Christian Man*, both of 1528) he allows nothing to stand between the suffering soul and God – and that suffering is so often metaphorized by him as either deep poverty or great illness, from both of which the gospel releases the ordinary man or woman or child, he insists, with glorious new and energetic liberty. Secondly, Tyndale translated the Bible for the ploughboy, as he famously remarked, that poor underprivileged, physically suffering creature. In no way am I saying that Shakespeare read Tyndale's books: but thirdly, Shakespeare *had* read Tyndale's translations of the four Gospels – Naseeb Shaheen has shown that they are easily Shakespeare's most-referred-to biblical books, and whether he read Geneva Bibles or the Bishops' Bible he is still largely reading Tyndale. The core of the Gospels is the removal of the religious rituals of exclusion: Jesus shocked the righteous by sitting down for meals with moral outcasts. His bodily presence, as a Messiah, someone with the greatest spiritual power who heals and teaches now and not in some future, was with fishermen and prostitutes and publicans. As Jesus says so often, the Kingdom of God is now. Any over-ritualized religion since the dawn of time can make its priests say that yes, it's rotten, and hard luck, but just do as we say, keep at the ritual, stick it out, give us your money and you'll end up with the angels in heaven for ever more. The Gospels do not say this. There is a future, but the world of the kingdom of God, as in so many of the parables, is now, not then. The finding of the lost sheep is now. The Prodigal Son returns now. The four Gospels are full of hard sayings, and the modern scholarly teasing-out of the relation between them as texts has been described as the most difficult problem in the humanities. Yet at the same time they are blazingly simple, being full of people, usually poor and suffering people, in the presence of an extraordinary teacher and healer. In the healing is the sudden dramatic conflict between humanity wrong (diseased, ill, deformed) and humanity right. Here, we might say, is Pauline Kiernan's 'presence'; what, as Deborah Shuger reminds us, William Perkins called 'a person of mine own self, under Christ . . .'.[18] Perkins continued what Tyndale brought to English readers from Luther, the strength of the inward, spiritual regiment, presence localized not only in the temporal and secular regiment but in the spiritual and subjective, psychologically represented, taken in to a body on a stage. The *mimesis* of the later humanists, Sidney and the rest, though Pauline Kiernan doesn't put it quite like this, pointed to some ethical value of art. Shakespeare is full of people, quite newly, and this came to him from fifty years of increasing subjectivity, particularly through everyone knowing the Bible in English, especially the Gospels, a Protestant thing.

Recent commentators express surprise about how new this was. Harold Bloom, in his introduction to his *Shakespeare: The Invention of the Human* (late 1999), writes 'In Shakespeare, characters develop rather than unfold, and they develop because they re-conceive themselves . . . [as in] no other writer . . .'.[19] Professor Shuger, three years before Harold Bloom, finely related this to Samuel Johnson's modernly maligned passage about the absolute newness of Shakespeare's 'persons' in the *Preface to Shakespeare*, which Bloom also uses. We might recall that something even more basic than the idea of a psychologically represented character came to us from Shakespeare: as the Arden 3 editor of *Julius Caesar*, I was often struck by the fact that the Rome the wide public knows is still the Rome that Shakespeare gave us in his Plutarch plays.

Shakespeare's theory of drama is of bodily presence, as Pauline Kiernan shows. That body

---

[18] Shuger, 'Subversive Faiths', p. 55.
[19] Harold Bloom, *Shakespeare: The Invention of the Human* (London, 1999), p. xvii.

is in interior, human, conflict. Of Edgar's bedlam beggar amd Lear's nakedness in the storm, Deborah Shuger writes:

Such characters acquire their psychological depth by assimilating the ancient Christian discourses of social injustice to the structures of the psyche . . . within the tragic protagonist, enabling a fundamentally new presentation of the self . . . Before Lear, kings did not hallucinate or run around half-naked with flowers in their hair, weeping over their unkind children.[20]

We could focus the phrase 'ancient Christian discourses of social injustice' to four narratives fully available to all English people, the Gospels.

It has for a long time been noticed that Hamlet's language borrows heavily from popular speech, his images being 'drawn from the most common aspects of everyday life . . . which ally him to the lower-class figures of the Moralities'.[21] Shakespeare had no need to walk to Coventry to see the mystery plays in order to meet ordinary people in dramatic conflict. He could find those everyday images, heavily pregnant with apparently infinite meaning, at home, in the Gospels. Of course Shakespeare inherited a great tidal wave of material from the ancient world, the European Renaissance and recent history. But the great shifting of tectonic plates in Europe which produced the Protestant *tsunami* (far greater than a 'tidal wave') which flooded Europe to such depth gave him, through the Bible in English, a Kingdom of Heaven which is immediate; bodily presence on stage. Here is a parable.

What woman having ten groats, if she lose one, doth not light a candle, and sweep the house, and seek diligently, till she find it? And when she hath found it she calleth her lovers and her neighbours saying: Rejoice with me, for I have found the groat which I had lost.[22]

What could be simpler? Language has changed: a groat is a coin to the value of a day's wage for an agricultural labourer, and 'lovers' now has only a sexual sense. Yet Jesus's story goes far beyond rational analysis. Luke tells it in the context of the Pharisees murmuring because Jesus is with 'sinners' and eats with them. The story is not, or not only, about moral outcasts: it is more fully about losing and finding again, an existential experience that can make one weep, like finding oneself unexpectedly at home again. Jesus uses it to parallel 'joy in the presence of the angels of God', and what *that* means cannot surely be put into rational words at all.

In Hamlet's last desperate words, he is fighting for time to tell vital things to the obtuse – and thus suddenly betraying – Horatio:

Had I but time – as this fell sergeant Death
Is strict in his arrest – O, I could tell you –
But let it be.   (5.2.328–30)

Shakespeare expresses what we feel we might say given less than a minute to live (unlike Ben Jonson, who expresses what we feel Ben Jonson might say). Notice in that simple language Hamlet's range of emotion and thought, and the sense of a vast revelation of what it could be like to die, beyond anything we expect. The extraordinary image of the fell sergeant strictly arresting suggests guilt, and martyrdom, and horror, and inevitability, and an arresting being who is both outside and inside the dying body, all in the end of someone's time on earth. Shakespeare is close to Tyndale in that sense of simple words bringing in a new kingdom of possibilities – 'This thy brother was dead, and is alive again; was lost, and is found': or 'Now abideth faith, hope and love, even these three: but the chief of these is love.'

Harold Bloom gets this wrong. He rightly says that only the Bible matches Shakespeare, but he finds that 'what the Bible and Shakespeare have in common actually is rather less than most people suppose . . . only a certain

---

[20] Shuger, 'Subversive Faiths', p. 57.
[21] Annabel Patterson, quoted in Shuger, 'Subversive Faiths', p. 57
[22] Luke 15, in *Tyndale's New Testament: A Modern-Spelling Edition of the 1534 Translation* with introduction by David Daniell (New Haven and London, 1989), p. 116.

universalism . . .'[23] Not so. What Shakespeare and the Bible have in common is that language, at the highest moments, of elemental simplicity, from the Gospels.

Our so-familiar Plutarchan Rome from Shakespeare blinds us to the extraordinary newness, even shockingness, of Plutarch. This is not the high political 'Twelve Caesars' Rome of the sixteenth-century schoolroom and educated man's study. Plutarch's is a Rome of streets and houses and people talking and running about, of a boy house-servant sent to run to the Senate house by a Portia too desperate to remember to give the message. Our so-familiar characters in Shakespeare, so many of them, are similarly 'shocking' in their psychological interiority and bodily presence. As Deborah Shuger stresses, it is suffering and poverty that are now interiorized by Shakespeare. In the Gospels it is 'one sick of the palsy' (whose friends, so dense is the crowd, break open the roof of the house and let him down) to whom Jesus says 'son thy sins are forgiven thee.' That paralysed man got up and went out.[24] A desperate woman ashamed of a secret sickness came behind Jesus in a pressing crowd and touched the hem of his garment and was instantly healed.

And Jesus said: Who is it that touched me? when every man denied, Peter and they that were with him, said: Master, the people thrust thee and vex thee: and sayest thou, who touched me? And Jesus said: Somebody touched me. For I perceive that virtue is gone out of me. When the woman saw, that she was not hid, she came trembling, and fell at his feet, and told him before all the people for what cause she had touched him, and how she was healed immediately. And he said unto her: Daughter, be of good comfort, Thy faith hath made thee whole, go in peace.[25]

Shakespeare had no need to walk all the way to Coventry to meet in a text those called, in that phrase rather shocking in its class-consciousness, 'the lower-class figures of the Moralities'. Shakespeare met suffering people, registered in the ordinary language of the people, in the texts of the Gospels in English, ultimately Tyndale's English. He interiorised their suffering, and put them on his stage. That is a great bequest of Protestantism.

---

23 Bloom, *Shakespeare: The Invention of the Human*, p. 3.
24 Mark 2, in *Tyndale's New Testament*, pp. 63–4.
25 Luke 8, in *Tyndale's New Testament*, p. 104.

DIVINE [ ]SENCES

GARY TAYLOR

> 'I am not here.'
> Thomas Middleton

How shall we represent God?

This question has preoccupied humanity far more often, and with far more consequence, than the question 'Does God exist?' Because 'How shall we represent God?' entails the question 'Who shall be God's representative?', and that question is as much political as theological;[1] how you answered it in early modern Europe determined not only whether you were Catholic or Protestant, but also what kind of Protestant you were (presbyterian or episcopal) – and which governments you would obey. 'How shall we represent God?' also entails 'Where shall we represent God?' and 'By what means shall we represent God?' The Reformation reformed divine representation: the personnel, texts, actions and artifacts, by which medieval Christianity had represented the divine. Protestant iconoclasts physically attacked the rood, the paintings, carvings, statues, stained-glass windows which had filled (or cluttered) medieval churches; they ended the ritual re-enactments of medieval biblical drama, and banned God, in both body and name, from the public stage. God is truth, the theatre is falsehood, falsehood cannot represent truth, the theatre cannot represent God.[2]

They banned God, but they did not ban gods. It is no violation of decorum for a false god to be represented by lies and disguises. Indeed, 'The Devil', Stephen Gosson declared, reiterating centuries of Christian diatribes, 'is the efficient cause of plays.'[3] Middleton's *The Black Book* begins with the stage direction '*Lucifer ascending, as Prologue to his own play*'; he has 'vaulted . . . Above the stage-rails of this earthen globe', and now intends to 'turn actor and join companies'.[4] Lucifer is here because he has been 'conjured up': as Celia Daileader argues, an arena theatre like the Globe – what Middleton in *The Revenger's Tragedy* calls 'this luxurious circle' – overlaps with the conjurer's circle, into which demons are summoned.[5] The lying theatre could be permitted to represent the Father of Lies and his dominions, and it did so, memorably: the damned Ghost of Andrea in *The Spanish Tragedy*, Mephistopholis and the other devils in *Doctor Faustus*, the demon Asnath conjured up in *The First Part of the Contention*, Jonson's Pug in *The Devil is an Ass*, the witches

---

[1] On the relationship between 'systems of representation' and 'systems of representatives' see Gary Taylor, *Cultural Selection* (New York, 1996), pp. 121–42.

[2] For an overview of these attitudes, see Jonas Barish, *The Antitheatrical Prejudice* (Berkeley, 1981).

[3] Gosson, *Plays Confuted in Five Actions* (c. 1582), cited in E. K. Chambers, *The Elizabethan Stage*, 4 vols. (Oxford, 1923), vol. 4, p. 215.

[4] *The Black Book*, Moral. 2–26. References to Middleton cite *The Collected Works of Thomas Middleton*, gen. ed. Gary Taylor (Oxford, forthcoming); the canon there defined as Middleton's is here assumed.

[5] Celia Daileader, *Eroticism on the Renaissance Stage: Transcendence, Desire, and the Limits of the Visible* (Cambridge, 1998), pp. 6–7, 73, 132–9, 141; Middleton, *Revenger's Tragedy*, 3.5.22.

in *The Tragedy of Macbeth* and *The Tragicomedy of the Witch*.

For the same reason, pagan gods were welcome where Jesus was not. What Shakespeare calls, in 1599, a 'wooden O' can easily accommodate what Middleton calls, in 1597, a 'wooden god';[6] in *Bartholomew Fair*, the god Dionysius, Defender of the False against the attacks of Zeal-of-the-Land Busy, is, like the other puppets, literally made of wood.[7] In the early polemical contests between Christian and pagan, the church fathers had declared that the gods of their rivals were all simply demons.[8] In Dekker's *If This be not a Good Play, the Devil is in it*, Lucifer and the other devils are subordinates of Pluto, god of the underworld, aka hell. In *Doctor Faustus*, Mephistopholis produces two Cupids as easily as he produces Helen of Troy.

More often, though, the classical deities are not mere pseudonyms or puppets of Satan; they are independent dramatic characters, apparently acting on their own initiative. And they pop up everywhere. Cupid appears on stage as a character in twenty-seven plays written and performed between 1576 and 1642; Venus in twenty, Mercury in eighteen, Apollo eighteen, Jupiter seventeen, Juno sixteen, Diana sixteen, Mars and Pallas ten apiece, Bacchus and Vulcan eight, Hymen and Saturn and Ceres seven; Pluto and Pan six, Neptune five, Iris four. These eighteen major deities furnish 210 characters in seventy-six different plays.[9] And of course there are other lesser divinities I haven't counted: Ate, Prosperina, many Muses, frequent Furies, innumerable nymphs. All these numbers would skyrocket if we added masques, pageants, and entertainments, where deities outnumber mortals. But even if we limit ourselves to the commercial theatres, the divine presence most often incarnate on the early modern English stage was not Protestant or Catholic, but pagan.

These same divinities people not just the stage, but the language. The words 'gods' and 'goddesses', and the names of the eighteen deities whose appearances I have just tabulated,

show up 370 times in Middleton's literary works; by contrast, in the same works the total for 'Christ', 'Jesus', or the singular capitalized 'God' of Christian adoration is only 115, less than a third of the pagan total.[10] Shakespeare is

---

6 Shakespeare, *Henry V*, Pro.13; Middleton, *The Wisdom of Solomon Paraphrased*, 15.200. *The Wisdom of Solomon*, which Middleton in his first published work paraphrased, was one of the texts most often cited in justification of Protestant iconoclasm: see especially chapters 13–15.

7 *Bartholomew Fair*, v.v., in *Ben Jonson*, ed. C. H. Herford, Percy Simpson, and Evelyn Simpson, 11 vols. (Oxford, 1925–52). Dionysius is repeatedly compared to objects made of wood: 'a beame' (v.v.6), a 'Hobby-horse' (38, 64, 119), and 'chariot wheeles' (78). Protestant iconoclasm routinely described pagan idols as 'puppets': see for instance 'The Sermon against Perill of Idolatrie', *Certaine Sermons or Homilies appointed to be read in Churches*, ed. Mary Ellen Rickey and Thomas B. Stroup (Gainesville, 1968), p. 71.

8 For an orthodox English recapitulation of this tradition, see for instance Richard Hooker, *Of the Laws of Ecclesiastical Polity*, ed. Arthur Stephen McGrade (Cambridge, 1989), p. 66. For this reason, some English Protestants objected to any literary representation of pagan gods: Douglas Bush cites numerous examples in *Mythology and the Renaissance Tradition in English Poetry* (Minneapolis, 1932), pp. 41, 71, 244–7.

9 Thomas L. Berger, William C. Bradford, Sidney L. Sondergard, *An Index of Characters in Early Modern English Drama: Printed Plays, 1500–1660*, rev. edn (Cambridge, 1998). All my figures for occurrences of deities or allegorical figures derive from this invaluable reference work; but I have altered the raw data. First, my list includes, under one name, all the names for a given deity: thus, 'Diana' includes 'Cynthia' and 'Phoebe', 'Jupiter' includes 'Jove', etc. Second, I have only counted plays for the commercial theatres (not masques, pageants, entertainments, or closet dramas). Finally, I have checked each text to make sure that the name actually represents a divine being: 'Diana' is apparently human in *All's Well*, 'Mercury' is a Duke of Anjou in *The Weakest Goeth to the Wall*, 'Hercules' is an Italian nobleman in Marston's *Parasitaster*, etc.

10 In compiling these totals I have drawn upon a computerized draft concordance to Middleton's works, prepared by John Lavagnino in 1993. I have not included in these totals Middleton's two specifically religious works, *The Wisdom of Solomon Paraphrased* and *The Two Gates of Salvation*; there is nothing comparable to these devotional works in the Shakespeare canon,

even more addicted to mythological allusion: he uses items in the heathen list 1,017 times – one hundred more occurrences than his Christian total.[11] And such arithmetic only scratches the verbal surface. Shakespeare knew Ovid as well as he knew the Bible.[12] In one of the most illuminating papers at the 1999 Lancaster conference, Alison Shell asked 'Why did Shakespeare *not* write religious verse?' His work lacks anything comparable to the poetic representations of the divine found in Donne, Herbert, Spenser, Sidney, or Edmund Campion. But although Shakespeare did not write Christian verse, he did write *religious* verse. He wrote, for instance, a long prayer to 'the goddess Venus':[13]

> Hail, sovereign queen of secrets, who hast power
> To call the fiercest tyrant from his rage
> And weep unto a girl; that hast the might,
> Even with an eye-glance, to choke Mars's drum
> And turn th'alarum to whispers; that canst make
> A cripple flourish with his crutch, and cure him
> Before Apollo . . . What godlike power
> Hast thou not power upon?

Like the divinity which most often appears on the Shakespearian stage, the divinity most often and most powerfully invoked on that stage is not Protestant or Catholic, but pagan.

Of course, we are not always asked to believe that those gods are in any sense real. In *The Tempest* Juno, Ceres, and Iris are characters in a masque, performed for an onstage bridal couple, as is Neptune in *The Maid's Tragedy*; in *As You Like It*, the entrance of Hymen is carefully explained in advance by reference to a magician, who may or may not be fictional, but who certainly does confuse the ontological status of the wedding god who 'peoples every town' (and keeps dress-makers, florists and photographers in business). We do not know who is playing Hymen, or Juno, or Ceres, or the Cupid who appears in the masque in a Middleton scene of *Timon of Athens*; but we do know that this is just playing, and the 'god' before us on stage is staged, stagey, stage-managed, a figure whose essence is the absence of essence. Elsewhere, any possibility of theological illusion

is punctured even more deflatingly. In the final scene of *Love's Labour's Lost*, we know that Hercules is being impersonated by Mote; in the final scene of *Women Beware Women*, we know that Livia is playing Juno. We see not a divine being, but a human being we have already watched for four acts – and one conspicuously ill-suited to the divine role they are attempting. Meta-theatricality relieves the audience of any burden of belief.

So does allegory. As Jean Seznec demonstrated in his classic account of *The Survival of the Pagan Gods*, the price of survival was conversion: just as the Roman ecumenical temple called the Pantheon was vandalized and converted into a monodenominational Christian church, so the pantheon of heathen deities was transformed into, and transfixed within, a grid of ethical equations, a collection not of divine beings but of household virtues and vices.[14] In an inset masque in Marston's *Parasitaster*, figures called Drunkenness, Sloth, Pride, Plenty, Folly, War, Beggary, and Laughter surround a figure called 'Cupid';[15] in an inset masque in Fletcher's *Wife for a Month*, 'Cupid' shares the stage with dancers called Fancy, Desire, Delight, Hope, Fear, Distrust, Jealousy, Care, Ire, Poverty, and Despair.[16] Obviously, in both plays Cupid is as allegorical as the company he keeps. A character

---

and I am interested here in the specifically literary competition between nominal paganism and nominal Christianity.

[11] I have compiled these figures with the aid of Marvin Spevack's *The Harvard Concordance to Shakespeare* (Cambridge, 1973). In Shakespeare as in Middleton, I count 'god' as pagan, 'God' as Christian.

[12] Leonard Barkan, *The Gods Made Flesh: Metamorphosis and the Pursuit of Paganism* (New Haven, 1986), 243–88; Jonathan Bate, *Shakespeare and Ovid* (Oxford, 1993).

[13] *The Two Noble Kinsmen*, 5.2.6–67.

[14] Jean Seznec, *The Survival of the Pagan Gods: The Mythological Tradition and its Place in Renaissance Humanism and Art*, tr. Barbara F. Sessions (New York, 1953).

[15] Marston, *Parasitaster, or The Fawn*, ed. David A. Blostein, Revels Plays (Manchester, 1978), 5.1.139.

[16] Fletcher, *Wife for a Month*, 2.6.45, in *The Dramatic Works in the Beaumont and Fletcher Canon*, gen. ed. Fredson Bowers, 10 vols. (Cambridge, 1966–96), vol. 6.

called 'Venus' or 'Cupid' could be interchanged with a character called 'Love' (who walks on stage in eight plays) or 'Desire' (who enters in four plays), without making much if any difference to text or staging; likewise, Diana might alternatively be called 'Chastity' (five plays), Apollo might as well be called 'Truth' (four plays), Mars could be 'War' (three plays), and Bacchus 'Drunkenness' (two plays). A character called 'Revenge' actually shows up more often (four plays) than his classical counterpart, 'Ate' (only two plays). Clearly, Christian allegories of psychomachia, which worked with vernacular abstract nouns like 'Love' and 'Chastity', could work equally well with classical proper names like 'Venus' and 'Diana'. This tactic allegorizes and domesticates divinity out of existence; it turns an ancient religious practice into an empty linguistic turn.

Which is why the paganism in these plays is, nowadays, almost invisible to critics and scholars, despite its conspicuous ubiquity: we regard it as a mere linguistic turn, an embarrassingly transparent affectation, or an affectation not transparent enough, an annoying patina of obscurity which we are obliged occasionally to explicate for bored or bewildered students, racking our brains to remember myths we memorized once for an examination; I am not Holofernes, nor was meant to be; all this Roman rhodomontade is just pedantry for pedants, a self-consciously 'literary' feature of texts which we are determined to rescue from the anachronistic and confining category of 'literature'; what is worse, a reminder of antiquated schools of criticism, like the multilingual digging-in-the-dirt source-hunting of Douglas Bush and T. W. Baldwin, or the mythological high-rise fantasies of Northrop Frye, those authorities once revered, but whose books now sit, musty and disgruntled, like some of the senior faculty in our own departments, muttering 'I was adored once', but now of no discernible use to anyone.

But then again, you never know what you may find in a secondhand clothing store. Maybe there are moments when the paganism in these plays is not a reflex reaction, not a compulsory convention drummed and beaten into unwilling boys in Tudor grammar schools, not allegory, not metatheatre. Maybe we cannot understand the Christianity of early modern Europe without understanding the unburied paganism that shadowed it.

What happens, for instance, when a play represents someone *worshipping* a pagan god? What if a play shows us a pagan god being worshipped by someone virtuous, someone that the play clearly demands that we admire, someone like Marston's *Sophonisba, The Wonder of Women*? What if this good person is asking these gods for something good, something which a demon would not provide? And what if her prayer is answered?[17]

Cornets and organs playing full music, enters the solemnity of a sacrifice; which being entered, whilst the attendants furnish the altar, Sophonisba [sings a] song; which done, she speaks

What she speaks is a prayer to Mercury and Phoebe, to protect her from imminent sexual violation. But before we even get to that prayer, the play asks us to take seriously 'the solemnity of a sacrifice' in an alien religion. The 'organs' called for in this stage direction are first heard, repeatedly, in the celebration of Sophonisba's wedding in Act I. Such organs are required in only two plays of the period, both performed by the Children of Paul's:[18] the organs are the organs of St Paul's cathedral, here being played to dignify a pagan religious ceremony. And Sophonisba herself is being played by one of the choristers of St Paul's, who is using that superb voice (trained to sing Christian hymns and psalms) to accompany instead a heathen sacrifice.

---

17 *Sophonisba*, 3.1.116, in *The Selected Plays of John Marston*, ed. MacDonald P. Jackson and Michael Neill (Cambridge, 1986).

18 Alan Dessen and Leslie Thomson, *A Dictionary of Stage Directions in English Drama, 1580–1642* (Cambridge, 1999), 155.

The gods to whom Sophonisba prays do not visibly respond; nevertheless, by the end of her prayer she has an idea, which she attributes to divine inspiration: 'Some stratagem now, let wit's god be shown; Celestial powers by miracles are known. I have't! 'tis done' (3.1.138–40). She immediately puts this god-given idea into practice, and it does indeed temporarily save her. But we do not have to believe in the god Mercury to credit this moment; her inspiration can be explained allegorically, as though instead of worshipping at the altar of the god Mercury she was simply invoking the figure called 'Wit' in half a dozen sixteenth-century plays, as though she was calling upon 'Chastity' rather than 'Phoebe'. Indeed, the very sentence in which Sophonisba names 'Mercury' and 'Phoebe' translates them into 'A worthy chastity and a most chaste wit' (3.1.123).

When the altar reappears, in Act 5, the evil character Syphax kneels to what he calls 'an altar sacred to black powers', and in answer to his prayer '*Out of the altar the ghost of Asdrubal ariseth*' (5.1.26–64). Despite Marston's daring use of the cathedral organs, the dramaturgy of the play is, in the end, Christian enough: the pagan prayer of the good character is allegorized as an invocation to her own spiritual faculties, the pagan prayer of the bad character is answered physically, by a frightening figure rising out of hell.

But Shakespeare and Fletcher's *The Two Noble Kinsmen* dares to do what Marston's *Sophonisba* did not. The sequence in Act 5, in which Arcite, Palamon, and Emilia pray in turn to Mars, Venus and Diana (5.1.34–5.3.37), is clearly by Shakespeare, and represents his very last surviving writing for the stage, a kind of literary last will and testament.[19]

They kneel before the altar.
Here they fall on their faces, as formerly, and there is heard clanging of armour, with a short thunder, as the burst of a battle, whereupon they all rise and bow to the altar.
Enter Palamon and his Knights with the former observance.

Here they kneel before the altar.
Here music is heard, doves are seen to flutter. They fall again upon their faces, then on their knees.
They rise and bow.
Still music of recorders. Enter Emilia in white, her hair about her shoulders, with a wheaten wreath; one in white holding up her train, her hair stuck with flowers; one before her carrying a silver hind in which is conveyed incense and sweet odours, which being set upon the altar, her maids standing apart, she sets fire to it. Then they curtsy and kneel.
Here the hind vanishes under the altar and in the place ascends a rose tree having one rose upon it.
Here is heard a sudden twang of instruments and the rose falls from the tree.
They curtsy and exeunt.

The rituals here are precisely prescribed, and elaborately detailed; kneeling, prostration before the altar, the burning of incense. Each god gives its devotee what the dialogue calls a 'sign' or 'token', which turns out to be an accurate omen; none of the three gods, and none of the three characters, is easily dismissed as evil. Their prayers might be described allegorically – Arcite invokes his own aggression, Palamon his sexual desire, Emilia her resistance to corporeality and incorporation; but if the characters are only verbalizing their own states of mind, if this is merely the trope of prosopopeia, how do we explain that clang of armour, the music, the fluttering doves, the vanishing hind, the rose tree, the falling rose? The characters believe they are worshipping a powerful intelligent being outside themselves, and we

---

19 Gary Taylor, 'The Canon and Chronology of Shakespeare's Plays', in Stanley Wells, Gary Taylor, et al., *William Shakespeare: A Textual Companion* (Oxford, 1987), p. 134; Eugene Waith, ed., *The Two Noble Kinsmen* (Oxford, 1989), pp. 4–23; Fredson Bowers, ed., *The Two Noble Kinsmen*, in *Beaumont and Fletcher Canon*, vol. 7 (1989), pp. 156–8; Jonathan Hope, *The Authorship of Shakespeare's Plays: A Socio-Linguistic Study* (Cambridge, 1994), pp. 83–89. Most editors describe this sequence as a single scene (5.1); those who give Fletcher any part of that scene assign him only the first 33 or 17 lines, before the prayers begin.

witness a powerful external material intelligent reaction to their invocations. If the altar in question were Christian, would we have any doubt that what we are witnessing, in each case, is a miracle? What does this pagan miracle mean? What could it have meant to a Jacobean audience?

One set of its meanings can be illuminated by comparing it with another scene, also performed by the King's Men, in the last act of the last play of another Jacobean playwright:

Music. An altar discovered, richly adorned, with tapers on it, and diverse statues standing on each side

This discovery is accompanied by a speech by the Black Knight –

> Hark! To enlarge your welcome, from all parts
> Is heard sweet sounding airs; abstruse things open
> Of voluntary freeness, and yon altar
> (The seat of adoration) seems to adore
> The virtues you bring with you. . .

– followed by '*a song*':

> May from the altar flames aspire!
> Those tapers set themselves a-fire.
> May senseless things our joys approve
> And those brazen statues move,
> Quickened by some power above,
> Or what more strange, to show our love.

On cue, the stage directions tell us, '*The statues move and dance*' (5.1.31.1–47.1).

This moment comes from the most spectacularly successful of all plays of the English Reformation, Thomas Middleton's *A Game at Chess*; the scene dramatizes the arrival of the White Knight and the White Duke in the Black House – or, if you prefer, the arrival of Prince Charles and the Duke of Buckingham in Madrid in 1623. Like the Latin oratory which precedes them (5.1.4–19), these properties and actions are all signifiers of Catholic ritual: the burning candles, the music, the statues, the richly adorned altar. Not for nothing is Eamon Duffy's chronicle of the English Reformation entitled *The Stripping of the Altars*. On 19 November, 1550, 'There were letters sent to every bishop to pluck down

the altars',[20] and John Stow records that 'shortlie after, all the aultars in London were taken downe, and tables placed in their roomes'.[21] Queen Elizabeth was officially indifferent to the distinction between altar and table, preferring altars in her own chapels, but her bishops systematically eradicated altars in parish churches; the visitation articles of 1560 and 1561 demand that 'all images, altars, holy-water stoups' be 'removed, defaced, and destroyed'.[22] The Elizabethan Homilies insistently attack altars, the rich 'decking' of altars, the burning of candles and incense, as a form of 'idolatry';[23] in extant plays, altars are either pagan (15) or Catholic (5).[24] In the 1630s, one of the controversies which helped precipitate the Civil War was Archbishop Laud's attempt to restore 'richly adorned' altars to a central place in the rites of the English church.[25] In 1639, the Fortune theatre revived a play called *The Cardinal's Conspiracy*, which they performed 'in as great state as they could, with *Altars, Images, Crosses, Crucifixes*, and the like, to set forth his pomp and pride'; as an observer commented, 'it was apparent that this play was revived on purpose in contempt of the cere-

---

[20] Thomas Fuller, *The Church History of Britain*, ed. J. S. Brewer, 6 vols. (Oxford, 1845), vol. 4, p. 58 (Fuller, Book VII, chapter xvi).

[21] John Stow, *The Annales of England* (1592; STC 23334), p. 1021.

[22] Eamon Duffy, *The Stripping of the Altars: Traditional Religion in England c.1400–c.1580* (New Haven, 1992), p. 571.

[23] 'Perill of Idolatrie', *Certaine Sermons*, pp. 18, 51–2, 67, 73–5. The verb 'deck' is used 34 times in this sermon, always pejoratively.

[24] Dessen and Thomson, *Dictionary of Stage Directions*, pp. 5–6. Leslie Thompson kindly informed me of an extra example in her database, left out of the printed account, in Brewer's *Lovesick King* (1617); other Catholic examples include Dekker's *Match Me in London* (1611), Fletcher, Field, and Massinger's *Knight of Malta* (1618), Fletcher's *Pilgrim* (1621), and *A Game at Chess* (1624).

[25] Fuller, *Church History*, VI, 110–11 (Book XI, cento xvii, para. 54–5).

monies of the Church', and the actors were summoned before the ecclesiastical courts.[26]

What his enemies perceived as the crypto-Catholicism of Laud was characterized, in the theatre in 1639, by both 'altars' and 'images'. The word 'images' here means 'statues'; indeed, what some texts of *A Game at Chess* call 'statues' other texts call 'images'.[27] Queen Elizabeth's Injunctions of 1559, the foundation of the Elizabethan settlement, had ordered the destruction of 'all images'[28] – that is, of the innumerable church statues of the Virgin Mary and the saints which had often been the focus of veneration, and the site of miracles, in traditional Catholicism. Although even the most recent editors of *A Game at Chess* seem not to realize it, the 'diverse statues' in the Black House, on either side of the 'richly adorned' altar, are not simply a bit of spectacle borrowed from the court masque; they are specifically Catholic properties, like everything else in the scene.[29] They are statues of the saints, perhaps even including the Virgin Mary. When the statues begin to move, the Black House claims they have been 'quickened by some power above', but of course in this context every Protestant spectator would intuit, without further evidence, that the moving statues are a typical Catholic fraud.[30]

Like the richly adorned altars, the moving statues characterize Catholicism in part by insisting upon its 'brazen' paganism.[31] For Protestants, Catholic 'Images, and idoles of the Gentiles bee all one', and the veneration of images 'first came from the Gentiles'; Catholi-

v, pp. 1300–1. For another theatrical example of Laudian ceremony criticized by conflating it with paganism, see *The Control and Censorship of Caroline Drama: The Records of Sir Henry Herbert, Master of the Revels 1623–73*, ed. N. W. Bawcutt (Oxford, 1996), p. 191 (17 February 1634, a fine 'for lending a church Robe with the name of Jesus upon it to ye players in Salisbury Court to present a Flamen a priest of the Heathens'). See also Martin Butler, *Theatre and Crisis 1632–1642* (Cambridge, 1984), pp. 234–7.

27 For the interchangeability of the two words see *OED*, image, n. 1a 'statue, effigy, sculptured figure. (Often applied to figures of saints or divinities as objects of religious veneration.)' In *A Game at Chess* 'Statues' is the reading in the Trinity, Archdale, Bridgewater-Huntington, and Rosenbach manuscripts; 'Images' occurs in the Lansdowne and Malone manuscripts and in both quartos (which also mention the 'tapers'). Only the Archdale manuscript specifies 'richly adorned', but Ralph Crane is unlikely to have made up the phrase; it probably stood in his copy (Middleton's papers), or at the very least it represented what he had seen on stage. For the complicated textual history of *A Game at Chess* see the extensive discussion in *Thomas Middleton and Early Modern Textual Culture*, ed. Gary Taylor (Oxford, forthcoming).

28 Duffy, *Stripping of the Altars*, p. 568.

29 Neither T. H. Howard-Hill, in his Revels Plays edition of *A Game at Chess* (Manchester, 1993), nor Richard Dutton, in his World's Classics edition of *Women Beware Women and Other Plays* (Oxford, 1999), specify what the statues represent, or call attention to all the other Catholic elements of the stage directions (or even cite the relevant variants in the directions).

30 See for instance Thomas Goad, *The Friers Chronicle: or, the true legend of priests and monkes lives* (1623; STC 11510), sig. B3v.

31 When the 'brazen statues move', Middleton suggests the meaning 'hardened in effrontery, shameless' (*OED* a.3), but also exploits the word's strong associations with idolatry: see 2 Kings 18:4 (the holy king Hezekiah 'broke the images' and destroyed the 'brazen' serpent which the people worshipped) and Revelation 9:20 ('idols of gold and silver and brass'). Pagan religion had been caricatured as the worship of 'brazen' statues by Tertullian (*Of Idolatry*) and Eusebius (*Church History*), among others; Calvin specifically linked the Babylonian worship of 'brazen' images to the Papacy (*Commentary on Daniel*, chap. 5).

---

26 Edmund Rossingham, whose letter of 8 May 1639 is one of two sources for this incident, specifies that 'the players' were fined 'for setting up an altar, a bason, and two candlesticks, and bowing down before it upon the stage'; they excused themselves on the grounds that it was 'an altar to the heathen gods', but Rossingham was not convinced, and concluded 'if my paper were not at an end I would enlarge myself upon this subject, to show what was said of altars': see G. E. Bentley, *The Jacobean and Caroline Stage*, 7 vols. (Oxford, 1941–68),

cism was simply a form of paganism.[32] In the antimasque of Beaumont's 1613 *Masque of the Inner Temple and Gray's Inn*, statues given 'an artificial life' by Vulcan, and descending from 'the altar of Olympian Jove', enter and 'dance for joy of these great nuptials'.[33] Moving statues are appropriate for pagan divinities, and dancing is central to the masque; but Middleton makes the same actions outrageously indecorous, simply by making the statues saints, and the altar Christian. For although Christians debated whether dancing was an image of divine order or a satanic celebration of fleshliness, no one advocated jigs in church, or imagined the Virgin Mary, or Saint Anne, kicking up their heels. Indeed, these very actions distinguished paganism from Christianity. In Shirley's 1639 play *Saint Patrick for Ireland*, in a temple represented on stage by an altar, candles, and incense, two characters named Ferochus and Endarius disguise themselves as '*idols*' (statues of Mars and Jupiter); after the king kneels at the altar and prays, '*A flame behind the altar*' signals divine approval; a song is sung to the idols, the seeming 'statue' of Jupiter '*moveth*' and then speaks, demanding the 'blood' of St Patrick. Afterwards, when their duped audience has left, Ferochus and Endarius come down from their pedestals, and are rewarded for their trick by being allowed to 'dance' with the Queen's two daughters 'i'th' temple'.[34] What is for Shirley an image of the grotesquery of paganism (fraudulently animated statues, dancing in church in front of an altar) is for Middleton an image of Catholicism – and probably also an image, closer to home, of the re-emergent ceremonialism of the increasingly visible Arminian episcopal faction of the English church.[35]

In Beaumont, Shirley, and Middleton the dancing is accompanied, unsurprisingly, by music. But music takes on a very different meaning when you move it from the context of a court masque, or a pagan temple, or secular song, to a Christian chapel. Calvin banished all instrumental music from divine service, arguing

that it belonged to the Old Testament, not the New;[36] under his influence, organs and choirs and polyphonic chant were displaced, in almost all English parish churches, by congregational psalm-singing.[37] The Elizabethan compromise preserved organs and choirs only in cathedrals, but that exception disgusted radical Protestants; in the early 1640s, triumphant Parliamentary armies spontaneously destroyed many cathedral organs, and in 1644 Parliament passed a law ordering destruction of the rest.[38] The use of the organs of Saint Paul's cathedral to accompany a ritual before a pagan altar, in Marston's *Sophonisba*, would have seemed to some not a moment of theatrical sacrilege, but a theatrical exposure of the sacrilegious ceremonialism of the cathedral itself.

The King's Men at the Globe did not have

32 'Perills of Idolatrie', *Certaine Sermons*, pp. 43, 46, 60.
33 Lines 196–215, ed. Philip Edwards, in *A Book of Masques*, ed. T. J. B. Spenser and Stanley Wells (Cambridge, 1967),
34 James Shirley, *St Patrick for Ireland* (1639), sig. E4v–F2; Act 2, Scene 2 in *The Dramatic Works and Poems of James Shirley*, ed. William Gifford and Alexander Dyce, 6 vols. (1833), IV, pp. 387–91. Shirley's play is not included in Dessen and Thomson's *Dictionary of Stage Directions*, because it was apparently acted only in Ireland.
35 For anti-Arminian anti-episcopal satire, see my introduction and commentary to *A Game at Chesse: An Early Form* in *Collected Works*.
36 For Calvin's condemnation of musical instruments (including organs) in church service, see William J. Bouwsma, *John Calvin: A Sixteenth-Century Portrait* (Oxford, 1988), 225, and *The New Grove Dictionary of Music and Musicians*, ed. Stanley Sadie, 20 vols. (London, 1980), III, pp. 360–2.
37 Nicholas Temperley, *The Music of the English Parish Church* (Cambridge, 1979), pp. 39–76.
38 Peter Le Huray, *Music and the Reformation in England, 1549–1660* (London, 1967), pp. 24–6; Stanford E. Lehmberg, *Cathedrals in English Society, 1485–1603* (Princeton, 1988), pp. 182–225; Kenneth R. Long, *The Music of the English Church* (London, 1991), pp. 62, 204–6. For the destruction of organs in cathedrals see particularly Margaret Aston, *England's Iconoclasts*, Vol. 1, *Laws Against Images* (Oxford, 1988), pp. 64–83, 94.

organs at their disposal, and the music for *A Game at Chess* has not survived. But we do know that the song is accompanied by instrumental music, that it is not a psalm, and that it is not sung by the congregation, but by an unidentified voice or voices. Since it is meant to characterize the Black House, it was probably polyphonic and melismatic.

This scene from *A Game at Chess* fits very well the model of institutional exchange, between the church and the theatre, described by Stephen Greenblatt in his influential account of the relationship between Shakespeare's *King Lear* and Harsnett's *Declaration of Egregious Popish Impostures*. Protestant churchmen 'try to drive the Catholic church into the theatre'; in order to 'demolish the experience of wonder', to show that what seemed to be miracles were just tricks, a 'sacred sign, designed to be displayed before a crowd of men and women, is emptied, made negotiable, traded from one institution to another'.[39] The 'one little altar' which Philip Henslowe recorded in his inventory of properties might, conceivably, have been salvaged from a church;[40] so might the altar which the King's Men began using as early as 1603.[41] Certainly the children of Paul's appropriated the cathedral organs for Marston's *Sophonisba* and for Middleton's *A Mad World, My Masters* (where they are thoroughly secularized, and parodically sexualized, as the latest fashionable acquisition of Sir Bounteous Progress).[42]

Greenblatt's essay is our most sophisticated critical account of the relationship between early modern religion and theatre, and it fits Middleton well, but I am not sure it fits Shakespeare. In *King Lear*, Greenblatt tells us, 'there are no ghosts, as there are in *Richard III, Julius Caesar,* or *Hamlet*; no witches, as in *Macbeth*; no mysterious music of departing daemons, as in *Antony and Cleopatra*'. The absence of such effects may distinguish *King Lear* from these other plays, but it does not demonstrate that *King Lear* is more typical of its author, or more typical of institutional exchanges between

church and stage. Greenblatt also claims that '*King Lear* is haunted by a sense of rituals and beliefs that are no longer efficacious, that have been *emptied out*. The characters appeal again and again to the pagan gods, but the gods remain utterly silent.' But isn't that what a Christian audience would expect to happen? that appeals to non-existent gods would remain unanswered? Greenblatt begins his essay by insisting on the importance of early modern struggles over what he calls 'the definition of the sacred'.[43] But the essay itself is devoted, not to the divine, but to the demonic. Of course, the two are related, but they are not identical. The absence from *King Lear* of real demonic possession, or real devils, does not prove that the essence of the divine has been emptied out of Shakespeare's theatre.

After all, the gods do not remain silent in the other plays Shakespeare wrote between 1605 and 1613.[44] The usual explanation for the

---

[39] Stephen Greenblatt, *Shakespearean Negotiations: The Circulation of Social Energy in Renaissance England* (Berkeley, 1988), pp. 104, 112.

[40] *Henslowe's Diary*, ed. R. A. Foakes and R. T. Rickert (Cambridge, 1961), App. 2, 70.

[41] The earliest extant evidence for the use of an altar by the King's Men is the elaborate altar-scene (5.4) in Jonson's *Sejanus* (discussed below).

[42] Middleton, *A Mad World, My Masters*, 2.1.42, 120, 170, 173.1 ('*The organs play*'), 175 ('How does your honour relish my organ?'), 2.1.179.2 ('*A song to the organs*'). For another reference to the playing of the cathedral organs, see *Civitatis Amor* 366 ('singing of divers anthems to the organs').

[43] Greenblatt, *Negotiations*, pp. 119, 95.

[44] The single exception to this chronological rule would be *Macbeth* (1606); but scholarly consensus since 1869 has agreed that the extant text represents a later theatrical adaptation by Middleton (Taylor, 'Canon and Chronology', pp. 128–9), and Nevill Coghill argues

difference between *King Lear* and the later plays is that Shakespeare lost his nerve, or regained his faith. Greenblatt himself provides no explanation. Instead, on the basis of this single play he generalizes about the relationship between religion and 'Shakespeare's theater'. What continues to be called 'New Historicism' is, of course, synchronic, not diachronic: time stands still, so that a single moment or a single text can represent an entire Foucauldian episteme.[45] Thus, chronological changes within one writer's oeuvre become irrelevant, and thereby invisible, and what is invisible does not require explanation. But Greenblatt's account of the institutional relationships between the church and the theatre is founded upon another, even more pervasive invisibility. By a slippage which is not limited to Greenblatt, or to anything which might be labelled New Historicism, 'Shakespeare's theatre' becomes synonymous with 'the Elizabethan theatre' or even 'the theatre'. Most readers of Greenblatt do not notice this slippage, because the same conjuring trick occurs repeatedly in almost everything we write and think; within our own institutions, *Shakespeare is the Renaissance*. But of course he was not. One cannot analyse the interests and strategies of a complex social institution by analysing the work of any one man. After all, both Middleton and Shakespeare belonged to the same institution; the company which performed Shakespeare's late plays also performed *A Game at Chess*. But *A Game at Chess* empties out the very rituals which Shakespeare's late plays validate.

Any satisfactory model of the early modern theatre, or its relationship to religion, has to be able to account for Shakespeare *and Middleton* – and Fletcher and Marlowe and Jonson and others. My own view is that between 1576 and 1642 the London theatres institutionalized 'the first large-scale, capitalized, routinized commodification of affect in human history'.[46] That commodified affect is 'portable', carried out of the theatre into the world, but also carried into the theatre from the world. Religion, in this

model, constitutes one of many affective sites and sources, which the theatre might mine. Except that religion is itself not a single affective site but several, and different theatrical entrepreneurs might mine different veins of religious feeling.

It would be easy, at this point, to pursue the binary opposition between Shakespeare and Middleton. Instead, consider how we might read the relationship between the church and the theatre if we were reading, or watching, a moment in Act 5 of Ben Jonson's *Sejanus his Fall* (performed in 1603, published in 1605): 'While they sound againe, the *Flamen* takes of the hony, with his finger, & tasts, then ministers to all the rest: so of the milk, in an earthen vessel, he deals about: which done, he sprinkleth, vpon the altar, milke: then imposeth the hony, and kindleth his gummes, and after censing about the altar placeth his censer thereon, into which they put seuerall branches of poppy, and the musique ceasing, proceed.'[47]

---

persuasively that the original text included an onstage scene dramatizing King Edward's miraculous healing of scrofula: see '*Macbeth* at the Globe, 1606–1616 (?): Three Questions', in *The Triple Bond: Plays, Mainly Shakespearean, in Performance*, ed. Joseph G. Price (University Park, 1975), pp. 223–39. For further evidence of Middleton's influence on the extant text, see the relevant sections of *The Collected Works of Thomas Middleton*.

[45] For a critique of Foucault's conception of time (which is implicit in all New Historicist criticism), see Gary Taylor, 'The Renaissance and the End of Editing', in *Palimpsest: Textual Theory and the Humanities*, ed. George Bornstein and Ralph G. Williams (Ann Arbor, 1993), pp. 121–50.

[46] Gary Taylor, 'Feeling Bodies', in *Shakespeare and the Twentieth Century: The Selected Proceedings of the International Shakespeare Association World Congress, Los Angeles, 1996*, ed. Jonathan Bate, Jill L. Levenson, and Dieter Mehl (Newark, 1998), p. 274.

[47] *Sejanus*, marginal stage direction opposite 5.177–210, covering action which takes place between 5.177–84, in *Jonson*, IV, 443–4. For Jonson's printed citations of his sources for this scene, see IV, 483. The printed text represents Jonson's revision of an originally collaborative performance script. In *Ben Jonson, Dramatist* (Cambridge, 1984), Anne Barton argues that the collaborator

The men we are observing are here worshipping at the altar of the goddess Fortune. That goddess appears in eleven other plays, but this is the first surviving commercial play that calls for an altar in its stage directions, or that reproduces a pagan ritual so elaborately.[48] In his marginal notes, Jonson authenticates every detail of the rite, thereby establishing his own humanist credentials and at the same time characterizing the religious ceremony as an historically alienated reconstruction; the annotation, as David Riggs observes, 'discouraged the reader . . . from connecting the play to the author's own situation'.[49] Nevertheless, Jonson was 'called befor the [Privy] Councell for his Sejanus & accused both of popperie and treason'.[50] Why?

Perhaps not for the rite itself, but for what follows it: 'See, see, the image stirres! — And turnes away! — *Fortune* averts her face!' (5.185–6). To explain the bad omen, the flamen conjectures 'Some pious rite We have neglected', but Sejanus contemptuously dismisses this explanation, condemning the 'scrupulous priest' and his 'iuggling mysterie, religion', with all 'these fumes, these superstitious lights, And all these coos'ning ceremonies' and 'peeuish gigglot rites' (5.107–206). Of course, as every spectator knows, Sejanus is wrong: Fortune has turned against him, and within a few minutes he and his children will be brutally murdered.

Jonson was a practising Catholic when he wrote this scene, where a female image in a chapel (worshipped by a priest with a censer to the accompaniment of offstage instrumental music) actually 'stirs' in an act of prophecy almost immediately vindicated. How Protestants reacted to such events can be illustrated by Thomas Goad: 'Concerning coozening deuices: Are not yet men liuing, that can remember the knaverie of Priests to make the Roodes and Images of the Churches in *England* in the dayes of Queen *Mary*, to goggle with their eyes, and shake their hands: yea, with Wiers to bend the whole body, and many times to speake as they doe in Puppet plays, and all to

get money, and deceiue the ignorant people?'[51] Goad's attitude toward moving statues reproduces Harsnett's attitude toward exorcisms: they are dismissed and ridiculed as Catholic theatrical tricks. But Jonson puts this orthodox Protestant attitude into the mouth of an atheist, murderer, would-be usurper, and (at this moment) fool, Sejanus. The sequence of emotions, the subordination of one to another, determines, here as elsewhere, the play's hierarchy of sympathies and allegiances.[52] In *Sejanus*, a moment of reverent (Catholic) affect is superceded by a moment of contemptuous (Protestant) affect, but the contempt of a contemptible character only reinforces the reverence of spectators.

---

was Shakespeare (92–4); I think this is plausible, but unprovable, and any discussion of the play must be based upon the printed text, which is Jonson's alone.

[48] For the eleven other appearances of Fortune, see Berger et al, *Index* – which does not include the appearance of Fortuna in *Sejanus*, presumably because she is not named in the dramatis personae list or in stage directions. But the statue was probably played by an actor; it has to move, and seems as much a 'character' as the image of the goddess 'Fortune . . . discovered upon an altar' in the second dumb show in Middleton's *Hengist, King of Kent; or, The Mayor of Queenborough* (which does appear in the *Index*). For altars in stage directions, see Dessen and Thomson, *Dictionary*, 5–6 (not in chronological order). It is always possible that an altar might have been used in other plays, without being specified in stage directions, but before *Pericles* (1607) no occurrence of 'altar(s)' in the dialogue of Shakespeare's plays implies an onstage property.

[49] David Riggs, *Ben Jonson: A Life* (Cambridge, 1989), p. 102.

[50] *Ben Jonson's Conversations with William Drummond of Hawthornden*, pp. 326–7.

[51] Goad, *The Friers Chronicle: or, the true legend of priests and monkes lives* (1623; STC 11510), sig. B3v. In subsequent paragraphs Goad cites specific examples involving 'the Image of our *Lady*' and another of 'the child' Jesus 'in our *Ladies* armes' (sig. B3v–B4). The Homilies likewise insist that a statue really 'is not able to stirre nor once to moove' ('Perill of Idolatrie', 64).

[52] For an analysis of the importance of affective sequencing and hierarchy in influencing a spectator's perspective, see Gary Taylor, *Moment by Moment by Shakespeare* (Basingstoke, 1985), pp. 162–236.

Shakespeare acted in Jonson's *Sejanus*, and his own late plays follow Jonson's lead: they give us, not a Brechtian emptying-out of Christian mythology, but the commodification of a specifically Catholic affect.[53] The statue in the chapel in *The Winter's Tale* (1609), which moves and speaks to the accompaniment of offstage instrumental music, is allegedly the work of the Italian artist and papal architect, Julio Romano; it represents a character the play calls a 'sainted spirit' (5.1.57).[54] Earlier in the same play, the pilgrimage to the temple of Apollo at Delphi, like the pilgrimage to the temple of Diana in *Pericles* (1607), presupposes that some places are holier than others – a Catholic tradition of veneration ridiculed by Protestants, who believed that God was accessible anywhere.[55] But, as in *Sejanus*, in *The Winter's Tale* and *Pericles* the veneration of such temples is vindicated by the accuracy of a prophecy unattributable to mere human agency. The pagan deities in the romances are not deceiving demons, but benevolent entities with real knowledge and real power, and as such easily understood as allegorical representations of Christian divinity.[56] Jupiter had been used to represent the Christian God on stage at least since John Heywood's *The Play of the Weather*; if audiences were in any doubt about how to interpret the Jupiter who descends from the heavens in *Cymbeline* (1610), those doubts should have been removed by the fact that Jupiter is summoned by four voices speaking in a metrical form conspicuously old-fashioned in the Jacobean theatre, but instantly familiar in another institutional context: it is the same ballad stanza used for most of the texts in the Sternhold and Hopkins psalter, the only religious music most English churchgoers in 1610 had ever known.[57] But what is most remarkable about Jupiter's theophany in *Cymbeline* is that he is not moved by the direct personal prayers of Posthumus himself, or any of the play's other living characters, as any good Protestant would expect; instead, the supreme deity, as Catholics

53 I would now include among the late plays *All's Well that Ends Well*. In 1987 I was not 'confident about its exact place in the period 1604–7' (*Companion*, p. 127). But MacDonald P. Jackson has since alerted me to the fact that the very rare name 'Spurio', used incidentally twice in *All's Well* (2.1.43, 4.3.161), is the name of a major character in Middleton's *Revenger's Tragedy*, performed by the King's Men in 1606; the Italian name is relevant to his identity in Middleton, and seems more likely to have been picked up by Shakespeare's acting in *Revenger* than by Middleton attending a performance of *All's Well*. Composition of *All's Well* in 1606 would also explain the play's reference to equivocation (5.3.252–3), and the stylistic tests by Oras, Lowes, and Brainerd I cited in 1987. *All's Well* fits the religious pattern of the other late plays in its dramatic validation of magic and 'miracle'. See particularly the speech by Lafeu (a character usually described by critics as 'sympathetic' or even 'choric'): 'They say miracles are past, and we have our philosophical persons to make modern and familiar things supernatural and causeless', etc. (2.3.1–6).

54 Shakespeare used the oath 'by saint X' more often than any of his contemporaries.

55 For objections to pilgrimage, see for instance 'Perill of Idolatrie', *Certaine Sermons*, pp. 49, 54. The religious politics of the romances is illuminated by comparison with Fletcher's play *The Pilgrim* (1621), where (as in *Pericles*) various characters are happily reunited in a final scene before 'An Altar' in 'the holy Temple' at Segovia. Unlike Shakespeare's characters, Fletcher's have been sent to this spot by a clever woman in disguise (not a goddess); the scene is devoid of religious affect or consequence, and instead conforms to the Protestant image of altar and pilgrimage as stage-managed trickery. Fletcher's play contains nothing comparable to Shakespeare's description of the temple 'surpassing', the 'celestial habits', and 'the sacrifice . . . ceremonious, solemn, and unearthly' (*Winter's Tale* 3.1.2–7); the entire scene with this dialogue by the two pilgrims Dion and Cleomenes, emphatically placed by Shakespeare at the beginning of an act, is superfluous to the narrative (and has usually been cut in performances since the eighteenth century).

56 Thomas Rist, *Shakespeare's Romances and the Politics of Counter-Reformation* (Lewiston, 1999), 123. Rist also argues that the romances were influenced by Ignatian meditation, and that the Shakespearian scepticism praised by many critics takes in fact a specifically Counter-Reformation form. Surprisingly, he omits *Kinsmen* from consideration, on the grounds that it does not show 'any . . . concern with Reformation issues' (226).

57 Temperley, *Music of the English Parish Church*, 45–9, 56–7.

would expect, responds to the intercession of dead souls.[58]

If Jupiter is easily understood as God the Father, Diana is as easily understood as the Virgin Mary;[59] indeed, in the early 1580s Puritan ministers in Kent complained about how easily parish churches could be reconverted to Catholic worship, thereby becoming 'like a Diana's shrine for a future hope and daily comfort of old popish beldames and young perking papists'.[60] The 'music of the spheres' heard just before Diana's appearance in *Pericles* would have been polyphonic vocal music, like a Catholic choir: the music was created by the angels who moved the spheres, and each sphere had a different pitch.[61] The temple of Diana (Sc. 22), venerated by 'nuns' like Thaisa, is easily understood as a convent; presumably that is how it was understood by the actors who performed *Pericles* for recusant audiences in Yorkshire in 1610, and by the Jesuits who read and perhaps performed it before 1619.[62] If Diana is the Virgin Mary in *Pericles*, she can serve the same function in *The Two Noble Kinsmen*. Indeed, in that scene where Emilia burns incense at the 'holy altar', unlike the two men who preceded her (and unlike Shakespeare's source) she never actually names the object of her devotions;[63] the play's climactic prayer invokes 'O sacred, shadowy, cold, and constant queen, / Abandoner of revels, mute contemplative, / Sweet, solitary, white as chaste, and pure / As wind-fanned snow' (5.3.1–4) – and when editing the Oxford Shakespeare we were perhaps too hasty to decide that the 'most modest queen' (5.3.21) being addressed here was Diana, rather than Mary. Certainly, as the contrast with *A Game at Chess* demonstrates, everything about the religious rituals of Act 5 of *The Two Noble Kinsmen* suggests a Catholic, not a Protestant, representation of the sacred.

And that is also, perhaps, why the gods in *King Lear* do not answer. What is absent from *King Lear*, but present in all these other late plays of Shakespeare? Ceremony, ritual, intercession: altars, candles, statues, priests, nuns,

[58] Contrast Fletcher and Field's *Four Plays in One* in *Dramatic Works*, gen. ed. Fredson Bowers, vol. 8 (1992): Anthropos directly prays to Jupiter ('Triumph of Time', i.116–29), who descends saying, 'Whose powerful prayers were those that reach'd our ears' (ii.2); later, 'Jupiter [is] *seen in glory*' (iv.50.4). Jupiter's transparence as an allegorical representation of the Christian God is apparent here; equally apparent is that he responds directly to an individual's prayer (as Protestants would expect), not to Catholic intercession or mediation.

[59] On these allegorical identifications, see also Peter Milward, *Shakespeare's Other Dimension* (Tokyo, 1987), pp. 131–2; he also records contemporary comparisons of papal decrees from Rome with oracles from Delphi.

[60] Duffy, *Stripping of the Altars*, p. 583.

[61] Kathi Meyer-Baer, *Music of the Spheres and the Dance of Death: Studies in Musical Iconology* (Princeton, 1970), pp. 35–41, 57–64, 127, 138–42, 206–7; Jamie James, *The Music of the Spheres: Music, Science, and the Natural Order of the Universe* (New York, 1993), pp. 71, 111–12. Perhaps most pertinent to Shakespeare's intentions for 'the music of the spheres' in *Pericles* (21.210–22) is the description in *The Merchant of Venice*: 'There's not the smallest orb which thou behold'st / But in his motion *like an angel sings*, / Still *choiring* to the young-eyed cherubins. / Such harmony is in immortal souls' (5.1.60–3; my italics). The music here is clearly vocal and choral.

[62] John L. Murphy, *Darkness and Devils: Exorcism and 'King Lear'* (Athens, 1984), 93–118; Willem Schrickx, '*Pericles* in a Book-List of 1619 from the English Jesuit Mission and Some of the Play's Special Problems', *Shakespeare Survey* 29 (1976), pp. 21–32.

[63] In *The Knight's Tale*, Emelye addresses 'Dyane' by name at 2364. She also invokes all 'thre formes' of the goddess (2313) – as patroness of chastity, the hunt, and childbirth, and 'Queene of the regne of Pluto derk and lowe' (2299); by contrast, Shakespeare's Emilia does not refer to hunting, childbirth, or hell, and does associate the 'holy altar' (5.3.28) with 'female knights' (4) in an 'order's robe' (6) and 'vestal office' (14). Moreover, in Chaucer Dyane is repeatedly associated with the colour green (2079, 2290, 2297), logically for a woodland huntress; in Shakespeare she has a 'rare green eye' (8), but is more insistently associated with 'white' (5.3.0.1, 0.3, 3) and 'silver' (0.4), as is Diana in *Pericles* (21.234, 22.27). Finally, Chaucer places the prayer to Dyane between those to Venus and Mars; Shakespeare makes it climactic. I cite *The Riverside Chaucer*, 3rd edn, gen. ed. Larry D. Benson (Boston: Houghton Mifflin, 1987), but I have checked *The Workes of our Antient and Learned English Poet, Geffrey Chaucer*, ed. Thomas Speght (1602: STC 5080), sig. B5v–C2.

hallowed and hallowing music, all the numinous synecdoches condemned by Calvinists as meaningless idolatrous fetishes, but revered by Catholics as necessary mediators between the human and the divine. In *King Lear*, in an England stripped of its altars, 'unaccommodated man' (11.97; 3.4.100) inhabits a world without any sign of that divine presence so unavoidable in Shakespeare's other late plays.[64]

At this point I have arrived at the conclusion I reached sixteen years ago: Shakespeare 'dyed a papist' – or at least wrote like one.[65] But as an explanation of the imaginative impact of the late plays that view seems to me, though true, not the whole truth. After all, Shakespeare's Catholicism has remained invisible for centuries; demonstrably, it is possible to interpret him in other ways. To read the late plays as allegories of Catholicism requires us to ignore their paganism, to act as though the signifier was transparent, and therefore irrelevant. Signifiers are never transparent. If the signified is Catholicism, the signifier is paganism. That signifier itself had many meanings. As a product of Latin culture, it belonged to the division of English society along lines of class, status, and gender which were defined, in part, linguistically. The Clown in *Titus Andronicus* is confused by an allusion to Jupiter, first mistaking it for 'gibbet-maker', and then confessing: 'Alas, sir, I know not "Jupiter". I never drank with him in all my life' (4.3.80, 84–5). His ignorance hangs him. Moreover, as Anthony Fletcher observes in his survey of the education of boys in early modern England, 'the most striking development of the period from 1660 to 1800' – that is, the period that canonized Shakespeare – 'was the insistence of the upper gentry . . . on sticking to schools which preserved the classical regime', even while most other schools were diversifying and modernizing their curriculums; Latin 'was the crucial foundation of a whole class and gender system'.[66] The mythology of the Latin world, which so saturates Shakespeare's texts, became the badge of England's male elite, a private language powerfully inflected with all the emo-

tional energies of adolescence and emergent adult identity.

If Shakespeare's pagan mythologies meant something to the men who would enshrine him as the most venerated idol of English culture, they also meant something to early modern audiences. If Diana were merely Mary, why in *Pericles* does she carry the bow of a huntress, why in *Kinsmen* is a hind sacrificed on her altar? If Jupiter were merely God the Father, why in *Cymbeline* does he 'descend in thunder and lightning, sitting upon an eagle' (5.5.186.1–2), the 'holy eagle' who 'preens the immortal wing and claws his beak' (209–12)?[67] Why does he insist that 'Our Jovial star' reigned at the birth of Posthumus (199)? There are no such particularities in the representation of Jove in Heywood's *Play of the Weather*. To read *Cymbeline*, or any of the late plays, *only* allegorically requires us to ignore too much of the text, too much of the imaginative texture. Allegory generalizes and rationalizes the experience of the play, which in performance is always particular and affective.

Consider, for instance, Act 4, Scene 3 of *Antony and Cleopatra*, where four Roman soldiers '*place themselves in every corner of the stage*';

---

64 For a reading of *King Lear* (and its relationship to Harsnett) quite different from Greenblatt's, see Gary Taylor, 'Forms of Opposition: Shakespeare and Middleton', *English Literary Renaissance*, 24 (1994), 283–314.

65 Gary Taylor, 'The Fortunes of Oldcastle', *Shakespeare Survey 38* (1985), 85–100. That essay was written and delivered in 1984, before E. A. J. Honigmann more generally re-opened the question of Catholicism in *Shakespeare's Lost Years* (1985). For the seventeenth-century claim that Shakespeare 'dyed a papist', see E. K. Chambers, *William Shakespere: A Study of Facts and Problems*, 2 vols. (Oxford, 1930), vol. 2, p. 256.

66 Anthony Fletcher, *Gender, Sex and Subordination in England 1500–1800* (New Haven, 1995), 301–2.

67 Peggy Muñoz Simonds cites St Ambrose and the Renaissance ornithographer Ulisse Aldrovandi to equate the eagle with Christ: see *Myth, Emblem, and Music in Shakespeare's Cymbeline: An Iconographic Reconstruction* (Newark, 1992), 294–5. But this will hardly explain the preening or the clawing, or why Jove/God is riding piggyback on Jesus.

shortly thereafter, another stage direction tells us that '*Music of the hautboys is under the stage*', and after their initial confusion one of them asks, 'What should this mean?' and another answers, ''Tis the god Hercules, whom Antony loved, Now leaves him'; mesmerized and curious, they follow the noise offstage; the last words of the scene (attributed to 'All' the soldiers) are ''Tis strange.'

Now it is true that Hercules was morally allegorized in the Renaissance, and that it was even possible to read Hercules as an emblem of Christ. But nothing in the scene itself – the text, or our theatrical experience of it – supports such an allegory here; the allegory depends upon exploding the significance of the one word 'Hercules' (by appending to it the testimony of many other texts) while ignoring the other 192 words of dialogue and stage directions which Shakespeare wrote here.

What the scene dramatizes is a communal human encounter with something powerfully not human. Not individual, but communal: a group of anonymous soldiers. Why a group? Because the testimony of one individual might be dismissed; the testimony of many is harder to ignore. Why soldiers? Because we expect soldiers to be men of the world, hardened, secular, suspicious, literally on guard, like the Roman soldiers who witnessed the crucifixion of Christ, like the soldiers who help rob the tomb in Middleton's *The Lady's Tragedy*.[68] In all three cases, soldiers' reactions create the sense of something outside ordinary experience, something holy. A group of soldiers, a community of non-believers, become believers, as a result of an undeniable encounter with the inexplicable.

Shakespeare's representation of the divine presence these soldiers encounter depends upon two signifiers: the music of hautboys, and their placement 'under the stage'. Those same signifiers had been twinned, to similar effect, in the dumbshow before the fourth act of *Gorboduc*: 'First the music of hautboys began to play, during which there came forth from under the stage, as though out of hell, three furies.'[69] But,

although this parallel confirms the association of hautboys with supernatural presences under the stage, it is difficult to read the Hercules of *Antony and Cleopatra* as demonic.

It is also difficult to read the scene as Catholic. Medieval and Catholic angels are sometimes pictured playing hautboys, and 'in the cathedrals of the English church, choirs were supplemented by organs, lutes, and hautboys';[70] in Dekker's *Match Me in London* (1611) and Middleton's *A Game at Chess* (1624) the instruments are associated with altars and Catholic rituals.[71] Thus, in the right context hautboys might arouse emotions metyonymically associated with Catholic or episcopal ceremony. But consorts of hautboys were regularly used on all sorts of public occasions (including royal entrances and masques), in the theatres, the city, the court, even for hunting in the country – in part because the instruments were particularly loud and shrill, creating a sound which could demand attention even in acoustically difficult circumstances and spaces.[72]

This scene in *Antony* is the only occasion in

---

[68] Middleton, *The Lady's Tragedy*, 4.2; this is the title given in *The Collected Works* to the play usually known by the (inept) editorial title, 'The Second Maiden's Tragedy'.

[69] Thomas Sackville and Thomas Norton, *The Tragedy of Ferrex and Porrex; or, Gorboduc* (performed 1561; edition of 1570), in *Early English Dramatists*, ed. John S. Farmer (London, 1906), p. 125 ('The Order and Signification of the Dumb Show before the Fourth Act'). This example is not included in the entry for 'hoboy' in Dessen and Thomson, *Dictionary*, pp. 115–16, because it predates 1580.

[70] Horton Davies, *Worship and Theology in England from Cranmer to Hooker, 1534–1603* (Princeton, 1970), p. 393. For angels with shawms (another word for hautboys), see Meyer-Baer, *Music of the Spheres*, fig. 67, 78, 79, 80, pp. 176–9.

[71] Dekker, *Match Me*, 5.3.0.1 ('*Hoboyes. Enter two Fryers setting out an Altar*' for a wicked marriage); Middleton, *Game*, 5.1.9.1 ('Hoboyes' in some texts just before entrance of Black King and his court to hear a Latin oration; this is the altar scene, analysed elsewhere in this essay).

[72] F. W. Sternfeld, *Music in Shakespearean Tragedy* (London, 1963), p. 225.

the surviving dramatic texts of the period when hautboys play 'under the stage'; in *Gorboduc*, they accompany an entrance from under the stage, but are not themselves placed there. Hence the unusual form and specificity of Shakespeare's stage direction: '*Music of the hautboys is under the stage.*' In Plutarch, the noises come from underground, but Plutarch describes many instruments and voices and the sounds of dancing;[73] Shakespeare chooses hautboys alone. And since he has changed so many other details of the scene, he could just as easily have changed the placement of the sound; it could have been heard 'in the air' (as music produced by invisible instruments is usually described) rather than 'under the earth'.[74]

Unless we are to believe that Antony is being abandoned by an evil demon, then the placing of the hautboys 'under the stage' is not an allegorical but a theatrical and experiential effect. The nature of that effect is suggested by stage directions in two other plays performed by the King's Men: in Jonson's *Catiline* (1611) twice 'A grone of many people is heard vnder ground' (1.315, 317), and in *Hamlet* (1601) the 'Ghost cries vnder the Stage' (1.5.151). In Jonson, there are *many* voices coming from under the stage, just as in *Antony* there are *hautboys*, not a single instrument but the usual consort, which included woodwinds of different size and pitch.[75] In *Hamlet*, the ghost is *moving* under the stage, creating a sound which cannot be localized, which invisibly shifts position.

From an acoustic viewpoint, the area under the stage has two effects: it reverberates and at the same time distorts. It reverberates in part because it is hollow. In *Titus Andronicus*, the trapdoor which enables actors to drop down below the stage is called 'this gaping hollow of the earth' (2.3.249); in *The Taming of the Shrew* barking hunting dogs 'fetch shrill echoes from the hollow earth' (Ind.2.45).[76] Not only hollow, but also – unlike modern theatres – a 'wooden O', a cylinder made of wood.[77] Wood has very different acoustic properties from concrete. In the musical conceit of Sonnet 128,

the 'dead wood' of the virginals is also 'blessed wood', indeed 'more blessed than living lips', because of the sound it makes when fingers 'walk' on it.[78] Transferring the metaphor from wooden keys to timbered platform, Achilles can delight 'To hear the wooden dialogue and sound' made by his own footsteps on the stage, ''Twixt his stretched footing and the scaffoldage'; the resulting sound is 'rich' (*Troilus* 1.3.154–6). Like the hautboy, the stage of the Globe – indeed, the entire Globe theatre – is a hollow wooden instrument. Within this reverberating wooden hollowness, Shakespeare places not one but several different musical instruments, and then he orders them to move around. The soldiers have been placed 'at every corner of the stage' in order to create a visibly geometric order, in the strongest possible contrast to the invisible ungeometric unlocalizable music of the hautboys. And the instruments are hautboys not only because of their metonymic

---

[73] For the passage in Plutarch, see Marvin Spevack's New Variorum edition of *Antony and Cleopatra* (New York, 1990), 449.

[74] Compare *1 Henry IV* 3.1.224. *Caesar* 2.2.22, *Macbeth* 2.3.56, 4.1.129, *Kinsmen* 1.5.6; even in this scene of *Antony* the sound is described as 'music i'th' air' (4.3.13). Music is often placed 'above' in stage directions: see Dessen and Thomson, *Dictionary*, p. 1.

[75] For the consorts see *New Grove Dictionary*, 17.237–43 (shawm); the word is always plural in stage directions (Dessen and Thomson, *Dictionary*, p. 115).

[76] Shakespeare often elsewhere describes the earth as hollow: *Titus* 5.2.35 ('hollow cave'), *Venus* 268 ('whose hollow womb resounds like heaven's thunder'), *Romeo* 5.3.4 ('Holding thy ear close to the hollow ground'), *Richard II* 2.1.83 ('hollow womb'), 3.2.136 ('hollow ground'), *Othello* 3.3.451 ('Arise, black vengeance, from the hollow hell'), 4.2.81 ('hollow mine of earth').

[77] For another reading of the importance of specifically wooden playing spaces, see Gary Taylor, '*Hamlet* in Africa, 1607', in *Travel Knowledge*, ed. Ivo Kamps and Jyotsna Singh (New York, 2000), pp. 211–48.

[78] Editors of the Sonnets have overlooked the idolatrous undercurrents of the conceit which blesses 'dead wood': it is not mentioned at all in the commentaries by Stephen Booth (Berkeley, 1980), pp. 437–41, John Kerrigan (New York, 1986), pp. 355–6, and Helen Vendler (Cambridge, 1997), pp. 544–8.

association with the formal rituals of royalty and the supernatural, but because hautboys produce sounds loud enough and shrill enough to penetrate the wooden barrier and reach every ear in the audience. What the audience experiences is a sense of invisible presence, something unseen and of indefinite size and shape, which keeps shifting location, something which asserts significance but cannot be easily interpreted, something familiar but also distorted. ''Tis strange', indeed.

Strange not least because no one in the original audience believed in the god here being so powerfully represented. No one left the Globe theatre and went to worship at the local temple of Hercules. Shakespeare represents the divine through the medium of a thoroughly dead religion; he challenges his audience to perform an act at least ethnographically sympathetic, at most vertiginously numinous. He creates religious affect without religious intellect, deus without dogma, theos without theology.

We might explain this anomaly by documenting, as Peter Platt does, the emphasis on the marvellous, on the affect of wonder, in sixteenth-century Italian critical theory;[79] as T. G. Bishop does, by citing Aristotle, Longinus, and medieval biblical drama;[80] as Leonard Barkan does, by relating it to the literal 'unearthing of the past' which took place in Italy in the fifteenth and sixteenth centuries, the resurrection of buried classical statues, made again to speak.[81] We might explain it as Shakespeare's Catholic resistance to what Max Weber described as the Protestant disenchantment of the world, 'the decline of magic' chronicled by Keith Thomas.[82] But these attempts at explanation themselves operate to disenchant, to explain and thereby comfortably domesticate our experience of something which is, and wants to be, alien.[83]

In A Game at Chess, the two most powerful players are those we never see, the invisible players who move the visible players; the black and white chess pieces are imagined as living puppets, created by the same playwright who so memorably animated inanimate puppets in The Revenger's Tragedy and Wit at Several Weapons. In A Game at Chess, the false god is represented by visible, palpable, moving statues; the real god is invisible, but irresistible. In Antony and Cleopatra, we encounter an invisible god, who becomes evident to our senses only at the very moment he departs. In the Gospels, the evidence for the resurrection of Jesus is the disappearance of his body from the tomb. For Greenblatt, 'emptying out' is what one religious institution does to its rival, or what the secularizing capitalist playhouse does to all religions. But 'emptying out' can itelf be a religious experience, is arguably the most fundamental religious experience. The believer empties himself, as the desideratum for being filled.

In his classic account of the psychology of religious belief, William James argued that its core was an emotionally charged 'consciousness of presence'.[84] But he might just as easily have called it 'a consciousness of absence', because that 'sense of divine presence' is apprehended

---

79 Peter G. Platt, *Reason Diminished: Shakespeare and the Marvelous* (Lincoln, 1997). Platt links Shakespeare's practice to the theory of Francesco Patrizi (a sixteenth-century Italian Catholic); he also recognizes the importance of wonder to Reformation iconoclastic debates (19–35); but he treats Shakespeare's practice as though it were only aesthetic, and not also religious.

80 Bishop, *Shakespeare and the Theatre of Wonder* (Cambridge, 1996).

81 Barkan at one point specifically relates this archaeological romance to *The Winter's Tale*: see *Unearthing the Past: Archaeology and Aesthetics in the Making of Renaissance Culture* (New Haven, 1999), p. xxv.

82 Weber, *The Protestant Ethic and the Spirit of Capitalism: The Relationships between Religion and the Economic and Social Life in Modern Culture* (New York, 1958); Thomas, *Religion and the Decline of Magic* (London, 1971).

83 See the critique of the all too familiar effect produced by 'post-psychoanalytic semiotics' and symbolic readings in H. W. Fawkner, *Shakespeare's Miracle Plays: Pericles, Cymbeline, and The Winter's Tale* (Rutherford, 1992), p. 15.

84 William James, *The Varieties of Religious Experience* (Cambridge, MA, 1985), pp. 51–70, 340–41, 383.

despite the absence of sensory corroboration. An invisible voice, a visible but impalpable body, a touch when there is no one there to do the touching. The divine essence is ex-sense, outside the senses, beyond understanding, nonsense; Erasmus, in praising folly, eventually equates it with Christ. Wisdom is folly, the truest being is not-being.

But these familiar intellectual paradoxes themselves reduce the complex weirdness of experience, the weird complexity of theatre, to a formulaic unanalysable marriage of binaries. The religious experiences James described, the theatrical experiences I have been describing, do not magically metaphysically combine presence and absence, being and not-being; instead, they represent moments of *proximity to presence*. Here as elsewhere, the concept of proximity enables an escape from dead-end binaries.[85] Because presence itself is multi-dimensional, it can be approached along multiple axes, which are themselves graduated and scalar; one can be more or less near, in one or more ways. Moses on Horeb heard a voice speaking from out of the burning bush: a voice but no bodily image, a vision of fire but no combustion. That obscure divine object of desire is not simply absent, or simply present, but almost present, or present in some ways and absent in others. At some moments, for some moments, God may be – as Celia Daileader would say – just offstage.[86]

This experiential complex is perfectly embodied in four numinous words of Middleton's *The Lady's Tragedy*, acted by the King's Men in 1611: 'I am not here' (4.4.40). In 1611, in a world without any audio recording technology, spoken words could not be separated from a speaking body. These particular spoken words echo those of the angel at Christ's tomb: 'He is not here.'[87] But Middleton's shift from 'he is' to 'I am', from visible angel to audible disembodied voice 'within', utterly transforms the utterance. 'He is not here' is a simple statement of absence; 'I am here' would be an equally simple statement of presence. But in Middleton's seemingly simple statement the divine 'I am' insists immediately upon its not-ness, not-local-ness; the sentence, in the very act of its articulation, contradicts its semantic content. *Mise en scene, mise en abime.* Logic collides with grammar; presence along one axis of sense coincides with absence along another axis. And because presence is associated with one affect (joy, or dread), and absence with another (grief, or relief), the unexpected uncanny coexistence of presence and absence compounds clashing emotional impulses. Feelings torque around a common axis, reflecting and intensifying each other, like two magnets with opposite charges: the closer you force them together, the more strongly you feel the invisible magnetic force pushing them apart. The emotional energy of such moments is a product of the degree of incompatibility multiplied by the degree of proximity: the less compatible two states are, the farther apart they want to stay, and the more energy is produced by bringing them together. In Shakespeare, in Middleton, the most powerful representations of divine essence are representations of the almost absolute co-presence of almost absolute incompatibles: theos and theatre.

---

85 For the concept of proximity developed here, see Gary Taylor, 'The Renaissance and the End of Editing', in *Palimpsest: Textual Theory and the Humanities*, ed. George Bornstein and Ralph G. Williams (Ann Arbor, 1993), pp. 121–50, and 'Theatrical Proximities: The Stratford Festival 1998', *Shakespeare Quarterly*, 50 (1999), 334–354.

86 Daileader, *Eroticism on the Renaissance Stage*, p. 18. My own interest in the collocation of divinity and the offstage is more generally indebted to Daileader's work on 'the limits of the visible'.

87 Matthew 28:6, Mark 16:6, Luke 24:6. (Noted by Lancashire, 221.)

'AN ALIEN PEOPLE CLUTCHING THEIR GODS'?: SHAKESPEARE'S ANCIENT RELIGIONS

ROBERT S. MIOLA

I CULTURAL DRIFT AND THE LOST ANIMA

Last year my Latin class and I were reading Ovid and came upon Pyramus' suicide: *demisit in ilia ferrum* (*Met.* 4.119): 'he plunged the *ferrum* (iron, sword, knife) into his *ilia*'.[1] Where, among the multiple dictionary possibilities for *ilia*, does Pyramus stab himself? 'Entrails', said one student cheerfully. (Golding had 'guts' by the way.) 'Chest' and 'breast' received solid support. I was a little uncomfortable; *ilia* actually are lower. But it was supposed to be a suicide and our conventions of self-stabbing support that location. The heart beneath has some sentimental resonance. And what about poetic licence, anyway? The pectoral group found themselves in the good company of the most brilliant English translator, Ted Hughes, and the most inept, that of Peter Quince and Nick Bottom: 'With bloody, blameful blade – / He bravely broached his boiling bloody breast' (*MND*, 5.1.145–6). No one, thankfully, wanted 'stomach', 'abdomen', or 'diaphragm', anatomically the more correct equivalents. Finally, pointing to a dictionary entry, Katelyn, a sophomore, ended the discussion: 'It's the groin! He's a lover, isn't he?'

Such lexical difficulty confronts every translator at every moment. Theoretically, one can find more or less correct and poetically acceptable equivalents for *ilia*; the word does not name an organ that has disappeared in human evolution; we all still have *ilia* somewhere. But

there is a larger, more pervasive problem that besets every effort at translating Latin or Greek, and every effort at reimagining antiquity: the problem of cultural drift. A few lines earlier Pyramus had said: *nostra nocens anima est* (*Met.* 4.110), 'My *anima* is *nocens*.' Lewis and Short will tell you that *noceo, nocere* means 'to do harm, to inflict injury' and, therefore, that the participle *nocens* means 'bad, wicked, harmful, culpable', and so on. Take your pick. But what can one do with *anima*? Our textbook accurately if not concisely, offered some possibilities: 'air, breath; soul, life; spirit, ghost'. 'My soul is guilty', the students overwhelmingly chose, with good reason, and in good company; this is essentially Golding's choice and that of many moderns. The translation is right and acceptable and it is also deeply wrong and unacceptable.

The Latin *anima* exists in creative tension with the *animus*, the principle of consciousness, the rational soul, the spirit as distinct from the body, translatable as the mind, intellect, sensibility, will, etc.[2] Ovid could never have meant by *anima* what we mean by soul, a concept freighted with millennia of intense theological

---

The quotation in the title is taken from T. S. Eliot, *Journey of the Magi* (1927).

[1] I quote Ovid from The Loeb Classical Library editions of the *Metamorphoses*, ed. and trans. Frank Justus Miller, 3rd edn, rev. by G. P. Goold (1977, rpt. 1994), and *Fasti*, ed. and trans. Sir James George Frazer, 2nd edn, rev. by G. P. Goold (1989).

[2] See Richard Broxton Onians, *The Origins of European Thought* (New York, 1973), pp. 168–73.

and philosophical discussion. We cannot think away the Bible and two thousand years of Western philosophy. *Anima*, then, remains permanently other, alien, untranslatable; we don't have *anima* any more. To an English speaking audience the rendering, 'My soul is guilty', carries the mythic moment across impossible divides; it translates the young lover into a fallen mortal composed of spirit and substance, soul and body; it transposes Ovid's fantastic world into a Judaeo-Christian universe where one's free will chooses moral or immoral action, where one's soul experiences guilt in its own sight and the sight of God, not gods.

Even the greatest translators must struggle with cultural drift, the clashing historicities of the signifier and the signified. At two important moments in the *Iliad*, for example, the deaths of Patroclus and Hector, George Chapman confronted these same two moving verses:[3]

psyche d'ek hretheon ptamene Aidosde bebekei
hon potmon gooosa, lipous' androteta kai heben.
                              (16.856–7; 22.362–3)

            his soul took instant wing,
And to the house that hath no lights, descended
   sorrowing
For his sad fate, to leave him young and in his
   ablest age.

His soul flying his fair limbs, to hell; mourning his
   destinies,
To part so with his youth and strength.

Both times Chapman renders Homer's *psyche* as 'soul'. Perhaps deriving from a word for breath and lying far behind the Latin *anima/us*, the Homeric *psyche* possesses substance, memory, emotion, and voice. Sometimes visible, it exits normally through a wound or opening in the body and appears in artistic images as a winged, small person. Here psyche laments *potmon*, the fate that befalls humans, that rolls towards all, cowards and heroes, the force that returns us to earth like so many generations of leaves. Chapman presents us with a different and modern drama of the soul and death. For him 'man is a living soul' and the body only 'her

shadow'. Contrarily, the first lines of Homer's epic describe the souls of brave warriors going to Hades while *autous*, 'themselves', become spoil. In Chapman's great Protestant *Iliad* the souls, not the bodies, are the essential persons; they suffer not *potmon*, but private death; they mourn individual destinies, not the fate that afflicts all mortals; and Hector's soul goes not to Hades but to hell.

Such cultural drift manifests itself pervasively in early modern encounters with antiquity and results in variously fruitful estrangements in Dante, the Pléiade, Spenser, Milton, and Shakespeare, especially his classical works. Put simply, the drifted humanist imagination apprehends the other as other and as itself.

The Rape of Lucrece, especially, embodies this paradox, as Shakespeare depicts the ancient *anima* and the act of Roman suicide, for him a signature gesture of alien antiquity. Lucrece's suicide makes sense as heroic sacrifice and expiation in the original setting of a shame/fame culture. In this culture the rape brings dishonour upon her, the husband, and family. The rape-victim suffers a pollution from without that infects her being and her descendants, regardless of personal choice. Lucrece, accordingly, assumes the interdependence of body and soul:

   Ay me, the bark peeled from the lofty pine
   His leaves will wither and his sap decay;
   So must my soul, her bark being peeled away.
                              (1167–9)

Lucrece rids herself of pollution by suicide. In death she cleanses herself of sexual dishonour by claiming a different kind of honour, that of the Roman warrior. Dead, she becomes, in Ovid's untranslatable phrase, *animi matrona virilis* (*Fasti*,

---

[3] For a fuller discussion of Chapman's Homer see my 'Death and Dying in Chapman's *Iliad*: Translation as Forgery', *International Journal of the Classical Tradition*, 3 (1996), pp. 48–64, from which I draw some phrasing and the quotations from Chapman. The paragraphs below on *Lucrece* revise and condense my discussion in *Shakespeare's Reading* (Oxford, 2000), pp. 29–32.

2. 847), 'a woman of manly [soul, spirit, mind, disposition, etc]'. By her suicide Lucrece earns the good afterlife available to the Roman, that offered by the memory of the living:

For in my death I murder shameful scorn;
My shame so dead, mine honour is new born.

(1189–90)

Later generations admired Lucrece but conceived the moral issues differently. Augustine queried succinctly: *si adulterata, cur laudata; si pudica, cur occisa*, 'if she was made an adulteress, why has she been praised? If she was chaste, why was she slain?'[4] Employing a postclassical ethics of guilt and sin, Augustine asks whether Lucrece was an adulteress or rape-victim. If an adulteress, then she can deserve no praise; if a victim, then her soul is stainless, not polluted, and the suicide must be morally unjustifiable, must be sinful despair rather than heroic assertion. Often unfairly reviled today, St Augustine shows himself a modernist and proto-feminist: he substitutes a later notion of soul for the earlier one; he rejects the classical gendering of virtue and vice; he regards Lucrece as an autonomous moral agent whose capacity for sin, like that of any man, resides wholly in her intellect, conscience, and will.

The poem outlines as well these Christian values, which undermine the logic of Lucrece's suicide. It evokes the later values first in the anachronistic imagery of Lucrece as 'earthly saint' and Tarquin as 'devil' (85), then in the depiction of Tarquin's inner struggle as a contest between 'frozen conscience and hot-burning will' (247). According to this conception of the action, Tarquin sins and pollutes his own soul, not Lucrece's. (There is no suggestion of this in Ovid.) Thus, Tarquin's 'soul's fair temple is defaced' (719), not his victim's; his soul is now a 'spotted princess' (721), hers immaculate. Precisely reversing herself, Lucrece at one point subscribes to the Christian sense of self and soul: '"To kill myself", quoth she, "alack, what were it / But with my body my poor soul's pollution?"' (1156–7). Only

Lucrece, not Tarquin, has the power to pollute her soul, which resides in some sense ontologically apart from the body and its misfortunes. And Fame, which in Ovid motivates her submission to Tarquin (*famae victa . . . metu*, 2. 810) and her suicide, becomes entirely irrelevant to the modern drama of sin and salvation within. The noisy approbation of the onlookers must yield to the silent judgement of an omniscient God.

This conflict in Shakespeare's poem between classical and Christian values, between *anima* and soul, remains unresolved. Brutus's final statement sounds more like criticism than praise: the 'wretched wife mistook the matter so / To slay herself, that should have slain her foe' (1826–7). Perhaps aware of the dissonances, Shakespeare belatedly introduces the idea of Lucrece's 'mind' as innocent, but this merely confuses the issues. The lost classical *anima* finds here habitation, temporary, unstable, and inhospitable.

II THE SACRAMENT OF VIOLENCE

As *Lucrece* illustrates, violence sickens and enthralls throughout Shakespeare's ancient Rome.[5] The conspirators stab Caesar, wash their hands and swords in his blood. Antony resolves to win battle, or to bathe his 'dying honour in the blood / Shall make it live again' (*Antony*, 4.2.6–7). Coriolanus returns from battle 'as he were flayed' (1.7.22); his shed blood qualifies him to stand for the consulship. Blood assumes a mystical quality in these plays as Romans spill, bathe, and revel in it to earn praise and effect transformation. This self-destructive ethos leads naturally to suicide in

---

4 Saint Augustine, *The City of God Against the Pagans*, trans. George E. McCracken, et al., 7 vols., The Loeb Classical Library (1957–68), vol. 1, pp. 88–9; for discussion see Ian Donaldson, *The Rapes of Lucretia: A Myth and its Transformations* (Oxford, 1982), esp. chapters 1, 2.

5 This section expands my earlier discussion in 'Shakespeare's Ancient Romans: Difference and Identity', *The Cambridge Companion to Shakespeare's History Plays*, ed. Michael Hattaway (Cambridge, forthcoming).

Shakespeare's Rome, even for Cleopatra, who resolves to do 'what's brave, what's noble . . . after the high Roman fashion' (4.16.88–9). Such rituals of violence enable Shakespeare's Romans to rise above ordinary limitations and touch the sacred.

Titus Andronicus represents Shakespeare's most sensational depiction of Roman violence. The spectacle of human sacrifice, mutilation, murder, and the Thyestean banquet defines the Romans as other, as an 'alien people clutching their gods'. But the line between antiquity and modernity fluctuates throughout the play. An invading Goth strays to 'gaze upon a ruinous monastery', fixing his eye upon the 'wasted building' (5.1.21, 23). Ancient Rome metamorphoses into the familiar landscape of contemporary England. Aaron demands that Lucius take an oath:

> I know thou art religious
> And hast a thing within thee callèd conscience,
> With twenty popish tricks and ceremonies
> Which I have seen thee careful to observe,
> Therefore I urge thy oath.   (5.1.74–8)

Aaron here appears as a reformer, scorning Roman Catholic 'ceremonies', a derisive Protestant term for superstitious beliefs and practices of Catholics (found, for example, in Article Nineteen of the original Protestant Thirty-Nine). Mocking Lucius's conscience, demanding an oath from a popish Roman, Aaron also enacts a cultural paradigm from the later wars of religion. The Elizabethan Act of Supremacy (1559) required an oath of subscription from all officers ecclesiastical and temporal, as well as from all persons suing livery of lands, taking holy orders, or proceeding to a degree at the Universities; James I required a milder Oath of Allegiance (1606).[6] Catholics agonized about their divided duties. Echoing throughout the generations, Thomas More's refusal to ratify the Act of Succession clearly articulated the terms and stakes of the conflict: 'in good faith my conscience so moves me in the matter, that . . . unto the oath that here is offered to me I cannot

swear, without the jeoparding of my soul to perpetual damnation'.[7] Aaron's anachronistic derision evokes a potent cultural paradigm which destabilizes and subverts: the villainous Moor acts the role of Tudor magistrate; he casts the victorious pagan Roman as defeated Roman Catholic.[8]

The barbarous action of *Titus Andronicus* evokes other contemporary paradigms. In Act 4 the hapless clown greets Saturninus: 'God and Saint Stephen give you good-e'en' (4.4.42–3). The jingle nods briefly to the most concrete and fully realized example of apostolic martyrdom, the first biblical saint to die for Christ. Stephen, memorialized in St Stephen's Alley and in two London churches, became an important Renaissance prototype for martyrs.[9] The discourse of martyrdom surfaces surprisingly throughout the Roman play. Lucius asks the ravished Lavinia, 'Speak, gentle sister, who hath martyred thee' (3.1.81). Titus notes sadly that

---

6 On the former see G. R. Elton, *The Tudor Constitution: Documents and Commentary* (Cambridge, 1960, rpt. 1968), pp. 363–8; on the latter, J. P. Kenyon, ed. *The Stuart Constitution: Documents and Commentary*, 2nd edn (Cambridge, 1986), pp. 165–71.

7 Peter Ackroyd, *The Life of Thomas More*, paper (New York, 1999), p. 361.

8 Writers in the period insist on conceptual distinctions between the two religions, though in practice, divisions between Catholics, Papists, Church Papists, Protestants of various stripes, and Puritans were unstable. See Peter Lake, 'Religious Identities in Shakespeare's England', *A Companion to Shakespeare*, ed. by David Scott Kastan (Oxford, 1999), pp. 57–84; Alexandra Walsham, *Church Papists: Catholicism, Conformity, and Confessional Polemic in Early Modern England* (Woodbridge, Suffolk, 1993).

9 See the entry in *The New Catholic Encyclopedia*, 18 vols. (New York, 1967–89); on Stephen in London see John Stow, *A Survey of London, Reprinted from the Text of 1603*, ed. Charles Lethbridge Kingsford, 2 vols. (Oxford, 1908, rpt. 1971), vol. 2, p. 102; vol. 1, pp. 283–4; vol. 1, pp. 227–8; on Stephen as martyr and model see John R. Knott, *Discourses of Martyrdom in English Literature, 1563–1694* (Cambridge, 1993), s.v. 'Stephen'. Jonathan Bate also notes the Reformation context of this play in his Arden edition (1995), pp. 18–21, but sees the Goths as prefiguring the reformers and the *translatio imperii* from Rome to Germany.

Lavinia has no tongue to tell 'who hath martyred thee' (3.1.107); he must interpret 'all her martyred signs' (3.2.36). Before cutting the throats of Chiron and Demetrius, Titus says: 'Hark, wretches, how I mean to martyr you' (5.2.179). The making, interpreting, and telling of martyrs occupied Protestants and Catholics alike in Shakespeare's England.[10] Displayed in Anglican churches, John Foxe's *Acts and Monuments* recounted gruesome tales of Marian persecution, including the burnings of the brave, eloquent Hugh Latimer and Nicholas Ridley. On the other side, Elizabeth herself oversaw the execution of at least 183 Catholics (including 123 priests) (thousands more were fined, imprisoned, tortured, and forced into exile). The horrific public deaths of Jesuits like Edmund Campion (1581) and Robert Southwell (1595) were themselves theatrical events which persecutors and victims struggled to invest with contrary meanings. They inspired writers like Thomas Alfield and William Allen, whose published accounts express their outrage and proclaim the victory of martyrdom.[11]

Ancient Roman barbarity thus affords the Elizabethan culture of martyrdom a disturbing reflection of its own religious discourses and practices. But neither Lavinia, a pathetic victim, nor Chiron and Demetrius, her tormentors, suffer, in any sixteenth-century sense, martyrdom. As Robert Southwell put it, recalling Augustine's dictum, 'the cause, not the punishment, makes the martyr'. A martyr must suffer for something, must give witness to a higher truth, to Christ. Before execution Campion on the cart quoted Paul: *Spectaculum facti sumus Deo, angelis, hominibus*', 'We are made a spectacle, or a sight, unto God, unto his angels, and unto men.'[12] The martyrological discourse in this play, interrogates the entire cultural practice of making martyrs. Removed from its theological foundations, such practice devolves to mere bloodsport and propaganda. It does not encourage the oppressed, light the way of the faithful, celebrate God's victory in human defeat. Instead, it turns the individual tragedy into a titillating spectacle that merely justifies hatred and more violence. The play exposes the dark side of the Elizabethan martyrdom industry, its hidden core of predatory self-interest. The martyr-maker Titus martyrs Chiron and Demetrius by slitting their throats on stage; and Titus himself, finally, plunges the knife into Lavinia.[13]

In *Titus Andronicus* the dismembered human body on stage also presents a barbarity that is familiar as well as alien. The display of *disjecta membra*, the cut-off tongue, heads, and hands, evokes the current controversy over relics. Article 22 of the Protestant 39 had flatly prohibited veneration of relics, as had Calvin and Luther. And no Catholic practice ever incited as much Protestant ridicule. Hugh Latimer scoffed at the relics that are actually pigs' bones. Anthony Munday took his reader on a sceptical tour of the relics in seven Roman churches, to

---

10 See John Foxe, *Acts and Monuments* (1563, often revised and reprinted); Thomas Alfield, *A True Report* (1582); William Allen, *Martyrdom of XII Priests* (1582). Helpful discussions include those of Anthony Raspa, ed., John Donne, *Pseudo-Martyr* (Montreal, 1993), pp. xiiiff.; Peter Lake and Michael Questier, 'Agency, Appropriation and Rhetoric under the Gallows: Puritans, Romanists, and the State in Early Modern England', *Past and Present*, 153 (1996), 64–107; and R. Po-Chia Hsia, *The World of Catholic Renewal, 1540–1770* (Cambridge, 1998), pp. 80–91, who supplies the figures below.

11 After reciting the grisly arithmetic and horrific stories, both sides still proclaim victory. I am deeply moved by the courage of Protestants and Catholics dying for their faith and deeply ashamed of both sides in their role as persecutors.

12 Robert Southwell, *An Epistle of Comfort*, ed. Margaret Waugh (Chicago, 1966), p. 215; Edmund Campion, as quoted by Alfield, sigs. B4v–C1.

13 It is always inconvenient to be more useful dead than alive: attending church in Suffolk, one Grimwood heard in the homily, drawn from Foxe, that his bowels had fallen out for giving false witness against a Protestant martyr, and that he had died a miserable death. Grimwood sued the preacher; he didn't win. Wood, *Athenae Oxonienses*, as quoted by Philip Caraman, ed., *The Other Face: Catholic Life Under Elizabeth I* (London, 1960), p. 29.

the 'old rotten crib' (supposedly of Christ) at Santa Maria Maggiore, for example. (That is another of Munday's lies; the crib is there today, old but certainly not rotten). Reverend James Pilkington wittily mocked the impossible logistics of Catholic credulity: 'If the relics, as arms, head, legs, scalp, hair, teeth, &c., were together in one place . . . some should have two or three heads, more legs and arms than a horse would carry.'[14] The Catholics were not amused. Veneration (*doulia*) of relics (as opposed to *latria*, worship) began as early as the second century, acquired theological justification in the works of Basil, Chrysostom, Ambrose, Augustine, Jerome, Aquinas and the Council of Trent, and flourished in the celebrations, pilgrimages and miracles of the middle ages. In the sixteenth century relics brought believers into direct, thrilling, and humbling contact with the saints. Hands and fingers were thought to have special powers; handkerchief-dipping was widespread.[15] Another Roman play, *Julius Caesar*, directly reflects the practice: Decius sees in Calpurnia's dream great men pressing 'For tinctures, stains, relics, and cognizance' (2.2.88–9); Antony imagines people dipping their 'napkins' in Caesar's 'sacred blood', bequeathing even a 'hair' as a 'rich legacy' (3.2.135–7).[16]

In 3.1 Aaron again plays contemptuous reformer to gullible and superstitious Catholics. He reports that Marcus, Lucius, or Titus may save the lives of Martius and Quintus Andronicus by chopping off a hand and sending it to the Emperor. After cutting off Titus' hand on stage, Aaron carries it away only to return it along with the heads of the two sons it was supposed to have saved. The Moor cruelly empties the body part of any meaning, emphatically denying to it any salvific power. The hand and heads on stage, however, galvanize the energy of the oppressed and become the centre of a religious ritual. The bereaved Andronici form a circle on stage and pledge future action:

> The vow is made. Come, brother, take a head,
> And in this hand the other will I bear.
> And, Lavinia, thou shalt be employed:

Bear thou my hand, sweet wench, between thy
arms.   (3.1.278–81)

The injured Andronici family reinvest the discarded relics with meaning; they take up the hand and heads as signs of their belief, love, suffering and identity.

Aaron's demythologization of relics may be gratuitously brutal but the Andronici's sanctification leads only to more brutality and revenge. The concluding banquet presents a final, parodic expression of the reliquary imagination. (It has nothing to do with the Eucharist, by the way, as is often alleged.) The commodification of human body parts leads here to the wilderness of tigers not the communion of saints. And believers always run the risk of bathos, a risk brilliantly courted and exploited in Deborah Warner's 1987 production.[17]

III SAILING TO AND FROM EPHESUS

Discovering Diana's temple at Ephesus in December 1870, British archaeologist J. T. Wood excitedly told a Turkish Mudir that he had found the remains of a great temple dedicated to worship of female, whose statue stood 40 or 50 feet high: '"Ah", said the Mudir, as if a

---

14 *Selected Sermons of Hugh Latimer*, ed. Allan G. Chester (Charlottesville, 1968), p. 23; Anthony Munday, *The English Roman Life*, ed. Philip J. Ayres (Oxford, 1980), pp. 45ff. (55); The *Works of James Pilkington*, ed. James Scholefield (Cambridge, 1842), p. 147.

15 For an overview of the history of relics see the entry in *The New Catholic Encyclopedia*; on Trent, *Canons and Decrees of the Council of Trent*, trans. H. J. Schroeder (St Louis, 1941), pp. 215–17. On Elizabethan practices see Keith Thomas, *Religion and the Decline of Magic* (New York, 1971), and Eamon Duffy, *The Stripping of the Altars: Traditional Religion in England c.1400–c.1580* (New Haven, 1992), s.v. 'relics'; David Kaula, '"Let Us Be Sacrificers": Religious Motifs in *Julius Caesar*', *Shakespeare Studies*, 14 (1981), 197–214.

16 Antony's prophecy of the commercial value of Saint Julius has proven true: in Rome today there are several restaurants located on the exact site of Caesar's assassination.

17 See Alan C. Dessen, *Shakespeare in Performance: Titus Andronicus* (Manchester, 1989), pp. 51–69.

new light had broken in on him, "they were Protestants".[18]

With some relief we may journey from the sanguinary, suffocating city of Rome to the far-flung shores of ancient Greece. Shakespeare's Rome usually hosts tragedy, his Greece, comedy and romance. This Greece is not centric but centripetal, in Sara Hanna's phrase, featuring the sea and characters who wander, through longing or expulsion.[19] The action of *Pericles*, for example, shuttles between exotic locales, Tyre, Antioch, Tarsus, Pentapolis and Myteline, before returning to Ephesus, specifically, to the temple of Artemis/Diana. This temple, the Artemision, stood for ages as an icon of Greek culture and civilization.[20] Destroyed and rebuilt several times, the temple's 127 marble columns, each sixty feet high, towered over our current Greek icon, the Parthenon in Athens. The Ephesian temple ranked as one of the seven wonders of the ancient world and received due notice in Renaissance handbooks, the lexicons of Estienne and Cooper. The Ephesians originally conceived the tutelary deity as the universal mother goddess, Isis for the Egyptians, Astarte for the Mesopotamians, Cybele for the Anatolians, Rhea for the Greeks. The Greeks later named her Artemis, the goddess who especially cared for women in their transitions (from *parthenos* to *gune*) and at childbirth. At Ephesus this Artemis combined with Anahita, the Persian goddess of waters, and Diana, Italian moon goddess, also associated with springs and fruitfulness. The surviving images of the goddess, regal, multibreasted (?), fantastic creatures adorning her person, reflect this complex syncretism and polytheism.

The celebrated Ephesian goddess undergoes further transformation in Shakespeare's *Pericles*. She loses Greek and Oriental accents to become Roman; more specifically, she is Ovid's Diana, goddess of the moon and chastity. Throughout his work Shakespeare consistently emphasizes these aspects of Diana.[21] This goddess, like Artemis, presides over female transformations

and childbirth. Accordingly, Thaisa invokes her upon awakening from the coffin; Diana herself appears to manage the final reunions between mother and daughter, wife and husband. This Diana is pre-eminently the goddess of chastity. Thaisa renounces the world, men, and sexual 'joy' (14.10) to become Diana's celibate votaress. Pericles proclaims later that his daughter, Marina, also wears the goddess' 'silver liv'ry' (22.27), meaning that she is a chaste virgin. Thinking of the moon, Shakespeare here changes Gower's 'black' to an appropriately cold symbolic colour. Thaisa describes her change in life as the donning of Diana's 'vestal liv'ry' (14.9). The reformed lord in the brothel leaves to hear the 'vestals' sing (19.7). Vestals? Unlike Gower and Twine, Shakespeare supplies the Ephesian goddess with vestal virgins, the celibate servants of another goddess, Vesta, from another place, another cult, and another time. Vestal virgins came by lot from Roman patrician families. Between the ages of six and ten

---

18 J. T. Wood, *Discoveries at Ephesus, Including the Site and Remains of the Great Temple of Diana* (Boston, 1877), p. 175.

19 Sara Hanna, 'Shakespeare's Greek World: The Temptations of the Sea', *Playing the Globe: Genre and Geography in English Renaissance Drama*, ed. John Gillies and Virginia Mason Vaughan (Madison, NJ, 1998), pp. 107–28. *Magna Graecia* provides a setting for a surprising number of works: *Venus and Adonis*, *The Comedy of Errors*, *A Midsummer Night's Dream*, *Troilus and Cressida*, *Pericles*, *The Winter's Tale*, and *The Two Noble Kinsmen*.

20 For accounts of Ephesus, the temple, and the goddess see Wood, *Discoveries*, note 15; the pertinent entries of *The Princeton Encyclopedia of Classical Sites*, ed. by Richard Stillwell (Princeton, 1976), and *Encyclopedia of Early Christianity*, ed. Everett Ferguson, 2nd edn, 2 vols. (New York, 1997); Rick Strelan, *Paul, Artemis, and the Jews in Ephesus* (Berlin, 1996); and, from a Turkish rather than Hellenic perspective, Ekrem Akurgal, *Ancient Civilizations and Ruins of Turkey*, trans. John Whybrow and Mollie Emre, 2nd edn (Istanbul, 1970), 142–71; Mehlika Seval, *Step by Step: Ephesus* (Istanbul, n.d.).

21 See Robert Kilburn Root, *Classical Mythology in Shakespeare* (1903; rpt. New York, 1965), pp. 51–6.

they entered on a thirty-year period of celibate service, during which they supervised the public festival and performed religious duties in exchange for public support and considerable privilege.

Shakespeare's anatopism continues the process of translation begun by the Greeks themselves six centuries BC. His representation is Roman in more ways than one. The chastity in Shakespeare's *Pericles* little resembles that of antiquity, a ritual requirement that protected the virgins and city from unscrupulous lovers. Ambrose, in fact, mocked vestal virginity as abstinence by contract. Heir to Roman Catholic traditions that celebrated celibacy as a victory over world, flesh and devil, as a gift of purity to the Almighty, Shakespeare here portrays chastity as moral virtue not legal requirement. Marina's purity in the brothel, as has been well remarked, refigures the similar suffering and victory of saints like Theodora, Serapia, Denise and Agnes.[22] Thaisa embraces one of Ambrose's three kinds of chastity, that of widowhood. John Gower conceives of the entrance into Diana's service as the entrance into a convent, *domum religionis*, where the widow takes a vow of chastity, *castam omni tempore vovit* (Bullough 6: 401). Twine consistently calls Diana's votaresses nuns. So, likewise, Shakespeare in his first encounter with the Apollonius story, *The Comedy of Errors*, turns the Temple into the Abbey or Priory, where Emilia, the celibate Abbess presides over the reconciliations. The common elements in all the early modern revisions – Gower, Twine, Shakespeare – are claustration for female religious (mandated by the Papal bull *Periculoso* (1298) and the Council of Trent, by the way) and celibacy. Greek *hiereia* becomes Roman vestal becomes, finally, Roman Catholic nun. Until we have better documentation of female religious life we can only guess at contemporary valences but our prejudices need disturbing. In England religious women achieved an impressive record of contemplative holiness and service to poor (often in defiance of Rome).[23]

Tim Supple's 1996 RSC *Errors* production, by the way, showed some possibilities: Emilia was not a cartoon but a woman who had suffered and who exercised spiritual authority and power.

The cultural transpositions in *Pericles*, like that of the Mudir, dozy the arithmetic of memory but are typical for Shakespeare. In another Greek play Theseus gives Hermia the choice of death or life as a 'barren sister', clothed in 'the livery of a nun', 'in shady cloister mewed', 'chanting faint hymns to the cold fruitless moon' (*MND*, 1.1.70–3). (The entire cluster of associations from *Pericles* appears here – nun, cloister, moon, livery, singing.) Theseus preaches the orthodox patristic position: 'Thrice blessed they that master so their blood / To undergo such maiden pilgrimage' (74–5). But the sermonizer lacks conviction; the church fathers did not see religious life as the rose withering on the virgin thorn. And the sermon, happily, fails. 'Single blessedness' (78) is not for everyone, certainly not for Hermia or Marina, and not ultimately for Emilia or Thaisa either. The latter two demonstrate the virtue of chastity in celibacy but end up with husbands. So too perhaps, *mutatis mutandis*, Isabella in *Measure for*

---

22 On Marina and the saints see Geoffrey Bullough, ed., *Narrative and Dramatic Sources of Shakespeare*, 8 vols. (London, 1957–75), vol. 6, p. 352; further references to Bullough are cited parenthetically in the text. On chastity and celibacy, see Peter Brown, *The Body and Society: Men, Women and Sexual Renunciation in Early Christianity* (New York, 1988); Suzanna Elm, '*Virgins of God*': *The Making of Asceticism in Late Antiquity* (Oxford, 1994); the entries in *The New Catholic Encyclopedia*.

23 See Elizabeth Makowski, *Canon Law and Cloistered Women: 'Periculoso' and its Commentators, 1298–1545* (Washington, 1997); Jo Ann Kay MacNamara, *Sisters in Arms: Catholic Nuns through Two Millennia* (Cambridge, 1996). Better understanding of these orders would also render untenable the view that the Reformation emancipated women from Catholic slavery. The long overdue re-examination of Catholic women in England and their roles should also attend to the organization and administration of gilds, the devotions to Mary and female saints, and the interesting evidence concerning female recusancy.

Measure. But there the ending disturbs and the display of fierce chastity reveals the lurking dangers of pride and self-love, the insidious threat of virtue exceeding the Aristotelian mean and becoming vice: 'More than our brother is our chastity' (2.4.184). Maybe, but that doesn't sound like anything in Matthew, Mark, Luke or John.

The relative marginality of Greek study in early Modern England makes Shakespeare's first romanization of Ephesus in *Pericles* natural enough – Artemis to Diana with vestal virgins. Ample precedent and practice also encouraged his second – the Catholicization of the town and temple. Shakespearian ontology, actually, recapitulates cultural philogeny. In the fourth century Christians razed the name Artemis from the colonnade of the Ephesian agora, carved crosses on the foreheads of Imperial statues, and erected a Cathedral to the Virgin Mary. Ephesus hosted a new universal mother, as Christians identified the city as Mary's home for the last nine years of her life and as the site of her dormition and assumption. Artemis yielded officially to Mary in 431 when the Council of Ephesus declared Mary *theotokos*, or the 'mother of God'. The city has been since then a centre of Marian pilgrimage and devotion.[24]

Early modern reformers found many additional reasons to associate idolatrous Ephesus with papal Rome. Protestant Bibles sometimes translated the Greek *naous* (Acts 19: 24) as 'shrines' instead of temples to equate pagan superstition with catholic reverence for saints. Thomas Cartwright defended the translation against Catholic objection by explaining that the word 'shrine' denoted 'a difference between places where men met for the service of God and wherein these puppets [ancient Diana and the Catholic saints] were set'. John Foxe compared the papist reverence for the mass to Ephesian worship of Diana, 'whom they thought to have come from heaven'. John Calvin saw Catholic superstition and venality in the Ephesus of Acts 19, specifically in Demetrius and the Ephesian silversmiths who

resisted Paul's preaching and continued to sell statues of Artemis/Diana: 'The Pope, the horned bishops, monks, and the whole dregs of the Papal clergy' likewise 'oppose the Gospel' and 'calmly ignore horrible blasphemies against God, so long as these do not diminish their income'. This view of the worldly papists appears in the gloss of the Geneva Bible for this episode. Elsewhere in his Commentary on Acts, Calvin compared the Ephesian exorcists to the fraudulent miracle workers of the Papacy. Both ancient and modern charlatans frequent market-places, deceive the public, and serve the devil.[25]

Shakespeare's Ephesus, where exorcisms and miracles figure importantly, reflects these controversies. In *The Comedy of Errors* Plautus's *medicus* becomes the schoolmaster/conjurer, Doctor Pinch, who attempts an exorcism on stage. 'I charge thee, Satan, housed within this man, / To yield possession to my holy prayers' (4.4.55–6). Pinch may or may not send up one R. Phinch, the author of a book explaining the false miracles and conjurations of Catholics (1590), but the episode clearly reflects the current exorcism debate, evident famously in *Lear*'s later reworking of Harsnett's *Declaration of Egregious Popish Impostures*. Outside of Ephesus, Pericles bids a 'priestly farewell' (11.68) to Thaisa before casting her coffin into the ocean. The Ephesian healer, Cerimon, a naturalist like Friar Lawrence, brings her back to life. Reunited with Thaisa at Diana's temple, Pericles thanks the gods and Cerimon for 'this great miracle' (22.81). The phrase pointedly evokes the Protestant–Catholic controversy. For Prot-

---

[24] Seval, p. 80; Marina Warner, *Alone of all her Sex: The Myth and the Cult of the Virgin Mary* (New York, 1976), pp. 87–8; Jaroslav Pelikan, *Mary through the Centuries: Her Place in the History of Culture* (New Haven, 1996), pp. 55–65, 206–7, 223.

[25] Thomas Cartwright, *A Confutation of the Rhemists' Translation, Glosses, and Annotations on the New Testament* (1618), p. 307; *Foxe's Book of Martyrs*, ed. G. A. Williamson (Boston, 1965), p. 123; Jean Calvin, *Calvin's Commentaries: The Acts of the Apostles 14–28*, trans. John W. Fraser (1966, 1984), pp. 161, 155–6.

estants, of course, miracles have 'ceased'; 'they say miracles are past' (*Henry V* 1.1.68; *AWW* 2.3.1); Catholics merely stage tricks to delude gullible spectators. Catholics argued that past and present miracles demonstrate irrefutably the authenticity of the Roman Church. The debate, Peter Milward reminds us, escalated in England and Europe around the years of *Pericles*: Justus Lipsius published a book about the miracle-working statue of the Virgin at Halle in 1604. In 1608 Robert Chambers Englished, with dedication to James I, Numan's account of Marian miracles at the shrine of Montaigue. Protestant preachers jeered at such superstition.[26]

The portrayal of religious chastity and the 'great miracle' at Ephesus, managed by Diana, Mary's Ephesian predecessor, may partly explain the attraction the play apparently held for early seventeenth-century English Catholics. *I Henry IV* may be the Shakespeare play that English Protestants, namely the descendants of Oldcastle, thought most offensively pro-Catholic in its irreverent portrayal of an early Lollard martyr. But the Catholics themselves showed more interest in *Pericles*. It formed part of the repertory (along with *King Lear*) for Cholmeley's Players, a touring recusant company which played for Catholic households. There was a performance on 2 February 1610, Candlemas, the feast that celebrated the purification of the Virgin. The quarto of *Pericles*, remarkably, appears in a 1619 catalogue of books from the English Jesuit mission in Saint-Omer, the only literary work amidst 124 devotional and polemical texts.[27] And yet, the play does not simply support either side of contemporary disputes. Spectators who witnessed Cerimon's medical skill could see in Pericles' 'great miracle' natural causality rather than divine intervention, pleasing improbability rather than wondrous impossibility.

IV THE WORD MADE ENGLISH

The revelation of divine will through an array of manifestations, artificial and natural, charac-

terizes ancient religion and modern conceptions of it. In *De divinatione* Cicero distinguished between two kinds of natural manifestation, oracles and dreams. Shakespeare supplies us with the first in *The Winter's Tale* and the second in *Cymbeline*.

So doing Shakespeare imagines antiquity as radically other. At the dawn of modernity Cicero began dismantling ancient belief as superstition, sceptically interrogating the nature of the gods, wittily debunking the art of divination. Continuing the disenchantment, Augustine declared the pagan gods to be false idols and judged the oracles to be the work of clever humans or devils. In his influential *Dictionarium* Thomas Cooper defined Delphos as the place 'where the devil gave answers by women'; Philemon Holland said much the same in his translation of Plutarch, himself a priest for thirty years at Apollo's temple at Delphi.[28] For most moderns, the oracles never were or at least had become silent, as John Milton put it, on the morning of Christ's nativity:

> The oracles are dumb,
> No voice or hideous hum
>   Runs through the archèd roof in words
>   deceiving.
> Apollo from his shrine
> Can no more divine,
>   With hollow shriek the steep of Delphos
>   leaving.

26 Peter Milward, *Religious Controversies of the Jacobean Age: A Survey of Printed Sources* (Lincoln, 1978), pp. 159–63.

27 See Charles J. Sisson, 'Shakespeare Quartos as Prompt-copies with some Account of Cholmeley's Players and a New Shakespeare Allusion', *Review of English Studies*, 18 (1942), 129–43; Willem Schrickx, "Pericles' in a Book-List of 1619 from the English Jesuit Mission and Some of the Play's Special Problems', *Shakespeare Survey 29* (Cambridge, 1976), pp. 21–32

28 Cicero, *De senectute, De amicitia, De divinatione*, tr. William Armistad Falconer, The Loeb Classical Library (1923, rpt. 1992), esp. *De divinatione* 2: 48ff.; Augustine, *The City of God*, 3: 114–29; 6: 214–31; Thomas Cooper, *Thesaurus Linguae Romanae et Britannicae* (1565; rpt. Menston, 1969), the *Dictionarium* is at the back; Philemon Holland, trans. Plutarch, *Moralia* (1603), the Explanation is also at the back.

No nightly trance or breathèd spell
Inspires the pale-eyed priest from the prophetic
   cell. (173–80)

Apollo and his pale-eyed priest are alive and well, however, in Shakespeare's Delphos.[29] In *The Winter's Tale* Cleomenes and Dion note the delicate climate and sweet air of the fertile isle. The remark the praiseworthy temple, the 'celestial habits' of the attendants, the 'solemn, and unearthly' ceremony of sacrifice (3.1.1–8). Far from being silent the oracle speaks in an 'ear-deaf'ning voice', 'kin to Jove's thunder' (9–10). In *Cymbeline* Jove himself 'descends in thunder and lightning' (5.5.186 *sd*). In Posthumus's dream vision mythological accoutrements become stage spectacle: the god descends on an eagle and throws a thunderbolt; fulminating thus, he ascends.

The vivid colour of these divinations portrays ancient revelation as alien and mysterious. Accordingly, productions of *The Winter's Tale* in the nineteenth century emphasized its ancient Greek setting. In 1856 Charles Kean, for example, precisely located the action in 330 BC and treated the oracle as the 'cornerstone' of the play.[30] And yet, Apollo functions in the familiar universe of a later dispensation, one featuring original sin, the 'hereditary' imposition (1.2.76–7), Whitsun pastorals, Judas Iscariot, the Prodigal son, and Leontes's 'saint-like sorrow' (5.1.2). The play departs from its source, Green's *Pandosto*, to conclude in a chapel where the Pauline Paulina restores Hermione, a 'sainted spirit' (5.1.57), to her penitent husband. Shakespeare's Apollo presides over Leontes's spiritual drama, imaged at least once in pointedly Catholic terms: Leontes says proleptically to Camillo: 'priest-like, thou / Hast cleansed my bosom, I from thee departed / Thy penitent reformed' (1.2.239–41). (Protestants emphatically denied the priest any sacramental function in Penance.) The ancient world of *Cymbeline* likewise includes mention of a chalice, holy water, orisons, and the prohibition against self-slaughter. Cymbeline, Posthumus, and Innogen

act in various dramas of sin and redemption. Jupiter himself echoes the Messianic prophecies (esp. Ezekiel 17.3–4, 22; 31.3–12) in a play set in the time of the Nativity and universal peace.[31]

These well-remarked transformations provide context for a more fundamental act of accommodation. Contrary to classical practice, the humanist imagination perceives the divine word as text, as the word written to be read. The ancient *oraculum*, from *ora*, mouth, was by definition, the word spoken, a divine utterance. The priestesses at Apollo's temples answered questions in viva voce.[32] Greene's priest, by contrast, instructs the questioners to pick up a scroll of parchment behind the altar, lettered in gold, and carry it sealed to Pandosto (Bullough, 8: 169–70). Shakespeare similarly redefines the oracle as an epistle with secret contents, 'sealed-up', 'by the hand delivered / Of great Apollo's priest' (3.2.126–7). An officer ceremoniously breaks the seal and reads the oracle aloud:

29 Terence Spencer, 'Shakespeare's Isle of Delphos', *Modern Language Review*, 47 (1952), 199–202; Spencer observes that Shakespeare views this Greek location (like Ephesus) through Roman lenses, this time through Virgil, *Aeneid* 3. On Apollo in the play see David Bergeron, 'The Apollo Mission in *The Winter's Tale*', *The Winter's Tale: Critical Essays*, ed. by Maurice Hunt (New York, 1995), pp. 361–79.

30 Dennis Bartholomeusz, *The Winter's Tale in Performance in England and America* (Cambridge, 1982), p. 82.

31 For tendentious enumeration of the Christian elements, see H. Mutschmann and K. Wentersdorf, *Shakespeare and Catholicism* (New York, 1952); see also Naseeb Shaheen, *Biblical References in Shakespeare's Plays* (Newark, 1999); for Christian readings in the critical history of the plays see Maurice Hunt, ed., *The Winter's Tale: Critical Essays* (New York, 1995), pp. 23–31; Henry E. Jacobs, *The Garland Shakespeare Bibliographies: Cymbeline* (New York, 1982), pp. xxxiii–xxxv.

32 See Joseph Fontenrose, *The Delphic Oracle: Its Responses and Operations with a Catalogue of Responses* (Berkeley, 1978), pp. 212–24; 'All records of responses that mention the Pythia represent her speaking directly and clearly to the inquirer' (212); evidence for replies copied and sealed is late and scanty (217–18). Of the 72 historically verified oracles at Delphi not one is obscure or ambivalent.

'Hermione is chaste, Polixenes blameless', etc. (132). The ancient dream vision, moreover, communicated divine will directly, through images, to the sleeping recipient. Jupiter, however, somehow delivers to Posthumus in *Cymbeline* a text, variously described as 'tablet' (5.5.203), 'book' (227), 'label' (5.6.432), and a lettered 'oracle' (452). Posthumus wakes and reads his dream vision: 'Whenas a lion's whelp shall, etc.' (5.5.232–8). The soothsayer later re-reads the text publicly (5.6.437–44).

Ancient divination here becomes holy writing, or Holy Writ, *scriptus* not *dictus*, in a word Scripture. Shakespeare is not so much alluding to the Bible as employing the pre-eminently available cultural category for the communication of the divine word. Biblical writing, of course, lay at the heart of every early modern religious controversy and itself engendered fierce dispute. This dispute sometimes turned out to be a matter of heresy, that is, a matter of life and death. Innogen evokes the charged contemporary context herself; she throws away Posthumus's letters: 'The scriptures of the loyal Leonatus, / All turned to heresy? Away, away, / Corrupters of my faith' (3.4.81–3). And one of Shakespeare's three allusions to burning heretics occurs in the ancient world of *The Winter's Tale*: Leontes threatens to have Paulina burnt: she retorts: 'I care not. / It is an heretic that makes the fire, / Not she which burns in 't' (2.3.114–16). Such slight fissures reveal the underlying categories of apprehension.

In these plays the word made text finds few apt readers. Leontes denies and blasphemes: 'There is no truth at all i' th' oracle . . . This is mere falsehood' (3.2.139–40). After coming to his senses, he shows no understanding of its prediction: 'the King shall live without an heir if that which is lost be not found' (134–5). Posthumus too reads uncomprehendingly: ''Tis still a dream, or else such stuff as madmen / Tongue, and brain not; either both or nothing' (5.5.239–40). In both plays Shakespeare depicts human incomprehension of revelation in lin-

guistic terms, as a problem of Latin translation. Before the word became text, before it became English, it was Latin. Paulina and Hermione in waiting understand, as Leontes does not, that Apollo's oracle refers to Perdita, Latin for 'the lost one' [feminine]. 'I, / Knowing by Paulina that the oracle / Gave hope thou wast in being, have preserved / Myself to see the issue' (5.3.126–9). In *Cymbeline* the Roman soothsayer uses Latin, his native tongue, presumably, for that excruciating bit of exegesis:

> Thou, Leonatus, art the lion's whelp.
> The fit and apt construction of thy name,
> Being *leo-natus*, doth import so much.
> (*To Cymbeline*) The piece of tender air thy
>   virtuous daughter,
> Which we call '*mollis aer*' and '*mollis aer*'
> We term it '*mulier*', (*to Posthumus*) which '*mulier*' I
>   divine
> Is this most constant wife.   (5.6.445–51)

We may well mutter with Cymbeline 'This hath some seeming' (454). Pope thought the vision and prophecy an interpolation, 'foisted in afterwards for mere show'; neither survived the adaptations of Thomas D'Urfey (1682), David Garrick (1761) and George Bernard Shaw (1937).[33] In both plays, however, the etymologizing essentially untranslates the word made English back into Latin: that which is lost becomes Perdita, the lion's whelp, Leonatus, and tender air, *mulier*, or Innogen. The Latin word becomes incarnate in the living flesh of the persons on stage. The process reveals what Socrates in *Cratylus* called *orthoteta tina ton onomaton* (383.1), 'the inner correctness of names', i.e. Latin names, here the essential coherence, intelligibility, and truth of divine language.

The soothsayer's explication in *Cymbeline* can be more comical than triumphant in

---

33 For Alexander Pope, see Brian Vickers, ed., *Shakespeare: The Critical Heritage*, 6 vols. (London, 1974–81), vol. 2, p. 418; on the adaptations see Ann Thompson, '*Cymbeline*'s Other Endings', *The Appropriation of Shakespeare: Post-Renaissance Reconstructions of the Works and the Myth*, ed. Jean I. Marsden (New York, 1991), pp. 203–20.

production. But the depiction of divine revelation as Latin Scripture translated problematically into English reflects the deepest religious realities and anxieties of the age. Gone forever were the mythical days of the Septuagint, when the seventy-two translators of the Hebrew Old Testament to Greek each produced in seventy-two days one and the same supernally correct text. Controversy over the text and meaning of the Vulgate lies at the epicentre of early modern religious dispute. Erasmus dared to apply Lorenzo Valla's notes and the new philology to Jerome's sanctified Latin. Fuelled by the Reformation, translations of Scripture into the vernaculars swept across Europe, hotly contested and defended.[34] In England More paradigmatically branded Tyndale's translation a corruption that should be burned. Tyndale turned church into congregation, charity into love, priest into senior, penance into repentance, grace into favour, confession into knowledge, idols into images, anointing into smearing, consecration into charming, sacraments into ceremonies, and ceremonies into witchcraft. To Tyndale's invocation of 'circumstances' as a defence, More retorted: 'For so he may translate the world into a football if he join therewith certain circumstances'; he may then say it is 'this round rolling football that men walk upon and ships sail on'.[35] Philology and theology clash constantly throughout period polemics, particularly at the times of biblical publication – the Geneva Bible (in England, 1576), the Rheims New Testament (1582), and about the time of these plays the King James version (1611), which, incidentally, restored some of the old readings under Bishop Bancroft's direct orders.

Deciphering the divine word, the English court in *Cymbeline* faces difficulties, hermeneutic as well as textual and linguistic. Its literal sense understood, the word made English continues to baffle auditors. No amount of Latin learning can explain the prophecy about the cedar, its lopped branches jointed to the old stock, and Britain's consequent prosperity. The Roman soothsayer, instead, must employ not another language, but another strategy of reading: the cedar and branches stand for Cymbeline and his sons, now restored. Such a strategy, of course, traditionally characterized biblical exegesis, the medieval four-fold schema (literal, moral, allegorical, anagogical) having yielded to the simple distinction between literal and figurative signification. As Gregory Martin put it, glossing Galatians 4: 24: 'the holy scriptures have beside the literal sense, a deeper, spiritual, and more principal meaning, which is not only to be taken of the holy words, but of the very facts and persons reported'.[36]

The reading of scripture in *Cymbeline*, so alien to us, stages a deeply pervasive and widely contested cultural practice. From Tyndale on Protestants revered 'the plain text and literal sense', but everyone, from time to time, looked beyond. (No one could read the erotic Song of Songs literally; it had to be a metaphor for something.) Like the Soothsayer, the Geneva Bible explained figuratively the Ezekiel passage echoed in Jupiter's prophecy: the plucked branch of the cedar stands for a king, Jeconiah; the replanted branch, for a restoration, that of the church. Calvin, who read the passage similarly, explained: 'God sometimes spoke enigmatically when unwilling to be understood

---

[34] See Eugene F. Rice, Jr, *Saint Jerome in the Renaissance* (Baltimore, 1985); Jaroslav Pelikan, *The Reformation of the Bible / The Bible of the Reformation* (New Haven, 1996); Debora Kuller Shuger, *The Renaissance Bible: Scholarship, Sacrifice, and Subjectivity* (Berkeley, 1994). One thinks of Luther's notorious translation of Luke 1. 28: 'gracious' or 'dear' Mary instead of Mary, 'full of grace'; and his addition to Romans 3. 28 : 'a person is justified by faith *alone* apart from works'. See Roland H. Worth, Jr, *Bible Translations: A History through Source Documents* (Jefferson, North Carolina, 1992), pp. 44–7.

[35] *The Confutation of Tyndale's Answer*, ed. by Louis A. Schuster, et al., *The Complete Works of Saint Thomas More*, 15 vols. (New Haven, 1963–90), vol. 8, pp. 144, 166; cf. *A Dialogue Concerning Heresies*, vol. 6, pp. 284–93.

[36] Gregory Martin, *New Testament* (Rheims, 1582), p. 508.

by the impious and disbelieving.'[37] People, of course, disagreed vehemently about what was enigmatic and who was impious. The transubstantiation controversy featured the period's most celebrated clash between literal and figurative readings. Reversing their usual positions, Catholics insisted that the words of the consecration, *Hoc est enim corpus meum*, 'This is my body', expressed literal truth; Protestants insisted that the speech was figurative. Thomas More attacked with characteristic brilliance and verve: Is it likely that despite his promises of guidance (Matthew 28.20: 'I am with you all your days'; John 16.23: 'The Holy Spirit will teach you all truth') Christ fooled men for 1,500 years into doing pointless good works and into believing in the Eucharist, only at last to reveal to Huskyn and Zwinglius, who both broke their vows of chastity, that the body and blood of Christ is nothing but 'very wine and therewith good cakebread alone'? The young, brilliant, and doomed reformer John Frith rose to the Lord Chancellor's challenge: 'How can the substance of Christ's body be in many places at once? Is it subject to mould and decay? Do you ingest your saviour into your bowels and pass him from your body? Christ says that he is a vine and a door too, and no one takes that literally.'[38] The man for all seasons had Frith burned at the stake.

For some the use of a Roman soothsayer, who has prayed and fasted, to adjudicate literal and figurative meanings and to explicate holy scripture may suggest preference for Catholic authority over Protestant democratization. And this may corroborate the current reading of Cymbeline's concession of tribute as expressing James's irenic wish for reconciliation with Rome. But the soothsayer is wrong about his own dream vision: the eagle flying into sunlight does not portend Roman victory. Human writing – Iachimo's frenzied scribbling and Posthumus' letter – requires explication, as well as divine. The play clearly distinguishes between the admirable ancient Rome of Augustus and Lucius and the modern corrupt

one of Iachimo. And though James may have been a pacifist who negotiated secretly with Pope Clement for Catholic support and who encouraged Catholic suitors for his children, he regarded the papacy with distrust and hostility. In the years following the Gunpowder plot, his *Triplici Nodo, triplex cuneus* (1608), *Apology*, and *Premonition* (1609) strenuously denied the Pope the right to intervene in temporal affairs. The response from Cardinal Bellarmine and ensuing debate attracted much attention, including John Donne's witty *Ignatius His Conclave*. In this context England in *Cymbeline* pays tribute to classical not Catholic Rome, particularly to its *virtus*, reincarnated in the princes, and to its culture and Latin language.

The drifted humanist imagination apprehends the other as other and as itself. The art of imagining the other in theatre begins with an intentional distancing that creates a space for contemporary epistemes to fill; it automatically entails investments of understanding and identification. So *Lucrece* sometimes has a Christian soul; *Titus* reflects the contemporary practice of making martyrs; *The Winter's Tale* and *Cymbeline* transform ancient divinations to Scripture. And so, at times, Catholic practices inform Shakespeare's ancient world: the Romans value oaths and relics; Diana's servitors practise a nun's chastity; in Ephesus a miracle occurs; authorities explain sacred writing to bewildered laity in *Cymbeline* and *The Winter's Tale*. Throughout Shakespeare's ancient world contemporary religious controversies inform

---

[37] *Tyndale's Old Testament*, ed. by David Daniell (New Haven, 1992), p. 8; *The Bible* (London, 1576), pp. 321–2; *Calvin's Commentaries 5: Ezekiel and Daniel* (Grand Rapids, Mich., 1970), pp. 261–71 (261). See also John Boe, '*Cymbeline* and Ezekiel', *NQ*, 42 (1995), 331–4.

[38] More, *The Confutation of Tyndale's Answer, Complete Works*, vol. 8, pp. 640–1; Cf. his *Letter Against Frith, Complete Works*, vol. 7, pp. 233ff.; John Frith, *A Christian Sentence*, rpt. as Appendix C, *Complete Works of Saint Thomas More*, vol. 7, pp. 428ff.; also his, *A Book . . . Answering unto M. More's Letter* (1533).

action. The forbidden, other religion here functions as a potent fund of myth, ritual, and concern that defines the ancient other, inflecting situation and charging conflict. The allusions do not amount to a manifesto of the playwright's personal belief – biographical Catholicity – or to a discursive body of dogma advocated openly or secretly – literary Catholicity. Instead they constitute a cultural Catholicity, which in Shakespeare's ancient Rome and Greece, has real presence.

'HE DREW THE LITURGY, AND FRAMED THE RITES': THE CHANGING ROLE OF RELIGIOUS DISPOSITION IN SHAKESPEARE'S RECEPTION

PÉTER DÁVIDHÁZI

For Garrick was a worshipper himself;
He drew the Liturgy, and framed the rites
And solemn ceremonial of the day,
And call'd the world to worship on the banks
Of Avon famed in song.[1]

There is no more vulgar mistake, so I was taught, than taking metaphors literally or trying to check the truth-value of a poetic statement, especially out of context. Yet reading these lines of William Cowper's *The Task*, one is tempted to make an exception to see whether their literal meaning, if such a thing can be construed from a poem at all, will stand up to close scrutiny, and in what sense Garrick might be considered the founder of a new quasi-religion, initiating a newly formed community into its liturgy and ritual. In other words the question is whether Cowper's lines can be used as a heuristic device to reveal the underlying quasi-religious pattern of the otherwise miscellaneous happenings at the 1769 Stratford Jubilee, and to discover the changing yet discernible role of latent religious attitudes omnipresent in our various dealings with Shakespeare ever since.[2]

In view of this question Garrick's religious sensibility deserves more attention than it usually receives. The most amply documented biography tells us that the Lichfield of his childhood was dominated by the army and the church, hence much of the intellectual life of this cathedral town centred in the cathedral close, complementing the yearly cycle of

services in the cathedral; we may also learn that Garrick inherited his place in this community because his mother was a granddaughter and daughter of vicars choral, he also had three uncles who were vicars choral and several of his acquaintances were sons of vicars, and his mentor, Gilbert Walmesley, was registrar of the ecclesiastical court and lived in the bishop's palace.[3] With this milieu in mind, it sounds much less convincing that Garrick's Huguenot origin 'meant far less to him and the community than that he was living in a garrison town, and that for thirty years his father was an officer in three of the top-ranking regiments in the aristocracy of the established army'.[4] This statement becomes even more doubtful when we are reminded (in the same biography) that family origins and familial loyalties were taken very seriously in eighteenth-century Lichfield.

---

[1] William Cowper, *The Task*, Bk VI, lines 678–82. *The Poems of William Cowper: 1782–1785* (Oxford, 1995), vol. 2, eds. John D. Baird and Charles Ryskamp, p. 254.

[2] As this paper does not allow room for tracing the genesis of the entire quasi-religious paradigm, which I tried to analyse comprehensively in my recent book *The Romantic Cult of Shakespeare: Literary Reception in Anthropological Perspective* (Basingstoke, London, and New York, 1998), it is restricted to some hitherto unexamined aspects of the Garrickian tradition.

[3] George Winchester Stone, Jr and George M. Kahrl, *David Garrick: A Critical Biography* (Carbondale, London, Amsterdam, 1979), pp. 7–9.

[4] Stone and Kahrl, *David Garrick*, pp. 3–4.

Though once in England the family apparently did not (or perhaps could not) keep in touch with any Huguenots in France, and young David seems to have learned his French at school rather than at home, we may still assume that the traumatic vicissitudes of his persecuted Huguenot ancestry left behind a haunting memory that turned into a family tradition, perhaps too deeply interiorized even to talk about. As is well known, the name Garrick is an anglicized form of its original Garrique, which in turn refers back to 'garrigues', the French name of the barren areas east of Bordeaux where David's grandfather was a wine merchant before the revocation of the Edict of Nantes in 1685 compelled him to escape to England, without his infant son who was too little for the dangerous journey over the sea and was brought to England secretly in 1687 by a courageous nurse. Garrick never referred to the sufferings of his persecuted family, not even in 1751 when he paid his first visit to France and recorded his experiences in his diary. But it is precisely the perfect unbrokenness of his silence that should make us suspect that he may have had something to be silent about. That he confessed in a letter to John Hoadly to have returned 'safe & sound from Paris & as true an Englishman as Ever'[5] was later interpreted as an indication that he had never exploited or even mentioned his French or Huguenot origin at home or abroad,[6] which is probably true, but one could also ask why did he feel the need (in an otherwise humorous letter) to reassert his Englishness after a journey which made him retrace the steps of his grandfather for the first time in his life.

His silence speaks volumes when we discover the religiosity implicit in some of his seemingly playful and profane works. Assuming an awareness of his Huguenot ancestry and remembering the milieu of his youth it is little wonder that many of Garrick's works rely on a latent system of religious analogies, and that even his letters are interspersed with allusions to the history of persecution. 'I heard Yesterday to my Surprize, that the Country People did not seem to relish our *Jubilee*, that they look'd upon it to be *popish* & that we shd raise ye Devil, & wt not', he complained to William Hunt in August 1769, 'I suppose this may be a joke, – but after all my trouble, pains labor & Expence for their Service & ye honor of ye County, I shall think it very hard, if I am not to be receiv'd kindly by them – how ever I shall not be the first Martyr for my Zeal.'[7] When similar analogies were made by somebody else, Garrick responded with a remarkably natural ease that reveals his familiarity with this mode of thinking. At the beginning of his acting career in 1741 he wrote a poem *Upon Mr Quin's saying that Garrick was a new religion, that Whitfield was followed for a time, but they would all come to church again*, in which one can see not only his playful readiness to think in terms of religious history about the rival schools of acting, but also his affinity to the explicitly Protestant role of a religious innovator.

> Pope Quin, who damns all churches but his own,
> Cries out that heresy corrupts the town;
> That Whitfield-Garrick has misled the age,
> And taints the sound religion of the stage;
> But soon they'll see their ignorance and sin,
> And then they'll all come back to Church and
>   Quin.
> Thou great infallible, forbear to roar,
> Thy bulls and errors are revered no more:
> When doctrines meet with general approbation,
> It is not heresy but reformation.[8]

There may be something in this lighthearted counter-attack, in this almost flippant treatment of a subject once so ominous for his family, that only a securely positioned third-generation

---

[5] David Garrick to The Reverend Doctor John Hoadly, July 1751. *The Letters of David Garrick*, eds. David M. Little and George M. Kahrl, 3 vols. (London, 1963), vol. 1, p. 167.

[6] Stone and Kahrl, *David Garrick*, pp. 293–4.

[7] David Garrick to William Hunt (August 16, 1769). *The Letters of David Garrick*, vol. 2, p. 660.

[8] David Garrick, *Selected Verse*, ed. J. D. Hainsworth (University of New England, Armidale, Australia 1981), p. 1.

refugee could afford. But we can easily imagine or even expect the author of this poem to draw the liturgy and frame the rites of a literary cult.

The first intriguing paradox to observe is that, in the quasi-religious context of the Jubilee, Garrick was facilitating a delicate retrieval of attitudes and gestures that had been stigmatized and condemned as idolatry by the Huguenot movement, this 'révolution symbolique' of French Calvinists who resorted to a 'construction théorique de l'iconoclasme' to underpin a 'politique de l'iconoclasme'.[9] Earlier manifestations of his religious sensibility had shown a similarly clear contrast with the austere Huguenot ideals. Visiting Paris in 1751, he lavished his superlatives mainly on those churches which offered beautiful statues and paintings to the eye. 'We went to *Notre Dame* the most splendid Church I ever saw & I think the *Mary wth ye Dead Christ* on her lap a most fine piece of sculpture I was not much struck with ye *Paintings* but was delighted with ye *Bas relieves* in wood which are above ye stalls in ye choir [. . .] Went to Chartreux & was much pleas'd with the paintings in ye Church & ye Cloister [. . .] then to *St Germain des Pres*, they have some good modern pictures & ye altar very elegant [. . .] *L'Eglise des Carmelites* is a most noble sight, I mean for the Pictures, particularly *Le Brun's Madgalen* & *Guido's Salutation*, the expression of ye first is admirable.'[10] Characteristically, he was eager to see the procession of the *Fête de Dieu* in Paris, by then a distinctly Catholic festival and pageant in honour of the Real Presence of Christ in the sacrament of the altar, and all his comment was that it was 'not so magnificent' as the one he had seen 'in Lisbon on ye same occasion'.[11] (It seems very probable that the Shakespearian procession and pageant both at the Stratford Jubilee and in its theatrical afterpiece version owe some of their characteristics to these foreign inspirations.) Bearing Garrick's iconoclastic ancestry in mind it is also paradoxical that he built a temple to Shakespeare in his garden at Hampton in 1755 to house Roubillac's statue of the Bard. It

is ironic that the Jubilee grew out of the Stratford magistrate's idea that Garrick should present the town with a statue of Shakespeare and a portrait of himself, and it is even more ironic when we read his ode (*An Ode upon Dedicating a Building and Erecting a Statue to Shakespeare*), especially the wording of its justification: 'To what blest genius of the isle, / Shall Gratitude her tribute pay, / Decree the festive day, / Erect a statue, and devote the pile? [. . .] 'Tis he! 'tis he! / The god of our idolatry!'[12] Perhaps his Huguenot ancestry explains, partly at least, why the last phrase, a paraphrase of Juliet's adoring invocation to Romeo, could haunt Garrick for so long, why it had to surface repeatedly in his correspondence,[13] before its variants were used by others for diverse purposes ranging from the affirmative to the subversive.[14] Despite all his attempts to tone it down playfully, Garrick himself must have felt something of the paradoxical nature of his position as founder of a quasi-religious liturgy and ritual his persecuted ancestors, presumably with less humour for such matters, may have considered either idolatrous practices or at best their dubious parody. His Mulberry tree ballad, sung both at the Stratford Jubilee and later in its Drury Lane version by several actors, begins with a momentous stanza that already contained (and sought to sanctify) the most essential doctrines and behavioural patterns of an incipient literary cult:

---

9 Olivier Christin, *Une révolution symbolique: L'iconoclasme huguenot et la reconstruction catholique* (Paris, 1991), pp. 35–61.
10 *The Diary of David Garrick: Being a Record of his Memorable Trip to Paris in 1751*, ed. Ryllis Clair Alexander (New York, 1928), pp. 8, 10, 13.
11 *The Diary of David Garrick*, pp. 12, 76.
12 D[avid] G[arrick], *An Ode upon Dedicating a Building, and Erecting a Statue, to Shakespeare, at Stratford upon Avon* (London, 1769), pp. 1–2.
13 See for example his letter to Jean Baptiste Antoine Suard, October 15, 1769. *The Letters of David Garrick*, vol. 2, p. 668.
14 See my *The Romantic Cult of Shakespeare*, pp. 53–4.

Behold this fair goblet, 'twas carved from the tree
Which, O my sweet Shakespear, was planted by
    thee.
As a relic I kiss it and bow at the shrine,
What comes from thy hand must be ever divine!

And this first stanza, like each of the following seven, was followed by a hymnic refrain, providing a blueprint of a new ritual, and urging everybody present to take part:

All shall yield to the Mulberry-tree,
Bend to thee,
Blest Mulberry,
Matchless was he
Who planted thee,
And thou like him immortal be!
           (Part 1, scene 3, lines 126–35)[15]

Bow at the shrine, *bend* to the mulberry tree, and *kiss* the mulberry goblet as a relic. The line 'What comes from thy hand must be ever divine!' originally referred to the goblet made of the wood of the mulberry tree planted by Shakespeare's own hand, yet its *must* and *ever* soon became the ultimate imperative of many interpretative strategies or evaluative acts in literary criticism as well. The same applies to the epithet of the refrain: 'matchless' and 'divine'. In the last third of the century more and more critics would declare that Shakespeare is beyond criticism and cannot be compared to any other artist. The ensuing tradition of a quasi-theodicy in criticism has been working on the unquestionable assumption that Shakespeare is always right, and that (therefore) we can give a seemingly flawed text the benefit of the doubt, based on our certainty about an unerring super-intellect. Theodicy is argumentative self-submission, the verbal equivalent to bowing, bending, even kneeling.

Unfortunately we don't know exactly how those singing the first stanza (Vernon in Stratford or Bannister in Drury Lane) did the bowing, neither do we know exactly what kind of bending (to the tree) Garrick sought to encourage. But most probably it is significant that Garrick did not propagate *kneeling* in his ballad. Not that bending, bowing, and kneeling

have no common denominator. Whatever their differences, there is a spatial movement of symbolic importance in all of them: lowering oneself in front of a respected other. To bend, and especially to bend the knee (or knees) in front of somebody is to present an emblematic self-portrait of humility, of not being on the same level, of admitting one's inferiority, submission, or obedience. In the Old Testament bending the knee or kneeling down expresses respect (Genesis 41. 43; 2 Kings 1. 13) or an acknowledgement of being conquered (Isaiah 45. 23). A traditional gesture of prayer, kneeling accentuates devout adoration and humble imploring with enhanced intensity (1 Kings 8. 54), and Solomon would kneel down on a high brazen scaffold to pray (2 Chronicles 6. 13). Bearing in mind the far-reaching implications of bowing versus kneeling in the context of a literary cult, it is important to remember that all the biblical gestures of kneeling (bowing or bending the knees, falling on one's knees, falling to the ground, falling on one's face) were to be preserved for revering God and/or his true representatives as opposed to idols. The Lord tells Elijah that he would spare the life of seven thousand people, that is 'all the knees which have not bowed unto Baal, and every mouth which hath not kissed him.' (1 Kings 19. 18). After Elijah proved by a miracle that he was a man of God, a captain 'fell on his knees before him' (2 Kings 1. 13). The God of the Old Testament prescribes the bending of knees for everybody in front of him: 'I am God and *there is* none else [. . .] unto me every knee shall bow, every tongue shall swear' (Isaiah 45. 22–3). In the New Testament this exclusive prerogative is extended to include Jesus himself: 'Wherefore God also hath highly exalted him, and given him a name which is above every name: That at the name of Jesus every knee

---

[15] *The Plays of David Garrick: Garrick's Own Plays, 1767–1775*, vol. 2, eds. Harry William Pedicord and Fredrick Louis Bergmann (Carbondale and Edwardsville, 1980), pp. 113–14.

should bow' (Philippians 2. 9–11). Nevertheless kneeling had been a sensitive and controversial issue in what has been recently called 'the body politic'[16] of post-Reformation England, and it had been no less problematic for the Huguenot refugees either. (When the French church of the Savoy chapel in London came into being in 1661 under the protection of King Charles, the new congregation was expected to submit to the Church of England, but it preserved such Calvinist forms of ritual as those practised in the island of Jersey, where the inhabitants received Communion standing, and were thought by the Anglican Peter Heylyn to be a 'stubborn generation, stiffer in the knees than any elephant, who will neither bow the knee to the name of Jesus, nor kneel to Him in His Sacrament'.)[17]

It is in juxtaposition with these biblical imperatives and Calvinist reservations that the suggestions of Garrick's Jubilee reveal their significance for the future norms of symbolic gestures in a literary cult. Decades later (20 February 1795) Boswell, who had heard Garrick's admonition to bend and had seen the kissing of the goblet as relic, would kneel before the Ireland forgeries and kiss them, imitating (perhaps unwittingly) a ritual pattern he had seen at the Jubilee, authorized by Garrick's quasi-liturgical text and accepted by the hundreds on the spot and many more afterwards at the 147 Drury Lane performances of the extremely successful stage version between 1769 and 1776.[18] Revealing his awareness of biblical analogies, Boswell reputedly performed this saying that 'I shall now die contented, since I have lived to witness the present day', adding that 'I now kiss the invaluable relics of our bard: and thanks to God that I have lived to see them!'[19] Boswell's exclamation has often been quoted, but as the whole episode has usually been considered merely as a curious attempt of deception with 'no significance for the history of the interpretation of Shakespeare',[20] it has passed unnoticed that Boswell alluded to the biblical Simeon's 'Lord, now lettest thou thy servant depart in peace, according to thy word:

For mine eyes have seen thy salvation' (Luke 2. 29–30), and that his allusion may epitomize latent transcendental analogies at work in late eighteenth-century attitudes to Shakespeare, attitudes significantly prevalent in contemporary (and later) interpretations of his works as well. Boswell's behaviour and words are closer to their biblical archetype than Garrick's had been, but the lasting impact of the Garrickian example is no less discernible than the difference. Whereas Garrick's ballad was initiating the audience into the quasi-ritualistic bending and bowing, Boswell, with his characteristic attraction to ritual symbolism and to all the spectacular forms of worship, actually knelt down, almost as if to illustrate that he had never been satisfied with the share of religious elements in the Jubilee. On 6 September 1769, on the first day of the celebrations, when Thomas Arne conducted his oratorio *Judith* in Holy Trinity Church, Boswell called the performance 'admirable' but added that he would have wished for prayers and a sermon as well. 'It would have consecrated our Jubilee, to begin it with Devotion, with gratefully adoring the Supreme Father of all Spirits from whom cometh every good and perfect Gift.'[21] As a biographer rightly observed, it was one of the main attractions of the Church of England for Boswell that 'its services possessed a liturgical

---

16 Lori Anne Ferrell, 'Kneeling and the Body Politic'. In *Religion, Literature, and Politics in Post-Reformation England, 1540–1688*, eds. Donna B. Hamilton and Richard Strier (Cambridge, 1996), pp. 70–92.

17 Quoted by Robin D. Gwynn, *Huguenot Heritage: The History and Contribution of the Huguenots in Britain* (London and New York, 1988), p. 98.

18 See *The Plays of David Garrick: Garrick's Own Plays, 1767–1775*, p. 333; *Boswell's London Journal, 1762–1763*, ed. Frederick A. Pottle (New York, 1950), pp. 256–7.

19 William Henry Ireland, *Confessions* (London, 1805), p. 96.

20 *Shakespeare: The Critical Heritage*, 6 vols., ed. Brian Vickers (London, Boston, and Henley, 1974–81), vol. 6, p. 65.

21 A letter published in *The Public Advertiser*, 16 September 1769.

and ceremonial drama (though not so highly pitched as in the Catholic Church)';[22] it was mostly his longing for grand ritual that motivated his attempt to convert to Catholicism as well, something Garrick with all his (not exactly Huguenot) love of processions and artistic church ornaments would have never contemplated.

When they travel abroad, the difference between their attitudes to Catholic ritual is telling. Whereas Garrick's 1751 diary reflects a detached curiosity about the regionally changing attitudes to religion in France,[23] and a keen aesthetic interest in the paintings and statues of the Paris churches, but no religious emotions of his own, Boswell's private papers during his 1765 tour in Italy (a few years before the Jubilee) explicitly, indeed eloquently testify that he was deeply moved by the High Mass in St Peter's and felt his own faith reassured. He mentions kneeling, whether that of himself or other people, without reservations, as the appropriate expression of reverence before God or the Pope. 'On Easter I was in St Peter's, and in that superb temple I saw noble and mystical adorations offered to the Supreme Being', he recalled in a letter to Rousseau on 3 October 1765, adding that he was overwhelmed by an ecstatic yet noble feeling he had never experienced before. 'I was penetrated with devotion. I was sure that the revelation given by Jesus was true; and when I saw the Christian High Priest with venerable magnificence elevate before the Eternal Justice a Sacrifice for the sins of the whole world, I fell to my knees among the throng of my fellow men who remained fixed in respectful silence; I struck my breast, and with all the ardour of which my soul was capable I prostrated myself at the feet of my Father "who is in Heaven", convinced that [. . .] he would one day lead all his creatures to happiness.'[24] Though he admittedly did not understand all its symbolism, he was greatly impressed by the procession on 25 March, the Annunciation of the Blessed Virgin Mary, when the Pope (Clement XIII) was first 'carried on a

magnificent chair decorated with a figure of the Holy Ghost', then the congregation 'knelt before his Holiness' and after 'he had performed certain sacred rites [. . .], people kissed his slipper'.[25] On his visit to the holy shrine at Loretto he felt the nearness of things sacred and miraculous so strongly that it prevailed over his otherwise sceptical disposition. 'I am in a most pleasing solemn frame and upon my soul I cannot refuse some devotion to this miraculous Habitation', he confided to John Johnston from Loretto, writing in the church itself; and although the house in which the virgin Mary had lived was said to have been brought to Italy from Nazareth by angels, he declared himself a sceptic devout enough *here* to accept its authenticity as a perfectly plausible example of divine 'interpositions'. 'The crowd of Pilgrims and the various sacred appearances now around me have made a strong impression upon my mind and fill me with a serious awe which I greatly preferr to all the levity of mirth.'[26] The lasting impact of the Catholic instruction Boswell received in 1760 was to be recorded in his journal of 20 March, 1768, the year before the Jubilee, in a way that testifies to an iconophile religious sensibility which uses the external as a means to perceive the spiritual. As he recalls, the dreariness of presbyterian ministers used to make him depressed, methodists shook his passions, and the sceptical thoughts of deists alarmed him, but the Catholic divines were always good 'lodgers' in the house of his mind: 'Romish clergy filled me with solemn ideas, and, although their statues and many movable ornaments are gone,

---

[22] Peter Martin, *A Life of James Boswell*, (London, 1999), p. 81.

[23] *The Diary of David Garrick*, pp. 4–5.

[24] *Boswell on the Grand Tour: Italy, Corsica, and France 1765–1766*, eds. Frank Brady and Frederick A. Pottle (London, 1955), p. 6.

[25] *Boswell on the Grand Tour*, p. 63.

[26] James Boswell's letter to John Johnston, 10 February 1765. *The Correspondence of James Boswell and John Johnston of Grange*, ed. by Ralph S. Walker (London, 1966), p. 157.

yet they drew some pictures upon my walls with such deep strokes that they still remain. They are indeed only agreable ones.'[27] Considering the wide gap between the religious sensibilities of Garrick and Boswell, it is a little more understandable that Garrick only bowed in front of Shakespeare's symbolic representation and Boswell fell on his knees. Yet what they had been doing in their respective ways at the Jubilee is essentially the same as everybody in any way relating to Shakespeare has been doing ever since: trying to renegotiate the relation of the profane and the sacred within the quasi-religious realm.

The symbolic actions of the Jubilee both in Stratford and in Drury Lane testify to Garrick's awareness of essentially religious needs lurking behind joyful secular celebrations. To illustrate this with one ritual episode from many: after the first day lunch in the Rotunda the merry company seized the goblet and (as an eye-witness reported) 'nothing would satisfy them till it was filled with the best of Wines, that they might have the pleasure to drink to the Memory of the immortal Bard', the goblet 'went around very freely indeed, and the enthusiastic Joy upon the Occasion was very remarkable'. One may suspect that the attraction of the event was much more than the sheer joy of drinking, because after the meal Garrick was halted on his way home by his friends who insisted on drinking some Shakespeare Ale from the goblet, which was filled again and 'every one did Honour to it', until they felt contented enough to end the celebration 'with three Cheers for the divine Bard, and three more to his truest Representative Mr. Garrick'.[28] In the light of its probable religious archetype this little episode reveals great, if subconscious, significance. Based on the atavistic revival of the belief in magic transfer by touch (Shakespeare planted the tree with his own hands, so he must be present in the holy wood of the goblet), the communal drinking by turns, from the same goblet, of wine (or, at the second time, its substitute) to the memory of the immortal

founder of the cult, in the presence of his elected or acknowledged representative, must have pointed, at least vaguely, to the well-known pattern of the Eucharist, the ritual Christ bequeathed to his disciples on the eve of his death, with its liturgy of transubstantiation. There is no explicit evidence that Garrick was fully aware of this biblical analogy, but he must have felt the episode significant because he incorporated it in the theatrical afterpiece as well, the little play he admittedly tried to make into a vivid replica of what actually had happened,[29] and not even this satirical, comedy-like version can conceal the solemn religious archetype of the merry moment. In Part 1, Scene 3 Bannister and Vernon enter, the latter with the Mulberry Cup in his hand, surrounded by a number of people.

VERNON: Hollo, boys! Don't let us selfishly and niggardly confine our joys to ourselves, but let every Jubilee soul partake of our mirth and our liquor, at least kiss the cup and be happy.
BANNISTER: With all my heart, my boy. [. . .] Let us take t'other taste of the dear mulberry juice.

$(120-5)^{30}$

There is no stage direction after this but presumably they drank from the goblet one by one and/or kissed the cup. In Garrick's Mulberry-ballad which is sung appropriately at this point in the play there are references to 'liquor' and 'mulberry juice' as well as to Bacchus, vine, and once even to 'wine', hence the audience could not be sure what exactly the goblet was supposed to contain; as a common denominator they probably thought of mulberry wine, a 1769 vintage from the mutual vineyard of the Shakespeare cult and Christianity. But whatever it

27 *Private Papers of James Boswell from Malahide Castle*, ed. Geoffrey Scott and Frederick A. Pottle, vol. 7, *The Journal of James Boswell 1765–1768: Corsica, Italy, France, England, Scotland* (London, 1930), p. 161.
28 *The Public Advertiser*, 16 September 1769, p. 3. col. 1.
29 David Garrick to the Reverend Evan Lloyd, 4 December 1769. *The Letters of David Garrick*, vol. 2, p. 675.
30 *The Plays of David Garrick: Garrick's Own Plays, 1767–1775*, p. 113.

was, in the last stanza of Garrick's ballad the newly acquired quasi-religious ritual was recapitulated in terms of patriotic duty: 'Fill, fill to the planter, the Cup to the brim, / To honor your country do honor to him.' (174–5)[31].

The theatrical version of the Jubilee was uniting the solemn and the satirical, but it was by no means blending the sacred and the profane. On the contrary, the characters are often anxious to distinguish them, and the chorus in the pageant (in Part 1, Scene 3) spells out a concern that is meant to be taken seriously: 'Hence, ye profane! And only they, / Our Pageant grace our pomp survey, / Whom love of sacred genius brings' (65–8).[32] A similar dividing line is drawn in the play between what Garrick considered appropriate and inappropriate in the worship of literary relics. In the first stanza of the Mulberry ballad the audience was to learn that it is the right thing to kiss the goblet as a relic, then in the second, a stanza Garrick liked so much that in a marginal note he ordered it to be repeated as stanza 6 as well, they learned more about the genealogical value of the tree whose wood was used to make the goblet. 'The fame of the patron gives fame to the tree, / From him and his merits this takes its degree.' (Part 1, Scene 3, 136–7).[33] This is contrasted in the same scene with the interlude of the two 'mulberry scoundrels' who try to outdo each other in their eloquence to sell fake objects allegedly made of the mulberry tree. But the ultimate incompatibility of the sacred and the profane is reiterated in a more sarcastic and almost subversive manner as well. As if to defend the wordly from the otherwordly, the lighthearted but revealing duet of Sukey and Nancy (in Part 2, Scene 3) refers to the fatal consequences of Shakespeare's divine omniscience for the world of human imperfection. First Sukey reminds Nancy of the verses a certain Parson Shrimp wrote upon 'him' who would see through everybody and know all the hidden vanities, sins and follies at once, then Nancy replies with great relief ('Though sins I

have none, / I am glad he is gone, / No maid would live near such a mon'), and finally they sing together:

> Let us sing it and dance it,
> Rejoice it and prance it,
> That no man has now such an art.
> What would come of us all,
> Both the great ones and small,
> Should he now live to peep in each heart.
>
> (70–8)[34]

All this refers to a Shakespeare of divine abilities, but the implied religious psychology of relief could just as embarrassingly refer to *any* divinity.

Cowper's poem was more sensitive to the potentially subversive, indeed blasphemous implications of such issues than the carefully guarded appreciation of the Jubilee might indicate out of context. The appraisive words about Garrick and his Jubilee are not decisive enough to let the reader forget about the lurking possibility of sacrilege, clearly the main concern of the narrator here as elsewhere. Despite the reassuring 'Ah, pleasant proof / That piety has still in human hearts / Some place, a spark or two not yet extinct', the suggestion that Garrick created the liturgy and ritual of a new type of worship sounds much less unambiguously endorsing when we realize that it was preceded by an explicit condemnation of a similar contemporary event. Indeed out of the poem's three examples of man's extravagant praise of man the Jubilee is the second, flanked by two other cases which are fiercely castigated. The first of the two, setting the tone for this triadic part within Book 6, refers to the Handel Commemoration (an event inspired by the memory of Garrick's Jubilee)[35] as a distasteful example of debasing Scripture to serve as the text of Handel's *Messiah*, an oratorio now listened to by the 'commemoration-mad' thousands for

---

[31] *Garrick's Own Plays*, p. 115.
[32] *Garrick's Own Plays*, p. 119.
[33] *Garrick's Own Plays*, p. 114.
[34] *Garrick's Own Plays*, pp. 123–4.
[35] Cf. *The Poems of William Cowper: 1782–1785*, p. 419.

remembering the musician and for sheer musical pleasure, 'to gratify an itching ear', thus for the wrong reasons. All this amounts to no less than 'sacrilege', the poem didactically concludes, something no heathen of ancient Rome would have dared to do, and we should remember that 'His most holy book from whom it came / Was never meant, was never used before / To buckram out the mem'ry of a man.'[36] (In Cowper's letters of the summer of 1784 his response to the Handel commemoration could hardly be more furious. 'A religious service instituted in honor of a Musician, and performed in the house of God, is a subject that calls loudly for the animadversion of an enlighten'd minister, and would be no mean one for a satyrist, could a poet of that description be found spiritual enough to feel and to resent the profanation.'[37] Writing to John Newton he calls the event foolish, preposterous and wicked,[38] and in a letter to William Unwin he illustrates his point by a mini-drama in which the verdict is finally summed up by an angel: 'So then – because Handel set Anthems to Music you sing them in honor of Handel – and because he composed the Music of Italian songs you sing them in a church? – Truely Handel is much obliged to you, but God is greatly dishonor'd.')[39] The judgement passed on the third example of man praising man in *The Task* is hardly less severe, though political caution tempers its wording: we see the 'statesman of the day' amidst a pompous pageant, adored by people in a way that is judged misplaced and inappropriate:

> Thus idly do we waste the breath of praise,
> And dedicate a tribute, in its use
> And just direction, sacred, to a thing
> Doomed to the dust, or lodged already there.[40]

This protest, and the indignant voice of its author, would reverberate in the century to come, and one of the rhetorical tasks would be to work out a defensive line of reasoning to legitimize the tercentenary celebrations. At the Stratford festival of 1864 the Sunday afternoon sermon of Charles Wordsworth, Bishop of St Andrews, in Holy Trinity Church revealed a painful awareness of the same conflicting loyalties. Feeling that the festival could far too easily and sinfully lose sight of the proper divine object of ultimate admiration, he began his sermon with the imperative to avoid the blasphemous error of idolatry, and argued that there was, luckily, enough of the divine in Shakespeare to justify reverence. Shakespeare was not just an example of intellectual superiority (which would not be recommended by the Bible for glorification) but also an example of things pleasing to God, moreover, he was a man with Christ-like meekness, thus one of the blessed who 'shall inherit the earth', and a man writing works 'plainly on the right side; [. . .] on the side of virtue and of true religion'.[41] This vindication of Shakespeare's impeccably Christian morality, both in his works and in his life, was a prerequisite of not considering his celebration a sacrilege. The initial problem of the clergyman, that is, how to refute possible charges of idolatry and how to negotiate theological objections to glorifying a man in the house of God, could be solved only by way of a long and apologetic meditation.

To illustrate that the problem is still with us both within and beyond the boundaries of

---

36 William Cowper: *The Task*. Book VI, lines 633–52. *The Poems of William Cowper: 1782–1785*, p. 253.

37 William Cowper to John Newton, 21 June 1784. *The Letters and Prose Writings of William Cowper*, vol. 2, *Letters 1782–1786*, eds. James King and Charles Ryskamp (Oxford, 1981), p. 254.

38 William Cowper to John Newton, 19 July 1784. *The Letters and Prose Writings of William Cowper: Letters 1782–1786*, pp. 264–5.

39 William Cowper to William Unwin, November 20, 1784. *The Letters and Prose Writings of William Cowper: Letters 1782–1786*, pp. 298–9.

40 William Cowper: *The Task*. Book VI, lines 711–14. *The Poems of William Cowper: 1782–1785*, p. 255.

41 Wordsworth, Charles, *Shakespeare's Knowledge and Use of the Bible: With Appendix Containing Additional Illustration and Tercentenary Sermon Preached at Stratford-on-Avon* (London, 1864), pp. 383–404.

Shakespeare's homeland, let us consider finally a twentieth-century case. Faithful to her childhood vow to herself, the Hungarian writer Magda Szabó *knelt down* at Shakespeare's grave in 1962. That vow had been made decades earlier by a little girl born (in 1917) and brought up in Debrecen, the foremost Calvinist stronghold of Eastern Hungary, where she was taught to be proud of her Calvinist faith and forefathers, one of whom had been sentenced to the galleys. As the adult recalls the motivation of the child, she was longing to go to Stratford 'so that I could kneel down once in my life as people of *other faiths* do'. Not that she was ever eager to complement, as a practising Christian, the ritual of her denomination: somewhat later, when the eighteen-year-old was sent to Vienna for a month, she was reluctant to pray in a nearby Catholic church, and would rather walk for hours to praise the Lord in a (well, second best) Lutheran church. The only other instance in her adult life of supplementary ritual was a repetitive symbolic action which could be practised without reservations because it was felt to be seamlessly continuous with the world of her Calvinist upbringing: on each New Year's Eve she and her husband celebrated the moment of midnight at home by standing up and murmuring together a solemn text composed by themselves while each drinking in turn a drop of wine from the same glass, as (her own simile) at the Lord's Supper. It is all the more significant that her naive childhood promise to kneel in Stratford turned (admittedly) into an obsession, something to be realized at all costs. This fixation of the child's desire to do at Shakespeare's grave something other denominations practise is a psychologically understandable response to the dominant non-kneeling tradition in early twentieth-century Hungarian Calvinism. (In 1911 the poet Endre Ady indignantly protested against the proposition of kneeling at prayer and maintained that Hungarian Calvinists should not kneel even if Calvin himself had done so.)[42] It also shows that the Shakespeare cult could provide a denominational no man's land where

a devoutly Calvinist child could sink on her knees in a church and yet without a bad conscience. When she eventually managed to go to Stratford, and in the church at last found a tourist-free moment at the grave, she became aware of her difficulties with performing the act of kneeling ('because I have never been taught to kneel' she says), but once on her knees, she felt overwhelmed by a mystical experience by which the moment, admittedly one of the greatest moments of her life, acquired weight and dimension, radiating a sense of eternity.[43]

Magda Szabó's case reveals that a Hungarian child in the 1920s could *sooner* realize that Shakespeare was somebody to be revered than she could possibly read his plays. Her example is typical of many others in the previous century: that of the Hungarian Lázár Petrichevich Horváth (1807–51), whose admiration for Shakespeare originated in the respectful words he had heard about Shakespeare in his childhood, at the beginning of the nineteenth century, when the seven-year-old boy (in his later phrasing) had 'no idea what kind of animal Shakespeare was';[44] or that of the Reverend John M. Jephson, who admits in the preface of his book *Shakespeare, His Birthplace, Home, and Grave: A Pilgrimage to Stratford-on-Avon in the Autumn of 1863* that from his childhood he has 'heard Shakespeare discussed, extolled, acted, and quoted', because 'an especial veneration' for the playwright has been 'hereditary' in his family.[45] As in both of the latter cases it was the early acquisition of a reverential attitude that led to serious works on Shakespeare in adult life; Magda Szabó's case also proves the lasting impact of learning this reverence in childhood.

---

42 Endre Ady, 'Kálvin hívei térdepelnek' in Endre Ady, *Publicisztikai írásai*, vol. 3 (Budapest, 1977), pp. 344–6.

43 Magda Szabó, 'Perc az időben: Angliai útinapló', *Kortárs*, 1962, June, pp. 891–902.

44 Lázár Petrichevich Horváth, 'Shakespeare és drámái', *Athenaeum*, 7 January 1838, pp. 19–20.

45 J. M. Jephson, *Shakespeare, His Birthplace, Home, and Grave: A Pilgrimage to Stratford-on-Avon in the Autumn of 1863* (London, 1864), pp. v–vi.

The lifelong imprint of her vow was to motivate not only the actual kneeling of the adult but it also *preformed* her attitude to Shakespeare's texts all her life, and contributed to making them (in her own words) her 'greatest literary experience', probably long before she translated *The Two Gentlemen of Verona* into Hungarian.

I remember analysing such cases in a lecture back in 1984, and being asked by a colleague why a seemingly normal person like me would bother to deal with such obviously idiotic behaviour that has nothing to do with literary scholarship anyway. Yet I thought, and still think, that there is no more madness here than in any of our own most respectable actions. More to the point, I am also convinced that the interpretative and evaluative procedures of literary scholarship 'proper', whatever that may mean, are secretly but inextricably interwoven with such quasi-religious acts of verbal and non-verbal reverence. It is still not easy to respond to this connection without premature hostilities. True, the unqualified acceptance of the line 'What comes from thy hand must be ever divine!' in Garrick's mulberry tree ballad would not only legitimate any apologetic argument, but in the last analysis it would *confine* the role of any scholarly reasoning, be it textual, interpretative or aesthetic, to justification. Symptomatically, the *Advertisement* preceding Garrick's *Ode* recommended Elizabeth Montagu's *An Essay on the Writings and Genius of Shakespeare* 'to those who are not sufficiently established in their dramatic faith', and explained the joint publication of his *Ode* and a selection of miscellaneous texts (ranging from Ben Jonson's and Milton's celebratory poems to appraisive passages by scholars like Theobald, Hanmer or Steevens) pointing to their common function: 'To strengthen and justify the general admiration of this astonishing Genius, it has been thought proper to subjoin to the Ode some undeniable Testimonies (both in prose and verse) of his unequalled original talents.'[46] However, Garrick's own offstage activity as a collector of books relating to early English drama, as a generous patron and relentless aid to a long row of scholars from Warton to Malone,[47] fostered a scholarly output far more valuable than such a merely vindicative rationale would make us expect, and that output probably owes at least as much to the Garrickian liturgy and ritual of quasi-religious self-submission as to any secular ideal of scholarly independence. And Garrick's legacy is paradigmatic. The changing, yet constant role of hidden religious needs in Shakespeare's scholarly reception has always had repercussions but it has not been entirely counter-productive. In our zeal to preserve or restore the methodological purity of our discipline, the absolute cleanliness that has never existed, we should be careful not to throw out the baby with the bathwater.

---

46 *Advertisement*. D[avid] G[arrick], *An Ode upon Dedicating a Building, and Erecting a Statue, to Shakespeare, at Stratford upon Avon* (London, 1769).
47 Stone and Kahrl, *David Garrick*, pp. 165–99.

JONSON, SHAKESPEARE, AND THE RELIGION OF PLAYERS

JEFFREY KNAPP

Scholars typically characterize the theatre of Shakespeare's England as a secular stage, and they have good reasons for doing so. By the time Shakespeare began to write plays, the biblical drama of medieval England had all but died, from causes not entirely natural. It had been censored by Protestant officials concerned with its Catholic provenance, and censorship appears to have hampered the depiction of religious material in the new public theatres as well.[1] Moralists such as Phillip Stubbes (1583) warned England that players allowed to dramatize the word of God would inevitably contaminate 'divinity' with their 'bawdy, wanton shows & uncomely gestures'.[2] Following a brief period (1588–9) in which church and state encouraged the theatres to vilify the radical puritan 'Martin Marprelate' for his attacks on bishops, the authorities did indeed recoil from the spectacle of 'divinity' handled, in their view, 'without judgement or decorum'; by a 1606 act of Parliament, moreover, players were forbidden to 'speak or use the holy Name of God or of Christ Jesus, or of the Holy Ghost or of the Trinity' profanely.[3] Whether or not these official strictures had any chilling effect, players in Shakespeare's day showed little interest in replacing the 'old Church-plays' with a biblical drama of their own.[4] 'Unchaste and wicked matters', as one exasperated Lord Mayor of London (1580) put it, seemed their preferred stock in trade: against the lonely example of Thomas Lodge and Robert Greene's *Looking Glasse for London and England* (c. 1590), which

includes the biblical figures Hosea and Jonah in its cast of characters, may be set the far more representative depiction of the city in Thomas Middleton's *A Mad World, My Masters* (c. 1604), the comedy of a London debauchee who repeatedly swindles his uncle until he accidentally weds his uncle's whore.[5]

It comes as some surprise, then, that a contemporary eulogist of Ben Jonson should claim that 'Grave Preachers' had been using the 'wit

---

1 See Eamon Duffy, *The Stripping of the Altars: Traditional Religion in England 1400–1580* (New Haven, 1992), pp. 579–81. As Paul Whitfield White observes, censorship cannot be the whole story of the miracle plays' demise: see his 'Theater and Religious Culture' in *A New History of Early English Drama*, ed. John D. Cox and David Scott Kastan (New York, 1997), p. 135.

2 Phillip Stubbes, *An Anatomie of Abuses* (1583; rev. edns 1583, 1584, 1595), ed. Arthur Freeman (New York, 1973), pp. L5r–L6r.

3 See E. K. Chambers, *The Elizabethan Stage*, 4 vols. (Oxford, 1923), vol. 4, pp. 306–7 and 338–9. For a challenge to the conventional view that the Marprelate ruling 'ushered in a new era of strict regulation' of the stage, see Richard Dutton's *Mastering the Revels: The Regulation and Censorship of English Renaissance Drama* (Iowa City, 1991), 77 ff.

4 Samuel Harsnett, *A Declaration of Egregious Popish Impostures* (London, 1603), p. 114.

5 Chambers, *Elizabethan Stage*, vol. 4, p. 279; unless otherwise indicated, the dates given for plays refer to their first performance, not publication. In her *Biblical Drama Under the Tudors* (The Hague, 1971), pp. 160–1, Ruth Blackburn lists only fourteen plays on biblical subjects performed in the public theatres between 1587 and 1602; all but two of these – the *Looking Glass* and George Peele's *David and Bethsabe* (c. 1587) – are lost.

and language' of Jonson's plays as 'golden Pills, by which they might infuse / Their Heavenly Physic' into their parishioners. This praise appears in *Jonsonus Virbius* (1638), a collection of memorial verse compiled six months after Jonson's death by the future bishop Brian Duppa, in which nearly a third of the thirty-one contributors had taken or would soon take holy orders – and three of these men too went on to become bishops.[6] If the Renaissance theatre was as secular a medium as modern criticism makes it out to be, why would clergymen not only draw on plays for their sermons but also proclaim their admiration for a playwright?

The answer, according to the Restoration commentator George Ridpath, is political. 'In King *Charles* I['s] Time', Ridpath writes in *The Stage Condemn'd* (1698), the theatre was 'necessary to ridicule the Puritans', and for that reason Archbishop '*Laud* and his Clergy became its Patrons'.[7] Most of the modern criticism that acknowledges at least some ties between church and theatre during the English Renaissance echoes Ridpath in judging those ties to be a matter of sectarian politics. The two finest books on the subject – David Bevington's *Tudor Drama and Politics* (1968) and Leah Marcus's *The Politics of Mirth* (1986) – make this stance clear in their titles.[8] It would be hard to deny the pertinence of such analysis to the Renaissance theatre: even the sympathetic Restoration observer John Aubrey reported that King James 'made' Jonson 'write against the Puritans'.[9] Yet a secularist view of religion as little more than politics mystified has led scholars to treat the historical record of dialogue between church and theatre more reductively than the presbyterian theatre-hater Ridpath does.[10] For Ridpath does not dismiss the claims of Jonson's clerical admirers, but instead notes with disgust how the Laudian 'Clergy became at last so enamor'd of the Stage' that 'it was too too frequent to have Sermons in respect of their Divisions, Language, Action, Style and Subject Matter, fitter for the Stage from whence they were borrowed, than for the Pulpit'.[11] What

began as a bond of mere expediency, according to Ridpath, ended as a world turned upside down. Thanks to Laud and the king, 'the Universities became infected with the Contagion of the Stage, and they being the Nurseries of Officers for the Church and State it was no wonder, if the Infection spread from them, all over the Kingdom'. Ultimately, the theatre 'grew *Rampant*, and as if it disdained to have any less Adversary than God himself, did boldly

---

[6] *Jonsonus Virbius: or, The Memorie of Ben Johnson Revived by the Friends of the Muses*, compiled by Brian Duppa (1638), in *Ben Jonson*, ed. C. H. Herford and Percy and Evelyn Simpson, 11 vols. (Oxford, 1925–52) [hereafter *HS*], vol. 11, pp. 438–9. The current or future clergymen are William Bew, Ralph Brideoake, William Cartwright, James Clayton, Samuel Evans, Henry King, Jasper Mayne, Thomas Terrent, and Richard West; Bew, Brideoake, and King later became bishops.

[7] [George Ridpath], *The Stage Condemn'd* (London, 1698), pp. 4 and 9.

[8] David Bevington, *Tudor Drama and Politics: A Critical Approach to Topical Meaning* (Cambridge, Mass., 1968); Leah S. Marcus, *The Politics of Mirth: Jonson, Herrick, Milton, Marvell, and the Defense of Old Holiday Pastimes* (Chicago, 1986). See also Donna Hamilton, *Shakespeare and the Politics of Protestant England* (Lexington, Ky., 1992).

[9] Quoted in *HS* vol. 1, p. 180.

[10] In *The Cambridge Companion to English Renaissance Drama*, ed. A. R. Braunmuller and Michael Hattaway (Cambridge, 1990), the sole essay to deal at any length with religious issues is Margot Heinemann's 'Political Drama'. Russ McDonald's recent *Bedford Companion to Shakespeare* (New York, 1996) is only superficially different. Of the eleven 'Illustrations and Documents' included in his chapter on 'Politics and Religion', only two are intended to represent religion, and they have clearly been chosen for their political charge: one is an excerpt from the foundational puritan tract, *An Admonition to the Parliament*, while the other is an excerpt from the anglican *Homily against Disobedience and Willful Rebellion*.

Marcus does note that 'most of the Laudian proponents' of recreations such as playgoing 'would not have seen themselves as operating on a purely political level', but she finds only 'inklings' of a 'sacramentalizing strain' in one play, Jonson's *Bartholomew Fair*, and she adds that Jonson 'was clearly wary of the trend even as he half espoused it' (p. 17).

[11] Ridpath, *Stage*, p. 11, paraphrasing William Prynne, *Histrio-Mastix* (London, 1633), p. 935.

usurp on the Sabbath Afternoons. And thus in the Year 1637 Masques were set up at Court on *Sundays*, by his Majesty's Authority, while at the same time *Laud* and his Faction forbad Preaching any oft'ner than once a day.'[12]

By Ridpath's time, this vision of the stage as supplanting the pulpit was a hoary antitheatrical nightmare. 'Do they not draw the people from hearing the word of God, from godly Lectures, and sermons?' Stubbes had asked; 'for you shall have them flock thither thick & threefold, when the church of God shall be bare & empty'.[13] The charge, nearly as old as Christianity itself, was laid at the time against other popular entertainments too: the alehouse, the whore-house, bear-baiting, card-playing, even piping. But by far the most disturbing of the preacher's rivals, for the godly, were the players.[14] Like many another theatre-hater in the period, Stubbes was appalled to report that some play-goers thought plays were not only more enter-taining than sermons but even 'as good as sermons' were; in the words of the clergyman John Northbrook (1577), people 'shame not to say and affirm openly, . . . that they learn as much or more at a Play, than they do at God's word preached'.[15] Stubbes concluded that plays were worse than atheistical, having been 'sucked out of the Devil's teats, to nourish us in idolatry[,] heathenry, and sin'. As the eminent puritan divine Richard Baxter (1673) later put it, 'the Devil hath apishly made these [theatres] *his Churches*, in competition with the *Churches* of Christ'.[16] And Ridpath was not the only writer to suggest that Charles's Sunday masques were the devil's *pièce de résistance*. By 1643, the puritan propagandist 'Mercurius Britanicus' could already claim that 'it has been an old fashion at Court, amongst the Protestants there, to shut up the *Sabbath* with some wholesome Piece of *Ben Jonson* or *Davenant*, a kind of *Comical Divinity*'; he predicted that the Cavaliers would soon 'go near to put down all *preaching* and *praying*, and have some *religious Masque* or play instead of Morning and Evening Prayer'.[17] Charging the king with treason six years later,

the parliamentary solicitor general wished that Charles had 'but studied Scripture half so much as *Ben Jonson* or *Shakespeare*'.[18]

In recent decades, such contemporaneous testimony to the theatre's idolatrous sway has begun to be taken seriously, in particular by the anthropological literary critics Stephen Green-blatt and Louis Montrose. Both scholars see the theatre as the beneficiary of a spiritual crisis in England sparked by the Reformation. Once 'the Elizabethan regime had suppressed most of the ritual practices and popular religious festivi-ties of late medieval Catholic culture', Montrose argues in his *Purpose of Playing* (1996), the English people had to look elsewhere for the 'symbolic forms' that might endow 'their material existence with greater coherence and value'. According to Montrose, they could turn to 'the spectacles of royal and civic power' that took the place of Catholic rites, or seek 'a

---

[12] Ridpath, *Stage*, pp. 114 and 12.

[13] Stubbes, *Anatomie*, sig. L8r.

[14] On the conventionality of the protest 'that the churches were empty and places of entertainment full', see Patrick Collinson, *The Religion of Protestants: The Church in English Society 1559–1625* (Oxford, 1982), pp. 203 ff. Drawing on the evidence compiled by the *Records of Early English Drama* series, Andrew Gurr maintains, however, that 'the strength of the hostility in most local authorities, including London, to professional playing was notably greater than it was to other crowd-pulling enterprises such as bear- or bull-baiting, or even to the smaller groups of entertainers like tumblers and acro-bats' (*The Shakespearian Playing Companies* (Oxford, 1996), p. 7).

[15] Stubbes, *Anatomie*, sig. L7v; John Northbrook, *A Trea-tise Wherein Dicing, Dauncing, Vaine Playes or Enterluds With Other Idle Pastimes etc. Commonly Used on the Sabboth Day, Are Reproved* (1577?), ed. Arthur Freeman (New York, 1974), p. 66.

[16] Stubbes, *Anatomie*, sig. L6r; Richard Baxter, *A Christian Directory* (London, 1673), p. 878.

[17] *Mercurius Britanicus* no. 12 (9–16 November 1643), p. 89; cited in Leslie Hotson, *The Commonwealth and Restoration Stage* (1928; New York, 1962), p. 9.

[18] John Cook, *King Charls [sic] His Case* (London, 1649), p. 13; cited in *The Jonson Allusion-Book: A Collection of Allusions to Ben Jonson from 1597 to 1700*, ed. Jesse Franklin Bradley and Joseph Quincy Adams (New Haven, 1922), p. 293.

substitute for the metaphysical aid of the medieval church in a welter of occult practices', but London's citizens may have found 'another alternative' to traditional religion in the 'collective and commercial, public and profane' experience of the theatre.[19] In *Shakespearean Negotiations* (1988), Stephen Greenblatt similarly portrays the Shakespearian theatre as appropriating the 'ritual' that 'the official religious and secular institutions' of Elizabethan England were in the process of 'abjuring'. Insofar as ritual thus became associated with the essentially 'fraudulent institution' of the theatre, this shift, according to Greenblatt, seemed to confirm the official Protestant position that ritual too was fraudulent. But for Greenblatt the theatre as fiction-maker 'evacuates everything it represents'; when a play such as *King Lear* (c. 1605) mimics the official critique of ritual, therefore, both ritual and the official critique are fictionalized, 'emptied out'. Freed of any doctrinal claims on it, ritual becomes theatre merely, yet as theatre it holds greater attractions for its audience, Greenblatt suggests, than a church now hollowed out and bare: 'evacuated rituals, drained of their original meaning, are preferable to no rituals at all'.[20]

The problem with these otherwise powerful accounts of the theatre as symbolically compensating for a lost Catholicism is that they take contemporary sectarian criticism of both pulpit and stage *too* seriously, and end up reproducing its partialities. Neither Greenblatt nor Montrose, in other words, credits the established church with any cultural capital of its own, nor *a fortiori* can either scholar imagine the church as investing the Shakespearian theatre with any religious purpose.[21] (Montrose goes so far as to omit the Protestant church from his list of 'metaphysical' alternatives to Catholicism.) In his recent essay on 'Theater and Religious Culture' in *A New History of Early English Drama* (1997), Paul Whitfield White counters that Protestantism must have figured significantly in the 'composition, performance, and reception' of plays because 'Reformation orthodoxy was,

by the midpoint of Elizabeth's reign, not merely the official doctrine of the national church but internalized as a major feature of the national consciousness.'[22] Debora Shuger (1996) makes a similar point, trying to strike a balance between the secular provenance of Renaissance drama on the one hand and the secularist biases of modern criticism on the other: 'if it is not plausible to read Shakespeare's plays as Christian allegories, neither is it likely that the popular drama of a religiously saturated culture could, by a secular miracle, have extricated itself from the theocentric orientation informing the discourses of politics, gender, social order, and history' at the time.[23]

An indispensable corrective to the historiographical blindspots of political and anthropological critics alike, this 'cultural saturation' theory of White and Shuger nonetheless concedes part of the secularist position it means to oppose, insofar as it depicts Renaissance playwrights as 'Christian' only subliminally or cognitively, rather than purposively and devotionally.[24] Not even this revisionist scholarship,

---

[19] Louis Montrose, *The Purpose of Playing: Shakespeare and the Cultural Politics of the Elizabethan Theatre* (Chicago, 1996), pp. 30–2.

[20] Stephen Greenblatt, *Shakespearean Negotiations: The Circulation of Social Energy in Renaissance England* (Berkeley, 1988), pp. 125–7.

[21] In *Staging Reform, Reforming the Stage: Protestantism and Popular Theater in Early Modern England* (Ithaca, 1997), Huston Diehl makes the same point about both Montrose (pp. 94–5) and Greenblatt (pp. 108–9).

[22] White, 'Theater and Religious Culture,' p. 146.

[23] Debora Shuger, 'Subversive Fathers and Suffering Subjects: Shakespeare and Christianity,' in *Religion, Literature, and Politics in Post-Reformation England, 1540–1688*, ed. Donna B. Hamilton and Richard Strier (Cambridge, 1996), p. 46.

[24] This is true even of Diehl's *Staging Reform*, which only appears to repudiate a secularist reading of Renaissance plays when it argues that the plays were 'both a product of the Protestant Reformation – a reformed drama – and a producer of Protestant habits of thought – a reforming drama'. Like Greenblatt and Montrose, Diehl bases her thesis 'on the insights of symbolic anthropologists who believe that religious practices help shape both individual consciousness and cultural forms' (p. 1).

in other words, allows the possibility raised by *Jonsonus Virbius* that Renaissance plays may have been intended and received as contributions to the cause of true religion.[25] And yet Jonson himself assured readers of *Volpone* (pub. 1607) that the poet is 'a teacher of things divine, no less than humane'; in 1619 he told William Drummond that he had 'a mind to be a churchman'; and it was as a churchman that he appeared to a (somewhat amused) young admirer who visited him in 1632:

> Great wearer of the bays, look to thy lines,
> Lest they chance to be challeng'd by Divines:
> Some future Times will, by a gross Mistake,
> Jonson a Bishop, not a Poet make.[26]

'They shame not to say and affirm openly, . . . that they learn as much or more at a Play, than they do at God's word preached.' To grasp how a theatre with little apparent religious content might ever have been regarded as spiritually edifying, it is necessary to take the theatre's contemporary defenders seriously too. So antithetical is that project to the secularist bent of modern criticism that scholars have largely ignored an otherwise striking fact about Renaissance English drama: the active participation of churchmen in its production.

When an anonymous respondent to Ridpath exaggeratedly proclaims in *The Stage Acquitted* (1699) 'that the *whole body* of the *Clergy* of the *Church* of *England* in the time of the *Martyr* [i.e., Charles I], did in an *extraordinary* manner encourage Plays', he means to highlight greater forms of encouragement than a single volume of eulogies.[27] Throughout the reigns of Elizabeth, James, and Charles, clergymen often undertook play-acting as part of their clerical training: 'in the Colleges', as the puritan Milton complained (1642), 'so many of the young Divines, and those in next aptitude to Divinity have been seen so oft upon the Stage writhing and unboning their Clergy limbs to all the antic and dishonest gestures of Trinculos, Buffoons, and Bawds'.[28] And acting was not limited to fledgling churchmen: according to Jonson's

friend Richard Corbet, a future bishop, the plays performed before King James at Cambridge in 1615 had 'a perfect *Diocese* of *Actors* / Upon the stage: for I am sure that / There was both *Bishop*, *Pastor*, *Curate*'.[29] Nor was acting the only form of clerical involvement in the drama: responding to an antitheatrical letter from his fellow Oxonian John Rainoldes, the Elizabethan cleric William Gager (1592) wished that Rainoldes had thought better of casting aspersions on 'those reverend, famous, and excellent men, for life, and learning, and their places in the Church of God, both of our house, and otherwise of the *University*,' who had been not only 'actors' in plays but 'writers of such things themselves'.[30]

Theatre histories generally treat the clergyman-dramatist as a phenomenon of the age before Shakespeare's, when the early reformers championed their cause with such straightforwardly religious plays as John Foxe's *Christus*

In other words, she does not claim that Renaissance playwrights consciously intended to comment on the religious issues their plays 'symbolically replicate and mediate' (p. 3 n. 6).

[25] This is not to say that all modern criticism of Renaissance drama is secularist. Some scholars do assert that 'the deepest inspiration in Shakespeare's plays is both religious and Christian' (Peter Milward, *Shakespeare's Religious Background* (Chicago, 1973), p. 274), but they have had little influence on recent Shakespeare scholarship, in large part because they tend to allegorize the plays crudely, as Shuger says. A thorough selection of such criticism may be found in *Shakespeare's Christian Dimension: An Anthology of Commentary*, ed. Roy Battenhouse (Bloomington, 1994).

[26] *HS* vol. 5, p. 17; vol. 1, pp. 141 and 113.

[27] Anon., *The Stage Acquitted* (London, 1699), p. 17.

[28] John Milton, *The Works of John Milton*, ed. Frank Allen Patterson et al., 18 vols. (New York, 1931–8), vol. 3, part 1, p. 300.

[29] Richard Corbet, 'A Certain Poem', *The Poems of Richard Corbet*, ed. J. A. W. Bennett and H. R. Trevor-Roper (Oxford, 1955), p. 15, lines 86–8. A marginal note in one manuscript copy of the poem reads 'Actores omnes fuere theologi [all the actors were theologians]' (quoted p. 111).

[30] William Gager, *The Complete Works*, ed. Dana F. Sutton, 4 vols. (New York, 1994), vol. 4, p. 273.

Triumphans (1556) or John Bale's *The Chief Promises of God Unto Man* (1538). By Shakespeare's time, this sort of godly drama had fallen out of fashion, but in fact more clergymen wrote plays during the second half-century of the English Reformation than during the first.[31] Gager himself was a renowned playwright, who published two of his efforts and had one performed before the queen. Other churchmen – Robert Gomersall, for example, and Samuel Harding – published closet dramas; still others, such as Thomas Goffe and Henry Killigrew, wrote plays that were first performed privately and then transferred to the public stage. James Shirley left the clergy for the theatre; conversely, some commercial dramatists went on to become clergymen: the best known of them is John Marston. Further kinds of trafficking between the pulpit and the stage have no doubt fallen from the historical record: according to George Buc, later Master of the Revels, Shakespeare informed him that an unnamed 'minister' had written the comic history play *George a Greene, The Pinner of Wakefield* (c. 1590) and 'acted the pinner's part in it himself'.[32]

Even more astonishing than the number and variety of clerical plays during this period is their almost exclusively secular subject matter.[33] Like the majority of his fellow clergymen–dramatists, Gager devised plays on classical themes, with titles such as *Dido* (1583) and *Ulysses Redux* (1592). Gomersall chose to dramatize a relatively contemporary secular topic in his *Tragedie of Lodovick Sforza Duke of Millan* (pub. 1628). But the most highly regarded clergymen–dramatists of their day produced comedies that, as G. E. Bentley delicately puts it, 'were not so pious as their [authors'] profession might suggest'.[34] The title setting of William Cartwright's *The Ordinary* (c. 1635), for instance, is a tavern filled with 'cheating Rakehells', while the chief difference between the heirs in Jasper Mayne's *City Match* (c. 1637) and Middleton's *Mad World* is that Mayne's debauchee swindles his uncle by staging the *uncle's* marriage to a *pretended* whore.[35]

How did these divinity students – not to mention the clergymen in their audiences – reconcile such coarse productions with their own high callings? Gager defended student acting on pedagogical grounds, defining its purposes as 'honestly to embolden our youth; to try their voices, and confirm their memories; to frame their speech; to conform them to convenient action; to try what mettle is in every one, and of what disposition they are of'.[36] A eulogist (1651) of the clergyman–dramatist Cartwright expanded this view of playing as a kind of rhetorical training to cover playwrighting as well: 'Thy Arts and Knowledge did but all prelude / That thou might'st *enter Orders*, not *intrude*.'[37] For another eulogist, however, Cartwright's theatre represented less the training he received than the extraordinary rhetorical capacities he always possessed:

What a rich Soul was thine! so soon knew'st how
To fill the *Stage*, the *Schools*, and *Pulpit* too;

---

31 Contrary to the picture of universal clerical support in *The Stage Acquitted*, most of the prominent clergymen-playwrights were in fact connected to Christ Church, Oxford, a 'playing' college from the days when Nicholas Grimald dedicated his biblical tragedy *Archipropheta* (pub. 1548) to the college's first dean. Other clergymen–playwrights associated with Christ Church include Robert Burton, James Calfhill, William Cartwright, Richard Edes, Richard Edwards, Gager, Goffe, Barten Holliday, Henry Killigrew, Jasper Mayne, and William Strode.

32 Buc wrote this information c. 1600 on the cover of his copy of the play; see Alan Nelson, 'George Buc, William Shakespeare, and the Folger *George a Greene*', *Shakespeare Quarterly*, 49 (1998), 74–83.

33 The sole exception I can find is a Latin play, John Hacket's *Loyola* (1623), which was twice performed before James I.

34 G. E. Bentley, *The Jacobean and Caroline Stage*, 7 vols. (Oxford, 1941–68), vol. 4, pp. 843–4.

35 William Cartwright, *The Ordinary* (c. 1635), *The Plays and Poems of William Cartwright*, ed. G. Blakemore Evans (Madison, 1951), line 2273; Jasper Mayne, *The City Match* (1636), ed. John Woodruff Ward, unpublished dissertation (Delaware, 1975).

36 Gager, *Works*, vol. 4, p. 263.

37 William Cartwright, *Comedies, Tragi-Comedies, With Other Poems* (London, 1651), sig. *13r.

Thy universal Wit
All Things and Men could fit.[38]

Rather than cast doubt on his piety, Cartwright's libertine plays actually help the eulogist see Cartwright as a latter-day St Paul, who, as Paul explained in his first letter to the Corinthians, made himself 'all things to all men' so that he 'might by all means save some'.

Nine years after writing *The City Match*, Mayne himself championed this Pauline conception of the ministry in his *Sermon Concerning Unity & Agreement* (1646):

by complying with the affections of those to whom he wrote, he [Paul] first transformed himself into their shapes, and became all things to all men, that he might the better transform them into his, and make all men become like himself. Thus to the Jews he became as a Jew; and put himself a while with them under the Law, that by insensible degrees he might take their yoke from them, and might beget their liking, and entertainment of the Gospel.

For Mayne, the truest Christians are what one might call the accommodationists – those who commit themselves, 'where our salvation, or the salvation of our neighbors is not concerned, charitably to comply, and sort with their infirmities; neither crossing them by our practice, though perhaps the better, nor perplexing them with our disputes, though perhaps the more rational'.[39] Making a similar call for moderation and religious harmony, Erasmus had celebrated Paul's accommodationism as a '*pia vafricie*' or 'godly wiliness', and Mayne in his own eulogy on Cartwright applies Erasmus's terms to Cartwright's ministry: 'How have I seen Thee cast thy Net, and then / With *holy Cozenage* catch'd the Souls of Men?'[40] In fact, Mayne invokes this Erasmian vision of Pauline accommodationism whenever he praises a playwright. Spectators who came to Beaumont and Fletcher plays 'to learn obsceneness', Mayne writes, 'return'd innocent, / And thankt you for this coz'nage'; in *Jonsonus Virbius*, Mayne recalls how Jonson 'ev'n sin didst in such words array, / That some who came *bad parts*, went out *good*

play.'[41] In short, Mayne portrays the apparent debauchery of the plays he admires as the rhetorical gambit that dramatists take in order to edify their audiences.

This artful conception of the ministry or ministerial conception of art is more plainly expressed by a nearer contemporary of Shakespeare and a playwright himself, Thomas Nashe, in his pamphlet *Christs Tears Over Jerusalem* (1593). Nashe blames a perceived resurgence of atheism in England on puritanical churchmen, 'ridiculous dull Preachers' who fail to recognize that an atheist will never be persuaded by anything but 'humane reasons': 'Vaunt you ye speak from the holy Ghost never so, if you speak not in compass of his five senses, he will despise you, and flout you.'

Men are men, and with those things must be moved, that men wont to be moved. They must have a little Sugar mixt with their sour Pills of reproof; the hooks must be pleasantly baited that they bite at. Those that hang forth their hooks and no bait, may well enough entangle them in the weeds, (enwrap themselves in contentions,) but never win one soul.[42]

---

38 Cartwright, *Comedies*, sig. B1v.

39 Jasper Mayne, *A Sermon Concerning Unity & Agreement* (Oxford, 1646), pp. 18 and 35.

40 Desiderius Erasmus, *Opera Omnia* (Amsterdam, 1969–), vol. 2, part 1 (1993), p. 201; trans. Richard Taverner, *Proverbes or Adagies* (London, 1545), fol. 51r-v; cf. Erasmus, *Collected Works*, ed. Peter G. Bietenholz et al. (Toronto, 1974–), vol. 31, p. 135. See also Erasmus, *Opus Epistolarium Des. Erasmi Roterodami*, ed. P. S. Allen, 12 vols. (Oxford, 1906–58), vol. 4, p. 493; trans. in *Collected Works*, vol. 8, p. 210.

   Mayne, 'To the Deceased Author of these Poems', in Cartwright, *Comedies*, sig. B5v; my emphasis. Mayne also echoes Erasmus in his *Sermon*: 'Like the Beast, of which *Pliny* speaks, which puts on the likeness of every thing next it, . . . so 'twas a piece of the Apostle's (Art shall I say?) or holy commission, to be *all things to all men*' (p. 19).

41 Mayne, 'On the Works of *Beaumont* and *Fletcher*, now at length printed', in *Fifty Comedies and Tragedies*, by Francis Beaumont and John Fletcher [London, 1679], sig. A3r; *HS* vol. 11, p. 453.

42 Thomas Nashe, *Works*, ed. R. B. McKerrow (1903–10), reprint ed. F. P. Wilson, 5 vols. (London, 1958), vol. 2, pp. 121–9.

The anglican preacher John Bury (1631) makes the same point in sermonizing on the Pauline text, 'Even as I please all men in all things, etc.': since 'we shall as soon catch fish with a *naked hook*' as convert the profane man 'with tart *invectives*', we must instead adopt the practice that made Paul so 'skillful' a '*fisher* of men', his 'holy art of *pleasing*'.[43]

This is just the advice that *Jonsonus Virbius* imagines preachers to be taking when they conceal their heavenly physic in Jonson's golden pills; it also helps explain why the clerical contributors to *Jonsonus Virbius* ever chose to fraternize with Jonson and then broadcast that fact in the first place. For rhetoric is only half the accommodationist program as both Nashe and Bury see it; the other half is ecclesiological – making oneself all things *to all men*. When the puritanical exclaim that they would rather '*defy*' the 'lewd and profane man' than '*please*' him, Bury argues, they effectively side with the '*Scribes* and *Pharisees*' who 'censured' Christ for 'eating and drinking with Publicans and Sinners'. Yet even 'the profanest worldling, the Turk, the Pagan have in them a *nature capable*' of that communion and fellowship' the saints enjoy in heaven.[44] Nashe puts the idea more drolly: he exhorts puritan preachers 'to love men of wit, and not hate them so as you do, for they have what you want. By loving them and accompanying with them, you shall both do them good and yourselves good; they of you shall learn sobriety and good life, you of them shall learn to utter your learning, and speak movingly.'[45] From this accommodationist perspective, the profane matter of a clerical play such as Mayne's *City Match* indicates that the author not only studied men of wit in order to improve his preaching but charitably consorted with the wits in order to improve them.

Jonson's insistence that the professional playwright as well as the clergyman can teach 'things divine' suggests that he may have regarded his ostensibly profane commercial art as a kind of 'holy cozenage' too. That case is emphatically made in a play Jonson co-wrote early in his career, *Eastward Ho* (1605). As the play begins, the prodigal apprentice Quicksilver urges the virtuous apprentice Golding to 'turn good fellow, turn swaggering gallant, and let the welkin roar, and Erebus also'; since these last words constitute a patchwork quotation of Shakespeare's Pistol, Quicksilver's debauchery is immediately associated with his playgoing. Condemning Quicksilver as 'a drunken, whore-hunting rakehell', Golding predicts that 'nothing' will 'recover' him 'but that which reclaims atheists, and makes great persons sometimes religious – calamity'. The prophecy proves true, in part. Released from his indentures, Quicksilver attempts a gold-hunting voyage to Virginia but is shipwrecked within a matter of minutes and then imprisoned as a vagrant felon. Pleading for mercy from his former master Touchstone similarly gets Quicksilver nowhere: 'Thou hast learnt to whine at the play yonder', Touchstone asserts, and turns his back on Quicksilver's presumed dissembling. But Golding, like a good accommodationist, comes to believe that Quicksilver has a nature capable of repentance.[46] Finding Touchstone intractable toward Quicksilver, Golding hits upon the 'device' of pretending to be imprisoned himself in order to make Touchstone a 'spectator' of Quicksilver's 'miseries'. And the plot succeeds: Touchstone both forgives Quicksilver and assures Golding, 'whose charitable soul in this hath shown a high point of wisdom and honesty', that his 'deceit is welcome'. Far from discrediting playgoing, in other words, *Eastward Ho* redefines it, exchanging a virtuous

---

43 John Bury, *The Moderate Christian* (London, 1631), pp. 11–13.

44 Bury, *Moderate Christian*, pp. 16–18.

45 Nashe, *Works*, vol. 2, p. 124.

46 George Chapman, Ben Jonson, and John Marston, *Eastward Ho*, ed. R. W. Van Fossen (Manchester, 1979), 1.1.125–7, 151–2, 168–71; and 4.2.350–1. As Touchstone's bad daughter sarcastically puts it to her pious sister, 'though thou art not like to be a lady as I am, yet sure thou art a creature of God's making, and mayest peradventure to be saved as soon as I' (1.2.52–5).

conception of the theatre for a debauched one. By analogy to Golding, the 'charitable' player only pretends to be one of the company of good fellows, in order to cozen playgoers into witnessing the true course of a prodigal life. This honest 'deceit,' the play implies, will have a doubly godly effect on the audience: as the 'spectacle' of Quicksilver's fall and conversion will help persuade them to become 'religious' (and without their having to experience actual 'calamity'), so it will also encourage their charity toward the 'lewd and profane man'.[47]

A later play of Jonson's, *The Magnetic Lady* (1632), underscores a further spiritual purpose to staging plays, and it is one that Erasmus, Mayne, Nashe, and Bury all associate with accommodationism: the promotion of Christian unity. Speaking almost autobiographically for Jonson (as a 'Scholar' and 'Soldier' who has 'been employed, / By some the greatest Statesmen o' the kingdom'), the character Compass begins the play by describing the social arena in which he exercises his 'wit':

> I'm lodged hard by,
> Here at a noble Lady's house i'th' street,
> The Lady *Loadstone's* (one will bid us welcome)
> Where there are Gentlewomen, and male Guests,
> Of several humors, carriage, constitution,
> Profession too: but so diametral
> One to another, and so much oppos'd,
> As if I can but hold them all together,
> And draw 'hem to a sufferance of themselves,
> But till the Dissolution of the Dinner;
> I shall have just occasion to believe
> My wit is magisterial.[48]

According to Master Probee in the play's opening chorus, such harmonizing of 'humours' is an undertaking not only conducive to 'the reconciliation of both Churches' but 'far greater' than that mission, 'the quarrel between humours having been much the ancienter, and, in my poor opinion, the root of all Schism and Faction, both in Church and Commonwealth' (chor.112–16). However whimsical it may sound to the modern reader, this reductive 'medicalization' of religious controversy would

become thoroughly conventional by the time of the Restoration, when fractiousness would be dismissed as the ravings of 'enthusiasm'.[49] The prologue to *The Magnetic Lady* thus asks us to see Compass as achieving more than one might otherwise think when he pacifies his dinner mates; and we quickly learn that he accomplishes his ultimately antischismatical work in familiar fashion, by making himself all things to all men:

> suiting so myself
> To company, as honest men and knaves,
> Good-fellows, Hypocrites, all sorts of people,
> Though never so divided in themselves,
> Have studied to agree still in the usage,
> And handling of me. (1.1.23–8)

That Compass should regard himself rather than his auditors as the beneficiary of their consensus seems to highlight a limitation to Jonson's imitation of Paul, who stressed that in pleasing all men in all things he was 'not seeking mine own profit, but the profit of many, that they may be saved' (1 Corinthians 10.33). Tension between Jonson's accommodationism and his notorious egotism becomes an explicitly theatrical issue later in *The Magnetic Lady*, when Probee declares that 'we come here to behold *Plays*, and censure them, as they are made, and fitted for us; not to beslaver our own thoughts, with censorious spittle tempering the *Poet's* clay, as we were to mould every *Scene* anew' (5.chor.14–17): according to Probee, in other words, the responsibility for a successful play

---

47 *Eastward Ho* 5.3.117–18, 5.5.112–15 and 216.

48 *The Magnetic Lady* (HS vol. 6, pp. 499–597), 1.1.19–21, 2–13.

49 I borrow the notion of 'medicalization' from Michael Heyd, who points out that major landmarks in the development of this discourse were Robert Burton's *Anatomy of Melancholy* (London, 1621 [1st edn]), Meric Casaubon's *A Treatise Concerning Enthusiasme* (London, 1655 [i.e., 1654]), and Henry More's *Enthusiasmus Triumphatus* (Cambridge, [1656]). See Heyd, *'Be Sober and Reasonable': The Critique of Enthusiasm in the Seventeenth and Early Eighteenth Centuries* (Leiden, 1995), esp. pp. 44–108.

rests less with the playwright who fits than with the audience who must submit to being fitted. Reporting how Jonson once 'fell down upon his knees' after one of his plays failed 'and gave thanks, that he had transcended the capacity of the vulgar', Edmund Gayton (1654) like many another contemporary playgoer faulted Jonson precisely for his elitist inability to suit himself to company: 'men come not to study at a Play-house, but love such expressions and passages, which with ease insinuate themselves into their capacities'.[50] Such criticisms, however, only highlight by contrast the intensity of Jonson's commitment to a dramaturgical theory he could not easily practise. *The Magnetic Lady* bears witness to his sense as he wrote the play that he could not justify his theatrical career without presenting Christian reconciliation as part of his purpose, and he could not lay claim to the role of reconciler without presenting himself as all things to all men.[51]

II

According to William Hazlitt (1818), Shakespeare possessed a special 'power of communication with all other minds' because 'he was the least of an egotist that it was possible to be': 'He was nothing in himself; but he was all that others were, or that they could become.' These lines echo and do not echo Paul: the difference, as Hazlitt understands it, is that when Shakespeare becomes 'like all other men', he has no rhetorical designs on them because he has no particular beliefs to peddle. Thus 'Shakespeare discovers in his writings little religious enthusiasm' and likewise has 'none of the bigotry of his age'.[52] George Santayana (1896) pushed Hazlitt's claims to their logical conclusion: Shakespeare 'is remarkable among the greater poets', he declared, 'for being without a philosophy and without a religion'.[53] This view has proven to be powerfully enduring. Extolling Shakespeare for the 'elusiveness of [his] personality' and his 'negative capability', so recent a biographer as Stanley Wells (1997) omits the

topic of religion from his analyses of Shakespeare's life and works.[54]

Comparison of Shakespeare to his fellow public-theatre playwrights does support Hazlitt to a degree. Little in Shakespeare's plays matches the anti-Catholic ferocity of Thomas Dekker's *Whore of Babylon* (1606), for instance, or the hatred of puritans expressed in Dekker's *If It Be Not Good, The Devil Is In It* (1611), which ends with hilarity about a deformed puritan soul burning in hell. But Shakespeare is not without polemical edge. The first two *Henry VI* plays (*c.* 1590) portray Cardinal Beaufort as a 'scarlet hypocrite' whose corrupt ambitions help to tear England apart. Even more inflammatorily, the king in *King John* (*c.* 1595) characterizes the pope himself as a 'meddling priest' who maintains his 'usurped authority' over English affairs only through the

---

50 Edmund Gayton, *Pleasant Notes upon Don Quixot* (1654), in *HS* vol. 11, p. 505.

51 As David Riggs notes, Jonson's surrogate in his final, uncompleted play *The Sad Shepherd* is Reuben the 'Reconciler' (*Ben Jonson: A Life* (Cambridge, Mass., 1989), p. 345).

52 William Hazlitt, 'On Shakspeare and Milton', *Lectures on the English Poets* (1818; 2nd edn 1819), in *The Collected Works of William Hazlitt*, ed. A. R. Waller and Arnold Glover, 12 vols. (London, 1902–4), vol. 5, pp. 47 and 56. Cf. Coleridge (1811) in *Shakespearean Criticism*, ed. Thomas M. Raysor, 2 vols. (London, 1960), vol. 2, pp. 66–7.

53 George Santayana, 'The Absence of Religion in Shakespeare' (1896), revised for *Interpretations of Poetry and Religion* (1900), ed. William G. Holzberger and Herman J. Saatkamp, Jr (Cambridge, Mass., 1989), p. 100.

54 Stanley Wells, *Shakespeare: A Dramatic Life* (1994), reprinted as *Shakespeare: The Poet and his Plays* (London, 1997); for the Romanticism of Wells's approach, see e.g. pp. 14–15, 20–1, and 229. Without citing the available biographical evidence on Shakespeare's possible religious views, Wells dismisses it as 'tenuous and therefore useless' (p. 12). His survey of Shakespeare's reading (pp. 12–14) does not mention the Bible; in a later list of Shakespeare's sources he places the Bible second to last, before 'accounts of foreign travels' (p. 33). But Wells does briefly refer to the presence of 'Christian paradox' and 'prayer' in *The Tempest* (pp. 369–70).

'sale' of 'corrupted pardon'.[55] Not even John's own mother, however, denies that John too rules illegitimately, and, as David Bevington points out, *1 Henry VI* weighs Beaufort's sins 'in the balance against other forms of opportunism'.[56] The same balancing act occurs when Shakespeare takes aim at puritans. In *Twelfth Night* (*c.* 1600), the puritanical Malvolio is offset by the toss-pot Sir Toby Belch, while in the two *Henry IV* plays (*c.* 1597) the equally unsavoury extremes of Malvolio and Belch meet, as it were, in the figure of the canting drunkard Falstaff. If Shakespeare's plays indicate that he sided with neither papist nor puritan, they also show him striving to resist identification with antipapists and antipuritans.

Recent years have witnessed a resurgence in efforts to shed light on Shakespeare's possible religious views from biographical evidence other than the plays themselves. This new research, the work of E. A. J. Honigmann and Eric Sams in particular, has persuasively demonstrated that Shakespeare was in all likelihood raised a Catholic.[57] Since Shakespeare was born only a few years after Protestantism had been restored as England's official religion, however, such an hypothesis is relatively unsurprising and, what's more, it tells us nothing about Shakespeare's adult beliefs: John Donne too was raised a Catholic, yet he went on to become Dean of St Paul's and a jewel in the crown of the Protestant church.[58] Extant records concerning the religious affiliations of Shakespeare's family and friends indicate only that Shakespeare, like Compass, was able to suit himself to all sorts of people. Whereas his father and daughter failed to attend services on occasion and were suspected of being 'popishly affected,' his partners and close friends Heminges and Condell were prominent office-holders in their parish church.[59] The silence of the records about Shakespeare himself suggests that he chose neither path: he seems to have conformed to the established religion, yet he also appears to have kept a low profile at church.

So quiet a devotional life does not make Shakespeare ipso facto an orthodox Protestant, as some scholars have maintained – many another of Shakespeare's contemporaries managed to reconcile a privately held dissenting faith with outward conformity – but it does add to the impression left by his plays that he deplored sectarianism. Shakespeare's puritanical characters are typically divisive figures, longing for a separation from their moral inferiors. Thus Malvolio hopes to 'wash off gross acquaintance'; the mock-puritan Falstaff continually gripes about the 'villainous company' to which he is subjected; and the 'precise' Angelo claims to have rejected Maria because 'her reputation was disvalued / In levity'.[60] Shakespeare's Catholic bishops and cardinals are more divisive still, sponsoring factiousness on a national and even international scale: the most dangerous of them, the papal legate Pandulph, causes a truce between France and England to be broken and promises sainthood to anyone who assassinates King John.[61]

Opposition to sectarianism can of course seem sectarian itself, as when Dekker punishes his schismatical puritan with deformity and hellfire.[62] Such antipuritan satire figures

---

55 William Shakespeare, *1 Henry VI*, 1.4.55 (Wells and Taylor oddly drop this Folio reading); *K. John*, 3.1.73–97.

56 *K. John* 1.1.40–3; Bevington, *Tudor*, p. 202.

57 See E. A. J. Honigmann, *Shakespeare: The 'Lost Years'* (1985; 2nd edn Manchester, 1998); and Eric Sams, *The Real Shakespeare: Retrieving the Early Years, 1564–1594* (New Haven, 1995).

58 For Donne's early Catholicism, see R. C. Bald, *John Donne: A Life* (Oxford, 1970). Neither Honigmann nor Sams makes the case that Shakespeare was Catholic when he wrote his plays.

59 Park Honan, *Shakespeare: A Life* (Oxford, 1998), pp. 38–40 and 354.

60 *Twelfth Night* 2.5.142; *1 Henry IV* 3.3.8; *Measure* 1.3.50 and 5.1.219–22.

61 For more on Shakespeare's depiction of bishops, see my 'Preachers and Players in Shakespeare's England', *Representations*, 44 (Fall, 1993), 29–59.

62 'Alack! / How can I choose but halt, go lame, and crooked? / When I pull'd a whole church down upon my back' (Thomas Dekker, *If It Be Not Good* (1611),

prominently in the plays of Jonson, Cartwright and Mayne; but Shakespeare, more careful to avoid provocation, equivocates about whether his puritanical characters are really puritans at all: in *Twelfth Night*, Maria alleges that Malvolio is 'sometimes' only 'a kind of puritan' (2.3.125), while Angelo in *Measure for Measure* (*c.* 1603) is again merely said to be 'precise'. The exception proves the rule: having aroused controversy by naming a comic character after the proto-Protestant hero Sir John Oldcastle, who also happened to be the ancestor of prominent puritan aristocrats, Shakespeare changed the character's name to Falstaff and ended *2 Henry IV* by insisting that the 'martyr' Oldcastle was a different man. In the context of these attempts to mute his criticism of puritans, Shakespeare's reluctance to preach Christian doctrine seems a mark not of his secularism, as most scholars have claimed, but rather of his fears regarding the potential divisiveness of his religious beliefs. As the moderate puritan Richard Sibbes puts it in his *Bruised Reede, and Smoaking Flax* (1630), 'In some cases peace by *keeping our faith to our selves*, is of more consequence, than the open discovery of some things we take to be true, considering the weakness of man's nature is such that there can hardly be a discovery of any difference in opinion, without some estrangement of affection.'[63] Such pious discretion coincides with the accommodationist advice of Shakespeare's one peace-loving bishop, Cranmer in *Henry VIII* (*c.* 1612), who also happens to be the only Protestant of the group: 'Win straying souls with modesty again', Cranmer urges the 'cruel' and 'bloody' Catholic Gardiner, 'Cast none away.'[64]

The most telling evidence of Shakespeare's own accommodationism is his surprisingly sympathetic treatment of friars, who 'speak with authority, within the sphere of their religious vocation, and command the respect of the other characters' in the plays they inhabit.[65] Gestures of reconciliation toward the Catholic members of Shakespeare's audience, the friars also act as reconcilers in the world of their plays: Friar Patrick in *Two Gentlemen of Verona* (*c.* 1591), Friar Laurence in *Romeo and Juliet* (*c.* 1595), Friar Francis in *Much Ado About Nothing* (*c.* 1598), and the various friars of *Measure for Measure* all help to arrange marriages. To ponder why Shakespeare should have assigned this unitive role to friars, rather than bishops, monks or priests, is to grasp more fully the religious aims that Shakespeare no less than Jonson seems to have regarded as compatible with his commercial efforts to 'please all men'. What first distinguishes friars from other Catholic clergy is their itinerancy, which, Shakespeare appears to believe, frees them from parochialness.[66] It also links friars with the itinerant players. From the 1570s, theatrical companies had in fact played in the 'liberty' once occupied by London's Black Friars; Shakespeare's company acquired Blackfriars property in 1596 and opened a playhouse there twelve years later (Shakespeare himself bought the Blackfriars gatehouse).[67] By making his most important peripatetic friar a pretender – the literally 'unreverend and unhallowed' Duke Vincentio of *Measure for Measure* (5.1.299) – Shakespeare indicates that he sees friars and players as performing a similar kind of spiritual

---

Dramatic Works, ed. Fredson Bowers, 4 vols. (Cambridge, 1953–61), vol. 3, pp. 113–223, 5.4.281–3).

63 Richard Sibbes, *The Bruised Reede, and Smoaking Flax* (London, 1630), p. 200.

64 *Henry VIII* 5.2.98–9, 163. For an alternative reading of Shakespeare as a 'moderate Catholic' who conceals his true beliefs because he fears persecution, see Gary Taylor, 'Forms of Opposition: Shakespeare and Middleton', *English Literary Renaissance*, 24 (1994), 283–314.

65 Milward, *Shakespeare's Religious Background*, p. 73.

66 Shakespeare highlights the itinerancy of friars in Petruchio's song – 'It was the friar of orders gray, / As he forth walked on his way' (*Shrew* 4.1.126–7) – and in contradistinction to the 'strict restraint' of *Measure for Measure*'s nuns (1.4.4).

67 A sense of professional camaraderie with friars helps explain why the only positive representations of friars in Elizabethan literature after 1563 appear, according to Stanley Satz, in the theatre. See Satz's 'The Friar in Elizabethan Drama', unpublished dissertation (Kent State University, 1972); Satz himself does not offer this explanation.

work, outside of 'precise' religious boundaries. Yet Vincentio's actions also imply that Shakespeare regards players as better suited to such an irregular ministry than friars are. For like Shakespeare's other friars, the 'Duke of dark corners' (*Measure*, 4.3.153) is addicted to a secretiveness and subterfuge that go against the grain of the friar's proper excursiveness; in *Romeo and Juliet*, Friar Laurence's unwillingness to be discovered even contributes to Juliet's death. Players, by contrast, enact the friars' cozenages on the open stage, in full view of the audience. This obligatory publicity appears to have made them more plausible sponsors of communal reconciliation, to Shakespeare's mind, than their huggermugger Catholic counterparts.

But how, aside from avoiding religious controversy, did Shakespeare think his players were to effect such reconciliation? The mere act of drawing thousands of people together on a weekly basis was unprecedented enough, outside of major church services, to make Stubbes fear the theatre as the church's rival. For other writers, conversely, the relative lack of occasions for mass sociability in Renaissance England made any such event seem a churchlike gathering: so William Fennor (1619) praises even the maypole and alehouse drinking for encouraging 'honest neighbourhood' and 'hearty fellowship,' no matter what 'factious' puritans may say about them.[68] Throughout the prologues to *Henry V* (*c.* 1598), Shakespeare appears to disclose his own belief that players can help forge a similarly congregational fellowship in the theatre by encouraging the imaginative participation of their audiences.[69] If this community must be fashioned without the aid of preaching, so much the better, Shakespeare's reticence about doctrine implies. Just as Nashe urged ministers to speak within the compass of the five senses and Jonson shifted the work of Christian reconciliation from doctrinal questions to the more uncontroversial and ordinary matter of 'humours,' so Shakespeare seems to have conceived that players could spiritually unite audiences through a shared examination

of human 'frailty' – especially erotic turmoil, the carnal simulacrum of Christian fellowship: 'for young Chairbonne the puritan and old Poisson the papist, howsome'er their hearts are severed in religion', jokes the clown in *All's Well That Ends Well* (*c.* 1604), their cuckold 'heads are both one' (1.3.51–4). What appears to have recommended friars to Shakespeare besides their itinerancy, in other words, is their association with confession, which Shakespeare presents as performed in his theatre the way Protestants argued it should be: not in 'private' or in 'secret', but before 'the open audience of the whole people'.[70]

Shakespeare's reference in *Romeo and Juliet* to the 'barefoot' friars (5.2.5) suggests one further source of his professional investment in them – their lowliness. More than egotism may have differentiated Jonson's attempts at accommodationism from Shakespeare's: no bishops published elegies on Shakespeare, and it may be that he kept his distance from such higher powers in order to avoid the partisan view of church affairs to which Jonson, along with an increasing number of younger playwrights, succumbed. Meaning to celebrate the era after Shakespeare's heyday and before the puritans closed the theatres, when bishops and theatre people supposedly worked together to teach religion and preserve Christian unity, a Jonson disciple

---

[68] [William Fennor?], *Pasquils Palinodia* (London, 1619), sigs. B3r–4r and D3v; see Marcus, *Politics*, and Ronald Hutton, *The Rise and Fall of Merry England: The Ritual Year, 1400–1700* (Oxford, 1994).

[69] See once again Knapp, 'Preachers and Players'.

[70] John Jewel, *Works*, ed. John Ayre, 4 vols. (Cambridge, 1845–50), vol. 4, p. 361; Jewel also affirms the efficacy of lay confession (p. 357). Cartwright's cheaters make a private confession public in *The Ordinary* 5.3.

Shuger reads *Measure for Measure* as dramatizing a 'penitential' conception of theatre in her forthcoming book, *The King of Souls*. For the communalism shared by the Shakespearian stage and the English church, see Ramie Targoff, 'The Performance of Prayer: Sincerity and Theatricality in Early Modern England', *Representations*, 60 (1997), 49–69.

(1653) instead unwittingly implicates players in the sectarianism that Shakespeare hoped his theatre could help cure:

> Time was, when Plays were justly valu'd, when
> Poets could laugh away the Crimes of men.
> And by Instructive Recreation teach
> More in one hour, than some in ten do preach.
> But Times are chang'd; and 'tis worth our note,
> Bishops, and Players both suffer'd in one Vote.

> And reason good, for [the puritans] had cause to
>   fear 'em,
> One did suppress their Schisms, and t'other jeer
>   'em.[71]

---

71 Alexander Brome, 'Upon the Ingenious Comedies of Mr. Richard Brome' (1653), in Roman R. Dubinski, ed. *Alexander Brome: Poems*, 2 vols. (Toronto, 1982), vol. 1, pp. 380–1, lines 15–22.

THE BARD AND IRELAND: SHAKESPEARE'S PROTESTANTISM AS POLITICS IN DISGUISE

PAUL FRANSSEN

In his curious science-fiction novel entitled *The Return of William Shakespeare*, Hugh Kingsmill shows a remarkable understanding of the cultural forces that determine our picture of Shakespeare, of how this image is constructed and how it is inextricably interwoven with questions of political power.[1] As a time-travel narrative, the book briefly holds out the promise of unmediated access to Shakespeare himself through the blessings of modern technology, but then proceeds to undermine the real possibility of ever recovering one authentic and objective truth, even within the fictional framework. In Kingsmill's novel, Shakespeare is transported from the year 1607 to the novel's present, the nineteen-twenties, by some unspecified process. As it turns out, however, the 'reintegrated' Shakespeare is depressed, and hardly presentable to the general public: he cries much of the time, speaks in 'an odd lingo, and accent you could cut through with a knife' (51), and worst of all, he does not remember anything. However, there are pressing reasons, not the least financial, for presenting Shakespeare to the public; and so a conspiracy is set up among the organizers of the time travel experiment to disguise one of them, a PR man, as Shakespeare. Unlike the real Shakespeare, the imposter 'corresponded roughly to the generalized impression the ordinary Englishman has of Shakespeare' (69).

It is through the contrast between the fake Shakespeare, acceptable to the modern audience, and the real one, nearly dumb and hard to communicate with, that the novel makes its main satirical points. The conspirators have to construct their own Shakespeare to present to the public, which leads to a lively discussion on which line to take. One possibility is to make him 'the lover broken by passion – the Frank Harris idea. Sex-exhaustion. To hell with women. The pity of it, Iago. But does the public want that? I doubt it. Not the big public anyway.'[2] The alternative is to 'try a Victorian Shakespeare on them . . . bland and mild, getting a little nest-egg together in London for the wife and kiddies down at Stratford' (75). Another suggestion is to make him a Catholic, which would appeal to both Protestants and Catholics in this time of secularization (76). And so the discussion goes on, whether to make him a democrat, a middle-class exploiter, or an aristocrat; a faithful husband or a philanderer. Always the discussion turns on what would be acceptable to the modern public at large; intrinsic likelihood or historical evidence play only a minor role.

Obviously, the plot is symbolic of real-life debates about the nature of the Bard: the silence of Kingsmill's Shakespeare corresponds to the lack of historical or biographical information

---

[1] Hugh Kingsmill, *The Return of William Shakespeare* (Indianapolis, 1929).

[2] Kingsmill, 75. Kingsmill knew Frank Harris personally, and later wrote his biography. See Charles Calder's entry on Kingsmill in the *Dictionary of Literary Biography*, vol. 149, and Michael Holroyd's introduction to his *The Best of Hugh Kingsmill* (London, 1970), pp. 10–11, 14–15.

about the real man, which gives clever and greedy opportunists a chance to substitute a whole range of fake Shakespeares, constructed with an eye to their marketability. The novel, then, satirizes the appropriation of Shakespeare, while suggesting that historical accuracy will always remain elusive, and would still be even if we really did have a time machine.

In one respect, Kingsmill's book has proved prophetic, in that currently the crypto-Catholic Shakespeare seems to be much in demand again: in particular with the recent Hoghton Tower conference, centring on evidence for Shakespeare's connections with a well-known Catholic family.[3] I am not suggesting, of course, that the scholars involved in that project were indulging in wishful thinking; but even if documentary evidence should ever emerge that the William Shakeshafte employed as a schoolmaster by the Hoghtons really was identical with William Shakespeare of Stratford-upon-Avon, that still would not prove that the mature dramatist held the same beliefs. With a playwright whose most famous protagonist fulfils the command of a ghost from a Catholic purgatory by most calvinistically resigning to the Divinity that shapes our ends, some uncertainty about his personal beliefs seems inevitable.[4]

Kingsmill's awareness of the near endless appropriability of Shakespeare, looking forward to much recent criticism,[5] is particularly applicable to that most pliable kind of Shakespearian appropriation, fictional representations of the Bard by novelists and dramatists. In so far as his religion is concerned, fictional Shakespeares seem to have covered nearly the entire range of plausible faiths. The one exception seems to be Puritanism, which for obvious reasons is not much in evidence. In most early fantasies of Shakespeare's life, the default assumption seems to be that the National Poet must have been a model Anglican. In Nathan Drake's *Noontide Leisure* (1824), for instance, Shakespeare is 'as remarkable for the piety as for the cheerfulness

of his disposition', and 'on principle, and after due enquiry, a firm believer in the truths of our holy religion'.[6] As these last words are spoken by a vicar, the religion in question must be Church of England. Later in the century, in *Shakespeare's Funeral* (1889) by Sir Edward Bruce Hamley, Shakespeare is relatively secular-minded compared to his bigoted Puritan relatives and townsmen at Stratford. That does not disqualify him, however, from becoming an object of bardolatrous veneration himself.[7] More remarkably, Louis Alexander's *The Autobiography of Shakespeare* provides Shakespeare with Jewish ancestry, without making him into a practising Jew himself.[8] Unsurprisingly, many recent authors find myriad-minded Shakespeare a natural agnostic: Philip Burton's *You, My Brother*, for instance, makes Will into a doubter among devout believers of different persuasions.

---

[3] The case for Shakespeare's Lancastrian connections was made most forcefully by E. A. J. Honigmann, *Shakespeare: The 'Lost Years'* (Manchester, 1985). For a survey of evidence concerning Shakespeare's Catholicism, see Gary Taylor, 'Forms of Opposition: Shakespeare and Middleton', *English Literary Renaissance*, 24 (1994), 283–314.

[4] Following an extensive survey of all the evidence regarding the religious affiliation of Shakespeare's Stratford surroundings, Patrick Collinson concludes that '[a]s for Shakespeare himself, we cannot say'. See his 'William Shakespeare's Religious Inheritance', in *Elizabethan Essays* (London, 1994), p. 252. For a comprehensive survey of recent research, see Donna B. Hamilton, 'Shakespeare and Religion', in *The Shakespearean International Yearbook*: 1. Where Are We Now in Shakespearean Studies, ed. W. R. Elton and John M. Mucciolo (Aldershot, 1999), pp. 187–202.

[5] Such as Gary Taylor, *Reinventing Shakespeare: A Cultural History from the Restoration to the Present* (London, 1990), and Terence Hawkes, *Meaning by Shakespeare* (London, 1992).

[6] Nathan Drake, MD, *Noontide Leisure: . . . including A Tale of the Days of William Shakespeare* (London, 1824), pp. 56–7; 327.

[7] Sir Edward Bruce Hamley, *Shakespeare's Funeral and Other Papers* (Edinburgh and London, 1889), esp. pp. 52–5.

[8] Louis C. Alexander, *The Autobiography of Shakespeare: A Fragment* (London, 1911).

He may occasionally envy the certainties of Puritan Anne Hathaway and Roman Catholic Ben Jonson, but refuses to settle for simple answers that cancel out others. Burton suggests that it is precisely this negative capability that enables Shakespeare to draw a broad array of characters with precision.[9] Other fictional Shakespeares have flirted with heretical beliefs: Peter Whelan's play *The School of Night*[10] portrays a young Shakespeare, son of a Catholic father, involved in a conspiracy to smuggle an atheistical Christopher Marlowe out of the country, whereas in Snoo Wilson's farce *More Light*, a female Shakespeare acknowledges s/he has been borrowing some ideas from the notorious heretic Giordano Bruno.[11] In both cases, Shakespeare acts as a peripheral figure, influenced by dangerous freethinkers, but not professing any strong religious views himself. In his classic novel *Nothing Like the Sun*, Anthony Burgess projects his own Manichean convictions onto the Bard, who gradually comes to believe in the reality of evil, 'an illness from beyond, gratuitous and incurable, . . . poison-[ing us] at source.'[12]

In our secularized world, the social force of representations of Shakespeare's religion is usually minimal. Still, occasionally we may be reminded that there was a time when religious issues were quite as important as politics. Indeed, as Deborah K. Shuger has argued, in the early modern era religion may well have been more important: 'Religion during this period supplies the primary language of analysis. It is the cultural matrix for explorations of virtually every topic: kingship, selfhood, rationality, language, marriage, ethics, and so forth.' However, '[r]eligion is not *simply* politics in disguise'.[13] That does not mean, of course, that the two can be easily disentangled; Donna B. Hamilton and Richard Strier speak of the 'near identity of religion and politics'.[14] In later centuries, in spite of the growing separation between church and state, religion has often played an important role as the spiritual side of state power, domestically and internationally. In

particular since the eighteenth century, a third factor has been added: the cultural domain, spearheaded by Shakespeare.[15] To some extent, bardolatry can be seen as an alternative for religion in an age of secularization, but in actual practice, the two often go together as complementary ways of projecting English values. If, according to the BBC, the Bible and the works of Shakespeare are essential equipment when travelling to a desert island,[16] this may well be a survival from the days of British colonialism, when Empire builders took not only their guns and their beads and baubles with them to the heart of darkness, but also their King James Bible and the Complete Works of Shakespeare: emblems of naked force, trade, the Protestant religion, and English culture respectively, as four different instruments in spreading English civilization. As I have argued elsewhere, the result may well be a blending of such symbols of English hegemony, so that we find in the works of Rudyard Kipling a fantasy of Shakespeare revising the *Authorized Version*, alongside a narrative of Shakespeare receiving the basic idea for *The Tempest* from some sailors newly

---

9 Philip Burton, *You, My Brother: A Novel Based on the Lives of Edmund & William Shakespeare* (New York, 1973).

10 Peter Whelan, *The School of Night* (London, 1992).

11 Snoo Wilson, *More Light: A Play about the Heretic Giordano Bruno* (Oxford, 1990).

12 Anthony Burgess, *Nothing Like the Sun: A Story of Shakespeare's Love-life* (London, 1992), p. 231.

13 Deborah K. Shuger, *Habits of Thought in the English Renaissance: Religion, Politics, and the Dominant Culture* (Berkeley, 1990), p. 6.

14 'Introduction' to Donna B. Hamilton and Richard Strier, eds., *Religion, Literature, and Politics in Post-Reformation England, 1540–1688* (Cambridge, 1996), p. 2.

15 As traced by Michael Dobson, *The Making of the National Poet: Shakespeare, Adaptation and Authorship, 1660–1769* (Oxford, 1992).

16 See John Drakakis, 'Theatre, Ideology, and Institution: Shakespeare and the Roadsweepers', in *The Shakespeare Myth*, ed. Graham Holderness (Manchester, 1988), 24–41; and Malcolm Evans, *Signifying Nothing: Truth's True Contents in Shakespeare's Text* (New York, 1986), p. 86.

returned from the New World. In both, the idea of the White Man's Burden, the imperial mission of civilizing the world, is not far off.[17]

Similar constellations, in which both Shakespeare and religion *do* become little more than 'politics in disguise', can be encountered in other fictions about Shakespeare's life. I will now turn to two antithetical examples, both relating to that most unfortunate island that was the first of England's overseas possessions, Ireland.

In 1872 a remarkable play was published, 'after the Elizabethan Model', as the title page proclaims, by Tresham D. Gregg, DD, entitled *Queen Elizabeth: or the Origin of Shakespeare*.[18] This pastiche of a chronicle play appropriates both Shakespeare and Bacon as symbols of English grandeur in the age of Elizabeth. For Gregg, however, that greatness was not so much secular as spiritual. Right before the entrance of her two greatest subjects, the Queen speaks prophetic words:

> It is my deep conviction that the Crown
> Is the true parent of those souls inspired
> Which to an age give immortality.
> The seeds of ill-doers are 'neath a ban,
> They never will be glorious or renowned;
> And so a state disloyal to the skies
> Is curs'd with mediocrity in its subjects.   (109)

Virtue, in this play, is primarily defined in terms of religious obedience and doctrinal correctness. God's reward for the monarch's righteousness is the genius of her subjects. Fittingly, in the prolegomena the preceding history is recounted in biblical phraseology: like Old Testament kings, Elizabeth did 'that which was right before the Lord', in particular when 'the temples of Baal she overthrew'. Antichrist, afraid of losing his influence in England, then caused the King of France to proclaim Mary Stuart the heir to the English throne. In Gregg's polemical language, redolent of the controversies of the Reformation era, the obvious referent of the Antichrist and Baal is Roman Catholicism. The

Queen's righteousness before the Lord is amply demonstrated in her piety, her addresses to the bishops and the peers of the realm, her refusal to marry the Catholic King of Spain, and most of all in the gift she receives from God to reward her for her virtue.

Small wonder, therefore, that Shakespeare, too, comes from an impeccably Protestant background. The poverty of his father, John, is the result of his generous financial support to an old doctor, to save him from the former government. The implication is that the doctor was in trouble for being a dissenter under Mary Tudor's reign. John Shakespeare's wife, Mary Arden, is transformed by Gregg into 'a parson's daughter, of the old Lollard stock, without a groat'. Obviously, without any monetary obstacle, and with such Protestant credentials on both sides, their marriage is bound to be an unqualified success. While John is happily sitting in his cell because of his debts, and his wife is giving birth to a son, he dreams that this son will be a 'leader in the way to Freedom', a kind of Moses figure. It is curious that, while Gregg writes such an explicitly anti-Catholic text, he cannot himself resist the temptation of a nearly popish idolatry of the Bard himself, casting him as the christological saviour of England.

Now that both the Queen and the Bard's family have been appropriated in the cause of good Protestantism, the stage has been set for their encounter. Shakespeare as well as Francis Bacon are still boys when they are both presented to Queen Elizabeth at the entertainment at Kenilworth, organized in her honour by the Earl of Leicester. Not unlike Christ teaching the elders in the Temple, Shakespeare is remarkably precocious. So is Bacon, but their styles are

---

17 Paul Franssen, 'The Bard, the Bible, and the Desert Island', in *The Author as Character: Representing Historical Writers in Western Literature*, ed. Paul Franssen and Ton Hoenselaars (Madison, 1999), 106–17.

18 Tresham D. Gregg, DD, *Queen Elizabeth: or the Origin of Shakespeare* (London, 1872).

dissimilar. Asked to give witty definitions of concepts such as life, death and twilight, Shakespeare wins on points, not in the last place because his definitions tend to be poetic and pious, where Bacon's are more scientific. Yet in their generosity, the two boys decline to compete for royal favour, founding a mutual admiration society instead. Shakespeare declares that Bacon is 'too noble . . . for [his] foe'. Having thus with remarkable foresight put the (future) Baconian heretics in their places, Shakespeare and Bacon dance with Queen Elizabeth, as a symbol of harmony, and Shakespeare speaks the epilogue in which he once more affirms that he was God's special gift to the righteous Queen.

Gregg's crude didacticism emerges throughout the play, which also includes a number of highly undramatic theological debates, such as an interview between John Knox and Mary Queen of Scots. Before dismissing this pious pastiche of a chronicle play as a mere curiosity written by an eccentric, however, it is advisable to enquire into the author's background. Tresham D. Gregg (1799–1881), Chaplain of St Nicholas Within, Dublin, was an Anglican clergyman working in Roman Catholic Ireland. 'Trashy' Gregg was well known in his own age as a prolific Protestant controversialist with a taste for polemics, writing in an abrasive style on topics ranging from the Psalms to Independency. Apart from his theological works, he composed a number of chronicle plays on subjects that lent themselves to controversy, such as Edward VI and Mary Tudor. In addition, he was a conservative political activist, and founded the Dublin Protestant Operative Association to agitate against the liberal Irish Nationalist Daniel O'Connell.[19]

This particular play, too, is informed by the politics of the moment. This emerges from Gregg's dedication to United States president Ulysses S. Grant, asking him to found a Church of America, meaning an established Church analogous to the Church of England. A mere three years earlier, in 1869, the Irish Church had been disestablished by Gladstone's liberal government, which suggests that this dedication is not so much aimed at the United States, as Maurice O'Sullivan has suggested, but can more profitably be read as a signal of protest against the policies of the English cabinet.[20] The disestablishment of the Church of Ireland was a particularly painful episode in the history of that institution, the more so as its main practical effect was its disendowment.[21] Debates in the English Parliament preceding the Act of Disestablishment centred on political questions rather than theological ones: whether the Catholic majority perceived the Church of Ireland as a 'badge of conquest', and whether disestablishment would appease Nationalist opposition to English rule. Even defenders of the status quo did not care to disguise the political dimensions of the issue. In June 1868, the Archbishop of Armagh, for instance, quite openly spoke of the role of the Church in subduing the Irish masses by peaceful means:

Do not imagine that if you overthrow the Irish Church there will not be an extensive emigration of Protestants who are the most loyal of her Majesty's subjects . . . If you will allow this, you will find Ireland so difficult to manage that you will have to depend on gibbet and sword; and you will regret having no longer the aid of the churchmen and the church, which kept the Irish people together and made English law, English authority, English freedom and an English Bible loved and respected. (Evans, *Disestablishment*, 155)

It is against this background that Gregg's play and its appropriation of Shakespeare and his era should be read. Its choice of setting, the Elizabethan period, reflects the Parliamentary

---

[19] *BBI* I 483, 190–3; *The Oxford Companion to Irish History*, ed. S. J. Connolly (Oxford, 1990), p. 230.

[20] See Maurice O'Sullivan's introduction to his *Shakespeare's Other Lives: An Anthology of Fictional Depictions of the Bard* (Jefferson NC and London, 1997), p. 10.

[21] My discussion of the disestablishment issue is based on Anna Laura Evans, *The Disestablishment of the Church of Ireland in 1869*, PhD thesis Columbia 1928 (Lancaster, PA, 1929).

debates of the eighteen-sixties: Gladstone, among others, had invoked the Virgin Queen, asking whether she would not have regarded the Irish state church, based on her Church settlement, as a failure if she could have seen it as it was in the nineteenth century: the Church of a tiny minority, paid for by a hostile majority (Evans, *Disestablishment*, 126). When Gregg's play opens with a discussion of the 'regiment of women', this would also have served to underline the parallel between past and present, in that another powerful Queen was ruling England and its overseas possessions. As such, part of the play's purpose may be reconstructed as hortatory praise of Queen Victoria, who was known to have little personal sympathy for the disestablishment carried through by her government (Evans, 222), asking her to intercede on behalf of the Protestant religion and English interests in Ireland. If she follows the example of her illustrious predecessor, the implication is, and persuades her government to reverse the disestablishment of the Irish Church, Victoria will be rewarded by God with a cultural and scientific Renaissance matching the glories of the Elizabethan age. As she did not, it is hardly surprising that, instead of another Shakespeare and Bacon, she got Charles Darwin, Thomas Hardy and Oscar Wilde.

The politics of Shakespeare's religion, in the context of the Anglo-Irish conflict, are made more explicit in the short play entitled *Shakespeare's End* (1912), by Conal O'Riordan, writing under the pen-name of Norreys Connell.[22] O'Riordan portrays Shakespeare as the prophet of Empire; yet, unlike Gregg, or contemporaries such as Rudyard Kipling, he takes an adversarial view, confronting rather than appropriating the bardic icon. The play's theme is the social and political function of art, seen from a radical perspective; Shakespeare, in O'Riordan's fantasy, comes to realize on the last night of his life that by glorifying material values, Protestantism, and English Imperialism,

he has failed to fulfil his proper function as an artist, and so he dies in bitter disillusionment.

The structure of the play is quite simple and didactic. Starting from the anecdote, recorded by John Ward, that Shakespeare died after some heavy drinking with Jonson and Drayton, O'Riordan imagines him celebrating his birthday in his Stratford house with a number of friends, when he receives two unexpected visitors.[23] The first, a beggarly sailor, represents the false ideals Shakespeare still believes in; the second, a Jesuit, represents the anti-imperialistic and anti-capitalistic values that he ought to have espoused. As a result of his confrontation with these two opposite characters, Shakespeare has an epiphany in which he comes to see the vanity of his life and values shortly before his death.

In his materialistic values and his desire for a knighthood, O'Riordan's Shakespeare owes much to Shaw's conception of him as a bourgeois upstart.[24] He does have a degree of kindness and hospitality, and feels outrage at cruelty; his weakness is due to his illusions rather than to utter wickedness. In a rare reversal of positions, Shakespeare is found inferior to Ben Jonson, with whom he is inevitably contrasted. Jonson is more modest than Shakespeare, who braggingly compares himself to Chaucer and slights the achievements of his predecessor Marlowe; and Ben knows the true value of poetry, unlike Will who regrets that he did not use his talents in a more lucrative employment like banking, or Empire building such as Drake's:

> . . . for the world at large
> I hold it to be nothing but a mine,

---

22 Norreys Connell, *Shakespeare's End and Other Irish Plays* (Adelphi, 1912).

23 Cf. Samuel Schoenbaum, *Shakespeare's Lives* (Oxford, 1993), p. 78.

24 Cf. George Bernard Shaw, *The Dark Lady of the Sonnets*, in *The Complete Plays of Bernard Shaw* (London, 1965), pp. 644–51, including the preface. O'Riordan seems to have been on good terms with Shaw: see Richard F. Peterson and Gary Phillips, 'W. B. Yeats and Norreys Connell,' *Yeats Annual*, 2 (1983), 46–58, (esp. 47).

Where men who have the strength may dig for
    ore. (105)

Shakespeare's world view is shaken by the
arrival of a character known as the First
Passenger, a beggar who asks for food and a
place to sleep. Though Ben recognizes the man
as a criminal, Shakespeare admits him when he
hears that he was once a sailor under Grenville.
In exchange for food and shelter, he asks the
beggar to recount some of his adventures,
obviously expecting to be confirmed in his
heroic view of the active life that he regrets
having missed. But the sailor's reminiscences are
far from glorious, and often downright
shocking. For the first time, Shakespeare hears
of English involvement in the slave trade, of the
grim realities of war, of the folly of com-
manders, and of the outrages committed by
English sailors during the sacking of a Spanish
town, such as raping nuns, murdering priests,
and acts of sacrilege.

Though Shakespeare now despises the sailor,
he has not yet discarded his illusions altogether.
Asked by Jonson for his reaction to such outrages, he regrets the cruelty as a necessary evil in
a basically good cause. He still believes in the
imperial project, in 'all the nations thirsting for
one rule', in spite of the inadequacies of the
tools that must be used to bring about this
desirable state of affairs:

> The law is terrible that histories teach.
> The path to empire leads through battle fields
> And fallen cities lined with charnel-houses.
> The pioneers must carry tiger-hearts
> That know not mercy, must be cruel men,
> Or they would fail and falter on the way.
> But in the end carnage shall have its day,
> And little England over-lord the world –
> Then comes the reign of Peace . . . (123)

Shakespeare's education in the ways of the
real world is completed by the second visitor,
who openly proclaims that he is a Jesuit (which
makes dramatic rather than historical sense).
The priest is an Irishman, on his way from Spain
to his native country, the prototype of all the
colonial victims of British expansionism. He
sees his aim as saving souls as well as 'Ireland
herself, if heaven's will it be / That she be
saved from England' (128). Shakespeare takes
exception to the priest's criticism of English
rule, only to be gradually defeated in a debate in
which the priest, of course, has all the best
arguments. Protestantism is equal to capitalist
exploitation, the Jesuit says. He hints at the
complicity of English poets in the exploitation
of the Irish by his own example: members of his
family were murdered, raped, and robbed of
their property by Edmund Spenser's soldiers.
This, taken together with the self-confessed
crimes of the sailor, at last convinces Shakespeare that Englishmen turn into swine when
they travel overseas. He donates some money to
the priest for the Irish poor, and even confesses
his sins to him.

Now that the wrongs of colonial exploitation
have been established, O'Riordan introduces
his main theme, which is political rather than
religious: that of the poet's stance with regard
to social injustice.[25] Is he to take up the sword
and take an active part in the struggle for
justice, or should he stick to his pen? This
question is symbolically represented by the
crisis that erupts when the priest has gone out,
carrying the money given to him by Shakespeare. The sailor follows the Jesuit, with the
obvious intention to rob, perhaps kill him; a
Jesuit is, after all, a legitimate prey, being outside

---

[25] That O'Riordan's main focus is secular rather than
religious is confirmed by his introduction. Though a
Catholic himself, he realizes the limitations of the
priesthood, though the Jesuits, in his view, 'have been
the worthiest of priests' and 'have more often fought for
liberty than against it'. His real interest is in social
justice (17). This political stance may be surprising,
coming from a man who tried to join the British Army
in 1914. O'Riordan's play *The Piper* (1908) had led to
riots in Dublin's Abbey Theatre, as it was seen as
mocking the Irish rebels. Cf. Peterson and Phillips,
'W. B. Yeats', *The MacMillan Dictionary of Irish Literature*, ed. Robert Hogan (London, 1980), 524–45; and
The Oxford Companion to Irish Literature, ed. Robert
Welch (Oxford, 1996), p. 455.

the law. Shakespeare feels the urge to follow them and stop the sailor, but he finds that his companions are unwilling to come with him. Some are afraid, others dislike the priest on principle: but it is Ben Jonson who comes up with the only legitimate reason to refrain from taking action, the superior moral function of art. He tells Shakespeare:

> The poet may see murder done before him,
> And never seek to stay it, even may
> Refuse to name the culprit to the judge:
> But murder he must paint so horrible
> That murderers reading his awful word
> Shall stand indicted by their consciences,
> And call red justice down upon themselves. (157)

This quotation reveals Jonson as the true artist, besides whom Shakespeare is a mere sycophant. O'Riordan openly announces his preference for the rival dramatist in his preface, stating that 'it is not the priest who speaks for me [O'Riordan], it is rather Ben Jonson' (17). Yet Shakespeare cannot accept Jonson's plea, and longs to emulate the priest's martyrdom. Again Jonson discourages him: this is just 'moonery', a new version of the earlier dreams of Empire. The true calling of the poet is to influence the world through indirect means, creating order out of chaos through his song. Shakespeare remains full of doubt and despair, and tries to drown his sorrows in drink. He bitterly sums up his career:

> God put good tools into my hand to make
> A world, and I have made a coat of arms
> And a trim house at Stratford. Ay, my friends,
> God chose me for His angel, but I chose
> Rather to be an English gentleman
> Who hopes, an he live long, to be a knight.

Shortly afterwards, he dies in Jonson's arms. Although Ben has been critical of his friend throughout the play, he now gives him generous praise, as the 'head [that] doth hold four continents' (165). This suggests that Shakespeare was a man of exceptional talent, whose ultimate failure is not the result of inability but of unawareness of the proper function of art:

not to enrich oneself, nor to glorify one's nation, but to further the causes of justice and equality.

Although O'Riordan's use of Shakespeare's putative religion for political ends is not in itself remarkable, what is exceptional is his strategy of confronting – or debunking – rather than appropriating Shakespeare; outside Baconian or Oxfordian fantasies, this is rare, and the only comparable case I know of is Edward Bond's *Bingo*.[26]

Shakespeare's religion has been appropriated in fictional form on both sides of the divide in the Irish question, where politics and religion are particularly entangled. One may well wonder whether the authors believed their strategy of appropriation to be effective, as they are so clearly dealing in fantasies, not in documented facts. Indeed, O'Riordan admits as much. In the prefatory letter addressed to Joseph Conrad, he explains that he does not pretend to any historical veracity: Shakespeare is simply a means to talk about different matters. A notice after the list of Dramatis Personae makes a similar point:

The object of the play is not to portray dead men but to set forth living ideas which, the author believes, may be associated with their names. (86)

In so far as O'Riordan is dealing with 'ideas . . . associated with [Shakespeare's] name', of course, we can only agree that, rightly or wrongly, Shakespeare and his putative Protestantism have often been appropriated by English hegemonic discourses, also in relation to Ireland, Gregg's play being a prime example. Although Gregg's plot of the presentation of Shakespeare and Bacon to Queen Elizabeth is a self-conscious fiction, too, Gregg would undoubtedly have defended his fantasy as essentially grounded in fact: in particular, that the Elizabethan Church settlement was followed by

---

26 Edward Bond, *Bingo: Scenes of Money and Death* (London, 1974).

a period of unprecedented cultural flowering, led by (as he believed) two Protestant figureheads, Shakespeare and Bacon. Although the particular plays and incidents are wholly fictional, therefore, the essential ideas – Shakespeare as God's reward for England's Reformation; Shakespeare as a symbol of English Protestant exploitation of Ireland – are taken much more seriously by their authors, and need to be painstakingly deconstructed.[27]

---

[27] On this point, see my 'Portraits of Mr W.S.: The Myth of Sweet Master Shakespeare in Asimov, Wilde, and Burgess', in *Reclamations of Shakespeare*, ed. A. J. Hoenselaars (Amsterdam, 1994), pp. 139–50; in particular p. 142.

'EVERY GOOD GIFT FROM ABOVE'
ARCHBISHOP TRENCH'S TERCENTENARY SERMON

RICHARD FOULKES

Falling, as it inevitably did, on 23 April 1864, the tercentenary of Shakespeare's birth co-incided with a period of exceptionally intense religious controversy. In 1859 Charles Darwin had finally committed *The Origin of Species* to print; *Essays and Reviews* (the contentious collection of seven essays on theological and scientific issues, whose contributors included the future Archbishop of Canterbury, Frederick Temple, Mark Pattison and Benjamin Jowett) appeared in 1860; Bishop Colenso's *The Penta-teuch and the Book of Joshua Critically Examined*, in which the author applied his mathematical skills to the Five Books of Moses with theo-logically disconcerting results, followed in 1862–3 and in January 1863 *Man's Place in Nature*, by T. H. Huxley – the Apostle of Unbelief, who coined the word 'agnostic' – was published. The two areas of dispute were firstly the implication of scientific discoveries of evo-lution for religion and secondly revisionist bib-lical scholarship, originating in Germany, but with its exponents in Britain. Shakespeare was pertinent to both these issues. Already estab-lished as England's greatest dramatist, his tercen-tenary gave rise to increasingly expansive claims on his behalf by his fellow-countrymen, thereby framing anew the question of how genius occurred. Could traditional religious doctrine on the subject withstand the challenge of new evolutionary ideas? As for the Bible, if its status as literally the word of God was in question and it was no longer considered to be directly 'inspired', what became of the fundamental distinction between it and even the greatest, but 'uninspired', works of human genius? For churchmen the Shakespeare tercentenary pro-vided an opportunity to enlist Shakespeare on the side of religion and to use him and his works to counter current scientific and theological ideas, which were threatening, as never before, to undermine traditional Christian belief and with it their authority.

Shakespeare's place in nineteenth-century religion might be categorized as (i) rejection, (ii) appropriation, (iii) substitution. Although this order does reflect chronological progression all three elements co-existed, but by the tercen-tenary (indeed stimulated by it) appropriation was very much in the ascendancy over rejec-tion. The battle had been extremely long and bitterly fought. The early Christian church had been virulent in its condemnation of the theatre with Tatian, Tertullian and St Augustine mounting forceful attacks. Of puritan opposi-tion in his own day Shakespeare was only too well aware. From 1817, for forty-seven conse-cutive years ('with but one single exception'), until 1864 the Revd Thomas Best of Sheffield 'delivered his annual protest against the amuse-ments of the stage from the pulpit of St James's'.[1] Equally forceful was the Revd John East of Bath who, in his evening sermon on 7

---

[1] The Revd R. E. Roberts ed., *Sermons on Theatrical Amusements Delivered in St James's Church Sheffield. by The Late Rev. Thomas Best, MA Oxon*, 2nd edn (London, 1864), p. iv.

January 1844, inveighed against *Hamlet*, which he avowed 'abounds in the most horrid and blasphemous imprecations . . . and in the grossest obscenities of language'.[2]

Such attacks did not go unanswered. In Birmingham in 1824 the Revd J. A. James of Carr's Lane Meeting House found himself confronted by the redoubtable Alfred Bunn, manager of the Theatre Royal in that city: 'The name of one individual is a name that, so long as one stone of the world is left upon another, and one man left to contemplate the ruins, can never be obliterated from his memory – Shakespeare.'[3] Another formidable advocate of the stage was dramatist James Sheridan Knowles whose 'A Controversial Correspondence with Four Clergymen in Defence of the Stage' appeared in the *Devonport Independent* of 30 July 1836. Knowles's claim for the drama was presumptuous in the extreme: 'The Almighty has employed the drama as a vehicle of Revelation. This fact which I presume they will not attempt to disprove, I follow up with the position – That the dramatist may plead Sanction of Revelation.'[4] To seek to elevate drama to the level of inspired scripture was excessive by most standards and may in part account for Knowles's subsequent renunciation of the stage in favour of the religious life.

It was at that later period of Knowles's life that in Devon the young Edmund Gosse 'was accosted by an old gentleman', dressed as a dissenting minister who took him to his house where in the dining-room hung two huge portraits 'one of a man, the other of a woman, in extravagant fancy dress. My old friend told me that the former was a picture of himself as he had appeared, "long ago, in my unconverted days, on the stage".'[5] Thus, Gosse recalled: 'It was from Sheridan Knowles's lips that I first heard fall the name of Shakespeare.' At Knowles's suggestion young Gosse asked his schoolmaster to read some of Shakespeare's plays with the boys. The project began well with Gosse reading Bassanio 'with ecstatic pipe', but came to an abrupt end, almost certainly at the insistence of Gosse's father, who 'prided himself on never having read a page of Shakespeare, and in never having entered a theatre but once'.[6]

Edmund Gosse's *Father and Son* (first published anonymously in 1907), in which these occurrences are recalled, is rightly regarded as a classic account of the clash between science and religion played out through the personal relationship of Edmund Gosse and his widowed father. Philip Gosse, a Plymouth Brother and eminent zoologist, had attempted to reconcile science and religion in his *Omphalis* (1857) in which he argued that God had created the world complete with evidence of previous stages of development: 'But alas! Atheists and Christians alike looked at it and laughed, and threw it away.'[7]

In April 1864 Philip Gosse took his son to London where 'some enormous Evangelical conference' was taking place, in the course of which 'an elderly man, fat and greasy, with a voice like a bassoon' denounced the spread of idolatry: 'At this very moment . . . there is proceeding, unreproved, a blasphemous celebration of the birth of Shakespeare, a soul now suffering for his sins in hell.'[8] Later, back at their hotel, Gosse senior confided to his son that he did not consider 'Brother So-and-So' justified in what he had said about Shakespeare, but this was prompted, not by any regard for the dramatist's work or desire to absolve him from the fate to which all contaminated by the theatre had

---

[2] The Revd. John East, *The Pulpit Justified and the Theatre Condemned* (London, 1844), p. 17.

[3] A. Bunn, *A Letter to the Rev J. A. James of Carr's Lane Meeting House* (Birmingham, 1824), p. 11.

[4] See also James Sheridan Knowles, *Lectures on Dramatic Literature Delivered by James Sheridan Knowles During the Years 1820–1850* (London, 1873) and Christopher Murray, 'James Sheridan Knowles: The Victorian Shakespeare?', in *Shakespeare and the Victorian Stage*, ed. Richard Foulkes (Cambridge, 1986), pp.164–79.

[5] Edmund Gosse, *Father and Son* (London, 1907), p. 242.

[6] Ibid., p. 244.

[7] Ibid., p. 120.

[8] Ibid., p. 322.

long been condemned, but by the possibility that Shakespeare might have made atonement before he died.

'Brother So-and-So's' vision of hell was of everlasting punishment (probably complete with fire and brimstone), but a decade earlier the Revd F. D. Maurice, theologian, educationalist and founder of Christian socialism had advanced a radically different idea in his *Theological Essays* (1853) in the preface to which he wrote: 'I admire unspeakably those who can believe in the love of God and can love their brethren, in spite of the opinion which they seem to cherish, that He has doomed them to destruction.'[9] Maurice's views caused a maelstrom of reaction, culminating in his dismissal from the chair of theology at King's College, London.

Going up to Cambridge in 1823, Maurice belonged to one of the most talented generations ever to attend that – or indeed any – university: John Mitchell Kemble (scion of the celebrated acting dynasty, destined to be a distinguished Anglo-Saxon scholar), William Bodham Donne (Kemble's successor as Examiner of Plays), John Sterling (with Carlisle for his biographer), John Spedding (editor of Bacon's *Works*), Richard Monkton Milnes (Lord Houghton) and Richard Chenevix Trench (Anglican divine, Spanish scholar and translator, philologist and poet). Alfred Tennyson and Charles Darwin (both born in 1809) were somewhat their junior.

Encouraged no doubt by the connection with the theatre through their friendship with John Mitchell Kemble, whose sister Fanny was the talk of the town as Juliet in 1829, these Cambridge contemporaries developed an interest in the stage, which for most of them was lifelong. Whilst still at Cambridge, Chenevix Trench wrote a play entitled *Bernardo del Carpio*, which he submitted to William Charles Macready, then in the early stages of his career as 'the Eminent Tragedian', who professed himself 'greatly delighted' with 'the piece as a whole',[10] though he did not perform it. In

1830 Trench took part in an ill-fated expedition to Spain in support of General José Maria de Torrijos and his (dismally) small band of political liberals, an experience which seemed to exhaust Trench's capacity for liberal causes for the rest of his life. Thereafter he confined his enthusiasm for Spain to its literature (particularly Calderon), combining his career in the Church of England with that of man of letters and teacher, helping Maurice with certain of his educational schemes (Queen's College – for training governesses – in Harley Street).

Like a number of other Victorian clerics, Trench was propelled from the relative obscurity of a parish priest (rector of Itchenstoke) to one of the high offices of the established church as Dean of Westminster in 1856. At the Westminster deanery Trench succeeded the geologist William Buckland, whose predecessor, Samuel Wilberforce, had held the office for what some considered an opportunistically brief period (March to October 1845) before being translated to the bishopric of Oxford. Significantly it was to Bishop Wilberforce that Trench wrote on 3 October 1856: 'Returning home this evening, I found a letter from Lord Palmerston offering me, as you had announced, the Deanery of Westminster, which of course I have gratefully accepted.'[11] In the words of his biographer, J. Bromley: 'Trench's career, in the professional sense, was made by Wilberforce.'[12]

The second of four sons born to William Wilberforce, the parliamentary leader of the abolition of slavery movement, Samuel attended

---

[9] F. D. Maurice, *Theological Essays* (London, 1853), p. xxvii.

[10] Miss M. M. F. Trench, ed., *Richard Chenevix Trench Archbishop Letters and Memorials* 2 vols., (London, 1888), vol I, p. 6. Trench (symbolically) destroyed *Bernardo del Carpio* prior to leaving London for his consecration as Archbishop of Dublin on 1 January 1864.

[11] Ibid., vol. I, p. 310.

[12] J. Bromley, *The Man of Ten Talents A Portrait of Richard Chenevix Trench 1807–86 Philologist, Poet, Theologian, Archbishop* (London, 1959), p. 61.

Oriel College, Oxford in the mid-1820s 'When the Senior Common Room contained an extraordinary galaxy: Thomas Arnold, John Henry Newman, E. B. Pusey, and Richard Whateley. John Keble had only just resigned for a curacy in Gloucestershire'.[13] Although as an undergraduate Wilberforce espoused some liberal causes, in manhood he was identified with conservatism and careerism (earning himself the soubriquet 'Soapy Sam'), contributing dismissive articles to the *Quarterly Review* on both Darwin's *The Origin of Species* and *Essays and Reviews*. However Wilberforce owes his place in the annals of the nineteenth century principally to his contribution to the evolution debate at the meeting of the British Association for the Advancement of Science held in Oxford at the end of June 1860. Intending to dismiss the evolutionists with facetious contempt, Wilberforce, 'turned with mock politeness to Huxley and begged to know "was it from his grandfather or his grandmother that he [Huxley] claimed his descent from a monkey?"'[14] Huxley whispered to the scientist beside him 'The Lord has delivered him into mine hands' and in due course delivered his own withering rebuke: 'If, then, the question is put to me, would I rather have a miserable ape for a grandfather or a man highly endowed by nature and possessed of great means of influence and yet who employs these faculties and that influence for the mere purpose of introducing ridicule into a grave scientific discussion, I unhesitatingly affirm my preference for the ape.'[15]

Owen Chadwick states that the exchange between Huxley and Wilberforce 'though it was talked about privately . . . did not become great matter of public interest until the publication of Darwin's biography (1887) and still more Huxley's biography (1900)',[16] but there can be little doubt that being bested by Huxley contributed to the decline in Wilberforce's fortunes. However, whilst his own ambitions were thwarted, Wilberforce nevertheless appears to have been instrumental in Trench's preferment to the archbishopric of Dublin in

1864, where his predecessor had been Richard Whateley, author of *Elements of Rhetoric* and editor of his uncle's (Thomas) *Remarks on Some of the Characters of Shakespeare.*

Prior to his arrival in Stratford-upon-Avon, as a leading contributor to the tercentenary celebrations, Archbishop Trench had not intervened publicly in the evolution debate, but his identification with the opinions of his mentor, Wilberforce, would have become evident to his congregation when he preached at Holy Trinity Church on Sunday 24 April 1864. At the banquet on the preceding day, in response to the toast 'The Archbishops, and the Bishops and Clergy', Trench had referred to 'the most intimate connection between all true art – and therefore, before all, between the art of Shakespeare – and that Christian faith whereof we are ministers.'[17] Trench thereby signalled that, in addition to whatever attention he planned to give to the evolutionary debate in his sermon, he would be considering the connection between Christianity and artistic genius, a topic which might abut on the current state of biblical scholarship as well as raising issues about the nature of the genius of the ancient authors and, since the ministers for whom he spoke were all Anglican, the nature of the genius of Roman Catholic authors whether they be pre- or post-Reformation. Other preoccupations were likely to be on Trench's mind; his position as Archbishop of Dublin, with the movement towards disestablishment gathering pace, must have given him a heightened awareness of national identity and the threat of Roman Catholicism. Finally as the eminent philologist, which the

---

13 Standish Meacham, *Lord Bishop: The Life of Samuel Wilberforce 1805–1873* (Cambridge, MA, 1970), p. 13.
14 A. N. Wilson, *God's Funeral* (London, 2000), p. 250.
15 Quoted in ibid., p. 251.
16 Owen Chadwick, *The Victorian Church*, 2 vols. (London, 1966 and 1970) , vol. 2, p. 10.
17 Robert Hunter, *Shakespeare and Stratford-upon-Avon Together With a Full Report of the Tercentenary Celebration* (London, 1864), p.182.

preface to *The Oxford English Dictionary*[18] testifies that he was, he knew the power of words and would use them carefully.

Trench's choice of text was from James 1.17: 'Every good gift and every perfect gift is from above, and cometh from the Father of lights'. It was of course an unequivocal assertion that 'all the wit, wisdom, intelligence, or goodness that any man has ever possessed, originally came [from God]', but Trench quickly moved on to assert God's munificence in framing 'the magnificence of that earth' as the 'dwelling-place' of 'his most excellent creature man'.[19] The Archbishop was therefore, at the outset, confronting the two key issues of evolution: the creation of the world and man's special place in it. The designation 'his most excellent creature man' carried with it the traditional Christian belief that man had been created by God in his own image and endowed with qualities not to be found in the rest of creation. This view was fundamentally at odds with recent scientific advances on evolution. Darwin delayed his account of man's evolution until 1888 when his *The Descent of Man* was published, but the work had already been done by Huxley in his *Man's Place in Nature* (1863). The book is amply illustrated with figures of which no. 21, showing the internal casts of a Man's and a Chimpanzee's skull, had been used by a Mr Marshall in his paper 'On the Brain of the Chimpanzee'. Huxley himself wrote: 'So far as cerebral structure goes, therefore, it is clear that Man differs less from the Chimpanzee or the Orang, than these do even from the Monkeys, and that the difference between the brains of the Chimpanzee and of Man is almost insignificant when compared with that between the Chimpanzee brain and that of the Lemur.'[20] A quarter of a century later, Darwin, who like Huxley was very well read, having compared the intellect of 'a Newton or Shakespeare' with that of 'a savage', concluded: 'Differences of this kind between the highest men of the highest races and the lowest savages, are connected by the finest gradations. Therefore it is possible that they might pass and be developed into each other.'[21]

One of the most sustained contributions to the expansion and dissemination of knowledge about evolution came from William (later Sir William) Flower, middle surviving son of Edward Fordham Flower, the moving force behind the tercentenary celebrations in Stratford and the town's mayor at the time. Huxley acknowledged Flower's contribution to the 1862 meeting of the British Association for the Advancement of Science in Cambridge at which Flower gave 'a public demonstration of the existence in the apes of those cerebral characteristics which had been said to be peculiar to man',[22] but he did not elaborate on the nature of Flower's intervention. Rising from the audience to reinforce Huxley against Richard Owen, Flower told the distinguished gathering: 'I happen to have in my pocket a monkey's brain.'[23] Supported by Darwin and Huxley in his election as a fellow of the Royal Society (at the age of thirty-one) in 1864, Flower succeeded in reconciling his scientific discoveries with his religious beliefs. He defended his brother-in-law, the Revd Professor Baden Powell, the author of 'On the Study of the Evidence of Christianity' in *Essays and Reviews*, against the charge of dying without ministration of religion, having been present at his death, as he was to be at that of the liberal

---

18 *The Oxford English Dictionary* (Oxford, 1933), 'Historical Introduction', *passim*.

19 Richard Chenevix Trench, *Every Good Gift From Above Being a Sermon Preached in the Parish Church of Stratford-upon-Avon on Sunday April 24 1864 at the Celebration of Shakespeare's birth* (London, 1864), pp. 5 and 6.

20 T. H. Huxley, *Man's Place in Nature and other Anthropological Essays* (London, 1897), p. 140.

21 Charles Darwin, *The Descent of Man* (London, 1888), p. 66.

22 Huxley, *Man's Place in Nature*, p. ix.

23 Charles J. Cornish, *Sir William Henry Flower KCB FRS DCL Late Director of the Natural History Museum and President of the Royal Zoological Society. A Personal Memoir* (London, 1904), p. 66.

churchman, Arthur Penrhyn Stanley, Trench's successor as Dean of Westminster.

Stanley and Trench represented the different extremes which the Church of England managed to contain within itself. From the pulpit of Holy Trinity Trench, having asserted man's special place in creation, delivered a riposte to the evolutionists commending 'men reconciled with God's scheme of the universe . . . accepting God's world, because it is his, with all its infinite perplexities' affirming Shakespeare as 'such a poet' on whose part 'there is no paltering with everlasting ordinances on which the moral estate of man's life reposes, no challenging of the fitness of these, no summoning of God to answer for Himself at the bar of man for the world which He has created'.[24] Thus in his sermon Trench sought to dismiss the evolutionists, not with the facile wit of his mentor Wilberforce, but with the poet's and philologist's precise command of language.

Similarly Trench's rebuttal of recent trends in biblical scholarship, though rather oblique, was telling. He referred to 'uninspired writers' and 'uninspired man',[25] the significance of 'uninspired' being that even geniuses such as Shakespeare were not directly inspired by God in the way that the authors of the Bible had been. The issue of divine inspiration had come under the scrutiny of Benjamin Jowett, Regius Professor of Greek at Oxford, in his contribution 'On the Interpretation of Scripture' in *Essays and Reviews*: 'The meaning of Scripture is one thing; the inspiration of Scripture is another. It is conceivable that those who hold the most different views about the one may be able to agree about the other. Rigid upholders of the verbal inspiration of Scripture, and those who deny inspiration of Scripture may nevertheless meet on the common ground of the meaning of words.'[26] In Trench's case this was decidedly over-optimistic, coming as it did from the man who had summarized his argument in the single precept: '*Interpret the Scripture like any other book*.'[27]

Trench had an ally in the vicar of Stratford,

the Revd G. Granville, as Sarah Flower, wife of Edward's eldest son Charles and a Martineau by birth, recorded in her diary: '1861 March. The publication of *Essays and Reviews* was now an engrossing subject. Mr Granville said one evening at dinner with us he did not like people's minds being disturbed by such books, he had signed a petition against it, but he had never read the book!'[28] Conservative though he was, Trench was unlikely to dismiss a book unread; his position was based on the fundamental supremacy of one book: the Bible. The origin of language was part of the evolutionary debate as the lectures on 'The Science of Language' delivered to the Royal Institution in 1861 and 1863 by Max Müller indicated. The German-born Orientalist and philologist, then Taylorian Professor of Modern Languages at Oxford, participated in the Stratford tercentenary celebrations alongside Trench whom he may well have regarded as one of those 'theologians who, in their zeal to vindicate the divine origin of language, were carried away far beyond the teaching of the Bible which they were anxious to defend.'[29]

In his book *On the Study of Words*, first published in 1851 and in its twenty-second edition by 1892, Trench affirmed the origins of language as given in the Bible: 'Here as in everything else that concerns the primitive constitution, the great original institutes of humanity, our best and truest lights are to be gotten from the study of the first three chapters of Genesis.'[30] Trench affirmed the biblical account that the whole world was peopled by 'a single pair' and claimed evidence 'in the proofs which

---

[24] Trench, *Every Good Gift*, pp. 8 and 9.

[25] Trench, pp. 13 and 18.

[26] *Essays and Reviews* (London, 1860), p. 351.

[27] Ibid., p. 377.

[28] Sarah Flower, *Great Aunt Sarah's Diary* (Stratford-upon-Avon, 1964), p.48.

[29] F. Max Müller, *The Science of Language* (London, 1899), p. 30.

[30] Richard Chenevix Trench, *On the Study of Words*, 4th edn (London, 1853), p.15.

are daily accumulating of the tendency of all languages, however widely they may differ [referring] themselves to a common stock and single fountain'.[31]

By the middle of the nineteenth century a powerful axis had been formed between a nation's language, literature and history. The development of English studies was partly a solution to the need to find an alternative to classics for the education of women, the middle classes and 'Working Men', but it rapidly assumed the function of creating a national identity and promulgating the notion that God's favourable predisposition to England was evidenced in his gift of its language, its literature and its history. Such a view was by no means the exclusive preserve of conservatives, liberals such as F. D. Maurice and Charles Kingsley repeatedly promoted such ideas in their lectures. Maurice's first appointment at King's College, London – in 1840 – was as Professor of English Literature and History and in his 'Introductory Lecture' he said: 'I am rather inclined to think that we shall find the study of words and constructions, the very link between literature and history' and through such studies 'we may interpret the purposes of God to our land'.[32]

Thomas Carlyle, whose lecture 'The Hero as Poet. Dante and Shakespeare' (12 May 1840) may stand for the third phase (substitution) of Shakespeare's relationship with religion, extolled this theme – 'He [Shakespeare] is the grandest thing we have yet done.'[33] – posing the question: which will you give up 'your Indian Empire or your Shakespeare'? In his sermon Trench, similarly, asked his congregation 'to imagine this England of ours without her Shakespeare'. As a nation England was the 'nursing mother of the foremost poet whom the world has seen, we are almost bold to prophesy, it will ever see'.[34] Such an assertion was indeed significant, placing Shakespeare above the ancient authors, Homer in particular, for whom the claim that they derived their genius from the Christian God could only be made with great ingenuity, if at all.

The relationship of the Victorian church to ancient Greece was close and complex, as Richard Jenkyns has observed: 'The Established Church had indeed forged a strange alliance with the ancient Greeks,'[35] with many a bishop receiving preferment on the strength of his Greek textual scholarship – hence the term 'Greek-play-bishop' – and Henry Alford, Dean of Canterbury, proclaiming the *Odyssey* as the greatest work of human genius. In his article on 'Archbishop Trench's Poems' Frederic W. H. Myers identified Pindar as Trench's strongest influence, showing that, though he was 'the very type and norm of Christian and Anglican orthodoxy', the English cleric showed 'profound affinity' with the 'hopes and creeds' of those pre-Christian times.[36] Trench no doubt subscribed to the orthodox account that God had selected ancient Greek as the most precise language in which the New Testament was to be written and as for Latin, he wrote: 'when the Church arose [she] required it to be the organ of her Divine word'.[37] In elevating Shakespeare above the ancient authors Trench went further than Sir Gilbert Scott, architect of the Albert Memorial, who, as Richard Jenkyns has pointed out,[38] denied Shakespeare the prime position on the literary frieze – 'directly beneath the feet of Albert' – in favour of Homer.

For Trench it was not simply a matter of Christianity against paganism, however civilized, but 'Shakespeare was the child of the

31 Trench, *Study of Words*, pp. 60–1.
32 In Alan Bacon, ed., *The Nineteenth-Century History of English Studies* (Aldershot, 1998), pp. 66 and 73.
33 Thomas Carlyle, *On Heroes, Hero-Worship and the Heroic in History* (Oxford, n.d.), p.148.
34 Trench, *Every Good Gift*, p. 16.
35 Richard Jenkyns, *The Victorians and Ancient Greece* (Oxford, 1980), p.67.
36 Frederic W. H. Myers, 'Archbishop Trench's Poems' in *The Nineteenth Century*, October 1877, p. 489. See Richard Chenevix Trench, DD, Archbishop of Dublin, *Poems* (London, 1874).
37 Richard Chenevix Trench, *Sacred Latin Poetry*, 2nd edn (London, 1864), p. 5.
38 Jenkyns, *The Victorians*, p. 192.

England of the Reformation. He was born in its spirit', despite this there was 'a noble absence' of attacks on Catholicism, which could be explained 'not in any lingering affection upon his part to Romish doctrines and practices, [as is] clear from the fact that he bears himself in exactly the same fashion towards the Puritans'.[39] As an authority on the Spanish dramatist Calderon – 'a zealous Romanist' who even wrote *autos*, religious plays – Trench took seriously the issue of whether God might bestow his gifts as – or even more – generously on a post-Reformation catholic as on a protestant. Typically Trench resolved the issue to his own satisfaction at least: 'Nationality, language, faith, made him [Calderon] very different and the same causes which have made the North of Europe the seat of the Reformation, the seat also of all the stronger thinking as well as the more earnest doing of modern Europe, have contributed to make our English poet far greater than the Spanish; our greatest (Shakespeare) greater than theirs!'[40] Trench brought the same scrupulous discrimination to his *Sacred Latin Poetry* in which he retrieved for 'members of our English Church' a selection of pre-Reformation sacred poetry from which the 'snares' of 'Romish doctrine' had been eradicated.[41]

Trench had seized the opportunity of the tercentenary sermon not only to affirm God as the only source of human genius, but also to counter new ideas about the creation, evolution and the Bible, and to claim Shakespeare as an English national and Anglican protestant. Sarah Flower and Andrew Halliday[42] complained of Trench's inaudibility, both of them catching only the word 'Shakespeare' from time to time, but, whatever the deficiencies of Trench's delivery, he has left posterity a trenchant statement of conservative Anglicanism at the period of fervent religious debate with which the Shakespeare tercentenary coincided and provided a prime example of what is now known as 'appropriation'.

Trench's was by no means the only sermon

preached on Shakespeare that day. Within an hour of the conclusion of the morning service, Charles Wordsworth, Bishop of St Andrews, nephew of the poet and author of *On Shakespeare's Knowledge and Use of the Bible* (1864), followed Trench into the pulpit of Holy Trinity. His text was 'All Thy works praise Thee, O Lord; and Thy saints give thanks unto Thee', Psalm 145.10. Wordsworth bracketed Shakespeare with Bacon in 'an age of giants (such was the bounty of God towards our land and people in the first half-century after the Reformation)' and in his allusion to 'the reverend author of the "Christian Year"' acknowledged the contribution of John Keble, to the inclusion of artists in Christian life.[43]

The Established Church did not enjoy a monopoly. At the Independent Chapel in Stratford R. W. Dale the prolific Congregationalist author and one time assistant minister at Carr's Lane Chapel, Birmingham preached on 'Genius The Gift of God'. Dale referred, more explicitly than Trench, to the evolution debate: 'the almost exclusive devotion of the cultivated classes in the community to the physical sciences', before going on to say that, though it had been 'the habit of religious orators to derive their most striking illustrations of the glory of God from the material universe', 'the genius of a great poet is a more wonderful product of the creative energy than the brightest constellation in the sky'.[44] At the other end of the religious spectrum Cardinal Wiseman, who had 'never in my life seen Shakespeare acted', prepared, at the

---

39 Trench, *Sacred Latin Poetry*, p. 12.
40 Richard Chenevix Trench, *Life's A Dream, The Great Theatre of the World from the Spanish of Calderon. With an Essay on his Life and Genius* (London, 1856), p. 72.
41 Trench, *Sacred Latin Poetry*, p. v.
42 Richard Foulkes, *The Shakespeare Tercentenary of 1864* (London, 1984), p.28.
43 Hunter, *Shakespeare and Stratford-Upon-Avon*, p. 214.
44 R. W. Dale, *Genius The Gift of God A Sermon on the Tercentenary of the Birth of William Shakespeare Preached in the Independent Chapel, Stratford-on-Avon* (London, 1864), p. 6.

invitation of the Royal Institution, 'A Lecture on Shakespeare', which he intended to deliver as a Catholic offering to the tercentenary, but was prevented from doing so by illness then death. Wiseman also addressed the origin of Shakespeare's genius, which was 'a gift, and not an acquisition . . . It must be congenital, or rather inborn to its possessor. It is as much a living, a natural power as is reason to every man.'[45] Like 'the very first germ of the plant' genius was part of God's purpose in the world. As the First Vatican Council (1869–70) was to show, the Roman Catholic Church recognized the seriousness of the evolutionary challenge.

The tercentenary pronouncements on Shakespeare by the Anglican Trench, the Congregationalist Dale and the Roman Catholic Wiseman – denominational differences notwithstanding – show remarkable congruity, partly no doubt because of the occasion, but also because of the common challenge which they all took the opportunity to address. Each asserted that Shakespeare's genius was the gift of God and each sought to use that assertion to reject current evolutionary ideas. However, though evolution was the greatest intellectual challenge ever to religious belief, evolutionists, as A. N. Wilson postulates with regard to Lord Morley or George Eliot,[46] might 'be surprised by the extent to which religion survives', an outcome which may well owe something to Shakespeare in whose work many experience some intimation of the divine.[47]

---

[45] Cardinal Wiseman, *William Shakespeare* (London, 1865), p. 25.
[46] Wilson, *God's Funeral*, p. 464.
[47] For example see Harold Bloom, *Shakespeare: The Invention of the Human* (London, 1999), 'Shakespeare's Universalism', pp. 1–17.

ANTHONY MUNDAY AND *THE MERCHANT OF VENICE*

DONNA B. HAMILTON

Scott McMillin is fond of saying that Anthony Munday was always in the middle of everything. However true that may be, Munday has never been at the centre of work on *The Merchant of Venice*. This situation has obtained despite the fact that Shakespeare seems to have used both versions of a narrative that Munday had handled once in *Zelauto* (1580) and again, though differently, in *The Orator* (1596), and that contains central features of the Shylock–Antonio bond plot as well as of the story of Jessica's elopement to marry the person she loves.[1]

While the source closest to *Merchant* is Ser Giovanni's *Il Pecorone*, Shakespeare's debt to *Zelauto* includes the doubling of suitors, the addition of a daughter for the usurer, the use of two women disguised as attorneys, and a son-in-law who will inherit the usurer's possessions. Two differences from *Zelauto* have not deterred critics from drawing these parallels, the fact that in *Zelauto* the usurer is a Christian rather than Jew and that the bond involves eyes rather than a pound of flesh. Further, like *Merchant*, the judge in *Zelauto* uses a plea for mercy that relies, like Portia's, on a religious argument. As for *The Orator*, its importance has seemed to lie in the arguments used on Shylock's behalf in the trial scene, especially the notions that in certain circumstances one might prefer to take flesh over money and that being treated as a slave is worse than losing a pound of flesh (4.1.89–99, and 4.1.39–41).[2]

Despite these similarities, not much has been of interest about Munday's narratives as sources other than the conclusion that Shakespeare found something useful to himself in them. Unlike the inspection of sources for *1 Henry IV*, a play contemporary with *Merchant*, there has been virtually no curiosity about whether Munday's materials represented or were participatory in any political or religious agenda.

Current interest in Shakespeare and religion creates an agreeable situation for looking more closely at the material from Munday that Shakespeare appropriated. Because the dates of those materials are 1580 and 1596, taking that look gives us an opportunity to traverse English history from the point at which, as Peter Lake has written, '"Catholics" represented a major, perhaps even . . . the predominant body of religious opinion' in England,[3] to the mid-nineties, by which time Protestantism had gained clear dominance. As Peter Lake and Michael Questier have argued, this same period

---

[1] For example, see Celeste Turner, *Anthony Mundy: An Elizabethan Man of Letters* (Berkeley, 1928), pp. 33–4; John Russell Brown, ed., *The Merchant of Venice* (London, 1955), pp. xxx–xxxi; Kenneth Muir, *Shakespeare's Sources: Comedies and Tragedies* (London, 1957), pp. 48–50; M. M. Mahood, ed., *The Merchant of Venice* (Cambridge, 1987), pp. 4–7; Geoffrey Bullough, ed., *Narrative and Dramatic Sources of Shakespeare*, 8 vols. (London, 1957–75), vol. 1, pp. 451–4; and Joan Ozark Holmer, *The Merchant of Venice: Choice, Hazard and Consequence* (New York, 1995), p. 68.

[2] See Mahood, ed., *The Merchant of Venice*, pp. 5–6.

[3] Peter Lake, 'Religious Identities in Shakespeare's England', in *A Companion to Shakespeare*, ed. David Scott Kastan (Oxford, 1999), pp. 57–84, p. 60.

offers an unusual opportunity to study how political circumstances either broaden the opportunities for ideas to enter the public sphere or narrow those opportunities almost to the point of elimination. According to Lake and Questier, in 1579 and 1580, the regime's 'major dislocations in policy-making' and the 'dissension within the privy council over what the queen should do' meant that 'religious engagés could start to open up and invade spaces . . . normally closed to them'.[4] As I shall argue, *Zelauto* was a product of that unusually open moment that was shortly to be followed by the arrest and execution of Edmund Campion. Tracking Munday all the way to 1596, a period that includes in the *Thomas More* play and in *Merchant* two different but nevertheless collaborative intersections with Shakespeare, allows us to speculate more knowledgeably about the adjustments Munday made to changing political circumstances. And the focus on *Merchant* allows us to look again at Shakespeare during 1596–7, when international relations, factionalism at court, and three changes in Lord Chamberlains were affecting the circumstances for public discourse.

Unlike Shakespeare, whose religion most earlier critics rarely questioned, there have nearly always been questions about Munday's religion. Certainly, Munday's Protestantism has been easy to assume. His visit in 1576 to the English College in Rome has been interpreted as his having joined Walsingham's spying operation, an interpretation that has seemed to fit neatly with his having served in the 1580s and in 1606 as pursuivant for Richard Topcliffe,[5] the notorious papist-hunter, puritan-hunter, and rackmaster. In 1582, Munday produced *A discoverie of Edmund Campion*,[6] his account of Campion's trial and execution, followed later that year by *The English Romayne lyfe*, a diatribe against the English College in Rome. All of Munday's writing about Campion and on related issues, printed during 1581 and 1582,[7] were dedicated to one or several members of the Privy Council or to the Queen and gave

relentless iteration to the government's position that Jesuit activity was justifiably characterized as not for religion but treason. Munday's five children were all baptized in the 1580s at St Giles without Cripplegate.[8]

Be that as it may, a case can also be made that Munday's religious and political identities – despite his report on Campion, and despite his visible conformity – were at this time that of a Romanist dissenter and, moreover, that he continued to write in sympathy with the Catholic cause throughout his career. In this scenario, the trip to the English College in Rome taken under the patronage of the crypto-Catholic Edward de Vere, Earl of Oxford,[9] signified allegiance to the Roman church. According to

---

4 Peter Lake and Michael Questier, unpublished abstract, distributed at the Folger Shakespeare Library seminar 'Stuart Catholicism', 24 September 2000, for Peter Lake and Michael Questier, 'Puritans, Papists, and the 'Public Sphere' in Early Modern England: The Edmund Campion Affair in Context', *Journal of Modern History*, 72 (2000), 587–627.

5 Turner, *Anthony Mundy*, p. 53; Mark Eccles, 'Brief Lives: Tudor and Stuart Authors', *Studies in Philology*, 79 (1982), 1–135, p. 99.

6 Munday's report on Campion was included in the second edition of Holinshed's *Chronicles of England, Scotland, and Ireland* (1587), an edition that Queen Elizabeth ordered expurgated in 1587 and 1590, at which later date, Munday's report on Campion was targeted for excision; for details of this excision (although without mention of the fact that the chronicler was Munday), see Cyndia Susan Clegg, 'Which Holinshed?: Holinshed's *Chronicles* at the Huntington Library', *Huntington Library Quarterly*, 55 (1992), 559–75, pp. 565–6; for the view that this account of Campion 'exposed both sides to public scrutiny,' see Cyndia Susan Clegg, *Press Censorship in Elizabethan England* (Cambridge, 1997), p. 141.

7 These works include STC 18259, 18259.3, 18261, 18262, 18270, 18272, and, for 1584, STC 18282; A. W. Pollard, G. R. Redgrave, Katharine F. Pantzer, et al., *A Short-Title Catalogue of Books Printed in England, Scotland, and Ireland and of English Books Printed Abroad, 1475–1640*, 3 vols., 2nd edn (London, 1976–91).

8 Mark Eccles, 'Anthony Munday', in *Studies in the English Renaissance Drama: In Memory of Karl Julius Holzknecht*, ed. Josephine W. Bennett, Oscar Cargill, and Vernon Hall, Jr. (New York, 1959), pp. 5–105, p. 99.

9 See Turner, *Anthony Mundy*, pp. 11–12.

Michael E. Williams, Munday was accepted at the English College as a scholar, but did not take the missionary oath; not convinced that Munday came as a spy, Williams suggested instead that Munday only later turned informant.[10] When Celeste Turner Wright arrived at her revised opinion that Munday was a Romanist, crucial to her new conclusion was his apprenticeship under John Allde and close association with John Charlewood, two printers friendly to Catholics. Charlewood, the printer to Philip Howard, first earl of Arundel, signed little of his presswork in 1584, the year printer William Carter was executed.[11] According to Richard Wilson, the report Munday wrote on the English College in *English Roman Life* can be understood as persistently ventriloquizing a Catholic critique of the Tudor protestant regime.[12] Also supportive of the notion of a Catholic Munday may be his book of consolation dedicated to Ferdinando Stanley in 1593 on the occasion of his father's death; *The Defense of Contraries* was a translation of a book by the French Catholic, Charles Estienne.[13] Certainly the *More* play figures in this version of Munday's religious orientation, as might Munday's translations of Spanish chivalric romances (1588–1619), his revisions of John Stow's *Survey of London* (1618, 1633), and his distinguished double-column octavo edition of Antonio de Guevara's *Diall of Princes* (1618), in which he reproduced the translation that Thomas North had dedicated to Mary Tudor in 1557.

Thus we confront with Munday what is so often the case in this period, the difficulty, often impossibility, of determining where someone's true religious allegiance lay. One could go the route of assuming that Munday's religious identity was no more fixed, no less porous, than that of many of his contemporaries.[14] And yet we need to reserve the option of considering that Munday's religious commitments might have been regularly on the Romanist side, but managed in ways that offered the most protection for changing circumstances.

However impossible or unsatisfactory labelling often is, *Zelauto* stands out as the work where Munday's projection of a Catholic identity is both most obvious and most dangerously present. Usually regarded as a pleasant-enough romance written in imitation of John Lyly,[15] *Zelauto* is better understood as addressing the threatened situation of English catholics in 1580, and as confirming Catholic resolve to remain true to the Roman faith. This book boldly appeared in England while Francis, duke of Anjou, was still suing for Elizabeth's hand and during the year that Campion and Parsons returned to England. And boldly too, *Zelauto* shares common ground with two of the most important Catholic books of this period, Gregory Martin's *A Treatise of Schism* (1578), for which the printer Carter would be executed, and Parsons' *A brief discours contayning certayne reasons why Catholiques refuse to goe to church* (1580). Both books proposed that Catholic resistance should take the form of rejecting outward conformity.[16]

---

[10] Michael E. Williams, *The Venerable English College, Rome: A History, 1579–1979* (London, 1979), p. 12.

[11] On Allde and Charlewood, see Celeste Turner Wright, 'Young Anthony Mundy Again', *Studies in Philology*, 56 (1959), 150–68; and Pantzer, ed., *A Short-Title Catalogue of Books Printed in England, Scotland, and Ireland and of English Books Printed Abroad, 1475–1640*, 3.40. On Carter, see A. C. Southern, *Elizabethan Recusant Prose, 1559–1582* (London, 1950), pp. 351–2; Clegg, *Press Censorship in Elizabethan England*, pp. 94–5.

[12] A point Richard Wilson argued during discussion of a paper I gave on Anthony Munday at the London Renaissance Seminar, October 1996.

[13] Munday translated Estienne's imitation of Ortensio Landi's *Paradossi*. For the Estienne family, see *The Encyclopedia Britannica*, 29 vols., 11th edn (Cambridge, 1910–11), vol. 9, pp. 798, 800.

[14] See Michael C. Questier, *Conversion, Politics and Religion in England, 1580–1625* (Cambridge, 1996).

[15] See Jack Stillinger, ed., *Zelauto: The Fountaine Of Fame* (Carbondale, Ill., 1963), pp. ix–xi. All quotations from *Zelauto* are from this edition.

[16] See Southern, *Elizabethan Recusant Prose*, pp. 136–42. In *Zelauto*, the names Giovanni Martino (pp. 24, 30–1), Roberto (p. 34), and Giulio di Pescara (p. 34) may be meant to recall the Catholic leaders Gregory Martin, Robert Parsons and William Allen.

Dedicated to the Earl of Oxford, *Zelauto* was printed by Charlewood but not entered in the Stationer's Register.[17] Establishing for the book a strong visual presence, Munday and Charlewood inserted twenty woodcuts into the first two-thirds of *Zelauto*, thirteen of which were from Stephen Bateman's *The travayled pilgrim* (1569).[18] What gave the inserted cuts a strong Protestant edge was that Bateman's book was a Protestant makeover of a Catholic book, the fifteenth-century French romance *Le chevalier delibere* by Olivier de la Marche.[19] La Marche's romance wrapped a spiritual allegory around a historical narrative that celebrated the triumphs of the Habsburgs. In his revision, Bateman had replaced the Habsburgs with an account of the glory of Tudor protestant rule. He had also eliminated the woodcuts that had pictured monks with rosaries, replacing them with cuts of gentlemen in plain clothes.[20]

Appropriating Bateman, Munday made *Zelauto* look like Bateman's book by reproducing many of Bateman's pictures. But he made Bateman's pictures available for meanings opposite to those Bateman had intended by inserting a different narrative. For a Catholic reader given sufficient prompting, the cuts of plainly dressed gentlemen could as easily represent the Catholic priests, Campion and others, who had come into England dressed so as to avoid detection. Munday encouraged such a reading not only by his narrative but also by a discussion, inserted at the beginning of Part 2, of the reading strategies required for understanding that his book was 'more meretorious' than it may first appear, and that to read it properly one must see 'behind' it, even as 'Many a good Captayne, may goe in a playne coate, and many an honest man, may walke simply arayed' (61).

The narrative that follows is divided into three parts, only the third section of which furnished materials for *The Merchant of Venice*. The first section presents Zelauto as the recipient of acts of charity as he recounts having been wounded by banditi, and then brought back to health by the hostess Ursula[21] who, in

the tradition of Saint Ambrose, saw that he was fed, his wounds dressed, and his feet washed. Munday juxtaposed this episode of charity in Naples to Zelauto's report on travelling to England where he had seen England's 'Mayden Queene' honoured by '*all true English harts*' (36, 38). And he accompanied this expression of loyalty to Elizabeth with Bateman's well-

---

17 The single extant copy is in the Bodleian Library.

18 Three cuts were originally from Thomas North's translation of *The moral philosophie of Doni* (1570); see Ruth Samson Luborsky and Elizabeth Morley Ingram, *A Guide to English Illustrated Books, 1536–1603* (Tempe, Ariz., 1998), vol. 1, pp. 586–7. Stillinger, ed., *Zelauto*, does not reproduce or discuss the cuts. Both Bateman's and North's books had been printed originally by Henry Denham in 1569 and 1570 respectively; Peter Blayney says that Charlewood probably rented the cuts from Denham. For the title page, Munday and Charlewood used a cut – featuring David with a lyre, Moses with the Ten Commandments – that was used in 1580 also for the second edition of Nathaniel Baxter, *The Lectures or Daily Sermons of J. Calvine upon the prophet Jonas*, by John Kingston for Edward White. The first edition had been printed in 1578, by John Charlewood for Edward White, with no woodcut on the title page.

19 La Marche's book had been printed in a Spanish translation in 1553 and 1555. See Olivier de la Marche, *Le Chevalier delibere, The Resolute Knight*, ed. Carleton W. Carroll, trans. Lois Hawley Wilson and Carleton W. Carroll (Tempe, Ariz., 1999).

20 For the history of translation and revision by Hernando de Acuña, Bateman, and Lewis Lewkenor, see Susie Speakman Sutch and Anne Lake Prescott, 'Translation as Transformation: Oliver de La Marche's *Le Chevalier delibere* and its Hapsburg and Elizabethan Permutations,' *Comparative Literature Studies*, 25 (1988), 281–317. For the cuts in the Spanish version adopted by Bateman, see Luborsky and Ingram, *A Guide to English Illustrated Books*, 1.67–9. For Lewkenor's having renounced Catholicism in 1594, the year he produced his version of de Acuña, see Anthony G. Petti, ed., *The Letters and Despatches of Richard Verstegan*, Catholic Record Society Records Series, vol. 52 (London, 1959), p. 221, n.7.

21 Ursula is most likely named for Saint Ursula, who was thought to have been martyred by the Huns along with 11,000 maidens; see Herbert Thurston and Donald Attwater, ed., *Butler's Lives of the Saints* (London, 1956), p. 165–8. For the Ursuline order, see Charmarie J. Blaisdell, 'Angela Merici and the Ursulines', in Richard L. DeMolen, ed., *Religious Orders of the Catholic Reformation*, pp. 99–136.

known picture of her in procession (M2r).[22] Next Zelauto reports on two pageants he has seen, the first of which shows England in a shipwrecked state of Babylonian confusion (38–9), and the second of which is a representation of the government's policy of equating religious conformity with loyalty, within which policy the loyal and conforming subject is the one who receives the mercy of the queen. Munday represented this set of ideas by way of an armed lady who chastises a knight for not loving the right woman. Dismayed at his recalcitrance ('your minde so misbeleeving that it wyll not be reformed', 45), the armed lady vanquishes him in battle, warns him that he will die if he does not submit, and elicits the admission that 'he had maintayned a wrong opinion' (48), but will now 'vowe . . dutifull alleageaunce' (49). Praising his submission, the armed lady directs the knight to 'homage her whose mercifull mind will not revenge with rigor' (50).

In its twin emphasis on conformity and loyalty, this first section implicitly articulates the effective means by which the concept of the royal supremacy was sustained. Part 2 critiques that concept and its implementation by way of a narrative that represents people who choose secrecy and risk death in order to follow the religion of their choice. In the process, Munday goes point-by-point through many issues crucial to Catholics at this time. This story occurs not in England but in Persia, where Zelauto's pagan host Manniko Rigustello meets secretly with him to learn about Christianity. Complication occurs when Mico Sheffola comes with the news that his sister is condemned to die for her Christian belief and that anyone who fights for her will himself be killed. Volunteering to defend her, Zelauto announces that if he were to lose his 'lyfe in defence of my faith, my Captayne Christe would purchase me the greater reward' (77), and that he will 'goe to the Combate for my conscience' (85).[23] When, on the day that Zelauto faces the champion, he finds that the lady is already bound to a stake, Zelauto denounces this 'aucthorytie, ruled by

rigor and not by indifferencie' (89, cf. 92) and insists on the Soldan's obligation 'not to pinche that partie, that avoucheth . . . dutifull loyaltie' (90). The lady is, after all, says Zelauto, 'your owne blood, and no enimie to your Majestie' (90); 'remember the race shee is descended of' (92).[24] If no other remedy is possible, 'put her in exyle' rather than kill her (92). None of these arguments works; Zelauto fights and kills Terolfo, and is sent to prison. On the next day, Rigustello is executed, his body parts 'dispersed about the streets' (102).[25] Aided by others, Zelauto escapes.

All of this material sets the stage for Part 3, where Munday inserted one more narrative which, albeit more symbolically, again juxtaposes the tyranny of persecutors to the value of being true to one's religion. The narrative is organized around two elements: the lady Cornelia insists that she not have to marry

---

[22] The *Zelauto* copy of this cut is reproduced in Carole Levin, *The Heart and Stomach of a King: Elizabeth I and the Politics of Sex and Power* (Philadelphia, 1994), p. 128. Deleted from the version in *Zelauto* are the captions at the top and bottom of the cut in Bateman's *The travayled pilgrim*, which read, respectively, 'The Author beholdeth the discourse of Dolor and Debilitie, Thanatos sitting and giveth judgement, Attropos giving place', and 'As they are at contention, the worthy Queene Elyzabeth passeth by, neyther Dolor nor Debilitie, as yet not able to resist.'

[23] The name Zelauto means 'zeal'. For the view that zeal was the quality that kept one from communicating with those of the wrong religion, see Gregory Martin, *Treatise of Schism* (C2r). For discussion of the zealous Romanist preacher ('*lo zelante concionatore*') willing to die for his beliefs and of Martin's use of this tradition, see Frederick J. McGinness, *Right Thinking and Sacred Oratory in Counter-Reformation Rome* (Princeton, 1995), p. 41.

[24] In his dedication to *A brief discours contayning certayne reasons why Catholiques refuse to goe to church*, Parsons argued that as representatives of the oldest religion in England Catholics should at least be tolerated equally with the rest.

[25] In his edition of *Zelauto*, Stillinger refers to the executions and imprisonments in Part 2 as being 'well enough detailed to have come from personal observation or experience' (p. xv).

someone she abhors (the material that critics have understood Shakespeare to have made over for the Jessica plot), and the usurer Truculento, who is pursuing her, insists on taking for his payment the eyes of the two young men (some of the material Shakespeare used for the Shylock plot). Here as elsewhere in *Zelauto*, the representation of power accompanies a representation of resistance. Despite all the power that Truculento holds, the others, through wit and will, keep what they hold so dear. Cornelia marries whom she chooses; her brothers keep their eyes. But the critique of a persecuting power is pointed. As the judge remarks, even a Turk would not be so cruel as Truculento, who respects 'cruelty: more then Christian civilitie' (174). Protesting enforced conformity, Parsons had made the same point in noting that, unlike the situation in England, 'amongst the very Turkes at this day, no man is compelled to any act of their religion'.[26]

As Lake and Questier have emphasized, Campion's insertion of himself into the public arena – his entry with Parsons and his issuing a series of politically radical challenges to government policy – was a great spur to the government's establishing harsher measures against Catholics. The Acts of the Privy Council document a series of moves against Catholics from June to December 1580, and in 1581 Parliament passed the act declaring it 'treason to be absolved from schism and reconciled to Rome', and increased 'the recusancy fine . . . to 20 pounds per month'.[27] In December 1580, the Earl of Oxford, Munday's patron, had recanted his Catholicism.[28] Clearly the tide had been turning for Munday too. Already in October 1580, Munday had taken on a new affiliation: the arms of the city of London appear in his anti-theatrical tract, *A second and third blast of retrait from plaies and theaters*.[29] Also suggestive of Munday's changing situation, but paid little or no attention, is the Stationers' Register entry on 13 February 1581 for the licensing to Charlewood of Munday's *The historie of Palmerin of Englande*, 'uppon Condicon that if there be anie

thinge founde in The booke . . . worthie of Reprehension . . . then all the Bookes shalbe put to waste and Burnte',[30] a reference which may also implicate *Zelauto*. In the dedication to *Zelauto*, Munday had promised Oxford that *Palmerin* would be forthcoming. Given the content of *Zelauto*, this threat to censor *Palmerin of England* may be evidence that Munday was being watched. But certainly we have here a superb example of the sudden closing up of the 'spaces for discussion and protest' that Lake and Questier have described as open just months earlier. Then virtually from the moment of the arrest of Campion, in July 1581, Munday began to testify in court (including against Campion), to write on behalf of the government, and to serve as pursuivant to Topcliffe.[31]

---

26 Dedication to *A brief discours contayning certayne reasons why Catholiques refuse to goe to church*.

27 J. R. Dasent, *Acts of the Privy Council of England, 1580–81* (London, 1890–), n.s. vol. 12, pp. 57, 59, 70, 75, 77, 90–2, 103–6, 124, 125, 132–3, 136–7, 142, 282, 285, 294–5; Christopher Haigh, *English Reformations: Religion, Politics and Society under the Tudors* (Oxford, 1993), p. 263. See also John J. Larocca, SJ, 'Popery and Pounds: The Effect of the Jesuit Mission on Penal Legislation,' in Thomas McCoog, *The Reckoned Expense: Edmund Campion and the Early English Jesuits* (Rochester, NY: Boydell Press, 1996), pp. 249–63.

28 B. M. Ward, *The Seventeenth Earl of Oxford, 1550–1604* (London, 1928), p. 207.

29 See Pollard and Redgrave, eds., *Short-Title Catalogue*, STC 21677.

30 Edward Arber, ed., *A Transcript of the Registers of the Company of Stationers of London, 1554–1640 A.D.*, 5 vols. (Gloucester, Mass, 1967), vol. 2 p. 383. Although Munday's translations of other romances would be printed beginning in 1588, in the context of the Spanish Armada, *Palmerin of England* was not printed until 1596, in the context of England's advance on Cadiz. The effort to get the romances into print seems to have begun in earnest in 1594, when *Primaleon* was entered in the Stationers' Register. Printers of the romances in 1594, 1595, and 1596, included John Danter, Thomas Creed, and Adam Islip, the latter of whom also printed *The Orator*.

31 For Munday's testimony at Campion's trial, see Richard Simpson, *Edmund Campion: A Biography* (London, 1867), pp. 298–305; for Simpson's view of Munday, pp. 311–12. For the comment of William

In assessing the implications of service that has such despicable dimensions, we nevertheless need to take full account of how great now was the risk of any action that might be interpreted as disloyalty.[32] We might recall that the laypeople and priests executed in the early 1580s included the printer Carter, the double agent William Parry, as well as John Alfield, author of the Catholic reply to Munday's report on Campion.[33] According to Christopher Haigh, the executions of priests alone in the early 1580s included 'four in 1581, eleven in 1582, two in 1583, six in 1584'; 'From 1586 to 1592, sixty-nine priests and twenty-eight laypeople' were executed, 'thirty-one of them in the second half of 1588'.[34] Munday's fate was different. In 1587, Queen Elizabeth granted him several 'leases in reversion of Crown property'; in 1588, he became Messenger of her Majesties Chamber.[35]

Despite the signs of seeming orthodoxy, the books Munday wrote in the 1580s are marked with some peculiar ambiguities. For example, when Munday brought out an edition of two sermons by Calvin,[36] he chose sermons exhorting people to suffer persecution and to avoid worshipping with people of wrong religion, sermons which we might read as sending veiled messages of encouragement to fearful Catholics. In 1588, his dedicating *The banquet of daintie conceits* to Topcliffe may be only an apparent compliment. Entered in the Stationers' Register in 1584 but not printed by Charlewood until 1588, this book contains some of the same cuts that had appeared in *Zelauto*,[37] accompanied by a collection of verses the theme of which is the transitoriness of life. I take that material as reminding the reader that this self-assured torturer Topcliffe will one day meet his own end. Dedicating such a book to Topcliffe does not praise him; it libels him.[38] Rhetorically adept, Munday, it would seem, thus continued his own moral battle while also managing – usually but not always – to stay out of trouble. In his dedication in 1602 of Philippe de Mornay's *The true knowledge of a mans owne selfe*, Munday asked John Swynnerton, a merchant

taylor and alderman who would become Lord Mayor in 1612, to accept this book as a replacement for one he had promised, 'my Paradox Apologie, which long since you should have had, but that the . . . misinterpretation of the worke by some in authoritie, was the only cause why it went not forward'.

Allen that Munday and his companions were 'salable for a sou and bought by the enemy to betray them [Campion and others]', see William Cecil, 'The Execution of Justice in England' and William Allen, 'A True, Sincere, and Modest Defense of English Catholics', ed. Robert Kingdon (Ithaca, N.Y., 1965), p. 85. Turner dated Munday's service to Topcliffe as beginning in 1581, after the 'ruin of his patron'; *Anthony Mundy*, p. 157. For Munday's testimony in 1588, see John Hungerford Pollen, ed., *English Martyrs, 1584–1603*, Catholic Record Society record series (London, 1908), vol. 5, pp. 60–1.

32 Allen and Parsons had made it clear that priests and lay Catholics would be absolved from hiding their Catholicism if revealing it meant risking their lives; see P. J. Holmes, *Elizabethan Casuistry*, Catholic Record Society Record series, vol. 67 (London, 1981), pp. 63–77.

33 See Haigh, *English Reformations*, p. 263. Alfield's *True report of the death and martyrdome of M. Campion Jesuite and preiste, & M. Sherwin, & M. Bryan preistes, at Tiborne the first of December 1581* had been printed by Richard Verstegan, who, after the book was seized, left for the continent; see A. F. Allison and D. M. Rogers, ed., *The Contemporary Printed Literature of the English Counter-Reformation btween 1558 and 1640*, 2 vols. (Aldershot, 1989, 1994), vol. 2, p. 3, no. 4.

34 Haigh, *English Reformations*, p. 263.

35 Eccles, 'Brief Lives: Stuart and Tudor Authors,' pp. 98–9.

36 Pollard and Redgrave, eds. *Short-Title Catalogue*, STC 4461, *Two Godly and learned sermons. Long since tr. out of Latine by R. Horne. Nowe published by A.M. [J. Charlewood] f. H. Car* [1584].

37 The book had been entered in the Stationers' Register in July 1584; see Pollard and Redgrave, eds., *Short-Title Catalogue*, STC 18260. Carter had been executed in January 1584; see Southern, *Elizabethan Recusant Prose*, p. 352. For the cuts, see Luborsky and Ingram, *A Guide to English Illustrated Books*, vol. 1, pp. 585–6.

38 On libel and Catholic propaganda, see Clegg, *Press Censorship in Elizabethan England*, pp. 32–3, 35, 69–70, 90–3, 94–5. On verse libel, see Arthur F. Marotti, *Manuscript, Print, and the English Renaissance Lyric* (Ithaca, 1995), pp. 92–4.

One reason it is important to establish that Munday occasionally got into trouble with the censor is that the evidence helps confirm our understanding not necessarily of his religious identity but of him as a writer with a strong ideological agenda that did not match that of the Crown. From this vantage point, his books on and related to Campion are the exception that proves the rule, while the *Thomas More* play represents yet another adjustment to the rhetoric of resistance at that crucial time when Robert Southwell and the Earl of Arundel were both in prison, Marlowe was threatened, and three Protestant nonconformists – John Penry, Henry Barrow, and John Greenwood – were hanged.[39] Through a representation of More's refusal to sign the articles of subscription, the *More* play, like *Zelauto*, certainly articulates a challenge to the royal supremacy. But, unlike *Zelauto*, *More* strategically omits any reference to religion, an omission which in combination with Shakespeare's lines about loyalty inserted into *More*,[40] allows the play to sidestep the more inflammatory subject of religion while not avoiding the opportunity to represent the distinction important to nonconformists of every stripe that loyalty be regarded as an issue independent of religious conformity.

The Orator, in which the *Zelauto* material recurs in 1596 is, as we know, constitutive of *Merchant*, but not entirely irrelevant to *More*, for, like *More*, *The Orator* directs attention to legal cases and so also to concepts of moral judgement. In this work – entered in the Stationers' Register on 15 July 1596, dedicated to John St John of Bletso,[41] and printed by Adam Islip – Munday used a variation on his regular strategy of adopting nearly an author-less[42] position. Not only presenting a translation of a book someone else had authored, this time he also used a pseudonym, Lazarus Pyot. We know Pyot was Munday,[43] and the pseudonym he used perhaps makes sense given the view of him offered in this paper. Lazarus was the name of a leper who returned from the dead; 'piot' is a word for the chattering magpie. In 'Lazarus

Pyot', Munday may have been merely describing his situation. A prolific writer, he was now bringing back to life some material closely associated with the English Catholic interests which were the source of his having been stigmatized in 1580.

In this instance, he had translated from the French a book by Alexandre van den Busche (also known as Alexander Silvain), *Epitomes des*

---

[39] *More* is usually dated 1593; see Vittorio Gabrieli and Giorgio Melchiori, ed., *Sir Thomas More: A Play* (Manchester, 1990), pp. 11–12. The Earl of Arundel had been tried for treason in 1589; Robert Southwell had been imprisoned in 1592, tortured during 1592–3, and would be executed in 1595. Marlowe was killed in 1593. Barrow, Greenwood, and Penry were hanged in 1593; for the latter, see Donna B. Hamilton, *Shakespeare and the Politics of Protestant England* (Hemel Hempstead, 1992), p. 8.

[40] See '*Sir Thomas More*, passages attributed to Shakespeare', in *The Complete Oxford Shakespeare*, ed. Stanley Wells and Gary Taylor (Oxford, 1986), p. 892, lines 108–54.

[41] That St John's daughter would marry the Lord Admiral's son within a few months has been thought to have been a factor in Munday's dedication; see Celeste Turner Wright, ' "Lazarus Pyott" and Other Inventions of Anthony Mundy', *Philological Quarterly*, 42 (1963), 532–41, p. 537. But using a pseudonym is a rather indirect way to give a compliment. St John had served on the commission for the trials of Mary Stuart and the Earl of Arundel, had had responsibility to identify recusancy, and in 1596 when England feared Spanish attack he would be asked to collect arms from the recusants. See P. W. Hasler, *The House of Commons, 1558–1603*, 3 vols. (London, 1981), vol. 3, p. 322. On St John's connection to the control of recusancy, see Dasent, *Acts of the Privy Council*, 23. 111, 256; on collecting arms from recusants, see William Raleigh Trimble, *The Catholic Laity in Elizabethan England, 1558–1603* (Cambridge, Mass., 1964), p. 156. St John was part of the machinery of state, and it may be there that as much or more of the signficance of the dedication lies.

[42] For this term applied to issues of nonconformist rhetorical positioning, see Lowell Gallagher, *Medusa's Gaze: Casuistry and Conscience in the Renaissance* (Stanford, 1991), p. 105.

[43] The decisive case for Lazarus Pyot being Munday is made in Wright, ' "Lazarus Pyott" and Other Inventions of Anthony Mundy', pp. 532–41.

cent histoires tragicques (Paris, 1581).[44] Unlike the episodic romance in *Zelauto*, Busche's collection of stories presents one hundred cases requiring legal judgement, with two speakers arguing different judgements for each case. In giving the book the title *The Orator*, Munday identified it as intended for practical use. Noting its differences from books containing 'models of oratory' for teaching Ciceronian rhetoric in grammar schools, T. W. Baldwin emphasized that 'Pyott was very well aware of the nature of this collection, and equally specific as to the classes of people whom he expected to attract by his translation.' Here Baldwin was referring to Munday's recommendations 'To the Reader': 'If thou studie law, they may helpe thy pleadings, or if divinitie (the reformer of law) they may perfect thy persuasions.' In other words, the book is aimed at readers with opportunities and responsibilities for action in the public sphere, and its method is to provide instruction in moral judgement by means of cases, which is another way to say that Munday's book presents cases of conscience, a category of legal, religious and moral discourse that had become of such importance to Catholics and Protestants but which was not limited to cases concerning religion.[45] The numbered Declamations of *The Orator* range widely in topic, for example, Declaration 1, 'Of Fulvius, who caused the Senators of Capua to be beheaded, without the consent of the Senate and people of Rome', Declamation 11, 'Of the wife of a Tyrant, who having slaine her husband, required his sonne for a recompence', Declamation 30, 'Of a knight of Rhodes, that would enter into Religioun again, after that he had given over his Order, to take a wife', Declamation 85, 'Of Agamemnon who first promised, and after would not sacrifice his daughter Iphiginia', Declamation 95, 'Of a Jew, who would for his debt have a pound of the flesh of a Christian.' Despite Munday's having dropped a veil over his own presence in this book, he nevertheless retained and exhibited his agency not by arguing a particular side of any-thing, as he had in *Zelauto*, but by making right action in the public sphere his topic.

Were we to describe the political context of summer 1596 in order to understand why this book by Munday might have come out at this time, the details would be similar to some of the material that affects our reading of *1 Henry IV*,[46] but with the addition of a French element. As in 1580 when *Zelauto* first appeared, France was coming to town again over a matter of alliance, this time in July 1596, 'to mark the ratification of the [English–French] alliance concluded at Greenwich in May'.[47] Partly at issue for the French was whether English action in Cadiz would draw too much attention away from France. At issue for Elizabeth was the need to prevent either France or Spain from dominating in Europe.[48]

---

[44] A native of Flanders and likely to have been Catholic, Bushe had served as an officer in the French army under Philip IX (1574) and Henry III (1584), and had written a number of moralizing works; see M. M. Michaud, ed., *Biographie universelle*, 2nd edn (Paris, 1880), vol. 4, pp. 520–1.

[45] On 'cases of conscience' as books presenting 'the resolution by expert minds of difficult moral cases', see Edmund Leites, 'Casuistry and Character', *Conscience and Casuistry in Early Modern Europe*, ed. by Edmund Leites (Cambridge, 1988), p. 119. See also Allen D. Boyer, 'Sir Edward Coke, Ciceronianus: Classical Rhetoric and the Common Law Tradition', *International Journal for the Semiotics of Law*, 10 (1997), 3–36; P. J. Holmes, *Elizabethan Casuistry*, Catholic Record Society, vol. 67 (London, 1981); Perez Zagorin, *Ways of Lying: Dissimulation, Persecution, and Conformity in Early Modern Europe* (Cambridge, Mass., 1990); Camille Wells Slights, *The Casuistrical Tradition in Shakespeare, Donne, Herbert, and Milton* (Princeton, 1981); and Gallagher, *Medusa's Gaze*.

[46] See Gary Taylor 'William Shakespeare, Richard James and the House of Cobham', *Review of English Studies*, 38 (1987), 334–54; Gary Taylor, 'The Fortunes of Old-castle', *Shakespeare Survey 38* (1985), pp. 85–100.

[47] David McKeen, *A Memory of Honour: The Life of William Brooke, Lord Cobham*, 2 vols. (Salzburg, 1986), vol. 2, p. 642. Cecil's father-in-law William Brooke, Lord Cobham, was in charge of welcoming the Duke de Bouillon, the leader of the French party; McKeen, *A Memory of Honour*, vol. 2, p. 643.

[48] See Paul E. J. Hammer, *The Polarisation of Elizabethan*

The tension around these international relations was matched by a crisis in factionalism at home. On 5 July, with Essex in Cadiz, Queen Elizabeth had appointed Robert Cecil as Secretary of State, and a year later, in October 1597, would also name him chancellor of the duchy of Lancaster.[49] Among other implications, Cecil's appointment to Secretary of State removed from Catholics and some Protestants the tolerance and protection that would have been anticipated had the appointment gone to Essex instead.[50] Finally, Lord Chamberlain Hunsdon, known to be in poor health, would die on 22 July 1596, to be succeeded immediately by Cecil's father-in-law William Brooke, Lord Cobham.[51] As Paul Hammer has documented, by late July and August, Cecil did tighten the rein on Catholics,[52] and, as Richard Dutton has emphasized, in late summer London officials made their move to shut down the playhouses.[53] Presumably Hunsdon had been the person at court in whose protection Munday had remained, a speculation consistent with the fact that Munday's final reference to himself as Messenger of her Majesty's Chamber occurred also in 1596, on the title page of *Primaleon*, Book II.[54]

When this context is brought to bear on *1 Henry IV*, at issue in part is the extent to which changing power relations at court would affect the conditions for public discourse, including conditions in the theatre. Like the dissension in 1580 over the Queen's marriage, dissension at court in 1596 again opened some new opportunities for discussion, an openness which would be challenged by the orders in 1597 and 1598 restricting theatre activities.[55] In *1 Henry IV*, primarily through Oldcastle-Falstaff, Shakespeare represented court factionalism – including the Cecils and Cobhams – by mocking that brand of Protestant rhetoric and practice that had as its end self-promotion and self-gain, and that included the blatant disregard of the public good as manifested in the taking of another's property.[56] The form of the critique in *1 Henry IV* has much in common with that in

Merchant, although critics rarely associate the two plays except for their utter closeness in date.[57] In taking up in *Merchant* a story Munday had told twice – dangerously in 1580 and quite safely in 1596 – Shakespeare was also, I would suggest, taking up where Munday and he had left off; the *More* play had ended, like the fourth act of *Merchant*, with an example of how legal and political systems work to the detriment of subjects not in power, although unlike *More*, *Merchant* is explicit about the tensions around

Politics: The Political Career of Robert Devereux, 2nd Earl of Essex, 1585–1597 (Cambridge, 1999), p. 261.

49 See Hammer, *Polarisation of Elizabethan Politics*, pp. 368, 355, 381. See also Paul E. J. Hammer, 'Patronage at Court, Faction and the Earl of Essex', in John Guy, ed., *The Reign of Elizabeth I* (Cambridge, 1995), pp. 77–83.

50 For Essex's sympathy for Catholics, see Hammer, *The Polarisation of Elizabethan Poltics*, pp. 174–8.

51 See McKeen, *Memory of Honour*, p. 644.

52 For the harsher measures the Cecil pursued in July and August, see Hammer, *The Polarisation of Elizabethan Politics*, pp. 369–70.

53 Richard Dutton, *Mastering the Revels: The Regulation and Censorship of English Renaissance Drama* (Basingstoke, 1991), p. 105; E. K. Chambers, *The Elizabethan Stage*, 4 vols. (Oxford, 1923), vol. 4, pp. 231–2, 322–3.

54 Turner, *Anthony Mundy*, p. 93; Gerald R. Hayes, 'Anthony Munday's Romances: A Postscript,' *Library*, 7 (1926), 35, 31–8. Vice-Chamberlain Thomas Heneage, who had paid Munday (Eccles, 'Brief Lives: Tudor and Stuart Authors', p. 99), died in 1595; no vice-chamberlain was appointed to replace him.

55 See Dutton, *Mastering the Revels*, pp. 107–11.

56 This reading is from Gary D. Hamilton, 'Mocking Oldcastle: Notes Toward Exploring a Possible Catholic Presence in Shakespeare's Henriad', unpublished paper presented at the Shakespeare Association of America meeting, 1–4 April 1999.

57 For the argument that *Merchant* was written right before or right after *1 Henry IV*, see Stanley Wells and Gary Taylor, *William Shakespeare: A Textual Companion* (1987; rpt. Oxford, 1997), p. 119. The reference in *Merchant* to the Andrew, a ship Essex captured in Cadiz, further confirms this dating; see Brown, ed., *Merchant*, pp. xxvi–xxvii. It is also possible that instead of writing *Merchant* during Cobham's tenure, Shakespeare wrote it in the freer time after Cobham's death when the theatre companies were once more controlled by the Lord Admiral and a Hunsdon; see Dutton, *Mastering the Revels*, pp. 106–7.

and risks of nonconformity in religion. Using both versions[58] of Munday's story, and repeating the power relations that Munday and he had represented in the *More* play, Shakespeare again produced in *Merchant* a critique of the physical and material advantages that intolerance gives to holders of power. As B. J. Sokol has written, Shakespeare succeeded in this critique partly by providing for 'Belmont's elite' to convey a 'mixture of bigotry and cruelty with social privilege and charm', products 'of Shakespeare's deeply intentional irony'.[59] Devoid of direct representations of either Catholics or Protestants,[60] *Merchant* nevertheless makes broadly the point that persecution for religion takes the form of, is motivated by, and is disguised within the most material of practices.

Whatever any of us concludes finally about Shakespeare's religion, putting Munday in the middle of our consideration of *Merchant* deepens our understanding of how religious issues informed Shakespeare's conceptualizations and articulations of what might constitute right action in the public sphere. Linking Shakespeare and Munday motivates us to consider again Dutton's suggestion that it was important to players and playwrights that by early in 1597 the theatre companies were once more controlled by the Lord Admiral and a Hunsdon.[61] And finally, Shakespeare's having given Munday the stage in *Merchant* proved to be an appropriate forerunner of the launching of the main part of Munday's stage career in December 1597.[62]

---

58 For example, see Brown, ed., *Merchant*, p. xxxi.
59 B. J. Sokol, 'Prejudice and Law in *The Merchant of Venice*', *Shakespeare Survey 51* (1998), pp. 159–73, p. 169.
60 For the dramatic tradition of representing Catholics as Jews, see Paul Whitfield White, '"Reforming Mysteries' End": A New Look at Protestant Intervention in English Provincial Drama', *Journal of Medieval and Early Modern Studies*, 29 (1999), 121–47, pp. 132–4.
61 Dutton, *Mastering the Revels*, pp. 104–7.
62 See Chambers, *The Elizabethan Stage*, vol. 3, 447–8.

PERFECT ANSWERS: RELIGIOUS INQUISITION, FALSTAFFIAN WIT

TOM McALINDON

I

Few would now deny that in *Henry IV* the character of Falstaff constitutes a deliberate and audacious caricature of a Protestant hero, the fourteenth-century champion of Wycliffe's doctrines, Sir John Oldcastle, the first Lord Cobham, 'Lollardus Lollardorum'.[1] Shakespeare's wicked joke, as Ernst Honigmann has called it,[2] gave offence in his own time not only to Cobham's distinguished titular descendants but also to earnest Protestants such as John Speed (1611), Richard James (*c.* 1625), and Thomas Fuller (1655),[3] to the authors of the anti-Catholic response play, *The first part of the true and honorable historie, the life of Sir John Oldcastle, the Good Lord Cobham* (1599), and no doubt to many playgoers of like persuasion. Defying the hagiographic efforts of John Bale and John Foxe, Shakespeare in effect took the Catholic side in a sectarian dispute about the character of the nobleman who was burned as a heretic shortly after his friend, the Prince of Wales, became Henry V; and although in Part 2 he changed his reprobate knight's name from Sir John Oldcastle to Sir John Falstaff, his contemporaries would still have recognized his original intention and treated the Epilogue's denial as tongue-in-cheek.

Apart from his friendship with the Prince of Wales, there are a number of parallels between the historiographic and the Shakespearian Sir John, some obvious, some teasingly oblique, most of them already noted by critics. The first

Sir John was a reformed sinner who publicly confessed that in his youth he offended grievously in pride, wrath, gluttony, covetousness, and lechery. The second Sir John, 'my old lad of the castle' (1:1.2.41), is a lecherous glutton and thief who repeatedly promises to reform and so is nicknamed 'Monsieur Remorse' (line 112). The first Sir John based all his religious beliefs on the Bible and according to Bale and Foxe had a masterful knowledge of both the Old and the New Testament; the second specializes in a Puritan idiom whose chief characteristic is an abundance of biblical quotation and allusion (no other Shakespearian character quotes so liberally from the Bible). The first Sir John was condemned for supporting Lollard preachers; the second flaunts his understanding of the godly art ('Well, God give thee the spirit of persuasion, and him the ears of profiting, that what thou speakest may move, and what he hears may be

---

[1] For a thorough consideration of the evidence in favour of Shakespeare's satiric intention, see Gary Taylor, 'The Fortunes of Oldcastle', *Shakespeare Survey 38* (1985), pp. 85–100. See also E. A. J. Honigmann, 'Sir John Oldcastle: Shakespeare's Martyr', in *'Fanned and Winnowed Opinions': Shakespearean Essays Presented to Harold Jenkins* (London and New York, 1987), pp. 118–32; Kristen Poole, 'Saints Alive! Falstaff, Martin Marprelate, and the Staging of Puritanism', *Shakespeare Quarterly*, 46 (1995), 47–95.

[2] 'Sir John Oldcastle: Shakespeare's Martyr', p. 126.

[3] For James and Fuller, see David Bevington, ed. *Henry IV, Part 1* (Oxford, 1987), pp. 6–8; for Speed, see S. Schoenbaum, *William Shakespeare: a Compact Documentary Life* (Oxford, 1977), p. 193.

believed' [lines 143–5]). One of the heresies for which the first Sir John was condemned was his denial of the value of pilgrimages, whether to Canterbury or to Rome; the second Sir John waylays pilgrims en route to Canterbury. Henry V tried hard to get his friend to renounce his Wycliffite beliefs, but he proved righteously immoveable; the second Sir John protests to the Prince that he will 'be damned for never a king's son in Christendom' (line 93). The first Sir John was executed for treason as well as heresy; in the play the Prince initially refuses to become a thief, and Sir John threatens: 'By the Lord, I'll be a traitor then, when thou art king' (line 137). The first Sir John was executed in a singular manner, being hanged in chains as a traitor and burned as a heretic; the Prince not only teases the second Sir John about being hanged but also calls him a 'roasted Manningtree ox' (2.4.457). After he was found guilty, the first Sir John escaped from prison and eluded the authorities for four years before being apprehended and executed; the second Sir John spends the whole of Part 2 engaged in a similar relation with the fangs and snares of the law.

To miss these parallels and the large parodic intention which they underscore is to miss the outrageously satiric dimension and some of the socio-political implications of Shakespeare's greatest comic character. In this article I shall be reinforcing the argument for parodic intent, for my purpose is to show that a central feature of Falstaff's complex comic art was probably inspired by Protestant hagiography's treatment of the way in which Oldcastle answered his theological accusers. As so often happens, parody will be seen as having metamorphosed the object of its mockery into something beguilingly attractive and even admirable.

What is the essence of Falstaff's comic character, what is it about him that most commands admiration and delight? Dryden was the first critic to address the question. 'That wherein he is singular', he explained, are 'those things he says *praeter expectatum*, unexpected by the audience; his quick evasions when you imagine him

surpriz'd'; and he added that Falstaff's unwieldy mass seems to intensify the unexpected and extremely diverting nature of his verbal evasions.[4] Subsequent attempts to define the essential Falstaff endorse this explanation and elaborate on it in ways which are useful for my purposes. In the nineteenth century, Henry Hudson emphasized the immense self-confidence with which Sir John handles himself when cornered by Hal and Poins; indeed he infers from Falstaff's incomprehensible lies that he deliberately invites being cornered, 'partly for the pleasure he takes in the excited play of his faculties, partly for the surprise he causes by his still more incomprehensible feats of dodging'.[5] In this century E. E. Stoll distinguished between Falstaff's evasions and those of other braggart soldiers such as Bobadill, noting that the latters' are 'mere excuses and subterfuges' whereas Falstaff's are 'gay, aggressive, triumphant . . . Falstaff carries things with a high hand, and expects to bear down all before him'.[6] H. B. Charlton asked, 'What then is . . . the ruling passion, the distinctive quiddity of Sir John Falstaff?', and in his answer he too stressed the immense self-confidence with which Falstaff courts and triumphs over the threat of censorious entrapment. 'Fundamentally, it is his infinite capacity for extricating himself from predicaments . . . So adept is he in this art of extrication that he revels in creating dilemmas for himself to enjoy the zest of coming triumphantly out of them.'[7]

There is no obvious model or archetype for Falstaff's primary characteristic and its associated tendencies. Critics looking at antecedents have variously and correctly noted that there is something in him of the mythical buffoon, the Vice, the picaro, the braggart soldier, and the

---

[4] The New Variorum *Henry the Fourth Part I*, ed. Samuel Burdett Hemingway (Philadelphia and London, 1936), p. 403.
[5] *Variorum, Part I*, p. 421.
[6] *Variorum, Part I*, p. 431.
[7] *Variorum, Part I*, p. 441.

Elizabethan clown, all of whom are adept in evasive trickeries of one kind or another. Nevertheless, as an extremely quickwitted and intelligent knight, equipped with a sumptuous store of biblical, theological, mythological, and literary knowledge, and majestically confident of his ability to confound his moralizing accusers, Shakespeare's Sir John seems remarkably unlike these prototypes. Nor do I detect his genius for the self-justifying smart answer either in Martin Marprelate, with whom he has also been compared, or in the colourless figure who shares his original name in the earlier *Famous Victories of King Henry the Fifth* (1594). So let us return to the first Sir John, or more precisely, to one of the first Sir Johns.

II

The most comprehensive account of Oldcastle's life and death, and the one we might assume was of most use and interest to Shakespeare, is that given in the expanded 1570 edition of John Foxe's *Actes and Monuments*. Together with much material from other sources, this account incorporates most of John Bale's pioneer treatise, *A brefe Chronicle concernynge the Examinacyon and death of the blessed martyr of Christ, Sir Johan Oldecastell the lorde Cobham* (Antwerp, 1544).[8] But what was of most interest to Bale, namely the interrogation of Oldcastle on the charge of heresy, constitutes less than a quarter of Foxe's lengthy account; moreover, as in the shorter narrative contained in the 1563 edition, where Bale's contribution is proportionately greater, Bale's explicitly defined *conception* of Oldcastle's examination is obscured.[9]

As he himself indicates, Bale's version of the examination is based partly on the brief and anonymous *Examinacion of the honorable knyght sir Jhon Oldcastell Lorde Cobham* (Antwerp, ?1530),[10] but mainly on the official report of the process made for Thomas Arundel, the Archbishop of Canterbury.[11] His own editorial hand, however, is at work from the start, guiding his readers' responses to question and answer in

accord with an interpretation of the whole procedure which he provides in his Preface. He refers briefly in the Preface to Oldcastle's career as a distinguished servant of the crown in Wales: 'In all adventurous acts of worldly manhood was he ever bold, strong, fortunate, doughty, noble, and valiant' (7). And after he deals with the examination, condemnation, and execration of Oldcastle he pays tribute to the great fortitude with which he met his cruel death. But his purpose is not to exalt the passive heroism of the martyr over the active courage of the soldier, nor even to focus intently on his final torment in the usual hagiographic manner. In his interpretation, Oldcastle's great triumph is oral, rhetorical, intellectual. Oldcastle, he says, was 'never so worthy a conqueror as in this present conflict with the cruel and furious frantic kingdom of antichrist' (7); and by this present conflict he means primarily the inquisition in which Oldcastle stands alone against a team of theologians led by the Archbishop of Canterbury: four bishops and twelve doctors of the church in all. In the end, Oldcastle allows his interrogators to prove him a heretic; but as Bale makes clear, he triumphantly demonstrates in his responses that what they call heresy is the true Christian faith as grounded in the scriptures. 'His courage was of such value that it gave him the victory over them by the clear judgment of the scriptures, what though the world's

---

8 An undated reprint was issued in London a few years later. This is contained in Bale's *Select Works*, ed. Henry Christmas, Parker Society Publications (Cambridge, 1849). My references are to this edition.

9 It is, however, *detectable* in Foxe; so it is just possible that Shakespeare acquired it indirectly from Foxe without having read Bale's original version.

10 *STC* 24045. It may have been edited by William Tyndale. No pagination.

11 Arundel's *Magnus Processus* is contained in the *Fasciculi Zizaniorum Magistri Johannis Wycliff cum tritico*, the only contemporaneous account of the rise of the Lollards. The *Fasciculi* is reprinted as vol. 5 of the Rolls Series, ed. W. W. Shirley (London, 1858). Bale and Foxe ascribe the authorship of this collection to Thomas Netter of Walden, a leading opponent of the Lollards.

judgments be far otherwise' (13). It is they who are outwitted and defeated, not he. Says Bale: 'He that hath judgment in the spirit shall easily perceive by this treatise . . . what influence of grace this man of God had from above concerning his answers' (6). In other words, prepare to read inspired answers to questions which are top-heavy with learning, authority and malicious intent. Nevertheless, suggests Bale, Oldcastle's surprising victory in this ostensibly one-sided battle of wits is exactly what the scriptures should lead us to expect. 'Most surely fulfilled Christ his promise in him which he made to his apostles: "Cast not in your mind aforehand . . . what answer ye shall make when these spiritual tyrants shall examine you in their synagogues . . . For I will give such utterance and wisdom in that hour, as all your enemies shall never be able to resist you"' (6).[12] Bale is here adapting and giving central significance to one of the secondary topoi of Christian hagiography, the wisdom derived from sanctity. The most famous example of this topos occurs in the legend of the virgin martyr, St Katherine of Alexandria, whose spectacular triumph over the physical torments with which pagans seek to break her faith in Christ is preceded by a display of divinely inspired eloquence in response to the arguments of a team of philosophers aimed at getting her to renounce her faith.[13]

Before Oldcastle is even brought to examination, the Archbishop publicly denounces him as 'that seditious apostate, that schismatic, that heretic, that troubler of the peace, that enemy of the realm and great adversary of all holy church'. But he is undeterred by these 'hateful names' (19) and, like St Katherine, answers his inquisitors with an air of serene and often disdainful self-confidence. His first response is a written exposition of what he believes, composed in reply to the official accusation of heresy. Before being examined by the theologians, he presents this document to the King as proof that he is a true Christian, assuring him that if he is taught a better belief he will most reverently and at all times obey it (22); thus

from the outset he seems to shift defiantly from defence to attack. When confronted by the theologians, he refuses at first to go beyond what he has written and state 'more plainly' his position on the eucharist, penance, pilgrimages, and the power of Rome. The implication is clear: anything not dealt with in his scripturally grounded confession of faith is irrelevant. Thus he informs them that he will gladly both believe and observe whatsoever the holy church instituted by Christ has determined, but he denies that popes, cardinals, and prelates have the power to determine such matters as stand not with God's word. With this aggressively evasive strategy, says Bale, the bishops and prelates 'were in a maner amazed and wonderfully disquieted' (26).[14]

---

[12] There is no hint of any of this in *The examinacion*. But Bale was clearly inspired by the defiance with which in this account Cobham responds to his inquisitors, and owes to it some of the more impressive retorts which he imputes to his hero.

[13] This legend in particular shows Bale's closeness to hagiographical tradition. Katherine is compared to the apostles armed with Christ's assurance that they should have no anxiety as to what they must say when brought before kings and princes; such indeed is the power of God's grace in her responses to the pagan philosophers who challenge her faith that they are filled with awe and completely overcome (*The Life of St Katherine . . . with its Latin Original*, ed. E. Einenkel, Early English Texts Society, No. 80 [London, 1884]), pp. 31, 58, 61–2; Jacobus de Voragine, *The Golden Legende*, trans. William Caxton [1493], sigs. Y3v–7). As Hippolyte Delehaye has shown, late-classical rhetoric played an important part in the growth of the martyr legend; he regards Katherine's debate with the pagan philosophers as an ingenious amplification of the standard interrogation of the martyr: see *Les passions des martyrs et les genres littéraires* (Brussels, 1921), p. 169. Having been a Carmelite friar, Bale was steeped in hagiography and had in fact compiled his own collection of saints' lives for the benefit of his fellow Carmelites. See Leslie P. Fairfield, *John Bale: Mythmaker for the English Reformation* (West Lafayette, Indiana, 1976), pp. 21–7

[14] In neither the *Examinacion* nor the *Magnus Processus* is there any warrant for Bale's repeated emphasis on the helpless confusion to which the inquisitors are reduced by Cobham's answers. This is a hagiographical motif which appealed to his dramatic instinct.

At the end of the first examination he is dispatched to the Tower, the frustrated bishops having determined to pin him down by giving him a precise list of the church's teaching on the disputed matters and requiring him to affirm or deny belief in each of them. Reading the document, 'he marvelled greatly of their mad ignorance. . . and deep errors' and perceived their malicious intent 'purposed against him howsoever he should answer' (28). He now decides, however, to put his trust in God and engage fully with their questions and accusations; and a few days later, says Bale, he is led from the Tower 'as a lamb among wolves, to his examination and answer' (29). But his assurance does not desert him and he matches thrust with counter-thrust. The Archbishop begins by telling him he stands accursed for his contumacy. 'Then spake the Lord Cobham with a most cheerful countenance, and said: 'God saith by his holy prophet, *maledicam benedictionibus vestris*".[15] Which may be construed as a succinct way of saying, 'I would rather be cursed by you and blessed by God than vice versa.' His Lordship is apparently discomfited by this retort, for he chooses to ignore it and tries a softer approach; but with no more success. Says Bale, 'The archbishop made then as though he had . . . not heard him' but 'continued forth in his tale', saying: 'Sir, at that time I gently proffered to have assoiled you, if ye would have asked it. And yet I do the same, if ye will humbly desire it in due form and manner as holy church ordained.' Adding injured innocence to audacity, Oldcastle responds, 'Nay, forsooth, I will not, for I never yet trespassed against you' (29).

He then proceeds to evaluate the Archbishop's offer of absolution in a surprising manner, and in so doing strikes obliquely at both the spiritual arrogance of his accusers and the sacrament of penance, one of the doctrines at issue. He gets down on his knees, raises his hands to heaven, and shrives himself loudly to the eternal living God, confessing that in his frail youth he offended most grievously in pride,

wrath, lechery and so on. This confession of a very sinful past is regularly noted by Shakespearian scholars (usually as a parallel with Falstaff's lifestyle), but its purpose and the spirit in which it is made are never remarked on. It is in fact a theatrical move in a rhetorical contest; and by no means does it signify defensiveness. For having made his public confession to God Himself (who alone, he implies, can absolve him), Oldcastle rises and turns to all those who have assembled to witness the inquisition, pointing out – 'Lo good people, lo' – that his accusers have condemned him for breaking their own laws and traditions but not for his grievous violation of God's great laws and commandments.[16] Whereupon, says Bale, 'the archbishop and his company were not a little blemished' (29–30).

They fare even worse when they try to catch him out on the the eucharist and transubstantiation. Questioned on this, he summarizes correctly all the relevant passages from the New Testament and on this basis affirms his belief that the consecrated host is Christ's body in the form of bread. But is it still bread? Yes, he answers, it is visible bread; the body of Christ is seen only by the eye of faith. 'Then smiled they each one upon other . . . And with a great brag divers of them said: "It is foul heresy"' (31). Some among them, however, feel it necessary to ask if he believes the bread to be material bread or not. 'The Lord Cobham said unto them: "The scriptures make no mention of this word material, and therefore my faith hath nothing to do therewith"' (32). When one of the bishops insists that after the sacramental words are spoken it is bread no longer, he

---

15 This answer is taken from the *Examinacion*. The 'most cheerful countenance' is Bale's characteristic addition, as is the following reference to the Archbishop's embarrassment. The original answer possibly marks the point at which Bale conceived the idea for his own version of Oldcastle's 'history'.

16 The confession is in the *Examinacion*, but the appeal to an audience is a typical example of Bale's theatrical heightening.

replies: 'Saint Paul the apostle was (I am sure) as wise as ye be now, and more godly learned: and he called it bread writing to the Corinthians.' 'Paule must be otherwise understood', they protest; to take him literally would be heresy. How can they justify this claim?, he inquires. Because, they reply, it has been so determined by Holy Church and its holy doctors. 'I know none holier than Christ and his apostle', responds the knight drily. 'A most Christian answer', exclaims Bale from the margin; but it is too much for the holy doctors: when Oldcastle proceeds to amplify his provocative point, 'Then asked they him, to stop his mouth therewith' (32).

When the interrogation resumes, the Carmelite prior engages with Oldcastle and makes the mistake of saying that Matthew 7 forbids judging one's superiors. But 'the same-self chapter of Matthew', explains Oldcastle, warns us against false prophets, appear they never so glorious; as does John 7 and 10, Deuteronomy 1, and Psalm 61. The Prior foolishly persists: 'Unto whom the Lord Cobham thus answered. It is well sophistried of you forsooth. Preposterous are your judgements evermore. For, as the prophet Esay saith . . .' When Oldcastle completes this crushing rebuttal, John Bale, as it were, cannot contain himself, and applauds once more from the margin: 'A perfect answer', he writes (34).

Repeatedly subjected to Oldcastle's masterful command of the Bible, the leaders of the English church are thus, says Bale, 'confounded in their learning'. In desperation, one of them plucks out of his bosom a copy of the document they had sent with him to Tower, 'thinking thereby to make shorter work of him. For they were so amazed with his answers . . . that they knew not well how to occupy the time, their wits and sophistry . . . so failed them that day' (37). They demand brief responses to what is written in this bill of belief. His answers are calm and sardonic; he knows they will inculpate him, but before his accusers condemn him he makes sure to treat them in kind. One of the last

questions put to him asks his view of the pope; and in attending to his answer we must note that his examination has been moved from the Chapter House in St Paul's to the Dominican Friary. 'The Lord Cobham answered . . . he and you together maketh whole the great antichrist. Of whom he is the great head, you bishops, priests, prelates, and monks are the body, and the begging friars are the tail, for they cover the filthiness of you both with their subtle sophistry' (38). Before bringing the proceedings to a conclusion, the Archbishop understandably accuses Oldcastle of having 'spoken here many wonderful words to the slanderous rebuke of all the whole spirituality'. Injured innocent to the last, however, Sir John loftily responds: 'Much more have you offended me than ever I offended you, in thus troubling me before this multitude' (40).

III

'You have misled the youthful Prince', says the Lord Chief Justice to Shakespeare's Sir John. 'The young Prince hath misled me', retorts the knight. 'Well, God send the Prince a better companion!', continues the Chief Justice. 'God send the companion a better prince! I cannot rid my hands of him', answers Sir John (2:1.2.145–47, 201–2).

This encounter provides a convenient point of return to *Henry IV* for a more exact reminder of Falstaff's characteristic comic procedure. In Part 1 as in Part 2, he is under attack from the outset, enduring Hal's good humoured but energetic denunciation of his sinful way of life, a diatribe prompted by his opening question about the time of day. By way of response, Sir John slides into a distractingly graceful conceit about Phoebus and the moon, but then counterattacks Puritan-wise with an accusation that will resonate in a two-part play dense with ideas about sin, redemption, and the lost grace or sanctity of kingship: 'God save thy grace – majesty I should say, for grace thou wilt have none . . . No, by my troth. Not so much as will serve to be prologue to an egg and butter' (1:1.2.17–21). Pertinent here is the fact that Falstaff not only poses from time to time as a godly, bible-quoting and self-righteous Protestant, but is also endowed with a secular form of the extraordinary grace which, according to Bale, inspired the first Oldcastle's responses (because of its concern with the nature of kingship and true nobility, there is in fact a notable continuity in *Henry IV* between theological and secular notions of grace). Says Sir John to the Chief Justice concerning one of his aggressively defensive rejoinders: 'This is the right fencing grace, my lord – tap for tap' (2:2.1.194–6). [17]

The scene in Part 1 which opens with Hal's indictment of Falstaff – 1.2 – concludes with preparations for the Gad's Hill escapade; and the whole purpose of that adventure is to create a situation in which Sir John will be compelled to admit that he is a coward and a liar. Occurring in most editions in 2.4, the scene of accusatory ensnarement – Falstaff on trial, as it were – constitutes the climax of the play's comic action. The gloating conviction of Hal and Poins that they can at last extract from him an abject confession of guilt, together with the presence of an excited on-stage audience (cf. 'Lo good people, lo'), generates suspense and focuses all our attention on the moment when Falstaff produces the answer that frustrates his accusers. The answer is too well known to quote here, but what I must quote is his answer when accused a second time in this same scene. In the playlet, Hal as King rebukes Falstaff as Prince: 'Swearest thou, ungracious boy? . . . Thou art violently fallen away from grace. There is a devil haunts thee in the likeness of an old fat man. . . Why dost thou converse with that trunk of humours, that bolting hutch of beastliness, that swollen parcel of dropsies, that huge bombard of sack, that stuffed cloak-bag of guts . . .' And so on, at length: Hal's demonizing invective, his catalogue of what Bale called 'hateful names' (cf. 'that seditious apostate, that . . . that . . . that . . .') is relentless. Nevertheless, Falstaff deflates it by responding with an air of exquisitely polite incomprehension which is innocence itself: 'I would your grace would take me with you. Whom means your grace?' (lines 443–4).

The centrality of this scene's chief comic procedure to Shakespeare's conception of Falstaff is confirmed in Part 2, where the same pattern of accusation and response is repeated with slight variation. As in 1.2 of Part 1, Falstaff in 1.2 here is under attack, this time from the Lord Chief Justice, Hal's mentor-to-be; and once again he relies on a general air of self-righteousness together with the right fencing grace of counter-thrust. The attempted shaming and condemnation again constitutes the climax of the comic action and occurs in the same position as before – 2.4 in most editions. Once again, too, the moralistic hubris of Hal and Poins and the presence of an eager audience maximize the effect of Sir John's responses to accusation. The charge of degeneracy, 'Why, thou globe of sinful continents, what a life dost thou lead', is cheekily deflated in one sentence (with a mock-contemptuous glance at Hal's disguise): 'A better than thou: I am a gentleman, thou art a drawer' (lines 290–1). His answer to the more damaging accusation of slandering a prince – a crime for which, as Hal points out, the statutory punishment was the loss of both ears – involves a wily assumption of both child-like innocence and adult wisdom, its effectiveness being greatly enhanced by Hal's sneering expectation that it will be a mere repetition of the cocksure answer given after the Gad's Hill affair:

---

[17] Cf. Baldassare Castiglione, *The Book of the Courtier* (1528), trans. Sir Thomas Hoby (1561) (London: Dent, 1966), p. 150: 'But among other merry sayings, they have a verie good grace, that arise when a man at nipping talke of his fellow, taketh the verie same words in the self same sense, and returneth them backe again, pricking him with his owne weapon'. Castiglione, it should be noted, likens perfect grace in speech and behaviour to divine grace: it is mysterious, not acquired by effort, 'the gift of nature and the heavens' (32, 44).

FALSTAFF (*to Prince Henry*) Didst thou hear me [abusing you]?

PRINCE HENRY Yea, and you knew me as you did when you ran away by Gad's Hill; you knew I was at your back, and spoke it on purpose to try my patience.

FALSTAFF No, no, no, not so, I did not think thou wast within hearing.

PRINCE HENRY I shall drive you, then, to confess the wilful abuse, and then I know how to handle you.

FALSTAFF No abuse, Hal; o'mine honour, no abuse.

PRINCE HENRY Not? To dispraise me, and call me 'pantler' and 'bread-chipper', and I know not what?

FALSTAFF No abuse, Hal.

POINS No abuse?

FALSTAFF No abuse, Ned, i'th'world, honest Ned, none . . . I dispraised him before the wicked that the wicked might not fall in love with him; (*to Prince Henry*) in which doing I have done the part of a careful friend and a true subject, and thy father is to give me thanks for it. No abuse, Hal; none, Ned, none.   (2.4.309–28)

Sir John's puritanism – dissociating himself from 'the wicked' – is not forgotten as he adroitly converts his sin to virtue.

In the end, of course, Falstaff's chief accuser, now the supreme figure of authority, condemns and passes sentence upon him. But there is a suggestion that he succeeds in doing so, not because he wins the argument, but because he prudently denies the accused the right of response. The new king's 'Reply not to me with a fool-born jest' (5.5.554) recalls what the holy doctors said in desperation when overcome by the sardonic fluency of the first Sir John: '[S]top his mouth.'

We are so familiar with Falstaff that it is difficult to imagine him other than he is. And yet if we had been in at the start of his creation and knew that Shakespeare intended to debunk the godly-Protestant view of Prince Henry's executed friend, our best guess would have been that he would caricature Oldcastle's biblical babbling (as Thomas Hoccleve conceived it in 1415)[18] and would present him as a Puritan hypocrite and a cowardly soldier;[19] which he does. But we would not have anticipated Falstaff's characterization as a reprobate who habitually wrongfoots his interrogators and accusers with incomparable rejoinders, perfect answers. That dominant characteristic, I suggest, follows from the felicitous marriage of Shakespeare's parodic imagination and John Bale's conception of the first Oldcastle as an apostle of truth whose answers had such 'influence of grace from above' that all the cunning and malice of his accusers was brought to nought. What results then is not a simple piece of anti-Puritan satire but a form of comedy which turns a Puritan butt into an exceptionally appealing character with a quicksilver mind and tongue.

---

18 'Hit is unkyndly for a knight / That shuld a kynges castel kepe, / To bable the Bibel day and night ' (Ballade). Cited in Wilhelm von Baeske, *Oldcastle-Falstaff in der englischen Literatur bis zu Shakespeare* (*Palaestra*, 1), p. 34.

19 Bale notes as a typical Romish slander Polydore Vergil's assertion in his *Anglica Historica* that Oldcastle 'cowardly fled' when he and other rebels were confronted by the King in person (*A Brief Chronicle*, p. 10).

WHEN SUICIDE BECOMES AN ACT OF HONOUR: *JULIUS CAESAR* AND *HAMLET* IN LATE NINETEENTH-CENTURY JAPAN

TETSUO KISHI

I wonder how widely it is realized that of all the Shakespearian characters who either kill themselves or think of killing themselves relatively few are overtly conscious of the sinfulness of the act. Both Romeo and Juliet are almost jubilant when they end their lives, and the same is certainly true about Pyramus and Thisbe, who can be interpreted as burlesque versions of the star-crossed lovers. Gloucester in *King Lear* is far from elated when he tries to kill himself, and his affliction seems to be simply too great to allow him time to consider the religious implications of the act he is about to perform. We are not quite certain about the state of mind Lady Macbeth and Goneril are in when they commit suicide as their deaths are not enacted on stage but only briefly reported to the audience. Still it would be safe to assume that their sense of guilt is far more overwhelming than any scruples they might have. We had better look elsewhere to encounter a Shakespearian character who thinks twice before proceeding to the act of fatal self-destruction.

One notable case is of course the central character of *Hamlet* with his reference to the everlasting fixing his canon against self-slaughter. Later in the play the priest talks disparagingly about Ophelia's death which he says is 'doubtful', but his remark does not really come as a surprise since he is professionally expected to be critical about suicide, and in any case Laertes's possibly sacrilegious attack against him might counterbalance the attitude the man holds. Still later in the play Horatio who claims

to be more an antique Roman than a Dane nearly kills himself. In this case suicide is clearly understood as a heroic and praiseworthy deed. Thus there is in this play a curious and interesting coexistence of two kinds of codes of behaviour, Christian and Roman or pre-Christian, or more generally, religious and secular.

In Roman plays, the situation seems to be much simpler. Both Antony and Cleopatra are deeply dejected, but to them killing themselves is in no way religiously unacceptable. To the Romans in *Julius Caesar* suicide is almost obligatory as the virtually only means to avoid humiliation. All this is rather surprising because Shakespeare after all was writing almost exclusively for a Christian audience in a Christian society. Although he was not one of the authors who adhere to historical accuracy, it may be argued that he changed his standards depending on what historical period he was dealing with. All the characters in Roman plays were born before Christ, and nominally at any rate *King Lear* is set in pre-Christian Britain. Perhaps this explains Gloucester's attitude towards suicide as well. He does not invoke Christian 'God' but 'gods'. But then there is *Hamlet* in which at least two different standards prevail, and apparently they are equally acceptable. It seems that the only point we can be absolutely certain about so far as Shakespeare's own attitude towards suicide is concerned is that it is neither consistent nor clearly defined.

Since this is so, it would be hardly surprising

if Shakespearian plays with suicidal characters are understood and appreciated in a considerably different fashion when they are transplanted to a non-Christian culture where suicide does not mean eternal damnation of one's soul. This is exactly what happened when Shakespeare's works were introduced to the late nineteenth-century Japanese audience.

The popular form of theatre in Japan at that time was *Kabuki*, which shares many artistic premises and conventions with another popular form, namely the puppet theatre *Bunraku*. Generally speaking, the repertoire of both *Kabuki* and *Bunraku* falls into two categories, *Jidai-mono* or history plays and *Sewa-mono* or domestic plays. The former deals primarily with a plight of people belonging to upper- and middle-classes of the society, court nobles and *samurai* warriors, for instance. The latter usually has to do with the tribulations of lower-class people such as farmers, artisans, merchants and prostitutes. In both history plays and domestic plays the basic dramatic conflict exists between two determinants of human behaviour, that is, *giri* which would mean social obligation and *ninjo* which would mean personal emotion. Just in case this combination sounds uniquely Japanese and exotic, I must hasten to say that such conflict is not dissimilar to the kind of conflict we recognize in a majority of tragedies in seventeenth-century France as well as Restoration England, that is, the conflict between a public principle and a private principle, between what one is expected to do and what one really wants to do.

Still there is probably a significant difference between the way dramatic conflict is solved in many Japanese tragedies and the way it is solved in French and English since all too often Japanese tragedies end with the suicide of one or more of the central characters. Certainly suicide figures far more prominently in these plays than it does in the plays of such authors as Racine and Dryden. It is almost mandatory, and no doubt cynics will regard it as too easy a way out.

A typical history play which ends with a central character's suicide might deal with a situation like this. A feudal warlord is insulted by a treacherous and totally unsympathetic court noble. The warlord tries to be patient, but when he feels it is just too much, he assaults the court noble. Under other circumstances this could be forgivable if not acceptable, but within the premises of the court where recourse to physical violence is strictly forbidden it is a very serious offence. The warlord is ordered to kill himself. He gave vent to his personal anger, and for this he has to pay with his own life. In this case suicide is an act of self-punishment, and by thus atoning for his offence he is elevated to an almost heroic status and gains the full sympathy of the audience.

In a domestic play a typical situation is likely to involve a married man who has an affair with another woman, very often a prostitute. The play usually ends with the man and the prostitute committing love suicides. The man's having an extramarital affair and being unfaithful to his wife is of course morally and socially wrong, but when he irrevocably sacrifices himself, the act somehow redeems his misdemeanour and makes him emotionally, if not rationally, acceptable and sympathetic.

One of the authors who dealt with such situations over and over again is Monzaemon Chikamatsu (1653–1724), arguably the greatest playwright Japan has ever produced. One of his best-known love suicide plays, *The Love Suicides at Sonezaki* (1703), describes the suicides in rather gruesome detail and then concludes with the following passage, 'No one is there to tell the tale, but the wind that blows through Sonezaki Wood transmits it, and high and low alike gather to pray for these lovers who beyond a doubt will in the future attain Buddhahood. They have become models of true love.'[1] Another play belonging to the same genre, *The Love Suicides at Amijima* (1720), ends with the

---

[1] *Four Major Plays of Chikamatsu*, translated by Donald Keene (New York and London, 1961), p. 56.

following tribute to the dead lovers, 'People say that they who were caught in the net of Buddha's vow immediately gained salvation and deliverance, and all who hear the tale of the Love Suicides at Amijima are moved to tears.'[2]

Chikamatsu was no Bertolt Brecht, and in no way was he prepared to alienate his heroes and heroines from his audience. Being an experienced and accomplished professional playwright, he knew how to sentimentalize his characters and draw the audience's sympathy to them. But no matter how competent he may have been, he would not have been able to achieve what he did without the Japanese frame of mind which does not harbour any religious reservation about suicide but regards it as a permissible solution to a desperate and apparently impossible situation, if not as a positively desirable and favourable act. When Shakespeare was introduced to Japan, Chikamatsu was long dead, but the mentality he so skilfully depicted and depended upon was still prevalent.

One of the earliest and most important Japanese translations of Shakespeare is that of *Julius Caesar* by Shoyo Tsubouchi (1859–1935), who is by far the most prominent figure in the history of Shakespeare in Japan. He was the first Japanese who eventually translated the complete canon of the playwright, and he published the translation of *Julius Caesar* in 1884 under the title of *Shiizaru Kidan: Jiyu no Tachi Nagori no Kireaji*. In English it would be something like 'The Strange Tale of Caesar, or The Lingering Taste of Sharpness of the Sword of Freedom'. This translation marked the beginning of his long and fruitful association with the Elizabethan playwright. It is both accurate and true to the original so far as it goes, but unlike his later attempts which include a more faithful rendition of *Julius Caesar* itself, it contains numerous descriptive passages which are not in the original at all. In order to understand why the translator added passages of his own, knowledge of the nature of traditional Japanese drama would be indispensable. A script of *Kabuki* and *Bunraku* consists of speeches which are meant to

be spoken by dramatic characters and descriptive passages which are meant to be recited or chanted by a narrator or narrators. The distinction between the two is not always clear, but one can safely say that a text of traditional Japanese theatre reads more like a piece of narrative literature than drama. In any case this is what 'a play' meant to the Japanese audience of the late nineteenth century. Hence Shoyo Tsubouchi's preface to his version of *Julius Caesar* in which he says, 'The original version of the present work is rather like a rough prompt-book and consists only of speeches. Therefore it cannot properly be called a play and it is quite different from full texts we are accustomed to. I have translated it using the style of such full texts for the sake of readers in this country'.[3]

A quotation from the scene of Caesar's death will give us some idea about the sort of metamorphosis which took place:

'If it comes to this' the conspirators say and they exchange glances, and as they planned in advance, Casca cries loudly from behind Caesar, 'But great Caesar'. 'Oh, don't be tedious' says Caesar and he turns back. Casca, trying to give him a deadly blow, grasps a dagger, points it downward and attacks him. Caesar dodges but he is hurt at the shoulder, and red blood begins to flow. 'How dare you' cries the astonished Caesar and twists Casca's arm. The pain makes him cry, 'Help me everybody'. 'Ready' they say, and everyone takes out a dagger which was hidden from sight, and attacks Caesar from all directions, flashing the daggers like wind-blown leaves in the moonlight or lightning in the dark. The desperate Caesar avoids them and kicks and stamps over the attackers as if he were a wounded lion. 'This is terrible' says everyone in the Capitol and is thrown into a great confusion like a great mountain assaulted by an enormous wave. Marcus Brutus who has been watching all this now runs towards Caesar and thrusts his dagger deep into his side. 'Oh Brutus, you too' says Caesar and after uttering these last words he covers his face with a mantle, and with more than twenty wounds all over his body falls under the

---

2 *Four Major Plays*, p. 208.
3 *Shiizaru Kidan* (Tokyo, 1884), p. xi (my translation).

statue of Pompey, conspicuous among many statues, and draws his last breath.[4]

This was Shakespeare for the late nineteenth-century Japanese readers. Of course this translator/adaptor is not always so elaborate and inventive. But the point I think is clear enough. By adding descriptive passages and commenting on what various characters do he can offer his own interpretation of the action and make explicit what is only inherent in the text. To put this differently, what Shoyo Tsubouchi gave his readers was Shakespeare's *Julius Caesar* with chorus played by Shoyo Tsubouchi.

It would be only fair to expect this chorus to say something about the suicides in the play. We are not disappointed, although the comments are rather brief. For example after the death of Titinius there is a line, 'His end is indeed brave.' As for the death of Brutus, the translator has added after the Japanese version of Lucilius' speech 'I thank thee, Brutus, / That thou hast proved Lucilius' saying true' a short passage, 'Friends and foes alike, they all wet their sleeves with tears.' They may well weep, but there is no stage direction to that effect in any English-language edition of Shakespeare. Titinius' end may indeed be brave, but the question here is, 'Who says it is brave?' The only possible answer is 'The translator'. Thus Shoyo Tsubouchi's version is far less ambiguous than Shakespeare's original, and perhaps considerably less profound.

In spite of all the additions this work is essentially a translation since virtually everything Shakespeare wrote is retained. But when his work is more freely adapted using a Japanese setting as well as artistic conventions of the chosen genre, the result can be even less ambiguous and less profound. In 1886, two years after the *Bunraku* script-like *Julius Caesar* appeared, a competent and prolific hack called Robun Kanagaki (1829–94) published an adaptation of *Hamlet* under the title of *Hamuretto Yamato Nishikie* which would mean 'Hamlet à la Japonaise' or more literally 'The Portrait of Hamlet Drawn in Japanese Style'. This was serialized in a newspaper, and although it reads like a script of *Kabuki* or *Bunraku*, it was never actually staged until 1991.

This 1991 production was mounted in Tokyo and was later brought to London. Intriguing as it was, it was in my opinion an artistic failure, simply because it was neither Shakespeare nor *Kabuki*. They used a text which was an adaptation of Robun Kanagaki's adaptation, and among other things they restored some of Hamlet's great soliloquies which the nineteenth-century adaptor ignored completely. Also they presented it as a vehicle for the young *Kabuki* actor Somegoro Ichikawa to show off his acting skill by playing not only Hamlet but Ophelia and Fortinbras as well. It is quite common for a *Kabuki* actor to play more than one role in a single play, but when this happens a quick change between the roles is usually involved. Unfortunately this was not the case with this production of *Hamlet*, and there was no direct confrontation between the prince and Polonius's daughter. I very much wish they had stuck to Robun Kanagaki's version. It is not a great work of art by any means, but it is at least artistically coherent, and perfectly makes sense as a piece of conventional *Kabuki*. More importantly, precisely because it is second-rate, a version like Robun Kanagaki's is likely to represent the cultural climate of its period more accurately, whereas a first-rate work tends to be somewhat exceptional and untypical, being very often a work of genius.

The adaptation in question is set in the middle of the fourteenth century. The action takes place in the northern county of Dewa which might be reminiscent of Denmark. This county has been ruled by feudal lords belonging to the Shiba family. Recently the former lord died mysteriously, and he has been succeeded by his younger brother who is now married to his dead brother's wife. So far the adaptation seems to be faithful enough to the original, but

---

[4] *Shiizaru Kidan*, pp. 135–6.

in reality a lot of funny things happened on the way from Denmark to Dewa.

It is not clear in Shakespeare's *Hamlet* exactly when Gertrude and Claudius became intimate. In the *Kabuki* version, as in John Updike's recent novel, there is absolutely no doubt about this. Gertrude was already sleeping with her brother-in-law when her husband was still alive. Not only that, she participated actively in the murder of her husband, the rightful ruler of the county. When Hamlet puts on the play-within-the-play, he is meticulous and explicit about this side of the event, and not surprisingly it is Gertrude rather than Claudius who is seriously disturbed and leaves the room. Claudius is more composed and can pretend to be more bored than annoyed and only after ordering Polonius to accompany him, does he follow his wife. Claudius in this version is just as great a villain as in Shakespeare's version, but there is a significant and conspicuous departure from the original in the characterization of Gertrude. She is far more villainous than Shakespeare's queen.

The real villain of the piece, however, is Polonius who is not a tedious old fool but a shrewd and cunning politician. For years he has been secretly planning to get rid of the ruling family and become the ruler of the county himself. For this purpose he skilfully tempted Gertrude and Claudius into starting an illicit affair, and eventually they killed the rightful ruler as he had hoped. Clearly both Claudius and Gertrude are manipulated by Polonius. Without Hamlet's intervention he may even have succeeded in getting rid of Claudius as well and achieved his goal. It is extremely relevant that this Hamlet, unlike Shakespeare's Hamlet, is well aware of what he is up to when he kills the old man. He admonishes his mother and tells her the reason why he *had* to kill Polonius, to eliminate the source of an evil to which Gertrude herself had fallen victim.

Thus the character of Polonius can expect absolutely no sympathy from the audience, but he has one weakness. He has spent most of his life as a soldier fighting in a series of battles and has had little time for liberal education. In fact he is semi-illiterate which he thinks (rightly) makes him less than a qualified contender for the position of a ruler of an independent county. This is why he sends his son to Kyoto, then the capital of Japan and the centre of high courtly culture, so that the well-educated son can support him and cooperate with him. The son suspects all this and, being an upright person, hates the father, which makes him deeply miserable. At the same time he realizes that he cannot openly oppose him, because in a feudal patriarchal society a son is supposed to obey a father no matter what the latter intends to do, which makes him even more miserable.

Ophelia suffers from a similar kind of dilemma. On the one hand she is expected to be loyal to her father, and on the other she is expected to be loyal to her lover, whom she knows killed her father. The only solution is the usual and obvious one, that is, suicide. It is true that Ophelia in this version is also mad, but she is not so mad as to be unable to understand what she is doing. She throws herself into a large pond in the castle garden. There is no 'doubtfulness' like that Shakespeare's priest suspects and condemns. Once again the Japanese version settles, by removing, one of Shakespeare's abundant ambiguities.

Hamlet and Ophelia are not the only characters in the play who know what they are doing. Gertrude is another. After Hamlet murders Polonius, Claudius decides to kill Hamlet. Gertrude stops him and suggests to him that they let Laertes kill Hamlet so that the former can revenge his father. What the audience does not learn until the last scene of the play is that Gertrude, after the admonition from her son, realized how guilty she had been and decided to make recompense for her past sins. The result is that although she realizes that Hamlet's death is imminent and unavoidable, she tries desperately to prevent it from happening too soon.

Thus the characterizations in the adaptation

are considerably different, but many of the dramatic devices in the original are retained. The use of the poisoned drink is one of them. Still there is a difference even in this case. Laertes has no inkling of the secret plot, and Claudius prepares the poison on his own. When Claudius believes (wrongly) that Gertrude sides with Laertes he tells her about the fatal drink. Yet again, an ambiguity is removed: unlike Shakespeare's Gertrude, this Gertrude knows everything about the drink before the duel begins.

This setting turns out to be crucial. Soon after Hamlet and Laertes start fighting, Gertrude stops them and drinks the poison. Dramatically this is her great moment, because she can indulge herself in playing a fallen woman finally doing the right thing, the kind of heroine we repeatedly encounter in nineteenth-century melodrama. She confesses that her heart belongs to her son, although nobody, certainly not Claudius, suspected it, and she tells the son to murder Claudius and then kill himself. Hamlet does exactly that. The reason for Hamlet's revenge would not require any explanation, but the reason for his suicide perhaps would. Claudius is a villain and traitor and it is perfectly justifiable to kill such a person, but to Hamlet Claudius is also an uncle. In a society where seniority matters a great deal, killing an uncle is an act which is 'less than kind'. To atone for this breach against a basic social code, Hamlet is expected to kill himself, as Gertrude told him to. In other words Hamlet's revenge has a double meaning. It is an act of justice as well as an unforgivable offence.

Hamlet's death is followed by the suicide of Laertes. The poor young man is in an even more complicated situation. Apparently it is all right for him to try to kill Hamlet who killed his father Polonius, but because Hamlet is his social superior Laertes's attempted revenge could be seen as a challenge, or even denial, of the accepted social hierarchy. What makes the situation even more difficult is that Laertes always knew that Polonius was a villain, and

now Laertes says to Hamlet that he did not really intend to kill the man who killed the villain, even though the villain was his father. If Laertes's confession had been made somewhat earlier, the play might have ended less unhappily, but now it is too late. During the duel, Laertes wounded Hamlet, which under these circumstances is extremely questionable. The only course Laertes can now take is suicide.

There are as many corpses in this scene as in the last scene of *Hamlet*, but the crucial difference from the original is that the deaths of as many as three of them, namely Gertrude, Hamlet and Laertes, were caused by themselves. Neither Laertes nor Hamlet consciously commits suicide in the original version. It is true that what Shakespeare's Gertrude does causes her death, but doubtful whether this can be called a suicide in the true sense of the word.

It is remarkable that none of the three characters (four, if we include Ophelia) has the least scruple about suicide. It is no less remarkable that Hamlet never for a moment stops and thinks about the act of revenge. *Hamlet* is not *The Spanish Tragedy* but the words 'vindicta mihi' simply could not find a place in this adaptation of *Hamlet*. It is only natural that this adaptor got rid of every single one of Hamlet's soliloquies. This version is anything but 'a tragedy of a man who could not make up his mind'. This prince is firmly independent and acts with a strong determination. He is ready to assume all the responsibility for his own deed.

If we read the original *Hamlet* after reading this adaptation, we would realize what an essentially religious play Shakespeare wrote. I do not mean to say it is a blatantly Christian play. But with its references to 'the everlasting' and 'providence', with the sense of man's helplessness, with the consciousness of the inscrutability of the universe, and more specifically Hamlet's revenge and other crucial events taking place almost by accident, the playwright seems to be well aware of an existence beyond human understanding.

This is not the case with the Japanese *Hamlet*.

The prince in this version would not dream of uttering, 'The readiness is all.' Virtually nobody is content to leave everything to fortune. So many people try to conclude their lives with their own will, as if they were eager to present the final interpretation of their existence. Is this uniquely Japanese? Certainly not. If we try to get rid of all the descriptive passages in the adaptation and then translate it *back* into English, then the result may read like one of the Restoration or eighteenth-century adaptations of Shakespeare.

To prove this point I will mention only one example, Dryden's adaptation of *Troilus and Cressida*. In Shakespeare's original neither Troilus nor Cressida dies, but in Dryden's version Cressida does. Not only does she die, she kills herself. It seems that she is more than ready to claim full responsibility for her own deeds. This, I think, is typical of the way Restoration authors appropriated Shakespeare.

Both their adaptations and the Japanese adaptation of *Hamlet*, and to some extent the Japanese adaptation of *Julius Caesar* as well, are trying to *rationalize* Shakespeare by getting rid of ambiguity and inscrutability, so that their audience can understand Shakespeare strictly in human terms. In these adaptations the heroes seldom let things go, as the original Hamlet does after a certain stage. Of course all tragic heroes are not passive, and it is true that Oedipus Rex, the archetypal hero of western tragedy, would not let things go either. But the tragedy of Sophocles would simply fall apart without the deep-rooted sense of human weakness and mysterious nature of the world. Perhaps it is not really important whether or not we can call such a sense 'religious'. What I think *is* important is that Shakespeare has been made 'fit' to modern sensibility by sacrificing such sense. It seems that modern sensibility cannot comfortably accommodate what Sophocles and Shakespeare took for granted. Perhaps it is highly significant that the central characters of both *All My Sons* and *Death of a Salesman*, two of the earlier works of Arthur Miller, kill themselves. Clearly they live in a 'godless' society.

The obscure adaptations of *Julius Caesar* and *Hamlet* which aimed at Japanese readers in the late nineteenth century seem to share a lot with their European counterparts, and are in fact two more eloquent examples of how Shakespearian tragedies without religious overtones are easier to understand, more logical, less unfathomable, and in the end less tragic.

RELIGION IN ARDEN

PETER MILWARD

It is strange how scant is the attention customarily paid to the precise locality of the Forest of Arden in Shakespeare's *As You Like It*. Agnes Latham, in her New Arden edition of the play (1975), expresses the general opinion that it is set in 'the Ardennes on the border of Belgium and Luxemburg', while allowing that Shakespeare and many in his audience 'could identify it easily with those parts of Warwickshire still known as Arden' (p. 8). This identification may be traced back to Edmond Malone, who identified the forest even more precisely as 'that in French Flanders, lying near the Meuse and between Charlemont and Rocroy' (quoted in the New Variorum edition of the play, p. 16). If for the source of these statements we go back to Shakespeare's source, Thomas Lodge's pastoral romance of *Rosalynde*, we find that the main setting is what he calls (like Shakespeare) 'the forest of Arden', but that the forest he has in mind is not so much that to the North-East of France as a vast unidentified forest between 'the province of Bordeaux', from which his hero Rosader (Shakespeare's Orlando) sets forth with his old servant, and the city of Lyons, to which they make their way. This is evidently to the South of the royal capital of Paris, where the usurping king Torismond has his court (Shakespeare's duke Frederick).[1]

When, however, we turn from *Rosalynde* to *As You Like It*, we are given no such clues as in Lodge's romance to the locality of Arden, whether in France or in England. It looks as if the dramatist has deliberately left the matter vague so as to suggest a locality not in France, whether to the South-West or the North-East, but in the English Midlands, where he himself was familiar with another Arden, both as place-name, of the ancient forest in his native Warwickshire to the North of the river Avon and as family-name of his mother and her ancient ancestry. It is indeed a suggestion that has long since been made by the Victorian scholar J. O. Halliwell with reference both to Shakespeare's play and to his friend Michael Drayton's *Poly-Olbion* XIII: 'The forest of Arden was no forest in far-away France, but was the enchanted ground of their own home' (quoted in the New Variorum edition, p. 18).

Now on the basis of these generally accepted considerations about the Forest of Arden as the setting of *As You Like It*, let me go on to explore that setting with reference not only to the meaning of the play but also to the personal involvement of the dramatist implied in his choice of setting. True, it is aptly said of Shakespeare's comedies that they are rarely set in his native England but look for the most part beyond the Narrow Seas to the sunny lands of the South. And so in *As You Like It* we may be excused for assuming that Shakespeare looks with Lodge beyond the seas to the Ardennes, whether of Belgium or Bordeaux. Yet, in virtue of the greater ambiguity the former puts into his play, he may well have felt free to indulge a

---

[1] Cf. D. Beecher's edition of Lodge's *Rosalind* (Barnaby Riche Society Publications 7, Ottawa, 1997), p. 141.

desire of injecting into it something of his own childhood background. True, again, we are well advised to avoid an autobiographical interpretation of any play of Shakespeare's, considering how enigmatic he is both as dramatist and as poet. Yet in this play we seem to be faced with something of an exception; and in the religion of Arden we may discern something of Shakespeare's own allegiance among the three religions recognised in his own time (by the Jesuit Robert Persons writing in 1592) as papist, protestant and puritan.[2]

As for the religion of Shakespeare's family at Stratford, let it suffice to say that a scholarly consensus has been building up over the past century in favour of their Catholicism, or loyalty to 'the old faith'. From the time of Elizabeth's accession to the throne in 1558 and the establishment of 'the new religion' by Act of Parliament the following year, they no doubt temporized in common with many who came to be known as 'church papists'; but the evidence we have seems to indicate a steady movement towards 'recusancy' culminating in the entry of John Shakespeare's name in the recusancy returns for 1592, however much he sought to conceal his religious reason by pleading 'fear of process for debt'.[3] More to the point of this article, however, is his origin in Arden, before settling with his wife Mary Arden in Stratford. Already in the village of Snitterfield to the North of Stratford, his father had been a tenant of Mary Arden's father Robert; and his forbears had evidently come from other villages further to the North, and well within the area of the Forest of Arden, Rowington and Wroxhall. In the latter village in pre-Reformation times there had been a nunnery, Wroxhall Abbey, now a ruin, which the poet may have had in mind in Sonnet 73, lamenting the 'bare ruined choirs, where late the sweet birds sang'. From this nunnery the names of two Shakespeares have come down to us, including that of the prioress earlier in the century, whose name Isabella may have suggested Shakespeare's

choice of name for the novice heroine of *Measure for Measure*.

This association with both Arden and 'the old faith' is no less evident in Shakespeare's mother Mary Arden, though her Catholic allegiance appears not so much in herself as in her father Robert's pious will, drawn up in Mary's reign in 1556, bequeathing his soul 'to Almighty God and to Our Blessed Lady'. Through her Shakespeare was connected at once with the old Saxon nobility of Warwickshire and with most of the Catholic gentry of the neighbourhood, the Catesbys, the Throckmortons, the Winters and the Grants, many of whose younger sons came to be involved in the Gunpowder Plot of 1605.[4] On the other hand, to the East of Arden were the great houses of the upstart family of Dudley: Kenilworth Castle, held by Elizabeth's favourite Robert, Earl of Leicester, and Warwick Castle, held by his elder brother Ambrose, Earl of Warwick. They were in turn assisted by the Puritan magistrate Sir Thomas Lucy, of Charlecote Park, not least in their envy of the older nobility of the Ardens. This envy found a practical outlet in the prosecution of the Somerville Plot of 1583, when the head of the family, Edward Arden of Park Hall near Birmingham, was implicated owing to his relationship with John Somerville (who had married his daughter Mary). Here already we may note a

---

[2] R. Persons, *Elizabethae Angliae Reginae Haeresim Calvinianam Propugnantis saevissimum in Catholicos sui Regni edictum . . . Cum responsione* (1592), had five editions in Latin, with translations into German and French, but none into English.

[3] The Catholic theory of Shakespeare's antecedents has been defended by H. S. Bowden, *The Religion of Shakespeare* (1899), based on notes left by the Victorian scholar R. Simpson; by J. H. De Groot, *The Shakespeares and 'The Old Faith'* (1946), though himself a Presbyterian; by H. Mutschmann and K. Wentersdorf, *Shakespeare and Catholicism* (1952), particularly valuable for its careful investigation into the poet's family and friends; and my own *Shakespeare's Religious Background* (1973), with more emphasis on the evidence of the plays.

[4] Cf. Genealogical table given by Mutschmann and Wentersdorf, *Shakespeare and Catholicism*, p. 422.

significant parallel between the tragic situation of the English Ardens and that of the exiled duke Senior in *As You Like It*.

Now let us turn to another village on the outskirts of the forest to the west of Stratford, Temple Grafton. As its name indicates, it was a commandery of the Knights Templars till their suppression in the fourteenth century under the rule of Philip the Fair of France, as it were foreshadowing the rule of Henry VIII of England. Then it passed into the hands of the Knights Hospitallers of St John till they were in turn suppressed by the latter monarch in 1536. It is mentioned in Shakespeare's application for a marriage licence from the diocesan authorities at Worcester during the season of Advent 1582, where his fiancée's name is given (in one of the two entries) as 'Anne Whateley of Temple Grafton'. Shakespeare's wife, we know, came not from Temple Grafton but from the nearby Shottery; but this association of her name with that village may be an indication of the church at which their wedding was to be held. And it so happens that the parson of that church was an old Catholic priest from Marian times, whose name is known to us as John Frith, from a Puritan survey of Warwickshire included in *A Parte of a Register* (1593).[5]

From this old Marian priest, with his 'unsound religion' (as he is described from the Puritan viewpoint of the survey), in the real Forest of Arden, we may turn to the old religious man (or are they two men?) who makes two interesting appearances in Shakespeare's play. First, there is the old religious uncle of Rosalind who has taught her a remedy of love, which (she claims) has worked so effectively on one patient as to make him 'forswear the full stream of the world' and 'live in a nook merely monastic' (3.2.404–5). This remedy Rosalind tries out on Orlando to such contrasting effect as to bring them both to a happy marriage. This uncle is subsequently described by Orlando as 'a great magician' who is still resident 'in the circle of this forest' (5.4.33–4) – as is Temple Grafton in relation to

the Forest of Arden. He may also be the 'old religious man' mentioned at the end of the play by Orlando's brother Jaques de Boys, as having met the usurping duke on his arrival with an army in the forest and as having converted him both from his enterprise against his exiled brother and even from the world.[6]

Then, we may ask, what about the other priest who turns up in Shakespeare's play to perform the wedding of Touchstone and Audrey? Doesn't Sir Oliver Martext, as has been suggested by certain biographers, correspond more closely to Sir John Frith, as 'vicar of the next village', than the above-mentioned religious man? And isn't he requested by Touchstone to officiate at his wedding with Audrey in much the same terms as, we may imagine, John Frith might have been requested by the young Shakespeare to officiate at his wedding with Anne? Well, unlike John Frith, Sir Oliver is repudiated by Touchstone and mocked in much the same way as the curate Sir Nathaniel in *Love's Labour's Lost* is mocked by the playful lords (5.2).[7] He is further contrasted by the melancholy Jaques with 'a good priest that can tell you what marriage is' (3.3.77–8), which may have been the reason why Shakespeare, if a Catholic, would have preferred the old Marian priest at Temple Grafton to perform his wedding with Anne rather than the Protestant vicar of the Holy Trinity church at Stratford.

Another reason, relating Sir Oliver rather to

---

5 The evidence for the wedding of William Shakespeare and Anne Hathaway at Temple Grafton is given at length by Park Honan, *Shakespeare: A Life* (London, 1998), pp. 81–5.

6 This strangely sudden conversion of the usurping duke is unique to Shakespeare, in contrast to Lodge's usurping king Torismond who is killed in battle.

7 The three parsons, Sir Oliver Martext in *As You Like It*, Sir Nathaniel in *Love's Labour's Lost*, and Sir Hugh Evans in *The Merry Wives of Windsor*, stand in interesting contrast to the three friars, Friar Laurence in *Romeo and Juliet*, Friar Francis in *Much Ado About Nothing* and Friar Lodowick in *Measure for Measure*, in that the former are mocked, the latter respected by those around them.

the puritans than to the papists, may be found in his surname of 'Martext'. Here is an obvious puritan connotation with the author of the Marprelate pamphlets of 1588–9, who is probably to be identified with another Warwickshireman and native of Arden, Job Throckmorton.[8] Just as Shakespeare himself was jeered at as 'Shakescene' (by Robert Greene in his *Groatsworth of Wit*) on his arrival in London, so we find Martin Marprelate derided by his episcopal adversary Thomas Cooper in the latter's *Admonition to the People of England* (1589) as 'not only Mar-prelate, but Mar-prince, Mar-state, Mar-law, Mar-magistrate and all together'. A similar Puritan character is glanced at in *The Merchant of Venice* both by Bassanio, as he reflects at a critical turning-point in the play on how 'In religion, / What damned error, but some sober brow / Will bless it and approved it with a text' (3.2.77–9), and by Graziano, who speaks of 'a sort of men whose visages / Do cream and mantle like a standing pond, / And do a wilful stillness entertain' (1.1.88–90). Such a wilful stillness is shown by Sir Oliver when, in response to the frivolity of Touchstone, he can only mutter, ''Tis no matter. Ne'er a fantastical knave of them all shall flout me out of my calling.' (3.3.96–8).

In addition to this contrast between the 'old religious man' in the forest and 'the vicar of the next village', there remains one more religious man to be considered, though he is rarely recognized as such. I refer to the man who goes under the name of Duke Senior (in the stage directions). He is the former duke – not king, as in Lodge's *Rosalynde* – unjustly banished from the court by his usurping younger brother Frederick, while he himself remains without a name.[9] He is seen as being, or having been, a secular ruler; but from his first appearance in the Forest of Arden he is introduced as a kind of 'convertite', as his usurping brother suddenly becomes at the end of the play. His impressive opening speech on 'the uses of adversity' and 'the good in everything' oddly echoes passages in the popular *Imitation of Christ* by Thomas à

Kempis (one of the best selling books of Shakespeare's time among Catholics and Protestants alike): one from 1.12 on this very theme: 'It is good for us to encounter troubles and adversities from time to time, for trouble often compels a man to search his own heart. It reminds him that he is an exile here, and he can put his trust in nothing in this world'; and the other from 2.4 on the wings of simplicity and purity: 'If your heart be right, then every created thing will become a mirror of life and a book of holy teaching. For there is nothing created so small and mean but reflects the goodness of God.' The same passages may also be heard echoed by Friar Laurence in his opening speech in Act 2 of *Romeo and Juliet*. Both their speeches are as it were sermons, the one by a duke and the other by a friar; and both look forward to other sermons preached by the duke-turned-friar, Duke Vincentio alias Friar Lodowick, in *Measure for Measure*.

I have already suggested a comparison between this exiled duke, suffering at the hands of his usurping brother, and the rightful ruler of the real Arden, Edward Arden of Park Hall, suffering at the hands of the upstart Earl of Leicester. Now I would like to suggest a further comparison between him in his religious character and another, spiritual ruler living in exile in the region of the other Ardennes beyond the sea. I refer to William Allen, ruler or president of the English College (or seminary) located from the time of its foundation in 1568 at Douai in the French Ardennes, but from 1578 onwards at Rheims (of which, it may be noted, explicit mention is made in *The Taming of the Shrew* 2.1, where Lucentio masquerades as a 'young scholar that has been long studying at Rheims'). For example, in the opening scene of *As You*

---

8 The identification of Martin Marprelate as Job Throckmorton has been authoritatively made by Leland H. Carlson in his writings on the Puritan authors of the sixteenth century.

9 In much the same way Edgar, in *The Tragedy of King Lear* 2.3, loses his identity on resorting to disguise: 'Edgar I nothing am.'

Like It, where the elder duke is first mentioned by Charles the wrestler as having been banished to the Forest of Arden and joined there by 'three or four loving lords', it is added that 'many young gentlemen flock to him every day'. Similarly, Allen was joined in his venture not only by several former colleagues from Oxford University, who formed the teaching body of his college, but also by a steadily growing number of young men, many of them from the gentry who could afford the expense, for their Catholic and priestly education. Such was a classmate of Shakespeare's, Robert Debdale, who left Stratford for Douai in 1575 in company with his and Shakespeare's master Simon Hunt, the latter going on to Rome where he entered the Society of Jesus. Such, too, was a distant cousin of Shakespeare's (on his mother's side), Edward Throckmorton, who also went on, like Hunt, to Rome and entered the Society of Jesus. All of them were from the Forest of Arden.[10]

Further, when Rosalind is in her turn banished from the court by her uncle, her protests are coldly answered: 'Thus do all traitors. / If their purgation did consist in words / They are as innocent as grace itself.' (1.3.51–3) His words interestingly echo those of the arch-persecutor of English Catholics, Lord Burghley, who in his pamphlet *The Execution of Justice in England* (1583) – itself written in response to Allen's *Apologie* for the two English colleges at Rheims and Rome (1581) – declares: 'It hath been in all ages and in all countries a common usage of all offenders for the most part, great and small, to make defence of their lewd and unlawful facts by untruths and by colouring and covering their deeds (were they never so vile) with pretences of some other causes of contrary operations or effects.' To this Allen responded with his famous *Defence of English Catholics* in 1584, maintaining that his students, so far from being the scum of the land, were most of them sons of Catholic gentlemen having chosen the path of exile for the sake of religion.

As for Allen himself, before founding his college at Douai, he had gone into exile with other Catholic scholars on the accession of Elizabeth and settled in the university city of Louvain, partly for the purpose of controversy with the Protestants. On account of ill health, however, he was recommended by his doctors to return home for a time to have the benefit of his native air. There, while recuperating in Lancashire and his home at Rossall, he did much to confirm the Catholic gentry and people in that region in their resolution to refuse all cooperation with the new state church. At that time, the gentleman who gave him most whole-hearted and financial support was the great landowner of the area, Thomas Hoghton, who was then engaged in the building of a stately mansion named Hoghton Tower (still to be seen there today). When he had to leave Lancashire, Allen spent some of his time at Oxford, where he had been principal of St Mary's Hall (subsequently absorbed into Oriel College), and also in the neighbourhood of Stratford, before moving into Norfolk and so back to Douai for the founding of his college.[11] It was in the following year, on the failure of the rising of the Northern earls in 1569, that Thomas Hoghton decided to go likewise into exile and to assist Allen in his new foundation.[12]

Hoghton's large estates in Lancashire were now entrusted partly to his younger brother Alexander, who resided at Lea Hall on the farther side of Preston, partly to his more reliable half-brother Richard, of Park Hall at Charnock Richard to the South. Meanwhile, two neighbours of theirs from the village of

---

[10] For Edward Throckmorton, who grew up at Coughton Court in the Forest of Arden and died as a Jesuit in Rome in 1582, see C. Devlin, *The Life of Robert Southwell* (London, 1958).

[11] There is an excellent article on William Allen in the *Dictionary of National Biography*, vol. 1 pp. 314–21.

[12] On Thomas Hoghton, who went into exile in 1569 and died in 1580, see B. Camm, *Forgotten Shrines* (London, 1910), pp. 183–6, with his poem, 'The Blessed Conscience', on pp. 185–6.

Dilworth, Thomas and John Cottam, were studying at Oxford University. Thomas went on to Douai and Rome to study for the priesthood; while John was later appointed schoolmaster at Stratford in 1579. (Thomas returned to England as a seminary priest in 1580 about the same time as the Jesuit Edmund Campion, but he was arrested soon after his arrival in London. He was arraigned with Campion and entered the Society of Jesus in prison while awaiting his execution in 1582.) It may have been on John Cottam's recommendation that the young William Shakespeare left Stratford to become, according to an old tradition emanating from his future colleague Christopher Beeston, 'a schoolmaster in the country', now identified as the county of Lancashire near Preston, in the household of Alexander Hoghton of Lea Hall. Here at least, according to a theory that has been gaining ground among Shakespeare scholars since the time it was broached by Oliver Baker in his book *In Shakespeare's Warwickshire* (1937) and seconded by Sir Edmund Chambers in his *Shakespearean Gleanings* (1944), we find a 'William Shakeshafte' mentioned in Hoghton's will, which was drawn up in August 1581 only to be followed by the death of the testator shortly afterwards, significantly in the immediate aftermath of the news of Campion's arrest towards the end of July and his torture in the Tower of London.[13]

Before that series of tragic events took place, there is good reason to suppose a meeting between the young Shakespeare and the Jesuit. Campion had not only come from Rome, where he must have met Simon Hunt, another English Jesuit resident there, but also entered England about the same time, the summer of 1580, as John Cottam's brother. He had, moreover, journeyed into the Midlands, staying (as we know from notes of his 'confessions' taken by Lord Burghley) with Sir William Catesby presumably at Lapworth, where Shakespeare with his father may well have gone to meet him. Then, after staying at several Catholic houses in Yorkshire during the winter of 1580–1, he had gone on to stay at other Catholic houses in Lancashire, including (as we also know from the above-mentioned notes) that of Richard Hoghton at Park Hall – and that at the very time William Shakespeare was probably in the household of Alexander Hoghton. It is indeed fascinating to speculate on what may have passed between the Jesuit, himself an expert in dramatic production from his five years at the College of Prague, and the future dramatist. May not Shakespeare have received his first lessons in dramaturgy from Campion, not to mention the Spiritual Exercises of St Ignatius, which it was a principal aim of Jesuits like Campion to introduce to promising young men like Shakespeare?[14]

Everything, however, must have changed for the young Shakespeare with the arrest of Campion in July and the news of his prolonged torture in the Tower (for the sake of eliciting from him the names of those at whose houses he had stayed on his journey),[15] and then the death of his patron Alexander Hoghton so soon after making his will. Campion was executed as a traitor in the December of 1581, and he was followed by Thomas Cottam to Tyburn some six months later. The situation must have made

---

[13] Other eminent proponents of this theory have been L. Hotson, *Shakespeare's Sonnets Dated* (1949), A. Keen and R. Lubbock, *The Annotator* (1954), R. Stevenson, *Shakespeare's Religious Frontier* (1958), and more recently E. A. J. Honigmann, *Shakespeare: The 'Lost Years'* (1985), where he successfully vindicates the theory against the criticism of S. Schoenbaum, *William Shakespeare: A Documentary Life* (1977).

[14] I have presented my own research into Shakespeare's Stratford schoolmasters, culminating in his probable meeting with Campion in Lancashire, in an article for *The Month* April, 2000 (261, 1588), entitled 'Shakespeare in Lancashire'.

[15] Cf. Burghley papers, Lansdowne MS 30 British Library, including the record of Campion's confessions under torture in the Tower: he stayed at the house of Sir William Catesby in the summer of 1580; he was in Lancashire between Easter and Whitsuntide 1581, staying (among others) with Bartholomew Hesketh and Richard Hoghton.

it dangerous for Shakespeare to remain in Lancashire; and so we find him returning to Stratford, wooing Anne Hathaway and maybe celebrating a quiet wedding at Temple Grafton, leaving their application for a wedding licence at Worcester till it became plain that Anne was with child. Then followed the births of Susanna in May 1583 and the twins Hamnet and Judith, named after their Catholic godparents Hamnet and Judith Sadler, in January 1585. Then arose the pressing problems of how to support this growing family, with the hopeful solution of a continued career, not so much as a schoolmaster with intervals of dramatic production but rather as a player and playwright in a more professional capacity. In his will of 1581 Alexander Hoghton had commended William Shakeshafte to the care of a recusant neighbour Sir Thomas Hesketh, who kept players for his entertainment; and Hesketh was well known to the Earl of Derby, whose son Lord Strange kept a larger and more professional group of players. So when Hesketh died in 1588, Shakespeare might well have been taken on by Strange's Men, in whose company he appears in London with the first recorded performance of *Titus Andronicus* in early 1594. In this play, I might add, there is a unique mention (among all Shakespeare's plays) of the epithet 'popish' in connection with 'conscience', as if echoing a poem written by Thomas Hoghton before his death in 1580 on the repeated theme of keeping his conscience. Thus, instead of proceeding (as Campion may have hoped) from Lancashire to Douai and the continental Ardennes, the young Shakespeare had to return to his native Arden and so evidently to London, with all the tests imposed by his new career on his loyalty to 'the old faith' and his resolve to 'keep his conscience'.

This loyalty and resolve of the dramatist we may find implied throughout the play of *As You Like It* – at least once we are aware of all this personal background that has gone into the making of it. We may think, for example, not only of the above-mentioned characters of the old religious man (or men) and the elder duke, but also of the feeling of nostalgia for the good old days that pervades the play.[16] It is what appears from the outset in the memory of 'the old Robin Hood of England' with his 'many merry men', as if connecting the Forest of Arden with that of Sherwood. It is what appears in Orlando's praise of the 'good old man' Adam – whose part is said by William Oldys to have been played by the dramatist himself – for his fidelity to 'the constant service of the antique world', in contrast to 'the fashion of these times' (2.3 58 and 60). It is what appears in the same Orlando's appeal to 'better days' when 'bells have knolled to church' (2.7.113–14), in contrast to the present days viewed by Shakespeare himself in Sonnet 67 as 'these last so bad'. Surely, we may well conclude, from the depths of his heart Shakespeare looks fondly back to the time before the far-reaching religious changes had been inaugurated by Henry VIII and ratified by his daughter Elizabeth, a time that had been realized in the old Forest of Arden near Stratford and was still present in the Ardennes overseas.

---

[16] I give a fuller treatment of Shakespeare's 'nostalgia' in *Shakespeare's Religious Background*, pp. 180–1.

A WEDDING AND FOUR FUNERALS: CONJUNCTION AND COMMEMORATION IN *HAMLET*

RICHARD C. McCOY

There are a lot of funerals in *Hamlet*: four, if you count the first for Hamlet's father, marred by that one hasty wedding, the 'hugger-mugger' (4.5.82) burial of Polonius, Ophelia's abbreviated obsequies, and finally the somewhat incongruous soldier's funeral for Hamlet himself. The first three leave the chief mourners bitterly disappointed, and both are almost as distressed by the funeral arrangements as they are by the deaths of their loved ones. Laertes is furious at the ignominious obscurity of his father's interment, and he is enraged at the priest for denying his sister 'sage requiem' (5.1.232). Hamlet is nearly mad with melancholy at the shocking brevity of his mother's mourning. From beginning to end, this is a play obsessed with getting a decent burial, and nobody seems to get one.[1] What constitutes a decent burial in Shakespeare's time? The answer is not clear because the Elizabethan religious settlement was so ambiguous on this point. A growing belief in predestination, the subordination of human works to faith alone, and the abolition of purgatory and indulgences made traditional Catholic funeral practices such as the requiem, the annual obit, and other intercessory rites and prayers unnecessary. Elizabeth's bishops, meeting in convocation in 1563, re-affirmed the Protestant position and denounced 'sacrifices of Masses . . . for the quick and the dead' as 'blasphemous fables, and dangerous deceits', and the requiem continued to be left out of the vernacular funeral service in *The Book of Common Prayer*.[2] Nevertheless, as Eamon

Duffy points out, 'Funeral practice was, inevitably, one of the areas where feeling remained most conservative' because mourners still wanted to retain contact and do something for their dead loved ones.[3] In an apparent concession to such feelings, Elizabeth authorized publication of a Latin prayer book in 1560, the *Liber Precum Publicarum* which included a requiem communion service or '*Celebratio coenae Domini, in funebribus, si amici & vicini defuncti communicare velint*' [i.e., the celebration of the Lord's Supper at funerals, if the friends and neighbours of the dead wish to communicate].[4]

This liturgical double-bookkeeping was a classic Elizabethan compromise, one whose inconsistencies and mixed signals were anticipated

---

[1] Cf. Michael Neill who says that 'No play is more obsessively concerned with funeral proprieties than Hamlet' in *Issues of Death: Mortality and Identity in English Renaissance Tragedy* (Oxford, 1997), p. 300. See also David Bevington, ' "Maimed Rites": Violated Ceremony in Hamlet', in *Critical Essays on Shakespeare's Hamlet*, ed. David Scott Kastan (New York, 1995), pp. 126–38.

[2] Article 31 in Edgar C. S. Gibson, *The Thirty-Nine Articles of the Church of England* (London, 1906), 2.687.

[3] Eamon Duffy, *The Stripping of the Altars: Traditional Religion in England, c.1400–c.1580* (New Haven, 1992), p. 578.

[4] *Liturgies and Occasional Forms of Prayer Set Forth in the Reign of Queen Elizabeth*, ed. William Keatinge Clay (Cambridge, 1847), pp. 433–4. See also G. J. Cuming, *A History of Anglican Liturgy* (London, 1969), pp. 124–5 and 368–9.

and encouraged from the beginning of her reign. An anonymous memorandum called the 'Device for the Alteration of Religion' began circulating shortly after Elizabeth's accession, advising a cautious and equivocal approach to religious reform for the sake of stability. More ardent reformers 'shall be discontented, and call the alteration *a cloaked papistry* or *a mingle-mangle*,' but 'better it were that they did suffer than Her Highness or commonwealth should shake, or be in danger'.[5] As predicted, Puritan opponents criticized her religious policies in precisely these terms. The Latin prayer book was justified by its use in collegiate chapels, but Cambridge students gagged at having '*the Pope's Dreggs*' forced on them, and the requiem service and prayers for benefactors were eventually dropped from a revised version of the *Liber Precum* in 1571.[6] Intercessory rituals gradually faded, and sermons, eulogies and monuments acquired increasing importance, but even these were denounced by more ardent reformers as worldly vanities, and many found *The Book of Common Prayer*'s promise of a 'sure and certain hope of resurrection to eternal life' too presumptuous.[7] In his studies of Reformation funeral practice, Ralph Houlbrooke traces a gradual shift from intercession to commemoration, but he contends that Protestants remained divided and uncertain about both functions: 'English reformers, after pulling down the structure of inherited observances, failed (partly because of their own divisions) to create a generally accepted way of death thoroughly imbued with their own spirit'.[8] As a result, Elizabeth's religious settlement was haunted by another spirit which was, in the words of Diarmaid MacCulloch, the 'ghost . . . of an older world of Catholic authority and devotional practice.'[9]

Hamlet can easily be seen as a text-book demonstration of the theological irresolution and liturgical failure of the Elizabethan compromise. It too is haunted by its own ghost from an older religious world, one claiming to return from a suppressed Catholic purgatory where his

'foul crimes . . . / Are burnt and purged away' (1.5.13–14).[10] Later in the play, the consolation of a requiem is briefly invoked and then withdrawn, leaving mourners with a sense of 'maimèd rites' (5.1.214).[11] Intercession for the

---

5 BL Cotton Julius F. VI, f. 161. This document is reprinted and discussed in Henry Gee, *The Elizabethan Prayer-Book and Ornaments* (London, 1902).

6 Cuming, *Anglican Liturgy* 124; Francis Procter and Walter Howard Frere, *A New History of the Book of Common Prayer* (London, 1958), p. 124; and William P. Haugaard, *Elizabeth and the English Reformation: The Struggle for a Stable Settlement of Religion* (Cambridge, 1968), p. 116.

7 David E. Stannard, *The Puritan Way of Death: A Study of Religion, Culture and Social Change* (New York, 1977), pp. 73–4 and 100–2; Patrick Collinson, *The Elizabethan Puritan Movement* (Berkeley, 1967), p. 370; and Duffy, *Stripping of the Altars*, p. 590.

8 Ralph Houlbrooke, *Death, Ritual and Bereavement* (London, 1989), pp. 40–2. In *Death, Religion, and the Family in England 1480–1750* (Oxford, 1998), Houlbrooke still speaks of a 'gap left by the abolition of Catholic intercessory rites' but concedes that 'private rites of commemoration' involving 'personal mementoes' help fill the void (374).

9 Diarmaid MacCulloch, *The Later Reformation in England 1547–1603* (New York, 1990), p. 6.

10 The play's ambiguous views of spirits and the afterlife has been the subject of much critical controversy, focusing primarily on the provenance and credibility of the ghost; is it actually the Hamlet's father's spirit or a demon from hell? See, among others, Roy W. Battenhouse, *Shakespearean Tragedy: Its Art and Its Christian Premises* (Bloomington, 1969) pp. 237–40; Sister Miriam Joseph, 'Discerning the Ghost in Hamlet', *PMLA*, 76 (1961), 493–502; Eleanor Prosser, *Hamlet and Revenge* (Stanford, 1971) pp. 136–7; Robert H. West, *The Invisible World: A Study of Pneumatology in Elizabethan Drama* (Athens, GA., 1939), pp. 162–200 and *Shakespeare and the Outer Mystery* (Lexington University of Kentucky Press, 1968), pp. 56–68; Arthur McGee, *The Elizabethan Hamlet* (New Haven, 1987), p. 112; and J. Dover Wilson, *What Happens in Hamlet* (Cambridge, 1967), pp. 62 and 184–5. Paul N. Siegel provides an excellent review of these arguments in ' "Hamlet, Revenge!": The Uses and Abuses of Historical Criticism', *Shakespeare Survey 45* (1993), pp. 15–26.

11 Dover Wilson discusses the play's requiem (298–9) as does Roland Mushat Frye, *Renaissance Hamlet: Issues and Responsibilities in 1600* (Princeton, 1984), p. 306. See also my 'Love's Martyrs: Shakespeare's "Phoenix and

dead subsequently degenerates into revenge and the ritual slaughter of the last act, aptly described as a 'black mass'.[12] Commemoration may be a more feasible alternative and 'Remember me' (1.5.91) a clearer imperative, but the strength of memory is doubtful throughout. Hamlet sarcastically entertains only a bleak hope that 'a great man's memory may outlive his life half a year. But, by'r Lady, a must build churches then, or else shall a suffer not thinking on, with the hobby-horse, whose epitaph is "For O, for O, the hobby-horse is forgot"' (3.2.125–9). Can 'a great man's' – or great woman's – memory survive without a church and its traditional intercessory practices? Hamlet suspects not, and in some ways, his own, the play's fourth and final funeral seems to confirm his suspicions. 'The rites of war' (5.2.353) ordered by Fortinbras seem at least vaguely menacing, even if his arrival is not staged as an invasion.[13] In some ways, the man ordering this rite seems more intent on asserting his own 'rights of memory in this kingdom' (5.2.343) than honouring Hamlet's. Yet, I want to argue that, regardless of his rival's intentions, Hamlet's own 'rights of memory' are powerfully vindicated by the last act. I also want to suggest, by invoking one of Shakespeare's typical puns, that Reformation rites and 'rights of memory' were more resilient and effective than many assume. My case will be partly historical, dealing with medieval and early modern funeral practices and it will include a post-mortem about where the bodies are buried. At the same time, I want to consider broader philosophical and literary questions, venturing larger claims about our ability to 'speak with the dead' – and their ability to speak to us.[14]

Building churches had been the preferred way to preserve a great man's memory for a long time, and the first Tudor, Henry VII, built one of the grandest of all. King Henry VII's Chapel stands as a magnificent dynastic monument, but it was actually built to enshrine another, less powerful king. Henry VII had originally intended to bury Henry VI in the

tomb where his own remains now rest, giving his predecessor pride of place.[15] Henry VI is recalled today, if at all, as the hapless victim of Richard III's villainy in Shakespeare's early history plays, but he was revered as a saintly martyr and prophet in his own time and quickly became the object of a popular cult. His tomb at Windsor began attracting more pilgrims than Thomas Becket's at Canterbury, and many reported miraculous cures.[16] Henry VII was eager to be associated with this holy king, and he began a campaign to have his namesake canonized and his remains 'translated' to the place of honour in his new chapel.

Henry's model for his chapel was England's most venerable royal sepulchre, the shrine of

---

Turtle" and the Sacrificial Sonnets' in *Religion and Culture in Renaissance England*, eds. Claire McEachern and Debora Shuger (Cambridge, 1997), pp. 188–208.

[12] Battenhouse, *Shakespearean Tragedy*, p. 250 and Robert N. Watson, *The Rest Is Silence: Death as Annihilation in the English Renaissance* (Berkeley, 1994), pp. 88–9.

[13] Fortinbras launches a surprise attack on Elsinore and topples the statue of old Hamlet in *Hamlet*, Dir. Kenneth Branagh (Castle Rock Entertainment, 1996), and his acquisition of the Denmark corporation is announced as a hostile corporate takeover in *Hamlet*, Dir. Michael Almereyda (Miramax Films, 2000). In Ingmar Bergman's production, Fortinbras executed Horatio at the end of the play; *Hamlet*, Dir. Ingmar Bergman (Brooklyn Academy of Music, 1988).

[14] Stephen Greenblatt, *Shakespearean Negotiations: The Circulation of Social Energy in Renaissance England* (Chicago, 1988), p. 1.

[15] See Jocelyn Perkins, *Westminster Abbey: Its Worship and Ornaments* (London, 1938), p. 2 for a comparison of the ground plans 'as completed by Henry VIII' and 'as intended by the founder'. According to Perkins, Henry VI was supposed to be placed in the chapel directly behind the altar with Henry VII's tomb placed in the choir, but Henry VIII buried his parents behind the altar instead.

[16] See Sydney Anglo, 'Henry VI: The Lancastrian Saint', *Images of Tudor Kingship* (London, 1992), pp. 61–73 and Brian Spencer, 'King Henry of Windsor and the London Pilgrim' in *Collectanea Londiniensia*, eds. J. Bird, H. Chapman, and J. Clark (London, 1978), pp. 235–64. Richard III moved the body from Chertsey Abbey to Windsor in 1484, placing it in a tomb across from that of his brother, Edward IV.

Edward the Confessor at the centre of the Abbey. King Edward had rebuilt Westminster in the eleventh century and was buried before its high altar. Following his canonization in the twelfth century, his body was moved or 'translated' to its own chapel by Henry II and Thomas Becket, and, a century later, Henry III erected a magnificent shrine above the tomb. Pilgrims flocked to it, hoping to be cured of their afflictions by Edward's posthumous royal touch, and those seeking even greater proximity to the saint crawled into the niches or 'squeezing spaces' in the tomb's foundation where they often spent the night.[17] Many later English monarchs sought their final resting place amidst its royal fellowship of death, and over the centuries, Edward's chapel, ringed with the tombs of five kings and three queens, became a sanctuary for a 'cult of English sacramental kingship'.[18] Within its precincts, the royal presence became a sacred presence whose healing powers survived death itself. In the older, medieval paradigm of sacred kingship, this thaumaturgic royal presence coexisted with and was enhanced by Christ's real presence in the sacrament of the altar. The Eucharist was revered by monarchs from Edward to Henry VII, and its daily sacrifice in the Mass was the main event in Westminster Abbey.[19] Royal patrons generously endowed its monastery in order to ensure a perpetual offering of commemorative Masses for the repose of their souls.

By the time Elizabeth came to the throne, the Reformation had destroyed this harmonious relationship of monarch, monk and Mass. When the Abbot and monks of Westminster greeted her first passage to parliament with tapers, incense, and holy water, the new queen dismissed them, saying 'Away with those torches, we see very well.' Inside the Abbey church, she gave precedence to her own chapel choristers who sang the litany in English, and a Marian exile delivered a sermon urging the abolition of monasteries.[20] Many Catholics found Elizabeth's attitude towards the Mass and the Eucharist even more shocking. For her

predecessor, Mary Tudor, 'the celebration of the mass' had been 'the centre of her spiritual life', and she died right after making the responses to the elevation of the host.[21] By contrast, as a good Protestant, Elizabeth regarded the elevation of the host as a form of Catholic idolatry, and she ordered the bishop who would preside at her coronation not to raise it.[22] Yet here as elsewhere, the Queen sent

---

17 Perkins, *Westminster Abbey*, 2.47 and Frank Barlow, *Edward the Confessor* (Berkeley, 1970), pp. 277–84.

18 Frank Barlow, 'The King's Evil', *English Historical Review*, 95 (1980), 25. See also J. G. O'Neilly and I. E. Tanner, 'The Shrine of Edward the Confessor', *Archaeologia*, 100 (1966), 129–54.

19 In one of the lives of Edward the Confessor, he is shown witnessing a Eucharistic miracle in which the Christ-child appears in the host; see Paul Binski, *Westminster Abbey and the Plantagenets: Kingship and the Representation of Power: 1200–1400* (New Haven, 1995), p. 146. The coronation ordo has Henry VII 'groveling afore the high aulter' and receiving the sacrament 'wt a great devocion'; see Leopold G. Wickham Legg, *English Coronation Records* (Westminster, 1901), pp. 220–39. Henry VIII also revered the Eucharist, defending it from Protestant attack in his *Assertio Septem Septorum* and making the denial of transubstantiation a capital crime, but the Reformation he launched eroded this devotion.

20 Norman L. Jones, *Faith by Statute: Parliament and the Settlement of Religion, 1559* (London, 1982), p. 83; cf. William P. Haugaard who contends that Elizabeth was not rejecting monastic superstition but simply giving precedence to her own choristers; *Elizabeth and the English Reformation: The Struggle for a Stable Settlement of Religion* (Cambridge, 1968), p. 82.

21 David. M. Loades, *Mary Tudor: A Life* (Oxford, 1989), p. 310.

22 Owen Oglethorpe, Bishop of Carlisle, had been celebrating Christmas Mass when she ordered him not to elevate the host. When he replied 'that thus he had learnt the mass, and that she must pardon him as he could not do otherwise', Elizabeth walked out after the gospel and replaced him at the next day's service with her own royal chaplain. Il Schifanoya to Ottaviano Vivaldino (31 December 1558) *Calendar of State Papers, Venetian (1558–1580)*, ed. Rawdon Brown and G. Cavendish Bentinck (London, 1890), vol. 7. For a discussion of the liturgical scandal surrounding Elizabeth's coronation, see my '"Thou Idol Ceremony": Elizabeth I, The Henriad, and the Rites of the British

deliberately mixed and confusing signals. Elizabeth went out of her way to assure otherwise scandalized foreign ambassadors that 'she differed very little from us as she believed *that God was in the sacrament of the Eucharist*, and only dissented from two or three things in the Mass'.[23] Her version of the *Book of Common Prayer* even dropped the notorious 'Black Rubric' of the previous version which explicitly denied 'any real and essential presence' in the Eucharist, and its communion liturgy combined the sacrificial and commemorative elements of the two preceding prayer books.[24]

As the compromises and evasions of her religious settlement fudged controversies over the real presence, the cult of Elizabeth increasingly overshadowed them, developing into a kind of 'state religion'.[25] Its pattern was established at her coronation, where the controversial religious service was effectively overshadowed by the civic progress the day before, an event better publicized in an official tract called *The Quenes Maiesties Passage*. This work carefully recorded and preserved the 'wonderfull spectacle, of a noble hearted princess toward her most loving people, and the peoples excading comfort in beholding so worthy a soveraign.'[26] By shifting attention from religious ritual to civic ceremony and courtly pageantry, her cult continued what John Bossy calls 'the migration of the holy' launched by her father's reforms in which 'the socially integrative powers of the host' were transferred 'to the rituals of monarchy and secular community'.[27] In this new, more exalted, Protestant version of sacred kingship, royal supremacy made the monarch responsible for 'the cure of souls' as well as the mystical embodiment of the realm.[28] As the Tudor reformations advanced, veneration for the royal presence almost supplanted adoration of the real presence. Rood screens above church altars were dismantled and replaced with royal insignia under Henry and Edward, and Elizabeth was carried in a canopied litter at her coronation and throughout her reign like the host in a Corpus Christi pro-

cession, a feast mocked under Edward and thoroughly suppressed under Elizabeth.[29]

Even in death, her royal presence loomed larger than the real presence. Elizabeth was the first English monarch to be buried without a requiem; Henry had arranged for one for himself, and Mary ordered one for Edward as well as herself.[30] By the end of Elizabeth's reign, both the Mass and the requiem had largely faded away.[31] The Venetian ambassador was

Monarchy', *Urban Life in the Renaissance*, eds. Susan Zimmerman and Ronald F. E. Weissman (Newark, DE., 1989), pp. 240–66 and '"The Wonderfull Spectacle": The Civic Progress of Elizabeth I and the Troublesome Coronation', *Coronations: Medieval and Early Modern Monarchic Ritual*, ed. by Janos M. Bak (Berkeley, 1990), pp. 217–27.

[23] de Feria to Philip (29 April 1559), *Calendar of State Papers, Spanish*, ed. Martin A. S. Hume (London, 1892–9), II.29: 62.

[24] A. G. Dickens, *The English Reformation* (London, 1989), pp. 243, 280–3 and Christopher Haigh, *English Reformation: Religion, Politics, and Society under the Tudors* (Oxford, 1993), pp. 179–81.

[25] Helen Hackett, *Virgin Mother, Maiden Queen: Elizabeth and the Cult of the Virgin Mary* (New York, 1995), p. 110. See also Frances Yates, *Astraea: The Imperial Theme in the Sixteenth Century* (London, 1975) and Roy Strong, *The Cult of Elizabeth* (London, 1977).

[26] *The Quenes Maiesties Passage through the Citie of London to Westminster the Day before her Coronacion*, ed. James M. Osborn (New Haven, 1960), p. 28.

[27] John Bossy, *Christianity in the West: 1400–1700* (Oxford, 1985), p. 145 and 'The Mass as a Social Institution, 1200–1700', *Past and Present*, 100 (1983), 59.

[28] J. J. Scarisbrick, *Henry VIII* (Berkeley, 1968), pp. 275–6. On Henry's 'mystical, even "thaumaturgical" idea', of royal supremacy, see G. R. Elton, *Studies in Tudor and Stuart Politics and Government* (Cambridge, 1974), vol. I, p. 105. I discuss this new Protestant notion of sacred kingship in my forthcoming book, *Alterations of State: Sacred Kingship in the English Reformation*.

[29] John Phillips, *The Reformation of Images: Destruction of Art in England, 1535–1660* (Berkeley, 1973), pp. 204–5. 103. For the suppression of the feast of Corpus Christi under Elizabeth, see Duffy, *Stripping of the Altars*, pp. 566 and 579–80.

[30] Haigh, *English Reformation*, p. 206.

[31] Haigh, 292. Haigh figures that the Mass continued to be celebrated in many parishes up through the 1570s; only

duly scandalized by a service where 'little else was done except the chanting of two psalms in English and the delivery of a funeral oration', but he was impressed by the 'immense sum' spent on the mourning garments of her funeral cortège.[32] He was also amazed by the honours paid to her embalmed corpse, noting how 'the Council waited on her continually with the same ceremony, the same expenditure, down to her very household and table service, as though she were not wrapped in many a fold of cere cloth, and hid in such a heap of lead, of coffin, of pall, but was walking as she used to do at this season, about the alleys of her gardens'.[33] For a time, these elaborate tributes provided the cult of Elizabeth with a vigorous afterlife.

Hamlet first appeared during the troubled final years of Elizabeth's reign, when fears of her imminent death were compounded by the lack of an heir and the prospect of an unsettled succession. Its portents of 'some strange eruption to our state' (1.1.68) and allusions to 'the late innovation' (2.2.333) are thought to be references to the Essex revolt of 1601.[34] Shakespeare's own attitude towards the cult of Elizabeth and the mystique of sacred kingship is profoundly ambiguous. *Hamlet*, after all, attributes the sonorous claim that 'There's such divinity doth hedge a king / That treason can but peep to what it would' (4.5.122–3) to a regicide and usurper. The emotions stirred by a pending 'cease of majesty' are similarly compromised by the characters' bad faith. Though it is one source of the hero's profound melancholy, the phrase belongs to Rosencrantz and Guildenstern. It occurs in their speech to Claudius in which they worry about their own dependence on this murderous usurper, cloaking their selfish apprehensions with unctuous piety:

GUILDENSTERN Most holy and religious fear it is
  To keep those many many bodies safe
  That live and feed upon your majesty.
ROSENCRANTZ The single and peculiar life is
    bound
  With all the strength and armour of the mind
  To keep itself from noyance; but much more

That spirit upon whose weal depends and rests
The lives of many. The cease of majesty
Dies not alone, but like a gulf doth draw
What's near with it.   (3.3.8–17)

Each speaker is primarily concerned with his own 'single and peculiar life', yet, for all their hypocrisy, their speeches really do express a 'most holy and religious fear'.[35] The venerable concept of the king's two bodies informs their claim that the monarch's well-being preserves his subjects' 'many many bodies'. This image is emblematically shown on the well-known title page of Hobbes's *Leviathan* by all those many little bodies making up the body of the king. As in Hobbes, the common 'weal depends' on the

---

in the 1580s did control of the universities and clerical training enable reformers to secure more thorough liturgical control (pp. 268–84).

32 Giovanni Carlo Scaramelli to the Doge and Senate (8 May 1603), *CSP, Venetian 1603–1607*, 10.22 Scaramelli declined to attend these 'heretic services' in order to avoid the 'inevitable scandal and a danger to myself' (10.23).

33 Scaramelli to the Doge and Senate (12 April 1603), *CSP, Venetian 1603–1607*, 10.3.

34 See the commentary by Harold Jenkins in *Hamlet* (London, 1982), pp. 470–2. For discussions of the play's context in the pending succession crisis, see Stuart M. Kurland, 'Hamlet and the Scottish Succession?' *Studies in English Literature*, 34 (1994), 279–300 and Steven Mullaney, 'Mourning and Misogyny: Hamlet, The Revenger's Tragedy, and the Final Progress of Elizabeth I, 1600–1607', *Shakespeare Quarterly*, 45 (1994), 139–62.

35 Cf. G. Wilson Knight who says that 'This fine speech, in the style of Troilus and Cressida, cannot be written off as sheer flattery' in *The Wheel of Fire: Interpretations of Shakespearean Tragedy* (1930; New York, 1958), p. 318. The speech is an excellent example of Norman Rabkin's principle of 'complementarity' which allows us 'at almost any point in the play to read its world as godless or divine'; *Shakespeare and the Common Understanding* (New York, 1967), p. 10. Stephen Greenblatt advances a similar notion of 'equivocality' which does not 'simply locate us in a disenchanted world of natural causes' because 'murky currents of invisible agency' are still perceptible; 'The Eating of the Soul', *Representations*, 48 (1994), 110–11. Both concepts involve variations on Keats's 'negative capability' as a kind of suspension between belief and doubt.

safety of the king, and older mystical notions of sacred kingship are given new urgency by *realpolitik*. At the same time, the royal presence becomes a sacramental real presence as the idea of the king as the collective body politic transforms an otherwise revoltingly parasitic image of those who 'live and feed upon your majesty' into a form of holy communion. This implicit comparison of the monarch to the host implies a process akin to transubstantiation. As Ernst Kantorowicz points out in his classic study of *The King's Two Bodies*, these two doctrines had been linked from their inception by a shared belief in the redemptive presence of an immortal corporate body that miraculously survives 'the cease of majesty' and holds the bereft community together.[36] According to the traditional response to the monarch's death, 'the king is dead, long live the king,' and this formulaic phrase assures continuity from one reign to the next.

In *Hamlet*, that continuity is undermined, of course, by the villainy of the successor and his followers' accurate fear that his death will 'draw/ What's near with it.' However, the play briefly holds out the prospect of an even more miraculous royal survival. The ghost of the legitimate king returns 'in his habit as he lived' (3.4.126) to expose his successor's treachery and demand retribution. The appearance of Hamlet's father at the beginning and midpoint of the play allows a kind of reunion of the king's two bodies, giving this supernatural spirit a visible shape. Hamlet is stunned by this apparition, and he hints at its extraordinary possibilities when he exclaims: 'His form and cause conjoined, preaching to stones / Would make them capable' (3.4.117–118). In a realm where so much is 'out of joint', such a conjunction might be 'a consummation / Devoutly to be wished' (3.1.65–6), but the meaning of this *hendiadys*, itself a rhetorical form of conjunction, is not immediately clear.[37] 'Form' can be taken as a synonym for the king's pitiful appearance, while the 'cause' of his return is presumably that 'foul and most unnatural murder' (1.5.25),

revealed only to Hamlet at their earlier encounter. In the first scenes, everyone else saw the ghostly form, but only Hamlet heard the cause, and he refuses to disclose it. Now the reverse holds true as Gertrude is told that the king was murdered but fails to see his form. Recognition of both form and cause could resolve these discrepancies and make the hidden truth manifest to others besides Hamlet. At the same time, the abstract, almost scholastic quality of both nouns suggests a more philosophic, even cosmic significance.[38] Rosemond Tuve's analysis of the links between image and cause in Renaissance poetics is pertinent here because it suggests the large intellectual significance of the latter word. Tuve defines 'cause' as an 'untranslatable Elizabethan term' bound up with occult meanings, the 'Aristotelian "final cause",' and ultimately, Renaissance philosophy's 'definition of the real'.[39] The reality that Hamlet hopes might be revealed by this conjunction occupies a comparably lofty plane.

Hamlet's reference to stones made capable certainly gives his hopes greater theological significance. It is an allusion to the gospel of Luke 19.37–40 where Christ is greeted by 'the whole multitude of the disciples' who spread

---

36 Ernst Kantorowicz, *The King's Two Bodies: A Study in Medieval Political Theology* (1957; Princeton, 1981), pp. 196 and 206.

37 'Form and cause conjoined' recalls – and might even recover – Hamlet's image of his father as a 'combination and a form indeed / Where every god did seem to set his seal/ To give the world assurance of a man' (3.4.60–2). This figure of speech, combining two proximate substantive nouns, abounds in Hamlet, as George T. Wright points out in 'Hendiadys and Hamlet' in *Critical Essays*, ed. pp. Kastan, 79–109. Yet, as Wright notes, all the play's conjunctions 'mask deeper disjunctions' (95).

38 According to F. C. Coppleston, these terms were adapted from Aristotle by St Bonaventure who claimed that 'almost all natural forms, at any rate corporal forms, are actualized through the action of a particular finite efficient cause'; see *A History of Medieval Philosophy* (New York, 1972), p. 164.

39 Rosemond Tuve, *Elizabethan and Metaphysical Imagery* (1947; Chicago, 1968), p. 12, n. 7 and pp. 24–6.

their garments on the road and rejoice 'with a loude voice, for all the great workes yt [i.e. that] thei had sene, Saying, Blessed *be* the King that cometh in the Name of the Lord'; told by the Pharisees to silence his disciples, Christ replies 'I tel you that, if these shulde holde their peace, the stones wuld crye.'[40] By invoking this passage, Hamlet indirectly identifies his father's ghost with the incarnate Christ at a moment of messianic triumph, and he wants his father to be recognized as another King who comes in the name of the Lord.

At the same time that he yearns for a regal apotheosis, Hamlet also wants a kind of sacramental miracle, suggested by that intriguing term 'conjoined'. The sacrament ordinarily connoted by the word is marriage, a connotation reinforced by references to Gertrude as the 'imperial jointress of this warlike state' (1.2.9) whom Claudius finds 'so conjunctive to my life and soul' (4.7.14). But here and elsewhere matrimonial implications acquire a mystical political significance when applied to a king. James I describes his relationship to England accordingly in one of his first speeches to parliament, declaring that 'God by his almighty Providence hath preordained . . . that union which is made in my blood . . . What God hath conjoined then let no man separate. I am the husband and the whole Island is my lawful wife.'[41] James, of course, is invoking the doctrine of the king's two bodies, and Edmund Plowden, the Tudor jurist who gave this doctrine its definitive formulation, uses the same term to describe this mystical union: 'For when the Body politic of King of this Realm is conjoined to the Body natural and one Body is made of them both, the Degree of the Body natural and of the Things possessed in that Capacity is thereby altered, . . . and the Body politic is thereby altered, . . . and the Body politic wipes away every Imperfection of the other with which it is consolidated.'[42]

Plowden describes a sacramental alteration of state akin to transubstantiation, and Hamlet clearly desires a comparable conjunction. In

fact, England's most influential theologians use the same term to define the Eucharist. In his *Short Treatise of the Lord's Supper*, John Calvin describes the sacrament as 'the presence and conjunction of reality and sign.'[43] His disciple and successor, Theodore Beza elaborates on its receptionist implications, explaining that Christ's 'body is truly joined (*coniungi*) with the bread and the blood with the wine, sacramentally and not otherwise, [and] this is not in a place or location, but because they efficaciously signify (*efficaciter significant*) what is given by the Lord to all participating with faith, and truly received by believers through faith'.[44] Richard Hooker, the greatest English theologian of Shakespeare's time, agrees that, while Christ's 'actuall *position*' cannot be 'restrained and tied to a certain place,' his presence in the sacrament 'by *waie of conjunction* is in some sort presence'; indeed, the Eucharist 'is by virtue of that conjunction made the bodie of the Sonne of God . . . [and] this giveth it a *presence of force and efficacie* throughout all generations of men'.[45]

In the closet scene, Hamlet desperately longs for a sacramental miracle along these lines, hoping for a supernatural conjunction of the

---

[40] *The Geneva Bible: A Facsimile of the 1560 Edition* (Madison, WI., 1969); hereafter cited in the text.

[41] C. H. McIlwain, *The Political Works of King James I* (Cambridge, 1918), p. 272.

[42] Edmund Plowden, *The Commentaries or Reports* (London, 1816), vol. 1, p. 238. Sir John Hawkins was the first to suggest that Shakespeare knew Plowden, suggesting that Plowden's summary of the torturous intricacies of 'Crowner's Quest Law' was an influence on the grave-digger scene (5.1.22), *A New Variorum Edition of Shakespeare: Hamlet*, ed. Horace Howard Furness (1877; New York, 1963), vol. 2, pp. 376–7.

[43] John Calvin, *Short Treatise of the Lord's Supper* (1541), *Theological Treatises*, trans. J. K. S. Reid (Philadelphia, 1954), 159.

[44] *Apologia Prima in Contra Claude de Sainctes* (1567), 298 in Jill Rait, *The Eucharistic Theology of Theodore Beza: Development of the Reformed Doctrine* (Chartersburg, PA, 1972), p. 39.

[45] Richard Hooker, *Of the Law of Ecclesiastical Polity, Book V*, ed. W. Speed Hill (Cambridge, MA., 1977), vol. 2, p. 234.

king's two bodies that, in the words of Plowden, 'wipes away every Imperfection' through what Hooker calls a mystical '*presence of force and efficacie*'. Unfortunately, no such miracle occurs. The ghost proves evanescent, confusingly sinister, and only partially visible. While it almost becomes a real presence for Hamlet, Gertrude sees nothing but 'vacancy' and 'incorporal air' (3.4.108–9). For her, the ghost of the legitimate king is no more substantial than Claudius is for Hamlet, a king who 'is a thing . . . of nothing' (4.2.27–9) and, despite the promise of his vision, form and cause are not firmly conjoined: 'The body is with the King, but the King is not with the body' (4.2.26–7).

The theatrical impact of the closet scene is profoundly unsettling. In some ways, it resembles the Eucharistic miracle of St Gregory as depicted by Albrecht Dürer (Illustration 1). In that scene, those sharing a space with the central figure remain oblivious to the supernatural action transpiring before his – and our – eyes. Yet, while Dürer's picture assures that we can believe what Gregory sees, since God and his angels also witness Christ's real presence on the altar, the ghost's reality in this scene is more dubious. Critical opinion is divided. Arguing that the ghost is an illusion, Robert Watson entitles his chapter on *Hamlet* 'Giving Up the Ghost', and he concludes that the play urges us to do just that because 'Calvinist theology created a blank wall between the living and the dead.'[46] Marjorie Garber gives her chapter the same title, but she concludes that 'giving up the ghost' is not so easy, citing Jacques Lacan to explain the uncanny hold of a 'presence without present of a present which, coming back only *haunts*. The ghost, *le re-venant*, the survivor, appears only by means of figure or fiction, but its appearance is not nothing, nor is it a mere semblance.'[47] The ghost is indeed 'not nothing', for it assumes a palpable and awesome form. Some sort of conjunction still occurs for Hamlet and the audience, permitting contact with things absent even if it does not make them a real presence.

A still more powerful conjunction occurs in the last act, as Hamlet supplants the ghost and acquires some of its uncanny powers. In a notorious syntactic impossibility, Hamlet twice declares that 'I am dead' (5.2.285 and 290). Tantalizing all who 'look pale and tremble at this chance, / That are but mutes or audience to this act' with intimations of what 'I could tell you' (5.2.286–9), he reprises his father's earlier role of a ghost come from the grave who 'could a tale unfold' (1.5.15) while declining to do so. Hamlet also repeats his father's categorical imperative, 'Remember me' (1.5.91); when Horatio tries to join him in death, Hamlet implores his friend to 'Absent thee from felicity awhile, / And in this harsh world draw thy breath in pain / To tell my story' (5.2.299–301). His dying appeal to 'Report me and my cause aright' (5.2.291) suggests that he too wants his own 'form and cause conjoined'. A report that could get Hamlet and his motives 'aright' would constitute an awesome conjunction of form and cause. It might even attain the force of what Michael Neill calls 'metamorphic narration', a 'persistent motif in the play'; as Neill notes, the closet scene and the last scene hold out the prospect of an 'untellable tale – one so astonishing and compelling that, could it only be told it would leave its audience utterly changed'.[48] Although Hamlet is pained by 'all that remains untold as though his life were an unfinished story still struggling for expression', the play itself has told that story and thus stands as a 'living monument' to Hamlet, and its conclusion provides, as Neill says, considerable 'consolatory power'.[49] In other words, the last act sustains the kind of conjunction described by Richard Hooker, making Hamlet 'a *presence of force and efficacie* throughout all generations of

---

[46] Watson, in Kastan, *Critical Essays*, p. 5.

[47] Jacques Lacan, 'The Art of Mémoires' in Marjorie Garber, *Shakespeare's Ghost Writers: Literature as Uncanny Causality* (New York, 1987), p. 172.

[48] Neill, *Issues of Death*, p. 225.

[49] Ibid., pp. 240 and 303.

1   Albrecht Dürer, 'Mass of St Gregory'

men'. However, before considering the impact of that conjunction we must turn to the forces arrayed against it.

Poor Horatio has been assigned a difficult, if not impossible, task. No eulogy or funeral rite could ever match Hamlet's own 'dying voice' (308), and Horatio's promised recitation of 'carnal, bloody, and unnatural acts' (335) could never achieve the intensity of all that we have seen.[50] In any case, his attempt to honour Hamlet's memory is quickly disrupted by the arrival of Fortinbras. The Prince of Norway, whose father was slain by old Hamlet in single combat thirty years earlier, has been intent from the start on recovering 'by strong hand / And terms compulsative those foresaid lands / So by his father lost' (1.1.101–3). Deflected from invading Denmark by his uncle's agreement with Claudius, he now returns victorious from battle in Poland only to find his opponents dead. The 'warlike noise' (5.2.302) of his approach interrupts Hamlet's request of Horatio to 'tell my story' (5.2.301) and it also disrupts the benediction begun by Horatio: 'Good night sweet prince, / And flights of angels sing thee to thy rest. – / Why does the drum come hither' (5.2.312–14). Such an approach suggests that Norway's original belligerence towards Denmark has not abated, as do the orders for Hamlet's somewhat incongruous military funeral:

> Let four captains
> Bear Hamlet like a soldier to the stage,
> For he was likely, had he been put on,
> To have proved most royally; and for his passage,
> The soldiers' music and the rites of war
> Speak loudly for him.   (5.2.349–54)

The likeliest occasion to put Hamlet to such a proof would have been a rematch over the contested lands, an aim Fortinbras may never have relinquished. Hamlet has given his 'dying voice' (5.2.308) to Fortinbras, and Horatio is eager to speak for his dead friend 'whose voice will draw on more' (5.2.346). However, before he can do so, Fortinbras asserts his own

authority, indifferent to any conferred by his dead rival: 'For me, with sorrow I embrace my fortune. / I have some rights of memory in this kingdom, / Which now to claim my vantage doth invite me' (5.2.342–5). Fortinbras is neither as coarse nor as murderous as Claudius, but his brisk self-assertion still recalls one who can 'with wisest sorrow think on him / Together with remembrance of ourselves' (1.2.6–7).[51] Whatever Horatio has to say, Fortinbras is now the man in charge, taking control in Denmark on the basis of his own ancestral claims.

Shakespeare thus treats the 'rights of memory' as 'rites of war' waged by survivors against those they succeed and motivated largely by 'remembrance of ourselves'. This cynical view of the rights and rites of memory was certainly confirmed by the ambiguous tribute paid to Queen Elizabeth by her successor. Elizabeth too had given a foreign monarch her 'dying voice', but James VI was eager to take possession of his new realm on the basis of his own ancestral claims and impeccable pedigree. He kept insisting to all his new subjects that his status as the 'next and sole Heire of the Blood royall of this realme' derived from his 'own lawful,

---

[50] Critical opinion is again divided. Barbara Hardy says that Horatio 'makes an intelligent, accurate, and fairly comprehensive summary of external events, and his capacity to tell is guaranteed by the preview' in 'Figure of Narration in Hamlet', Robert Druce, ed. *A Centre of Excellence: Essays Presented to Seymour Betsky* (Amsterdam, 1987), p. 14. By contrast, Terence Hawkes says that Horatio's oration cannot possibly comprehend 'the subtleties, the innuendoes, the contradictions, the imperfectly realized motives and sources for action that have been exhibited to us' in 'Telmah', *Shakespeare and the Question of Theory*, eds. Patricia Parker and Geoffrey Hartman (New York, 1985), p. 311.

[51] Anthony B. Dawson's discussion of theatre as a 'conduit for "social memory"' (55) is pertinent here, as is his account of the struggle between Fortinbras and Hamlet's ghost in this last scene, especially in its emphasis on how 'the performance of memory . . . ignites a struggle for control of interpretation'; see 'The Arithmetic of Memory: Shakespeare's Theatre and the National Past', *Shakespeare Survey 52* (1999), pp. 54–67.

unstained, and unblemished' descent from the Tudor line.[52] Moreover, once enthroned, James I acted as belligerently as Fortinbras to assert his own 'rights of memory' in a kingdom responsible for his parent's death, in his case, his mother rather than a father.

Hamlet begins and ends with state funerals, and, as Shakespeare shows, these are often delicate affairs, demanding a precarious balance of 'delight and dole' (1.5.13). Within a few years, the death of Elizabeth placed many of her powerful subjects in a comparable predicament. Thomas Dekker's *Wonderful Year*, a lurid chronicle of 1603, makes the moment of transition sound nerve-wracking indeed: 'Upon Thursday it was treason to cry God saue king *Iames* king of *England* and uppon Friday hye treason not to cry so. In the morning no voice hearde but murmures and lamentation, at noone, nothing but shoutes of gladnes and triumphe.'[53] For some, the division of loyalties between the old and new regimes proved fatal. Robert Devereux, the Earl of Essex, sided prematurely with James VI two years earlier. They had been conducting a secret correspondence for more than a decade, and, shortly before his abortive coup in 1601, the Earl wrote to assure James that he 'shall be declared and acknowledged the certain and undoubted successor to this Crown and shall command the services and lives of as many of us as undertake this great work'.[54] The failure of this revolt threw James into a panic, but Robert Cecil, the late Earl's rival, quickly took up the secret correspondence and managed to allay the king's anxieties.[55] Cecil proved no less adept at managing the succession itself, summoning the Privy Council after Elizabeth's death and reading the proclamation declaring James I king of England. Cecil accused other rivals, Sir Walter Ralegh and Lords Gray and Cobham, of conspiring to block James's accession in the so-called Bye Plot, and he made certain that James was immediately informed of Cobham's 'ordinary axiom both since the death of Essex and before . . . That it was not possible for any

man to be a loyal subject to his gracious mistress, that respected King James in any degree, either present or future.'[56] By contrast, Cecil himself was a virtuoso at managing these divided loyalties, but, even for him, there were awkward moments. Funeral protocol and the doctrine of the king's two bodies required that the late monarch be buried before the successor arrived; Elizabeth's reign lasted as long as her mortal body remained on earth. In explaining these arrangements to James, Cecil and the other privy councillors declared that 'we are a little troubled when we consider how it will stand together in one letter that we should both profess our infinite longing for you and yet in the same propound some courses to retard your coming hither'.[57] Even the most adroit politicians sometimes found it hard to balance 'delight and dole'. James agreed to hang back

---

[52] Howard Nenner, *The Right to Be King: The Succession to the Crown of England* (Chapel Hill, 1995), pp. 95 and 59. See also D. Harris Willson, *King James VI and I* (London, 1956), pp. 140–1; James was the grandson of Henry VII.

[53] Thomas Dekker, *The Wonderful Year* in *Non-Dramatic Works*, ed. by Alexander B. Grosart (London: 1884), vol. 1, p. 97.

[54] Willson, 152.

[55] P. M. Handover, *The Second Cecil: The Rise to Power, 1563–1604, of Sir Robert Cecil, later, first Earl of Salisbury* (London, 1959), pp. 235–40. James initially demanded that Elizabeth 'give out a plain declaration, which must be enacted in her own records, that I am untouched in any action or practice that hath ever been intended against her, especially in this last [i.e., the Essex revolt]', and he reminded her of her 'old promise, that nothing shall be done by her, in her time, in prejudice of my future right'; James to the Earl of Mar and Edward Bruce (8 April 1601), *The Secret Correspondence of Sir Robert Cecil with James VI of Scotland*, ed. David Dalrymple (Edinburgh, 1766), pp. 5–6. Cecil, in turn, urged James to forego 'needles expostulations' and 'generall acclamation' in *The Correspondence of King James of Scotland with Sir Robert Cecil and others*, ed. John Bruce (London, 1861), p. 7.

[56] Lord Henry Howard to Edward Bruce (4 December 1601), *Secret Correspondence*, p. 46.

[57] Lords of the Privy Council to James (8 April 1603), *Historical Manuscripts Commission, Salisbury*, ed. by M. S. Giuseppi (London, 1930), vol. 15, pp. 39–40.

until Elizabeth was interred, proceeding only as far as York, but he still demanded that enough regalia be delivered to permit a properly majestic entry into 'the second city of our kingdom', and he required Cecil to deliver it.[58]

King James himself strove for a decorous blend of 'delight and dole,' vowing to abstain from any 'ceremony of our own joy . . . as long as her body is above ground', and promising to have 'all things observed which may testify the honour we bear to her memory'.[59] Once she was buried, however, he moved aggressively to assert his own 'rights of memory in this kingdom'. Elizabeth was originally interred, as Julia Walker has shown, closer to her grandfather, Henry VII and her step-brother, Edward VI. The last Tudor monarch chose to be buried at the centre of Westminster Chapel, the chapel constructed by the first. King James, however, had other designs on this space, and he pursued them with a shocking disregard for hers. He dug up Elizabeth's casket from its original grave site and placed her in a side chapel with her Catholic step-sister, Mary.[60] He then erected a monument with marble effigy and canopy, but he also built a more expensive, attractive and loftier memorial for Mary Stuart directly across the nave. His mother's remains were 'translated' from the site where Elizabeth had her buried at Peterborough after her execution, to Westminster 'where the kings and queens of this realm are usually interred'.[61] Walker convincingly argues that James aimed to marginalize his predecessor by relocating her in a side chapel with her childless step-sister and making their burial site into an architectural dead end.[62] In his most brazen move, James claimed Elizabeth's original grave site for himself, placing his tomb behind Henry VII in the middle of the Chapel (Illustration 2). Aligning himself with the patriarch of the Tudor dynasty, he aimed to establish his central place as the head of a reinvigorated and more fruitful royal line.[63] James intended, as Jennifer Woodward explains, to transform Henry VII's chapel into 'a royal necropolis for the Stuart dynasty', and it gradu-

ally acquired 'an impressive collection of Stuart heirs', including Prince Henry, Princess Elizabeth of Bohemia, the children of Charles I as well as the remains of Charles II and his offspring.[64] James planned an especially grand monument for himself at the centre, but it was never built.[65] Indeed, James's ambitious designs went awry well before his demise, thwarted in part by the tomb he built for Elizabeth. That memorial ultimately affirmed the surprising autonomy of the 'rights of memory'.

James's reign was initially greeted with great enthusiasm because he was Protestant, male,

---

[58] James to the Earl of Mar and Edward Bruce (12 April 1603), HMC, Salisbury, 15.44. See also Willson, King James VI, p. 166. Cecil travelled to York to greet his new sovereign on 18 April and remained in the royal entourage until 25 April (Handover, 299–300). Even as he hastened to join his new master, Cecil remained concerned with his duties to his old mistress, writing to the Privy Council that 'if his Majesty should hold on his journeys thither with such speed as he has begun, he would be near London before the funerals, or at the very time. So as the State could not attend both the performance of that duty to our late Sovereign, and of this other of this Majesty's reception' (18 April 1603), HMC Salisbury 15.53.

[59] James to the Earl of Mar and Edward Bruce (12 April 1603), HMC Salisbury, 15.44.

[60] Julia M. Walker, 'Reading the Tombs of Elizabeth I', English Literary Renaissance, 26 (1996), 510–30.

[61] James I to Dean of Peterborough (September 28, 1612), Letters of Kings of England, ed. J. O. Halliwell Philips (London, 1846), vol. 2, p. 119.

[62] Walker, 'Reading the Tombs', 515–16

[63] For a discussion of Stuart efforts to propagate this patriarchal image, see Jonathan Goldberg, 'Fatherly Authority: The Politics of Stuart Family Images', Rewriting the Renaissance: The Discourses of Sexual Difference in Early Modern Europe, eds. Margaret W. Ferguson, Maureen Quilligan, Nancy J. Vickers (Chicago, 1986), pp. 3–32.

[64] Jennifer Woodward, The Theatre of Death: Ritual Management of Royal Funerals in Renaissance England (Woodbridge, UK, 1997), p. 136; Walker, 'Reading the Tombs', 523–4.

[65] Woodward attributes this not to a lack of funds, arguing instead that the continued display of James's funeral effigy as well as other posthumous portraits and statues precluded the need for a memorial (pp. 202–3).

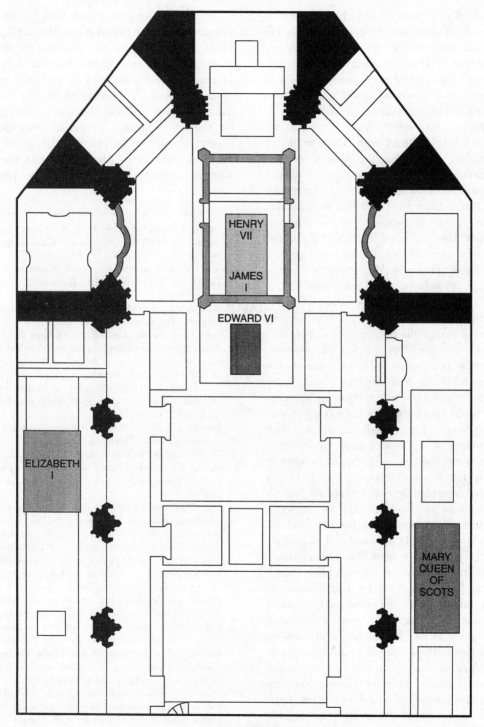

2   Henry VII's Chapel

and married with three healthy children, and, in the words of one contemporary, 'the people were generally weary of an old woman's government'.[66] Over the course of his reign, however, his popularity diminished and nostalgia for the days of 'good Queen Bess' increased. By his last years, discontent with his rule sparked a so-called 'blessed revolution', when renewed tensions with Spain fuelled a sabre-rattling ardor for the glories of the Armada defeat, and James found himself stalked by a number of Elizabethan ghosts.[67] Tracts like *Robert Earl of Essex His Ghost Sent from Elizium* and *Sir Walter Rawleighs Ghost, or Englands Forewarner* were published in 1624 to sound the call to arms against Spain. Portraits of Elizabeth as a celestial spirit and Amazonian St George with the Armada in the background circulated.[68] An especially striking image of Elizabeth's tomb appears in a book published during James's last year on the throne, Samuel Purchas's *Hakluytus Posthumus or Purchas his Pilgrimes* (Illustration 3).[69] James and Charles are shown on the left, the heir apparent confidently straddling the realm. On the right, an astonishingly Hamlet-like portrait of James's other son, the late Prince Henry, meditates upon a skull and mourns at the monument of his true kindred spirit. Revered as the Stuart paragon of chivalric heroism and Protestant zeal, Henry had been regarded by opponents of James's foreign policy as a worthier heir to Elizabeth than either his father or his brother, and his death left many deeply bereaved.[70] The appearance of all these ghosts 'sent from Elizium' must have been somewhat unsettling. The king's sleep was also disturbed by bad dreams of George Buchanan, his old tutor and a defender of popular resistance, 'who seemed to check him severely as he used to do', and cannons fired at Gray's Inn during the Christmas revels in 1622–23 so frightened him that he awoke shouting 'Treason! Treason!' putting 'the city . . . in an uproar'.[71] These revenants from James's past clearly retained considerable power.

Elizabeth's monument itself took on an odd prominence in the events of the Blessed Revolution. In 1621, a petition lamenting the abuses of James's reign was placed 'into the hand of Queen Elizabeth's statue in Westminster by an unknown person'.[72] Addressed to 'the blessed Saint Elizabeth of famous memory' and signed by the late Queen's 'perpetual and faithful beadsmen, and daily orators, the poor distressed Commons of England', it asks for her help in seeking celestial relief from courtly

---

66 Bishop Goodman cited in G. P. V. Akrigg, *Jacobean Pageant or, The Court of King James I* (Cambridge, MA, 1962), p. 17.

67 See Thomas Cogswell, *The Blessed Revolution: English Politics and the Coming of War, 1621–24* (Cambridge, 1989).

68 Roy Strong reproduces the Jacobean portraits in *Gloriana: The Portraits of Queen Elizabeth I* (London, 1987). See also my 'Old English Honour in an Evil Time: Aristocratic Principle in the 1620s' in *The Stuart Court and Europe: Essays in Politics and Political Culture*, ed. Malcolm Smuts (Cambridge, 1996), pp. 133–55.

69 See Arthur M. Hind, *Engraving in England in the Sixteenth Centuries: The Reign of James* (Cambridge, 1955), vol. 2, p. 387.

70 Roy Strong, *Henry, Prince of Wales and England's Lost Renaissance* (London, 1986), pp. 72 and 222–4.

71 Joseph Mead to Sir Martin Stuteville (30 March 1622) and (25 January 1623), *The Court and Times of James I*, ed. by Thomas Birch (London, 1848), vol. 2, pp. 301 and 360.

72 'The Coppie of a Libell put into the hand of Queen Elizabeth's statue in Westminster by an unknown person, Anno dni 1610 [corrected to] – 1621. Ultimo die Martii. 1623' [Bod. Malone 23/32]. 'This copie was founde in the hand of Queen Elizabeths tombe at West. February [erased] 22 of june 1623' [Folger MS v.a.275, Commonplace book of George Turner]. Alastair Bellamy has transcribed this petition which appears in different versions in several ballad collections and commonplace books of the 1620s and reappears in 1642. I am very grateful to Professor Bellamy for alerting me to its existence and kindly sharing his transcription with me. Elizabeth's reply combines admonitions to subject and sovereign, warning that 'Princes are gods on earth, and subjects' eyes / Upon their actions must not stand like spies', while condemning the dispersal of the 'revenues of the Crown . . . to favourite or friend'.

3   Samuel Purchas, *Hakluytus Posthumus or Purchas His Pilgrimes* (1624)

corruption.[73] The verse proposes to 'make the name of great Eliza / Equal the name and glory of Maria' by building a monument that 'shall make proud Rome / On pilgrimage to come, and at thy shrine / To offer gifts as to a thing divine.' Those who composed and placed the 'Petition of Long Afflicted England' on Elizabeth's tomb self-consciously evoked older intercessory practices long associated with Westminster's royal sepulchre, but they are also mocking Romish superstition; few petitioners presumably spent the night squeezed into the base of her tomb. The older medieval system of sacred kingship had been shattered by the Reformation's assault on monastic foundations and intercessory prayers, the cult of the saints and pilgrimages, shrines and even sacred space itself. A few Catholic stalwarts kept hoping for its revival; on hearing of Mary Stuart's new monument, a Scottish seminarian wrote from Bologna that 'I hear her bones, lately translated to the burial place of the Kings of England at Westminster, are resplendent with miracles.'[74] James certainly disappointed such hopes for he had no interest in cultivating his mother's legend or supporting her religion; once again, he was more intent on asserting his own 'rights of memory in this kingdom' rather than hers.[75]

Elizabeth's tomb never became a site of pilgrimage or miracles either, but it remained an object of veneration, perpetuating the cult of Elizabeth beyond the grave in a less spectacular fashion. According to Thomas Fuller, a seventeenth-century church historian, copies of her 'fair tomb in Westminster' spread throughout the realm, 'the lively draught whereof is pictured in most London and many country churches, every parish being proud of the shadow of her tomb, and no wonder, when each loyal subject erected a mournful monument for her in his heart'.[76] Something like a reversal of the process described by Walter Benjamin occurs here, as the mechanical reproduction of 'the shadow of her tomb' preserves and disseminates its aura rather than dissipating it.[77] These pictures of Elizabeth's 'fair tomb in

Westminster' extend 'the migration of the holy' by displacing older notions of sacred space and real presence from an actual site while preserving the feelings they arouse through the circulation of images and other mementos. Indeed, memorial objects of this sort permit a sustained if tenuous connection between the living and the dead, allowing commemoration to acquire some of the power of intercession.

The image of Hamlet has maintained a much stronger hold on our imaginations long after his last act, and he overwhelms all his rivals, including those claiming their own 'rights of memory'. Fortinbras has the last word, but who leaves the play thinking of him? Moreover, Hamlet replaces and surpasses his father's ghost, making the paternal imperative, 'Remember me', wholly unnecessary. Indeed, this figure has so dominated modern memory that he has acquired a kind of palpable historical power. The great Romantic critic, William Hazlitt, eloquently describes the extraordinary impact of what is finally a fiction: 'Hamlet is a name; his speeches and sayings but the idle coinage of a poet's brain. What then, are they not real? They are as real as our own thoughts. Their reality is in the reader's mind. It is we who are Hamlet. The play has a prophetic truth, which is above that of history.'[78] A prophetic truth beyond history sounds like religious transcendence, but Hazlitt describes a 'reality' firmly anchored in 'our own thoughts'. He offers a reception theory of a real presence resulting not from

---

73 'The Coppie of a Libell.'

74 Thomas Dempster, *History of the Scottish Church* (1627), vol. 2, p. 464.

75 James refused to have the Earl of Northampton's florid epitaphs describing his mother as a martyr for her faith placed on her tomb; see James Emerson Phillips, *Images of a Queen: Mary Stuart in Sixteenth Century Literature* (Berkeley, 1964), pp. 226–7.

76 Thomas Fuller, *The Church History of Britain* (Oxford, 1845), vol. 5, p. 258.

77 Walter Benjamin, *Illuminations*, ed., Hannah Arendt, trans. Harry Zohn (New York, 1969), pp. 222–3.

78 William Hazlitt, *The Complete Works*, ed. by P. P. Howe (London, 1967), p. 233.

transubstantiation but from a meeting of minds over time. Although Hazlitt describes a conjunction more literary than sacramental, the reception theories of Calvin and Beza are still pertinent. Protestant arguments over the real presence reached an impasse at Marburg in 1529 when Luther insisted on Christ's substantial presence in the sacrament (hence consubstantiation) and Zwingli allowed only a symbolic presence.[79] Calvin objected to both positions, accusing Luther of encouraging fantasies of a 'local presence that the papists dream about', while criticizing Zwingli for denying 'the reality and efficacy' of the sacraments.[80] Beza charged Luther and Zwingli more succinctly with reducing the sacrament to either 'transubstantiation or a trope'.[81]

The bleak binary that Beza describes still confronts us because post-modern thought is still struggling with this pivotal issue of early modern theology. Contemporary theory, most notably deconstruction, has done a brilliant job of demolishing naive notions of presence, but it often does so at the risk of reducing truth to a trope and reifying absence.[82] New Historicism is no less intent on escaping delusions of presence. In her essay on 'Renaissance / Early Modern Studies', Leah Marcus spurns any thought of 'communion' with the past, emphasizing 'disjunction' over 'intellectual continuity'.[83] Reformation theology, in some instances, brings more rigour and sophistication, not to mention impassioned engagement, to these questions. In outlining his position on the real presence, Calvin insists that 'we maintain no other presence than that of a relationship'.[84] Beza concedes the intellectual modesty of the concept but emphasizes its interpersonal validity: '*Relata* have, I confess, the least of Being, as they say in the schools, but they are nevertheless maximally efficacious according as

they have true and solid subjects and objects in wholly natural things, as father and son, Lord and servant.'[85] Seen from this less transcendent perspective, *Hamlet*'s conjunctions permit contact with things absent even if they do not make them a real presence. While true communion with God, or his saints, or even with one another may prove an impossible hope for many, relationships with the living and the dead, with the actual and the imaginary, are, willy-nilly, inescapable – and the source of much that matters in literature and in life.

---

79 For a discussion of this theological summit meeting, see G. R. Potter, *Zwingli* (Cambridge, 1978), pp. 325–31.

80 Jaroslav Pelikan, *Reformation of Church and Dogma, 1300–1700* (Chicago, 1984), pp. 186 and 192–3. See also Kilian McDonald, *John Calvin, the Church, and the Eucharist* (Princeton, 1967), pp. 224–5.

81 Pelikan, *Reformation*, p. 201.

82 Paul de Man attempts to complicate 'the assimilation of truth to trope', but he reaches the, by now, banal conclusion that truth is power; see *Rhetoric and Romanticism* (New York, 1984), pp. 239 and 242–3. Geoffrey Hartman says that 'the "work" of art, then discloses Being as this absent presence: it allows us to stand on absence, as it were', but the qualifying 'as it were' does not preclude a certain complacency at taking such a bravely precarious stand; see *Criticism in the Wilderness: The Study of Literature Today* (New Haven, 1980), p. 167.

83 Leah Marcus, 'Renaissance / Early Modern Studies', in *Redrawing the Boundaries: The Transformation of English and American Literary Studies*, eds. Stephen Greenblatt and Giles Gunn (New York, 1992), p. 45. In *Shakespearean Negotiations*, Stephen Greenblatt jokes about 'literature professors' as 'salaried, middle-class shamans', making literary scholarship sound like a branch of magical thinking (1). I am arguing here that discourse with the dead does not require communion or shamanism.

84 Calvin, *Institutes of the Christian Religion*, ed. by John T. McNeill, trans. by Ford Lewis Battles (Philadelphia, 1960), vol. 2, p. 1374.

85 Beza, *De Controversius in Coena Domini* (1593), 38 in Raitt, *Christian Spirituality*, pp. 64–5.

BETWEEN RELIGION AND IDEOLOGY: SOME RUSSIAN *HAMLETS* OF THE TWENTIETH CENTURY

BOIKA SOKOLOVA

In 1911, looking back at an epoch, which had come to an end with Leo Tolstoy's death, and forward, to an already palpable time of change, the philosopher, critic and poet Vyacheslav Ivanov wrote:

From the religious and moral point of view we can distinguish three types of cultural attitudes: the relativist, the ascetic and the symbolic. The first denies the religious basis of culture as a system of relative values. The second (to which Tolstoy belongs), lays bare the moral and religious basis of cultural work, denies all derivative, symbolic or irrational cultural values; it inevitably subjects the instinctive, the playful, the artistic to moral utilitarianism . . . identifies the necessary with the useful and the morally correct. The third attitude to culture is according to us the only sound and correct one . . . It lies on the heroic and tragic path of liberating the world soul. Those committed to it have sworn . . . to turn the inherited legacy of human culture into a symbolism underpinning all spiritual values, and to relate them to the hierarchies of the divine world, to justify the relativity of human art through its symbolic correlation with the absolute. In other words, the task is to bring all culture, and together with it, nature, into a Church mystical, the principles of whose creation coincide with those of the Creation itself.[1]

Ivanov's tri-partite typology profoundly reflects the state of the cultural debate in Russia at the turn of the twentieth century in circumstances of dramatic transition. The mighty imperial structure was unwillingly giving under the social pressures urging for democratization. The century began with student unrest and activities of leftist organizations. While the European fringe of the Empire was strengthened by counterproductive russification policies, the frontier in the Far East was crumbling. The crucial defeat by Japan in 1905 triggered off massive popular unrest and the sweep of radicalism released by this first revolution triumphed in 1917. The decade between these cataclysms was bridged by the ravages of the First World War. The disorientation and disintegration in the whirl of history pushed a major strand of the cultural debate in the direction of religion. A political instrument for the government, it was for the radically minded an ideology to be challenged and fought. For Tolstoy, it showed the path to preserve the very soul of Russia against foreign pollution. For intellectuals like Ivanov, it offered a way to transcend the Russian reality by envisaging a brotherhood of Christian spirituality and peace.

On its part, the Shakespearian debate had been energized by Tolstoy's controversial essays on the state of culture: 'What is Art?' (1898) and 'On Shakespeare and the Drama', published in 1906 but written in 1903–4. Both of these undeniably fascinating works put forward the thesis that moral content is at the hub of artistic merit and that moral teaching is what Russia needs. Tolstoy, who had turned to fundamentalist religion and populism, believed that

---

[1] Vyacheslav Ivanov, *Sobranie sochinenii*, 4 vols., (collected works), edited by D. V. Ivanov and O. Dechart (Bruxelles), vol. 4, pp. 601–2 (translation mine).

the root of evil lay 'in the non-acceptance of Christ's teaching in its real, that is, its full, meaning'.[2] Being tools for educating the masses, art, as well as drama, had to offer sound moral lessons and guidance. In Shakespeare, Goethe, Schiller, as well as most of contemporary Russian drama, he found no other purpose than a wish to titillate the emotions with shallow immorality, a dangerous legacy, which could only be denounced.

Viewed from this angle, Shakespeare was nothing short of 'pernicious'. Indeed, for a young person to assimilate the 'immoral view of life which permeates all Shakespeare's works' is to lose 'the capacity to distinguish between good and evil'. Tolstoy's Shakespeare is 'an insignificant, inartistic, and not only not moral, but plainly immoral writer' aiming 'only at distracting and amusing the spectators'; he is an author who 'cannot possibly serve to teach the meaning of life'.[3] At this stage, Tolstoy's aesthetic agenda could only brook moral plays and his view of Shakespeare was that for Russia he was no good; to use Ivanov's term, his stance was truly ascetic.

Tolstoy's opinion, like the man himself, was quite exceptional. It was also antiquated and more in line with the fundamentalist Orthodoxy of the past century. The large and influential group of younger religious philosophers, one of whose voices was Ivanov, had a more inclusive view. The Symbolist poets and publicists, who were attracted by it, embraced the idea of Shakespeare's genius, whereby he could easily fit into their universalist project.

Like Tolstoy, Ivanov had a particular interest in the theatre, which, he believed, held the key to the meaning of life. The theatre was a place of communion, the stage the site where a poet's inspired dream acquired a physical reality to be fed back into real life. He believed that the dramatist, like a high priest of the noblest cult, forged a mystical link between stage and life. This Church mystical embraced all forms of life, artistic and natural, through the symbols of Christian religion.

Ivanov considered drama an intermediary between earthly and transcendental reality where the tragic hero is a mediator of higher truths. He slightly modified Nietzsche's model in *The Birth of Tragedy* and gave the opposition between Apollo and Dionysus an overtly Christian meaning. Dionysus, the source of tragic inspiration, is equated with Jesus Christ, while the Apollonian element is external, reflecting the inescapable trappings of art necessary to captivate the imagination of non-believers and take them into the higher reality of the Godhead.

In a 1916 article entitled 'Shakespeare and Cervantes', Ivanov interprets Shakespeare in the light of his hierophantic scheme:

The answer to the question about the meaning of life has been almost lost and we would in vain look for it in Shakespeare as we would in vain look for that cathartic cleansing, which, according to the ancients, should blossom in the soul of the audience at the end of tragedy; such cleansing can only be achieved on the basis of a religious synthesis of life's contradictions. Shakespeare offers no such synthesis, but postulates one . . . Shakespeare solves the problem of life by postulating his religious views in a purely tragic form, by entering madness and recognising the irrational or supra-rational beginnings in the world that surrounds us, a world which cannot ever be completely explained, since it embraces, as he tells Horatio, so much 'that is not dreamt in your philosophy'. In presenting madness, Shakespeare reveals his profoundest achievement, his transcendence of his own time's absurd [assertion] of the . . . power of the human mind . . . Hamlet's and Lear's thoughts reveal to us his spiritual work. Human life is steeped in lie and violence; in itself, it resembles a senseless sacrilegious travesty; it is a show where poor actors play out an endless bloody drama, whose peripeteia are marked by Fate, lethally slashing through its serpent knots. The moral character travels through life wrapped in heroic purity and

---

[2] Leo Tolstoy, 'What is Art', in *Tolstoy on Art*, edited by Aylmer Maude (London, 1924), p. 308.

[3] Tolstoy, 'On Shakespeare and the Drama', in *Tolstoy on Art*, p. 463.

honour; his person is incommensurate with the life, which stupefies and destroys him.[4]

For all his admiration for Shakespeare, like Tolstoy, Ivanov finds his religion incomplete in the Christian sense. His Shakespeare, however, is blessed with a metaphysical dimension lying beyond sanity and philosophy, transcending the boundaries of everyday existence, the mark of genius. Hamlet emerges as the essential christological tragic hero, who, wrapped in a mantle of purity, eyes on the beyond, faced with the task to set the times right, opens the eyes of the audience to a transcendental truth, unveils nothing less than the symbolic subtext of the absolute and brings the theatrical viewer in touch with another reality. Shakespeare's genius is thus harnessed into a typical *fin-de-siècle* idealist aesthetic agenda, positing art as the teacher of life.

In the theatre, the Shakespeare debate was enlivened not only by philosophical opinion but also by the current experimental wave. The Symbolists of the Ivanov circle were fashionable and widely influential, which affected the practice of theatres with platforms radically different from theirs.

In 1898, Konstantin Stanislavsky and Vladimir Nemirovich-Danchenko, had created the Moscow Art Theatre (MAT). Set up with the aim of accommodating the Chekhovian type of drama, MAT favoured a realist–psychological method of acting, careful attention to atmosphere, and, originally, a meticulous circumstantial realism. Depending on the play, the theatre would send designers to Italy, France or Denmark, to sketch from nature models for the sets.

In spite of the original success, the limiting nature of the naturalistic stage was sensed by Stanislavsky himself, who, by 1905 had begun to feel the pressure of the Symbolists' criticisms. Following his sound businessman's sense (it was after all the profits from his family factory that sustained the theatre), he realized the need for other approaches. He even suggested that his former student Vsevolod Meyerhold should start up a studio specializing in stylized, expressionistic acting.

The need to survive in the conditions of competition made Stanislavsky look far afield. Partly by chance, he was put in contact with Gordon Craig, who was then making his name in Germany and Italy. Their liaison engendered the 1911 *Hamlet*, which became the most influential production of the play in the pre-Soviet period. It is also of particular interest to the theatrical historian, not only because it brought into focus the aesthetic tendencies of the time, but for the significant influence it has had on the Russian tradition of dealing with the play as well.

Craig's vision of Hamlet was modelled on his own theory of monodrama, where audience reaction is manipulated by directing the attention to a single character. Similar ideas had already been aired in Russia, independently of Craig, by N. N. Evreinov and the ground for experiment in this direction had been prepared. In an early letter to Stanislavsky, Craig describes his vision of the hero: 'He is no ordinary man; his words and looks and action are so extraordinary, so superfine, that men whisper . . . that he is mad. So was Dionysus mad, Christus mad: they were Gods: here Hamlet is a man who is so full of the intoxication of love that no one can understand him.'[5]

The meticulous minutes taken at the discussions at MAT render a wealth of material on what Craig wanted Hamlet to be. The court should not be shown as it is, but as *perceived* by Hamlet. Indeed Craig wanted to keep him on stage all the time, so that the play could be shown as happening in his own mind. To achieve this effect he composed Act 1, Scene 2 as Hamlet's nightmare. The King and Queen were placed on a raised platform representing 'the feudal ladder' of subordination, with the

---

4 Ivanov, *Sobranie sochinenii*, vol. 4, pp. 103–4 (translation mine).

5 Laurence Senelick, *Gordon Craig's Moscow 'Hamlet'. A Reconstruction* (Westport, Connecticut, 1982), p. 36.

court statically arranged in descending order around them. All in lavish overlapping mantles of gold, frozen as a 'monolithic golden pyramid', they resembled 'a phantasmagorical many-headed hydra'. The effect was further enhanced by a diagonal beam of light cutting the scene in two. In a greyish-blue garment, decorated with embroidered geometric ornaments, instead of the traditional black, Hamlet stood out and outside this mass. His black wig, parted in the middle, and an ubiquitous book which he clasped 'suggested to most Russians a monk in a cassock.'[6] The contrast of stylish grey set against the gaudiness of the gold was a visual analogue of the conflict between the intellectual aesthete and the barbaric world he lived in.

Craig also envisaged a Gertrude knowing about the murder of her husband, and a beautiful but stupid Ophelia.[7]

To strengthen Hamlet's position in the play, he modelled the King as a formidable antagonist. His Claudius was, 'energetic, blunt', possessing an 'unearthly strength', an archvillain.[8] In the great public scene (1.2) Claudius's power had to be conveyed by representing his full control of the court to which he speaks like an automaton, his jaws snapping mechanically.[9] Against such an enemy Hamlet would come across as Craig wished him to be 'the first STRONG Hamlet the world has seen'.[10] His strength had to be underlined by a dignified calmness and he had to refrain from romantic shouting, since 'there is no need for Hamlet to howl, shout, get excited'[11], he is a saviour figure, and has to avoid theatrical cliché.

Craig defined three tones for the performance: abstraction for the inner experience, semirealism where the tragedy begins to develop and realism for the comic scenes.[12] The set consisting of movable pale screens of varying shades was functional in providing the level of symbolic abstraction with a visual backing by creating a non-specific, timeless ambience. In spite of this and the comparisons with Christ, Craig did not see Hamlet as a religious character in the traditional sense but rather as a brilliant

aesthete set in tragic opposition to a primitive world.

How did Stanislavsky take all this? The same minutes, which give us a glimpse of Craig, tell us that at one point he uttered in an aside: 'This is another play . . .' Yet, he agreed to go ahead with Craig's central idea. The dichotomy between a corrupt court and a Hamlet who purifies the world was in tune with his own conception and, uncannily, he had had the same vision for a cloth-of-gold scene, even before he had met Craig.

For Stanislavsky *Hamlet* was a play about mystical human experience and the impossible difficulty of one's mission to relieve the sufferings in a netherworld, while moving among the complexities of life. He further elaborated the metaphysical framework, proposed by Craig, by casting Fortinbras for the final scene as an Archangel Michael-like character, his ponderous shield slung across his shoulder, followed by a mighty troop waving spears and flags. A sea allusion brought the beginning and the end together. The sound of crashing waves, heard at the opening of the play, was transformed into a visual image in the last scene – the long wavy flags, carried by the soldiers, were piled upon the dead hero, burying him as if under a mound of white foam. They covered the 'smiling face of the great purifier of the earth who had finally discovered the secret of life in the arms of death'.[13] His triumph at the end of his Golgotha at the Court was complete.

Nemirovich-Danchenko, who, after complications with Craig began, was also involved as a director for some time, voiced strong reservations. He wrote: 'There is an obvious danger in Stanislavsky's interpretation – I don't know,

---

6 Ibid., p. 157.
7 Ibid., p. 73.
8 Ibid., p. 67.
9 Ibid., p. 157.
10 Ibid., p. 142.
11 Ibid., p. 142.
12 Ibid., p. 46.
13 Ibid., p. 173.

maybe it's Craig's – that the theatre might become a commentator . . . I am terrified of ideologies: Hamlet = Christ. This might uplift and inspire the actor, but it is alarming.'[14] Indeed, the play had been given a specific slant, but it had also been prepared with utmost respect for the text. Except for last-minute cuts called for by technical reasons, the rich suggestiveness of its poetic texture was fully preserved. The performance lasted nearly five hours and finished well after midnight on the first night.

Stanislavsky prevented major distortions of the play. To 'shade everyone else in dark colours', he said, was to turn 'all the rest of the characters into toads, buffoons' with 'nothing human'.[15] He gave a compassionate reading of Ophelia and Gertrude and his insistence on psychological coherence made Hamlet, as acted by Vladimir Kachalov, extremely appealing to the Russian audiences and critics.

At that stage, critical evaluation was mostly positive. Russia, with its mystical turn and Symbolist tastes in full swing had no problem with a saviour Hamlet. What some, like the poet Valery Bryusov found problematic, was the mixture of styles. As he put it:

A house without windows, doors and ceilings, the monochromatic denuded walls, even the stone graveyard itself with its square pillars would not have seemed strange and inappropriate, if we had seen them filled with substantially 'conventionalised' creatures, with conventionalised gestures and vocal intonations.'[16]

Yet the shrewd St Petersburg critic Alexandr Kugel saw the rich potential of the marriage of abstraction and psychological realism and their consequences for the interpretation of the play. 'The tragedy, as presented by Kachalov', he wrote, 'has no personal, and for that matter *no passionate* [my italics] nature. This is a *tragedy of lofty thought* [my italics], for which personal fate, personal problems, even the avenging of a father's death, Ophelia's destruction and a mother's dishonourable behaviour, are the core and sharp reason for revealing depths of thought

and doubt. After Kachalov, all other Hamlets seem theatrical, as if cardboard . . . All of Kachalov's attractive features, his moderation and elegant movement, the pale face, the thoughtfulness, the absent-minded, good-natured, short-sighted eyes, the nobleness of his speech, the very sound of his voice – bright, rich, melodious – have blended together in the character of Hamlet.'[17]

It is thanks to Kugel, that we have something close to a pithy definition of the twentieth-century Hamletian synthesis. The ultimate strength of Russia's hero, his greatest attraction and power, is his intellectualism. This, and his remoteness from personal problems, made him slightly larger than life and he entered history poised between the mystical and the self-assertively intellectual. The drastic visual and character oppositions, the memorable symbolic images, the mixture of abstraction and psychological realism of the 1911 Stanislavsky/Craig production proved a flexible enough model which survived more than mere changes in taste. For further history was full of unexpected turns.

About the time when this Hamlet was strutting the stage, one Vladimir Ulyanov, otherwise known as Lenin, was on his way to becoming Russia's ruler. Under him, the country would lose its name and transcendental pursuits would be viewed solely as a bourgeois weapon for the suppression of the masses.

Lenin's anti-religious and anti-aestheticist views were a leading element in his ideology. In 1913, he took the poet Maxim Gorki to task for what he considered a serious ideological lapse. In a newspaper article Gorki had suggested that the pursuit of God should be *temporarily* suspended because there were more urgent issues

14 Ibid., p. 131.
15 Ibid., p. 131.
16 Ibid., p. 180.
17 Quoted after *Shekspir i russkaya kultura* [Shakespeare and Russian Culture], edited by M. P. Alekseev, (Moscow, 1965), p. 780 (my translation).

at hand. Lenin's reaction reveals not only his ideas but his typical vicious paranoid style:

I can't believe it . . . It seems you want to suspend 'the pursuit of God' only 'temporarily' . . . Isn't this pursuit the worst form of self-denigration?? Isn't any man taken by the pursuit of God, or even only admitting the possibility of such a pursuit, his own worst self-denier, because instead of being engaged in *action* [my italics] one falls into a state of *self-contemplation* [my italics], whereby one contemplates the filthiest, stupidest, most slavish features of one's 'I', the ones most praised in the pursuit of God. Not from the personal, but from the social point of view, [this pursuit] is an act of self-indulgent self-contemplation of the stupid philistinism, molli-coddled vulgarity, dreamy self-deprecation of the philistine petty bourgeois . . .[18]

In another, later letter, also to Gorki, Lenin gave a comprehensive materialist-Leninist definition of God:

It is not true that God is a complex of ideas serving to awake and organise social feelings. This is [Bogdanovian] idealism, which covers up the material origins of ideas . . . God is (historically and socially) a complex of ideas, which have arisen from the drudgery of human oppression by external nature and class – ideas which attempt to solidify this oppression and blunt the edge of class struggle . . . At this stage of history, in Europe and Russia, any, even the finest and most well-meant defence or justification of the idea of God is a justification of the reactionaries.[19]

In the wake of an ideology which found God deficient of active materialist self-assertiveness, the likes of Tolstoy, who thought Shakespeare deficient of God, or those proffering him as a channel of transcendental illumination, like Ivanov, were doomed to condemnation or exile. After Lenin seized power in 1917, his version of materialism became law. While churches were blown up as an act of relieving social oppression, the literary and theatrical world was faced with the imperative necessity to make sense of the new aesthetics, which held that the major organizer of social feelings is class struggle. Hamlet's fortune was markedly affected by this portentous change.

Theoretical studies, which rode the new ideological wave, were quick to appear and fill the ideological vacuum. By 1923, the critic V. Volkenshtein had devised a new model of tragedy, which argued that tragic characters are strong personages whose strength is action, thus putting Lenin's imperative into practice. According to this new provision, Hamlet is strong because he acts all the time, though, alas, not always successfully. He attempts to murder the King three times, cleverly plots to corrobo-rate the revelation of the Ghost, eliminates Rosencrantz and Guildenstern, defeats Laertes in the final duel. The monologues where he accuses himself of inaction and irresolution are not to be taken at face value; they, rather, voice the dissatisfaction of a self-exacting fighter with what he has already achieved. Hamlet is cer-tainly not devout. His unwillingness to kill Claudius at prayer is a discrete and incompre-hensible scene, a mere accident.

This 'progressive' interpretation became a model for the staging of *Hamlet* by the Second Moscow Art Theatre (MAT2), in 1924.[20] Originally a studio of the old MAT, master-minded by E. Vakhtangov, it had taken on board many of the people who had worked together with Stanislavsky and Craig on the 1911 production. The celebratory volume, dedicated to its twelfth anniversary in 1924, makes it clear that there were serious worries concerning the implications of choosing Shake-speare's play. This is how the theatre tried to justify its decision in its own publication:

The very nature of the ethical problem in *Hamlet* represents the world-view of the intellectual with its inherent idealism, and is, by its philosophical concept, alien to the new vision of the world. The

---

[18] V. I. Lenin, *Za religiyata* [On Religion], (Sofia, 1957), pp. 40–2 (my translation).
[19] Lenin, *Za religiyata*, p. 45 (my translation).
[20] Quoted after Lev Semenovich Vygotosky, *The Psychology of Art*, Introduced by A. N. Leontiev, commentary by V. V. Ivanov (Cambridge, MA, 1971), p. 172.

cruel duality and mysticism, which permeate the tragedy, are remote and alien to the progressive revolutionary generation! This gesturing towards *Hamlet* could have badly damaged the theatre's reputation as an institution orientated to contemporary reality.[21]

It seems that the old Tolstoyan moralism had crept up from under the rubble of history disguised as political expedience. The only question was reformulated as, 'Is Shakespeare right for our time?' MAT2 was a major experimental venue. As with many other pre-revolutionary establishments, it had hailed the political overturn as an encouragement for further experiment. Was not the revolution itself the breaking of fresh ground? This naive belief was soon crushed by reality.

The tone of the three directors, V. Smyshlyaev, V. Tatarinov and A. Cheban, suggests that they were strongly conscious of the explosiveness of the situation and took all precautions to explain their concept in the light of the new expectations, a task which was far from easy. They define their approach as an exploration of only one side of Hamlet's character, not surprisingly, 'the protesting, heroic, fighting' side of his character, perceived as relevant to the moment.[22] In search of this new Hamlet, as they admit, they 'had to shorten considerably the text of the tragedy and eliminate from it all that could possibly interfere with the whirl of events . . . As early as the middle of the second act Hamlet takes up his sword and does not let go of it until the end of the tragedy . . .' 'We have also underscored Hamlet's activity by condensing all the obstacles, which he encounters in his path. He was our guideline in the treatment of the King and all the other characters . . . King Claudius personifies everything that attempts to thwart the heroic Hamlet . . . To highlight the shades and colour of the play we found it necessary to transfer the action to the Middle Ages . . .'[23]

Much of what the directors tried to do would have been to Craig's liking. Indeed, MAT2 was putting to yet another test the idea of *Hamlet* as

a monodrama, as well as some of the basic principles of his concept. All this however, had been done at a considerable expense to the text, with a clear political aim.

This post-revolutionary Hamlet, acted by Mikhail Chekhov, was an active, but rather erratic hero. The directors imagined him, to use Lenin's words, as relieved of 'the filthiest, stupidest, most slavish features of one's 'I', the ones most praised in the pursuit of God', the spiritual image of new humanity. Yet, stylistically, he was steeped in abstraction, which could be read as a search for a mystical rather than political truth in spite of the fervent claims.

In the strongly distorted play, evil towered out of proportion, epitomized by the King, clad in a Japanese-style medieval military costume. Polonius was a mask of 'a hateful, cunning, servile and cruel courtier',[24] Gertrude had a 'pale, drawn expression' behind which lurked 'a fierce temperament.'[25] The characters were set against each other in a kind of psychomachia, their faces frozen in exaggerated, strained, mask-like expressions. The set suggested the vast inside of a church where light seeped through stained-glass windows creating a mysterious out-of-time atmosphere. The Craigian pyramid of power was also there. Hamlet's determination to kill the usurper was underlined by the way he always kept to his sword. The fixedness of the mask was straightforwardly aggressive, but also deadeningly restrictive and morbid.

This production belongs to a line of attempts to minimize and modify the presence of the supernatural on the Soviet stage. His face contorted, Mikhail Chekhov's Hamlet 'as if in a

---

21 *Moskovskii hudozhestvennii teatr vtoroi* [Moscow Art Theatre Two] (Moscow, 1925), pp. 32–3 (translation of all further quotations mine).

22 Vygotosky, *The Psychology of Art*, p. 172.

23 Ibid.

24 *Moskovskii hudozhestvennii teatr vtoroi*, p. 43.

25 Ibid., pp. 40–2.

trance, whispered the speech of his father's ghost'.[26] In spite of the fervent assertions of the directors, the production was considered ideal-istic, steeped in mysticism and pessimism, out of touch with reality, focused on incomprehen-sible 'other worlds' which seemed accessible only to the hero.[27]

The general tendency to schematization gave secondary characters, such as Marcellus, Horatio, the gravediggers, more prominence, a tendency that was to grow in the following years. The stylized eclecticism of MAT2, though ideologically reaching for the radical, was mostly disapproved of by Soviet critics. However, productions of this kind marked the direction in which the interpretation of the play would go. 'The Soviet cut' of *Hamlet* focused on several basic situations, taking as the play's central theme the lines: 'Time is out of joint; O, cursed spite / That ever I was born to set it right.' This, in the words of Marco Mincoff, is 'the single tag' for 'those whose interest centres on social reform',[28] a focus, not invalid, but, if abused, potentially reductive.

The way ahead traversed the unforeseen dangers of ideological pressure and political recriminations of unimaginable scope. The 1930s set in motion the nightmarish mincing machine of Stalinist reprisals. Fear ruled the lives of millions. In conditions of excessive ideo-logical pressure, directors desperately groped for ways of bringing their productions close to safe political platforms and tuned carefully into the latest news spread by the Party press.

In this atmosphere, in 1932, the Moscow Vakhtangov Theatre mounted N. P. Akimov's production of *Hamlet*. The director did his best to subscribe to a political agenda and declare war on idealism, again by massively cutting the play in the already familiar fashion. His Hamlet's one and only aim is starkly political: to come to the throne. He and his friend Horatio are astute spin-doctors, authors of the Ghost hoax, needed to captivate the imagination of the simpler characters and attract them to their side. Hamlet himself played the trick by speaking into an

earthen jar, which amplified and threateningly distorted his voice.[29]

The monologue 'To be or not to be' was given a new, so far unforeseen meaning. It was rehashed into a dialogue between Horatio and Hamlet, where Hamlet toyed with a metal pot, putting it on and taking it off as a mock crown, his ironically played dilemma being to become a king or not.[30] References to 'fear after death', 'dream of death', 'pale cast of thought', and the list of iniquities borne by mankind were erased.

This was supposedly a Hamlet close to the new times, about whom there was no religious nonsense, no idealistic dithering over uncertain-ties. All speeches where characters refer to the beyond, God, or moral compunction, such as Claudius at prayer, consideration of suicide, the graveyard scene with Yorick's skull, etc., were removed. What mattered was the political con-flict, which devoured and dominated all others.

In spite of its correctness on the matters of religion, the production was criticized for debasing with gimmicks the stature of the fighter for social right, and for erasing some of the pithiest phrases of social criticism to be found in the play. Akimov's operation on the text, though pointedly political, had missed the chance of suggesting the horrors of the world Hamlet lived in and, in this way, hinting at the happiness of the circumstances in which his audience was living. He had also reduced Hamlet to someone pursuing his own interest, not a cause larger than a throne. In the idiom of the times, this was a major lack of realism.[31] The Great Heroes, institutionalized by the

[26] Sergei Yutkevich, *Shekspir i kino* [Shakespeare and the Cinema] (Moscow, 1973), p. 38 (translation mine).

[27] Sofya Nels, *Shekspir na Sovetskoi stsene* [Shakespeare on the Soviet Stage], (Moscow, 1960), p. 58 (all transla-tions from Nels mine).

[28] Marco Mincoff, *A History of English Literature from the Beginnings to the Close of the Seventeenth Century*, 2 vols. (Sofia, 1970), vol. 1, p. 370.

[29] Yutkevich, *Shekspir i kino*, p. 38

[30] Nels, *Shekspir na Sovetskoi stsene*, p. 288

[31] Ibid., pp. 58–64; 288.

system, such as Hamlet, had to be treated with respect.

Akimov's production appeared at a moment when considerations of aesthetic quality were becaming more prominent, as the 1930s shook off the last remains of Proletkult organizational structures together with the 'fellow travellers', as the non-party writers were called. All art and literature were brought into the fold of socialist realism. In the same year, 1932, at the First Congress of Soviet Writers, the newly defined method of Soviet literature and art was proclaimed.[32]

Four ideas stand out as its basic tenets: realism, populism, historicism and class. To define what these terms meant in relation to *Hamlet* and Shakespeare, who had entered into the list of the progressive Great Precursors of Communism, was the task of anointed critics.

In the theatre, the first of these terms, realism, little by little came to be identified with Stanislavskian psychological and circumstantial realism. Populist requirements were also satisfied by Stanislavskian principles. Ensemble work and attention to the delineation of smaller personages, the impressive handling of crowd scenes, were all useful in underlining 'the role of the people' in plays from any period. As Soviet criticism focused on Shakespeare's realism and populism, their stage version in the Russian tradition was equated with the MAT acting style. As a consequence, other forms of theatrical expression were suppressed for a long time.

Historicism was a harder nut to crack. Some directors responded to this requirement by experimenting with lightly constructed stages in the style of the Elizabethan theatre. At the important 1939 Moscow Shakespeare Conference, a biannual gathering of theorists, critics and directors, a production of *Twelfth Night* was attacked for its 'primitive' methods, which did not give a clear sense of location but for minor changes in detail.[33] A process of trial and error slowly licked into shape the concept of the 'historical' stage, as opposed to the naturalistic and the symbolist, basically as a mixture of the

two, with predominant elements of the former. As for the Elizabethan stage and the exploration of its potential, criticism soon made it clear that the latter type should be avoided.

A History of West-European Theatre, published in 1941, influentially argues that the seventeenth-century stage was blatantly unrealistic, and, since boys played women, the drama of characters, especially the female ones, could not be adequately conveyed. To the critics, it was perfectly clear that Shakespeare did not write for this rather backward stage, for 'contemporary acting was way below the standard of his dramaturgy'. Another inadequacy foisted upon the Elizabethan theatre was its alleged tendency to omit most statements of social criticism, which explains Shakespeare's own critical attitude to the theatre. It is taken for granted that audiences were not allowed to reach into the depth of the poet's philosophy and his social critique.[34] Only the new Soviet stage could adequately take care of these deficiencies. Shakespeare had at last found his true home.

Thus, in the 1930s and 1940s, Soviet Hamlet was finally born in the monitored dialogue between stage and criticism. Invariably, he was strong and had one clearly defined task: to fight social iniquity. This made him a friend of the people. From his predecessors he had inherited a visionary intellect and since no mystic power lurked behind his prophetic mind, it became emblematic of quintessentially self-sufficient humanity. He inhabited a somewhat diffuse historic past, which safely locked him in

---

32 Alexander Shurbanov and Boika Sokolova, *Painting Shakespeare Red: An East-European Appropriation* (Delaware, 2001), especially chapter 3, pp. 83–114.

33 This was V. M. Ipatov's production at the Irkutsk Theatre where the stage contained 'a mere table and a bed, two chairs and two screens' as reported by Nels, *Shakespeare in the Soviet Theatre*, p. 75.

34 A. Djivelegov and G. Boyadjiev, *Istoriya zapadnoevropeiskogo teatra ot vozniknoveniya do 1789* [A History of West European Theatre from the Beginning to 1789] (Moscow, 1941), p. 253, quoted by Nels, *Shekspir na Sovetskoi stsene*, p. 72.

previous history. He was allowed to plunge into some well-controlled doubt only to underline the triumph of his final resolution. The carefully doctored scripts from which he spoke suggested, among other things, that conscience is not religion-based. Stanislavskian acting never failed this Hamlet, though, in the long run, it became stultifying. What he was not allowed to do was to address the present.

The years after Stalin's death in 1953 and Nikita Khruschev's revelations of Stalinist atrocities before the Twentieth Congress of the Communist Party of the Soviet Union in 1956 brought in a breath of fresh air. They not only ushered a new generation into the cultural scene but also sustained a brief hope for a liberalization of cultural life. The parts of Central and Eastern Europe, which had been added to the Soviet empire after the war, showed the first strong signs of resistance, which were ruthlessly suppressed. However, by 1960 the dramatic practice in many East-European countries had swerved from pre-scribed models. Versions of *Hamlet* pointed the lines of social criticism in the play towards the world around the theatre, focusing on its sub-versive potential. In 1961, Jan Kott published *Shakespeare Our Contemporary*, which by 1964 had appeared in English and French. His grim view of history as a repetitive cycle of senseless violence, supported by current theatrical prac-tices, became a challenge to the optimistic message propounded by socialist realism.

Suspended between the hopes and fears of this period are the best *Hamlets* of the socialist-realist tradition in the Soviet Union. The most notable of them, Grigory Kozintsev's 1964 film, transcends the model, which it completely absorbs and reworks, by grafting onto it ele-ments of the Stanislavsky/Craig legacy. Interest-ingly, in *The Space of Tragedy*, the director denies consciously evoking or even thinking of the earlier production at the time when he started shooting the film, yet discloses a con-sciousness of his profound internalization of Craig's designs.[35]

Kozintsev had first staged the play in 1954, at the Leningrad Pushkin Dramatic Theatre, a production which turned into a blueprint for the film. The theme, as defined by critics, was the clash between two worlds. To achieve such 'a historicist-materialist point of view on the problems of Shakespeare's time',[36] the director had taken serious liberties with the text. He had brought forward the popular theme by introdu-cing a silent scene in which 'the people' showed their compassion for Hamlet's loss and by including them in Laertes's rebellion. Claudius's narrow-mindedness was in sharp contrast with the hero's intelligence. Hamlet's prominence was achieved by cutting down on Fortinbras and Ophelia; Gertrude was evil. The hero, played by B. Freindlikh, was serious, collected, rational. The shape of the play, as well as some of the character interpretation, strongly recalls the 1911 production, though the effects were achieved by a more drastic operation. Accents were reshuffled so that Act 3, Scene 2, where Hamlet taunts Rosencrantz and Guildenstern to play the recorder, acquired a climactic position.

Kozintsev's approach to the stage business too, novel as it was in the realist context, is strongly reminiscent of the earlier production. He combined the mandatory circumstantial realism with powerful symbols. Black funeral flags at the opening created a sombre atmo-sphere, uncannily reversing elements of the ending of the 1911 production. A sea crashed in the background. The heavy sculpted mass of Elsinore's towers framed the stage and suggested the material solidity of power. They were so different from the light pale screens of Craig's design, and at the same time so similarly sug-gestive of the nature of the conflict. Craig's hero was offered escape into an airy beyond, Kozintsev's, was to stay enclosed in an oppres-sive materiality of subdued, leaden, colours.

---

[35] G. Kozintsev, '*King Lear*': *The Space of Tragedy. The Diary of a Film Director*, trans. by M. Mackintosh (London, 1977), p. 155.

[36] Nels, *Shekspir na Sovetskoi stsene*, p. 292.

A clock, with little figures coming out on the stroke of the hour to play an allegory of life and death, and a figure of the Goddess of Victory, Nike of Samothrace, which stood in Hamlet's book-filled study, served as two contrapuntal symbolic foci. In the final scene, as Hamlet lay dead, a beam lit the striking clock, which played its repetitive drama while the image of the Goddess of Victory rose above the hero in an optimistic finale. By excluding Fortinbras, this ending further narrowed the focus on the protagonist, whose legacy was communicated to the audience in the words of Sonnet 74.

Some of these elements Kozintsev brought to the film, where he could give full scope to his pictorial imagination. The somewhat indefinite Danish world belongs to a past on the verge of Christianity. The monochromatic film and the slow pace of the action throw into sharp relief the dynamic features of Hamlet's character and enhance the impact of the ensuing violence. As in the theatre production, Kozintsev used Boris Pasternak's translation, which takes liberties with the original, obliterates some of the decorative and bawdy aspects of the language and gives a profound seriousness to the text.

The costumes are a mixture of strictly historical ones and others which were historical in contour rather than in detail.[37] The Ghost's presence is carefully reduced to one, though mighty, visual encounter and the text in 1.5 is cut so that all references to purgatory, or a heaven to be entered with one's reckoning made, or a power which will pass judgement on Gertrude, are removed. The ghost is a pagan force, come back to seek its right, without imposing moral limitations on the son. Hamlet's references to God are also dramatically minimized. To give only one example of many: in 1.2, the little that remains of his speeches elides 'the everlasting', 'God' or meeting 'one's dearest foe in heaven'. The only religious outburst in the film belongs to Claudius, and is provoked by fear. Nor is it composed as a prayer proper by kneeling at an altar. The King rather considers his chances to obtain a pardon only to

find that he is not up to it. Hamlet is not present, and as a consequence, does not have to consider his actions in a religious context. The only altar ever seen is the one where Laertes pledges silently to avenge his father's death and the only priest is the one who refuses to give Ophelia full funeral rites.

Religious reference was not the sole element, which Kozintsev suppressed. His approach was also monodramatic, which resulted in a major slashing of parts: Ophelia, Gertrude, Horatio, Marcellus, Bernardo, the players, the gravediggers are consigned about one-third of their text. Gertrude is not a traitor to her son and, though Ophelia is left with few words, her treatment as a fragile girl, mercilessly turned into a mechanical plaything, is profoundly moving.

To make up for the loss of popular voices, well-controlled mass scenes were introduced, where a sad people in rags watches the ravages of a bloody history played without its participation. Kozintsev strengthened the popular level by turning Fortinbras into a general who marches along with his foot soldiers and an admirer of Hamlet. The way he draws the curtain over the tragic scene promises the rule of decency, which Hamlet would have offered 'had he been put on', and negates the Claudian greed for power. He is the right man brought to the fore by the objective powers of history, corroborating the Marxist thesis of the logic of its workings.

The spirituality of Kozintsev's reading does not depend on God, but originates in the active qualities of the hero played by Innokentii Smoktunovsky, whose magnificently controlled performance shuns emotionalism. Hamlet's 'explosive force of thought'[38] sets the pace of the action and forms the danger threatening Claudius' government. Unflinching intellectualism, not splashes of Stanislavskian psychology,

---

[37] Kozintsev, *Shakespeare: Time and Conscience* (London, 1967), p. 235.

[38] Ibid., p. 250.

is for the audience the sole guide through the shapeless crumbling dungeon of Denmark whose doors, windows and walls are spying holes.[39] Thought, like the sea and the open air, is beyond the reach of the crushing stone grasp of Elsinore. Uniquely, Kozintsev's hero dies in the open, the sea crashing at his feet, a solitary gull gliding freely away.

On the level of symbol, this ending is much richer than that of the theatre production, while still remaining a statement of hard-earned optimism. However, the climate in which the film appeared suspended this optimistic image on the edge of another, modern, truth. Hamlet could be seen not as the mandatory victor in a struggle of olden times, but as the ultimate Soviet intellectual, destroyed but undefeated, both a solitary and a public figure lying before the eyes of the stunned nation. Such is the elusive nature of symbols.

How fragile any hope for freedom was, was soon proved by events. In October 1964, a few months after the release of the film, an in-party coup toppled Nikita Khruschev and brought to power Leonid Brezhnev who restored the Stalinist principles of government in a modified form. Almost ten years into Brezhnev's rule, in 1973, Kozintsev thought of another finale for his film – armed men take all the important points in the kingdom; Fortinbras settles in Claudius's study; the frightened ministers crawl out of their hiding places; breaking the lock of Claudius's filing cabinet with his knife Fortinbras casually asks where the scene of the accident is, then, looking absent-mindedly through the window, orders Hamlet's funeral.[40]

Such an ending would have given us a different, Kottian, *Hamlet*. Yet, back in 1964, Kozintsev blended the visionary Russian hero and the Soviet fighter against social evil into something uniquely his own and of his own

time, a synthesis that has given us the masterpiece we have. Though, as any great artist, he was led by his own instinct and experience, Kozintev himself recognized the liberating influence of Craig when in *The Space of Tragedy* he wrote:

While I was still a boy, I was astounded by Craig's sketches; space, devoid of any recognizable landmarks, the unification of the emptiness of night and the coldness of ice, sea mist in which anything can be imagined. Lonely figures in the midst of unfamiliar worlds of stone. There is not one detail, not one feature which you can grasp onto in order to find your way to that place, so strongly does the void beckon you . . . Craig was the first to insist that Shakespeare's tragedies are concerned not only with human passions and the relations between the main characters in the plays, but first and foremost, with the conflict of some sort of mighty visual powers; you cannot restrict the poetry within the confines of the subject matter, it goes far beyond those bounds – it is a whole universe.[41]

History had gone full circle – from Stanislavsky and Craig to Kozintsev, from Kachalov to Smoktunovsky, whether with eyes set on the beyond, or on 'the oppressor's wrong', the great Russian Hamlets of the twentieth century carry in themselves the painful knot of 'the very age and body of the time his form and pressure'. As for the 'angels and ministers of grace', in later history they mostly had to take their chances.[42]

---

[39] Ibid., p. 25.

[40] Mark Sokolyansky, *Perechitivaya Shekspira* [Re-reading Shakespeare] (Odessa, 2000), p. 167, has reminded me of this idea of Kozintsev's, for which, as well as for his book, I am grateful.

[41] Kozintsev, '*King Lear*': *The Space of Tragedy*, pp. 155–7.

[42] I wish to thank Dr Carol Rutter for much kindness, helpful advice and her love for Ophelia. See Carol Chillington Rutter, *Enter the Body: Women and Representation on Shakespeare's Stage* (London, 2001).

OF SHADOWS AND STONES: REVERING AND TRANSLATING 'THE WORD' SHAKESPEARE IN MEXICO

ALFREDO MICHEL MODENESSI

Para Sarah, alma mía

Jan Kott recalls in *Aloes* that, during one of his many encounters with Peter Brook, the British director was very excitedly discussing what the shadow (or ghost) of Hamlet's father should do to an audience. After insisting 'this ghost must make you shiver with fear, it must', Brook showed Kott a pair of stone figurines – small reproductions of 'demons from Sumatra' – and asked: 'Don't they make you afraid?' They didn't, says Kott; actually, they looked a bit ridiculous. But then,

Peter turned out the lights and placed the larger figure against a window so that it cast a long shadow in the middle of the room. Then he aimed a lamp from another direction. The figure, the shadow, grew in stature; its head was horrible; the shadow was terrifying and disgusting. I shivered. I started to feel afraid.[1]

Despite its evident emphasis on religion and mind (on providence, doubt, scepticism, procrastination, and the like), to me, *Hamlet* is Shakespeare's most provocative engagement with *shadows* – the *darkest* shadows. For the shades, dreams, images and ghosts that appear in other plays seem less dense, less obscure and threatening when compared to the shadows that populate Elsinore. Every character in *Hamlet* becomes a shadow, or the shadow of another. Following Shakespeare's own example, it is possible to say that the characters of *Hamlet* are *translated* into shadows: Hamlet senior stalks Hamlet junior as much as Polonius shadows

him and orders Ophelia to play a similar game, while Hamlet drops in on Claudius, who has Polonius, Rosencrantz *and* Guildenstern play the clownish detectives shadowing Hamlet's every move, and so on. Above drinking, incest and procrastination, prying into somebody else's business seems to be the favourite sport in Shakespeare's rotten Denmark. Additionally, this process also translates us, the spectators of *Hamlet*, into universal busybodies.

Of course, this obsessive mutual shadowing does not merely amount to the silly description above. At one important level, it has to do with the very Shakespearian problem of the old not letting go of their grip on the young. Hamlet senior haunts Hamlet junior rather conspicuously, but he is certainly not the only one (or *thing*) keeping a jealous hold on those underneath. Everything that is young in this play is one way or another the object of a

This paper derives from a lecture delivered at the Symposium 'Hamlet and the Mind' held at the University of New Mexico in April 1999, and includes material from a paper presented at the 1997 SAA seminar 'Critical Contexts for *As You Like It*', as well as information from an entry forthcoming in the *Oxford Companion to Shakespeare Studies*, edited by Stanley Wells and Michael Dobson. My gratitude to Barry Gaines, Christy Desmet, Fran Teague, Ton Hoenselaars, Inga-Stina Ewbank, Peter Holland, Maria Sten, Lucas Gómez, Gilberto Jerónimo and Juan Carlos Arvide.

[1] Jan Kott, 'Encuentros', *La Jornada Semanal*, 11 November 1998, translated into Spanish by Maria Sten and Alfredo Michel Modenessi, pp. 4–5 (my translation into English).

profound desire of control by the old, and ends up either materially or spiritually destroyed. In turn, the young one who is not destroyed seems to be the least shadowy of all, a sort of stone god, an inevitability that, given the demise of mind, arrives to rule as pure substance over a stage now populated by the freshly dead flesh and blood of those who had earlier turned into shadows – or, to go back to my original proposition, who had been translated.

Translation is but a shadow of literature, some say. And I agree: doubtless, the ephemeral nature of translation is its greatest asset. But this fact is frequently misinterpreted, and at times makes some others wish that the 'substance' of literature kept a stern, Hamlet-senior-type of hold on translations. Still, translating literature remains a dynamic endeavour in so far as it makes no claims at permanence but constitutes a testimony of cultural exchange *and change*. Although often targeted by criticism that seeks to constrain its universe of textual and performative choices – mostly in the name of 'faithfulness' – translation remains fairly unconfined, free to try, discard, or apply a variety of solutions to the problems of artistic realization posed by the multiple energies[2] inscribed in the source texts *within* particular space–time frames. When all is done, the shadow remains difficult to keep under cultural control. This, in turn, makes translating a search for *otherness* through affinity and not a search for *identity* with respect to the source text – or the source culture, for that matter. Translation is, or so I prefer to think of it, a performative art, then: an interpretive actualization of shadows in permanent, critical and creative contingency with its sources.

I will not strictly focus on issues arising directly from the dramatist's complex inter-action with religion, doubtless crucial to the task of translating his works. Instead, I have chosen (an ambitious notion) to write from an alternative understanding of the subject 'Shakespeare and Religions'. As suggested in my title, I wish to present some ideas con-cerning the specific significance and impact of 'the Word' Shakespeare as an object of reverence in Mexico and, ultimately, in Latin America.

Translating whatever 'the Word' Shakespeare may signify in/to Spanish-speaking Latin America involves important issues concomitant to the process of 'translation proper',[3] especially if we consider that, in a region where Spanish *and* English coexist as [post?]colonial languages, translating Shakespeare entails not only bringing him/it into Spanish but also into *other* cultures and *other* literatures, often but not always expressing themselves *in* or *through* Spanish. In my view, therefore, translating Shakespeare in such a context demands regarding and under-taking translation as a way to deal with the *other(s)* in mutually creative – as opposed to suppressive or repressive – ways, which in turn requires considering what Shakespeare evokes and provokes in our context beyond strictly linguistic or restrictively 'literary' boundaries. Three examples, I hope, will serve to suggest why translating this revered word demands special awareness from the Spanish-speaking Latin-American translator.

The history of Shakespeare in Spanish goes back only to 1772. The first Spanish Shakespeare ever was (inevitably?) a version of *Hamlet*, by Ramón de la Cruz. His was not a direct translation, however, but a derivative of Ducis' translation into French. Hence, the first direct version of Shakespeare into Spanish was, yes, a *Hamlet* translated in 1798 by 'Inarco Celenio', the rather ugly pen-name then used by Leandro Fernández de Moratín. Since our cultural history is indissolubly tied to Spain, the history

---

[2] I am thinking of the word as employed by Stephen Greenblatt in *Shakespearean Negotiations* (Los Angeles, 1988), p. 3.

[3] Or 'Interlingual translation', as defined by Roman Jakobson: 'On linguistic aspects of translation', in Reuben Brower ed., *On Translation* (Cambridge, Mass., 1959), p. 233.

of Shakespeare in Spanish-speaking Latin America is roughly as old.

Whether in English, or in French or Italian translations, or in the few but steadily growing Spanish versions available, a handful of Shakespeare plays were known in Latin America immediately before and at the beginning of the independent era. In Argentina and Uruguay productions began as early as the mid-1810s (some translated and staged by Luis Morante, who later worked in Chile), while in Mexico the first play ever produced was, of course, *Hamlet*, in 1821. As a cultural token of our shaky independence, throughout the nineteenth century productions by European companies were relatively frequent – mainly Spanish, although a cross-gendered Italian *Hamlet* played by Giacinta Pezzana successfully toured the subcontinent in 1878. Among the Spaniards who staged Shakespeare in Mexico, Leopoldo Burón produced two different versions of *Hamlet*, the first in 1880, the second in 1886; it is worth noting that the latter was translated by the local writers Manuel Pérez and Francisco López, one of the earliest native versions to enjoy a favourable response from Mexican audiences and critics.

In the first half of the twentieth century, interest in other plays grew. In 1903 Emilio Thuillier staged *The Taming of the Shrew*, perhaps for the first time in Mexico, and in 1924 the Argentine company of Vittore-Pomar produced a *Tempest* that would tour every major city in our sub-continent south to north. In the following decades *Hamlet*, *Othello*, *Macbeth*, and *King Lear* continued to be frequently staged, but other plays – e.g. *A Midsummer Night's Dream*, *The Merchant of Venice*, *The Tempest* – began to attract Latin-American theatre-makers and theatregoers with an appeal that is yet to cease. Unsurprisingly, in the second half of the twentieth century Shakespeare has been a favourite with the professional, community, and middle and higher education theatres.

Most translations of Shakespeare in Spanish-speaking Latin America, however, remain the unpublished – and often undocumented – result of performative need rather than the outcome of editorial projects; in fact, an overwhelming majority of Mexican productions still rely on translations made in Spain, whether slightly or thoroughly adapted.[4] Perhaps the only systematic effort to translate and publish Shakespeare in Spanish-speaking Latin America is the 'Proyecto Shakespeare' of the Universidad Nacional Autónoma de México (UNAM), which aims at issuing the entire canon in individual volumes, introduced and annotated. Since 1982, sixteen plays have been released, thirteen of which are the work of María Enriqueta González Padilla, head of the project;[5] two more are finished and either awaiting printing or being prepared for publication,[6] and another three are in progress.[7]

While the academic aims and standards for UNAM's 'Proyecto Shakespeare' are made clear in its basic document,[8] policies for actual translation are nowhere overtly stated. Instead, the versions published so far reflect a tacit subscription of the unwritten and widely applied rule that rendering Shakespeare into Spanish 'naturally' demands the use of European Spanish norms and forms with a somewhat

---

4 For instance, among the many plays by Shakespeare staged in Mexico City during the past five years or so, only two have been expressly commissioned to Mexican translators, of which only one is programmed for publication. The rest were adapted mainly from Luis Astrana Marín's standard edition of Shakespeare's 'Complete Works' into Spanish (Madrid, 1929).

5 *Richard II*, *1Henry IV*, *2Henry IV*, *Richard III*, *The Winter's Tale*, *The Merchant of Venice*, *Julius Caesar*, *Coriolanus*, *King Lear*, *The Tempest*, *A Midsummer Night's Dream*, *Romeo and Juliet*, *Macbeth*, and *Hamlet*. The other two are *Twelfth Night* by Federico Patán, and *Timon of Athens* by Marcel Sisniega.

6 María Enriqueta González Padilla's *Othello* and my version of *Love's Labour's Lost*.

7 *Measure for Measure* by Marcel Sisniega, *As You Like It* by Gabriel Linares, and my version of *Henry V*.

8 María Enriqueta González Padilla, 'Noticia sobre el *Proyecto Shakespeare*', typed ms, 1994 (my copy revised and updated 2000).

archaic colour. For the Mexican readers, theatre-makers, and audiences, then, the UNAM volumes do not constitute a distinct alternative to the better-known, less expensive, and more effectively marketed versions from Spain. None of the translations published to date have been used on the Mexican stage, despite the fact that they might serve the conventional purposes as efficiently as the more popular Spanish versions. Conversely, only one, as yet unpublished, originated as a translation specifically commissioned for the Mexican stage. This version has provoked a small controversy which may illustrate how this project – as well as many other Latin American versions of Shakespeare in Spanish – is not free from 'revering the Word' in ways that favour, perhaps inadvertently, a concept of translation seeking an evidently impossible (and pointless) identity with the source texts and the cultural assumptions that gravitate around them from both their English and Spanish ends.[9] Such reverence, consequently, does not favour translations aiming at otherness through affinity, which, I believe, could be more interesting in the context of post-colonial Latin America.

To illustrate further, allow me to introduce the hypothetical case of someone in Latin America translating *As You Like It*. To begin at the beginning, a title would be required, even if only a 'working' one. And to add a bit of critical thinking, this observation could be brought into play:

[Shakespeare's comedies] are powered by their commitment to unfolding forms of life liberated from whatever forbids the free play and shared satisfaction of justified desires. . . . [The titles of the comedies] alert us to the fact that the plays, which they describe, occupy a privileged realm beyond the reach of the attitudes that ordinarily programme and discipline people's lives.[10]

Now, the title by which most Latin Americans know *As You Like It* is *A vuestro gusto*, recognizably the choice, though not the coinage, of Luis Astrana Marín, a Spaniard

whose long endeavour spans across the early twentieth century. In our Spanish-speaking world, this title has become a historical reference, an authority, maybe even a version of 'the thing itself'. There is a reason for this: Astrana Marín remains the only translator in the Spanish language to have written versions of the entire canon – i.e. the canon that was in his time, including the poems – albeit all in prose.[11] Since the publication of his 'Complete Works', all over the Spanish-speaking world his texts have often been the automatic choice of general readers and literature teachers; of crooked publishers looking for versions to plagiarize; of theatre performers whom habit, lack of interest in textual nuances, or low budgets have kept from obtaining more appropriate or specific versions; and, yes, even of translators looking for help.

A sort of reaction against this dominance in Spain may be construed from the title employed, say, by the team from the Shakespeare Foundation of Valencia. Their rendering

---

[9] Since the actual controversy involved my translation of *Love's Labour's Lost*, I would rather deal with it in this note. Although I was asked to write a version of the play (and later, a very liberal adaptation) specifically for the stage, my first draft was made with both the performers' and the readers' needs in mind. More importantly, however, I pointedly avoided the use of European Spanish norms and the usual conventions of 'colour' from the start, something I had earlier done with Marlowe's *Edward II* for similar ends, and I am currently applying to *Henry V*. Needless to say, my work reflects a conscious search for otherness that caused some doubts with regard to its inclusion in UNAM's collection. The case is now settled and my version will be published as soon as I finish writing the prologue and notes, provided that a certain issue, which will become more relevant below, is finally cleared.

[10] Kiernan Ryan, *Shakespeare* (London, 1995), pp. 110, 112.

[11] Astrana Marín's versions were also published in individual volumes by Espasa-Calpe. That collection is currently being replaced with the outstanding translations into verse by Ángel Luis Pujante. To be fair, mention must also be made of the work of José María Valverde, who likewise translated the complete plays into prose, though not the poems.

of *As You Like It* as *Como gustéis* suggests a possibly conscious effort to shun Astrana Marín's authority, a kind of statement of differentiation, even if within the same cultural context there seems to be little contrast between the two titles.[12] On the other hand – that is, on the other shore of the Atlantic – this issue probably demands a more complex approach. Here the mechanical adoption of a Spaniard's choice for the title of *As You Like It* automatically binds the entire process to the use of European Spanish norms in denial of native linguistic, cultural and literary history – let alone creative writing.

In the titles cited above, the use of an exclusively European Spanish second person plural (which also applies to the archaic formal second person singular) is definitive: '*vuestro*', '*gustéis*'. In Latin America there is not one form of actual use of this second person plural, although almost everyone in our schools *learns* to conjugate according to European norms; that is, nearly all Latin American users of Spanish are enabled to read and understand European Spanish from early in their lives, and hence, to receive texts written thus as 'naturally' as their own, something that does not quite apply the other way around.[13] This, I believe, though simple, should not be deemed trivial, for it is only a token of numerous differences, extending to other markers of address, verb tense variations, vocabulary, rhythms of speech, and so on. A hypothetical Latin-American *As You Like It* starting with a title bearing exclusively European Spanish markers would be entirely affected by such a non-choice, I insist, since to begin by adopting those norms in the title would imply a resort to them automatically, and perhaps to fake archaism, everywhere, contradicting a critical stance aware and in favour of de-centring.[14]

Other, more practical, objections may also be made. Mexican, Spanish, Uruguayan and Cuban actors, for instance, employ very different rhythms of speech and verse-delivery in their individual interpretations; moreover,

due to radical differences in pronunciation, the training and the mature formation of their vocal organs will be quite different, even if, given the occasion, they might adapt to need and circumstance; and finally, a performer confronting a fundamentally alien text is always under greater pressure to meet additional demands, and consequently at risk of dividing his concentration between creative and pointlessly mechanical tasks. Thus, if the Latin-American translator begins by thinking of his text as ruled by Astrana Marín's or another Spaniard's title, he will be renouncing his own and his primary receivers' Spanish in favour of a close, yes, but clearly alien one.

An alternative approach to translating Shakespeare in, from, and for Latin America could consist in stimulating detachment from the languages and cultures of power – from *any* of them, that is. A Latin-American translator could adopt an alternative, critically post-colonial, approach and look for ways to temper and foreground his/her experience and practice of the received tongue by means of preventing

---

12 It may be interesting to note that *Como gustéis* is also Ángel Luis Pujante's choice.
13 The notable exception to this may be found in the Canary Islands, which were colonized around the same time as our countries and have a long history of exchange with Latin America. Their norms *and conditions of textual reception and production* are practically the same as ours.
14 What remains to be solved concerning my version of *Love's Labour's Lost* is precisely that I have been asked to consider publishing it not under the name that I gave it, *El vano afán del amor*, but as *Trabajos de amor perdidos* – Astrana Marín's title. Moreover, his was the title originally appearing on posters, newspaper inserts, and playbills. After a while, *both* titles were advertised, separated by a slash, and something similar was done in the latest update of 'Noticia sobre el *Proyecto Shakespeare*'. My opinion was not requested in either case, though my objections were evidently considered. I will not accept publication under any other title but my own, of course, and this will undoubtedly be accepted. By the way, the case of *As You Like It* is a bit less hypothetical than I would like it to be. The translator now in charge will use the title *Como gustéis* – fittingly.

total assimilation of the pragmatic content of the source text into the fabric of the target language; that is, to aim at modified (or covert) estrangement effects. A translation could be written adopting native norms while constantly counterpointing or even undermining the expectations they promote even from the title. This strategy has proven effective in the case of several other playwrights and plays which, once translated into a form of unplaceable but clearly not European Spanish, still 'read naturally' while, inconspicuously, from time to time the rhythms of speech are slightly off beat, perhaps syntax suddenly demands a bit more attention than usual, and occasionally the lexical fabric is decidedly but not overtly unfamiliar. Of course, similar effects sometimes occur in productions, although frequently not as the outcome of design but maybe of a performer's improvisational wit or, alas, a translator's incompetence. Unlike the religious art of the indigenous craftsmen who during colonial times would infuse the newly assimilated Catholic imagery and architecture with their particular – and at times highly critical – visions, published versions of Shakespeare in our midst rarely, if at all, shun the inherited reverence for the unwritten but hardly unquestioned dictate that Shakespeare must speak to us as if from a fake sixteenth-century Spanish pulpit. Acquaintance with Shakespeare-as-text in Spanish-speaking Latin America, therefore, is still very much ruled by former rules and rulers.

This is not, however, the only form of Shakespeare translation that reflects a problematic reverence for 'the Word' in our midst. What else may also be called 'Translating Shakespeare', whether in/to Latin America or any other place? Translating 'Shakespeare' in/to post-colonial contexts cannot be conceived without political implications. The forms that such translation takes are not exclusively verbal or literary. In here translating Shakespeare – creating shadows of, on, off, and from Shakespeare – may involve seemingly innocuous but very revealing attitudes.

A headline in Illustration 4, 'Shakes-peare [sic] in Chiapas', is the lead to an article in the Fall 1996 issue of the tabloid-style literary quarterly *Diario de Poesía*, published simultaneously in three cities of Argentina and Uruguay. The cover summary features a photograph of the now mythical 'Comandante Marcos', the mysterious and ambiguous leader and bard of the Zapatista National Liberation Army, a guerrilla force that has been fighting a war-without-an-open-war since January 1994 in Chiapas, the southernmost state of my country. Just what exactly was 'Shakes-peare' doing in Chiapas? This is not the headline to a note announcing, say, a performance of one of his plays, nor a series of talks about him or his work. And despite first impressions, it is not, either, an attempt at transporting the worn-out controversy over the 'true' identity of the English poet to the tense battlefield of Chiapas, to suggest that Shakespeare has been re-invented or re-fashioned as Marcos, the masked paladin of post-modern guerrilla and literary cliché.

At first sight, then, this could be just another instance of what Shakespearians have more or less agreed to call 'the uses (and abuses) of Shakespeare'. Here, his name is employed as a hook to call the reader's attention to an otherwise very predictable interview with the Mexican poet Juan Bañuelos, a native of Chiapas. In fact, the editors slyly highlighted a comment made by Bañuelos during the interview. While describing the situation in his native state, he referred to it as 'enveloped in a darkness that turns Chiapas into a perpetual scene from Shakespeare, grown nationwide. It's all Renaissance politics at the peak of its bloody stage.'[15] There is hardly anything interesting or new in this. It is, at best, an invocation of the Word to support a pseudo-

---

15 *Diario de Poesía*, 37 (Fall 1996), 35. All quotations from this article come from the same page (my translations into English).

4 'Shakes-peare in Chiapas', cover of *Diario de Poesía* 37.

dramatic characterization of an otherwise complex and challenging conflict.

But that is not all. Bañuelos carried on and added what unwittingly amounts to a thought-provoking twist to his trite invocation by delivering one of those rhapsodies that always invite critical interpretation. In another segment of the interview, he predicts: 'A great literature will emerge from the vast field of experimentation that Chiapas has become.' And further

on, being one of the many fans of Marcos's myth and (mostly self-replicating) literature, Bañuelos proceeded to make his personal contribution to them, uttering a vision of angelical proportions in which Marcos becomes the seed of redemption through knowledge, the origin of that 'great literature that will emerge:'

Marcos is a very cultivated man – he speaks [more literally, he *masters*] three or four languages. I don't know who he is, but I guess that he descends from colonizers who came from the north, looking for new lands. They traveled two thousand miles or more, moving from the desert to the jungle, and arrived in Chiapas in the 50s or early 60s. [. . .] He makes the [indigenous] people read Shakespeare or reads to them from the works; he translates pieces from Baudelaire to them, and gives them poems by Latin American poets such as Neruda, Vallejo, and Benedetti. [. . .] The Mexican government hates his guts, the fact that he makes fun of them all the time.

Except for the accuracy of his last remark, Bañuelos's mythologizing smacks of a mixture of condescension and pathetic fallacy that could make anyone cry over the power of the sacred Western Canon to redeem an irredeemable and stubborn part of humankind. It also brings to mind many an infamous debate during colonial times whether the native Americans were human or not, and hence worthy of religious education, mercy, and assimilation, or merely of exploitation and extermination. All of these 'solutions' to the 'problem' are frankly Eurocentric, anyway – like Bañuelos's approach. Who or what are those he relishes to characterize as 'colonizers who traveled two thousand miles from the north, looking for new lands'? A race of northern saviours coming to rescue illiterate Calibans from their ignorance of Shakespeare, Baudelaire and Latin American poets, in that particular order?

Here is a vision of the apostle of the down-trodden, indeed: the cultivated white man from the north who 'masters' four languages and fights for freedom as he quotes Shakespeare while sowing the seeds of a new literature in mellifluous Spanish in the midst of half-users of that tongue. Is there any significance, perhaps, in the fact that the catalogue of linguistic virtues of this freedom fighter does not seem to include the knowledge of an indigenous language?[16] Given this attitude, is there any chance for Shakespeare to shake some scenes – or pears at least – in the world of these thousands who are seemingly more in need of salvation from themselves than in search of an effective solution to their indeed unbearable plights, one

that may pay respect to their cultural identities, including their views on Christianity, a religion they have so passionately adopted *and* transformed, that is, *translated*?

I, for one, find it inevitable to read Bañuelos's 'colonizers from the north', poets, and poet/teacher/army commander as the protagonists of a deeply prejudiced and self-betraying subtext where western poetry implies the redemption of the poor, dirty and ugly to a life of canonical bliss. And I wonder whether Bañuelos, or many others like him who are prone to this kind of fashionable mythologizing of the Zapatista struggle and its leader, ever turn their talking heads back to reassess their words and realize that their contents are suspiciously similar to the narratives of reformation and improvement of the un-Christian savages employed by, say, founders and defenders of apartheid in South Africa.

What use or translation of Shakespeare has been made here? The quick answer is correct, for all I know, though not complete: Shakespeare has not been translated at all, not made free from the constraints that keep the Word captive within the premises of 'high-culture'. There has been no actualization of anything other than Shakespeare-the-commonplace, the worn-out equation of his work with quintessential goodness. In his invocation of Shakespeare as a shadow behind the mask of the freedom fighter, Bañuelos and those like him unwarily deliver whatever we call Shakespeare not as a set of multiple opportunities for delight, critical thinking, and profitable, intelligent performance, creativity, study, or even simple conversation – all of which could be acts of liberation – but as a colonial commodity, a culturally dead all-purpose glue that brings cohesion to claims at this or that through the prestige of four hundred years of genius.

With regard to texts written from a

---

16 Bañuelos himself 'never learned the native language [. . .] because it's so very hard'. But which language?, one may ask, as there are several in the state of Chiapas.

Shakespeare play either for the page or the stage that remain faithful to the 'saviour-from-the-north' vision exemplified by Bañuelos's rhapsody, the best and rest is . . . well . . . silence. But something may yet be said about versions of Shakespeare that, wittingly or unwittingly, move away from reverence towards a more interesting form of conversation with the powerful set of energies labelled 'Shakespeare'.

My last example is a translation of *Hamlet* into P'urhepecha, an indigenous language of Mexico, staged in 1990 and published in 1992. The P'urhepecha are the native Mexicans of the state of Michoacán, on the west coast of my country, neighbouring Jalisco and Colima. The book is called *Hamlet P'urhepecha*, and contains an adaptation of Shakespeare's play into that language and context.[17] Its cover (Illustration 5) shows a painting by Alfredo Zalce, one of the many fine artists to come out of the Mexican state of Oaxaca. It is a fitting illustration, for it features our main icon of the shadow of death, the Lord or Lady of Bones, a familiar presence around the time of All Saints and the coming of winter.

This adaptation and production went a long way from design to staging and publication. Juan Carlos Arvide, a native of Mexico City living and working in Morelia, the capital of the state of Michoacán, came up with the idea of staging a classic in the P'urhepecha language, in an effort to bring together very dissimilar historic and artistic experiences. Arvide has worked in the theatre since very early in his life as announcer, actor, producer and director. When asked why he finally decided on *Hamlet*, his answer was simple: its plot is very similar to a chronicle that he once heard from a man called *Tata* (Father) Felipe, a *Petamuti* or keeper of oral tradition among the P'urhepecha. Like many other native ethnic groups, until recently the P'urhepecha did not have a writing system but relied entirely on oral transmission for the preservation of their historic and artistic

consciousness. Starting in 1939, several efforts were made to study and apply this language outside its original context. The first translation of a western standard into P'urhepecha was, as might be expected, biblical: the New Testament.[18] A few decades ago, the Regional Institute for the Study of the P'urhepecha Culture developed a script for their language by adjusting its phonetics to the Latin alphabet. Lucas Gómez and Gilberto Jerónimo, the translators of the play, both P'urhepecha, work at that institute now. It must be noted that *Hamlet P'urhepecha* was not translated from an 'original' text but from several of its many Spanish shadows. To my knowledge, at this point there are no translators into P'urhepecha working from English.

Tata Felipe's chronicle is roughly as follows. About one hundred years before the arrival of the Spaniards, in one of the four kingdoms into which the ancient realm of the P'urhepecha was divided, a young prince witnessed how his uncle smothered his father to death, thus managing to take over his estate and wife. There is no ghost urging revenge in this narrative, the case stands by itself. The boy grew up hating the usurper until, in due time, he took his uncle's life and recovered his place as legitimate ruler. These overt coincidences with *Hamlet* were enough to make Shakespeare's play meaningful to the mind of the P'urhepecha. They approved of the plan to stage a story of power and betrayal, of the righting of a wrong, befitting their experience of royal politics.

But the literature of the mestizo and the conqueror is too indirect for the mind of the

17 *Hamlet P'urhepecha*, translated at the Centro de Investigación de la Cultura P'urhepecha by Lucas Gómez and Gilberto Jerónimo with the contribution of Felipe Chávez and Rafael Ambrocio from an adaptation by Juan Carlos Arvide (Morelia, Michoacán, 1992).

18 The original project for the translation of western standards into P'urhepecha, dating back to the 1940's, was finally discontinued – among other reasons – because it was combined with an effort to convert the native population into Protestantism. Michoacán has Mexico's largest Protestant population, however.

P'URHEPECHA

HAMLET

ADAPTACIÓN DE LA OBRA DE WILLIAM SHAKESPEARE

5   The cover of *Hamlet P'urhepecha* (1992), 'an adaptation of William Shakespeare's play', painting by Alfredo Zalce.

P'urhepecha; for them, western literature creates a glow around things to make them proper for the overt expression of emotion. Among the P'urhepecha such indirections are a waste of words. For example, where Ophelia, in the Spanish version used as the basis for the translation, is something like a 'poor wretch pulled from her melodious lay to muddy death', the P'urhepecha language, disdaining rhetoric, calls her 'flower drowned in the pull of water'.

For the P'urhepecha, Hamlet cannot be a man who hesitates, but one who must wait. His pain is as sharp, but his resolution cannot be doubted. His rank demands sobriety, and his character definition must find an equivalent in the brevity of his speech. The P'urhepecha translation, hence, included only what was left after editorial work in pursuit of a text matching this cultural framework.

The use of different versions of the play in

Spanish was surprising to the translators, who, at first, could not make sense of the fact that in some texts it was a mouse that would not stir, while in others it was a fly. For an idea of the difference in conciseness and emphasis between the two languages, suffice it to say that the introductory speech to the performance in Spanish would usually take about sixty-five to eighty seconds, while its equivalent in P'urhepecha lasted barely forty-five to fifty.

A shadow of a shadow, the P'urhepecha text was then adapted to their native land, time, uses, and mind. The play was re-set in the area of Zacapu, 'the place where there are stones', one of the old regions of the P'urhepecha kingdom, supposed to be the place of their first settlement. It was also adapted to the era of *Tata* Felipe's narrative. Furthermore, each character was given a native name. The list is long, but I trust it may be of interest. Hamlet is *K'uiiusïnari*, the one with the eyes or glance of the eagle. His name implies alertness and nobility: he is an *Irecheri*, the son of a great lord. Horatio is *Kuamba*, the firm companion, best friend in terms of solidarity, not love. Claudius's name is *T'ipujpeti*, the traitor, now an *Irecha*, or Lord, of Zacapu. *Irecha* has the connotation of the one who protects, the one who keeps the house intact – the contradiction between his name and his new title were enough to show that he would be condemned. Gertrude is *Ireri*, Chief Woman, the Lady. Polonius is *Umbarpeti*, the gossip, the one who talks much, harmless but with an inclination towards mischief. Ophelia is *Tsïpata*, the flowering flower. Laertes is *Miotspentsti*, the vengeful one. Rosencrantz is *Tekari*, a carpenter, and Guildenstern was given the name of the snowy mountain, *Ts'irati*.

Translating the ghost became quite a problem. For all its meanings in Shakespeare's English, to the P'urhepecha the word 'shadow' means simply shadow, the darkness always by you. That is a good phrase, indeed, one that has, we might say, metaphoric potential. But the use of metaphor in P'urhepecha is minimal, and so the ghost became a *Pitsentsti*, a dead one

wandering in grief. Still, a material dimension had to be added to this chiefly abstract notion. Hence, the figure finally on stage was an eighteen-feet tall *Guaricha*, an external power or spirit that haunts, scares and ultimately takes you, thus completing what may be viewed as a successful process of translation by fusion. Finally, the troupe of players in Shakespeare's text were equated with what may be the only kind of show close to being theatre among the P'urhepecha, the tradition of the *Ch'anach'anandirecha*, the ones who play with their mouths, or more literally, the witty clowns with the obligation to make you laugh through mimicry. The *Ch'anach'anandirecha* were compelled to criticize the great lord by mocking his bad actions; if the great lord did not receive heavy criticism from these jesters, they might be severely punished, even sentenced to death. Tradition also dictates that these clowns be men only. Finally, Arvide and his translators added the figure of a *Petamuti*, to lock on to the oral traditions of their people.

The already shortened text became even shorter in production. Arvide's calculations indicate the use of approximately 60 per cent of Shakespeare's lines in the published text, and maybe 15 per cent below that in the performance text. His original plans, which included a multi-levelled stage, had to be adjusted to unexpected conditions. In the end, the scenery was the frontal representation of a ruined palace. Costumes, weapons and featherwear were designed according to the old Chronicles of Michoacán; music was a mixture of ancient instruments with martial rhythms. Being one of the few non-P'urhepecha members of the production team, Arvide relied on the translators to communicate with the players.

The actor playing the title role was a gifted speaker whose talent was used to advantage by Arvide. In a defective but complete videotape of one performance, after the vigorous performance and exit of Claudius/T'ipujpeti and his train, Hamlet/K'uiiusïnari delivers the 'sullied flesh' speech with great determination and little introspection, illustrating *both* the limitations and merits of these inexperienced players who, without the benefit of training, made the best of a powerful means of expression, a language rich in intonation and rhythms. The published text of this soliloquy also provides a token of their approach to one of the play's crucial religious matters. A rough re-translation of it from P'urhepecha to Spanish to English may read as follows:

God of mine, why are the creatures of nature and the world like this? I am disgusted. This sort of thing only strengthens the ways of the world. Why is the landscape so? He is not quite two months dead, a man of utmost respect, the best of best in town and realm, who loved my mother. I don't want to remember. One month only, and you are bound to another! Heavens! A stupid animal would have waited in pain. There is no explanation, none. Holy Heaven, Father Heaven, that woman has married my uncle, my mother married that man, who never was like my father – only a month later, when tears are not yet dry. It is not good, it cannot be good, but it is not about now; this is not a reality, and all may end up wrongly, it cannot be but bad. Yet I'll remain silent, will not show feelings.

As mentioned earlier, after a long and painful process, most native Mexicans embraced the Catholic faith with passion – not least because of the charity they found from many mission-aries. But they also transformed it by infusing its premises and art with their magic, values and creativity. Thus, the very strict interpretation of some aspects of doctrine by the P'urhepecha became a major factor in preparing the text. The absence of Hamlet's death wish in this soliloquy, for instance, responds to its being a notion unacceptable in the P'urhepecha under-standing of Christianity: it was erased on grounds of cultural difference *from* a historical appropriation of cultural difference. Arvide, Gómez and Jerónimo had to be extremely cautious where such notions were involved. In general, then, the text reveals a Hamlet not of inaction and despair – much less from any sort

of religious disillusion – but a man in grief and angry wait, distraught but never lost; rather, a noble mind who can master his anger to reveal his innermost self only when justice is to be achieved, even to the cost of life. Hamlet/K'uiiusïnari is therefore closer to being 'Heaven's scourge' than 'loosed out of Hell', 'passion's slave', or a mere 'instrument'. Under-standing translation as a performative form of writing, then – the translator as a performer of the target text – *Hamlet P'urhepecha* is a full translation, a shadow newly, if ephemerally, cast in stone that 'marks the ripening process in a foreign language and the pulse of changing life in its own'.[19]

In spite of this, the translators of *Hamlet P'urhepecha* insist that in undertaking the task they were seeking to prove that a version of this 'immortal play' in their native language could be as 'universal' as any other. More interestingly, however, they supplement this nearly reverential view by adding that they accepted the challenge because the P'urhepecha language could *host* the foreign dramatist – a self-explanatory nuance. To meet that challenge, moreover, they decided to coin words and phrases in P'urhepecha, wherever necessary, to avoid borrowing from Spanish – another act opposed to mechanical and passive solutions, like translation. Two texts from the western world, then, the New Testament and *Hamlet*, have become part of the recent tradition of the *written* P'urhepecha language: shadows and stones that prove their culture capable of hosting much revered Words.

Still, I suspect that *Hamlet P'urhepecha* displays more explicit signs, specifically political, inviting questions beyond its translators' explicit purposes. Before the early sixteenth century, the P'urhepecha had never been vanquished by invaders, whether Mexican or Spanish. Instead, the kingdom of Michoacán – with its ancient capital at Tzintzunzan, near the lake of

---

19 Walter Benjamin, 'The Task of the Translator', trans-lated by J. Hynd and A. M. Valk, *Delos*, 2 (1968), 82.

Pátzcuaro – welcomed the pale foreigners after learning that they had defeated their traditional enemies, the Aztec Empire. Calzonzin, then High Lord of the P'urhepecha, sent messengers to seek the friendship of Cortés. In turn, Cortés delighted the ambassadors and the ruler of Michoacán with an impressive show of horsemanship and fireworks. Calzonzin opened the door to the invaders, and for a short time the high lords enjoyed their friendship. Later, however, everybody felt the full force of the conquerors. Only then there was a war. As a result of earlier blindness, betrayal and internecine strife, the newcomers triumphed and, according to many natives, continue to hold this realm in their power. Is there something of this narrative in *Hamlet P'urhepecha*, just as there is something of it in *Hamlet*? The entrance of Fortinbras marks the arrival of power from without to a world undermined by shadows from within, a world, perhaps, that could not help falling prey to its own decay and corruption, as well as to its own innocence and misguided faith. Was there any of this in the minds of those who played a part in *Hamlet P'urhepecha* or watched it?

To this question another could be added. The 1994 *World Shakespeare Bibliography* refers to *Hamlet P'urhepecha* as written in 'Tarascan'. The P'urhepecha, however, find this term derogatory.[20] In their language, 'Tarasco' means 'brother in law'. But the English translation does not suggest what the Spanish *'cuñado'* implies in the macho wordplay of my country. Calling a man *cuñado* without being 'in law' with him indicates that you have had, or wish to

have, sex with his sister, thereby severely challenging his manhood. In spite of this, 'Tarasco' has become the name given to the P'urhepecha all over Mexico, if for the most part now unwarily. This term, adopted from their own language by the conquerors as a humiliating form of address, bitterly reminds the P'urhepecha of the violent destruction of their world, and of the contempt with which the indigenous population is regarded by most *criollos* (Mexicans who descend from Europeans) and *mestizos* (even those from Michoacán, most of whom descend from the P'urhepecha). Octavio Paz's fame owes much to a book where he suggested that Mexicans are the children of rape.[21] Tarasco *means* rape to the P'urhepecha: it is an echo of the taking of their sisters *and* of their Gertrudes by force or deceit. Did *Hamlet* bring any of this back to the minds of those who played a part in *Hamlet P'urhepecha* or watched it?

One of Peter Brook's 'demons from Sumatra', a figurine of stone translated by light into a powerful shadow, made Jan Kott shiver with fear. Among the many shadows that haunt the stages of my homeland are strong shadows of cultural, historical and political identity still unacknowledged or concealed in the words of Shakespeare translators. A light aimed from critical awareness of otherness might help to cast them over.

---

[20] I am sorry to say that I unwittingly used the phrase 'P'urhepecha, also known as *Tarasco*' when submitting the entry to *WSB*.

[21] *El laberinto de la soledad* (México, 1950).

MINISTERS, MAGISTRATES AND THE
PRODUCTION OF 'ORDER' IN
MEASURE FOR MEASURE

PETER LAKE

I

I want to start with a tableau taken from the cheap print of the period. It features a condemned felon on the gallows performing a good death, repenting his (or her) sins, admitting his guilt and throwing himself on the mercy of God in Christ. All this takes place under the eyes of the attendant minister and the presiding magistrate, as well as of a large, socially mixed (popular) audience. In the murder pamphlets from which it is culled, this scene was usually represented as the culmination of a heavily stylized, providentialized narrative which had started with an initial, often demonically sponsored, temptation, continued with a lapse into some master sin or other and a consequent descent down a chain of sins which ended in an often morally or physically gross and disgusting murder. This led to the often providential, or even frankly miraculous, capture of the felon and was followed by the trial, condemnation and usually (but not always) more or less repentant death on the gallows of the perpetrator. Sometimes that death was a really good one, the felon having been converted to a true faith and a full and frank confession not only of the particular crime that had brought him (or her) to the scaffold but also more generally of his or her sinful course of life. When such happy endings occurred the credit went first to the secular magistrate who had allowed various clerics to insert themselves into the interstices of the judicial process and then to the ministers

themselves who had conferred with the felon in prison, instructed and converted him and then taught him the outward forms of a good death, which he then performed on the scaffold.

Such outcomes were thus presented as the result of the collaboration of three agents; first the presiding operation of God's providence, bending events in the world to the purposes appropriate to his justice and mercy and then the activities of the secular magistrate (acting primarily as the agent of justice) and the minister (acting primarily as the agent of mercy). Here, in microcosm, could be observed that collaboration between magistrate and minister that contemporaries (and in particular perfect protestant contemporaries) saw as the means through which reformation would be achieved, both on the collective, social and political levels, in the punishment of crime and suppression of sin and, on the personal, spiritual, religious levels, in the conversion of individual Christians to true religion and a saving faith. As the murder narratives showed, this outcome was to be achieved through a scrupulous division of labour between the two officers of God's will. The role of the magistrate was to capture, try, convict and execute the felon. No matter how repentant that felon became or appeared there was no room here for the exercise of human mercy in the form of a reprieve or pardon. Capital crimes deserved capital punishment. The two both traditional and pseudo scriptural saws around which the murder stories were often organized – that 'murder will out' and 'the murderer must die the death' – demanded as much. There remained room, however, for the exercise of mercy, even on the magistrate's part. This consisted in leaving room in the judicial proceedings for the pastoral efforts of the clergy, the efficacy of whose ministry was, however, dependent on the felon's death being absolutely certain. There must be no prospect of pardon, no chink of hope of secular mercy left or else the condemned would remain in the thrall of this world, rendered unable to confront the enormity and consequences of his or her own sin by lingering hopes of reprieve. Only when death was certain would felons really and finally confront the extremity of their spiritual condition, admit their fault, repent their sins and throw themselves on the mercy and grace of God in Christ.

Such endings served a number of both temporal and spiritual purposes. They saved the soul of the criminal. They provided a potentially saving, and certainly an edifying, staging of the capacity of an entirely gratuitous divine mercy and grace to save, at the last, even the most desperate of sinners. They vindicated the justice of the verdict that had brought this particular felon to his or her death. And, finally, by the public doing of exemplary justice, fitting the punishment to crying sins and notorious crimes otherwise likely to bring down the providential punishments of God on the society that had produced them, they knit up the rent in both the social fabric and the relations between the wider society and its God caused by the enormity of the initial crime.[1]

Such stories were not, of course, simple descriptions of how the judicial system worked. As Cynthia Herrup and others have pointed out, not all capital offenders died the death; the workings of the judicial system were mediated through the operation of communal values, through collective apprehensions of the reputation, social status and wealth of the accused and the often seemingly arbitrary operations of the pardon system.[2] Again, as Tom Lacqueur has shown, many felons went unrepentant to

desperate or drunken deaths, in executions left largely unscripted by the authorities.[3] But, particularly in the case of notorious crimes, which attracted the attention of a wide public, such scenes did happen; they were first acted out in the gaols and on the scaffold then told and retold, sold and resold, in cheap print and sometimes theatrical performance. Arguably they contained widely held assumptions about how the world should be, if not how it was; assumptions and claims about sin and providence, the nature of human and divine justice and order, and about the distinct but complementary roles of the minister and magistrate. While many of the moral and narrative assumptions and conventions encoded in these stories were commonplace, many of them dating from well before the reformation and all of them circulating widely throughout the social order, they

---

[1] The preceding paragraphs summarize the argument of P. Lake, ' "Deeds against Nature": Cheap Print, Protestantism and Murder in Early Seventeenth Century England' in K. Sharpe and P. Lake, eds., *Culture and Politics in Early Stuart England* (Stanford, 1993), pp. 257–83 and P. Lake, 'Popular Form, Puritan Content? Two Puritan Appropriations of the Murder Pamphlet from Mid-Seventeenth Century England' in A. Fletcher and P. Roberts, eds., *Religion, Culture and Society in Early Modern Britain* (Cambridge, 1994), pp. 313–34; for the background, both conceptual and generic that underpinned the cheap pamphlets upon which these articles are based see A. Walsham, *Providence in Early Modern England* (Oxford, 1999). For the alliance between magistrate and minister as the engine of reformation in post reformation England see P. Collinson, 'Magistracy and Ministry; A Suffolk Miniature' in his *Godly People* (London, 1983), pp. 455–66 and more generally his *The Religion of Protestants* (Oxford, 1982)

[2] C. Herrup, *The Common Peace* (Cambridge, 1987); for the socio-cultural mechanics and dynamics of convictions for murder see M. Gaskill, *Crime and Mentalities in Early Modern England* (Cambridge, 2000), part III.

[3] T. Lacqueur, 'Crowds, Carnival and the State in English Executions, 1604–1868' in A. Beier, D. Cannadine and J. Rosenheim, eds., *The First Modern Society* (Cambridge, 1989), pp. 305–55. Also see the seminal article by Jim Sharpe, ' "Last Dying Speeches": Religion, Ideology and Public Execution in Seventeenth Century England', *Past and Present*, 107 (1985), 144–67.

were subject to appropriation for a number of distinct, even mutually incompatible purposes. Certainly they could be and were appropriated for perfect protestant and even puritan purposes; in these renditions of the basic narrative emphasis was placed on the role of providence in bringing the felon to book and to repentance, on the role of divine grace in saving even such desperate sinners and thus on the true repentance and good deaths achieved at the end by the felon. Other versions of what remained essentially the same narrative template paid little or no attention to the good death, concentrating instead on the gory details of the crime itself, on the shocking nature of the sins, impulses and behaviours that had produced it and/or on the miraculous means whereby the crime or the perpetrator were brought to light and to book. My interest in this material started here, and it was from this perspective that I approached *Measure for Measure*, for *Measure for Measure* contains many of the elements and themes at the centre of these narratives, only in the play they have been split apart, disaggregated, removed from their usual order, deprived of their usual outcomes and then reworked and recombined.[4]

Thus in the Angelo/Isabella plotline we have two thirds of the conventional chain of sins narrative: temptation via master sin – in Angelo's case a mixture of spiritual pride and lust – into corruption, fornication and murder. In the Angelo/Claudio plotline we have a godly magistrate ardently applying the law to someone formally guilty of a capital crime, claiming, in the process, just as the pamphlets said he should, that to yield to the siren song of mercy would undermine the demands of justice and the wider interests of the common weal. In the friar/duke we have a priest haunting the gaols, reconciling convicted felons to their fate, mitigating the demands of human justice by the application of divine grace and mercy – again just as the pamphlets said he should. His efforts with Claudio are, of course, undermined by the hope of pardon brought by Isabella, again just as the conventional view held they would be. Again,

just as in the pamphlets, these pastoral efforts reach their height in the meeting between the friar duke and a convicted and confessed murderer, Barnardine.

But, of course, in the play none of these plotlines follow on naturally one from the other and all are denied their conventional or expected ending or resolution. Angelo only gets part of the way down his chain of sin; despite his best efforts, he fails to commit murder; he neither dies on the scaffold nor repents. The magistrate (Angelo) does not bring the felon (Claudio) to a deserved death on the scaffold nor does the minister (the friar/duke) convert him (or indeed anyone else, save perhaps Juliet) to a true repentance or a good death. Barnardine, the only convicted and admitted murderer in the play, is not only neither converted nor executed but pardoned. The minister in question is not a real minister at all but a secular magistrate in clerical drag and his pastoral efforts in gaol are – with the possible exception of Juliet – a complete bust. Moreover, the play ends with a series of capital sentences which are then immediately pardoned; no one dies, no one (with the partial exception of Isabella) repents and everybody gets married.

Coming at the play from the perspective provided by the pamphlets, all this seemed rather weird – and interesting. Perhaps the elements of the murder pamphlet template, scattered throughout the action, provide us with a clue to the ways in which the play might have engaged with the conventional narrative expectations and moral assumptions of the audience; first by inviting them to regard the play as a known quantity, about to make a regular progress down well-grooved narrative tracks, and then denying them their expected

---

[4] Lake, 'Popular Form, Puritan Content?'; also see P. Lake and M. Questier, 'Agency, Appropriation and Rhetoric at the Foot of the Gallows: Puritans, Romanists and the State in Early Modern England', *Past and Present*, 153 (1996), 64–107.

outcomes before coming to rest in an altogether unconventional happy ending and moral resolution? Might this provide a more finely historicized account of the entirely conventional observation that the play, having started out looking like a tragedy, ends as a comedy? Beyond providing a clue to the way the play may have worked on, frustrated, reframed and finally gratified the expectations of its audience, did all this, if not inversion, then certainly severe disruption, of the standard narrative expectations and outcomes attached to these themes and plotlines bring with it a critique of the assumptions that underlay those conventional expectations and outcomes? If it did, precisely what sort of critique was the play providing and what were its wider political, cultural or religious resonances? Moreover, in *Measure for Measure* we had precisely the sort of theatrical appropriations of and playings about with narrative, cultural and emotional materials from the wider society that were calculated to further enflame godly and godly sounding critics of the theatre. Here were materials which, within the conventional moralized and providentialized frameworks which usually contained them, might be expected to lead the audience/readership to conventionally edifying, morally improving, conclusions. But now those moralized and providentialized frames were being disrupted, some bits of the narrative were being attenuated, others played up, in ways that, far from edifying the punters, might be taken to titillate, delight and even, on some accounts, to deprave them. Finally, all this was taking what looked like an overtly anti-puritan form which was designed explicitly to speak not only to the particular politico-religious, the political and polemical, circumstances attendant upon the accession of James I but also to a number of issues particularly dear to James himself.[5]

II

So I started to look at the play as an exercise in anti-Puritanism deliberately pushed at the situa-

tion created by James's accession. The anti-puritan bit seemed straightforward enough. Angelo is called 'precise' – a well-known contemporary term of abuse for the godly – twice in the play (1.3.50; 3.1.92). He is also referred to more than once as a 'saint' or as 'saint seeming' and, of course, while the godly did intermittently refer to one another in such terms, this was also a term used in ironic derogation of the godly by their enemies. The subsequent account of his descent from pharisaical pride in his own godliness into lust, corruption, fornication and judicial murder fits contemporary anti-puritan stereotypes and libels as well as wider notions of the nature of a false faith. It was a commonplace that – as Angelo himself at various points as good as admits both to himself and Isabella – a godly affect and reputation as often as not acted as a mere front or cover for the pursuit of sexual or monetary gratification and self interest. That was the essence of the hypocrisy, that, to their enemies at least, was typical of the godly. Again it was a commonplace amongst the godly themselves that a false, pharisaical faith was often the result of a failure, typical of the unregenerate, truly to appreciate the depths of their own sinful depravity and, of course, Angelo's own spiritual pride is based precisely on his own failure to recognize his own fleshly lusts and sexual impulses. These are set off by the sight of another very differently constituted 'saint', Isabella. When the centrality of the idea of the mutual love of the godly for one another to the self image and wider reputation of the puritan godly is added to the equation, the depth of the satire intended here emerges all the more clearly. Angelo is done in by an altogether

---

[5] I should add that in order for this claim to work it is not necessary that the play should have been written expressly for court performance, still less directly addressed to the king, but only that it should have espoused a certain topicality, seeking to excite and exploit the interests of a wide variety of contemporaries in central issues attendant on the accession of the first Stuart.

too literal minded and carnal love for 'the saints'.[6]

Angelo then is a puritan whose spiritual pride and investment in his own righteousness as an elect saint, someone who cannot fall from grace, means that when he does fall, he does not, having been shown the extent of his own corruption and depravity, repent and amend. Rather his identity as a godly person collapses, leaving him to rush down the slippery slope of sin in pursuit of sexual gratification and the defence of his own reputation as a godly man and magistrate.

The critique of Angelo's puritanism offered by the play transcends the details of his spiritual pride and hypocrisy to encompass a whole style of rule, whereby the deputy's self righteous godliness is translated from the private sphere of godly conversation and affect to the public domain of the godly magistrate. Here his moral and religious rigourism produces a view of the magistrate as someone who is bound to enforce the law. By the law in this context is meant not so much the necessarily imperfect, sometimes necessarily arbitrary and mutable human law but human law assimilated to and informed by, indeed sometimes equated with or collapsed into, an increasingly draconian version of divine and sometimes even of Mosaic law. This law binds the conscience and constrains the room for manœuvre of the magistrate. It rigidly defines order. For only through the strict application and enforcement of that law can order be maintained, sin punished, the wrath of God appeased and his judgements removed from the land. It is precisely this version of godly magistracy that is staged in the play by Angelo's attitude to and treatment of Claudio. The assumptions that underpin it are laid bare in his defence of that treatment in a number of exchanges with both Escalus and Isabella.

Again the play's image of the extremity and rigour of Angelo's style of rule echoes and parallels contemporary anti-puritan stereotype and polemic. Many conformist polemicists saw a propensity to view the law of Moses as a

model or prototype for the law of the land as a puritan characteristic. Puritans were also accused of wanting to introduce the death penalty for adultery, of viewing the breach of the sabbath as the moral and, therefore, in an ideal, properly reformed world, the legal, equivalent of murder, indeed even of wanting to enact the full Mosaic law as the law of the land. Such claims were typically exaggerated but they were not baseless. Radical puritans and presbyterians like Dudley Fenner did indeed write treatises seeking to apply the mosaic law to contemporary practice and the godly did wax lyrical about the moral enormity of sabbath breaking, swearing, drunkenness and a whole variety of sexual offences.[7] All of which is paralleled in the play by Angelo's equation of bastard-bearing with murder.

Now, the critique or caricature of puritanism thus set up is then inserted by the play into the particular circumstances both before and after James's accession. For those years did indeed see a level of puritan agitation for further reformation unseen since the 1580s. James was a Scot,

---

[6] For a recent account of the dynamics of anti-puritan stereotyping see K. Poole, *Radical Religion from Shakespeare to Milton: Figures of Nonconformity in Early Modern England* (Cambridge, 2000). Also see P. Collinson, *The Puritan Character: Polemics and Polarities in Early Seventeenth Century English Culture* (Los Angeles, 1989); 'Ecclesiastical Vitriol: Religious Satire in the 1590s and the Invention of Puritanism' in J. Guy, ed., *The Reign of Elizabeth I* (Cambridge, 1995), pp. 150–70; 'Bartholomew Fair: Theatre Invents Puritans' in D. L. Smith and R. Strier, eds., *The Theatrical City* (Cambridge, 1995), pp. 157–69. Also see P. Lake, '"A Charitable Christian Hatred": The Godly and their Enemies in the 1630s' in C. Durston and J. Eales, eds., *The Culture of English Puritanism, 1560–1700* (London, 1996), pp. 145–83.

[7] On the issue of the death penalty for adultery see, for instance, M. Sutcliffe, *An Answer to a Certain Libel Supplicatory* (London, 1592), p. 173; on the sabbath see Bancroft's chaplain Thomas Rogers's commentary on the thirty-nine articles of 1607, *The Catholic Doctrine of the Church of England*, ed. S. J. Perowne, The Parker Society (Cambridge, 1854), pp. 17–20. For Fenner see M. McGiffert, 'Covenant, Crown and Commons in Elizabethan Puritanism' *Journal of British Studies*, vol. 20, (1980), 32–52, esp. 40–1.

who had made warm gurgling noises at the godly before coming to the throne. He had even given them a formal hearing at Hampton Court. Many contemporaries as well informed as Bancroft and Whitgift feared that James's reign would see a distinctly pro-puritan shift in royal policy and many of the godly briefly got their hopes up at the outset of the reign. All of this was compounded by a more general sense that, with the death of the queen, one era was ending and another beginning and that the war, dearth, plague and corruption of the 1590s, when the governing clique had shrunk to tiny proportions, needed a new regime to reform the church and commonwealth and reconstitute the governing elite. James, of course, had sought to exploit such hopes and expectations to his own advantage and in the process exacerbated them by appearing to offer a new and more sympathetic dispensation not only to puritans but but also to catholics, not only Cecil but also to Henry Howard.[8] All of this is, of course, evoked in the play with talk of a period of magisterial lassitude and moral decay, of war, poverty, dearth and plague stretching back variously fourteen or nineteen years; that is back to the late 1580s when the war with Spain had started. The play also features peace or rumours of peace and war, just like those that attended James's accession.

I want now to cite a document (found by Nick Tyacke) to show what I mean. It is a petition in the state papers, one of a number of reforming proposals set before the king. It is headed 'things grievous and offensive to the commonwealth which may be reformed by your highness or by a parliament'. It starts with secular grievances, detailing monopolies, pluralities of office, abuses of the court of wards, extortion by purveyors, packing of parliaments, impositions of new fees, restraints of grain. It reads like a wish-list of commonwealth grievances left over from the parliaments of the 1590s, compiled by someone excluded from the narrow Cecilian clique at the centre of power in the late Elizabethan and early Jacobean regimes.

It then passes on to an equally conventional list of moderately puritan ecclesiastical grievances comprising the usual suspects of conformity, unpreaching ministers, profanation of the sabbath, pluralities, bribes, extortion of money from poor ministers, insufficient penalties for popish recusants.[9]

Here, then, is the basis for contemporary hopes and/or fears of a newly puritan, reforming regime coming in with James to meet the moral, ecclesiastical and political messes bequeathed by Elizabeth. And, of course, just such a regime is set up in the play, occasioned not by the change of one ruler for another but established on the duke's behalf by Angelo who enjoys the same relation to the previous laxity of the duke as some hoped James would adopt towards the state of affairs he had inherited from Elizabeth. In the play, of course, the result is not so much a definitive switch from one regime to another, as a controlled experiment in puritan rule, con-

[8] For the destabilizing both domestic and international effects of the accession see J. Hurstfield, 'The Succession Struggle in late Elizabethan England' in S. T. Bindoff, J. Hurstfield and C. H. Williams, eds., *Elizabethan Government and Society* (London, 1961), 369–96 and Paul Allen, *Philip III and the pax hispanica, 1598–1621* (New Haven, 2000), chapter 5. For the range of reforming petitions and initiatives put before the new king in 1604 see R. C. Munden, 'James I and 'the Growth of Mutual Distrust'; King, Commons and Reform, 1603–4' in K. M. Sharpe, ed., *Faction and Parliament* (Oxford, 1978), pp. 43–72. The literature on Hampton Court is both large and uneven; for selected highlights see M. H. Curtis 'The Hampton Court Conference and its Aftermath', *History*, vol. 46, (1961), pp. 1–16; P. Collinson, *The Elizabethan Puritan Movement* (London, 1967) part 8, chapter 5; F. J. Shriver, 'Hampton Court Revisited; James I and the Puritans', *Journal of Ecclesiastical History*, vol. 33, (1982), pp. 48–71; P. Collinson, 'The Jacobean Religious Settlement; The Hampton Court Conference', in H. Tomlinson, ed., *The English Civil War; Essays in Early Stuart Politics and Government* (London, 1983), pp. 27–51.

[9] Public Record Office State Papers Domestic, 14/1, 129r.–132r. I owe my knowledge of this fascinating document to the kindness of Nicholas Tyacke, who is currently preparing an article setting it in its full contemporary contexts.

ducted, on the duke's authority, by Angelo and observed in secret by the friar/duke.

Now, of course, the puritan agitations of the period concerned themselves with traditional issues of ecclesiastical reform – with the details of church ceremony, of conformity and government – rather than with issues concerned with the reformation of manners of the sort which define and embody Angelo's puritanism. Not that these issues were not sometimes associated with one another. The petition in state papers to which I just referred has a third section concerned with issues of sexual regulation and marriage. This starts with a complaint 'about license to marry without publication . . . of the contract and in lawless places whereby parents are defrauded of their children and the children cast away in unfit marriages'. It then proceeds to the issues of fornication and adultery which the petition laments were only punished 'after the canon law', 'by commutation into money or by a white sheet and wand . . . by means whereof this sin increaseth and overfloweth the land'. The remedy suggested was condign punishment: 'if not that punishment which God proportioneth to that sin [i.e. death] . . . yet some other sharp and desperate punishment together with the censures of the church to bring the offenders to their repentance'. Finally it turned to the enormity of noblemen not cohabiting with their wives, here citing the breakdown of the marriage of the earl of Essex's sister, Penelope, the wife of Sir Richard Rich, who was now notoriously living with Lord Mountjoy, a sin connived at by royal authority 'for want of due reverence to the state of marriage and toleration of wanton and licentious living which followeth the neglect of the ordinance of God'.[10] Here, then, is a remarkable echo of the concerns for moral reformation shown in the play by Angelo, here associated with an elaborated programme for the reformation of both church and commonwealth.

More generally the issue around which Angelo's moral and legal rigourism defines itself – the issue of the nature of a true legal marriage

and the offence of bridal pregnancy – did represent an area of contemporary moral and legal concern and dubiety, if not controversy. Certainly as Martin Ingram and Eric Carlson have shown the offence of bridal pregnancy had only come to be prosecuted in the church courts relatively late on in the sixteenth and early seventeenth centuries, often as part of campaigns to discourage the poor from entering into marriages and conceiving children, they could not, in fact, sustain. The element of class bias inherent in such campaigns is perhaps critiqued by the play's transposition of the issue of fornication and bridal pregnancy from the people and the poor to the elite.[11] For the trouble starts when Angelo starts treating members of the gentry (Claudio and Juliet) just as the church courts were increasingly treating ordinary mortals. Again issues of clandestine marriage and breach of promise, consequent upon legal and moral doubts about what constituted a true marriage, were also common in the church courts during this period. These, however, were far from being 'puritan' issues. What was at stake was a redefinition of marriage and a reform of popular attitudes and behaviours undertaken through the church courts and prosecuted by people we have no need or warrant to call any sort of puritan. This was no more a distinctively puritan issue than the similar contemporary campaigns to suppress or regulate ale houses, brothels or the theatre.

But that, of course, was and is the whole point. On a whole series of such socio-moral issues there was no free-standing, distinctively or exclusively puritan agenda. Rather, as often as not, on those issues the godly were pursuing far more widely held ends: what were in certain circles more or less conventional notions of order. They were merely doing so with a

---

[10] *State Papers Domestic*, 14/1.

[11] M. J. Ingram, *Church Courts, Sex and Marriage in England, 1570–1640* (Cambridge, 1987), part 2, esp. chapters 6 and 7; Eric Carlson, *Marriage and the English Reformation* (Oxford, 1994), part 3.

peculiar zeal, a particular moral and emotional ferocity based on their own experience and style of piety and laced with or prompted by reasons culled from the scripture that might indeed set them apart from even the more reforming of their contemporaries. It was this situation and these relationships that enabled the godly to burrow so effectively inside the Elizabethan and Jacobean establishments of church and the local and national state. Indeed, it was this that enabled them, in certain circumstances and on certain issues, when order was taken to be particularly under threat and the need for zeal and discipline peculiarly pressing, to place themselves at the head of far wider bodies of opinion and feeling.[12]

And that, of course, is precisely what happens to Angelo in the play. For he is pictured there not as some wild-eyed oppositional figure, some prophet of doom welcomed into the inner circle from the periphery, but as a courtier, an intimate of the duke and a member of the governing class, a man whose reputation for virtue, self control and severity, whose reputation, in other words, as a 'puritan' – the 'precise Angelo' – has led the duke to place him in power ahead of the elder and more experienced Escalus. The duke has done so precisely because he feels that prevailing circumstances require a dose of puritan zeal to make up for the years of laxity and moral decline over which he and the likes of Escalus have just presided. Moreover, when he comes to power Angelo does not have to innovate to institute his new regime; he merely has to enforce a long-standing and long-neglected statute – with which, of course, early modern England was littered. It was a contemporary commonplace, dear to the godly and many others, that what was needed was not so much new laws as the strict and proper enforcement of such laws as already existed. All this, of course, fits perfectly with recent scholarship on the relationship of what one might term moderate puritans with the contemporary establishment in church and state and on the penetration of perfect protestant attitudes into a number of canons of contemporary orthodoxy.[13]

But if puritan notions of moral reformation were in some sense conventional, serving to attach the godly to, rather than to distance them from, wider bodies of opinion, that does mean that they were uncontroversial, particularly when turned into harshly uncompromising practice by driven godly magistrates and their clerical helpers. At times further reformation or the reformation of manners could create ructions and conflict, not so much between social groups or cultural layers but in ways that cut diagonally across such horizontal divisions. This situation is again faithfully reflected in the play's depiction of the impact of and reaction to Angelo's reforming regimen which unites neither the social elite nor the magistracy. The first and most notorious objects of Angelo's reforming regime, Claudio and Juliet, are themselves members of the social elite; persons of good moral reputation, they seem entirely unaware of having done anything wrong until the reforming zeal of Angelo apprehends them. Again, Escalus, praised by the duke in the opening scene as a master of the conventions of 'common justice', clearly has a very different style of rule to Angelo, differences which are played out in his scenes with Pompey and Froth and his discussions with Angelo about the fate of Claudio. While the close relation between Angelo's reasoning and contemporary orthodoxy compels Escalus' agreement, that agreement is grudging. He makes it quite clear that if he were in control, Claudio would get off (no doubt with a rebuke) in the blink of an eye.

But if Angelo's puritan rigour cannot unite the social elite or indeed even magistracy, it does strike a chord with elements of the people.

[12] P. Lake, 'Defining Puritanism – Again?' in F. Bremer, ed., *Puritanism: Transatlantic Perspectives on a Seventeenth Century Anglo-American Faith* (Boston, 1993), pp. 3–29.

[13] P. Collinson, *Religion of Protestants*; P. Lake, *Moderate Puritans and the Elizabethan Church* (Cambridge, 1982); Lake, 'Defining Puritanism – Again?'

The very offence for which Claudio is facing death – having sex with his intended bride before they have been formally married – elicits horror from the very plebeian figure of Elbow when he is accused of having done precisely the same with his wife. This he takes as an affront to both his and her honour and wants to pursue the matter at law. Thus the same social values and moral judgements that animate Angelo's reform campaign can be found circulating amongst the lower orders – and the play goes out of its way to inform us that Elbow is not of the parish elite, not even, that is, a member of the most prosperous elements of the middling sorts. This, of course, is entirely in line with the findings of recent research (by Laura Gowing and others) on the importance of usually sexually based notions of honour and reputation to the lower orders.[14]

But if there are popular aspects to the reforming agenda being pushed by Angelo, there were also elite elements at the centre of that which most needed to be reformed. Of course, Claudio and Juliet are themselves gentle. Not only that, but the milieu of the brothels and alehouses of the city which stands in the play as a figure for those elements in the commonwealth that most need to be controlled and reformed, may be run by plebs like Pompey or Mistress Overdone, but they are patronized by gentlemen like Lucio, Froth or the range of social types satirized by Pompey on his first arrival in gaol. Neither the behaviours nor attitudes being reformed and punished by Angelo are restricted to the people. Rather, what is involved is an extreme extrapolation or development of what remain conventional notions of order, virtue and vice, being given external form and force in a reform campaign that cuts across and reveals the contradictions and strains within the attitudes and expectations, the notions of order, honour and shame, held by a number of social groups and of both sexes.

The wider point to be made here is that the picture painted in the play of Angelo as puritan constitutes a remarkably accurate reflection both of contemporary anti-puritan stereotype and polemic and the 'real' relations pertaining between puritans and the contemporary social, ideological and political orders and orthodoxies as modern research has revealed it.

III

Having established as much, one could then go on to read the rest of the play as the untangling of the mess made by Angelo's ducally sponsored but disastrous experiment in puritan godly rule by the friar/duke. Here the first, tragedy-like, part of the play corresponds to the puritan-dominated part; the second, comedy-like, part to the undoing of Angelo's ducally sponsored puritan mess by the friar/duke. In so doing the duke has to address or redress two main areas of confusion and disorder created by Angelo. These involve the nature and proper division of labour between the magistrate and the minister and the proper relation between a variety of laws – divine, natural and human and the prerogative powers of the prince. The nature and extent of the confusions created by Angelo's puritan experiment in godly rule are revealed in a number of exchanges about the fate of Claudio between him and Escalus and Isabella.

In response to Isabella's pleas for mercy for her brother Angelo's first line of defence is that his hands are tied: the law will not allow it; Claudio has been tried and condemned by the law and now there is nothing for Angelo to do. She will have none of this and insists that he could pardon Claudio if he would and, of course, we know that he could do precisely that since, before his departure, the duke had expressly conferred power of life and death in Vienna on his deputy. 'Your scope is as mine

---

[14] L. Gowing, *Domestic Dangers: Women Words and Sex in Early Modern London* (Oxford, 1996). Gowing draws on and develops earlier work on defamation, for which see the seminal study by Jim Sharpe, *Defamation and Sexual Slander in Early Modern England: The Church Courts at York* , Borthwick papers, 58 (York, 1980).

own, / So to enforce and qualify the laws / As to your soul seems good' (1.1.64–6). Angelo can plausibly make this claim only because the law he is referring to seems to be not merely the law of Vienna but that law glossed by, indeed collapsed into, God's law. The law by which he is bound is not the imperfect, inherently arbitrary and mutable law of the land, the application of which to shifting circumstances not only can but should be mitigated and altered by the supervening sovereign authority of the prince. This claim is rendered explicit when Angelo tries to explain to Isabella that bastard-making and murder are morally equivalent offences. As she replies ''Tis set down so in heaven, but not in earth' (2.4.50). In other words, in the eyes of God they may be equally serious sins, since before God's justice all sins are mortal. But in the eyes of God all sins are equally mortal because of the perfection and omnipotence of the person whom they offend and the perfect justice of the law they break, not because they are simply the same. And so human law can and must distinguish both between sin and crime and then again between crimes, leaving the apprehension and punishment of sin to God, while designating certain externally knowable offences and behaviours as crimes and then distinguishing between and punishing them according to demands of natural justice and human order.

In taking the line he does, Angelo is, in fact, usurping the role of the Calvinist god in his dealings with fallen humanity. This shows most clearly when, again under pressure from Isabella, he claims that 'what I will not, that I cannot do' (2.2.53). Here he is speaking like the Calvinist God whose will was his law and whose law was his will. There could be no distinction between what God willed and what he did or what he was. To ask if God's actions were just was thus both tautological and blasphemous. Omnipotent and immutable, God defined what was just by willing it and always, therefore, did precisely what he willed and what was just. By claiming a congruence between the human law

he was enforcing and the divine law, Angelo was thus placing himself, as a human magistrate, in the same relationship to fallen humanity as that enjoyed by the Calvinist God or rather the Calvinist God in his just and judgemental, rather than in his merciful, mode. Small wonder, then, that they spoke the same language.

These parallels are noted in the play by Claudio's response to news of his condemnation by Angelo when he cites 'The bonds of heaven. On whom it will, it will / On whom it will not, so; yet still 'tis just' (1.2.114–15). This is an appropriate response to the exercise of divine justice by an omnipotent and absolutely just and merciful God over a fallen humanity, but it scarcely fits the dispositions of a fallible human magistrate applying an inherently imperfect and mutable human law to the shifting circumstances of earthly existence. Transposed to that arena, such language smacks of tyranny, as Claudio, almost in spite of himself, acknowledges later in the same exchange when he says 'Whether the tyranny be in his place / Or in his eminence that fills it up- / I stagger in.' (1.2.151–3)

Isabella, of course, notices the consistent slippage in Angelo's discourse between human and divine law, justice and authority, ridiculing the deputy's pretensions to a divine power and justice;

> Could great men thunder
> As Jove himself does, Jove would never be quiet,
> For every pelting petty officer
> Would use his heaven for thunder, nothing but
>   thunder   (2.2.113–16).

Then, however, pursuing the logic of Angelo's own argument she follows him into the realm of divine rather than human justice and mercy. Here she makes two main claims. The first is based on Angelo's own spiritual condition as a fallen, sinful creature: if he has ever felt the promptings of lust and concupiscence in his own heart he should exercise mercy towards her brother who has, after all, been convicted for the same crime.

Go to your bosom;
Knock there, and ask your heart what it doth
    know
That's like my brother's fault. If it confess
A natural guiltiness, such as is his,
Let it not sound a thought upon your tongue
Against my brother's life   (2.2.140–5)

This is a claim, of course, based on the equivalence as sins, offences against the law of God, of both evil thoughts or intentions and acts. Secondly, she has recourse to the general sinfulness of fallen humanity before the justice of God and to the equally general extent of the compensatory sacrifice of Christ for the sins of the world.

Why, all the souls that were, were forfeit once,
And He that might the vantage best have took
Found out the remedy. How would you be
If He, which is the top of judgement, should
But judge you as you are? O, think on that,
And mercy then will breathe within your lips,
Like man new made.   (2.2.75–81)

In other words, if Angelo really is a regenerate saint, he should act like one showing the same mercy toward Claudio as God in Christ showed toward a fallen humanity. He should, as she puts it elsewhere, condemn the sin but forgive the sinner.

But this, of course, is to make the same mistake as that just made by Angelo, fatally confusing the workings of human with those of divine justice, if not mistaking the human magistrate for God himself, then, at the very least, conflating and confusing the roles and prerogatives of the magistrate with those of the minister. Angelo, of course, immediately sees and seizes on the fallacies created by her deployment of these arguments to this purpose. He points out that the limitations and ends of human government and justice are very different from those of God. Before human law, if not before God, there was all the difference in the world between thought and action. The human law could only try and punish offences known to it.

'Tis one thing to be tempted, Escalus
Another thing to fall. I will not deny

The jury passing sentence on the prisoner's life
May in the sworn twelve have a thief, or two
Guiltier than him they try. What knows the law
That thieves do pass on thieves? What's open
    made to justice
That justice seizes. 'Tis very pregnant:
The jewel that we find, we stoop and take't,
Because we see it, but what we do not see
We tread upon and never think of it.   (2.1.17–26)

Again Angelo is able to deride Isabella's recourse to the general nature of human sin and of the atonement and her consequent claim that he condemn the sin but pardon the sinner. Such an approach would render all human justice nugatory; 'Mine were the very cipher of a function / To fine the faults, whose fine stands in record, / And let go by the actor' (2.2.39–41). After all, human justice was not just concerned with the guilt or innocence, the moral desert, of the individual, it was also concerned to preserve order in a fallen world. Thus to Isabella's reiterated demand that he show pity he retorts

I show it most of all when I show justice,
For then I pity those I do not know
Which a dismissed offence would after gall,
And do him right that, answering one foul wrong,
Lives not to act another. Be satisfied.
Your brother dies tomorrow.   (2.2.102–7)

By thus switching back to the realm of human sublunary government and justice, reverting from the domain of God and the minister to that of the magistrate, from his general calling as a Christian to his particular calling as a magistrate, Angelo is able to win this part of argument hands down, just as Isabella had prevailed earlier when she had exposed his confusions over the nature of the same divide. But he does not actually ever abandon his pretensions to godly rule and the semi-divine transcendence of the limits inherent in human law justice and government. On the contrary, he persists in conversation with Escalus to equate the justice of the sentence passed on Claudio with his own moral spiritual purity.

You may not extenuate his offence
For I have had such faults; but rather tell me,

When I that censure do so offend,
Let mine own judgement pattern out my death,
And nothing come in partial. Sir, he must die
                                    (2.1.27–31).

On this basis, Angelo's law-bound version of magistracy renders the ruler's personal conduct, no less than his subjects' subject to the laws of the land. It is a sustainable position only because of his own conviction of his own sinlessness. On this basis he is a 'puritan' indeed. And here it is worth recalling that it was a commonplace of anti-puritan discourse that the puritans were justly so called precisely because they did indeed regard themselves as purer than others; indeed, on some renditions of this charge, because they simply regarded themselves as morally and spiritually pure. As always these charges were quite inaccurate and unfair and yet one can also see precisely what they meant.

All these discussions between Isabella and Angelo, and indeed Angelo and Escalus, take place on the abstract, totalizing plain of what one might term absolute justice and mercy. Moreover, in the course of their debates it becomes clear that both the play's two 'saints', Angelo and Isabella, have got their laws crossed; both are congenitally incapable of distinguishing consistently between the realms of human and divine law, justice and mercy, between, if you like, religion and politics, the realm of the divine and that of the judge and the ruler. Confronted by the other's conflations and confusions each is capable of making sharp observations and arguments based on these divisions, but both always lapse back into versions of those same confusions and conflations that suit their argumentative needs of the moment. Neither deigns, with Escalus, to discuss the issue of Claudio's guilt and fate in a middle ground of prudence, policy and equity, taking the surrounding circumstances into account, categorizing his offence as 'a fault' rather than a heinous crime or a damning sin.

Theirs is an extreme position echoed and paralleled by the subversive commentary on the action maintained by the low-life characters of the play who intermittently (and for equally self serving reasons) point out the imperfect, somewhat arbitrary, mutable, morally quixotic, class-based and sometimes corrupt nature of human law and justice. The point is made most forcibly by Pompey's comparison between usury and whoredom – the former 'worser' sin allowed by the law, the latter 'merrier' one outlawed – or again, even more explicitly, by his observation to Escalus that his profession as a bawd would be legal if the law would allow it. Here, of course, Elbow is merely reiterating, in a *bon mot*, a more general point made by the play's careful juxtaposition and comparison between Angelo and Claudio's treatment of Mariana and Juliet. According to one view of the matter, a view accepted not merely by Claudio and Lucio but by the duke himself, Angelo was the 'combinate husband' of Mariana, just as much as Claudio was the legal spouse of Juliet. Angelo, for purely self-serving financial reasons, cold-bloodedly first abandons and then slanders Mariana as a loose woman, the better to cover up the real reasons for his appalling treatment of her. He escapes scot-free, being subject neither to the sanctions of the law nor the moral opprobrium of his peers. It is after all five years after he jilted Mariana that the duke chooses him as a man of virtue and honour as his deputy. Claudio, on the other hand, being more subject to the promptings of the flesh than the preternaturally cold blooded deputy, sleeps with his wife, merely putting off the formal wedding ceremony in order the while to arrange a better dowry. But merely because of the accident of a human law, which happens to define Claudio's conduct as 'fornication' – as he says at one point he is condemned for 'a name' – Claudio finds himself dragged in disgrace through the public streets, reviled by his own sister as a sex monster and condemned to death by the very man whose conduct towards his own 'wife', Mariana, has been so much worse than his own towards Juliet. There could scarcely be a more carefully constructed exemplification of Pompey's claim that the demands of natural justice and morality very often diverged from the demands and definitions of human law.

But if the low-lifes are capable of a certain moral perspicacity on the subject of the arbitrary and often unjust nature of human law and justice, they are no more capable of establishing a middle ground between the absolute demands of divine law and godly rule, on the one hand, and their own relativist libertinism and sarcasm, on the other. Thus when Lucio imagines the returning duke as a source of solace and pardon for the condemned Claudio, he does not envisage a prince using his prerogative powers to mitigate the letter of the law according to the demands of equity and natural justice, but rather a ruler as mired in the sins and impulse of the flesh as he is and therefore likely to view all such offences not only with complacence but even with approval.

It is, of course, these conflations and confusions, laid bare by the exchanges between the play's 'two saints' and their very different notions of true religion and godly rule, and by ironic moral commentary provided by the likes of Pompey and Lucio, that the duke sets to rights in the second half of the play, through the series of condemnations, pardons and mitigated punishment/rewards and marriages with which the action concludes. None of these resolutions are worked out solely through the powers and prerogatives of the secular prince but rather through those powers guided by the insights, the inside knowledge, culled by the duke through his exercise in the goal of the spiritual prerogatives and powers of a priest or minister. It is only his pastoral ministry in the gaols, reconciling a variety of felons to their ends, that allows the duke to gain the information necessary to frustrate Angelo's evil schemes and then perfectly to make the punishment fit the crime, as he repeatedly does at the play's end. One might well see this as an explicitly anti-puritan vindication of that odd mixture of the erastian and the sacerdotal that made up the English royal supremacy; taking it as a confirmation of

James's famous anti-presbyterian claim that princes were not 'mere laics' and thus as a refutation of the overly severe and complete puritan separation between the secular and the spiritual, the minister and magistrate, the church and the state, which reached its logical conclusion in the presbyterian platform.

But, of course, even masquerading the while as a priest, the duke does not pull it off on his own: all his intricate plans to frustrate Angelo, pardon Claudio, spiritually educate Isabella, all the while remaining, as it were, behind the curtain disguised as a friar, fail. And they fail, moreover, because of his own failure in his assumed role as a priest to reconcile Barnadine to death, thus freeing up this condemned murderer for execution and making his severed head available for substitution for that of Claudio. He is rescued from the resulting impasse by a direct divine intervention, a genuine providence, defined with wonderful economy here as 'an accident that heaven provides'. Again, one might see this confluence of both divine and royal power and cunning as confirming the view of direct divine sponsorship and protection of both the Stuart monarchy and the person of James I propagated throughout the reign by myriad court preachers and divines, who continually presented first the Gowry conspiracy and then the gunpowder plot as near miraculous divine interventions to save Great Britain's Solomon from the machinations of his enemies.[15]

But, of course, the duke who does all this is precisely not the duke who entered the action lamenting years of his own regime's laxity and complacence and calling on Angelo for a dose of puritan rigourism to put things right. Rather it is a duke now morally educated by having watched the awful consequences of the experiment in godly rule that, through his

---

[15] L. Ferrell, *Government by Polemic: James I, the King's Preachers and the Rhetorics of Conformity, 1603–25* (Stanford, 1998). On providentialism more generally see Walsham, *Providence*, chapter 5.

hand-picked deputy, his own folly has visited upon his realm. Having thus directly experienced, seen through, in a sense, triumphed over the false claims to purity and rigour of the godly, the duke has been enabled to achieve that balance between justice and mercy, rigour and temperance that is staged by the end of the play. Perhaps here we might imagine some contemporaries detecting or reading in a reference to James's own treatment of the puritans at Hampton Court where, against the advice of his English bishops, he had given the puritans their head and a hearing, and having heard their best arguments, made his definitive determinations about the future of the church and realm.

The duke does all this through the use of his royal prerogative which, *pace* Angelo's entirely law bound version of royal power, he uses to mitigate the application of the law according to the demands of equity and natural justice as his own conscience has been able to discern them. He does so, of course, by breaking all the rules laid down not merely in the murder pamphlets but in myriad assize and Paul's Cross sermons which cried up the need for judicial severity and decried the deleterious moral and social effects of a promiscuous use of the power of pardon.[16] For in the final scene the duke dishes out capital sentences and pardons with dizzying speed and ends up by formally punishing no one. Even Barnardine, the convicted, admitted and sentenced murderer, gets off. Thus is the absolute authority that the duke had ceded to Angelo at the play's start freed from the tyranny-inducing subjection to the letter of the law, which the deputy had placed upon it; thus is recreated a supra-legal prerogative authority which is able to respond, via the promptings of the conscience of the king, to the demands of divine and natural law and justice, and thus to mitigate the impact and course of human law and justice by finally making the punishment fit the crime.

The sort of moral resolution or balance thus achieved at the play's conclusion is, of course, figured through marriage. Throughout the play the issue of order or rather of that which has to

be controlled in order to establish order, has been figured by sex. Sex, particularly when mixed with money or the market, through prostitution or the pursuit of larger and larger dowries – in the argot of the pamphlets, lust when mixed with covetousness – has throughout been the source of moral breakdown and disorder. It lay behind Claudio and Juliet's fornication and bastard bearing; it prompted first Angelo's abandonment of Mariana and then, via his obsession with Isabella, his subsequent descent into corruption, deceit, fornication and judicial murder; it lay behind the libertinism, the moral and physical corruption, of Lucio and the other habitués of Pompey's brothel, and even arguably behind the strident, even hysterical, chastity and consequent spiritual pride and lack of charity displayed by Isabella. The question of how to order and control, without denying or repressing, the lusts and pleasures of the flesh thus hangs over the play and in the final scene it receives the entirely predictable, for the comedy the play by this point has turned into, indeed, the inevitable answer: marriage. Here is the way to foster the procreative, life giving aspects of sex without giving reign to its corrupting, disease and death-ridden resonances and consequences.

The high point of these marriage-centred resolutions is, of course, provided by the union proposed between the duke and Isabella. The duke, after a life time immune from the pleasures and allurements of the flesh, gives final expression to and proof of the completeness of his moral education while in hiding as a priest, by deciding to marry Isabella, the would-be nun, over whose own moral and spiritual education he has just, rather violently, personally presided. Under his tutelage, she has been forced to announce herself unchaste before half of Vienna, before begging for mercy for the man who tried to seduce, if not to rape her, a

---

[16] See, for instance, John Lawrence, *A Golden Trumpet to rouse up a Drowsy Magistrate* (London, 1624) or Sampson Price, *Ephesus' Warning Before her Woe* (London, 1616).

man whom, at that point, she still thinks has killed her brother. Thus, having been broken of her chastity-based spiritual pride she is rewarded by having whatever aspirations she may have retained towards the consolations of the cloister dashed by marriage to the prince. Thus might James be pictured seeing through the false claims to spiritual purity and power advanced by both puritan (Angelo) and catholic (Isabella) religious *engagés*.

IV

As I said earlier one could read the play as just such a paean of praise to a morally educated anti-puritan Jacobean absolutism, with everything ending happily ever after, through the wisely and moderately exercised prerogative powers of a truly and temperately godly prince. There are indeed elements in the play that allow, even elicit, perhaps even demand, such a reading but I think that it would, for fairly obvious reasons, be ill-advised to end on that note. For having offered such a happy ending, the play, if it does not take it away again, certainly severely qualifies it.

To begin with, most of the marriages with which the action concludes are as much punishments as they are rewards or likely sources of pleasure or gratification. Clearly Claudio and Juliet are as pleased as punch; Mariana too, and perhaps even Kate Keepdown, get a good deal of what they want. Lucio certainly does not; notoriously, for him marriage to a whore is 'pressing to death, whipping and hanging' (5.1.520–1). As for Angelo, his last words are a plea for death. This in itself is rather a bad sign for his current spiritual condition and perhaps even for his likely destination in the next world. Just as his first discovery of his own internal corruption and sin and his subsequent fall from grace had not led him to repentance or amendment but rather to a renewed pursuit of sexual gratification and a ruthless defence of his own position as a man of exemplary godliness, so now the discovery to the world of his crimes

and subsequent reprieve at the duke's hands has not led to a humble expression of repentance and amendment of life but rather to a desire for immolation, a wish that the ground almost literally and definitively should open up and swallow him. His is a typically proud determination to both judge and punish his own sin and thus avoid the (at least potentially edifying indeed saving) social and moral consequences of disgrace and marriage. On this evidence, Angelo, even now, is still not capable of true repentance. Judged according to the puritan godly's own criteria – criteria which they routinely applied both to their own and others' conversation – he might well be thought to be reprobate. To the, in this case at least, bitter end, the play appears to retain its razor sharp anti-puritan edge.[17] The plays other 'saint', Isabella, comes off rather better. Her newly found spiritual humility and charity having found expression in her plea for mercy for Angelo, her reward – the final stage of the play's taming of the nun – remains the duke's offer of

---

[17] The key phrase here, of course, is 'judged according to the godly's own criteria' for in and through his disgrace and rehabilitation, and, of course, his marriage to Mariana, the play or rather the duke continues to offer Angelo the possibility of moral growth and saving repentance. Again, his stubborn desire to die might be seen as the product of a certain stiff-necked moral and intellectual honesty which demands the same fate for himself as that which earlier he had tried to impose on Claudio. On this reading, since he is the person upon whose fall, upon whose *felix culpa*, the 'happy ending' or resolution achieved at the close of the action depends, the possibility of Angelo achieving a genuine repentance and redemption might be thought to be crucial to the play's overall Christian and indeed its anti-puritan messages. The fact that the play enables us to take either a sanguine or a pessimistic view of Angelo's chances in the repentance stakes may be designed to tell us not so much about puritans and what we ought to think of them, as about our own propensity, when handed the sort of moral advantage that the play hands its audience over Angelo, to adopt precisely the same sort of uncharitable and vengeful assumptions about the spiritual state and chances of salvation of erring brethren as those habitually used by the godly themselves. I owe these points to A. D. Nuttall.

marriage which, of course, she famously greets with silence. Even if she may not (yet) quite want him, Isabella gets the prince.

If these matrimonial outcomes are at best ambiguous, the means whereby they are achieved are by no means triumphs for princely power and temperance. The union between the roles of magistrate and minister achieved in the person of the duke/friar is, as we have seen, by no means stable. After all, the apologists for the royal supremacy agreed that while the prince was the supreme governor of the church he or she could never exercise the spiritual functions of a priest or minister. Nor, of course, does the duke: he is either a friar or a duke but never both. His attempts to manage affairs in character as the friar fail because of his own pastoral failure with Barnardine. Providence having saved his bacon, he is still forced to half-resume his real persona as a prince to get his way with the provost and spends the rest of the play hopping from one persona to the other until he is accidentally unmasked as the duke by Lucio.

The play clearly gestures throughout at temperance and moderation as the key princely virtues and moral qualities. It suggests a number of *via media*s between mercy and justice (both human and divine), between the laxity and complacence of the first incarnation of the duke and the unforgiving rigourism of Angelo, between the different but complementary domains of the minister and the magistrate, between the pleasures and exorbitances of the flesh and the demands of social order, between the different (catholic and protestant?) styles of religious rigourism personified by Isabella and Angelo, but the precise nature of these various middle ways remains consistently illusive and unstable. Having gestured at a powerful endorsement of the transcendent claims to godly rule made by Jacobean absolutism (at least in its more buoyantly theoretical moments), the play backs off. The best we can do when confronted by a number of rival claims to godly rule and spiritual purity is to trust to the prince and his temperate exercise of his supra-legal prerogative

powers to mediate between the demands of divine and natural law, justice and mercy, on the one hand, and fallen humanity, with all its necessarily arbitrary, imperfect and mutable laws, and its necessarily partial approximations to justice, on the other.

Having started out as a critique of puritan pretensions to godly rule the play ends, if not by undercutting, then certainly qualifying the very similar pretensions of Jacobean absolutism. That it does so, I would argue, is a function of its initial anti-puritan project. For the claims and assumptions, the moral nostrums and commonplaces labelled puritan in the play were not only or even mainly puritan or even protestant in provenance. To return for a moment to the narrative forms and framing assumptions of the murder pamphlets with which I started, and which the play so radically reorganizes and reshapes, while they were certainly susceptible to perfect protestant appropriation and gloss, they were never anything like distinctively puritan in provenance or tone. The implication of puritanism in the ideological and institutional, the social and political fabric of post reformation England, which the play so wonderfully stages, ensured that if you had a real go at puritanism you ended up laying bare and confronting some of the central, the most complex, over determined and controversial political, religious and socio-cultural cruxes in early modern England and that, I would argue, is precisely what *Measure for Measure* does.[18]

---

18 Of course, to come to the conclusion, as, at the most general level, this article does, that *Measure for Measure* is a play about the relations between human and divine justice and mercy, between 'law' and prerogative, a play that gestures at but never quite resolves a number of moral and theological cruxes, a play that, despite the decidedly anti-puritan (and perhaps even anti-Calvinist) inflection of much of its language and argument, ends ambiguously, is scarcely novel. But in my own defence let me explain that my purpose in this paper has not been to offer a novel interpretation of the play so much as to seek to ground the perhaps rather unsurprising reading offered here in certain historical contexts and circumstances. But that is not an end in itself, but rather

a means to a further historical rather than literary, or perhaps historical as well as literary, end. And that end is, having set the play in a series of contexts, having run a series of contemporary issues, arguments and identities through the grid provided by the play's structure and argument, to then reinsert those categories, identities and issues, as they have been illuminated and critiqued, problematized and confirmed by that process, back into the wider history of the period. It is, thus, to use a literary text as a form of historical evidence with which to address questions – about puritanism, about Stuart absolutism and the relations between law and prerogative, between 'religion' and 'politics', about con-temporary notions of order (moral, social, political and religious) – that are, and are likely to remain, at the centre of the historical writing on the period. The point here is not merely to use literary texts as a source of examples or evidence for things that one already knows or suspects, but rather to exploit what I take to be the peculiar relations pertaining between the theatrical and the wider society during this period to shape and deepen our overall view of that period. This is a task that I undertake on a larger scale in a book written with Michael Questier, *Antichrist's Lewd Hat; Papists, Puritans and Players in Post Reformation England*, forthcoming from Yale University Press.

THE HEBREW WHO TURNED CHRISTIAN: THE FIRST TRANSLATOR OF SHAKESPEARE INTO THE HOLY TONGUE

HANNA SCOLNICOV

The first two translations of plays by Shakespeare into the Holy Tongue were the work of a convert, a Hebrew who did indeed turn Christian. He not only converted, but became a Presbyterian minister and a missionary to the Jews. It is thanks to his unique life-story that the first translations of complete plays were made directly from the English rather than from Russian or German, the languages more familiar to nineteenth-century Jewish intellectuals, and from which most of the early Hebrew and Yiddish translations were made.[1]

In this article, I shall investigate the connection between this translator's personal religious biography and the first Shakespeare play he chose to translate. I shall argue that this translation reflects his own spiritual journey and forms an integral part of his missionary work. Furthermore, I shall suggest that the clue to its appreciation is viewing the transformation of Shakespeare into biblical Hebrew as a textual conversion. So, it is within the religious discourse of conversion that I shall consider the first translation of Shakespeare into Hebrew.

Isaac Edward Salkinson was born in a small *shtetl* in Belorussia, within the Jewish Pale of Settlement, in 1820.[2] His parents were orthodox and he received a traditional Jewish education. He was orphaned young, but carried on his religious studies in various yeshivas. He studied in Wilna, at that time an important centre of Jewish studies. It was there that he studied the Bible with its glosses, becoming an expert in Hebrew grammar, and also took up German

and read German literature. He then left for America to pursue his Jewish studies there, but never reached the United States. Instead, he

I am grateful to my colleague Harai Golomb for sharing with me his thoughts and some bibliographical references on Shakespeare translations into Hebrew. Ruth Morse read an earlier draft with her usual enthusiasm and made many helpful suggestions.

[1] A comprehensive account of Shakespeare translations into Hebrew is given by Dan Almagor, 'Shakespeare in Israel: A Bibliography, 1950–1965', *Shakespeare Quarterly*, 17 (1966), 291–306; and 'Shakespeare in Hebrew Literature, 1794–1930: Bibliographical Survey and Bibliography', in *Festschrift for Shimon Halkin* (Jerusalem, 1975), pp. 721–84 (in Hebrew).

For a more recent, analytical discussion see Harai Golomb, '"Classical" vs. "Contemporary" in Hebrew Translations of Shakespeare's Tragedies', *Poetics Today* (Theory of Translation and Intercultural Relations issue), 2 (1981), 201–7, and 'Shakespearean Re-generations in Hebrew: A Study in Historical Poetics', in *Strands Afar Remote: Israeli perspectives on Shakespeare*, ed. Avraham Oz (Newark, 1998), pp. 255–75.

See also Leonard Prager, 'Shakespeare in Yiddish', *Shakespeare Quarterly*, 19 (1968), 149–63.

[2] Biographical information on Salkinson is scarce. The fullest account is Israel Cohen, *Monographies*, vol. 3 (Tel-Aviv, 1976), 'Isaac Edward Salkinson: His life and Literary Works', pp. 333–420 (in Hebrew). Some contemporary material can be found in John Dunlop, *Memories of Gospel Triumphs Among the Jews During the Victorian Era* (London, 1894), pp. 373–87. This Jubilee report of the British Society for the Jews was compiled by the Revd John Dunlop, its Secretary, and published about ten years after the death of Salkinson. It includes a 'Brief Autobiographical Sketch', pp. 373–5, covering the years 1849–79. See also the short entry on Salkinson in the *Encyclopedia Judaica*.

stopped in London on his way and was converted by the London Missionary Society.[3]

In 1849 he entered the British Society's College, where he studied for four years. Later, he attended Divinity Hall in Edinburgh and was ordained in Glasgow in 1859. Salkinson was engaged as a missionary to the Jews by the Jewish Society in Scotland, which was subsequently incorporated into the United Presbyterian Church, and later by the euphemistically named British Society for the Jews. He was stationed first in Glasgow, then in Pressburg, and in 1876 moved to Vienna, where there was a large Jewish community, numbering about 70,000. He died in Vienna in 1883.

In the short autobiographical sketch published by Dunlop, Salkinson stated that his mission was to live among 'his brethren', i.e. the Jewish community, be in personal and intellectual intercourse with them, correspond with them and, especially, write treatises, in Hebrew, on their behalf.[4] Apparently, he was not too successful in converting other Jews, but set his heart instead on the literary aspect of his mission, which he regarded as his real vocation. He decided, therefore, to 'translate classical pieces into Hebrew', saying that

Hebrew translation seems to be the only talent given me, and it I have consecrated to the Lord. It is my alabaster box of precious ointment which I pour out in honour of my Saviour, that the fragrance of His name may fill the whole house of Israel.[5]

From his first attempt at translating Paul's *Epistle to the Romans* (1855), through *The Philosophy of the Plan of Salvation* (1858),[6] Milton's *Paradise Lost* (1871), and C. A. Tiedge's *Urania* (1876),[7] and up to his crowning work, the translation of the *New Testament*, begun in 1877 and published posthumously in 1885, all his translations were serviceable to his vocation. The exception was Shakespeare, whom he claimed to have translated 'in my hours of recreation'.[8]

Salkinson was well aware of his peculiar position as a translator who was a baptized Jew. In a published Hebrew correspondence, he states that, in his translation of *Paradise Lost* into Hebrew, he has not attempted to judaize the book by removing its foreskin, that he has refrained from circumcizing the text by excising anything from it. Instead, he says, he has attempted to present *Paradise Lost* to the Hebrew reader exactly as it issued from its author's womb, adding or subtracting nothing.[9] In the very act of denying its relevance to his translation of Milton, Salkinson had created the self-conscious metaphor of the Hebrew translator as a mohel circumcizing the text by cutting out references to Christian doctrine.

In the translation of the New Testament, Salkinson had to exercise even greater caution. He attempted to render it into strictly biblical Hebrew, without, however, compromising its Christian message. In its consistent use of the biblical linguistic register, Salkinson's translation was judged by many to be superior to that of Frantz Delitzsch, published not many years earlier.[10] The British missionaries believed the New Testament would have a special appeal for the People of the Book if it could stand side by side with the Old Testament, as though it too were handed down on Mount Sinai. They also

[3] On the remarkable role of the idea of Jewish conversion in Protestant England in the nineteenth century, see Michael Ragussis, *Figures of Conversion: 'The Jewish Question' and English National Identity* (Durham, 1995).

[4] See Dunlop, *Memories of Gospel Triumphs*, p. 373.

[5] Ibid., p. 382.

[6] Attributed to 'an American citizen' by the Revd Principal Davidson in his assessment of the translation, in Dunlop, *Memories of Gospel Triumphs*, p. 376.

[7] Some of the publication dates given in the Autobiographical Sketch are mistaken.

[8] Dunlop, *Memories of Gospel Triumphs*, p. 374.

[9] Letter by Salkinson to Alexander Halevi Langebank, in 'Critical letters', *Beit Otzar ha-Sifruth*, Magazin für hebräische Literatur und Wissenschaft, vol. 1, ed. Eisig Gräber (Jaroslau, 1887), p. 32 (in Hebrew).

[10] The New Testament, tr. Frantz Delitzsch (Leipzig, 1877). On some contemporary evaluations of Salkinson's translation, see Dunlop, pp. 383–6. To this day, the standard Hebrew translations of the New Testament are those of Delitzsch and Salkinson, superseding two earlier ones.

realized that, for the observant Jew, the New Testament was the forbidden book, but that, with the spread of Enlightenment and secularization among the Jews, there was growing interest in some circles in reading it.

The English Evangelical Revival coincided with the Jewish Enlightenment movement.[11] In the nineteenth century, the East-European Jews were increasingly eager to restore a national, historical and cultural identity for the demoralized Jewish people. The bonding of the dispersed Jews could only be achieved through the revival of Hebrew with its treasure house of literary and historical associations.[12] The struggle to bring about the re-birth of the ancient tongue formed part of the national movement, which culminated in the founding of the State of Israel.

Thus the Jewish national revival movement shared with the British mission a common interest in Hebrew as a viable language for translation.[13] Salkinson received praise and encouragement from both Church circles and Jewish intellectuals. The latter, however, while they appreciated the quality of his work, distanced themselves from its missionary aims.

Despite the critical acclaim with which they were initially received, Salkinson's translations of Shakespeare never became the classics they were meant to be. Modern Hebrew developed so rapidly and with such revolutionary fervour that they dated very quickly. They have come to be seen as no more than historical curiosities and are generally ignored by scholars of Hebrew literature.

It was a key figure in the Jewish Enlightenment movement, the writer Peretz Smolenskin, who persuaded Salkinson to take up the translation of Shakespeare. In his Hebrew foreword to the translation of *Othello*, Smolenskin celebrated the publication of the first Shakespeare play in Hebrew as an act of cultural retaliation:

Today we shall revenge ourselves on the Britons. They have taken our Holy Scriptures and done with them as they pleased, translating and disseminating them into the four corners of the earth, as though they belonged to them. Now shall we pay them back, take the books they hold no less than Holy Scripture – Shakespeare's plays – and bring them into the treasure house of our holy tongue. And is not this revenge sweet?[14]

Smolenskin saw the Hebrew appropriation of Shakespeare as a counter-measure to the English appropriation of the Old Testament, and expected it to do no less for Jewish culture. He perceived the first step in translating the works of Shakespeare as an important move towards restoring the self-confidence of the Jews in their ancient culture at the moment in which they were being enticed away from it by the European Enlightenment.

Othello was followed by *Romeo and Juliet* (1878), but Salkinson's work on Shakespeare was halted by a complaint lodged against him to the Church authorities, that he was using the Holy Tongue for translating secular literature, Shakespeare's licentious plays. Salkinson was banned from office for a year, in which time he was required to finish his translation of the New Testament.[15]

The issue of baptism and conversion in which *Othello* is steeped must have been of great personal interest to the Hebrew who turned

---

11 On the English Evangelical Revival, see Ragussis, *Figures of Conversion, passim.*
12 For the different views within the Jewish Enlightenment movement on biblical Hebrew, see Shimon Federbush, *The Hebrew Tongue in Israel and the Nations* (Jerusalem, 1967), p. 342 (in Hebrew).
13 For the views of the Jewish Enlightenment on translation, cf. Golomb, 'Shakespearean Re-generations', pp. 259ff.
14 Peretz Smolenskin (Peter Smolensky), 'Foreword' to *Ithiel the Moor of Venice*, tr. from English into Hebrew by J. E. S [Isaac Edward Salkinson] (Vienna, 1874). My translation of the paragraph differs considerably from that of Golomb, who quotes it in 'Shakespearean Re-generations', pp. 255–6. The difference in translation reflects our different interpretations of the tone and meaning of the paragraph, which I take to be only half-serious.
15 See Cohen, *Monographies*, pp. 359–60, 411.

Christian and missionary. Like Othello in Venice, Salkinson was an outsider in England. Yet, his very otherness, the knowledge he brought from his earlier, pre-baptismal existence, made him uniquely serviceable to his new, chosen faith. The wheeling stranger Othello was sent by the Venetian Senate to fight the Turks in Cyprus; similarly, the foreigner Salkinson was sent by the British mission to convert the Jews in Vienna.

Salkinson was interested in the Moor's religious conversion, not in his colour.[16] Like Desdemona, he saw Othello's visage in his mind. Salkinson would feel especially close to Othello if he understood him as a convert from Islam, rather than from paganism.[17] He could then see in Othello his own dual nature as both circumcized and baptized. One can perceive a dynamics of baptism being set in motion between the conflicting factors that make up both Salkinson's person and his work. His vocation was to baptize the circumcized, but, by translating this play into biblical Hebrew, Salkinson was judaizing the text.

Despite his open embrace of the Christian message and his commitment to it, Salkinson was always regarded as a Jewish convert, whose translations needed Church endorsement on their rendering of doctrinal matters. Thus, for example, J. J. Stewart Perowne, the Dean of Peterborough, approved the translation of *Paradise Lost*:

I have examined many portions of the translation, and especially those in which there is a reference to the Divinity of the Messiah, and I have no hesitation in saying that the translator has rendered the work faithfully.[18]

Conversion was perceived as a profound change of identity, perhaps akin to today's change of gender or change of sex. And like them, it was looked upon with suspicion by Christian society, which questioned the possibility of such a profound transformation and always anticipated recidivism.

Conversely, Jewish society traditionally viewed converts with great animosity. Salkinson was well aware of this Jewish attitude, which he expounded to his fellow missionaries:

The thoughts of the Jew are like the following: Here is one who brought shame upon his parents, betrayed the national faith, rebelled against God; and this great sin is light to him, so that he now seeks to cause Israel to sin. Then, again, measuring others with themselves, they suppose it is impossible for a Jew ever to become a true believer in the Saviour of the Gentiles; hence the missionary is regarded as a hypocrite, given to filthy lucre.[19]

So great was Jewish dislike of converts, and especially of missionaries, that Salkinson and his publisher found it expedient to hide the identity of the translator of *Othello* behind an acronym.

Because biblical Hebrew constitutes a closed linguistic continuum, frozen in time, encapsulating a religion and a culture, it is not a 'neutral' language that can easily accommodate new ideas. It carries with it a whole built-in world of associations, beliefs, stories and prayers, which are intertexts of the language itself. Every word and phrase has its own precise reference and meaning, so that the educated Jew could be expected to identify quotations and even the contexts of particular words.

Within this historical layer of language, any reference to Christianity would sound anachronistic and incoherent. Even Christian interpretations of the Old Testament have necessarily been allegorical or anagogic, rather than literal.

Salkinson had to find ways of dealing with the abundance of Christian concepts in *Othello*

---

[16] On the nineteenth-century English perception of 'the African character of the Jew', see Ragussis, *Figures of Conversion*, pp. 24–6. On the controversy on Judaism as race or faith in relation to Shakespeare, cf., e.g., James Shapiro, *Shakespeare and the Jews* (New York, 1996), p. 84.

[17] Cf. Julia Reinhard Lupton, 'Othello Circumcised: Shakespeare and the Pauline Discourse of Nations', *Representations*, 57 (1997), 73–89.

[18] Dunlop, *Memories of Gospel Triumphs*, p. 377.

[19] Ibid., p. 385.

without violating the boundaries of biblical discourse, which has no equivalents for 'baptism', 'redemption', or 'Christian shame'. Unlike his New Testament (which required the closest possible word-for-word translation), his Shakespeare invited a different kind of fidelity. It seemed to demand a re-creation of the work within the target language and culture. Salkinson searched for idiomatic biblical expressions that would convey the meaning of the original without becoming enslaved to the religious doctrine implicit in the source language, and substituted some of the Shakespearian imagery with biblical allusions. He described his translation of *Othello* as a transmigration of the soul of the play into Hebrew.[20]

In the second part of this paper, I look at Salkinson's treatment of some of the passages that relate to theology and religion. There is a certain irony in discussing in English a translation into Hebrew; however, as much of Salkinson's translation is directly based on Scripture, my task is simplified through the handy assistance of the King James Version.

Salkinson substituted the names of the characters, and even the name of the play itself, with biblical equivalents. This was the fashion at the time, but a close examination of Salkinson's names reveals his underlying ideology.[21]

'Othello' became the phonetically similar 'Ithiel' (Proverbs 30.1; Nehemiah 11.7), a Hebrew name meaning 'God is with me'. This meaning must have contributed to Salkinson's attraction to the character and his spiritual biography. But the choice of the name may also have to do with the context in which it appears, in Proverbs. Ithiel is one of the addressees of Agur's words, strangely reminiscent of Othello's 'Rude am I in my speech' (1.3.81):

Surely I am more brutish than any man, and have not the understanding of a man. I neither learned wisdom, nor have the knowledge of the holy.

(Proverbs 30.2–3)

Although all the characters bear biblical names,

practically all are, unlike Ithiel, the names of gentiles. Thus, for example, Desdemona is called Asenath, after the bride given to Joseph by Pharaoh, the daughter of Poti-phera, priest of On (Genesis 41.45). The one exception is Raddai, i.e. Roderigo, who is called after David's fifth brother (I Chronicles 2.14), whose name was obviously chosen for homophonic reasons alone.

Salkinson isolated Ithiel by giving him a Hebrew name that emphasizes his faith in God and surrounding him with Venetians carrying gentile names. Through the allocation of names, Salkinson re-defined the position of the protagonist as that of a Jew within gentile society, thus emphasizing the religious tensions in the play.

Especially interesting is the transformation of Iago into Doeg. The biblical Doeg was an Edomite. For the children of Israel, the Edomites were a long-standing foe. Edom became synonymous with the enemy of Israel: in post-biblical literature, Rome is frequently called Edom. By naming Iago, in the biblical context, 'Doeg', Salkinson set in motion a train of associations that makes him, in the subtext, the equivalent of the Christian Enemy.

In the Bible, Doeg the Edomite is an especially reprehensible figure. It was he who betrayed to King Saul Ahimelech, the priest who had given shelter to David in Nob. None of Saul's servants was prepared to execute his revenge order, except Doeg, who killed first all eighty-five members of Ahimelech's family, then the rest of the inhabitants of the city of Nob and even its livestock (1 Samuel 22). That his name became a by-word for ill-repute can be learned from its use by the psalmist:

To the chief Musician, Maschil, A Psalm of David, when Doeg the Edomite came and told Saul, and said unto him, David is come to the house of

---

[20] 'Translator's letter to the publisher', printed as a second foreword to *Ithiel*, p. xxxiii. See also Cohen, *Monographies*, p. 375.

[21] See Appendix, below.

Ahimelech . . . Thy tongue deviseth mischiefs; like a sharp razor, working deceitfully. Thou lovest evil more than good; and lying rather than to speak righteousness. (Psalms 52.1–3)

This could easily be a character-sketch of Iago. The felicitous choice of the name 'Doeg' was intended to carry these unpleasant associations, including the easy wielding of the sword in the service of mischief.

Iago is perhaps the character most aware of theological issues. He asserts that Desdemona has such a strong influence on Othello that it would be easy for her 'to win the Moor' and even make him 'renounce his baptism, / All seals and symbols of redeemèd sin' (2.3.334–5). 'Renounce his baptism' becomes in Hebrew: 'to be separated from the congregation of God' (Ezra 10.8). 'Renounce. . . all seals and symbols of redeemèd sin' is changed into 'cast his soul',[22] or, in the King James Version, 'adventured his life far', as in Jotham's Parable of the Bramble (Judges 9.17). After recounting his parable, Jotham rebukes the people of Shechem for their ingratitude, for having forgotten how his father, Jerubbaal, i.e. Gideon, delivered them from their enemies. Jotham's highly emotional evocation of his late father who cast his soul for the people of Shechem is a figure for Christ's having died for man's sins. Thus Salkinson indirectly preserves the signification of the 'symbols of redeemèd sin'. Although he substituted the Old Testament story of Jotham for Iago's theology of hell, Salkinson succeeded in keeping the Christian subtext.

Jotham's parable is also used for the translation of the image of the net that Iago promises to make out of Desdemona's own goodness, 'that shall enmesh them all' (2.3.353). The diabolical net is replaced by the biblical 'fire [that] will come out and devour them all' (p. 76), deriving from the bramble's threat: 'Let fire come out of the bramble and devour the cedars of Lebanon' (Judges 9.15).

Iago also promises to turn Desdemona's 'virtue into pitch' (2.3.351). Doeg recalls Isaiah's prophecy on Edom, that 'the streams thereof shall be turned into pitch, and the dust thereof into brimstone, and the land thereof shall become burning pitch' (Isaiah 34.9). Translating back from Hebrew, what Doeg says is: 'And her goodness shall turn into brimstone and all her grace into pitch' (p. 76). In this example, Salkinson has planted Iago's words within Isaiah's apocalyptic vision. However, this infernal landscape manages to remain within the imagistic boundaries of the play, outlined by Othello's 'Fire and brimstone' oath (4.1.231).

Iago's graphic description of the coming together of Othello and Desdemona as a bestial copulation takes off from the image of the Barbary horse:

. . . you'll have your daughter covered with a Barbary horse, you'll have your nephews neigh to you, you'll have coursers for cousins, and jennets for germans. (1.1.113–15)

In Hebrew, the Barbary horse is transformed into an ass, 'hamor' (p. 7). The image of bestiality and its monstrous progeny is used metaphorically by Ezekiel, who chastises Aholibah for doting on paramours 'whose flesh is as the flesh of asses, and whose issue is like the issue of horses' (Ezekiel 23.20).[23]

Even more forceful are the narrative and structural parallels evoked by the translation, for Hamor is also the proper name of the father of Shechem, whose story is told in Genesis 34. It is the story of the rape of Dinah, the daughter of Jacob, by Shechem, the son of Hamor. By implication, Desdemona is being raped by a beast, just as Dinah was by the son of Hamor.

Dinah's brothers, Simeon and Levi, revenged the rape by deceiving the people of Shechem into being circumcized, then, 'on the third day, when they were sore' (Genesis 34.25), attacked the city and killed all the males. Obviously, this allusion is totally uncalled for by the Shakespearian text. But Salkinson used the biblical association because of the meaning of

---

22 *Ithiel*, p. 75.
23 My thanks to Harai Golomb for drawing my attention to this verse in Ezekiel.

Hamor's name, combining the innate bestiality of the ass with the story of the rape of Dinah by an uncircumcized stranger. The multiple references to Brabanzio's bestial progeny, who will neigh to him, were replaced by the reference to the seed or semen of the ass. Thus the grossness of Iago's language found its parallel in this biblical myth of defilement.

Salkinson's allusion to this story can be deconstructed to reveal his fascination with the dynamics of circumcision: the uncircumcized defiles the circumcized, but the circumcized retaliates by persuading the rapist and his relatives to undergo circumcision, then, taking advantage of their being incapacitated, slays them.

Brabanzio mourns the loss of his daughter: 'Gone she is' (1.1.162). This is translated into the excruciatingly simple language of Reuben's sorrow, when he returns to the pit where Joseph was cast, and, not finding him, says to his brothers: 'The child is not' (Genesis 37.30), or, as in the original Hebrew (for lack of a neuter), 'the boy is not'. Except for the change of gender, 'the girl is not' (p. 9), Salkinson makes Brabanzio's sorrow echo that minimalistically expressed, archetypal mourning.

After she has eloped, Desdemona is a girl no longer, and first her father, then her husband, try to contain her sexuality. Through his use of biblical terminology, Salkinson charged their definitions of her with different religious overtones.

Trying to ascertain what has happened, Brabanzio asks Roderigo: 'Are they married, think you?' (1.1.169). There is no biblical word to express the reciprocity of marriage: the husband weds a wife, but she remains a passive figure, wedded to her husband. Therefore, Brabanzio's question is turned into the sexually explicit: 'Do you think, Roderigo, that she has lost her virginity?' (p. 10). The word Salkinson uses here is 'be'ulah', i.e. she who has been tilled or deflowered, cognate with the word for 'husband' or 'master', 'ba'al'.

In the Hebrew, there is both consonance and

assonance between 'be'ulah' and 'bethulah', the word for virgin. Brabanzio's question thus highlights the critical debate over whether the marriage of Othello and Desdemona is ever consummated.

That Salkinson was using this word advisedly can be learned from his translation of the story of the immaculate conception in Matthew. Delitzsch had translated 'Joseph her husband' (Matthew 1.19), using the word 'ba'al' for 'husband'. If 'be'ulah', a passive, feminine form, is she who has lost her virginity, 'ba'al' is the masculine, active form, husband in the sense of he who has deflowered the woman. With his greater sensitivity to etymology, Salkinson felt the absurdity of using that word in defining the relationship between Joseph and Mary, and used the Hebrew for 'her man', to avoid the sexual connotation.[24]

Like her father, Othello too tries to ascertain Desdemona's chastity. His accusation that she is a whore (4.2.74, 89) is translated as 'kedesha' (p. 147), playing on the implicit ambiguity of 'kedesha' as holy prostitute. Othello speaks in the language of an Old Testament prophet, chastising the Children of Israel for leaving their God and prostituting their faith. When Othello asks Desdemona, 'Are not you a strumpet?' (84), she responds: 'No, as I am a Christian' (85). Salkinson makes her swear instead by her faith in God her saviour: 'be-emunati be-elohei yish'i' (p. 148). She uses a common biblical expression, but Salkinson was surely punning on 'yesha', the word for 'salvation' or 'delivery', and 'Yeshua', the Hebrew name of Jesus. In this case too, Salkinson has pushed the Christian meaning into the subtext so as not to disrupt the Old Testament conceptual texture. Another consideration may have been trying to avoid giving offence to his intended Jewish readership.

The Holy Land is actually invoked towards the end of the play by Emilia, who 'know[s] a lady in Venice would have walked barefoot to

---

24 See Cohen, *Monographies*, p. 410.

Palestine for a touch of [Lodovico's] nether lip' (4.3.36–7). 'Palestine' is naturally translated as 'the Holy Land'. Picking up that theme, Salkinson evokes the Jewish longing for the Land of Israel in his translation of Barbary's song (4.3.38–55): the willow of the refrain appears in the plural (p. 161), as in the Song of the Exiles:

By the rivers of Babylon, there we sat down, yea, we wept, when we remembered Zion. We hanged our harps upon the willows in the midst thereof.

(Psalms 137.1–2)

The unhappiness of Desdemona, of Barbary and of all jilted young women is thus tied to the archetypal mourning for the lost homeland and to the nationalist sentiment of the nineteenth-century Jewish Enlightenment. So intent is Salkinson on this analogy, that he changes 'An old thing 'twas' (4.3.28) into *shirath kedem* (p. 160), which means both 'ancient song' and 'song from the East'.

The willows of Babylon bring us back to what is, perhaps, the ultimate source of the association of willows with mourning. The associations with the Holy Land heighten the power of the image, but also, at the same time, distract the reader from the dramatic issue at hand. Salkinson's handling of the Willow Song demonstrates both the strength and the weakness of his art of translating: here as elsewhere, Salkinson's stake in Christian religion and Jewish nationalism overshadows the romantic aspects of the play.

Salkinson's treatment of Othello's final speech (pp. 196–7), with its notorious crux of 'Indian' or 'Judean' (5.2.356), deserves special attention.[25] Ithiel compares himself to 'that Jew' – not 'the base Judean' – who 'threw a pearl away, / Richer than all his tribe' (5.2.356–7).[26] In Hebrew, there is no difference between 'Jew' and 'Judean' – both are 'Yehudi', and 'Yehudi' means from the tribe of Yehuda, i.e. Judah, or Judas. This linguistic feature served, for many centuries, as fuel for antisemitism, making Judas into the archetypal Jew. Reading the passage as Othello's self-comparison to Judas, Salkinson could not help but infuse the words with echoes of the Gospel story of Judas' betrayal of Christ.

It is a precarious and loaded dramatic moment not only for Othello, but also for Salkinson, reviewing in a poetic flash the whole narrative of the rift between Christianity and Judaism. The 'turbaned Turk [who] beat a Venetian' (5.2.362–3) becomes, in Hebrew, a 'turbaned . . . Ismaelite [who] hit one of our brethren' (p. 197). It is a moment in which both Ithiel and Salkinson take upon themselves the weight of centuries of theological debates. So, whatever Shakespeare wrote and whatever the meaning of this heroic speech, it becomes, in Salkinson's version, a convert's manifesto, an expression of the inherent duality of the convert's consciousness. The integration of both sides of his personality is achieved symbolically, and tragically, in his suicide, when the baptized man finally kills 'the circumcised dog' (364) within himself.

Salkinson's translation brings out forcefully the drama of the Moor's conversion but also introduces his own, Jewish convert's parallel. By translating all this into the religious language of his forefathers, he set in motion a dialectic of circumcision and baptism that, but for Ithiel's suicide, would remain unresolved. Like its author, the translation remains ambiguous, both baptized and circumcised.

---

25 See, e.g., Richard Levin, 'The Indian/Iudean Crux in *Othello*', *Shakespeare Quarterly*, 33 (1982), 60–7; Naseeb Shaheen, *Biblical References in Shakespeare's Plays* (Newark, 1999), pp. 600–3.

26 See *Ithiel*, p. 197. On p. 200, Smolenskin, the publisher, adds a note: 'The translator wrote, "richer than all the tribes of Israel", but I changed his translation and wrote, "richer than all the wealth of Israel". I believe I was right in making this change, for the English "richer" denotes both "wealth" and "honour", and I chose the first meaning. So too did the German translator, for he translated not "besser als sein Stamm" but "reicher als sein Stamm". There is a vast difference between these two translations, as any perceptive reader will note' (my translation).

APPENDIX: A LIST OF THE PARALLEL BIBLICAL CHARACTERS IN SALKINSON'S TRANSLATION

Othello	Ithiel	Nehemia 11.7 (one of the exiles returning from Babel to Jerusalem); Proverbs 30.1 (One of the addressees of Agur's 'confession of faith')
Brabanzio	Phichol	Genesis 21.22, 26.26 (Abimelech's chief captain)
Cassio	Chesed	Genesis 22.22 (son of Nahor, Abraham's brother, and Milcah)
Iago	Doeg	1 Samuel 21.8, 22.9, 18, 22, Psalms 52.2 (King Saul's chief herdsman)
Roderigo	Raddai	1 Chronicles 2.14 (one of David's brothers)
Montano	Kenaz	Genesis 36.11, 15, 42; 1 Chronicles 1.36, 53 (Esau's grandson); Joshua 15.17, Judges 1.13, 3.9, 11, 1 Chronicles 4.13 (father of the judge Othniel); 1 Chronicles 4.15 (son of Elah the son of Caleb)
Lodovico	Lud	Genesis 10.22; 1 Chronicles 1.17 (Shem's son); Isaiah 66.19, Ezekiel 27.10, 30.5 (a gentile people)
Graziano	Gether	Genesis 10.23; 1 Chronicles 1.17 (Aram's son and Shem's grandson)
Desdemona	Asenath	Genesis 42.45, 50, 46.20 (Joseph's wife)
Emilia	Milcah	Genesis 11.29, 22.20,23,24 (Nahor's wife); Numbers 26.33, 27. 1, 36.11, Joshua 17.3 (Zelophehad's daughter)
Bianca	Anah	Genesis 36.2, 14, 18; 1 Chronicles 1.38, 40, 41 (Esau's wife)

SHAKESPEARE AND ENGLISH PERFORMANCE STYLE: THE EUROPEAN CONTEXT

JANETTE DILLON

Records show that Shakespeare's plays were performed in Europe during his lifetime; but no extant records, to my knowledge, show what those performances were like or how European audiences received them. I propose in this paper to use contemporary records and our wider knowledge of European performance traditions to build up a picture of the kinds of emphasis that may have prevailed in performing Shakespeare to mainland European audiences in the late sixteenth and early seventeenth centuries and to assess how far these kinds of emphasis accorded with contemporary performance styles in England. The materials I cite here are not newly discovered; instead they are assembled largely from the neglected work of older scholars in a way that creates, I think, an unfamiliar emphasis in the study of Shakespeare.

The best-known comment on Shakespeare from a European witnessing a contemporary performance of one of his plays is the Swiss Thomas Platter's account of a visit to the Globe in London in 1599, when he witnessed, he says,

an excellent performance of the tragedy of the first Emperor Julius Caesar with a cast of some fifteen people; when the play was over, they danced very marvellously and gracefully together as is their wont, two dressed as men and two as women.[1]

The description is notable for its concentration on the excellent dancing that follows the play, rather than on the text or narrative of the play itself; and the prominent place of music and dance generally following the performance of plays in London at this time is confirmed by another foreign visitor in the previous year, Paul Hentzner, who writes that:

Without the city are some theatres where English actors almost every day represent Tragedies and Comedies to very numerous audiences, these are concluded with excellent music, variety of dances and the great applause of the audience.[2]

Platter and Hentzner are of course responding to performances given in England; but the earliest evidence of English players abroad confirms the widespread familiarity of Platter's perspective via an overwhelming emphasis on the non-verbal elements of performance. One of the earliest records, for example, is the observations of an Englishman, Fynes Moryson, who saw a group of English players under Robert Browne performing in Frankfurt in 1592:

---

[1] *Thomas Platter's Travels in England*, ed. Clare Williams (London, 1937), p.166.

[2] Quoted in Albert Cohn, *Shakespeare in Germany in the Sixteenth and Seventeenth Centuries: An Account of English Actors in Germany and the Netherlands and of the Plays Performed by them during the same Period* (London, 1865), p.xvii. One might note, by contrast, the Englishman Fynes Moryson's scorn for the unsophisticated dancing by Germans he witnessed in Germany, where, he said, 'they vse no kynd of Art', but sometimes 'playnly walke about the roome with grauity inough and to spare, which kynde of dauncing they iustly call Gang, that is going' (*Shakespeare's Europe: Unpublished Chapters of Fynes Moryson's Itinerary* (London, 1903), p. 326).

I remember that when some of our cast dispised Stage players came out of England into Germany, and played at Franckford in the tyme of the Mart, hauing nether a Complete number of Actours, nor any good Apparell, nor any ornament of the Stage, yet the Germans, not vnderstanding a worde they sayde, both men and women, flocked wonderfully to see theire gesture and Action, rather then heare them, speaking English which they vnderstoode not, and pronowncing peeces and Patches of English playes, which my selfe and some English men there present could not heare without great wearysomenes.[3]

In the same year as the visit to Frankfurt recorded by Moryson, Röchell's Chronicle of Münster confirms the English practice of dancing and playing music at the beginning and end of their plays.[4]

As Moryson's comments (again confirmed by Röchell's Chronicle) make clear, one of the factors working to foreground non-verbal elements in the English players' performances abroad was the fact that they performed in English, which most of their audience did not understand. Not until the seventeenth century is there evidence that the English actors had begun to perform translated versions of their plays.[5] It is self-evident, however, that in either case, whether English players performed Shakespeare's plays abroad in English or in translation, Shakespeare's original words were not the primary focus of attention or attraction.

The two most prominent elements in the responses cited above, the emphasis on non-verbal aspects of performance and the high degree of admiration for English performers, especially for these same non-verbal skills, are echoed by a German writer writing in 1605 on the playing careers of English actors in Germany:

England thus produces numerous and outstanding musicians, and tragedians most experienced in histrionic art, among whom some formed congregations and for some time left their homes and went abroad, and they used to present and exhibit their art above all at ducal courts. Several years ago, the English musicians came to our Germany . . . and having stayed for some time at the courts of great princes, they gained – through their musical and histrionic art – so much favour that they returned home generously rewarded and loaded with gold and silver.[6]

Cellius scarcely distinguishes between musical and theatrical activity, which suggests the degree to which music was integrated into English performance at this date; and numerous other records demonstrate not only the high number of musicians in English companies travelling abroad, but the extent to which playing routinely incorporated some degree of musical skill and physical agility and the falseness in many instances of attempting to distinguish between musicians, dancers and other players. When the Earl of Leicester took English military aid to the Netherlands in 1585 he laid on after-dinner entertainment, possibly by his own players, which combined 'dancing, vaulting, tumbling, and an exhibition, probably of a pantomimical character, termed 'The Forces of Hercules', which gave great delight to the strangers'.[7] Englishmen in the service of the Elector of Saxony in 1586 are described in the

---

[3] *Shakespeare's Europe*, p. 304. English actors are first recorded on the continent in 1417, but records of their visits are especially frequent in the first two decades of the seventeenth century (before the outbreak of the Thirty Years' War) and fairly regular for some years on either side of that period. See Cohn, *Shakespeare in Germany*, and Jerzy Limon, *Gentlemen of a Company: English Players in Central and Eastern Europe 1590–1600* (Cambridge, 1985).

[4] Cohn, *Shakespeare in Germany*, p. cxxxv.

[5] Cohn cites the requirement of the Dresden court in 1659 that the English players provide German translations for their plays; but the existence of German printed versions from earlier in the period may suggest that the performance of translated texts, even if not perhaps by English players, predates this.

[6] Erhard Cellius, *Eques Auratus Anglo-Wirtembergicus*, cited in Limon, *Gentlemen of a Company*, pp. 7–8.

[7] Cohn, *Shakespeare in Germany*, p. xxii, citing Stowe's *Chronicle*, which in turn is reliant on the eye-witness account of Segar, the herald. Cohn points out that a letter of Philip Sidney's names 'Will, the Lord of Leicester's jesting player', as accompanying Leicester to the Netherlands.

court documents as instrumentalists, but include the players Thomas Pope and George Bryan, and are called 'comedians' by Thomas Heywood in his *Apology for Actors*.[8] The Elector's decree of appointment makes it clear that the Englishmen are expected to deploy a variety of skills in entertaining the court: they are to 'play music, and amuse and entertain us also with their art in leaping and other graceful things that they have learnt'.[9] The Chronicler of Nuremberg in 1613 describes the English comedians continuing to offer 'graceful dancing, lovely music, and other entertainments' besides comedies and tragedies; and English actors themselves are similarly inclusive in their own descriptions of what they offer in their petition to the Council of Rostock in 1606 'to execute our music and plays'.[10] Charles Harris notes a company of eighteen at Frankfurt in 1605, of whom seven seem to have been musicians; one at Königsberg in 1611 with nineteen players and sixteen musicians; and one at Frankfurt in 1614 with nineteen players and fifteen musicians.[11] Even the celebrated clown Will Kempe is described in the Danish court records as an instrumentalist.[12] Players and companies typically combined a range of skills in this period, as Kempe's own dance to Norwich, following his career as a clown with the Chamberlain's Men, demonstrates. The same Robert Browne whose company Fynes Moryson saw in Frankfurt had 'dogges, Beares and Apes' as well as players with him when he travelled abroad; and as late as 1630 a touring solo Italian performer in England was licensed 'to dance on the ropes, to use interludes and masques and to sell his powders and balsams'.[13]

An emphasis on music, dance and visual spectacle, together with a highly gestic form of acting, however, was no novelty imported to Europe by English actors, as this last example of an Italian player should remind us. Both elite and popular genres of performance were already deeply imbued over a long period with music and other non-verbal emphases all across Europe. Performed in Latin, the earliest religious drama throughout Europe had to signify to most of the congregation other than through the semantic meaning of its text. An appeal to the eye through costume and tableau, and to the ear through music and song as well as through the sound and texture, as opposed to the meaning, of language, was central to it from its earliest beginnings. Its origins, furthermore, were musical, beginning in the polyphonic decoration of simple tropes. Vernacular religious drama across Europe retained an emphasis on visual spectacle and a strong musical element, including some dance as well as instrumental music and song. Occasionally, as in the case of the sixteenth-century Spanish *Danza del Santísimo Nacimiento*, religious drama was conceived primarily in the form of dance.[14]

Secular forms were equally reliant on pleasing the eye and ear, and sometimes totally free of text. Courts across Europe cultivated a variety of dramatic or quasi-dramatic entertainments which went by different names (disguising,

8 *An Apology for Actors* (1612; rpt London, 1841), p. 40.

9 Cohn, *Shakespeare in Germany*, p. xxvi.

10 Ibid., pp. lxxxvii, lxxxi.

11 'The English Comedians in Germany before the Thirty Years' War: The Financial Side', *PMLA*, 22 (1907), pp. 455–6.

12 Charles Read Baskervill, *The Elizabethan Jig and Related Song Drama* (1929; rpt New York, 1965), p. 129. Cohn argues that these terms are in use because professional actors were unknown in Germany and no current term was available for designating an actor (p. xxvi), but the records he cites everywhere make clear that music, dance and acrobatics are germane to the acting profession at this time.

13 The animals are mentioned in a travel warrant granted to Browne on leaving England for a later tour in 1604. See K. M. Lea, *Italian Popular Comedy: A Study in the Commedia dell'Arte, 1560–1620 with Special Reference to the English Stage*, 2 vols. (Oxford:, 1934), vol. 2, p. 351. For the record of the Italian performer's licence, see Lea, vol. 2, p. 361.

14 See J. E. Gillet, '*Danza del Santísimo Nacimiento*, a Sixteenth-Century Play by Pedro Suárez de Robles', *PMLA*, 43 (1928), pp. 614–34. Gillet notes a few further Spanish plays in which dancing is central on pp. 623–4.

entremets, interlude, triumph, mask, *ballet de cour*) but were characterized above all by the integration of different elements, including music, dancing and visual spectacle, while the tournament became less of a military event and increasingly a part of court revels, until by the reign of James I the barriers had become a form of masque. Even where forms we would call 'plays' were incorporated into these entertainments, thus seemingly giving more prominence to verbal text, the need to punctuate them with interpolated music, dancing, disguising or dumb-show allowed for the creation of a new and highly influential form, first developed in Italy: the *intermezzo*. At the Este court in Ferrara, where the first performance of Plautus's *Menaechmi* in 1486 set a fashion for classical plays across Italy, Isabella d'Este's boredom on an occasion when there seemed to her too little music and dancing interspersed in the comedy offers some indication of the degree to which these elements were indispensable.[15] A shared vocabulary of spectacle was widely understood across Europe, and new fashions spread quickly and widely. Edward Hall's recording of the English court's shock on Twelfth Night, 1512, at a new style of disguising 'after the maner of Italie, called a maske, a thyng not seen afore in England' underlines both the copying of new fashions and the extent to which Italy led the way in such matters in the early part of the sixteenth century.[16] By the latter end of the century, however, France was contesting that pre-eminence. The splendours of the Medici festivals were known all over Europe, and Inigo Jones copied both Italian and French models in designing his masques.[17]

Enid Welsford, noting the cross-fertilization of dramatic forms across Europe, comments that 'the distinctions between various types of revelling at this period seem to have been social rather than national'.[18] Writers on early modern court entertainment rightly emphasize the combination of a political with an aesthetic agenda in the mounting of such integrated spectacles, and Sydney Anglo has been the pioneer in this respect with regard to the early Tudor English court. As Mark Franko puts it in relation to French ballet: 'Clearly, one should look to Renaissance thought on politics and music when seeking to understand the nature and necessity of collective unity in early modern *Gesamtkunstwerk*.'[19] Early choreography, as Franko shows, uses the body to enact a metaphor of harmony derived from musical theory and applied to social and cosmic thinking. Each element of these integrated spectacles, from music, dance and the allegorical conceits of pageantry, to the later development of the perspective stage, expresses through its own internal order and symmetry an affirmation of

---

[15] See Enid Welsford, *The Court Masque: A Study in the Relationship between Poetry and the Revels* (1927; rpt New York, 1962), p. 88. This was not, however, the first performance of a Plautus play in Renaissance Europe. An earlier performance of his *Aulularia* took place in Rome in 1484.

[16] *Hall's Chronicle*, ed. by Henry Ellis (London, 1809), p. 526. Despite the excitement evident in Hall's text about a new direction emerging under Italian influence, however, Gordon Kipling rightly points out that many of the most striking innovations in the disguising were the work of William Cornish at the court of Henry VII, and that the debt in that period was more directly to the Burgundian court (*The Triumph of Honour: Burgundian Origins of the Elizabethan Renaissance* (Leiden, 1977), especially chapter 5).

[17] The Medici name is associated with both French and Italian court festivals, of course, from the time of Catherine de' Medici's marriage to Henry II of France. The Valois court festivals of the second half of the sixteenth century were very much her creation, and these fêtes, together with the *intermezzi* mounted by the Medici in Florence in 1589, were milestones in the development of sixteenth-century European spectacle.

[18] *The Court Masque*, p. 130.

[19] *Dance as Text: Ideologies of the Baroque Body* (Cambridge, 1993), p. 32. On the neo-platonic philosophical principles underlying this development of integrated spectacles, see Günter Berghaus, 'Theatre Performances at Italian Renaissance Festivals: Multi-Media Spectacles or *Gesamtkunstwerke*?', in *Italian Renaissance Festivals and their European Influence*, ed. by J. R. Mulryne and Margaret Shewring (Lewiston, Queenston and Lampeter, 1992), pp. 1–50.

political order radiating outwards from the centre of the monarch.[20]

But the emphasis on social distinction, with its conventional binary formulation of popular and elite, also has a misleading dimension. As Welsford herself demonstrates, court masques, mummings, disguisings and moriscos incorporate elements of popular festival, from mumming to morris-dance. A morisco at court is a morris-dance by another name; and the elegant dancing Platter describes in the public playhouse may not have been so very different from the dancing of court masque. While clearly court revels of the fifteenth, sixteenth and seventeenth centuries have moved a long way from village entertainments in terms of sophistication and elaboration, the prominence of music, dance and gestic display remain common to dramatic entertainment at all levels. Jigs, ballads, acrobatics and clowning may have been primarily popular forms of entertainment, but it was not uncommon for clowns and acrobats to perform at court. Italian *commedia dell'arte* toured across the courts as well as the towns of Europe; and the English players who were followed from town to town also performed before European princes, just as in England they played both at court and in the public theatres.[21] Entertainments devised at the highest level, for the honour or diversion of monarchs, whether royal entries, coronation pageants or tournaments, were either routinely or occasionally open to all-comers or to a restricted number of the public, which meant that ordinary people were exposed, though much less frequently, to the same type of drama (visual, spectacular, often allegorical, almost always interspersed with music and song) as the ruling elite.[22] The sameness, of course, is not complete, which is where the argument returns to social distinction. Though elite and popular practices interact with and influence each other, each makes its own recognizable identity within different bodily paradigms, social spaces and cultural practices.[23]

To return to specifically English performance style, then, what was notable about English actors was not a difference in their style of

[20] On both the political thinking underpinning drama and festival and the influence of European courts on each others' spectacles, see also Roy Strong, *Splendour at Court: Renaissance Spectacle and Illusion* (London, 1973) and, the revised version, *Art and Power: Renaissance Festivals 1450–1650* (Woodbridge, 1984).

[21] Fynes Moryson notes how the English players were followed from town to town (*Shakespeare's Europe*, p. 476); and the preface to a published anthology of English plays printed in Germany in 1620 confirms the appeal of the 'English Comedians' to 'persons both of high and low condition' (cited Cohn, *Shakespeare in Germany*, p. civ).

[22] Much more work remains to be done on the composition of audiences for court spectacles. While one might assume that, whereas street pageantry is open to the widest possible audience, court masques and disguisings would be attended only by an invited elite, this may not be an accurate picture. Sydney Anglo suggests, for example, that Henry VIII's entertainment of the French ambassadors at Greenwich in 1527 was probably more open to the public at large than Hall's account indicates, and that, not only would the open-air tournament have been open to the public (as was routinely the case), but ordinary subjects may also have attended the indoor evening celebrations ('La Salle de Banquet et le Théâtre Construits à Greenwich pour les Fêtes Franco-Anglaises de 1527', in *Le Lieu Théâtral à la Renaissance*, ed. J. Jacquot (Paris, 1964), pp. 287–8). Anglo's view is presumably based on sneering remarks elsewhere in Hall's *Chronicle* about the attempts by lower-class spectators to strip revels costumes and pageants for souvenirs, as in February 1511: 'After the kyng and his compaignions had daunced, he appointed the ladies, gentelwomen and the Ambassadours to take the letters of their garmentes, in token of liberalitie, which thing the common people perceyving ranne to the kyng, and stripped hym into his hosen and dublet, and all his compaignions in likewise' (*Hall's Chronicle*, p. 519). The Venetian ambassador's account of the 1527 entertainments, which suggests rather a small and select attendance, may indicate that the audience for some spectacles was more carefully monitored than for others, or may arise out of the ambassador's wish to present the event in a particularly impressive light to those reading his report at home.

[23] On the social distinctions and different codes of movement at different social levels characterizing dance forms in early modern England, see, for example Skiles Howard, *The Politics of Courtly Dancing in Early Modern England* (Amherst, 1998), especially the introduction.

performance, but their developed artistry and their numbers. According to Fynes Moryson again, whose evidence must be somewhat suspect on account of his own nationality, England's swarms of travelling entertainers were 'rare in other Kingdomes'.[24] Certainly Moryson's view of English artistry, though widely shared, must be set alongside equally widespread recognition of the artistry of Italian players, who were popular at the French, Spanish, English and Bavarian courts.[25] But English players seem to have made a greater impression in Germany and Central and Eastern Europe, where several English companies were retained by the ruling elite. Jerzy Limon notes the patronage of the Hohenzollerns, Electors of Brandenburg, the Vasas, rulers of Poland, and the Habsburgs in Austria and Bohemia.

Far from differing from the rest of Europe in respect of performance tradition, English modes of performance grew out of similar practices at both popular and elite level. As in other European countries, physical skill, spectacular visual effects, song and dance, clowning and improvisation, were as much a part of touring performance as of court revels, and the same performers were often doing both kinds of entertainment. The main effect of the professionalization of theatre that came with the establishment of fixed theatre buildings in England was that an increasingly large number of Londoners could see the shows that were 'rehearsed' in the public theatres before being taken to court. The early Tudor situation, in which court and noble households almost certainly saw more dramatic entertainments than popular, paying audiences, was effectively reversed, so that now London audiences could see a different play every day of the week except Sunday, while only a fraction of those plays was ever taken to court.

Professional playing remained true to tradition by bringing together a variety of skills in the playhouse. Afterpieces such as Platter describes were standard in the public play-houses, as an epigram by Sir John Davies (written by 1594) confirms:

> For as we see at all the play house dores,
> When ended is the play, the daunce, and song;
> A thousand townsemen, gentlemen, and whores,
> Porters and serving-men together throng.[26]

Plays themselves, furthermore, were routinely constructed along lines that allowed for great variety within the dramatic structure itself, accommodating fools, songs, dances, subplots, dumbshows, plays-within-plays and so on into tragic as well as comic form. Even university-educated, 'intellectual' dramatists who set great store by verbal text held on to the pleasures of variety in performance: the inclusion of such stage directions as 'Perim danceth' and 'Milo tumbleth' in Lyly's *Campaspe*, for example, seems to exemplify this principle of inclusive diversity.[27] Writing to showcase the skills of specific performers was common, as was improvisation by particular performers seeking a bigger outlet to demonstrate their own skills, as Hamlet famously complains. And plays might be revised to accommodate a change in company personnel, so that the loss of one particular talent or the arrival of another might be compensated for or exploited. *Twelfth Night* is long thought to have been revised to show off Robert Armin's musical talents to best advantage.

An emphasis on music, dance and spectacle becomes even more marked in English performance following the accession of King James in

---

24 *Shakespeare's Europe*, p. 476.
25 Thomas Coryat, whose views must be as suspect as Moryson's for the same reason of his nationality, thought the Italian actors he saw could not compare with the English 'for apparell, shewes & musicke' and dismissed the Venetian playhouse he visited as 'very beggarly and base in comparison with our stately play-houses in England' (quoted in Lea, *Italian Popular Comedy*, vol. 2, p. 345).
26 Epigram 17, *The Poems of Sir John Davies*, ed. by Robert Krueger (Oxford, 1975); also cited in Baskervill, *The Elizabethan Jig*, p. 106.
27 *Campaspe*, v.i.4, 12, in *Campaspe and Sappho and Phao*, ed. by G. K. Hunter and David Bevington (Manchester and New York, 1991).

1603, due mainly to the growing prestige of court masque under the patronage of James's queen, Anne. Whereas, under Elizabeth, plays provided the regular entertainment during the holiday season at court, with masques figuring only occasionally, and often outside the routine festivities organized by the Master of the Revels, under Stuart patronage they became spectacular, at least annual, events, which, while not outnumbering plays performed at court, clearly outclassed them in terms of prestige.[28] Elizabeth had initially encouraged the invitation of professional companies to play at court because that was so much cheaper than producing court entertainments from her own resources; but the new monarchs willingly paid out the thousands of pounds necessary for one masque on a regular basis, much to the disgust of many of their subjects. In such circumstances they could scarcely fail to make invited plays by professionals, paid for at £10 each, look like cheap alternatives in every sense.

Court masques provide a clear case of text and professional acting subordinated to music and spectacle, as Ben Jonson knew to his chagrin. The climax of the masque, as all those present understood, was the point at which the masquers descended to dance with members of the court; and what merely reading a masque text tends to conceal is the length and dominance of this part of the event. The four hours of dancing after midnight (which may indicate a total dancing time including some hours before midnight) noted by the Venetian ambassador in 1625 may be worthy of comment by virtue of its exceptional length, but extended dancing of itself was part of the expectation of the genre.[29] Comments on court masques by those in attendance, both English and foreign, echo Platter's dominant interest in elegant dancing. All the spectators of *Tethys' Festival* (1610), for example, were struck by the dancing skill of the child performers, including the young Duke of York (aged nine); while Antonio Correr found the *Masque of Oberon* (1611) 'most remarkable for the grace of the Prince's every movement'.[30]

William Trumbull, an Englishman also commenting on *Oberon*, took care to specify the sequence of dances by name:

They entered dancing two ballets intermingled with varied figures and many leaps, extremely well done by most of them. The prince then took the queen to dance, the Earl of Southampton the princess, and each of the rest his lady. They danced an English dance resembling a pavane. When the queen returned to her place the prince took her for a coranta which was continued by others, and then the gallarda began, which was something to see and admire. The prince took the queen a third time for *los branles de Poitou*, followed by eleven others of the masque. As it was about midnight and the king somewhat tired he sent word that they should make an end. So the masqueraders danced the ballet of the sortie, in which the satyrs and fauns joined. With vocal and instrumental music the masqueraders approached the throne to make their reverence to their Majesties.[31]

Nor were such variety and skill in the level of dance performance, and such knowledge and discrimination in the spectator, unusual. Orazio

---

28 On masques under Elizabeth, see Stephen Orgel, *The Jonsonian Masque* (1965; rpt New York, 1981), part 1. Masques had of course played a much more prominent and integrated part in the life of the court during the early part of Henry VIII's reign, a factor which had in turn influenced the earlier development of theatrical tradition.

29 The comment was made of *The Fortunate Isles and their Union*, and is cited in *Inigo Jones: the Theatre of the Stuart Court*, ed. by Stephen Orgel and Roy Strong, 2 vols. (London, 1973), vol. 1, p. 370.

30 Orgel and Strong, vol. I, pp. 192, 205. Jeremy Maule, in a paper given to the Early Modern Women's Writing Seminar in Nottingham in 1998, shortly before his sad and sudden death in 1999, demonstrated the importance of dance in an aristocratic upbringing, citing children as young as two performing in a seventeenth-century household masque. Cf Barbara Ravelhofer, '"Virgin Wax" and "hairy men-monsters": Unstable movement codes in the Stuart masque', in *The Politics of the Stuart Court Masque*, ed. David Bevington and Peter Holbrook (Cambridge, 1998), pp. 244–72, which reproduces a delightful picture painted *c.* 1596 of children practising their dancing.

31 Orgel and Strong, vol. I, p. 206.

Busino's account of the dancing in *Pleasure Reconciled to Virtue* (1618) also refers to 'all sorts of ballets and dances of every country, such as passemeasures, corantos, canaries, Spanish dances, and a hundred other beautiful turns to delight the fancy'.

Interestingly, Busino's account is much better known because of its narrative of the King's own intervention to complain when the dancing seemed to lag as the dancers tired: 'Why don't they dance? What did you make me come here for? Devil take all of you, dance!', an outburst which inspired his favourite, the Marquis of Buckingham, to dance 'a number of high and very tiny capers with such grace and lightness that he made everyone admire and love him'.[32] It is James's only recorded response to a masque. But the king's temper, reminiscent as it is of Isabella d'Este's boredom in fifteenth-century Ferrara, may show something of a more widely shared appetite for dancing as the focus point of the whole spectacle, one deep-rooted and widespread across Europe. Certainly John Chamberlain's comment in relation to *The Lords' Masque* (1613) seems to share the king's preference: 'That night was the Lords maske wherof I heare no great commendation, save only for riches, theyre devises beeing long and tedious, and more like a play then a maske.'[33] The wording is instructive: a masque that is more like a play than a masque is, in the English court of 1613, likely to be dismissed as inferior to one that is truly masque-like. And presumably the 'true' masque is by implication distinguished by fewer words and hence a greater emphasis on music, tableau, song and dance.

It was shortly prior to this date, of course, that Shakespeare was writing his late plays. His company, licensed as the King's Men within two months of the new monarch's accession in 1603, was called to perform at court much more in the first decade of the seventeenth century than under Elizabeth, and thus had even greater opportunity to observe the fashions and preferences of the court.[34] What is sometimes forgotten by Shakespeare scholars is that the King's Men also took the speaking parts in court masques. So masques were not just spectacles that they observed or heard tell of when they came to court, but shows in which they were full participants. It is scarcely surprising, then, that Shakespeare's late plays show, as scholars have long noted, a strong receptivity to the influence of court masque.[35]

When the King's Men began to play at the Blackfriars as well as the Globe, from about 1609, jigs were not standard, as in the public theatres, but music per se, and musical elements in plays, became even more conspicuous. The Blackfriars was renowned for its musicians, who entertained audiences while the candles were trimmed between the acts as well as supplying an increasingly prominent place in Shakespeare's later plays. Indeed the Blackfriars seems to have cultivated the musical and spectacular aspect of its provision as enhancing its pretensions to greater elegance than the amphitheatres. While all Shakespeare's late romances show the development of masque-based elements, *The Tempest* in particular shows tableau, dance and song making extended pauses in the narrative to the point where they are evidently intended to be at least as central to the experience of spectatorship as any engagement with narrative.

---

[32] Orgel and Strong, p. 283.

[33] Ibid., p. 242.

[34] Leeds Barroll rightly points out that their more frequent invitations to court are partly the result of the fact that James had a family, and hence several courts to entertain, and partly due to the increased number of foreign visitors requiring to be honoured by appropriate festivities, especially in the first years of the reign, when dignitaries were still arriving to pay their countries' respects to the new monarch (*Politics, Plague, and Shakespeare's Theater* (Ithaca and London, 1991)).

[35] Alan Brissenden notes that while dancing figures in a maximum of eight of Shakespeare's plays written up to about 1605–6, almost all of those written from 1607 on contain dancing (*Shakespeare and the Dance* (London, 1981), p. 17).

Again, a too-rigid separation of theatre into courtly and popular strands seems to miss the point of theatrical practice. *The Tempest* was almost certainly performed at the Globe as well as the Blackfriars and Whitehall (*Pericles, Cymbeline* and *The Winter's Tale* were probably also performed at both the King's Men's theatres and at court), thereby bringing elite performance style to popular theatre. The non-verbal in its various forms is as central to popular as to elite theatre. Dumb-shows or speaking pictures may be explained as suitable for groundlings or for courtiers, depending on the terminology used. The rhetoric of social difference within a given form, of course, is crucial to the kinds of meaning it constructs. Though masque, for example, an elite form by definition, comes routinely to incorporate an anti-masque, thereby bringing a more jigging and popular vein into court theatre, it does so within a shape that sets the grotesqueness of anti-masque alongside the forceful harmonies of masque's own resolutions. Similarly, while song, dance, music and clowning may be more translatable across cultures and countries than verbal text, and ingrained in European performance over centuries and across different countries, the forms are differently nuanced in different places and at different times.[36] Even so, however, it remains the case that England is not marked out from the rest of Europe in the late sixteenth and early seventeenth centuries by any difference in style or taste with respect to its admiration for, and cultivation of, the non-verbal and spectacular in performance. What marks it out in this period is the acknowledged pre-eminence of its performers.

Much more famously, of course, in later history, the England of this period comes to be known for the plays of Shakespeare; and Shakespeare is renowned above all with later readers and audiences for his words. There is thus an element of paradox about Shakespeare's place in cultural history. He is known for the brilliance of his text, but the context of his writing was a culture that set an especially high value on non-

verbal elements of performance, and that almost certainly performed his works in line with a performance style based on this cultural valuation. Even more paradoxically, despite the relatively widespread accessibility and popularity of Shakespeare and others like him, whose plays, with their wonderful words, were performed within their lifetimes at court, in several London theatres, at venues across England, and abroad at least as far afield as Eastern Europe, the broad movement from the late sixteenth to the mid-seventeenth century in English theatre was towards an increased emphasis on the non-verbal in performance, one that culminates in the development of opera. It is following the closing of the theatres in 1642 that the beginnings of opera may be found in England, in Sir William Davenant's *Siege of Rhodes* (1656). On the other hand, opera seems to mark the point at which the development of musical theatre has gone so far that it needs to be recognized as something requiring separate definition. Once an implicitly integrated performance style separates into opera and theatre, making a distinction between the two, it is likely not only that the two will develop differently from then on, but that past practice will be differently valued and differently understood. It may be that the separation of opera from other forms of theatre allows verbal text in theatre to acquire a higher cultural currency. Once the successive adaptations of Davenant and Shadwell have rewritten *The Tempest* as opera for an audience that is expected to recognize this as different from, and co-existent with, the Shakespeare play that goes by the same name, the space has been created for Shakespeare to be valued especially for his

---

[36] See, for example, Susan McClary's discussion of the clear distinctions between French and Italian styles and their implications in 'Unruly Passions and Courtly Dances: Technologies of the Body in Baroque Music', in *From the Royal to the Republican Body: Incorporating the Political in Seventeenth- and Eighteenth-Century France*, ed. by Sara E. Melzer and Kathryn Norberg (Berkeley, Los Angeles and London, 1998), pp. 85–112.

words. After that, there is no looking back. The association of Shakespeare with verbal excellence continues and grows down to our own day. But we should recognize that, however remarkable the words may seem to us now, Shakespeare's plays were conceived within a culture that valued picture, sound and movement in performance very highly indeed and responded to Shakespeare from within that milieu all over Europe.

ALL AT SEA: WATER, SYNTAX, AND CHARACTER DISSOLUTION IN SHAKESPEARE

WILLIAM POOLE

Character, personality, its threatened loss and its restitution, are issues habitually discussed in Shakespeare using metaphors of water, tears and melting. Moreover, when Shakespeare's characters use such language, their very syntax tends to float, to become inexact or ambiguous. What can this tell us about the characters that possess this language? Many of these watery sites can also be located in a larger mechanism of symbols, specifically ports, shipwreck and the story of the falling Icarus. How are these two mechanisms of watery syntax and watery symbols connected? Though not a collocation of Shakespeare's invention, I shall suggest in this essay that this cluster of associations nevertheless proves particularly complex in his work.

The corollary to this enquiry works with the converse of the above contention, and now and then this twin breaks the surface. This second thesis is that, while the operation of melting undoes character or personality, the operation of naming fixes it. A famous example will show how these two ideas are connected.

When Richard II decrowns himself in the fourth act of his play, his language flits melodramatically between a search for various names or roles which can be used to fix his sense of identity, and an opposing tendency to think about various unfixing, mobile, liquid actions. He names, retracts, and melts, renames, restates, fixes, melts again:

God save the King! Will no man say 'Amen'?
Am I both priest and clerk? Well then, Amen.

God save the King, although I be not he.
And yet Amen, if heaven do think him me.
                              (*Richard II* 4.1.163–6)

Now is this golden crown like a deep well
That owes two buckets filling one another,
The emptier ever dancing in the air,
The other down, unseen, and full of water.
That bucket down and full of tears am I,
Drinking my griefs, whilst you mount up on
      high.   (174–9)

Though some of you, with Pilate, wash your
      hands,
Showing an outward pity, yet you Pilates
Have here delivered me to my sour cross,
And water cannot wash away your sin.   (229–32)

            I have no name, no title,
No, not that name was given me at the font,
But 'tis usurped.   (245–7)

O, that I were a mockery king of snow,
Standing before the sun of Bolingbroke
To melt myself away in water-drops!   (250–2)

This mirror-smashing king oscillates between named and watery roles. When he is a bag of tears, he is losing his role, even, he claims, his name, given him first at that notably wet place, the baptismal font. When he gives himself a name – 'I', 'Richard', Christ, 'king' – he regains grip. Richard holds up various names like

I am grateful to Professor A. D. Nuttall, Mr Richard Scholar and Mr Jeremy Noel-Tod for commenting on various versions of this paper. An earlier version was delivered in the Oxford English Faculty, Michaelmas 1999, at the invitation of Professor John Carey.

talismen, and then, when he worries about how these particular names relate to each other, his grip on identity slackens again. As he finally confesses:

> Thus play I in one person many people,
> And none contented. (5.5.31–2)

So naming and water have a symbiotic relation and, although the latter is here primarily discussed, the arguments produced have this other index, the act of naming.

This is by no means an exhaustive enquiry; metaphors of melting are so common in Shakespeare that only sites in which imagery of water is specifically related to the characters under analysis are discussed. Nor is this the first discussion of water imagery in Shakespeare.[1] What is offered as fresh is the emphasis on close syntactic analysis of plays not commonly examined in the context of water or tempests. The place of watery speeches in the confusing world of *The Comedy of Errors* is first discussed; then, various permutations of these ideas are followed through other plays, in particular *Timon of Athens*. Finally, some preliminary remarks are offered on the late plays.

THE COMEDY OF ERRORS

The confusions caused by mistaken identity in *The Comedy of Errors* are quite different from those generated by the twinnings of its Plautine sources, the *Menaechmi* and the *Amphitruo*. In the *Amphitruo*, for instance, Mercury impersonates Amphitryon's servant in the fourth act, denying the real Amphitryon access to his own house;[2] this is the source for the similar scene in Shakespeare's play. The comedy thus generated relies on complicit deception: Jupiter and his audience know that not only is Mercury not Amphitryon, but he is not even a mortal being. Person and impersonator are poles apart. But Shakespeare's play is based on a more real possibility of confusion: Antipholus is shadowed not by a god but by something much closer – his identical twin brother. Moreover,

after the model of the *Amphitruo*, Shakespeare adds to the twins of the *Menaechmi* similarly twinned servants, the Dromios. *The Comedy of Errors* also doubles the length of the *Menaechmi* and mathematicizes it into a gleaming symmetry, only to subvert this heightened sense of order by creating a similarly heightened sense of disorder, of heterodoxy. The minor character Angelo the goldsmith, for instance, embroiled in an argument between Antipholus of Ephesus and his wife, finds that his own experience contradicts not one but both of the stories spun by the wranglers. Having formerly agreed with Adriana and Luciana, in the final act he suddenly hears them claim that they dined earlier with Antipholus. The audience knows it was the other Antipholus, but Angelo doesn't, commenting in an aside:

> O perjured woman! They are both forsworn.
> In this the madman justly chargeth them.
> (5.1.213–14)

The goldsmith's role here serves not to clarify but to complexify the action. The women have their truth; Antipholus of Ephesus has another; Angelo a third. In this way, the simple device of one block of characters disagreeing with another is converted into the suspicion that truths are as many as men. Had Antipholus of Syracuse been present, he would have added a further fiction to those on offer; his Dromio, a further version still.

Antipholus of Syracuse is the most obvious psychological aberrant in his play. For *The Comedy of Errors*, Shakespeare creates a pattern of hard, sunny clarity by extracting an almost geometric regularity from his sources; but he

---

[1] See G. Wilson Knight, *The Shakespearian Tempest* (Oxford, 1932), *passim*; Caroline Spurgeon, *Shakespeare's Imagery* (Cambridge, 1968), pp. 24–5, 47–8, 91–100, 337–8; Wolfgang Clemen, *The Development of Shakespeare's Imagery* (2nd edn) (London, 1977), pp. 159–60, 182–7.

[2] See *Amphitryon* Act IV in the Loeb Plautus vol. I (London and Cambridge, Mass., 1916), pp. 102–6.

then complicates this by populating it with characters that do not behave in quite the confident fashion of their Plautine ancestors. Antipholus of Syracuse's Plautine prototype – Menaechmus Sosicles – regards the mysteries of his port of call with disbelief, then materialistic glee, and finally wiliness. In William Warner's 1595 translation, as Sosicles says, '. . . the best way for me is to faine my selfe mad indeed, so I shall be rid of them'. At every juncture he is quite sure of his own sanity: 'Surely this fellow is mad', he says of the cook Cylindrus' bewildering remarks; 'I know thou art mad.'[3] Menaechmus Sosicles is a boisterous, cynical merchant; his brother is a boisterous, cynical citizen.

Antipholus of Syracuse is nothing like this, quite opposite in three ways. First, he is given many more lines than his brother. Secondly, he is constantly worrying about his sanity. (This is vaguely ironic, because the Syracusan *is* a genuinely different kind of thinker from his brother, whereas the Plautine Menaechmi, so confident of their separability, nevertheless come across as virtually interchangeable people.) Finally, Antipholus, 'the mistaken Lover/Wanderer', as the Folio occasionally suggests ('Erotes', 'Errotis'),[4] shipwrecked as a child, and now voyaging over the sea to Ephesus, biblically the site of magic, where, upon the arrival of St Paul, in the words of the Geneva Bible, 'the whole citie was ful of confusion' (Acts 19.29) – this Antipholus expresses his confusion in a language of water-drops:

> I will go lose myself,
> And wander . . .
> I to the world am like a drop of water
> That in the ocean seeks another drop,
> Who, falling there to find his fellow forth,
> Unseen, inquisitive, confounds himself.
> (1.2.30–1, 35–8)

The language of watery dissolution is syntactically mimetic: who is referred to by 'Who'? Antipholus or the droplet? And whom does 'Unseen, inquisitive' qualify? Pursuer or quarry? Antipholus and the water-drop become syntactically intertwined, and the linguistic confusion mirrors the real confusion of Antipholus, given dramatic articulation in this scene as he proceeds to address the *wrong* Dromio as 'the almanac of my true date' (1.2.41). Again, this oddly talismanic use of Dromio's age is similar to Richard II's obsession with tokens of exactitude. The Syracusan's twin happily repeats the Plautine trope of accusing everyone but one's self of madness ('How now? A madman?' (4.1.93)) – but the wanderer is less sure:

> The fellow is distraught, and so am I,
> And here we wander in illusions. (4.3.42–3)

He is 'Known unto these, and to myself disguised!' (2.2.217). This is slightly more complex than the confusion of an outsider. What worries Antipholus is not his foreignness but his apparent ability to function in a manner acceptable to others, and yet without any personal canons of identity – 'to myself disguised'. He indeed confounds himself, but he is not unseen: it is the fuzzy collective consciousness of the town, relentlessly assimilating him, which acts as a solvent for his personality. What threatens the Syracusan's sanity is not the way in which things aren't working, but the way in which they *are*, happily independent of his comprehension. Indeed, we feel that Antipholus, like an intentionally

---

[3] In Geoffrey Bullough, *Narrative and Dramatic Sources of Shakespeare* (London, 1957), vol. 1, pp. 31, 18.

[4] See Wells and Taylor, *William Shakespeare: A Textual Companion* (Oxford, 1987), p. 267. Shakespearian 'etymologies' are more often suggestive than exact; in the present case, I suggest a Latinate complex of 'erraticus' ('wanderer', 'mistaken one') and 'eroticus' ('lover'), both significations being relevant to the Syracusan; Plautus' Courtesan was helpfully called Erotium. (These etymologies are also available through the Greek.) Bullough thinks that 'Antipholus' ('Antiphilus' = 'mutual affection') may be an ironic glance towards Sidney's *un*faithful Antiphilus from the second book of *Arcadia*. See Bullough, *Sources*, vol. 1, p. 9.

incompetent detective, lets his comprehensive faculties go slack in a manner designed to generate rather than to explain seeming irrationality.

Even the Syracusan's language seems to be communal. Having delivered his watery soliloquy, he comes across a stranger who bizarrely identifies herself thus:

> I am not Adriana, nor thy wife. (2.2.115)

Adriana intends sarcasm but, ironically, the latter half of her statement is true: she is not the Syracusan's wife. Again, we see the third or middle position coming into existence, the space that Angelo the goldsmith occupied: the sense that things are never entirely a hard either/or as they are in the Plautine version. Adriana then, quite basically, proceeds to rewrite a soliloquy she cannot have heard:

> For know, my love, as easy mayst thou fall
> A drop of water in the breaking gulf,
> And take unmingled thence that drop again
> Without addition or diminishing,
> As take from me thyself, and not me too.
>
> (2.2.128–32)

A stranger reproduces the Syracusan's idiolect. Moreover, Adriana produces an implicit commentary on the earlier soliloquy. Antipholus had said he was going to lose himself, that is, walk around, and that he felt like a drop of water. Adriana says that water drops in oceans become assimilated, their identity erased. We infer that people like them will likewise lose themselves in a different metaphorical sense – that of madness.[5] In other words, although Adriana means 'get a grip', her imagery, because of Antipholus' earlier speech, turns the argument round in the opposite direction: it suggests that a man who speaks like Antipholus had done is going to lose his wits. And upon scrutiny of Adriana's imagery, it is itself not entirely coherent. 'Fall' is initially heard as an intransitive verb: not only is the intransitive sense dominant in this period (*OED* 1.a.), but Antipholus's earlier likening of himself to a water drop will help us to expect intransitivity. But this gives us

a strange visual picture in which Antipholus falls as a drop and then somehow duplicates himself, leaving one body on the cliffs wielding a device for the restoring of single water-drops from the ocean. In order to make visual sense of the image, Antipholus has to come apart. Of course, mislikers of ambiguity will retrospectively reinterpret the verb as transitive – a sense now obsolete but witnessed in this period (*OED* 49. a., citing *Richard III* 5.5.88–9: 'Tomorrow in the battle think on me, / And fall thy edgeless sword.') – but it is a readjustment caused by the mind being led into visual paradox. The initial effect can only be adjusted, not undone. This double syntax – intransitivity metamorphosing into transitivity as we listen – is the linguistic equivalent of the large-scale character confusions.

The third time the water-drops appear, they are once again in Antipholus' mouth, speaking to Luciana, who considers him quite mad. She is not entirely unjustified.

> O, train me not, sweet mermaid, with thy note
> To drown me in thy sister's flood of tears;
> Sing, siren, for thyself, and I will dote.
> Spread o'er the silver waves thy golden hairs,
> And as a bed I'll take thee, and there lie,
> And in that glorious supposition think
> He gains by death that has such means to die.
> Let love, being light, be drowned if she sink.
>
> (3.2.45–52)

Once again, this cloying, luxurious verse hides basic problems. As the Arden editor notes, one kind of dissolution is rejected for another: the 'weeping sister' Adriana is cast off in favour of an equally liquefying Luciana, and the language in which he chooses to emphasize his choice itself wishes for death by water. Although he melodramatically plays on the worn pun of 'dying', the obstinate literal tendency of the

---

5 See R. V. O'Brien, 'The Madness of Syracusan Antipholus', *Early Modern Literary Studies*, 2.1 (1996) 1–26.

verse is to beg the sleepy grave of the ocean. Paradoxically, Antipholus is actively employing a system of imperatives – 'train . . . sing . . . spread' – to insist upon his *passive en*chantment. In fact, after the imperative 'spread', Antipholus shoulders himself in, and first-person pronouns assume control. This, as we shall see, is the peculiar property of much of Shakespeare's watery language: his speakers tend unwittingly to manifest a control over their verse that belies their supposed sentiments of passivity. The sanity of Antipholus of Syracuse is probed: the entire play has hanging over it the possibility of Egeon quite literally losing his head; meta-phorically, his son is in a similar predicament. Almost the last line he says shows that he is still not confident whether his senses are suppositions, or reality:

If this be not a dream I see and hear. (5.1.379)

But for all this, the Syracusan's problem is not quite what he claims, as his syntax belies him. He likens himself to water, is told that such a likeness will confound his individuality, and then goes on to woo Luciana in exactly the drunken tones he was warned against. However, I have suggested that, despite his fantasy of sex as personal extinction, he retains too much control to be a genuinely melting man. As with Richard II, the ego controls syntax with a stronger grip than is pretended. Antipholus's real problem is that he wants to dissolve, and can't.

HAMLET AND RICHARD

Concerning Antipholus of Syracuse, then, I contend that an egotistic presence survives in and directs his language, thereby undermining his dreams of passivity. Richard II behaves in a similar fashion. Let us re-examine one of his speeches already quoted:

O that I were a mockery king of snow,
Standing before this sun of Bolingbroke,
To melt myself away in water-drops!

(4.1.250–2)

Once again, it is visual rehearsal that reveals the flaw. The image pretends to be of the sun melting a snowman. But that is not quite what Richard says. He wishes himself a snowman *that melts itself* – 'To melt myself' – rather than the familiar model, which tends to be melted by the sun. He usurps the standard metaphysical explanatory scheme for active/passive: Richard not only stage-manages his own deposition but controls the sun, imparting it its virtue *as a result of* his melting. Richard is a grammatically surreal being: he is actively passive. This use of overactive syntax was Antipholus's stumbling block:

O, train me not, sweet mermaid, with thy note
To drown me in thy sister's flood of tears.
(*The Comedy of Errors* 3.2.45–52)

– the vocative and ablative interjections shield his underlying syntax which shuns external agency: 'me' drowns 'me'. Hamlet also proves too egotistic to melt (note how the argument of this paper makes it easier to resist the famous emendation 'sullied'):

O that this too too solid flesh would melt,
Thaw, and resolve itself into a dew.
(*Hamlet* 1.2.129–30)

Attempting to escape his role as revenger, Hamlet desires fleshly deliquescence, and this has the larger correlative of his sea-voyage. It is striking that Hamlet stops soliloquizing after his return from the sea, as if the wonted fleshly deliquescence has become mental, Hamlet having lost or suppressed his ruminative faculties. But in this early stage, the desired melt-down is again that suspicious thing: actively passive. Hamlet wishes his flesh to 'melt . . . *itself*', not 'be melted' by some external force. Reflexivity usurps passivity. Again, scientific processes are envisaged as spon-taneous, working in a kind of causal loop sealed off from external agents. But what scientific process is this? Flesh melts, then thaws and then resolves itself. Now this process described is very hard to imagine. Once something is melted, it scarcely needs to thaw, unless it has rehardened.[6] And 'resolve' is not what we expected – 'dissolve': 'resolve' sounds like 'return to an original condition'. This metaphoric suggestion of human life as a brief rupture in a non-human continuum looks forward to Prospero's 'our little life / Is rounded with a sleep' (4.1.157–8), that is, surrounded by a sleep. Milton, for one, treats melting in a manner similar to Hamlet when Adam remembers his first dream:

> . . . there gentle sleep
> First found me, and with soft oppression seis'd
> My droused, sense, untroubld, though I thought
> I then was passing to my former state
> Insensible, and forthwith to dissolve.
> (*Paradise Lost* VIII.287–91)

– interestingly, C. S. Lewis suggested that the ambiguous syntax used here mimes the 'crumbling of consciousness' described.[7] But to return to Hamlet, the point is that, on the evidence of this speech, his consciousness does not crumble. He should have said something like:

> O, that this too, too solid flesh would thaw,
> Melt, and be dissolved back into a dew!

But he doesn't, supplying us instead with another piece of hard-to-imagine science. Like Antipholus, like Richard, Hamlet unwittingly interferes with his own language in a manner which reveals the movement of a strong ego, even in, even through, his assertions to the contrary.

So far, then, the characters discussed typically don't quite manage to do what they promise with water. The three foregoing texts, *The Comedy*, *Richard II*, *Hamlet*, all belonged to the first half of Shakespeare's writing career. The remainder examined will date from the latter period, and in them some changes in the way water works will be observed, as well as some continuities.

TIMON OF ATHENS

Timon of Athens is perhaps an unfinished play, but the character of Timon nevertheless is constructed with intellectual coherency, although this coherency is based on an almost mathematical, inhuman conception. Moreover, the language of this play contains some of Shakespeare's most complex resonances, especially of the type under examination.

Timon of Athens is underpinned by a myth that is not explicitly announced, but manifests itself in the metaphorical structure of the play, and this myth also has a larger relevance for this enquiry. When the Steward dissolves Timon's bankrupt household, a suitably anonymous servant comments:

> Leaked is our barque,
> And we, poor mates, stand on the dying deck
> Hearing the surges' threat. We must all part
> Into this sea of air.
> (4.2. 19–22)

This evocation of oceanic and aetherial expanses is typical of *Timon of Athens*, set in an Athens only fleetingly tangible. The walls upon which the senators appear to beg mercy of Alcibiades in the final scene have nothing about them of the sturdy polis of the Roman plays.

The servant's conflation of sea and air, moreover, parallels a textual crux in the first scene of the play. There, the Poet is describing his vocation to the Painter, and, as poets are wont, he uses language so obscure and contrived that emendation has frequently been sought:

> My free drift
> Halts not particularly, but moves itself
> In a wide sea of wax. No levelled malice
> Infects one comma of the course I hold,
> But flies an eagle flight, bold and forth on,
> Leaving no tract behind. (1.1.45–50)[8]

---

[6] Compare Donne:

> So mankind feeling now a generall thaw,
> A strong example gone equall to law,
> The Cyment which did faithfully compact
> And glue all vertues, now resolv'd, and slack'd.
> ('An Anatomy of the World', lines 47–50)

[7] C. S. Lewis, *A Preface to Paradise Lost* (London, 1942), p. 46.

[8] Wells and Taylor unnecessarily accept the emendation of 'wax' to 'tax'.

Here, Shakespeare's first thought is historical – he imagines Greek wax writing tablets, and so his Poet is expressing the plenitude of a poet's – this poet's – talent. Tablets become seas of wax, so propulsive is his muse. But the idea of an eagle's flight lends the metaphor independent development: something is seen flying over a waxy sea. Such a mixed, evolutive metaphor has prompted textual doubts, but, as Armstrong first recognized, 'wax' and 'eagle flight' are unified by the myth of Icarus, he who, flying mindlessly high on his wax-bound wings, drowned himself.[9] Accordingly, the surface metaphor is of a powerful, disinterested talent, the supple imagination of which lends wings to the pen. But the cohesion of the terms of the extended metaphor relies upon the myth of Icarus the foolish boy for unity. Other Shakespearian juxtapositions of wax, melting and feathers can be found. Armstrong supplies the following from *Richard Duke of York*:

> The proud insulting Queen
> With Clifford and the haught Northumberland,
> And of their feather many more proud birds,
> Have wrought the easy-melting King like wax.
>
> (2.1.168–71)

Most importantly, however, there is a famous Marlovian precedent:

> Till swolne with cunning, of a selfe conceite,
> His waxen wings did mount aboue his reach,
> And melting heauens conspirde his ouerthrow.
>
> (*Dr. Faustus*, Chor. 20–2)

Nor is this an inert source. A. D. Nuttall has recently identified in this passage what he called 'metamorphic grammar'.[10] In the second line of the above extract, the expected pronoun and verb – 'he fell' – is ousted by an unexpected pair of wings. As the heavens melt, so does Faustus's power over his flight. As we shall see, something very similar to this happens to Timon when he discusses his grave. Nor is this the only Marlovian precedent[11] – he appears to have been as obsessed as Shakespeare was with melting, and the Icarus myth is the one Dido invokes:

> Ile frame me wings of waxe like *Icarus*,
> And ore his ships will soare vnto the sunne,
> That they may melt and I fall into his arms.
>
> (*Dido, Queen of Carthage* 5.1.243–5)

Typically, Marlowe is making Dido reinterpret the myth – in Dido's mouth, the high flight becomes deliberately, orgasmically suicidal. Again, six lines from damnation, Icarian Faustus cries:

> O soul, be changde into little water drops,
> And fal into the *Ocean*, nere be found.
>
> (5.2.195–6)[12]

Returning to the Poet from *Timon of Athens*, I suspect his Icarian subtext evokes a specifically Latinate diction. His concluding phrase – 'Leaving no tract behind' – sounds like a periphrasis for 'trackless', Latin *avius*, away from the road, pathless. It is also, I suspect, the idea behind the similar phrase from *The Tempest* 'Leave not a wrack behind' (4.1.156) This touch of classicism in the Poet's speech drives us back to the *locus classicus* of the Icarus story in Book VIII of Ovid's *Metamorphoses*. Ovid describes the fall thus:

> Oraque caerulea, patrium clamantia nomen
> Excipiuntur aqua, quae nomen traxit ab illo.[13]

(lit. 'Crying the father's name, his lips were drawn into the azure sea: which took the [i.e. either 'its' or 'his'] name from him.')

The bold agent gradually loses active power to the sea. Icarus dwindles to a pair of lips shouting

---

[9] Edward A. Armstrong, *Shakespeare's Imagination* (Lincoln, 2nd edn, 1963), pp. 37–8.

[10] A. D. Nuttall, *The Alternative Trinity* (Oxford, 1998), pp. 31–3.

[11] Apart from the many Donnean examples of melting, Walton's *Life* of Donne describes how, as a preacher, Donne 'did so work upon the affections of his hearers as melted and moulded them . . .' – a casual collocation of melting and wax (Oxford, 1927), p. 52.

[12] See also *The Tragedie of Dido*, 4.4 (through line no. 1268–9); *The Conquests of Tamburlaine* (I Tamburlaine), 3.1 (t.l.n. 926–9); 5.2.237; *The bloody Conquests of mighty Tamburlaine* (II Tamburlaine), 5.3 (t.l.n. 4393).

[13] Ovid, *Metamorphoses* VIII. 229–30, in the Loeb edition, ed. and trans. by F. J. Miller (London and Cambridge, Mass., 1960), vol. I, pp. 422–3.

a name – lips that are drawn by a passive verb – 'excipiuntur' – into the ocean. Moreover, 'excipiuntur' is closer to 'they were seized, and 'traxit' – note how the sea now assumes possession of the active verb – is nearer to 'hauled' or 'dragged' than simply 'took'. The sea drowns Icarus, and captures his name. Loss of self and name are conflated in a syntax that transfers verbal potency from Icarus to the sea. These two lines, therefore, rehearse in a remarkably concise manner the very framework I have been throughout proposing.

Timon's loss of self is similarly caught up in watery dissolution. He enters and exits his text in a uniquely staggered manner: initially he is presented in the formal ecphrasis of the Painter's canvas; and his last traces are likewise the two epitaphs he leaves behind him. The repeated epitaph may be a consequence of textual problems, but it is strangely fitting that the secluded centre of this cerebral work appears, so to speak, before his bodily presence and lingers on after his bodily exit. This conception of Timon is stretched between two theoretical points, attenuated benevolence and attenuated misanthropy. Famously, he is lent the abstraction of a mathematical proposition:

> The middle of humanity thou never knewest, but
> the extremity of both ends.   (4.3.302–3)

Timon, like Icarus, appears overwhelmed by marine forces outside his control: as his Steward tells him:

> I have
> Prompted you in the ebb of your estate
> And your great flow of debts.   (2.2.137–9)

The symbolic crux of water in the play is Timon's final dinner party, that strange mixture of Christian symbols. In the old *Timon* play, Timon serves up 'Stones painted like to' artichokes;[14] in Shakespeare's play he serves up bowls of 'lukewarm water', steaming a little (3.7.88), perhaps also filled with stones.[15] Just as Timon is performing a reverse Last Supper, as some lone Christ figure, he is also doing something that reminds us of Pilate and his

bowl of water, as well as the rite of absolution. Mixing these latter two ideas together, he says:

> This is Timon's last,
> Who, stuck and spangled with your flattery,
> Washes it off, and sprinkles in your faces
> Your reeking villainy.   (3.6.89–92)

It is in many ways, as Timon says, his last communication. After this washing-of-the-hands, he slowly falls into the faceless ocean of invective, cursing repeatedly until he has almost emptied language of its meaning. Of course, his words still have definitions, but his discourse ceases to cohere. His statement that he is washing off their flatteries with which he is 'stuck' and 'spangled' may operate once again on the idea of feathers. Timon, losing his artificial plumage, ends up, quite literally, considering his final resting-pace, all at sea. Marlowe's Dido similarly had wished her own Icarian fall; Richard II was also keen on Pilate. He had called the deposers Pilates, but contrasted by maintaining that water could not wash away their sins. Richard, as ever, has a good grip on his stories. Timon is altogether more unstable. His dinner-party is a farrago of religious echoes, all discordant, none announced, Timon a pagan blundering the wrong way through rites yet to be created. His actions intersect with some well-known ones performed by Christ, Pilate or a priest, but the signals are all wrong. Timon's eucharist terminates communion; his bowls of water incriminate; his absolution damns. Apemantus,

---

14 Anon, ed. by Bulman and Nosworthy, *Timon* (Oxford 1978/80), line 2065 s.d.

15 Most editors, including Wells and Taylor and Oliver for the Arden edition, read the old play back into Shakespeare's, and have Timon's dishes also containing rocks, which indeed seems to be supported by the last line of the scene 'One day he gives us diamonds, next day stones' (3.7.114). But it is interesting that, up until that point, the only evidence we have is of Timon throwing water at the guests and beating them with his fists. Both ingredients, however, would emphasize the eucharistic non-parallel, as bread and wine become stones and water.

that harmless, gregarious side-show of a Diogenes, finds himself wrong-footed by Timon in his recursive misanthropy. Apemantus had once railed that he was proud

> Of nothing so much as that I am not like Timon.
> (1.1.193−4)

But Timon's collapse throws this back at Apemantus with one small change. He is proud, he tells Apemantus, 'that I *am* not thee' (4.3.279, my italics). The easy sentiment that one would not like to be a similar kind of person to Timon is replaced by Timon's statement that he doesn't want to be a human at all. Timon washing his hands is Timon trying to wash his hands of humanity. And, just as he leaves two connected epitaphs behind him, so he makes two watery predictions of his death:

> Then, Timon, presently prepare thy grave.
> Lie where the light foam of the sea may beat
> Thy gravestone daily. (4.3.380−2)

The underlying idea of a gravestone being slowly worn away is continued in his second prediction:

> Timon hath made his everlasting mansion
> Upon the beached verge of the salt flood,
> Who once a day with his embossed froth
> The turbulent surge shall cover. (5.2.100−3)

Timon chooses the least solid place he can think of for his everlasting mansion, which cannot be presumed to last as long as he claims. (Incidentally, that shadowy historical precursor of Timon, the seventh-century BC invective poet Archilochus, likewise, according to the *Palatine Anthology*, wished to be buried *parapontios*, on the sea-shore.)[16] Moreover, 'grave' itself is etymologically connected with the act of writing. This can be seen either through the Greek verb *graphein* − 'to write' − or the Old English *grafan* − 'to dig' − and 'gravestone' is thus 'inscribed stone'. Shakespeare, if he lacked these precise facts, could easily have made the connection through the word 'engrave'. The sea, however, will gradually unwrite all Timon's detail, smoothing flat

and ultimately smoothing away his not-so-long-lasting mansion. All inscriptions, in the grasp of the sea, become unwritten. Water, as Keats once almost said, is not a particularly durable writing tablet. Although Timon is outlasted by his two textual traces, the epitaphs, his locating of his grave on the border between solid and liquid states will be the ultimate victor. It is surely an ironic moment at the end, when the Messenger enters to Alcibiades:

> My noble general, Timon is dead,
> Entombed upon the very hem o' th' sea;
> And on his gravestone this insculpture, which
> With wax I brought away, whose soft impression
> Interprets for my poor ignorance. (5.5.66−70)

One imagines the hot Athenian sun bending the wax around the Messenger's outstretched hands; as Icarus might have told him, wax is scarcely an ideal material for preserving constructions, whether mechanic or linguistic.

The second prediction of death Timon made bears striking comparison with one of the Antipholan speeches previously examined:

> Timon hath made his everlasting mansion
> Upon the beached verge of the salt flood,
> Who once a day with his embossed froth
> The turbulent surge shall cover. (5.2.100−3)

> I to the world am like a drop of water
> That in the ocean seeks another drop,
> Who, falling there to find his fellow forth,
> Unseen, inquisitive, confounds himself.
> (*The Comedy of Errors* 1.2.35−8)

Now Antipholus and Timon are using eerily similar syntax. In both cases, the word 'Who' momentarily floats, it being not apparent which antecedent governs the relative. Is the 'Who' Antipholus or the water-drop? The turbulent surge or the salt flood or even, momentarily, Timon? In both cases the possibility of mixture lingers on after the grammatical moment, because in both cases Shakespeare personifies

---

16 See *Palatine Anthology* 7.71, quoted in the Loeb *Greek Iambic Poetry*, ed. and trans. by Douglas E. Gerber (London and Cambridge, Mass., 1999), pp. 50−1.

the non-human element(s), so that no easy delineating choice between 'who' and 'which' is available. '*Which* falling there to find its fellow forth', '*which* once a day with its embossed froth' – these would have been unambiguous. But 'His fellow', 'His embossed froth' – these lend the constructions an inherently mixed meaning, a floating syntax, as distinctions between genders and agents are disabled.

Yet there are differences too. Antipholus possesses his language with a sure first-person pronoun, and although he and his water-drop intertwine, by the end of his speech he has become free again, as 'another drop' and 'his fellow' argue together to free Antipholus from the initial entwinement. Timon, however, despite the similarities in syntax, is a less secure unit. He refers to himself not as 'I' but as 'Timon' – the device of 'illeism' or externalizing one's public identity into third-person address that unites him with Shakespeare's other classical characters. It is, however, a very dangerous habit. Brutus, for instance, in splitting himself up into an 'I' and a 'Brutus', talks himself into schizophrenia. Timon, however, loses all control: although he could be referred to by 'Who', it swiftly becomes apparent that the real battle for possession of 'Who' is between 'salt flood' and 'turbulent surge'. Timon is ousted by two highly mobile forces of water fighting for him. He is, in a manner quite different from the other characters I have discussed, drowned out of identity. As Alcibiades says:

> . . . his wits
> Are drowned and lost in his calamities.
>
> (4.3.89–90)

One of the critical preoccupations with this play has been the 'inadequacy' of Timon's character. Precisely: from ephemeral painting to melting epitaph, from attenuated benevolence to attenuated hatred, Timon is strung out between two morally opposed points, and as he approaches his destination of total hatred – not just misanthropy, a far lesser condition than that

from which Timon eventually suffers – he breaks up, becomes an invective machine, and finally shattered epitaphs. Admittedly, he is shaken in his misanthropy by his faithful steward, but one can see him performing the same linguistic alchemy on this problem as he had performed on Apemantus:

> . . . Had I a steward
> So true, so just, and now so comfortable?
> It almost turns my dangerous nature wild.
> . . . You perpetual sober gods! I do proclaim
> One honest man – mistake me not, but one,
> No more, I pray – and he's a steward.
>
> (4.3.491–3; 497–9)

The Folio reads 'wild' as I do. Hanmer's conjecture, followed confidently by Wells and Taylor, and hesitantly by the Arden editor, emends to 'mild'. But surely the Folio is correct. For the fanatic, the exception *enrages* the rule. A prescriptive misanthrope will not like nice people, as they flaunt and offend his prescription. So Timon tries to rename him not 'man' but 'steward', vainly trying to create a separate category of being from man which can be populated by such an annoyingly loyal, but thankfully singular, steward. This is what really animates Timon as a character: he actively propels himself into extinction. Antipholus, Richard and Hamlet dearly wished to do what Timon does; but their language betrayed a residual egotistical presence. Timon, in an almost 'meta-egotistic' way, manages to propel himself out of humanity into extinction. Good people are annexed into separate things from 'people' seemingly by will-over-language alone; Timon's second prediction of death manages to award verbal power to the sea in a way which the other watery men had ultimately failed to accomplish. I talked earlier about Richard's active passivity; Timon shares this ability, but he has managed to shift the alloy into a passivity Richard's masterful syntax belied. Timon genuinely dissolves. First, invective conquers his idiolect; next, he surrenders power to the sea; then his body dies; and in a final, surreal achievement, his traces multiply, the last of which only survives in wax, melting, as the wings of Icarus had done, and with them taking his name, his identity and his life. Timon is Shakespeare's genuine melting man.

LAST DIRECTIONS

There is, I suggest, much work still to be done in this vein on the use of water in the late plays, but this is made difficult at this late point by water's now confusing ubiquity. Generally speaking, however, water, if it interferes with character, ultimately heals: though the seas threaten, they are merciful. In *Pericles*, for instance, Marina, 'this fresh-new seafarer' (Scene 11, line 41), etymologically the sea, sea-changes those around here. Lysimachus, her future husband, is initially, *pace* the Arden editor, a rather nasty piece of work, gloating as he enters the brothel 'How now, how a dozen of virginities?' (Scene 19, line 28). But his coarse vaunt when he sees Marina for the first time –

Faith, she would serve after a long voyage at sea.
(Scene 19, lines 49–50)

– is unwittingly prophetic, and strangely sublimating. For Marina has come from a long voyage, and will serve both to regenerate her father, and quite literally to serve Lysimachus as a wife. When Pericles recognizes her, he uses language like Antipholus. But Antipholus had brooded over his identification with the sea, and had used it to articulate his sense of things falling apart. For Pericles, however, at last everything is coming together, and Pericles holds off the waves, imagining himself as the land, not the sea:

O Helicanus, strike me, honoured sir,
Give me a gash, put me to present pain,
Lest this great sea of joys rushing upon me
O'erbear the shores of my mortality
And drown me with their sweetness!
(Scene 21, lines 178–82)

The sea is not destructive, but a more complex machine, a whirligig of time:

Thou that begett'st him that did thee beget,

Thou that was born at sea, buried at Tarsus,
And found at sea again! (Scene 21, lines 183–5)

Pericles does talk of melting when he regains his wife –

. . . you gods . . . you shall do well
That on the touching of her lips I may
Melt, and be no more seen. – O come, be buried
A second time within these arms.
(Scene 22, lines 62, 63–5)

But here, melting is opposite from earlier uses. Dramatically, Pericles, like the unwitting Hamlet, is resolved, not dissolved. He regains what he has lost; he does not drown his wits. Thaisa does not become buried in his arms but, like some fresh Venus, resurrects herself from the sea into which she had been cast as a corpse in a bitumened coffin.

Indeed, it is fitting that the use of water becomes less a personalized device of isolated characters, but a more universal substance in the Late Plays, as, following its own nature, its properties become multifarious, operating on rather than being operated by characters, variously depriving or restoring, melting or even turning apparently drowned fathers into even harder stuff: 'Of his bones are coral made' (*The Tempest* 1.2.401). In *The Tempest*, Miranda talks of '. . . the sea, mounting to th' welkin's cheek' (1.2.4), anthropomorphizing the marine expanse; later, Prospero performs the converse operation, likening all human cognition to the action of the sea on the shore:

Their understanding
Begins to swell, and the approaching tide
Will shortly fill the reasonable shores
That now lie foul and muddy. (5.1.79–82)

By *The Tempest*, that which had destroyed Timon becomes common cognition. Thus, we can propose a general shift in Shakespeare's use of water as a psychological metaphor. In the first half of his career, water was for individuals to commandeer, often with ambiguous results. At the end of the third quarter of his career, *Timon of Athens*, the apex of water's corrosive power, portrays the final and, I suggest, unique success of a character in managing to surrender himself to the sea. But after Timon, the tide turns, and water, the sea, its actions of transport and restitution become ubiquitous and ultimately merciful. The plunge, the immediate switch of states typified by Icarus disappears, and is replaced by more time-consuming processes in which the bright, frequently harsh Ovidian metamorphosis is itself changed into the slower, circular, restoring currents of the Greek Novel.[17]

---

[17] See Carol Gesner, *Shakespeare and the Greek Romance: A Study of Origins* (Lexington, 1970), esp. pp. 80–142.

KING JOHN, KÖNIG JOHANN:
WAR AND PEACE

LAURENCE LERNER

Friedrich Dürrenmatt's *König Johann*, published in 1968,[1] is described as a *Bearbeitung* (reworking or adaptation): it departs considerably from Shakespeare's original, inventing and modernizing freely, and sometimes inserting material from *The Troublesome Reign of John, King of England*.[2]

Dürrenmatt's version is certainly more cynical (or at least more openly cynical) than Shakespeare's. There is, for instance, the arrival of the Archduke of Austria as ally to the French at the beginning of Act 2. Since he was responsible for the death of Richard Coeur de Lion, he might not seem an appropriate person to help restore the English crown to Richard's nephew Arthur: in Shakespeare we are told, by the French king, that he is doing this to make amends (no doubt this is the official version); in Dürrenmatt the French king remarks:

> Österreichs Zug
> Hierher ist nur ein Vorwand, unser Land
> Zu plündern.

(Austria's campaign is just a pretext to plunder our country.)

A more complex example is the bargain that ends the battle, by which France abandons Arthur's claim to the English throne in return for receiving the English possessions in France. In Shakespeare, the governor of Angiers proposes that further fighting be avoided by means of a match between Blanche of Spain, John's niece, and the Dauphin, which is accepted once John has offered 'Anjou and fair Touraine,

Maine, Poitiers, / And all that we upon this side the sea . . . / Find liable to our crown and dignity.' (2.1.488–91) In Dürrenmatt the kings strike this bargain themselves, with no mention of the marriage, *before* the battle begins:

KÖNIG JOHANN Wenn in Angers das bürgerliche Pack
  Zum König mich erwählt, gibst du dann nach?
KÖNIG PHILIPP Ich gebe nach. Und wenn es Arthur wählt?
KÖNIG JOHANN Ich gebe ihm Touraine und Anjou dir.
KÖNIG PHILIPP Nicht viel.
KÖNIG JOHANN Mein Heer ist stärker . . .
KÖNIG PHILIPP Einverstanden.

K JOHN If the crowd of citizens in Angers choose me as king, will you give in?
K PHILIP I'll give in. And if they choose Arthur?
K JOHN I'll give him Touraine, and you Anjou.
K PHILIP That's not much.
K JOHN My army's stronger . . .
K PHILIP Agreed.

The Austrian archduke, overhearing this, decides to sabotage it ('This stinks of rotten

---

[1] Friedrich Dürrenmatt, *König Johann (nach Shakespeare)* (Zürich, 1968).

[2] *The Troublesome Reign of John, King of England* was published in 1591. The controversy about its relation to Shakespeare's play will probably never be settled: the majority view is that it preceded *King John*, and was, along with Holinshed, his main source; a minority view claims that it is a corrupted text of Shakespeare's play. Settling this question is, fortunately, not relevant to the argument of this essay.

peace, I'd better act') by launching an attack on the rear of the English army, whereupon Philip indicates with a shrug that the bargain is off:

> Es tut
> Mir Leid, Johann, doch gib es zu: Es wäre
> Ein Wahnsinn, meinen Vorteil nicht zu nutzen
>
> I'm sorry, John; but you must admit
> It would be madness not to use this advantage.

Even more nakedly cynical is the fate of Angiers. In Shakespeare, the governor's proposal is made in self-defence, even desperation. After the drawn battle between the two armies, the Bastard suggests to the two kings that they join forces to destroy 'this peevish town', then resume their contest, and it is in response to this that Hubert, the governor, proposes his diplomatic solution – which succeeds. In Dürrenmatt the diplomatic solution also succeeds (i.e. the battle is not then resumed) but the kings then decide, out of annoyance, to destroy the town after all ('Doch weil ihr keine der Parteien wähltet / Und weder warm noch kalt war, laue Hunde, / Seid jetzt bestraft': All the same, because you wouldn't take sides, and were neither hot nor cold, you lukewarm dogs, you'll now be punished). The town is attacked, and the cathedral destroyed.

The other principle discernible in Dürrenmatt's changes is pacifist: the question of war v. peace is made, over and over, the centre of attention. Cynicism, pacifism: the two cannot always be distinguished.

Wars are arranged by kings but fought by ordinary people: this is perhaps the first and most striking point that will occur to the modern reader of Renaissance plays with their heroic value-schemes. In *The Humorous Lieutenant* of Beaumont and Fletcher, for example, the kings whom Demetrius has defeated in battle refuse to give up their 'cities, forts and frontier countries', protesting indignantly that they would then be 'Traitors to those that feed us'. Demetrius is so impressed by their spirit that he tells them they can keep the lands; whereupon they in turn, not to be outdone in

generosity, declare 'You shall have all our countries – All, by heaven sir!' – an offer which Demetrius naturally refuses.[3] Completely absent from this generosity contest is any awareness that these 'countries' have inhabitants, to whom it might matter who they are ruled by, or whether their land becomes a battlefield: the 'cities, forts and countries' have become tokens for royal gestures, nothing more.

The obvious antidote to this concern with heroic gesture is to bring the ordinary people into the play, as Shakespeare most famously and successfully does in *Henry V*; but Dürrenmatt refuses this easy method, explaining (in a note) that this is a play dealing with the murderers, not the victims. Instead, he uses a brilliant device which in the theatre is very powerful: the royal families greet one another effusively, and sit down to dinner together with a good deal of bonhomie, while soldiers drag corpses away in the background. During the battle they wear plastic aprons, which they later remove when covered with blood. When Shakespeare's kings discuss the battle it is an argument about who's winning –

> England, thou hast not saved one drop of blood
> In this hot trial more than we of France;
> Rather, lost more   (2.1.341–3)

– whereas Dürrenmatt's are as proud of their armies' performance as a football manager of his players' skill:

> Gib's königlicher Bruder, zu: Der Angriff
> Des rechten Flügels unsrer Reiterei
> In deine linke Flanke, das war Klasse.

Come on royal brother, admit it: that attack by the right wing of our cavalry on your left flank, that was real class!

When the two kings argue about Arthur's claim to the throne, and then move to settling it by battle, the *Troublesome Reign* had John say:

---

[3] Beaumont and Fletcher, *The Humorous Lieutenant*, Act 3, Scene 7 in *The Dramatic Works in the Beaumont and Fletcher Canon*, ed. by F. Bowers, vol. 5 (Cambridge, 1982), pp. 363–4.

'What wants, my sword shall more at large set down.' *My* sword: the convenient fiction that the kings themselves do the fighting is vividly undermined by Dürrenmatt's device.

This representation of war as a game for the kings is further underlined when John breaks the 'rules' and threatens Philip personally: Philip is shocked.

> Du bist beleidigt? Nimmst persönlich,
> Was unumgänglich durch die Politik?
> Das kann nicht Ernst sein, mein lieber Freund.

You're offended? Such things are unavoidable in politics, and you take them personally? You can't be serious, old man.

The kings' detachment is, however, not altogether successful, since Chatillon, the Herald, later comes in hobbling on a crutch, and reveals that none of the French royal family has escaped unscathed (though Philip's injury was only indirectly the result of the war: he fell off his horse). Most interesting of all is Chatillon's reproach to King John that he didn't handle the negotiations very well: he could easily have avoided the battle by appearing to give in to the cardinal's demands (in Dürrenmatt, the cardinal Pandulph intervenes before, not after, the battle):

> Als Diplomat habt ihr nicht sehr vernünftig
> Gehandelt. Ich bin offen, Sir, verzeiht.
> Der Krieg war leicht vermeidbar. Was
> Der Kardinal von Euch verlangte, nun,
> Ein Kloster weniger geplündert, sei's
> Zum Scheine nur, die Antwort bloss ein wenig
> Konzilianter, und zufrieden wäre
> Der Kardinal nach Rom zurückgereist.

You didn't handle the diplomacy very well. Excuse my frankness, sir. It would have been easy to avoid this war. What the Cardinal demanded – well, plundering one cloister less (or pretending to) – a slightly more conciliatory answer – and the Cardinal's on his way back to Rome, quite satisfied.

The interminable negotiations for peace in Northern Ireland have kept stumbling over the question of decommissioning: will the IRA give up their weapons? If Chatillon could be brought into that situation, one can imagine him pointing out to the IRA negotiators that a gun or two handed over, a slightly more conciliatory answer, and Senator Mitchell is on his way back to America, quite satisfied. The parallel is tempting – not least because it shows once again how close to each other pacifism and cynicism can come in politics.[4]

Dürrenmatt inserts into his version constant small reminders of the difference between war and peace. His citizens of Angiers are much more explicit than Shakespeare's governor in declaring

> Wir lieben Frieden, weil wir Frieden brauchen
> Zu unserer Geschäften

We're for peace, since we need peace for our business affairs

No doubt that too could be seen as cynical; but there is also the blunt riposte which Konstanze receives when urging Philip not to agree to the bargain: 'Du, Vampir, willst nur Blut!' Shakespeare's Constance is excessively rhetorical, building her concern (and later her grief) for Arthur into mountainous structures of paraded emotion, and is rebuked precisely for her rhetoric: 'You are as fond of grief as of your child' (3.4.92–3) – to which she (inevitably) delivers an extended reply – 'Grief fills the room up of my absent child' – that can be regarded as a confirmation of the accusation. Since Dürrenmatt's dry modernism removes a good deal of the concern with rhetoric, judgement on his Konstanze is passed not in terms of how she speaks but in terms of what she is proposing.

The character whom Dürrenmatt most strikingly changes is Blanche, King John's niece, the subject (the victim?) of the diplomatic marriage that is intended to end the fighting. In his notes, Dürrenmatt informs us, without further explanation, that it became clear, in the course of the rehearsals, that she needed to be changed.

---

4 It is of course common to see *King John* as cynical (e.g. M. M. Reese, *The Cease of Majesty*, p. 280: 'the most cynical and disillusioned among the histories'); the point that the present essay seeks to add is the close link between cynicism and pacifism.

Instead of the 'touchingly naive creature' depicted by Shakespeare, he makes her into a self-aware, rich millionaire heiress ('zu einer selbst-bewussten reichen Millionenerbin'). Taking a detail from the *Troublesome Reign* he introduces a possible match between Blanche and the Bastard, which is now abandoned. In the *Troublesome Reign* it was an opportunity for the Bastard to acquire wealth and land, in Dürrenmatt it is a love affair, and Blanche objects to the arranged match with the Dauphin on the grounds that she is not a piece of goods to be traded, to which the Bastard replies in what is perhaps the most interesting speech in the play, informing her that though they spent hot nights together and he loves her 'von ganzem Herzen / Wie Redensart' (with all my heart – as one says), her body was not made for enjoyment but as a bargaining counter which she now needs to take into bed with Louis, 'diesem fetten Gockel' (this fat slob, this old goat). Even this violently cynical moment has its pacifist touches, since he explains that the purpose of the disgusting bargain would be to bring peace, and the result of her refusal would be the spilling of a sea of blood from thousands of poor devils. ('Wenn nicht, vergiesst Ihr Meere roten Bluts / Von vielen Tausend armen Teufeln'.) When therefore Angiers has been destroyed and the war is about to be resumed, she is given perhaps the most violently bitter speech in the play, pointing out that she has been sacrificed for nothing, and when lying like a whore in the Dauphin's bed she'll think of the Bastard as the biggest fool there is ('Im verhurten Bett des Dauphin denk ich Euer / als aller Narren allergrösster').

How relevant to our understanding of Shakespeare's play is this brilliant, controversial modern adaptation? The question it opens, and to which it provides such an illuminating answer, can be stated as: How will a pacifist read *King John*? No doubt the question itself needs defending: to some it will seem not only an improper question, but the very model of an improper question. It will seem to treat a work of literature not as something from which we can learn, but as an examination candidate who has to conform to our expectations. And if the literary work is four hundred years old, this would be to assume that its concerns are the same as our concerns: to assume the unchanging human nature, the timeless values, that our new historicists have tirelessly denounced as (this has become one of the newer terms of reproach) humanist.

The terminology of E. D. Hirsch's *Validity in Interpretation* will be useful here. Hirsch distinguishes between *meaning*, attained by means of understanding, the criterion for which is authorial intention (and of course historical knowledge on our part), and *significance*, attained by judgement, which relates the author's verbal meaning to ourselves, to history, even to the author himself and his other works.[5] A historical reading of a literary text, attempting to attribute to it the meaning which the author intended and contemporary readers understood, guarding against the temptation to assume that our concerns today were its concerns then, would clearly be an example of what Hirsch called understanding, the attempt to find the meaning. The historical critic will then go on to assert that if we find the concerns, or the values, of an earlier work to be different from ours, we must then read it 'as Elizabethans', granting it a willing suspension of disagreement. Since few people, other than scholars (and not all of them), are prepared to suspend disagreement, this will mean that there is almost always an alternative way to read, not historical but immediate, or committed.

Hirsch's distinction is a valid and even necessary one, but it should not blind us to the fact that the process of responding to literature involves a constant traffic between understanding and judgement – a fact which Hirsch does not deny, his aim being to draw a theoretical

---

[5] E. D. Hirsch, *Validity in Interpretation* (Yale, 1967), especially pp. 61–7, 139–63.

distinction. Only the most austere Dryasdust will be able to devote himself exclusively to the establishing of meaning without allowing any concern with significance to cross his mind. This will be particularly difficult in the case of a work like *King John*, not only because it deals with issues that can hardly fail to be of concern to the modern reader, but also because it is a play: that is, a theatrical event.

We need to remind ourselves of the situation in a theatre today. The ideological gap between modern audience and Renaissance text is, as I have already remarked, immense. It is not only impossible to recreate the situation of the 1590s: it is arguable that the more conscientiously a production strives for authenticity (apron stage, no scenery, Renaissance acting style, even sixteenth-century pronunciation) the more aware the audience will become of the gap. If therefore there are elements in the production which draw attention to this gap (such as the plastic aprons) they are, arguably, simply methods of making explicit what is already and inevitably there. The usual rule of thumb in the English theatre today for stating what should and should not be modernized is that you must not monkey with the text: even outrageous production effects are allowable but the words must be Shakespeare's. That rule is of course not available to a German production. When the play is performed in translation, the question of how far the production should be modernized has already been anticipated by the question how far the language should be modernized.

When Shakespeare's John, in the opening scene, asks the French herald what will happen if he refuses King Philip's demands, he receives this reply:

The proud control of fierce and bloody war,
To enforce these rights so forcibly withheld.

(1.1.18)

In Dürrenmatt this becomes a single word, 'Krieg'. This is almost like an announcement, at the very beginning of the play, that war is also being declared on rhetoric. The reduced language is ready to receive reductive accounts of political motives. This is to make articulate an awareness that political language is the better for shedding its rhetorical dress, and this is an awareness the audience have brought into the theatre with them.

Just as they have brought with them an awareness that the difference between war and peace is important; and it is this awareness which enables me to describe the value of *König Johann* as a guide to our reading of *King John*. If in experiencing *King John* we are aware both of our own values and of historical understanding, then the experience will involve constant shifts and tensions between the two, and Dürrenmatt's version offers us a series of goads that remind us of our values. By calling these values 'pacifist', and using the shorthand term 'pacifist reading' I do not of course mean to claim that all modern readers are pacifists, but to call attention to the crucial point about political conflict, that it presents us with two sides, each claiming to be in the right, and each trying to defeat the other. A conventional representation of this invites us to decide which side we support; in contrast, what I have called a pacifist reading directs our attention to how the dispute is to be settled. Settling it by war could cause more suffering than the victory of either side. The crucial moments in such a reading, then, will not be the moments of choice between the two sides (should John or Arthur sit on the English throne?) but the moments of choice between ways of settling the matter (war or diplomacy, war or compromise).[6]

There are two episodes in *King John* which present us with this choice: the encounter of the two kings outside the gates of Angiers in Act 2, and the French invasion of England in Act 5. Act 2 brings the contrast between war and diplomacy in front of us. Angiers (technically an English town) is invested by both the French

---

[6] I have developed this position further in 'Peace Studies: A Proposal', *New Literary History*, 26, no. 3 (1995), 641–65.

and the English armies, each of which demands entrance; Hubert the governor tells them to sort out who is really king of England, and then he will open the gates. They fight, the result is indecisive, and the Bastard suggests that they join forces to destroy 'this contemptuous city', and then resume their fight against each other. They agree, and prepare to attack the town; whereupon Hubert proposes a way to 'win this city without stroke or sound' by means of a compromise: if Blanche, King John's niece, marries the Dauphin, the war can end. John agrees, and offers all the English possessions in France as dowry. This means he is giving up part to retain the whole: his title to England itself will now be recognized. The agreement is presented as consequent on the marriage, and there is some public insistence that Lewis the Dauphin and Blanche need to declare 'I love', but the fiction is transparent: asked if he can love Blanche, Lewis replies, 'Nay, ask me how I can refrain from love.' It is very tempting for the actor to deliver this with a smile, since it can so obviously mean 'Because I'm being ordered to'. Blanche too disposes of any possibility of taking 'love' seriously, declaring 'My uncle's will in this respect is mine.' It is a purely political marriage.

Constance, of course, objects, regarding the agreement as a betrayal:

> You are forsworn, forsworn!
> You came in arms to spill mine enemies' blood,
> But now in arms you strengthen it with yours.
>
> (3.1.27–9)

This is a most convenient pun: the contrast between arms as weapons and arms as what one embraces with contains the issue that has lain under the surface of the whole encounter: that the open conflict between France and England, which culminated in a stage battle and has remained undecided, can be replaced by a different kind of conflict, the argument about means: should it be settled by fighting, or patched up by diplomacy? The more carefully we look at the scene, the more prominently this second conflict appears. Austria announced near the beginning:

> The peace of heaven is theirs that lift their swords
> In such a just and charitable war.   (2.1.35–6)

Religious language here is not applied to earthly situations by analogy: the love of God is not a way of bringing us to love one another, the peace of Heaven is not a path to peace. This sums up what has been said in the first twenty-five lines: Austria's intervention in the war is presented as an act of love towards Arthur, on whose cheek he lays 'this zealous kiss', but the vocabulary of love is used to justify fighting. The idea that religious vocabulary can contradict ordinary usage is of course familiar in Christianity, the religion of paradox. The purpose of such paradox is to shock us out of the familiar onto a higher plane of thinking – from the values of this world to the contrasting values of the kingdom of God; but every shock is not necessarily an elevation, and we see here that religious language can be seen as duplicity: 'peace' does not really mean peace.

There is a parallel between this linguistic trickery and the crucial evasiveness of Hubert's response to the demands of the two kings. Both France and England demand entrance to Angiers as a matter of right, since Angiers belongs to the English king: it's just a matter of deciding who, as a matter of right, *is* the English king. 'He that proves the king, To him will we prove loyal', declares Hubert, delicately playing on two meanings of 'prove': he that advances evidence to show his right, or he that *turns out* to be king. A moment later he declares

> Till you compound whose right is worthiest,
> We for the worthiest, hold the right from both.
>
> (2.1.281–2)

'Compound' here means 'come to an agreement about' (*OED* 6 or 7 if transitive, 10 or 11 if 'whose right is worthiest' is used adverbially). Hubert says nothing about how the proving or compounding will be done: that is left to the kings, just as the application of 'Heaven's peace' to earthly situations is left to God – or His interpreters! Is Hubert being evasive? Does he not know perfectly well how the matter will be settled? When the battle takes place and is indecisive, Hubert's language is franker:

> Blood hath bought blood, and blows have
> answered blows,
> Strength matched with strength and power
> confronted power.
> Both are alike, and both alike we like.
> One must prove greatest. While they weigh so
> even,
> We hold our town for neither, yet for both.
>
> (2.1.329–33)

Both the vocabulary of Hubert and that of the kings hover on the edge of an open admission: that might is right, and the language of justice is only a rhetoric that conceals. Such would be the cynical reading; but we are faced with the realization that the cynical and religious interpretation can be equated. Either 'Cut the cackle and admit that it's just a matter of who is stronger', or 'Cut the tortuous evasions of human lawyers and leave the decision to God.' Two contrasting ways of saying the same thing. There is a parallel to this in the opening of *Macbeth*. The question of legitimacy is important in *Macbeth*, as it is in all Shakespeare's political plays: Duncan's murder is 'deep damnation' because he is the rightful king, Macbeth's claim to the throne is illegitimate, he is a usurper. Yet the first act of the play makes it clear that Duncan has only retained his throne because Macbeth and Banquo *fought better* than the Norwegian invaders. Is this a reminder that might is right and illegitimacy only a rationalization, or that God ensures, as in trial by combat, that the right side wins? Trial by combat can always be presented in religious terms.

To raise such questions is precisely the function of a political play; in this scene the Bastard's intervention offers an answer. He proposes that the two kings should join forces to destroy the town and then resume their battle. This is a response to Hubert's prevarication in general, and to his invoking of Divine Justice in particular, since he has just declared 'A greater power than we denies all this.' The suggestion that God approves of his refusal to take sides appears to be the last straw for the Bastard:

> By heaven, these scroyles of Angers flout you,
> Kings,
> And stand securely on their battlements
> As in a theatre, whence they gape and point
> At your industrious scenes and acts of death . . .
>
> (2.1.373–6)

Including the theatre audience in his contempt might set up an ironic cheer – true, we spectators are enjoying the battle scenes in safety, but that, after all, is our function, whereas Hubert *could* decide to join in: ergo, he's as bad as us. And now the Bastard is offering us more scenes and acts of death (the vocabulary rubs home the point) to gloat over.

One thing is certain about the Bastard's suggestion: that there is nothing religious about it. Perhaps it *could be* made in religious terms – we must never underestimate the possible ingenuity of the casuist; but it is quite clear that it isn't.

> I'd play incessantly upon these jades,
> Even till unfencèd desolation
> Leave them as naked as the vulgar air.
>
> (2.1.385–7)

> An if thou hast the mettle of a king,
> Being wronged as we are by this peevish town,
> Turn thou the mouth of thy artillery,
> As we will ours, against these saucy walls.
>
> (2.1.401–4)

'Saucy', 'peevish', 'contemptuous': there is no suggestion that Angiers is defying Heaven, only that they're defying *us*. 'Playing incessantly' presents the attack as offering the pleasures of destruction, not the moral satisfaction of acting as God's instrument.

The Bastard has traditionally been regarded as the most sympathetic figure in the play,[7] and

---

[7] Ornstein (*A Kingdom for a Stage* p. 95) even speaks of his 'fundamental innocence' – a view that can only be reconciled with the present essay if we use the wordplay of Maria ('He hath all the good gifts of nature' – 'He hath indeed almost natural') and say he is almost an innocent.

since he delivers the choric commentary that ends this long scene, there is clearly some kind of special relationship between him and the audience. But this may also suggest a gap between audience and dramatist: the dramatist is showing them – or some of them, the more jingoistic and more bloodthirsty part – the real nature of their enjoyment. An audience is no more uniform than a play, and one function of the Bastard may well be to excite cheers from some spectators, and invite others to reflect on what is going on. The famous concluding soliloquy, about 'commodity' (which could be glossed as 'self-interest') observes that France has been drawn

From a resolved an honourable war,
To a most base and vile-concluded peace.
(2.1.586–7)

Since he immediately goes on to ask 'Why rail I on this commodity?' and answers 'But for because he hath not wooed me yet', we can interpret 'honourable war' as meaning a war that gives *me* chance to shine, and 'base and vile-concluded peace' as meaning one that takes it away from me.

Act 2, Scene 1 is explicitly about war, and also the scene in which it takes place; in the following scene (3.1) peace and war are explicitly opposed. Hubert's suggestion has prevailed, Lewis has married Blanche, and 'John, to stop Arthur's title in the whole, / Hath willingly departed with a part.' (2.1.563–4) What undoes the treaty is the arrival of Cardinal Pandulph, that wily and evasive rhetorician. Pandulph's demand for the reinstatement of Stephen Langton as Archbishop has nothing to do with the question of succession, and can be seen as quite irrelevant to the concerns of the play: it no doubt provided an opportunity for the audience to hiss at this example of Papal interference, and to cheer when John denounces Popish practices ('By the merit of vile gold . . . Purchase corrupted pardon') as a form of commodity. Whether they went on cheering when the French king joined in the denunciation of Pandulph is not easy to decide.

That would, in Hirsch's terms, be a question about meaning only, perhaps merely about partial meaning; when, shortly afterwards, the scene reverts to the question of peace and war, it is very difficult, if we get interested in the argument, to exclude significance. The war party now consists of Constance, Pandulph and the Dauphin (plus, of course, the Bastard), and the very fact that they all want war for different reasons necessarily focuses our attention on the question of war itself. And the peace party? Well, of course, there isn't one. The only person who speaks unequivocally for peace as desirable in itself is Arthur, who in Act 2 says:

Good my mother, peace.
I would that I were laid low in my grave.
I am not worth this coil that's made for me.
(2.1.163–5)

No one takes any notice of him. The two who speak against war in Act 3, Blanche and King Philip, do not do so out of principled objection. Blanche is distressed that her wedding feast should be 'kept with slaughtered men', and that her husband should war against her uncle; Philip now finds slaughter distressing for much the same reason, and feels no inconsistency between his ordinary kingly belligerence in Act 2 and his politic change of position now. There is no one like Burgundy, who in the last act of *Henry V* delivers his wonderful speech on the horrors of war as such (and of course even on this the cynical remark is possible that this is the way one speaks once the war is over).

But the fact that there is no principled pacifist in this scene should neither surprise nor worry us. We cannot expect such principles to be formulated in the thirteenth century, and perhaps not in the sixteenth either; what we can expect – and do find – is the experience of the horror of war causing a reaction in those who suffer from it, a turning towards a position that has not yet been formulated as a principle. That is, after all, the way literature reaches towards the future.

'Peace' and 'war' are not only underlying

ideas in the play, they are also active as words; and to look at how the words behave is always illuminating when considering how the ideas operate.

> The grappling vigour and rough frown of war
> Is cold in amity and painted peace. (3.1.30–1)

Why does Constance describe peace as 'painted'? Paint presumably refers here to make-up, and peace is regarded as deceptive, a painted face being a sign of hypocrisy. But what is the difference between real peace and hypocritical peace? To accuse apparent peace of not being genuine is one of the commonest strategies of the bellicose idealist: if true peace means peace in which all conflicts have been resolved and there is no longer any possibility of war, then true peace is not possible in human society: a war party can *always* denounce peace as 'painted'. Just as it can always declare its belligerent strategy through the syntax of 'peace if': Philip's speech in 2.1.235 is the best example of this, telling Hubert that he will 'leave your children, wives and you in peace' *if* they yield to his demands, and followed inevitably by the balancing syntax 'but if . . .'

Austria attempts to interrupt Constance in Act 3 with 'Lady Constance, peace!'; she replies: 'War! War! No peace! Peace is to me a war.' (3.1.39–40) When Austria said 'peace' he meant, of course, 'silence', as in 'hold your peace', and Constance's word-play can be seen as rebounding back on her, as evidence of her bad faith: the case for war is made by a disputant who will not 'hold her peace' and will not let others speak.

And finally, Act 5, which is almost universally regarded as clumsy: either a botched rewriting of the *Troublesome Reign* or a sign that Shakespeare had lost interest by this stage. This common judgement may well be correct, but it is of course not always easy to distinguish clumsiness from a deliberate undermining of conventional expectation. John's poisoning by wicked monks, so prominent in the *Troublesome Reign*, is played down in Shakespeare's version in order to concentrate on the invasion of England by the Dauphin, who seems at first set for an easy victory: the islanders are shouting 'Vive le roi', he has 'the best cards for the game', and there seems to be little resistance. Here is another opportunity to address the question of war *v.* peace, but it is not taken – or not explicitly taken. Pandulph's exhortation to 'tame the savage spirit of wild war' (5.2.74) is never elaborated into anything like Burgundy's vision of peace and its blessings – and Pandulph is by now thoroughly tainted by his duplicity (we see the great advantage of introducing a wholly new character as the peacemaker in *Henry V*). Once again, the treatment of the word 'peace' is revealing. It is used five times in 5.2, and only once (line 76) in its primary sense, as the opposite to war. The other uses are John 'making his peace with Rome' (line 92 twice, and line 96), where it means 'recognizing Rome's authority', and line 159, where it means 'silence'. No attention is paid to the word because no attention is paid to the concept.

In contrast to this, the Bastard's military zeal is very prominent. He uses the very rhythms and thoughts of Henry V's more famous defiance:

> Be stirring as the time, be fire with fire;
> Threaten the threat'ner, and outface the brow
> Of bragging horror. (5.1.48–50)

> Now set the teeth and stretch the nostril wide,
> Hold hard the breath, and bend up every spirit
> To his full height. (*Henry V* 3.1.15–17)

Similarly, in the following scene, the Bastard's flyting expresses a lengthy contempt for 'This apish and unmannerly approach, / This harnessed masque and unadvisèd revel' (5.2.131–2) before working up to the threat of 'warlike John' (since John is dying of poison, he is only 'warlike' in the Bastard's vocabulary: but vocabulary is itself a weapon.

The rhetoric of Act 5 makes it clear that war has all the best tunes, just as the Bastard (as everyone seems to agree) got the cheers of the groundlings – perhaps of everyone. This would be decisive as a reading of the last act, if it were not for Shakespeare's talent in leaving us with an aftertaste. The Bastard's famous concluding speech ('Naught shall make us rue / If England to itself do rest but true') certainly leaves him as the patriotic hero. This conclusion is not as bellicose as some of his earlier speeches, since it puts the case for security through strength, a position he had already adumbrated in 5.1.73–6:

> Let us, my liege, to arms!
> Perchance the Cardinal cannot make your peace,
> Or, if he do, let it at least be said
> They saw we had a purpose of defence

– and reasserted in 5.7.87–8, when he remarks that the Dauphin is more likely to sue for peace

> when he sees
> Ourselves well-sinewed to our own defence.

And how is peace finally achieved? Not, certainly, through a principled rejection of war; but not through defiance either. The war simply fizzles out; there is no decisive battle, no concluding treaty. Count Melun is slain, the English traitors revert (presumably with their soldiers) to John again, and Lewis' reinforcements 'are cast away and sunk on Goodwin sands'. (5.5.13) It is all very cursory, as if we are being shown that Nature does not go in for high-flown climaxes and splendid victories. This may mean that Shakespeare botched the ending of an indecisive play; it may also mean that he ended it with great subtlety.

THE TEMPEST'S FORGOTTEN EXILE

JANE KINGSLEY-SMITH

But he that cannot abide to live in companie, or through sufficiencie hath need of nothing, is not esteemed a part or member of a Cittie, but is either a beast or a God.[1]

The popularity of Aristotle's maxim in English Renaissance literature seems partly due to its vagueness. Who is Aristotle's solitary man? Can he remain in society and yet be considered an outcast? Is he one who has chosen to live outside society or one who has been forced out? We might also ask who decides whether the subject is beast or God, and consider whether he can occupy those identities simultaneously. Aristotle's riddling definition of the solitary man was repeatedly quoted because it expressed an ambivalence understood by contemporary historians, philosophers, poets and dramatists as central to the experience of exile. In *Coriolanus*, Shakespeare exploited the dramatic possibilities of this ambivalence. The protagonist's banishment is partly incurred through his virtues; he is both the beast and god of Aristotle's dictum.[2] Perhaps more unexpected is the influence of Aristotle's *Politics* and other paradigms of exile on *The Tempest*. Prospero's self-exile in his library allowed Antonio to usurp the kingdom; banishment brought Prospero to the island; alienation dictates his actions there. It is my contention that critics of *The Tempest* have not taken Prospero's banishment, or the identity crisis that it inspires, seriously enough. The competing discourses surrounding banishment at the time can be seen to shape not only Prospero's posturing as an exile but also, more startlingly, his identity as a magician and colonialist.

There were two major interpretative frameworks within which to understand banishment in the sixteenth and seventeenth centuries, one emphasizing the liberty, hedonism and creativity of exile, the other focusing on its attendant confusion, self-loss and even death. Both perspectives had their roots in classical literature. The Stoic consolation for exile recognized banishment as one of Fortune's cruellest blows. In his *Consolatio ad Helviam*, Seneca described the 'poverty, disgrace and contempt' incurred by exile, and conceded that death might seem preferable.[3] But the philosophy which promised to transform the banished man's condition required a self-abnegation almost equally harsh. Seneca urged the exile to renounce love, hope, pity and fear, severing all ties with the external world for a life of pure contemplation and self-sufficiency. Senecan Stoicism informed many sixteenth-century consolations for exile such as Erasmus' letter to Canidius in *De conscribendis epistolis* (1522) and Justus Lipsius' *De constantia*

---

[1] *Aristotles Politiques, or Discourse of Government. Translated out of Greeke into French, with Exposition taken out of the best Authours . . . By Loys Le Roy, called Regius. Translated out of French into English. At London printed by Adam Islip Anno Domo: 1598*, p. 15.

[2] See F. N. Lees, '*Coriolanus*, Aristotle and Bacon', *RES*, 1 (1950), 114–25.

[3] *Ad Helviam* in *Seneca's Minor Dialogues* tr. by A. Stewart (London, 1889), pp. 325, 342.

libri duo (1585),[4] but scepticism about such inhuman detachment was also widely expressed. In Marston's *Antonio's Revenge* (1600–1), Pandulfo responds to the news of his banishment with Senecan imperturbability,[5] but then declares 'Man will break out, despite philosophy [. . .] I am the miserablest soul that breathes' (4.2.69–76).

The alternative to this Stoic detachment (or its failure) was a consolation for exile based on Epicurean ideas. Plutarch's *Of Exile or Banishment* urged the exile to transform his fate through imagination. Exile could become one's liberation from social duties and civic restrictions, a voluntary journey taken for pleasure and profit, and a philosophical and artistic vocation. With this perspective it was possible to turn even Ovid's experience of exile into a comedy. The latter's sufferings on the island of Tomis were familiar to Renaissance England through the *Tristia* and *Ex Ponto*, texts frequently quoted in sixteenth-century representations of banishment.[6] Here, Ovid mourned the annihilation of his identity, in particular the loss of his name and of his poetic vocation. But in *Cardanus Comforte* (1576), Jerome Cardan argued that Ovid's poetic career had been enhanced by exile, for he had written more in six years on Tomis than during the previous fifty-four years in Rome. Similarly, in *As You Like It*, Touchstone cites Ovid as his poetic forefather (3.3.5–6) but in a context which undermines the tragic associations of the Roman's exile. Touchstone's wit is *not* unappreciated by the banished courtiers, and the satirical context of his remarks deflates the stature of both poets.[7]

Comic and tragic representations of banishment on the English Renaissance stage emphasize the importance of keeping one's place. At the end of the comedy, the exiles return to society without a backward glance. Tragedy tends to confirm the suffering of its outcast hero and kills him with exile. Hence, the representation of banishment can be seen as a response to contemporary anxieties about displacement and self-loss, connected to conduct books warning of the dangers of travel, sumptuary laws which tried to restrict people to the clothing appropriate to their station in life, and anti-theatrical polemic which argued that neither audience members nor actors were where they should be. But within this fundamentally conservative structure, these two perspectives on exile are played out according to genre. Thus, pastoral comedy encourages its exiles to forget the initial trauma of expulsion in order to embrace the possibilities for change. Metamorphosis becomes a kind of play, which does not threaten the character's identity so much as allow for its fuller expression. Tragedy explores more deeply the sense of loss incurred through expulsion, and the individual's dependence upon society for selfhood. This outcast is characterized by his inability to play a different part, which, combined with the intransigence and ruthlessness of society, leads to his destruction.[8]

At the beginning of *The Tempest*, Miranda does not know how to respond to her father's revelation that he was once prince of Milan: 'What foul play had we that we came from thence? / Or blessèd was't we did?' (1.2.60–1). Their banishment seems most easily aligned with the comic/pastoral pattern represented in the Shakespearian canon by plays such as *The*

---

4 See *The Collected Works of Erasmus*, vol. 25, ed. by J. K. Sowards (Toronto and London, 1985), pp. 151–5; and *De constantia libri duo* trans. by Sir John Stradling (London, 1592), STC 15696.

5 Pandulfo quotes Seneca's *De providentia* and *De remediis fortuitorum* in response to banishment (2.1.152–62), and the death of Mellida (4.2.33–42). Moreover, the book of philosophy that Antonio brings onto the stage in 2.2 is Seneca's *De providentia*.

6 In Thomas Nashe's *The Unfortunate Traveller* (1594), the banished English Earl quotes Ovid's *Tristia* III.3.53, as he tries to explain to the hapless Jack the penalties of exile.

7 T. W. Baldwin has argued that echoes of the *Tristia* in *As You Like It* and *Richard II* suggest that Shakespeare read Ovid's lament for exile in the Latin, *William Shakespere's Small Latine & Lesse Greeke* (Urbana, 1944) 2 vols., vol. 2, pp. 427–30.

8 For an extended treatment of this subject see my PhD thesis *Banishment in Shakespeare's Plays*, University of Birmingham, 1999.

Two Gentlemen of Verona, *As You Like It*, *Henry IV* and *The Winter's Tale*. It has brought Prospero magical and colonial power and has facilitated the marriage between Ferdinand and Miranda. And yet exile is also a torment and a shame that, even after twelve years, Prospero has been unable to transform philosophically or imaginatively.

Prospero's account of exile is tragic and accompanied by much weeping and lamentation. His description of their enforced departure through the gates of Milan at dead of darkness, when the three year-old Miranda wept, is greeted with fresh tears (1.2.127–35). On the sea journey which followed, it was apparently Prospero who sobbed and groaned (155–6). But as far as Prospero is concerned, the tragedy is ongoing. In *Romeo and Juliet*, Romeo declares 'There is no world without Verona walls / But purgatory, torture, hell itself. / Hence banishèd is banished from the world, / And world's exile is death' (3.3.17–20). Though older, wiser, and at the other end of the Shakespearian canon, Prospero too dismisses his years of exile in yearning for the past. Despite the fact that he has recently raised a tempest and caused a shipwreck in which no one was harmed, Prospero insists upon his present insignificance:

> I have done nothing but in care of thee,
> Of thee, my dear one, thee, my daughter, who
> Art ignorant of what thou art, naught knowing
> Of whence I am, nor that I am more better
> Than Prospero, master of a full poor cell
> And thy no greater father.   (1.2.16–21)

Prospero's fantastical magic power is nothing to the revelation that he once held political sway in Europe:

> Twelve year since, Miranda, twelve year since,
> Thy father was the Duke of Milan, and
> A prince of power.   (53–5)

I have suggested that Prospero's banishment needs to be taken more *seriously*. To do thus, is not simply to recognize its tragic status, but to appreciate how banishment shapes *The Tempest* at the most basic level. The protagonist uses his magical power to subdue the island and his enemies. But he does so, not in pursuit of Gonzalo's prelapsarian innocence, not from a dispassionate desire for justice or a passionate desire for revenge, and not even to practise tyranny in a ritual exorcism of his previous political failure, but to reverse the sentence of exile. This reversal does not alone require his physical removal from the island and his reinvestiture as Duke of Milan. Rather, it demands that the banishers, Antonio, Sebastian, Alonso, and the banished man himself, recognize Prospero's humanity.

This need to prove humanity is apparent in Prospero's various pedagogic projects. Jonathan Bate considers Prospero a failed humanist in that his liberal arts have inspired evil not virtue in Antonio. When the Duke's efforts to educate Caliban also result in the pupil's wrong-doing, the blame must fall on Prospero himself:

Learning language should be what makes man god-like as opposed to beast-like, but since the first effect of Caliban's education is his desire to rape Miranda, one wonders whether there is not in fact something devilish about the way in which Prospero has taught him.[9]

But this 'something devilish' about Prospero has already been implied by his banishment from Milan. In the Aristotelian terms invoked by Bate, banishment defines Prospero as either bestial or divine. Hence, education is not the source of his alienation but a possible solution to it. If Prospero can inspire civility, he will prove his own commitment to civilization; if he can fashion a citizen out of the base substance of a Caliban, he will differentiate himself from the savage.[10]

---

[9] Jonathan Bate, 'The Humanist *Tempest*' in *Shakespeare: La Tempête: Etudes Critiques* (1993), ed. by Claude Peltraut, pp. 5–20, 12–13.

[10] Prospero's need to prove his civility may also inform the pains he takes with Miranda's education. By making her eligible for marriage with Ferdinand, this education indirectly ensures that Prospero's credentials as an Italian prince and humanist scholar will never again be in doubt.

Thus, when Prospero's education of Caliban fails, the Duke undermines his own fitness for society, and experiences the same pattern of betrayal and stigmatization begun in Milan. Rather than allow this rejection to identify him once again as an outcast, unfit for human society, Prospero designates Caliban as monstrous, unnatural, and inhuman, and finally banishes him (1.2.345–6).

This strategy of displacing exile and monstrosity onto others is repeated with the shipwrecked men. On one hand, Prospero performs a civilizing function by confronting his enemies with the evil they have perpetrated, forcing them to feel guilt and finally offering reconciliation. But more blatantly, Prospero uses his magic to reverse the positions of banisher and banishèd. In *Coriolanus*, the protagonist declared 'I banish you' (3.3.127) in vengeance at his own expulsion. Prospero has the opportunity to banish those who banished him by forcing them to experience the full horrors of self-loss he has known.[11] In a powerful reworking of his own guilt and insecurity about what banishment implies, Prospero sets about to create on the island a landscape of exile. It is a place beyond civilization, perhaps even hell itself. The shipwrecked men hear noises that might be wild beasts or damned spirits, and meet monstrous shapes that might be islanders but they cannot be sure. If this exposure to 'strange shapes' makes the shipwrecked men feel vulnerable and leads them to question their position in the hierarchy of creation, that is exactly Prospero's intention.

More specifically, Prospero's exiles are made to identify with beasts. Thus, Stefano and Trinculo are hunted by Ariel, driven into a filthy-mantled pool and wracked with cramps and pinches (4.1.256–60). Alonso, Antonio and Sebastian are deprived of their wits. As they become more beast-like, so Prospero appears increasingly divine. The scene in which Ariel plays the harpy, interrupting the banquet to remind the shipwrecked men of their guilt, implicitly identifies Prospero as a god, for if

Ariel and the other spirits are 'ministers of fate' (3.3.61), he is Providence itself. The curse of 'ling'ring perdition' and of banishment upon the shipwrecked men (77), echoes God's curse upon Cain in Genesis 4.10–12, once again identifying Prospero with the divine.

But although Prospero may seem to enjoy this power, divinity still necessitates alienation from humanity according to Aristotle's dictum. The last scene of the play represents Prospero embracing mankind. The magus who had earlier declared himself human by the expression of pity (5.1.21–8), pointedly weeps with Gonzalo: 'Mine eyes, ev'n *sociable* to the show of thine, / Fall *fellowly* drops' (63–4, italics mine). Moreover, when he enfolds Gonzalo in his arms, Prospero is literally embracing humanity. This action proves first of all that he is of mortal flesh, unlike a spirit or a ghost. It proclaims his reconciliation with humankind (and with particular men). But it also symbolizes Prospero's acceptance of human limitations, for he rejects the beast/God dichotomy represented by magical and colonial power in favour of human ambivalence and vulnerability. He drowns his books, liberates his servants and relinquishes possession of the island.

In 'Prospero's Empty Grasp', John S. Hunt describes the magus as

a dreamer trapped in the nightmare of past experience, a mind painfully detached from the life

---

[11] Harry Berger Jnr suggests that Prospero uses his power on the island to stage a reconstruction of past events, particularly the conspiracy that led to his downfall, in 'Miraculous Harp: A Reading of *The Tempest*', *Shakespeare Studies* 5 (1969), pp. 253–84, 271. Peter Hulme sees this pattern of repetition working on a larger scale: 'The courtiers must repeat Prospero's primary suffering: the distress at sea, the absence of food, and the powerlessness in a hostile environment. Prospero takes pleasure in their suffering and then, when the moment is right, brings the suffering to an end in order to obtain his final purpose', *Colonial Encounters: Europe and the Native Caribbean 1492–1797* (London and New York, 1986), pp. 89–136, p. 121.

of the body, a self contemptuously separate from the entanglements of society, a cultivated person cultivating nothing.[12]

According to Hunt, Prospero's alienation is only increased by authoritarian power (303), hence he must renounce magical sway and colonial mastery in order to end his exile. And yet there is a deeper connection between the powers that Prospero abandons and his banishment. Earlier it was suggested that Prospero forgets or ignores his metamorphosis into a magician and a colonialist, in order to elegize his former power. These new roles cannot compensate the exile for what he has lost. But Prospero's case is complicated by the fact that these roles actually *reinforce* his identity as an exile for, as I will show, both the magician and colonialist were identified as banished men at this time. Shakespeare torments his character and introduces a bitter irony to the play by insisting that even in his supposed metamorphosis Prospero remains an exile.

Magic is the attainment of the scholar who has dedicated a great number of hours to the contemplation of various texts. The practical demands of study, not to mention the illicit nature of conjuring at this time, require withdrawal and solitude. We first see Dr Faustus (1592) in his study pursuing 'concealèd arts' and from there he removes to a 'solitary grove' (1.1.104, 155). In Robert Greene's *Friar Bacon and Friar Bungay* (1589), characters refer to 'Bacon's secret cell' (2.9). Moreover, this physical withdrawal might reflect a psychological alienation from the world. In his *De Occulta Philosophiae* (1533), a text referred to in *Dr Faustus*, Henry Cornelius Agrippa argued that the magus must isolate himself from the 'vulgar' uncomprehending masses and from worldly ambitions.[13]

In *The Tempest*, Prospero describes himself as both physically and psychologically detached from his kingdom. He willingly withdrew from Milanese society, 'being transported / And rapt in secret studies' (1.2.76–7), to the neglect of 'worldly ends' (89). Given that the pursuit of

magic requires a state of exile, Antonio's banishment of the Duke facilitates the latter's apprenticeship in magic. Prospero's precious books go into exile with him and there is abundant time and liberty for their perusal on an island replete with spirits.[14] The continuity in Prospero's fate, his movement from the isolation of his library to an island, has led to his exile being interpreted as a kind of wish-fulfilment, or an expression of his essential nature.[15] But Prospero should be careful what he wishes for; the practice of magic may be seen as dangerously transgressive and anti-social.

The Aristotelian paradox about the solitary man also describes the choice made by the magician, for the art of the Neoplatonist operates on the same vertical scale. In his *Oration on the Dignity of Man*, Pico della Mirandola famously described man as suspended between god and beast. Prospero's studies offer him a glimpse of transcendence, of something like

---

[12] 'Prospero's Empty Grasp', *Shakespeare Studies*, 22 (1994), 277–313, p. 297.

[13] Agrippa described this work as deliberately elusive: 'for we have delivered this Art in such a manner, that it may not be hid from the prudent and intelligent, and yet may not admit wicked and incredulous men to the mysteries of these secrets, but leave them destitute and astonished, in the shade of ignorance and desperation'. See *Three Books of Occult Philosophy* tr. by J. F. (1651) (Hastings, 1986), 3 vols., vol. 3, ch. 65, p. 555.

[14] In at least two other magician plays, banishment is the *cause* of the character's initiation into magic. In *The Rare Triumphs of Love and Fortune* (1589), the former courtier, Bomelio, seems to have discovered magic during the course of his woodland exile. He has taken up residence in a 'darksome sell', with books condemned as 'vile' and 'blasphemous' by Hermione (3.609, 1356). *The Maid's Metamorphosis* (1600) also represents the transformation of Aramanthus into a magician through exile.

[15] David Sundelson suggests that Prospero is aware of his inadequacies as Duke and longs to escape his own shame and weakness, 'So Rare a Wonder'd Father: Prospero's *Tempest*' in *Representing Shakespeare: New Psychoanalytic Essays*, ed. by C. Kahn and M. Schwartz (Baltimore and London, 1980), pp. 33–53, p. 36. Berger suggests that his removal to an island externalizes Prospero's 'self-sufficient insularity', 'Miraculous Harp', 258.

divinity, and yet always with the possibility that he will fall towards bestialism, for Neoplatonic magic was with difficulty extricated from its associations with witch-craft and demonism.[16] If, therefore, Prospero is regarded as a man acutely troubled about the significance of banishment, the practice of magic can only confirm his self-doubt, particularly since magic *incurs* banishment in the play.

In 1.2, Prospero relates, not for the first time, the banishment of Sycorax:

> This damned witch Sycorax,
> For mischiefs manifold and sorceries terrible
> To enter human hearing, from Algiers
> Thou know'st was banished.   (264–7)

This fable is significant for a number of reasons. Prospero assumes here that exile is a fitting punishment for Sycorax's 'sorceries'. He recognizes the anti-social nature of magic through its anti-social fate, namely expulsion to an uninhabited island. However, contemporary European practice when Shakespeare was writing his play was to burn the magician or witch at the stake. Banishment was most often applied to the magician figuratively, as a metaphor for his state of damnation.[17] Hence, Sycorax's exile seems deliberately written in to the play to reflect upon Prospero's banishment. Her history contaminates Prospero's, to the extent that we might ask, with Geraldo de Sousa, whether Prospero was himself banished for practising witchcraft.[18] The magus contrasts Sycorax's 'earthy and abhorred commands' with his own art. But Shakespeare's audience must still have had doubts about the legitimacy of Prospero's 'rough magic'. The magus's description of himself waking the dead and raising storms (5.1.41–9) echoes not only the black arts of Medea in Bk 7 of Ovid's *Metamorphoses*, but the Scottish trials of 1590–1 at which a number of 'witches' were accused of raising storms to drown James VI.[19]

And yet, it is not just Sycorax's association of magic and exile that disturbs Prospero. Both magicians have used their power to seize control of a territory and to bend it to their will. Indeed, there was a clear association between magic and colonialism in the magician plays of the 1580s and nineties:

> O, what a world of profit and delight,
> Of power, of honour, of omnipotence
> Is promised to the studious artisan!
>
> (*Dr Faustus*, 1.1.55–7)

There is a sense that the world now lies open to the philosopher, a rich, fruitful and virgin territory which will yield him secrets denied to other men. Most frequently, this plunder is envisaged as material treasure. Faustus imagines fetching gold from India and orient pearl from the ocean. He will 'search all corners of the new-found world / For pleasant fruits and princely delicates' (86–7). Friar Bacon too promises his dignitaries a great feast of 'candy' and 'spices' brought from Egypt, Persia and Africa (9.256–64). Yet the magician was also motivated by nationalist and imperialist aims, so that his plunder might include Egypt or Persia themselves.[20] In *Dr Faustus*, the magician

---

16 For a consideration of Prospero's relation to Neoplatonic magic see Walter Clyde Curry, *Shakespeare's Philosophical Patterns* (Louisiana, 1937), pp. 141–59, 163–99 and Barbara Howard Traister, *Heavenly Necromancers: The Magician in English Renaissance Drama* (Columbia, 1984), pp. 125–50.

17 In *Dr Faustus*, Mephistopheles repeatedly attests to the agony that is absence from God and from heaven (1.3.78–81, 2.1.121–6). See also the account of Lucifer's banishment from heaven in *The History of the Damnable Life and Deserved Death of Doctor John Faustus* (the English Faust-book) tr. by P. F. (1592), reprinted in *Christopher Marlowe: The Plays and Their Sources* ed. by Vivien Thomas and William Tydeman (London and New York, 1994), pp. 186–238, p. 199.

18 *Shakespeare's Cross-Cultural Encounters* (London, 1999), p. 160.

19 *Shakespeare's Cross-Cultural Encounters*, pp. 209–10, n. 2.

20 Faustus's nationalist ambitions include military expansion, the construction of a wall of brass around Germany, and the eviction of the Prince of Parma, a Spanish governor-general reviled in England for his oppression of the Netherlands, 1.1.94–5. John Dee offers an example of a 'real life' contemporary magician whose scientific and genealogical studies were dedicated

describes the alterations to the map of the geographical and political world that he will effect through Mephistopheles:

> By him I'll be great emperor of the world
> And make a bridge through the moving air
> To pass the ocean with a band of men;
> I'll join the hills that bind the Afric shore
> And make that land continent to Spain,
> And both contributory to my crown.
>
> (1.3.105–10)

Thus before the Virginia project and before Shakespeare's *Tempest*, magical power was conventionally linked with territorial expansion and foreign conquest.

Through Sycorax, Prospero finds not only his identity as a magician tainted with exile but also his identity as a *colonialist*. Sycorax's exile proves her unfit to live in society. Hence, the society that she creates upon the island is a kind of hell which in turn reinforces her exclusion from civilization. Prospero feels it necessary to relate, time and again, the island's improvement under his dominion because his exiled status makes such an improvement doubtful. But *The Tempest*'s association of colonialism and exile is not simply a by-product of the links between magic, exile and colonialism expressed in Sycorax's career. The colonialist had long been marked as a banished man.

The association between colonialism and exile can be traced back to the anti-travel polemic of the sixteenth century, which deplored the metamorphosis and self-loss entailed by the voluntary renunciation of one's family, property, language and nation. It is also related to the various connotations of the term 'wandering'. A system of licences or passports had been applied within English boundaries to try to control the movement of displaced peoples such as gypsies, beggars, various kinds of entertainer, soldiers, sailors and agrarian workers. Such 'wandering' placed one outside the restrictions of law and of society, and therefore marked one as capable of all kinds of crime.[21] In the *Politics*, Homer is quoted describing the solitary man as 'tribelesse, law-lesse, houselesse', a liberty that makes him dangerously unpredictable and self-willed.

Exiles in English Renaissance drama invariably bewail the need to travel and specifically to *wander* outside familiar boundaries. In *The Rare Triumphes of Love and Fortune*, Bomelio addresses himself as an exile: 'Goe walke the path of plaint, goe wander wretched now / In uncoth waies, blind corners fit for such a wretch as thou . . .', (3.613–14). Similarly, in *The Maid's Metamorphosis*, Eurymine describes her fate: 'Banisht to live a fugitive alone / In uncoth paths and regions never knowne'. But the exile is not simply forced to become a traveller or a wanderer of dubious virtue. The enforced exploration of unknown and possibly uninhabited regions also suggests his/her identity as a colonialist.

The association between banishment, wandering and colonialism is made explicit in Peter Martyr's *De Orbe Novo Decades* (1516), an account of Spanish colonialism, translated into English by Richard Eden in 1555.[22] Of particular interest is the passage in which Martyr describes the encounter between the Spanish *conquistadores*, and the native Americans under King Comogrus. The Indians have given the Spanish a sum of gold, a gift that has driven them into an undignified frenzy. Their behaviour inspires wonder and even pity in Comogrus' eldest son who asks:

---

to the realization of what he considered Elizabeth's imperial destiny. His conversations with angels, like Bacon's hopes for the brazen head, were directed to the discovery of some secret that might be to England's benefit. See William H. Sherman, *John Dee: The Politics of Reading and Writing in the English Renaissance* (Amherst, 1995), pp. 14–15, 148–200.

21 On the connotations of the word 'wandering' in terms of vagrancy see A. L. Beier's *Masterless Men: The Vagrancy Problem in England 1560–1640* (London and New York, 1985), especially chapter 4, pp. 51–68.

22 I am indebted for the discovery of the following passages to Andrew Hadfield's study, *Literature, Travel and Colonial Writing in the English Renaissance* (Oxford, 1999), ch. 2.

What is the matter [with] yowe Christen men, that yow soo greatly esteeme soo litle a portion of golde more then yowr owne quietnes [. . .] If yowre hunger of goulde bee soo insatiable that onely for the desyre yowe have therto, yowe disquiete soo many nations, and yow yowre selves also susteyne soo many calamit[i]es and incommodities, *lyving like banished men owte of yowre owne countrey*, I wyll shewe yowe a Region floweinge with goulde, where yowe may satisifie yowr raveninge appetites.[23]

The colonialist and the exile are seen to share a number of basic characteristics, for example both behave as if they had no home. Martyr himself describes the Spanish as 'thys wandrynge kynde of men [. . .] lyvynge onely by shiftes and spoyle' (116). Moreover, like Aristotle's solitary man, the Spanish colonialists evince a kind of restless desire, an anti-social exorbitance, implied not only by their 'raveninge appetites' for gold but also by the fact that they destroy the peace of other nations through such 'raveninge'. The prince has given the Spanish a quantity of gold lest 'they shuld handle hym as they dyd other[s] whiche sought noo meanes howe to gratifie theym' (116). Indeed, such is the colonialists' innate transgressiveness, according to the prince, that they resemble 'cruell Canybales a fierce kynde of men, devourers of mans flesshe, *lyvyng withowte lawes, wanderinge, and withowte empire*' (117, italics mine).

Perhaps this encounter between Spanish colonialists and Amerindian prince is chiefly remarkable for its reversal of the conventional positions of European and Other, noble and savage, for Comogrus' son not only lectures the Spaniards in civility, he is also described by Martyr in terms reminiscent of Christ.[24] But Comogrus' son also questions the most basic assumptions about the colonialist project here. The avowed intention to civilize hides the restless wandering and insatiability of the banished man.[25] One might object that this is Spanish not English colonialism. The English began their colonial adventures much later than the Spanish and distinguished their humanist intentions from the so-called pure greed and viciousness of

Spanish imperialism. Although we are familiar with the price paid by English colonists – starvation, disease, execution by English martial law or massacre by the natives – we do not tend to associate colonialism with the shame and self-loss of banishment. But there is evidence that the connection between colonialism and exile was already conventional in sixteenth-century England.

Before colonialism in North America became a reality, Catholics were fleeing Elizabethan England to join communities abroad, in particular the seminaries at Rome and Douai.[26] The association of this migration with the shame of exile was one of the rhetorical weapons at the government's disposal as it tried to prevent Catholics from leaving the country. William Cecil, who was responsible for many of the punitive measures taken against them, wrote a

---

[23] Reprinted in *The First Three Bookes on America*, ed. by Edward Arber (Edinburgh, 1885), Book 3, p. 117 (italics mine).

[24] Martyr describes the prince's response to the contention among the Spaniards. He was seen 'commynge sume what wyth an angery countenaunce towarde hym whiche helde the balences, he strooke theym wyth his fyste, and scatered all the golde that was therein, abowte the porche, sharpely rebukynge theym with woordes in this effecte . . .' Perhaps Martyr is remembering the scene of Christ rebuking the moneylenders in the temple in Matthew 21.12–13.

[25] Paul Brown also makes the connection between colonialism and the discourse of wandering or masterlessness. In '"This thing of darkness I acknowledge mine": *The Tempest* and the Discourse of Colonialism', he examines the identification of the native with the European masterless man and savage, both associated with a 'directionless and indiscriminate desire', *Political Shakespeare: New Essays in Cultural Materialism*, ed. by Jonathan Dollimore and Alan Sinfield (Manchester, 1985), pp. 48–71, p. 52.

[26] There were also plans for English Catholics to establish colonies in the New World. Two Catholic noblemen, Sir George Peckham and Sir Thomas Gerard, proposed such a migration in the early 1580s and found some supporters in Elizabeth's government, though their plans eventually came to nothing due to Spanish opposition. See David Beers Quinn, *England and the Discovery of America 1481–1620* (London, 1974), pp. 364–86.

letter on 28 December 1574 to one Thomas Copley, a man who had turned Catholic and was planning to seek sanctuary abroad. Cecil wrote to dissuade him by describing the shame of voluntary exile. He warned Copley that he would lose 'the sweet benefit of your native soil, your friends, your kindred'. More gravely, he asked if Copley were willing to incur

the infamy that wilful exile doth bring, to be accompted, if not a traitor, yet a companion of traitors and conspirators, a man subject to the curses and imprecations of zealous good subjects, your native countrymen, yea, subject to lack of living by your own and thereby compelled to follow strangers for maintenance of livelihood and food? The cause must needs be of great force to induce you thereto.[27]

Cecil's image of exile is based upon his jaundiced impression of the Catholic refugees abroad. In *The Execution of Justice*, written nine years after the letter to Copley, Cecil denied that the exiles were heroes, sacrificing everything for their faith. He insisted rather that they were rebels, traitors and vagabonds whose departure from England had nothing to do with religious persecution. The same ambivalence between exile as a divine, heroic vocation, and as an expression of dissoluteness and treachery, appears in the context of English colonialism.

In a sermon published in 1610, William Crashaw justified the exclusion from Virginia of atheists, players and papists.[28] The Jesuit, John Floyd, responded with *The Overthrow of the Protestants Pulpit-Babels* (1612) in which he reminded Crashaw that if it had not been for papists, Britain would never have been converted to Christianity in the first place, and warned that Virginia's conversion too might depend upon Catholic intervention. According to Floyd, the Protestants are shamefully lacking in evangelical zeal:

No *M. Crashaw*, the miseryes which the enterprize of converting Savages doth bring with it, the wanting your native soyle, friends and Gossips, wherwith now after Sermon you may be merry, the enduring hunger, cold, nakednes, danger of death, and the like, but specially the want of the new

Ghospells blessing, a fayre wife, too heavy a lump of flesh to be carryed into *Virginia*; these be such curses, & such hinderances, as you may speake of.[29]

Floyd subsequently distinguishes between two kinds of banished colonialist. First, there is the priest who willingly endures the sufferings concomitant with this divine vocation. Then there is the colonist who has his mission thrust upon him. Floyd declares that those Protestant priests who do become colonists are in many instances 'the refuse of their [the Church's] Realme, whome they terme the very excrements of their swelling State' (324). Virginia's conversion depends on men presented with the choice of banishment to Virginia or the gallows. They are men conscripted in taverns, at plays, even in hedges. It was Crashaw himself who condemned the purgation of England by the deportation of such 'ruffians' to Virginia. But Floyd suggests that the Protestant Church actively promotes this. To leave England for Virginia may be a heroic expression of religious commitment but it is also an indication of one's superfluousness to the state and even of criminality.

Prospero has bemused, irritated, and confounded critics by his apparent uninterest in colonialism, an attitude in stark contrast to critics' own fascination with the colonial aspects of *The Tempest*.[30] After twelve years of exile, he

---

27 Cecil's letter is reprinted in *The Other Face: Catholic Life under Elizabeth I*, collected and edited by Philip Caraman (London, 1960), p. 141. This book includes a chapter of exile writing, pp. 140–6.

28 'A Sermon Preached in London before the right honorable the Lord Lawarre, Lord Governour and Captaine Generall of Virginea', STC 6029.

29 *The Overthrow of the Protestants Pulpit-Babels*, STC 11111, p. 321.

30 This observation is also made by Ben Ross Schneider who examines Prospero's anger within a Stoic context in 'Are we being historical yet?: Colonialist Interpretations of Shakespeare's *Tempest*', *Shakespeare Studies*, 23 (1995), 120–45, p. 123; and by Jeffrey Knapp who examines English colonialism within a context of national trifling in *An Empire Nowhere: England, America, and Literature from Utopia to the Tempest* (Berkeley and Oxford, 1992), p. 221.

still lives in a cave by a fen and is dependent upon Caliban for providing the basic necessities of life. Even if we remind ourselves not to expect empire-building from the seventeenth-century colonialist who was primarily concerned with establishing trade routes,[31] Prospero is at best negligent in his colonialist duties and at worst hardly a colonialist at all. A more obvious reading of his failure to civilize the island might be suggested by the discourses of exile. As a banished man, Prospero's ability to cultivate anything has been profoundly affected. Shamed by exile, he directs all his earth-shattering, sea-fraughting magic towards exorcizing this curse and returning home.

And yet, like Prospero, many of the Virginia colonists had been banished to the New World. Prospero's apathy and anxiety towards the island might yet reflect the experience of seventeenth-century English colonists. In fact, colonialism and exile are profoundly implicated with one another. The discourse of colonialist-as-exile, invoked by Martyr, Floyd and others, challenges the image of a self-assured, patriarchal, even tyrannical colonialist (the archetype which does not fit Prospero's attitude to the island), and replaces it with a figure more anxious, self-doubting, and above all more marginal than has hitherto been appreciated.[32]

Shakespeare's Prospero, like Aristotle's solitary man, and Floyd's colonialist, is suspended between the god and beast,[33] uncertain whether his actions on the island are to his credit or to his shame. Like Thomas Gates and other apologists for the Virginia company, Prospero defends his usurpation of power from the natives. He insists upon the providential nature of his safe arrival on the island and extends this divine sanction to his tyrannical rule (1.2.263–94). Like Gates and his associates, Prospero also denies responsibility for his failures. Caliban's inherent baseness renders him irredeemable. The fact that the island remains uncultivated is implicitly blamed on the laziness and obstinacy of Prospero's subject i.e. Caliban, just as the Virginia company blamed the colonists' laziness and lack of motivation for their slow progress.[34]

But just as the Virginia company's rhetoric was formulated in response to public criticism of the colonial enterprise, so Prospero defends himself against detraction. This questioning of the colonialist project is not alone expressed or embodied by the two slaves, Ariel and Caliban. As we have already seen, Caliban does not reject the idea of colonialism per se. He simply resents the fact that it is not he who holds power. Rather, we might argue that Prospero himself is the location of this colonialist dialectic. If we attribute to the magus, as I have done, some sense of the contemporary association between colonialism and exile, his violence and frustration might be expressions of this conflict.

---

31 See Palmira Brummett's *Ottoman Seapower and Levantine Diplomacy in the Age of Discovery* on sixteenth-century conquest and the emphasis placed on expanding trade routes and exploiting resources rather than redrawing national boundaries (New York, 1994). *A True and Sincere Declaration* describes the aims of the Jamestown colony as the conversion of natives to the Christian faith, the creation of a 'Bulwarke of defence' against the Spanish, and the appropriation of all kinds of goods which England had previously been forced to import at great expense, 3–4.

32 There have been various challenges to this stereotypical colonialist. One of the most impressive is that of Meredith Anne Skura who examines the multiple and dissonant expressions of 'colonialism' and their possible relationship to *The Tempest* in 'Discourse and the Individual: The Case of Colonialism in *The Tempest*', *Shakespeare Quarterly*, 40 (1989), 42–69.

33 Aristotle's beast/God dichotomy is also a feature of much colonialist literature with the colonialist identifying himself as a god, and damning the Indians as beasts. But again, the opposition between beast and God does not hold. See Karol Ordahl Kupperman's *Settling with the Indians: The Meeting of English and Indian Cultures in America 1580–1640* (London and Toronto, 1980), pp. 119–40.

34 *A True and Sincere Declaration of the purpose and ends of the plantation begun in Virginia* (London, 1610), STC 24832, p. 35. See also Hulme's examination of the paradox that though the colonists were sometimes figured by the natives as magicians because of their firepower, those colonists were yet unable to feed themselves or to be in any way self-sufficient, *Colonial Encounters*, pp. 127–32.

Shakespeare's audience, familiar with the polemical war waged on this subject, might themselves have attributed such meanings to Prospero's bewilderment.

But at a more obvious and fundamental level, at the level of plot, *The Tempest* can be seen to take an active role in the stigmatization of the colonialist project, again through its references to banishment. The wreck of the Sea Venture, which left Sir Thomas Gates and a number of colonists stranded in an alien landscape, was more than once described as exile.[35] This disaster was perceived by some as an expression of God's wrath at the greed and hubris underlying the colonialist enterprise. In *The Tempest*, the shipwrecked men imagine that their shipwreck/exile is also divine vengeance for a similar act of 'extravagance'. Alonso has pursued a ruthlessly expansionist foreign policy by marrying his daughter, Claribel, to the prince of Tunis, neglecting not only Claribel's feelings but also national and European concerns. As Sebastian puts it:

> Sir, you may thank yourself for this great loss,
> That would not bless our Europe with your
> daughter,
> But rather loose her to an African,
> Where she, at least, is banished from your eye,
> Who hath cause to wet the grief on't.
>
> (2.1.129–33)

Claribel's banishment beyond the known world has incurred their own exile on an unmapped island and it is Alonso's anti-social ambition which is to blame.

A related plot which perhaps reinforces the immorality of colonialist ambition, is Caliban's attempt to rape Miranda. The native's motive was not lust but colonialism: 'I had peopled else / This isle with Calibans' (1.2.352–3). If we recall Peter Martyr's description of the encounter between Spaniards and Comogruans it is clear that a ravenous appetite, whether for female flesh or gold, could be synonymous with colonialist ambition and the anti-social nature of the exile. The moral of the story appears to be

that colonialism is dangerous, even inhuman, and it derives some of this inhumanity from its associations with exile. It might be argued then that one of the ways in which Prospero proves himself worthy of the Milanese dukedom is his rejection of this proposed union between Miranda and Caliban, despite its possibilities for extending Italy's dominions into the New World. Instead, Prospero marries her to the Neapolitan heir, training his gaze as always on the Western horizon.

One of the values of reading *The Tempest* through the glass of exile is that instead of narrowing our perspective on the text, it allows us to discuss simultaneously the play's magic, humanism and colonialism. Because ideas of exile feed into such discourses, banishment allows us to make connections which enrich and perhaps defamiliarize *The Tempest*. In a recent article, Jerry Brotton has also pursued this aim of defamiliarization. He challenges post-colonialist stereotypes and turns our attention to the Old World contexts of the play. In particular, Brotton aspires to recapture some of Prospero's ambivalence and liminality, arguing that the latter's roles as traveller, magician and Italian suggest 'a distancing of audience identification with Prospero'. He is one whom English audiences would arguably have regarded with 'fascination, but also unease'.[36] However, Brotton fails to mention Prospero's identity as an exile, despite the fact that the play consistently suggests that what is most strange and self-estranging about Prospero is his exile, an identity that encompasses these other roles. Only when we understand the centrality of exile in *The Tempest*, will Prospero be for us the truly marginal and alien figure that Shakespeare created.

---

35 See *A True Declaration*, p. 34.
36 ' "This Tunis, sir, was Carthage": Contesting Colonialism in *The Tempest*' in *Post-Colonial Shakespeares* ed. by Ania Loomba and Martin Orkin (London and New York, 1998), pp. 23–42, p. 30.

THE OLD LADY, OR ALL IS NOT TRUE

THOMAS MERRIAM

The third scene of Act 2 of *All Is True* rewards particular consideration as it is almost literally, and certainly symbolically, central to the play. The scene is described by R. A. Foakes as follows,

For her [Katherine's] divorce follows the brief scene between Anne and an Old Lady – the only scene in the play devoted to Anne – in which Anne, as it were, is 'queened': it is a scene of rich and complex meaning, of bawdry and high spirits, in which Anne's promotion as Marchioness of Pembroke foreshadows her further elevation. Out of Anne's pity for Katherine grows the Old Lady's series of quibbles, playing always on the idea of Anne becoming queen (or 'quean'),

> ANNE   By my troth and maidenhead,
>   I would not be a queen.
> OLD L   Beshrew me, I would,
>   And venture maidenhead for't, and so would you
>   For all this spice of your hypocrisy.   (2.3.23–6)

The placing of this gay little scene of Anne's rise before the trial lends added poignancy to Katherine's refusal to yield.[1]

Foakes's synopsis is of an innocuous and amusing exchange; he regards Anne Boleyn's expression of sympathy for Queen Katherine, soon to be supplanted by Anne herself, as genuine despite the Old Lady's allegation of Anne's hypocrisy.[2] *Hypocrisy* is not a word which Shakespeare uses without deliberation.[3] How seriously then are we to take remarks of the Old Lady whose speech is riddled with ambiguous ironies?

To answer the question one must consider the Old Lady's indelicacies in the wider context of Shakespearian usage. Anne's swearing by her maidenhead is uniquely paralleled in Shakespeare by Juliet's nurse in *Romeo and Juliet* 1.3.2, 'Now, by my maidenhead at twelve year old,' – a sardonic expression which links the pairing of Anne and the Old Lady with Juliet and her near toothless Nurse. The Nurse's reminiscences of Juliet's childhood are spiced with *double entendres* – as are Juliet's mother's.

Count has a similar usage in *Romeo and Juliet* 1.3 and *All Is True* 2.3. Juliet's mother employs a *triple entendre*: 'By my count / I was your mother much upon these years / That you are now a maid' (*Romeo* 1.3.73–5). The Old Lady says, 'Pluck off a little; / I would not be a young count in your way / For more than blushing comes to' (*All Is True* 2.3.40–2). The dialogue between Anne and the Old Lady is reminiscent not only of the exchanges between Juliet and her nurse, but also of the women-only exchange

---

[1] *King Henry VIII*, ed. by R. A. Foakes (London, 1957), pp. l–li.

[2] 'Her professions of concern for Katherine ring sincere, but her insistence that she would not change places with her does not.' *King Henry VIII, or All is True*, ed. Jay L. Halio (Oxford, 1999), p. 30. This discrepant observation should have alerted the reader to the trenchancy of the Old Lady's accusation.

[3] See *Othello* 4.1.5–6. 'Naked in bed, Iago, and not to mean harm? / It is hypocrisy against the devil.' Shakespeare references are to the Oxford *Complete Works*.

between the French Princess Catherine[4] and Alice, 'an old gentlewoman', in *Henry V* 3.4. Alice pronounces the English word *gown* so as to sound like *cown/coun*, a homophone of *count*,[5] thereby shocking the Princess. However, the authenticity of Catherine's protestation at 'les mots de son mauvais, corruptible, gros, et impudique, et non pour les dames d'honneur d'user'[6] is laid open to question by her readiness to memorize the offending words, – the recitation of which meets with approval and encouragement from Alice.[7]

Je ne voudrais prononcer ces mots devant les seigneurs de France pour tout le monde. Foh! *De foot et de cown*! Néamoins, je réciterai une autre fois ma leçon ensemble. *D'hand, de fingre, de nails, d'arma, d'elbow, de nick, de sin, de foot, de cown.*[8]

(*Henry V* 3.4.50–5)

Audiences are bemused by the wit and playful bawdiness of the scene. Catherine affects a refinement which charms by virtue of the audience's unfamiliarity with foreign linguistic insouciance. Her denial 'pour tout le monde' is word-for-word Anne Boleyn's 'I would not be a queen / For all the world' (*All Is True* 2.3.45–6). Shakespeare deftly (perhaps too deftly) casts doubt on the sincerity of both young women. The parallelisms suggest that he may have consulted his previous history play before contributing to *All Is True*.

The most searching meditation on 'for all the world' with its biblical echo,[9] and its consideration of conscience, is found in the dialogue between Othello's wife Desdemona and Iago's Emilia. Desdemona's values are compared with Emilia's 'situational ethics', thereby shedding light on the respective morals of Catherine and Anne Boleyn. The contrast between Desdemona and Emilia parallels the contrast between Queen Katherine and Anne Boleyn.

DESDEMONA

   Dost thou in conscience think – tell me, Emilia -
   That there be women do abuse their husbands
   In such gross kind?

EMILIA   There be some such, no question.

DESDEMONA

   Wouldst thou do such a deed for all the world?

EMILIA

   Why, would not you?

DESDEMONA   No, by this heavenly light.

EMILIA Nor I neither, by this heavenly light. I might do't as well i'th' dark.

DESDEMONA

   Wouldst thou do such a deed for all the world?

EMILIA The world's a huge thing. It is a great price for a small vice.

DESDEMONA In truth, I think thou wouldst not.

EMILIA In truth, I think I should, and undo't when I had done. Marry, I would not do such a thing for a joint ring, nor for measures of lawn, nor for gowns, petticoats, nor caps, nor any pretty exhibition; but for all the whole world? Ud's pity, who would not make her husband a cuckold to make him a monarch? I should venture purgatory for't.

DESDEMONA

   Beshrew me if I would do such a wrong
   For the whole world.

EMILIA Why, the wrong is but a wrong i'th' world, and having the world for your labour, 'tis a wrong in your own world, and you might quickly make it right.

DESDEMONA

   I do not think there is any such woman.

EMILIA

   Yes, a dozen, and as many
   To th' vantage as would store the world they
   played for.   (*Othello* 4.3.59–84)

Juliet's nurse complains of a sore back. 'My back – [*Juliet rubs her back*] a' t'other side – ah my

---

[4] Catherine is later addressed in 5.2 as 'Kate', 'a name associated with promiscuous women', *Henry V*, ed. Gary Taylor (Oxford, 1982), p. 270, n. 107.

[5] The *First Folio* spells the word *count* (3.4.47, 48, 52, 55), thus making the connection with 'cunt' less ambiguous.

[6] 'Words of evil sound, corrupting, gross, and immodest, and not for ladies of honour to use.'

[7] The old gentlewoman was as aware of the *double entendres* as Catherine.

[8] 'I would not wish to pronounce these words in the company of the lords of France for all the world! Fie! *De foot* and *de count*! Nonetheless I shall recite once again my whole lesson: . . .'

[9] Luke 9. 25.

back, my back!' (*Romeo* 2.4.50). And later reminds Juliet 'I am the drudge, and toil in your delight, / But you shall bear the burden soon at night' (*Romeo* 2.4.75–6). The Old Lady warns Anne, 'If your back / Cannot vouchsafe this burden, 'tis too weak / Ever to get a boy' (*All Is True* 2.3.42–4).

The *innuendo* in the Old Lady's converse is more barbed than the Nurse's. When the Old Lady says of Anne,

> You, that have so fair parts of woman on you,
> Have, too, a woman's heart which ever yet
> Affected eminence, wealth, sovereignty;
> Which, to say sooth, are blessings; and which
>   gifts,
> Saving your mincing, the capacity
> Of your soft cheveril conscience would receive
> If you might please to stretch it.
>
> (*All Is True* 2.3.27–33)

she employs *saving your*, *mincing*, *cheveril conscience*, and *stretch*, all of which have indicative and pejorative meanings in their previous Shakespearian contexts. 'Saving your mincing' is plausibly a translation of the Latin stock phrase, *salva reverentia*. Shakespeare uses *saving your reverence* as a mock disclaimer of what follows directly by one in conversation with a social superior.[10] With Launcelot Gobbo the phrase is addressed to the Devil. 'To be ruled by my conscience I should stay with the Jew my master who, God bless the mark, is a kind of devil; and to run away from the Jew I should be ruled by the fiend who, saving your reverence, is the devil himself.' (*Merchant* 2.2.20–24) *Conscience* and the Englished *salva reverentia* are within 33 words of each other in the scene with Gobbo, and within six words of each other in the scene with Anne and the Old Lady.

In *Henry V*, Fluellen addresses the King in a speech containing the *salva reverentia* formula as well as *conscience* and *glove* (made of cheveril). The expression *saving your majesty's manhood* recalls Mistress Quickly's bawdy speech 'A comes continuantly to Pie Corner – saving your manhoods – to buy a saddle . . .' (*2 Henry IV* 2.1.26–7).[11]

FLUELLEN Your majesty hear now, saving your majesty's manhood, what an arrant rascally beggarly lousy knave it is. I hope your majesty is pear me testimony and witness, and will avouchment that this is the glove of Alençon that your majesty is give me, in your conscience now.   (*Henry V* 4.8.34–9)

In the same play, Alice employs the *salva reverentia* formula in French, 'Sauf votre honneur' (*Henry V* 3.4.34 and 44) in a scene whose bawdy *double entendres* between future bride and her elderly noble companion parallel those in *All Is True* 2.3. 'Sauf votre grace' (addressed by Alice to Henry) and 'sauf votre honneur' (addressed to Henry by Catherine) occur in a later scene with Henry V's wooing of Catherine, *Henry V* 5.2.[12]

As with Gobbo's speech in *The Merchant of Venice*, the *salva reverentia* in *1 Henry IV* has a darker association.

PRINCE HARRY That villainous, abominable misleader of youth, Oldcastle; that old white-bearded Satan.
SIR JOHN My lord, the man I know.
PRINCE HARRY I know thou dost.
SIR JOHN But to say I know more harm in him than in myself were to say more than I know. That he is old, the more the pity, his white hairs do witness it. But that he is, saving your reverence, a whoremaster, that I utterly deny.
        (*1 Henry IV* 2.5.467–75)

Saving your mincing is richer in meaning than a straight rendering of *salva reverentia*. Shakespeare's most striking use of *mince* is spoken by Lear.

---

[10] The expression was also abbreviated to 'sir-reverence' and by the seventeenth and eighteenth centuries came popularly to be used as synonymous simply with 'turd'.

[11] See *Henry V* 5.2.137–40: 'If I could win a lady at leap-frog, or by vaulting into my saddle with my armour on my back, under the correction of bragging be it spoken, I should quickly leap into a wife.'

[12] The following occur in *Much Ado* 3.4: 'troth' used by the bawdy Margaret (6, 8, 17, 74), 'gown's/gown' (14, 17), ''Twill be heavier soon by the weight of a man' (25), 'Saving your reverence' (30), 'gloves' and 'Count' (57).

. . . Behold yon simp'ring dame,
Whose face between her forks presages snow,
That minces virtue, and does shake the head
To hear of pleasure's name.
The fitchew nor the soiled horse goes to't
With a more riotous appetite. Down from the
    waist
They're centaurs, though women all above.
But to the girdle do the gods inherit;
Beneath is all the fiend's. There's hell, there's
    darkness,
There is the sulphurous pit, burning, scalding,
    stench,
Consumption . . .   (*Lear F* 4.5.116–26)

There are parallels between 'yon simp'ring dame' and Anne Boleyn, difference of age notwithstanding. Anne expresses a virtuous sympathy for Queen Katherine, remarking that it would have been better for her never to have known the pomp of high station. Yet Anne tenders her thanks and obedience to the King for making her Marchioness of Pembroke, 'as from a blushing handmaid'. She denies wishing to be queen as emphatically as Sir John Falstaff/Oldcastle denies being a whoremaster. Sir John, once disguised as 'an old, cozening quean',[13] however, is no less a whoremaster, and Anne later embraces the pomp of her regal coronation. Even the words spoken to the Lord Chamberlain,

Beseech your lordship,
Vouchsafe to speak my thanks and my obedience,
As from a blushing handmaid to his highness,
Whose health and royalty I pray for.
              (*All Is True* 2.3.70–3)

are ambiguous, and especially so in the final suspended four-beat line, last of a series of eight lines with feminine endings: does Anne pray for acquiring royalty for herself?[14] In addition, the ambiguous word 'blushing' echoes its previous sexual context, 'I would not be a young count in your way / For more than blushing comes to' (*All Is True* 2.3.41–2).

There is resonance of a similar ambiguity in Cressida. Lord Pandarus stage-manages the pivotal encounter between Cressida and Troilus, imagining himself the controller of his niece's life.

PANDARUS She's making her ready. She'll come straight. You must be witty now. She does so blush, and fetches her wind so short as if she were frayed with a spirit. I'll fetch her. It is the prettiest villain! She fetches her breath as short as a new-ta'en sparrow.   (*Troilus* 3.2.28–32)

But Cressida, 'false Cressid', is no 'new ta'en sparrow', – nor is Anne Boleyn. Pandarus returns twice to Cressida's blushing.

PANDARUS Come, come, what need you blush? Shame's a baby.   (*Troilus* 3.2.38–9)

And again:

PANDARUS What, blushing still? Have you not done talking yet?   (*Troilus* 3.2.97–8)

Cressida is no innocent. She is too knowing.

CRESSIDA
Perchance, my lord, I show more craft than love,
And fell so roundly to a large confession
To angle for your thoughts. But you are wise,
Or else you love not – for to be wise and love
Exceeds man's might: that dwells with gods above.
              (*Troilus* 3.2.149–53)

The Old Lady's accusation – 'all this spice of your hypocrisy' – may be dismissed as no more than an expression of her general cynicism. Her own hypocrisies have not gone unremarked: before recommending the pursuit of courtly preferment to Anne, she patently lies, 'Our content / Is our best having' (*All Is True* 2.3.22–3). The interpretative crux of the Act 2, Scene 3 is the reliability of the Old Lady's witness. Those who see the exchange between Anne and the Old Lady as 'a gay little scene' construe its sexual *innuendos* as light-hearted. This view is not borne out by its verbal and contextual antecedents. Like Cressida, Anne's naivety is more art than nature.[15]

---

13 *Merry Wives* 4.2.158.
14 I am indebted to Dr Leo Daugherty for this perception.
15 'By contrast to Wolsey's machiavellianism, Anne's behaviour in the next scene is utterly naïve.' Halio, *Henry VIII*, p. 30.

The stretching of 'the capacity of your soft cheveril conscience' is a case in point. *All Is True* is the only Shakespeare play which plainly conflates conscience with genitalia. Some have questioned whether Shakespeare's view of conscience is consonant with Christian teaching. A formulation of Christian doctrine in 1994 reads:

It is by the judgement of his conscience that man perceives and recognizes the prescriptions of the divine law: . . . The dignity of the human person implies and requires *uprightness of moral conscience* . . . Man has the right to act in conscience and in freedom so as personally to make moral decisions.[16]

The divine law includes the Decalogue.

Shakespeare's negative formulation alludes to that law: (Numbers of the Commandments are added in brackets.)

SECOND MURDERER I'll not meddle with it [conscience]. It makes a man a coward. A man cannot steal but it accuseth him. (VII) A man cannot swear but it checks him. (II) A man cannot lie with his neighbour's wife but it detects him. (VI and IX) 'Tis a blushing, shamefaced spirit, that mutinies in a man's bosom. It fills a man full of obstacles. It made me once restore a purse of gold that by chance I found. It beggars any man that keeps it. (Beatitudes) It is turned out of towns and cities for a dangerous thing, (Beatitudes) and every man that means to live well endeavours to trust to himself and live without it.

(*Richard III* 1.4.131–41)

Or in another context:

AARON
Yet for I know thou art religious
And hast a thing within thee called conscience,
With twenty popish tricks and ceremonies
Which I have seen thee careful to observe,
Therefore I urge thy oath; . . .   (*Titus* 5.1.74–8)

There is every indication that Shakespeare was conversant with the notion of conscience and valued it very highly. Supporting evidence lies in the negative appraisal of Richard III which anticipates Nietzsche and Hitler.

RICHARD
Conscience is but a word that cowards use,
Devised at first to keep the strong in awe.

Our strong arms be our conscience; swords, our
law.   (*Richard III* 5.6.39–41)

The Old Lady's identification of conscience and pudendum is prefaced just prior to Act 2 Scene 3, when King Henry exclaims, 'But conscience, conscience – / O, 'tis a tender place, and I must leave her' (*All Is True* 2.2.143–4). Act 2 Scene 3's first words, spoken by Anne, 'Not for that neither.' are uncannily relevant to these last words of the previous scene.'[17]

Editors of the play have not drawn attention to the conflation of conscience and pudendum as worthy of note. This may be because conscience is regarded as problematical in contemporary thinking, – owing to the Freudian super-ego, to post-Victorian reaction against prudery, or to the difficulty of reconciling conscience with the biological mechanisms of evolutionary survival. More plausibly it is because the substance of the Old Lady's ribald turn of phrase is seen merely as a figurative commonplace for a flexible conscience. Fletcher entertained a less scrupulous notion of conscience than Shakespeare.[18] There is a looseness of tone characteristic of Fletcher which pervades *All Is True*. Semantic diffuseness is reinforced by editors' footnotes. Foakes advises that *cheveril* is 'kid-leather, proverbial for its stretching capacity, especially as applied to conscience'.[19] Humphreys reminds one 'The phrase 'cheveril conscience' was quasi-

---

16 *Catechism of the Catholic Church* (London, 1994), pp. 396–7.
17 'Conscience' may be pronounced 'cunt-science'. McMullan has suggested that if, in performance, the dialogue with which 2.3 begins follows directly after the last words of 2.2, Anne's words 'Not for that neither' can sound as if they apply not to an unheard remark by her interlocutor in 2.3, but rather to Henry's hypocritical explanations in 2.2. See *Henry VIII*, ed. by Gordon McMullan (London, 2000) p. 289, n. 23.
18 There is no evidence that Fletcher would have concurred with Newman in regarding conscience as 'the aboriginal Vicar of Christ'. Shakespeare's agreement, on the other hand, is more likely.
19 Foakes, *King Henry VIII*, p. 71 n. 32.

proverbial'.[20] A minimum of emphasis is placed on sexual metaphor, modestly veiled as 'quibble'.[21] Schoenbaum clarifies 'saving your mincing' as 'despite your coyness'.[22] In the process of elucidating the unfamiliar, the scholarly apparatus dilutes the meaning.

Examples of Fletcher's use of *conscience* illustrate his semantic slackness and studied light-hearted mockery. In *The Woman's Prize* there are fourteen occurrences of *conscience*, eleven of which are in the form of the stock expression 'o' my conscience', 'upon my conscience', 'on my conscience', and so forth. The word *conscience* has little meaning in these phrases. In two of the remaining occurrences, *conscience* is something to swear by, comparable to *honesty* or *Heaven*. One usage is worth quoting.

ROWLAND Shall I have liberty of conscience
    Which by interpretation, is ten kisses?
    Hang me if I affect her: yet it may be,
    This whoreson manners will require a struggling,
    Of two and twenty, or by'r Lady thirty.

The tenor is swashbuckling and debonair. The tone may seem to resemble that of the Old Lady's remarks, but it is verbal buckshot rather than well-aimed rifle fire. Another example is found in *The Island Princess*.

Take a good draught or two of wine to settle ye,
'Tis an excellent armour for an ill conscience,
    Uncle.

The expression 'the capacity of your soft cheveril conscience' is Shakespearian in its boldness of juxtaposition of a non-trivial conscience with the earthiness of *capacity*, *soft cheveril*, and *stretch*, contextually belonging to the female pudendum.[23] The Old Lady's words are neither diffuse nor charming; hers is the voice of unrelieved, if not unadulterated, experience.

The verbal antecedents of *cheveril* illustrate its sexual meaning.

But the latter image – stretching in order to receive – appears elsewhere in Shakespeare in an explicitly sexual sense, for the opening up or stretching of female sexuality to 'fit' whatever it receives – in the image of the chevril glove ('Here's a wit of cheverel, that stretches from an inch narrow to an ell broad! – I stretch it out for that word "broad"') in *Romeo and Juliet* (II.iv.83–5) and in the old lady's reference, in *Henry VIII*, to the ambivalent 'capacity' of Ann Bullen ('The capacity / Of your soft cheveril conscience would receive, / If you might please to stretch it', II.iii.31–3). The image of the chevril glove is linked to female wantonness in the scene in *Twelfth Night* where Feste invokes it in lines that refer to making his sister 'wanton'. But it is also explicitly summoned for Diana's duplicitous 'angling', in the final scene of *All's Well* when, in her riddling double entendres, she begins to look perilously close to the prostitute or 'common customer' (v.iii.276) Bertram seeks to portray her as ('This woman's *an easy glove*, my lord, she goes off and on at pleasure.' 5.3.277–8).[24]

Even the word *capacity* has a sexual connotation.

O spirit of love, how quick and fresh art thou
That, notwithstanding thy capacity
Receiveth as the sea, naught enters there,
Of what validity and pitch[25] so e'er,
But falls into abatement and low price
Even in a minute!   (*Twelfth Night* 1.1.9–14).

Act 2, Scene 3 is not the 'gay little scene' overflowing with 'high spirits' of Foakes's

---

20 *King Henry the Eighth*, ed. by A. R. Humphreys (Harmondsworth, 1971), p. 216 n. 32.

21 See, for example, Foakes, *King Henry VIII*, 72 n. 47, '. . . with a quibble carrying on from the puns in lines 37, 41, 45.' The ordinary sense of *quibble*, 'evasion', 'pun', or 'gibe', is used by Foakes and Humphreys as well.

22 *The Famous History of the Life of King Henry Eighth*, ed. S. Schoenbaum (New York, 1967), p. 89, n. 31.

23 See Sonnet 151 for a parallel juxtaposition, involving the other sex.

24 Patricia Parker, *Shakespeare From the Margins: Language, Culture, Context* (Chicago, 1996), p. 342, n. 35. Shakespeare's father was a glover, 'and a wealth of gloving images in the plays suggests that William knew his father's craft well'. Park Honan, *Shakespeare: a Life* (Oxford, 1998), pp. 28–9.

25 For *pitch* in this context, see 1 *Henry IV* 2.5.414 ff. 'There is a thing, Harry, which thou hast often heard of, and it is known to many in our land by the name of pitch. This pitch, as ancient writers do report, doth defile.'

reading. Anne swears three times that she does not wish to be queen. First 'By my troth and maidenhead', secondly 'good troth',[26] and thirdly 'I swear again'. Directly following the third denial, the lord Chamberlain arrives and offers her a thousand pounds a year to be Marchioness of Pembroke.[27] She accepts.[28] The writing makes clear the connection between becoming a queen and a prostitute for hire.

OLD LADY

   'Tis strange. A threepence bowed[29] would hire me,
   Old as I am, to queen it.   (*All Is True* 2.3.36–7)

The Old Lady's 'How tastes it? Is it bitter? Forty pence, no.' (2.3.90) spoken after Anne's acceptance of the King's favour suggests the price of another betrayal for a sum between forty pence and a thousand pounds. Bitter taste evokes vinegar mingled with gall.

There are echoes of Christ's second temptation in the Old Lady's urging that 'eminence, wealth, sovereignty', the kingdoms of the world ('for all the world / 'pour tout le monde'), . . . 'to say sooth, are blessings' (2.3.29–30). The nomenclature Old Lady, is reminiscent of another character, the 'old mole' of *Hamlet* (1.5.164) or 'my old lad of the castle' (*1 Henry IV* 1.2.41), Oldcastle, 'that white-bearded Satan', jester and devil.

The Lord Chamberlain as a substitute Archangel Gabriel creates a vignette of the Annunciation. He speaks of 'heaven'ly blessings'. Anne's response to the King's favour reflects the Virgin's Fiat: 'Behold the handmaid of the Lord: be it unto me according to thy word.'[30]

               Beseech your lordship,
   Vouchsafe to speak my thanks and my obedience,
   As from a blushing handmaid to his highness,
              (*All Is True* 2.3.70–2)

Mary's 'the low estate of his handmaiden'[31] is echoed and gone several better by Anne's 'More than my all is nothing; nor my prayers / Are not words duly hallow'd' (2.3.67–8).

This Anne-nunciation is an intentional parody of its scriptural archetype. To the Lord Chamberlain's, 'What were't worth to know / The secret of your conference?' Anne divulges only, 'Our mistress' sorrows we were pitying' – a matter, by her own admission, not worth the asking. The Lord Chancellor commends the women for their apparent virtue: 'It was a gentle business, and becoming / The action of good women' (2.3.54–5). In light of his embassy, his earnest, 'There is hope / All will be well' joins ambiguously in the pretence of concern for the queen.

Anne does not reveal her previous banter about queenship; she warns the Old Lady to conceal her ennoblement from Katherine. Candour is not the keynote.

Interpretation of Act 2, Scene 3 is baffled by two things: first, the forceful bawdiness of the Old Lady's *double entendres* is confusingly importunate; Shakespeare used the technique in *Henry V* with Catherine and Alice as a smokescreen – in French – to conceal doubts about the marriage of Henry and Catherine.[32] Second, the intervention of the Lord Chamberlain alters the focus of the scene. The irony of the dialogue between the women is interrupted by his courtly formality.

               That you may, fair lady,
   Perceive I speak sincerely, and high note's
   Ta'en of your many virtues, the King's majesty
   Commends his good opinion of you, . . .
              (*All Is True* 2.3.58–61)

---

[26] The word *troth* combines meanings of truth as veracity, and truth as faithful promise, both of which are present in the title *All Is True*.

[27] £1,000 a year would be equivalent to between £80,000 and £100,000 in present day terms.

[28] The parallel with Peter's questioning by the serving maid and servants of the High Priest and his three denials of his master is implicit in a scene in which Anne betrays her mistress.

[29] 'Bowed' pronounced 'bawd', one who lives off the earnings of prostitution.

[30] Luke 1. 38.

[31] Luke 1. 48.

[32] Catherine was the great-grandmother of Henry VIII by her second marriage to Owen Tudor. The connection was not as far-fetched to Shakespeare's contemporaries as to modern readers.

His personal commendation is in the major key.

> I have perused her well.
> Beauty and honour in her are so mingled
> That they have caught the King, and who knows yet
> But from this lady may proceed a gem
> To lighten all this isle.   (*All Is True* 2.3.75–9)

The importance of this speech lies in its prophetic allusion to the birth of Elizabeth, whose christening is the culmination of the play. As the celebration (5.4) is free of irony, the Lord's Chamberlain's reference to Elizabeth's birth can only be read in like vein. The quality of Anne's honour ('beauty and honour in her are so mingled') lies at the root of the exchange between the two women. Having been misinformed that the women were solely engaged in pitying Katherine, the Lord Chamberlain is unaware of the Old Lady's probing of Anne's 'honesty', and so judges the young woman's honour by what he has gathered from her own lips. Foakes comments, 'It is notable that this reference to Elizabeth, foreshadowing v.iv, appears in a scene generally allowed to Shakespeare.'[33] Fletcher is generally agreed to be the author of 5.4; Shakespeare is generally agreed to be the author of 2.3.[34] Researches of mine confirm this to be the case, excepting lines 2.3.50–81, which, in light of the evidence, were apparently written by Fletcher under Shakespeare's guidance.

The discrepancy between 2.3.1–49 and 2.3.82–108 on the one hand, and lines 50–81 on the other, is a key to the play's collaborative strategy. There is no trace in the Lord Chamberlain's four speeches in 2.3 of the mordant word-play which characterizes the dialogue before and after his appearance. While he is present, the Old Lady is silent. To regard the Lord Chamberlain's intervention as seamlessly integral with the rest of Act 2, Scene 3, – even allowing for difference in characterization and for the situation of feminine dialogue exclusive of a male presence, – is to limit the scene and the play to a superficial level.[35] The

Lord Chamberlain's 'gem / To lighten all this isle' is not ironic, and yet is situated deliberately within an ironic framework. This incongruity is fundamental to the play's conception.

Logometric analysis, employing the relative frequencies of *all, are, dare, did, 'em, find, for, hath, in, it is, -ly, little, must, no, the, them, these, they, too, to the, sure, where/there, which,* and *ye* statistically combined, suggests that Fletcher wrote the prologue (TLN 1–33), Shakespeare the first two scenes, 1.1 and 1.2 (TLN 34–568), and Fletcher 1.3, 1.4, 2.1 and most of 2.2 (TLN 569–1114). Shakespeare wrote 2.2.74–144 (TLN 1115–99), 2.3.1–49 and 2.3.82–108 (TLN 1200–61 and 1299–1330). Fletcher wrote 2.3.50–81 (TLN 1262–98). Shakespeare then completed the second act, 2.4.1–238 (TLN 1331–1613).[36]

The Lord Chamberlain's intervention was composed by Fletcher within an envelope of Shakespeare's writing, – under Shakespeare's direction. The collaboration of the two playwrights at this juncture was pivotal. Shakespeare created the context of Lucianic irony within which the Lord Chamberlain's bland words and Anne's protests of modesty articulate themselves. The parody of the Annunciation would be clear to those who regularly prayed the Angelus 'Domini nuntiavit Mariae.

---

[33] Foakes, *King Henry VIII*, p. 74, n. 79.

[34] See Jonathan Hope, *The Authorship of Shakespeare's Plays: A Socio-Linguistic Study* (Cambridge, 1994), pp. 70–83 and Table A5.1 on p. 163. See also Thomas B. Horton, *The Effectiveness of the Stylometry of Function Words in Discriminating between Shakespeare and Fletcher* (Edinburgh, 1987), p. 344. Horton assigns the final scene to Fletcher but leaves 2.3 unassigned, as does Hoy.

[35] Schoenbaum, *The Famous History*, p. xxxix, 'The contrastingly intimate scenes, in which a young maid of honour is shown royal favour while her defeated elders confront isolation and imminent death, appeal more directly to the emotions, if on no very profound level.'

[36] 92.4 per cent of these ascriptions agree with the consensus concerning the authorship of Act 1 and 2 of *All is True*. The discrepancies are TLN 1115–99 and TLN 1262–98.

Et concepit de Spiritu sancto'[37] thrice daily, and would have alerted them to the transition from Shakespeare's biting irony to the compliant hypocrisy distinctive of Fletcher's off-hand sense of irony. The reference to Elizabeth in the 'gem / To lighten all this isle' is delivered as straight discourse within a framework which is either satirical, or is nothing. That nothing has beset interpreters of the play.

Without this division of labour, interpretation of *All Is True* is constrained by an unconvincing tameness of conviction over which editors have expressed unease.[38] The play has two contrapuntal ironies. The first (Shakespeare's) is the injustice of Henry's divorce of Katherine and her replacement by Anne;[39] the second (Fletcher's) is the paradox of the wheel of fortune, encompassing the fall of Buckingham, Katherine, and Wolsey, and the rise of Cranmer, Cromwell, and Anne.[40] The second and more superficial of the two ironies carries sufficient weight to obscure the skilful counterpoint and allow the play to assume its place as pageant among the lower rank of Shakespeare plays.[41] The first and second ironies mesh in Act 2, Scene 3. What editors for the most part have done is interpret the exchange between Anne and the Old Lady from the Lord Chamberlain's point of view (the second irony); that is the only way in which to maintain an instinctive sense or Gestalt of the play's unity, congruent with its triumphal finale. But the authors of *All Is True* have left the choice of counterpoint melody to the audience.

R. A. Foakes follows Frank Kermode[42] in seeing in *All Is True* an embodiment of the eternal cycle of rise and fall, suffering and joy. His interpretation further elevates the 'irony' of fortune's wheel to the plane of natural religion. Foakes finds a naturalistic appreciation of the alternating seasons of humanity in late Shakespeare.

All moreover suggest something of the cycle of suffering and joy which is found in *Henry VIII*. It is embodied in the masque of Ceres in *The Tempest* and in the allusions to the Ceres-Proserpine myth in *The Winter's Tale*, the legend of the daughter of the corn-goddess who is forced to spend six months of the year in the underworld, and is restored to earth for the other six; these correspond to the seasons, winter and summer, which reflect in their interchange her mother's endless alternation between grief and joy, and relate also to the sowing of the seed, placing it in the ground, and the rising of the crop to harvest. In *The Winter's Tale* the cycle relies on a break of sixteen years, in *The Tempest* it is compressed to a day, and in *Henry VIII* the action oscillates from pole to pole, joy gradually predominating through a historical sequence of events.[43]

---

[37] 'The angel of the Lord announced unto Mary. And she conceived of the Holy Spirit.'

[38] 'It is as though the dramatists, having set out to extol Henry and, through him, England, were nevertheless unable – or unwilling – entirely to suppress undercurrents of motive and policy inconsistent with so simplified a view of him. The effect is of a disturbing ambiguity of character.' Schoenbaum, *The Famous History*, p. xxxviii. 'My own opinion is that this is a collaborative play and that Fletcher is one of the collaborators, but that the authors worked closely enough together to achieve at least a superficial unity of tone for most of the play.' Stanley Wells, *Shakespeare: A Dramatic Life* (London, 1994), p. 381.

[39] The most searching modern legal analysis of the injustice is probably that of Henry Ansgar Kelly, *The Matrimonial Trials of Henry VIII* (Stanford, 1976).

[40] 'Fortune, the blind goddess, raises her favorites high upon her wheel, then capriciously flings them to earth. It is an old theme,' Schoenbaum, *The Famous History*, p. xxxiii.

[41] A prejudice against Katherine was enshrined constitutionally by the 1533 Act of Restraint of Appeals, which rendered the Queen's appeal to Rome illegal, and was overruled only in living memory with Britain's recognition of the European Court of Justice as court of final appeal. By according the solemnity of the law to prejudice against Katherine, Thomas Cromwell ensured that judging her to have been a victim of injustice was tantamount to contempt of Crown and Parliament.

[42] Frank Kermode, 'What is Shakespeare's *Henry VIII* About?', *Durham University Journal*, NS, 9 (1948), pp. 48–55.

[43] Foakes, *King Henry VIII*, pp. lxiii–lxiv.

Although Schoenbaum largely agrees with Foakes's idea of the structure of the play,[44] he draws attention to places at which the unifying scheme breaks down.[45] Injustice is seen as a part of Nature's recurrence that transcends human morality, and it is difficult to see how *conscience* fits within Foakes's naturalistic theme.[46] Foakes proposes the notion of 'patience in adversity' as a bridge between morality and the cycle of nature.[47]

Shortly before the arrival of the Lord Chamberlain the Old Lady says to Anne,

> If your back
> Cannot vouchsafe this burden, 'tis too weak
> Ever to get a boy.   (*All Is True* 2.3.42–4)

The chance remark 'to get a boy' is underlined in the following scene in which Henry makes clear to the ecclesiastical court that his conscience was primarily troubled that he 'stood not in the smile of heaven' owing to the fact that Katherine's sons died in infancy. This seeming judgement of heaven made him doubt the legitimacy of his marriage to Katherine.

The Old Lady returns in Act 5 to bear tidings of the birth of a royal child. The biblical allusion is to the angels announcing the Nativity of Christ.

> The tidings that I bring
> Will make my boldness manners. (*To the King*)
>   Now good angels
> Fly o'er thy royal head, and shade thy person
> Under their blessed wings.
>   (*All Is True* 5.1.159–62)

When Henry urges her to say the news is that of a birth and the birth of a boy, – 'Say, "Ay, and of a boy."' the Old Lady enigmatically obliges,

> Ay, ay, my liege,
> And of a lovely boy. The God of heaven
> Both now and ever bless her! 'Tis a girl
> Promises boys hereafter.   (*All Is True* 5.1.164–7)

The irony is as pointed as in Act 2, Scene 3. The Annunciation of the earlier scene is followed by a Nativity whose angel of glad tidings is the same Old Lady present at the conception.[48] She tells the King what he wants to hear, modulates her words to urge a blessing on the mother (or daughter), and then says that the birth of a girl promises boys to follow. The playwright assumes the audience's shared knowledge that Anne produced no male children, nor her daughter Elizabeth. The Old Lady's prophecy of future sons is false. Her stated motive for misleading the King is earning a larger reward for bearing good news.

One critic has read the Old Lady's announcement of the birth of a boy as evidence of obtuseness.[49] This interpretation is understandable in light of the incorrect assumption that she is a semi-historical character apposite to the genre of chronicle plays – *All Is True*. The Old Lady, jester, fool, superannuated court wanton, is the voice of the playwright Shakespeare subverting the play's celebration of the Tudor (and Stuart) monarchies. The Old Lady's false announcement of the birth of a boy and her false prophecy of boys to come contradict the proposition that *All Is True*, and are to be seen in light of her earlier observation regarding Anne's back, "'tis too weak / ever to

---

44 Foakes's unifying scheme is his rejoinder to the major adverse criticism of the play, 'that *Henry VIII* has no controlling and unifying plan, but is only a series of loosely connected scenes strung together to offer an attractive stage spectacle.' Foakes, *King Henry VIII*, p. xlviii.

45 Schoenbaum, *The Famous History*, pp. xxxvii–xxxix.

46 *Conscience* occurs more often (24 times) in *All Is True* than in any other Shakespeare play.

47 See Foakes's extended discussion of patience, pp. lviii–lx.

48 'I shall not fail t'approve the fair conceit (conception) / The King hath of you' (*All Is True* 2.3.74–5). The Magnificat (Luke 1.46–55) is based on the song of Hannah (Anne) in thanksgiving for the granting of her prayer for the gift of a male child (1 Samuel 2.1–10). I suggest that the chances of Shakespeare being aware of the parallel are greater than the chances that he intended obtuseness as a characteristic of the Old Lady, see below.

49 Wells, *Shakespeare*, p. 379. '. . . the Old Lady who brings him the news (and obtusely says at first that the child is a boy)'.

get a boy.' The 'tender place' of the Tudor monarchy was its inability, despite the lengths to which Henry went to alter the fact, to ensure a lasting male dynasty. The Old Lady rubs in the salt most calculated to sting Tudor wounds. Having done so, she departs in the guise of perverse venality, inviting the audience or reader to dismiss her barbs as cantankerousness.

There is confirmation of this view in Paulina's announcement of the birth of a female child to Leontes in *The Winter's Tale*. Foakes remarks, 'There is a remarkable similarity between the trials of Hermione and Katherine, who defend themselves in similar terms, and both appeal finally to an external religious authority, Hermione to Apollo, Katherine to the Pope.'[50] The parallel between Leontes and Henry, and Hermione and Katherine, is more extensive than Foakes suggests.[51] Act 2, Scene 2 of *The Winter's Tale* shows Paulina volunteering to inform Leontes of the birth of his daughter, Perdita. But first she is informed of the birth:

EMILIA   On her frights and griefs,
   Which never tender lady hath borne greater,
   She is, something before her time, delivered.
PAULINA
   A boy?
EMILIA   A daughter, and a goodly babe,
   Lusty, and like to live.
                 (*The Winter's Tale* 2.2.26–30)

Paulina's 'A boy?' hits the same nerve as Henry's 'Is the Queen delivered? / Say, "Ay, and of a boy"' (*All Is True* 5.1.163–4). There is no paramount rationale for underscoring the child's sex in *The Winter's Tale*; Leontes already has a son Mamillius. The reason lies rather in the underlying connection with the issue of a Tudor male heir. Paulina's determination to inform the king presupposes Leontes' negative reaction.

PAULINA   He must be told on't, and he shall.
   The office
   Becomes a woman best. I'll take't upon me.
   If I prove honey-mouthed, let my tongue blister,
   And never to my red-looked anger be
   The trumpet any more.
                 (*The Winter's Tale* 2.2.34–8)

Paulina's resolve not to be 'honey-mouthed' is echoed by the Old Lady's 'The tidings that I bring / Will make my boldness manners.' The Old Lady says of the baby Elizabeth, ''Tis as like you / As cherry is to cherry'. Paulina expatiates,

PAULINA   Behold, my lords,
   Although the print be little, the whole matter
   And copy of the father; eye, nose, lip,
   The trick of's frown, his forehead, nay, the valley,
   The pretty dimples of his chin and cheek, his
     smiles,
   The very mound and frame of hand, nail, finger.[52]
                 (*The Winter's Tale* 2.3.98–103)

The Old Lady in *All Is True* is an extra-historical invention, subversive of the play's chronicle genre and its triumphal climax. She emerges from and retires into the margins of nowhere,[53] threatening to undo her report of the baby's likeness to Henry. Part-Falstaff, part-Sycorax, she is an image of self-reflecting, retrospective

---

[50] Foakes, *King Henry VIII*, p. lx, n. 1. 'Rome is sometimes compared by Protestant controversialists to the oracle of Apollo at Delphi.' Peter Milward, *The Catholicism of Shakespeare's Plays* (Southampton, 1997), p. 96.

[51] In *All Is True*, the king uses the characteristic expletive, 'Ha?' nine times. In *The Winter's Tale*, Leontes uses 'Ha?' in a circumstance similar to those in *All Is True* (*The Winter's Tale*, 1.2.231). This is one detail among a number of parallels.

[52] *The Winter's Tale*, ed. by J. H. F. Pafford (London, 1966), p. 49 nn. 98–9: 'Paulina is, of course, here paying the usual flattery to a parent. Cf. *All Is True* 5.1.168–75: "as like you / As a cherry is to cherry. . . / Said I for this girl was like to him?"' The 'usual flattery to a parent' misses the tone of Paulina's 'red-looked anger', a sharpness made apparent by the concluding lines of her speech in which she expresses the hope that the child will not inherit her father's paranoia. Furthermore, her care in pointing out the likeness of the child to the father must be related to the lines in Rowley's previously performed play, *When You See Me You Know Me*, in which the King says, 'Who first brings word that Henry hath a son / Shall be rewarded well.' Upon which his jester adds, 'Ay, I'll be his surety, but do you hear, wenches, she that brings the first tidings, however it fall out, let her be sure to say the child's like the father, or else she shall have nothing' (286–90).

[53] See Parker, pp. 1–19.

Shakespeare mirrors. Of all the characters in the play based on Holinshed or Foxe, the Old Lady is not a naturalistic historical person. All is not true (faithful) in *All Is True*, and the Old Lady bears eloquent witness to the fact, not least by her own faithless intensity. The final word remains her own, 'What do you think me – ' (2.3.108).

SHAKESPEARE PERFORMANCES IN ENGLAND, 2000

MICHAEL DOBSON

In 1966 John Lennon caused an uproar by suggesting that Jesus Christ was less popular than the Beatles: in the year of the said Messiah's official two thousandth birthday it appeared as though the profile of the man from Nazareth had been eclipsed instead by that of a man from Stratford, but no one, in Britain at least, seemed to be at all shocked. Shakespeare, chosen as Man of the Millennium by listeners to BBC Radio 4, featured at least as prominently in public celebrations of the year 2000 as did Christ: supposedly the last safe symbol of common culture for a nation increasingly committed to religious diversity, his complete plays were even acted in abbreviated versions by schoolchildren in a number of British cities (notably at the Millennium Dome in London, an edifice whose souvenir book, *The Official Commemorative Album for the Millennium*, devotes nearly as much space to Shakespeare as it does to religion). Shakespeare plays were selected as millennial offerings, too, by an unusually large range of theatre companies, amateur and professional. Both the RSC and the Royal Exchange responded to the apocalyptic tone of autumn 1999 by staging *King Lear* during the closing weeks of the twentieth century (and the RSC threw in a brooding *Macbeth* for good measure); the Almeida company put together a suitably grand enterprise in the spring of 2000 by setting up a large temporary theatre in the cavernous shell of Alfred Hitchcock's old Gainsborough Film Studios in Shoreditch, where Ralph Fiennes appeared as Richard II and as Corio-

lanus; in the summer the National produced the most religious *Hamlet* anyone can remember, and the same play (voted 'Masterpiece of the Millennium' in another Radio 4 poll) appeared for the first time at Mark Rylance's Globe, which also offered Vanessa Redgrave as a new-age Prospero; and in Stratford the RSC inaugurated a grand-scale national millennial project of reviving both tetralogies of histories under the heading 'This England', beginning with *Richard II*, the two parts of *Henry IV*, and *Henry V*. In between, a number of the comedies – notably *As You Like It*, performed by no fewer than three major theatre companies and BBC radio – were called upon to set a positive and inclusive mood for the new century. In the great tradition of this slot in *Shakespeare Survey*, I am going to group the year's productions by genre, but in order to respond to what was a particularly seasonal grouping of revivals (predominantly tragedies in the winter, comedies and histories in the spring and summer), I will adopt the uncanonical sequence of tragedies, comedies and histories.

TRAGEDIES

'I am very pleased that, in celebration of the millennium, the Royal Shakespeare Company, a jewel in our cultural crown, has visited Japan with this production of *King Lear*', wrote the Rt Hon Tony Blair, MP, in the programme to Yukio Ninagawa's *Lear*, a programme unusually full of such well-meaning messages from

6 *King Lear*, RSC, Barbican Theatre, 1999, directed by Yukio Ninagawa, 3.2. A vaguely Japanese *Lear*: during the storm
Lear (Sir Nigel Hawthorne) sermonizes, while the Fool (Hiroyuki Sanada) watches for falling boulders.

governmental and corporate patrons. This was, indeed, a very expensive undertaking, heavily reliant on the generosity of HoriPro Inc and Point Tokyo Co Ltd: all but one of the cast (Hiroyuki Sanada, the Fool) were flown from Britain to Japan to begin rehearsing with Ninagawa in August 1999, and after a short season at the Saitama Arts Theatre the entire production traversed the globe to reopen at the Barbican in October and thence transfer to Stratford in December. In its programme's terms – those of international corporate diplomacy – it was, no doubt, a great success, and the presence in the title role of an actor as well known to television and cinema audiences as to theatregoers, Sir Nigel Hawthorne, guaranteed that it did very well at the box office. But however this Anglo-Japanese collaboration may have worked in terms of funding, it never seemed to have been fully thought-through artistically. Yukio Horio's impressively simple black-lacquered set – consisting almost entirely of a pair of double doors decorated with a classical Japanese motif of pine trees, which could open to reveal a stage that seemed to extend backward beyond them almost indefinitely – came to function less as the productively 'empty space' borrowed from Noh theatre which Ninagawa intended than as a costly, non-committal vacuum, within which the cast's disparate performances struggled in vain for significance.

Given Ninagawa's track record of directing Shakespeare forcefully and distinctively in Japanese, this seemed very surprising, and one suspects that the rehearsal process may have been hindered by the difficulty of working for once with Anglophone actors and with Shakespeare's untranslated text. Despite the Japanese costumes, set and Fool, there was nothing to suggest that the play had been comprehensively reimagined in a Samurai-period setting, or directed with any particularly Japanese perspective in mind: indeed there were times, particularly during the early scenes, when it barely seemed to have been directed at all, so out-of-scale were the performances. While Robin Weaver's quiet, slightly prissy Cordelia showed some concern for psychological naturalism, Sian Thomas and Anna Chancellor played Goneril and Regan as mere pantomime monsters, matched by a revoltingly over-greasy, hobbling Oswald from Nicolas Tennant; William Armstrong's Edmund, however, apparently more anxious not to make any very conspicuous mistakes than to give a strong performance, seemed hardly naughty, let alone evil, and a very incongruous object for these Gothic ugly sisters to squabble over. The one convincing relationship on the stage was that between John Carlisle's Gloucester and Michael Maloney's Edgar, touchingly detailed studies in recognizable and forgivable panic and weakness: these two actors, with much of Act 4 to rehearse together, had evidently collaborated to make the sort of decisions about the style and size of their performances which Ninagawa had failed to make for their lost-looking colleagues.

At the centre of this unfocused ensemble, Hawthorne's Lear, visibly deprived of coherent directorial guidance, alternated precariously between siding with the over-players and with the under-players. His first entrance, striding at tremendous speed all the way downstage through the opening double doors with his court struggling to keep up, looked marvellous, but this choreography, coupled with his delivery of his opening lines, gave a strong

impression that he was already irritated with his family and associates before his trajectory from surprise to anger to madness even began. The king's successive responses to Cordelia's truthfulness, Kent's attempted intervention, Goneril's demand that he reduce his train, Regan's siding with her sister and even the storm itself never varied very far, vocally, from the same note of general annoyance, and Hawthorne was not helped, either, by Sanada's youthful, cartwheeling Fool, whose lines, not always easily distinguished through his accent, were twinklingly delivered as if he thought they were uniformly funny. Underpowered in delivery, Hawthorne was mercifully spared the customary shouting-match against the storm, which Ninagawa, clearly more interested in providing visual novelty than in letting the audience concentrate on Lear's lines, chose (bizarrely) to render as a spotlit trickle of sand and an unnerving intermittent barrage of boulders dropped onto the stage from the flies. This aspect of the production was greeted, understandably, with unanimous derision by the critics, and is sadly the one most likely to be remembered.

Perversely determined not to repeat any aspect of the brilliant, intricate, tragicomic performance as another mad king, George III, which had earned him the role, Hawthorne resorted after the storm to a sing-song Anglican sanctimoniousness that managed to seem less like any of his own best work than like a disappointing imitation of Robert Stephens: this rendered the last scene of the play as unmoving as I can remember it. There was just one splendid moment in Hawthorne's performance that hinted at how effective he might have been in a different production, a tiny incident in 1.5: having sent a servant to prepare his horses for the journey to Regan's house, Lear, on the servant's dutiful return, was momentarily unable to recall who this man was or what he was doing there. His recollection, the tiny glimpse of his relief and even self-congratulation at re-grasping the plot, was quite beautifully

7   *King Lear*, Royal Exchange Theatre, Manchester, 1999,
    directed by Gregory Hersov, 2.2. A Victorian *Lear*.
    On 'O reason not the need' Lear (Tom Courtenay)
    turns on Regan (Ashley Jensen).

registered: but it's a sorry comment on a *King Lear* that the most affecting line of the evening should be 'How now, are the horses ready?' This was clearly a performance to file away with Derek Jacobi's Macbeth of a few seasons ago, further proof that the RSC's most commercially successful shows, in which famous actors play famous roles, are sometimes their least artistically assured.

Gregory Hersov's simultaneous production at the Royal Exchange in Manchester, with Tom Courtenay as Lear, offered a different approach entirely. Despite the round, glass-walled auditorium's perpetual feel of late 1960s futurism, this production was carefully grounded in the play's native Victorian performance tradition, its medieval-cum-Pre-Raphaelite robes and furred gowns a mass of green, gold and russet curtain fabrics that might have come from the costume department of Irving's Lyceum – or, indeed, from the trunks of the fictitious wartime troupe for which Courtenay dressed Albert Finney's 'Sir' to play Lear in *The Dresser*. It was striking, indeed, how closely Courtenay's performance during the first half of the play resembled the mock-Wolfit display staged by Finney in that film, such a mass of long, open, moaning vowels and trembling lower lip that the audience, right to the end of the storm scenes, were for the most part unwilling to take Lear's grandiose histrionic tantrums very seriously. They were supported in this regard by Hersov's strangely static rendition of 1.1 (it is possible that the court were trying to look too scared or dumbfounded to register their shock at the king's behaviour, but they came across as unimpressed by it); by the success with which Ian Bartholomew (a middle-aged, authoritative Fool) made his criticisms of the king's conduct funny; and, of course, by Courtenay's close association with roles, like the one he played in *The Dresser*, that may be poignant but are in essence comic, characterized by a fussy Northern domesticity. Some of his Mancunian fans, indeed, seemed to find it as hard to believe in Courtenay as an egotistical absolutist monster as they would have found it to accept Alan Bennett as Othello, and as a result I have never seen the sequence of Lear's mounting wrath and eventual departure from Goneril's castle get so many laughs. This king's anger was registered less as titanic than as comically inappropriate, a grossly unconvincing display of self-important petulance: it wasn't until Courtenay began to show compassion, on 'Poor naked wretches . . .', that he seemed to be working securely within his proper range.

What nonetheless prevented the first half of the play from dwindling to a situation comedy was some superb work from the rest of the cast: however mannered Courtenay's lowing rendition of the curse on Goneril may have been, for example, Helen Schlesinger's response to it – suppressing sobs of horrified recognition that after years of frustrated competition for her father's attention and approval, she could now never again hope to attain it – was entirely convincing, a key moment in one of the most acute and precisely observed Shakespearian performances of the year. This was a Goneril who abruptly tried turning to evil only after unrewarded years of trying terribly hard to be good, and her desperate and ultimately murderous pursuit of Edmund's sexual complicity seemed the more shocking for being pathetically out of character. Ashley Jensen's Regan, meanwhile, was just as visibly afraid of her father, dwindling in misguided self-protection into a tyrannical caricature of him, and both sisters were clearly drawn to Adam James's Edmund as much in pursuit of the self-confidence he appeared to embody as for his sheer sexual charisma. As this swaggering bastard's father, David Ross offered a more rueful version of the family smugness (allowed unusual space in which to claim the audience's serious attention during the first movements of the play by Courtenay's initially shaky grasp on it), and this smugness was beautifully exhibited, too, by David Tennant's Edgar – if only for the few eloquent moments between his too-tardy first entrance in 1.3 (having evidently got up late with the complacency of an elder brother) and the busy Edmund's feigned revelation of Gloucester's anger. From here Tennant made far more sense than do most Edgars of his alienated progress from outcast to masked avenger, carefully marking its phases and its levels of pretence phonetically – RP for his own asides, Glaswegian as Poor Tom (very effective without ever tempting the audience to forget that this was a disguise), and a rustic accent as the supposed fisherman who kills Oswald, which

gradually faded to RP for his final interviews with Gloucester and his confrontation with Edmund. This was a performance of exemplary lucidity in a remarkably clear, well-cut, narrative-driven rendition of the play.

By the time of Edgar's final unmasking, however, Courtenay had wholly re-established himself at the centre of the production. He may find it hard to be very terrifying, but few actors alive are as skilled at eliciting pathos, and his performance as the exhausted, purged Lear of Acts 4 and 5 was extraordinarily moving. The reunion with Cordelia (Gillian Kearney, back from France in modish Virgin Mary blue) was staged with arresting and irresistible simplicity. With the sounds of the sea washing around the exterior of the auditorium (and Scott Myers' sound design was excellent throughout: the off-stage battle in 5.2 was a good deal more impressive than are most onstage ones), Lear was carried on asleep, bolt upright in a chair, and set down close to one edge of the circular acting area. At the moment he awoke – his eyes abruptly opening wide, but with no other movement – he found himself looking directly across the diameter of the circle into Cordelia's face, and it is a mark of how saggily expressive Courtenay's face has become that he was then able to rivet the auditorium with no movement of his head or body at all but just an impression of his eyes coming into focus and then slightly widening again, in a disbelieving recognition that quickly faded into the conviction that he was already dead. Somehow one had the illusion of having even seen his pupils narrow and widen and then narrow again: it wasn't an intrusive or tricksy effect, and can't have taken more than a second to perform, but it gave the scene an absolute, almost biological conviction which in other productions – Ninagawa's, for one – it sometimes lacks. Lear's eventual death was staged no less powerfully, the round acting area used to full, dreadful, symmetrical effect: he finally collapsed centre stage with the bodies of his three daughters pointing towards him like spokes of the wheel to which he had

8 *Macbeth*, RSC, 2000, directed by Gregory Doran, 2.2. Harriet Walter as Lady Macbeth, Anthony Sher as Macbeth.

earlier imagined himself bound. Despite its programme's topical gestures towards eclipses and apocalypses, this was almost an unassuming production of Shakespeare's bleakest tragedy, more concerned with the play's affective impact than with developing an intellectual interpretation: it wanted to look the way its audience would expect *King Lear* to look, and its main priorities were to tell them the story and to make them care about the characters. In this it was, by the end of Act 5, remarkably successful: the tragedy may at times have been weak on terror, but it was overpoweringly strong on pity.

The winter's two productions of *Macbeth* were small-scale affairs by comparison (alike in this as in many other respects), despite having equally well-known actors – Antony Sher and Corin Redgrave, for the RSC and the Battersea

Arts Centre respectively – in the title role. Gregory Doran directed Sher, with Harriet Walter as Lady Macbeth, at the Swan (the production transferred for a sell-out run at the Young Vic in London), in a modern-dress production (mainly combat gear and bayonets) which was blithely uninterested in Scotland but which came with a heavy-handed programme note needlessly underlining the play's resonances with recent power-struggles in the Balkans. Mercifully, the production itself wasn't about to trivialize *Macbeth* and the Balkans alike by pursuing this analogy in its details, and its cast stuck with RP instead of replacing stage-Scots with stage-Serbian. Tom Morris's production in Battersea, with Amanda Harris as Lady Macbeth, was also more-or-less modern dress (though, deliberately eschewing any narrowly topical application, it advertised itself as being about 'militarism' *per se*), and it was played on a similarly shaped acting area (rectangular, with audience on three sides). If anything it was slightly better blocked than its Stratford counterpart, where Doran for once seemed to forget the audience on either side of the stage and directed predominantly forwards as if from under a proscenium arch.

Both designers (Stephen Brimson Lewis and Ti Green respectively) had sought the kind of uncluttered dark-toned simplicity remembered from Trevor Nunn's Other Place production of 1976, and both had largely found it, though Brimson Lewis made some clever use of the Swan's trapdoor (having the witches discovered already lurking under the banquet's table, for example, at the opening of the apparition scene), and was able to supply some impressive, rather cinematic apparitions (what had appeared to be part of a plain brick wall at the rear of the stage proved to be artfully camouflaged latex, through which the successive visions bulged). Ti Green, meanwhile, used a working fireplace at the back of the Battersea stage to good effect, unobtrusively suggesting both the fires of the hearth and those of Hell, and had no apparitions at all (in near-darkness Redgrave economically feigned a visionary headache). The two directors had each streamlined and even elaborated the script in comparable ways: both, for example, combined the roles of Seyton and the Porter (even if Battersea's smaller budget required more cutting – no Young Siward – and more doubling – most conspicuously, Lady Macbeth with Third Witch), and both allowed their Porters to extend their roles considerably. For the RSC Stephen Noonan supplied various topical impersonations as glosses on his 'hell gate' speech (notably a very good rendering of the Rt Hon Tony Blair, MP, to illustrate 'equivocator'), while in Battersea a bullish Jonathan Coyne repeated and paraphrased his favourite lines, and menaced the first rows with protracted displays of his buttocks. Despite Noonan's revue routine, though, neither production had very much to say about politics –

anxieties over devolution aren't making it any easier to stage a celebration of the Anglicization of the Scots as a play for our times, however one undercuts Malcolm's triumph by showing Fleance among the witches at the play's conclusion, or repeats the blocking of 1.4 (Duncan receiving the victorious Macbeth after the opening battle) for the end of 5.11 (Malcolm receiving the victorious Macduff after the closing battle) to underline the similarities between Macduff's position at the story's end and Macbeth's at its beginning (as did both of these versions). What the two productions principally offered were contrasting domestic portraits of a married murderer.

At Stratford, Sher continued to develop the considerable extension of his range revealed two seasons ago by his Leontes in *The Winter's Tale*'s last act: no longer solely an impersonator of deranged megalomaniacs, he has at last found ways of achieving genuine-looking intimacy with other players, and his scenes with Lady Macbeth, particularly 1.7, were among the most impressive of this production. Although the stocky Sher and willowy Walter don't look like a natural couple, they worked conscientiously together to produce a persuasive account of a long-established marriage. Dismayed by Macbeth's attempted withdrawal from their conspiracy to kill Duncan, Lady Macbeth's 'I have given suck . . .' clearly wasn't the first time she had played the card of reminding him about their dead child, nor the first time it had succeeded in bringing Macbeth back across the room to comfort her (it was just the first time this ploy had persuaded him to agree to commit murder); with their intimate collusion thus restored, Macbeth's 'Bring forth men children only . . .' became almost a piece of foreplay towards attempting to conceive again, and both recited 'False face must hide what the false face doth know' together, as if it had become one of those childish catch-phrases in which childless couples specialize. This was *Macbeth* seen through the lens of *Who's Afraid of Virginia Woolf?*, and it worked. Walter particularly excelled at finding the element of comedy of manners in Lady Macbeth's subsequent social discomfitures. Her momentarily visible sense that Macbeth's dismissal of her among his other courtiers in 3.1 (before his first interview with the murderers) was something of an affront, as well as a dreadful personal blow, was funny as well as poignant, as if she were brought up short by a memory of her mother's repeated warnings that she was marrying beneath her class. Walter's leading ladies are always nervy at the best of times, so her excellent rendition of the sleepwalking scene came as no surprise: what particularly impressed was the self-denyingly rapid pace at which she took it. Similarly, Sher has always been wonderful as paranoid tyrants, so that his brilliant rendition of cowering angrily with Seyton in Dunsinane in Act 5 (in what appeared to be the castle's attic) was only to be expected: what surprised was his sudden switch back to a remembered, lost warmth and sense of social belonging for 'Tomorrow, and tomorrow, and tomorrow', an effect he could never have achieved in the flashier, narrower days of his Richard III. Even if Sher's arrival in 1.2 – borne in triumph with Banquo on their soldiers' shoulders – had him still looking rather more like a wild-eyed Tamburlaine or Rasputin than would be compatible with ever convincing a real Duncan that Macbeth would happily have remained a subordinate to anybody, his performance was nonetheless another milestone in the maturing of a major Shakespearian actor. Doran, responsible for shaping both this performance and Sher's Leontes, should be congratulated, too, on an atrociously vivid depiction of the murder of young Macduff (as should Diane Beck, a Lady Macduff already achingly hurt and angered by her husband's apparent desertion): this ultimate violation of domesticity was nicely underlined by the white clothes which, drying around the room, wound up bloodstained as if in a grimly earnest parody of a detergent advertisement.

Corin Redgrave's Macbeth, it has to be said, suffered cruelly by comparison with Sher's.

Redgrave never gave the impression that he was actually seeing anyone else on the stage at all, swallowing his lines introvertedly and unmetrically in a style which seemed like a composite of all the worst vocal mannerisms of Richard Harris, Peter O'Toole and Alan Howard, and the sense that one was in the presence less of a soldier than of an actor of a certain age was only reinforced by a costume which belonged more to the dressing rooms of the past than to the stage of the present – usually a collarless shirt with a sort of dark-coloured, thespian cravat under it. His Macbeth's marriage to the much younger Lady of Amanda Harris looked plausible despite this self-involved quality, but on very different lines to the equal, confiding partnership of Sher and Walter: it was as if Macbeth had finally married, quite recently, only on the eve of a longed-for retirement, and was now dismayed to find that his pretty young bride was intensely bossy and had all sorts of unpleasant work in mind for him still to do. Harris was terrific at being doggedly persistent, forcing Macbeth to ignore his own scruples without remotely understanding them herself, but as a result she rather gave the impression that Lady Macbeth wouldn't be clever enough for the moral consequences of her actions really to dawn on her even in her dreams, so that the sleepwalking scene, for which she wasn't able to find a different register, came out of nowhere. This was a serviceable, plain-dealing little production, but at such crucial moments as this it lacked all punch, never successfully inducing its audience to share the imaginative worlds of either Macbeth or his queen.

Morris's *Macbeth* was, however, streets ahead of the squalid, monotonous, indistinctly spoken *Troilus and Cressida* which arrived in London soon afterwards (directed by Dominic Dromgoole for the Oxford Stage Company), which really merits attention only for the glib, blazer-clad Pandarus of Darragh Kelly, ingeniously played with the suspect professional Irish charm of a Terry Wogan. By comparison with the winter's other tragedies, Dromgoole's production might be called concept-driven, in so far as Anthony Lamble's design seemed definitely to have been imposed on the play rather than chosen to help it: the desired effect seemed to be to make the Trojan War resemble a feud on a scruffy Mediterranean campsite between rival gangs of British yobs. But if this was a concept, it was one which unfortunately left the play almost without substance. With its characters unable to make their elaborate rhetoric comprehensible, never mind interesting, and Greeks and Trojans alike deprived even of any vestigial pretensions to heroism, there was nothing left for Shakespeare's antiheroic play to be anti-heroic about. Perhaps West End audiences need to regain some idealism from somewhere before the cynicism of *Troilus and Cressida* can look anything other than stale and conformist, as it did here: at very least, if the play's conflicts are to grip, it might be a good idea for the lovers and warriors to look and sound rather less like so many additional versions of Thersites.

All this was a far cry from Sam Mendes' wonderful *Troilus and Cressida* of 1989, remembered for, among other things, Ralph Fiennes's inventive, nuanced performance as an insecure Troilus; but then so, unfortunately, were the two Shakespeare productions in which Ralph Fiennes appeared in 2000. There is comparatively little to be said about Jonathan Kent's *Richard II* and *Coriolanus* for the Almeida company at Gainsborough Studios, once one has recorded that the near-derelict, warehouse-like playing space, with a great artfully placed crevice up the back of the old brick wall behind the stage, was wonderful (despite some sightline problems from the side galleries) and that the presence of Fiennes in the title roles was quite sufficient to fill it, his enormous following among admirers of *The English Patient* providing a needed commercial safety-net for the risk involved in taking on two such contrasting and challenging roles at once. *Richard II* opened at the end of March (to take one history out of turn), and was joined in repertory by *Coriolanus*

in June: by then the productions' audiences included such high proportions of American cinemagoers that United Airlines might as well have run a shuttle bus service between Shoreditch and Heathrow. As one would expect, Fiennes was considerably more at home in the ex-Gielgud role of Richard than in the ex-Olivier one of Caius Martius, but even here he was betrayed by some curiously uninspired direction. Beyond covering the stage with grass and supplying some taped bird calls (so that even the deposition scene seemed unaccountably to be taking place out in Essex somewhere), Kent appeared to have had no ideas about *Richard II* at all, unless one counts the notion that it was all about a neurotic-looking leading actor in white medieval robes who held forth under a follow-spot while a semicircle of deferential fellow-players in black looked impassively on. This was *Richard II* on autopilot, an abnormally strong company (Barbara Jefford, Angela Down, Emilia Fox, Oliver Ford-Davies, David Burke, Linus Roache) reduced to so many supporting players, apparently told not to risk distracting the audience from a dazzling star turn that in the event never came. One kept hoping for Fiennes's performance to change gear and break through into something less or at least differently mannered, if only for his last scene, but it never did, and the only real surprise of the evening was that David Burke decided to play Gaunt's 'This royal throne of kings . . .' through an unhelpful fog of shaking and gasping, as though the point of the speech wasn't its patriotic rhetoric but the opportunity it provided for a naturalistic simulation of mortal illness. Like Courtenay, Fiennes got some unintended laughs from admirers unwilling to accept the more unsympathetic behaviour of his character at face value, and the evening's best comment on the extent to which his film work has now typecast him for an endlessly repeated performance of decorous pathological melancholy was perhaps the indulgent guffaw that greeted the Gardener's diagnosis of Richard's condition in 3.4:

FIRST MAN: What, think you then the King shall
be deposed?
GARDENER: Depressed he is already . . .

Fiennes is still potentially a fine classical actor,
and potentially a splendid Richard, but he needs
a lot more help out of his current rut than Kent
was willing or able to provide.

The *Coriolanus* was more interesting, though
on balance less effective, if only because
Fiennes, hardly anyone's obvious first choice for
a muscle-bound instinctive dictator, had at least
to find some justification for playing it regardless. In stylized modern dress, the play initially
looked more at home in this auditorium than
had its medieval companion-piece, almost
fatally so: at the start of 1.1 the citizens, discussing their grievances around a table, looked
so admirably like a workers' revolutionary
committee meeting surreptitiously in a factory
that it was hard to work out what the patrician
Menenius was doing when he arrived there, or
ever to accept the playing space as a fully public
area thereafter. Fiennes, however, dressed in a
dark, tailored jacket buttoned up to the neck
around a sort of white stock – which made him
look more like an inhibited Barchester cleric
than a warrior – seemed as unlike either the
assured right-wing consul or the epic soldier
imagined by his mother and by Menenius as
could have been imagined, persuasive only as
the comically self-conscious, self-disgusted elec-
toral candidate in 2.3's garment of humility. But
this miscasting in the end was what the production came to be about: just after the close of
Volumnia's last plea in 5.3 (splendidly delivered
by an implacable Barbara Jefford in a magnificent 1930s-style dress), Fiennes, at last unable to
sustain his twitchy immobility any longer,
moved his hand uncertainly towards hers, and as
she took his wrist he collapsed slowly to his
knees crying 'O mother, mother!' in a hitherto
wholly unused vocal register that conveyed
terrible anguish but also the most profound
sense of relief. All that stiffly unconvincing
machismo, all those repeated tremulous equine

sneers at the tribunes, all that half-hearted business with Aufidius, hadn't been the real him at
all, but the symptoms of some dreadful feat of
denial: now at last he could give in and have the
nervous breakdown he had evidently been
pining for since well before the start of the play.
It was a very affecting moment, and retrospectively it offered some kind of explanation for
Fiennes's behaviour up to that point – this
hadn't just been an unconvincing performance
as Coriolanus, but a performance as an unconvincing Coriolanus. But four and three-quarter
acts is a very long time to have to wait for a
central performance to start making sense, and
to say that what was achieved was a belatedly
interesting performance of Coriolanus-as-
Fiennes, rather than a consistently interesting
performance of Coriolanus by Fiennes, is not
exactly wholehearted praise.

David Tennant, by contrast, having already
given one consistently interesting performance
as Edgar at the Royal Exchange in the autumn,
went on to give three more in the RSC's spring
and summer repertory in Stratford, in Sheridan's
The Rivals, in *The Comedy of Errors* and, most
impressively, in the only tragedy proper of the
season, Michael Boyd's *Romeo and Juliet* in the
RST. Here, by contrast with Kent's efforts, was
a show firmly under the control of a director
able to elicit distinctive and cogent work from
his leading players, a director with, if anything,
too much in the way of organizing ideas rather
than too little. If Romeo seemed unusually
central to this reading of the play it wasn't solely
because Tennant – hitherto a lively Touchstone
whose destiny seemed to lie with Mercutio at
best – here extended his own range quite as
dramatically as Sher has been developing his.
Quite apart from anything else, Romeo, or
what in retrospect proved to have been his
regretful ghost, got on this occasion to speak the
Prologue, passing ethereally from the auditorium and through the temporarily frozen
opening brawl to the strains of airy music. This
was his story before it was anyone else's.

The design of Boyd's production had hinted

9   *Romeo and Juliet*, RSC, Royal Shakespeare Theatre, 2000, directed by Michael Boyd, 2.3. A boys' *Romeo and Juliet*:
Romeo (David Tennant) joking homosocially with Mercutio (Adrian Schiller) and Benvolio (Anthony Howell) in 2.3.

at a preoccupation with the male side of the
play even before this. Tom Piper's set was quite
a restrained one for him, from which nothing
popped up at all except an instant herb garden
for Friar Laurence, and its only other surprise
was the priest-hole in which the Friar concealed
the banished Romeo (known, unfortunately, to
the police, who, rightly suspicious of Laurence
as a potential troublemaker, had searched it just
before Paris's visit in Act 4). It consisted mainly
of two curving and inhospitable grey walls, one
of them splattered with blood from the brawl
onwards, with a narrow curving passageway
between them: the suggestion was of a rather
bleak playground, or perhaps the space in front

of a military installation. In any case, we were
for once in a *Romeo and Juliet* which never
looked like turning out as a comedy. Boyd took
both the play's fatalism and its bawdy jokes very
seriously, indeed in his interpretation the two
were closely connected. He placed the action in
a violent, adolescent milieu where, from Samson's remarks about raping the Montague
women onwards, sexual desire was pervasively
stalemated into aggression, both verbal and
physical. Thus the Chorus's sonnet at the start
of Act 2, 'Now old desire doth on his deathbed
lie', for once uncut, was intoned by Gregory
and Sampson as a further piece of obscene
male jeering. Verona *can* seem like one of

Shakespeare's more pleasant holiday destinations – somewhere which might be a lovely, sunny place to live, if only the authorities were a bit more efficient at dealing with the odd fight, and if only Juliet would have the sense to marry Paris. But on this set, and presided over by Alfred Burke's old and infirm Prince, it was visibly a dead end.

Although even in these unpromising surroundings Anthony Howell did a splendid job of personifying goodwill and common sense as Benvolio, he was easily eclipsed by Adrian Schiller's seamy and angry Mercutio, who, so far from being a carefree jester tragically caught up in a quarrel which has nothing to do with him, was in this production the very personification of what was rotten in the state of Verona. (His kinship with the Prince was stressed accordingly: in this production the Capulets felt obliged to bow to him when at the end of their ball he revealed his identity as a way of securing his friends' unmolested exit.) Possessively jealous over Romeo, Mercutio was unable to express this emotion except in the form of smutty taunts – and it was a jealousy which his friends seemed uneasily to be realizing might be sexual, even if he himself didn't. Benvolio's 'Stop there, stop there' in 2.4, after Mercutio's 'Now art thou sociable, now art thou Romeo . . .' speech, wasn't amused at all, but anxious and embarrassed. For Boyd the story of the play was primarily of Romeo's escape from all this, the story of how he ceased to resemble the troubled and vicious Mercutio and became instead the calmed apparition who spoke the Prologue. Hence Tennant's Romeo, despite his forebodings, was at first unusually cocky at the Capulets' ball, and his initial approach to Juliet with 'If I profane with my unworthiest hand . . .' wasn't dreamily rapturous but a half-swaggering come-on. This was clearly the only way he and his peers knew of approaching women, even those that hung upon the cheek of night like a rich jewel in an Ethiop's ear. Romeo, however, was rapidly surprised out of this mind-set by Juliet's willingness and ability

to join in the same game. Instead of blushing and casting her eyes to the floor, Alex Gilbreath's fearlessly confident Juliet answered him as readily and wittily as would Mercutio. From here onwards these two were launched into an accelerating trajectory of fully mutual desire, but it was one which in this production was literally haunted by the figure it excluded. Passing invisibly across the stage with a ghostly Tybalt while Juliet was about to take the Friar's potion, the malevolent shade of the slain Mercutio took up the place on top of the stage-right wall which earlier served as Juliet's balcony. From here he helped to pass Romeo the apothecary's lethal drugs in 5.1, in a deliberate reprise of the lovers' hand-clasp in the balcony scene, and it was he who spoke Friar John's lines to Friar Laurence in 5.2, so that the plague Mercutio had wished on both their houses explicitly materialized as the plague which prevented the banished Romeo hearing that Juliet was really alive. Denied the love which Romeo and Juliet fleetingly enjoy, Mercutio avenged his own death on them both.

The problem both with this set and with the original and usually viable reading of the play which it supported is that they didn't leave very much room for Juliet. Instead of being *Romeo and Juliet*, the play nearly became *Romeo and Mercutio (Deceased)*, a story to which the set seemed slightly better suited. The space worked beautifully for the fight scenes, but our sense of the Capulet household remained dangerously vague: it was symptomatic that the rack of saucepans glimpsed during the preparations for the ball was on wheels and was in rapid motion to nowhere in particular. Very little was made of Juliet's arrival at the ball (for which she was already dressed on her first appearance in 1.3, so that we weren't shown any distinction between her private and public spaces within the household); and the dancing, instead of being focused in a particular location, largely took the form of a sort of conga-line which passed inconsequentially on and off the stage and accidentally allowed Romeo and Juliet to meet in limbo rather than specifically within her parents' social world. Though Juliet necessarily got a bed on which to lose consciousness after taking the potion, her privacy – quite apart from her hold on the audience's undivided attention – was of course wholly compromised by the unexpected arrival of the dead Mercutio and Tybalt during her best soliloquy of the night. Even this nominal bedchamber remained pretty sketchy, since the servants puzzlingly threw logs to each other across her sleeping form the following morning. Lady Capulet and the Nurse were both beautifully acted in this production (by Caroline Harris and Eileen McCallum), but Boyd and Piper didn't really have a place for them either, and Gilbreath's courageous Juliet – though tremendously strong in the love scenes and particularly affecting in 3.2, on the news of Romeo's banishment – sometimes seemed to be functioning almost as an honorary man, forced in this production to compete with Mercutio on his own terms.

Boyd's resolutely unfairytale approach certainly made the bulk of this show one of the most closely reasoned and least sentimental *Romeo and Juliet*s I've seen, though the regrettable concomitant was that it was also one of the least lyrical (sufficiently careless about the verse, for example, for all of the cast except the Prince habitually to have pronounced the heroine's name as if it had three syllables, the stress on the last, so that we didn't hear it metrically until the very last line of the night). Even in death these Capulets didn't get a fully realized space of their own, the tomb reduced to a mere shallow grave with a hinged lid, so that Romeo's most beautiful speech in the play, his last farewell to the supposedly dead Juliet, was in the event upstaged by his efforts to lift her into view (rather like an untrained dancer rehearsing the Macmillan/Prokofiev ballet). Juliet's suicide, though, was staged with real clarity and force: on the last painful sexual pun of the evening, 'This is thy sheath: there rust, and let me die', she used the weight of Romeo's body to press the dagger down into hers. But this cruelly

powerful and shocking effect was immediately thrown away: disappointingly, in death Juliet was obliged awkwardly to fall back into the grave, dragging Romeo with her into invisibility. I was struck by how cheated I felt by this: perhaps the full emotional impact of this play depends on the audience being allowed the same proper contemplative inspection of the corpses as is forced upon the remaining members of the cast during the impromptu inquest conducted by the Prince. This is, retrospectively, their public wedding as well as their funeral, and we have been anticipating one or both for some time. But I was more disappointed still by the way in which Boyd's studied unsentimentality failed him completely during the Prince's last speech, when the dead lovers were allowed to rise from the grave and, looking pityingly at their surviving relatives and at the darker ghosts of Mercutio, Tybalt and Paris who remained in limbo on the upper level, moved serenely out of this stagnant Verona via the ramp into the auditorium. This final interpolated stage direction completely neutralized the play's determinedly secular tragedy by a facile and incongruous injection of pseudo-religion. It will, however, make it very easy for people to remember what was uniquely Michael Boyd's about Michael Boyd's production of *Romeo and Juliet*, and perhaps that was half the point.

If the casting of Tennant as Romeo came as something of a surprise, both of the year's two English Hamlets had long been on the cards. The world had been waiting for Simon Russell Beale to play the role for some time (at one point Sam Mendes was to have directed him in the part, but in the event that job fell to John Caird at the National), while Mark Rylance had played the Prince successfully before (in pyjamas, for the RSC) and was sooner or later bound to cast himself in it again in his capacity as the Globe's *de facto* actor–manager. Apart from this, though, and the fact that both shows opened in the summer (Caird's at the Lyttleton in July before touring to Malvern and Elsinore and thence back to London, with further visits thereafter to Brighton, Glasgow, Dublin, Stockholm, Sheffield, Bath and Aberdeen – how chances it they travel, with a vengeance), the two productions had nothing in common except that both surpassed most people's expectations of them – expectations which had, in the case of Caird's production, been very high indeed.

Caird's *Hamlet*, to the satisfaction of some and the disdain of others, was director's Shakespeare to the core: meticulously choreographed; expensively lit (if that's quite the word for the darkness visible in which so many key scenes took place); equipped with an impressive, reverberating sound system and sumptuous incidental music; glossily designed; and informed by a single, powerful vision – a vision which those critics who were unwilling to be persuaded by it predictably dismissed as a mere striving after novelty. This was a *Hamlet* set either in Purgatory or very near it, with its dramatis personae – all beginning the play in a semi-circle of niches, to the singing of a single choirboy, lit like so many votive or commemorative images – perhaps doomed to re-enact these events for eternity. From this initial tableau the actors moved to sit on a ritual circle of steamer trunks; above what were by now whole church choirs, the sentries' opening dialogue became audible, and through a brilliant vertical fissure of light opening in the centre of the stage's rear wall (joined at what became literally crucial moments later on by a horizontal fissure, to make a vast and dazzling sign of the Cross) came a suitcase-bearing stranger. This was Horatio, whose presence as witness and future narrator seemed to be the stimulus for the play proper to begin, the rest of the cast filing away into the shadows. (This sequence, complete with fragments of the sentries' dialogue, was recapitulated as a sort of prologue to the final stages of the tragedy when the pirate arrived through the fissure to bring Horatio Hamlet's letter in Act 4: Hamlet himself re-entered the play from that glaring beyond in 5.1, and the vertical fissure

also admitted other key figures from elsewhere, the players and the Ghost.) The set was composed throughout the play of different arrangements of these same trunks: this may sound like Brechtian minimalism, but above the actors' heads dangled a changing array of ornate metal crucifixes and brass chandeliers (the latter lowered for cleaning to provide a more informal court setting for Ophelia's mad scene), so that this flexible but ever-present array of luggage occupied not a blank empty space but something with the aura of a Byzantine cathedral. These people, we gathered, were passing through nature to an eternity that wasn't far away, and they were encumbered on their journey by various forms of literal and metaphysical baggage.

In keeping with this, Caird's Denmark was as much a theocracy as a monarchy: Peter McEnery's suave, tactful Claudius wore what resembled a cope and mitre rather than a robe and crown in 1.2, and his first speech led the court in an incense-scented prayer for the dead King Hamlet (as if we were witnessing the closing stages of his state funeral) rather than initiating a secular business meeting. (The secular business was in any case greatly curtailed: more interested in a family's souls than in a nation's foreign affairs, Caird cut the Fortinbras plot entirely, thus allowing the play to end, or at least to move into repose before its next repetition, with flights of angels singing Hamlet to his rest.) Prayer, indeed, set the tone for much of this production, certainly for its central performance. With a self-discipline which made the speech more dramatic than any pacing and gesticulating could have done, Simon Russell Beale played the whole of 'O that this too, too sullied flesh . . .' kneeling motionless, facing the audience as if across an altar rail, and his meditative, beautifully spoken delivery of this soliloquy struck a keynote of quiet but intense moment-by-moment concentration and attention which would characterize the whole production. By now it was quite clear that what was on offer was a sacramental *Hamlet*, its cast priests as much as comedians. In almost complete darkness the audience listened to the play's holy words spoken once again, but spoken on this occasion with such articulacy and nuance that it was, to resort to a cliché for once made true, like hearing them for the first time.

Hushed, intimate, exquisite stillness characterized many of this production's most distinctive moments. In 3.2, for example, the Players listened to Hamlet's advice as if to an oracle, and after their departure 'Horatio, thou art e'en as just a man . . .' was delivered apart in a moment of intense quiet, the two men pausing from the task of lighting ornate metal red-shaded footlights for the players which wouldn't have looked out of place around the sanctuary of an Eastern Orthodox church. This hush was ingeniously extended to provide the interval: having assembled the court's impromptu theatre, Hamlet and Horatio sat on a raised area behind it, contemplating the empty stage in silence as if savouring the last possible peaceful interlude before events swept them onwards into violent action. The lights slowly faded on this tableau to initiate the interval, and when they came up again for the second half there the two men still were – only now at the front of the stage, their backs to us, so that we knew we were now looking at the same space and the same moment from an angle 180 degrees altered. Sometimes such intimacies were shared by characters not usually privy to them: Ophelia lingered after the play to hear the ensuing dialogue between Hamlet and Horatio, for example (a slightly uncertain performance by Cathryn Bradshaw, her mad games of dressing as Polonius intrusive rather than poignant), and Horatio remained for 'Now is the very witching hour of night . . .', which became a confidence between friends rather than a melodramatic self-exhortation.

The tiny, still moment which will surely haunt most of the people who saw this production, though, came in the closet scene, which had already been unusually tender even before the arrival of either Hamlet or the Ghost. Sara Kestelman's sympathetic Gertrude, upset by *The Murder of Gonzago*, had been rummaging through her trunks to find, for the first time in years, Hamlet's baby shoes, some love letters from his father and the veil she had worn at her first wedding, so that the Prince's lecture found his mother unusually predisposed to hear it (her fleetingly downcast eyes and rueful, apologetic smile when he mentioned his distrust of Rosencrantz and Guildenstern were marvellous, suggesting memories of flirtatious games in Hamlet's boyhood as well as convincingly re-establishing their intimacy on the Prince's terms). But the scene's most striking moment, visually at least, came just after 'But look, amazement on thy mother sits . . .', when for the briefest moment Hamlet found himself between Gertrude and the Ghost, touching both of them, poised yearningly between this world and the next. For a tiny second this family triad was and was not reunited, and Russell Beale's expression eloquently conveyed his sense of all that had been lost: his frustration that Gertrude could not see the ghost was almost unbearable. As the picture fleetingly formed and dissolved again, many members of the audience – certainly including me – audibly took an intake of breath: this is the sort of effect – so simple and powerful that one wonders one has never seen it achieved at this moment in the play before – that keeps audiences coming back to this most undead of tragedies.

To some, this production was a little too tender: a few critics found Hamlet's sobbing remorse over Denis Quilley's dead Polonius, and indeed Quilley's return from the dead to play a companionable Gravedigger (popping up in a trunk, punningly singing 'Resurrexit' from the requiem mass which haunted this production's soundtrack), merely sentimental, attempts to compensate for Russell Beale's unconventionally rotund appearance as the Prince by making him unusually attentive to the feelings of others. It has to be admitted that Russell Beale did look momentarily self-conscious as he took off his cloak to undertake the swordfight, at last fully revealed as fat and scant of breath just

10   *Hamlet*, Royal National Theatre (Lyttleton auditorium), 2000, directed by John Caird, 3.4. A quiet, intimate closet scene:
Sara Kestelman (Gertrude), Simon Russell Beale (Hamlet).

in time for his mother to underline the point, but the duel itself never lacked conviction, and the fact that the audience were briefly uncertain as to whether this Hamlet actually would kill Claudius when the moment came – when the usurper made the same smiling gesture of spreading his arms defencelessly wide which had successfully charmed Laertes into submission earlier on – made the play's finale seem more rather than less dramatic and shocking and painful. But these deaths were there to be contemplated as much as to be enacted: the corpses didn't stay supine at the production's close, but the whole cast returned to the circle in which they had first become visible, again candle-lit in their niches, before filing away outwards through that brilliant fissure into the beyond, some one way, some another – some to Heaven, some to Hell? Or merely to separate compartments of Purgatory to await the next rueful re-enactment? This was a *Hamlet* to meditate upon for a long, long time after the house lights came back on.

If the National's *Hamlet* was all quiet contemplation, more melancholy than madness, the Globe's – necessarily *sans* brooding lighting effects – was both simpler and altogether more frenetic. This production marked a major landmark in the history of its theatre, in that so far from being continuously embarrassing, as so many of the Globe's shows have been, it was actually watchable. This was in part because the 'Master of Play', Giles Block, had seen fit to surround the stage with a little knee-height wooden rail like the one on the *Roxana* illustration, so that for once one had a secure sense of where the boundary was between audience and acting space, but not entirely. It's true that, with the honourable exceptions of Penny Layden as Ophelia and Mark Lockyer as Laertes, most of the supporting cast offered nothing very special in the way of performances – in their standard Elizabethan clothes, they could have come from just about any standard touring B-production of the early twentieth century, and neither Tim Woodward's Claudius nor James Hayes's Polonius even seemed to have a particularly secure grip on their lines (at one performance I saw, Polonius had to be prompted by a member of the audience). It's true, too, that as Hamlet Mark Rylance offered what was in essence the same performance he gave as Hamlet at the RSC ten years ago, and much the same performance that he has given on many previous occasions and nominally in many different roles at the Globe – a helpless Norman Wisdom-like little-boy-lost, always on the edge of either comic or melodramatic hysteria, desperately needing to be looked after, and peering out of whatever play he happens to be in to appeal pitifully to the audience as if to the only possible source of tea and sympathy left in the world. But in *Hamlet* this performance just about works, and it's a play which can even thrive on a supporting cast cardboard enough to look like figments of the Prince's imagination: here the stiff stooge-like qualities of Claudius, Polonius and the Ghost (not an easy part to play in daylight before a modern audience, but a ludicrous orange plume didn't help) only set off Rylance's weird, damaged charisma to better advantage.

While Russell Beale wanted to stay in his black cloak to the last possible moment, Rylance, tellingly, couldn't wait to get out of his, losing it entirely after his first interview with the Ghost to reappear at first in a soiled white nightgown (the equivalent of his RSC pyjamas, only in what the Globe calls 'recreated clothing of the period') and then, to welcome the Players, in what was practically motley. This was a Hamlet who extravagantly over-acted his madness with a wild frivolity, his laughter constantly bordering on hysterical despair, until in the nunnery scene he began to feel that he was no longer pretending – 'Go to, I'll no more on't, it *hath* made me mad', he sobbed. Chased in 4.2, he pretended to have Polonius' head in a bag, which he repeatedly stabbed (it turned out to be a cabbage), and in 5.1 he refused to give Yorick's skull back to the gravedigger, clutching it with him as he left the stage after his confrontation with Laertes as if seeking comfort from a teddy bear. It was all very clear, and very outward, Rylance nicely pacing his alternations between dealing with his fellow cast-members and dealing directly with the audience. His easy collusion with the latter may forever incline him to comedy, not always helpfully – predictably, he took the rhetorical questions in 'O what a rogue and peasant slave am I' as if in a panto, insisting on getting actual shouted replies to 'Am I a coward? . . . Who does me this? Ha?' – but this intimate complicity can at least produce some pleasantly novel readings. Here 'guilty creatures *sitting* at a play' drew a satirical moral distinction between those who had paid up to be out of the rain and those who preferred to be closer up in the yard at £5 a head, and in the players' scene Rylance playfully feigned to turn against this favourite constituency, nicely timing the Prince's more snobbish theatrical advice: '. . . to split the ears of the groundlings', (turning from the Player to the yard), 'who are for the most part capable of nothing but inexplicable dumb shows' (pauses for expected laughing groans of protest, about which his next words then become an afterthought) ' – and noise'. In the major soliloquies, one never really felt that this Hamlet was in full control of what he was saying – he threw off their profound truths as if by accident – but this never made them undramatic: they became a sort of frantic verbal pacing of Rylance's cage, as did his behaviour on the rail-bound stage. The sword-fight was the best-staged I have ever seen – Lockyer and Rylance actually gave the impression that they wanted to hit each other rather than just each other's rapiers – and Heaven knows that the Globe's real cannon, already showed off to good effect during Claudius' offstage carousing in Act I, gave Fortinbras' final line far greater impact than is usual, the audience hurriedly covering their ears and waiting to be sure the salute was over before they dared to start applauding. This show never offered serious emotional competition to John Caird's exceptional production – nor, come to that, to Peter Zadek's eclectic German *Hamlet*, with Angela Winkler in the title role, which visited the Edinburgh Festival, so that at the end of the summer there were briefly three rival productions of the Masterpiece of the Millennium running in Britain at once. But it was at the very least a thoroughly respectable, entertaining *Hamlet*, and it's a relief at last to be able to say that about a show performed in this playhouse, a space in which so many people have invested so much hope – and money – with hitherto such small rewards in the way of convincing theatre.

COMEDIES

The Globe's other two Shakespearian offerings of the summer, though, were very much the mixture as before, even though one of them was in its own way another landmark, the first Globe production to feature an internationally renowned major actor – Vanessa Redgrave – somehow induced to play Prospero in an incoherent and often inaudible production by her friend Lena Udovicki. However, this turned out to be such an underwhelming performance that it is hard to know whether to call it misguidedly laid-back or just plain lazy: Redgrave simply adopted the wistful half-smile she always uses when no one has any better

ideas, briefly affected an Irish accent for the early scenes which she forgot later on, twirled her staff a little (looking half-dangerous only once, when compelling Ariel to re-enact her imprisonment in the cloven pine), and in general played the Duke of Milan as a bland New Age healer rather than a potentially vengeful magus. This show never looked as if stealing it would be difficult for any actor even half-awake, but the only one who bothered to try – Jasper Britton, a scatalogical, low-comedy Caliban – used a steamroller to crush this fly, mugging with the groundlings, throwing dead fish into the yard, and adding obscene pieces of business to his scenes with Stephano and Trinculo so that they dragged on to what were in every sense grotesque lengths. But there was no real dramatic conflict even here: Redgrave's Prospero, forgiving her slave as perfunctorily and unthinkingly as she did her brother, even let Caliban wear her hat at the end of the play, cosily adjusting its angle on his head for better effect. It ought to be possible to say something interesting about the consequences of casting a woman as Prospero, but this production didn't go in for coherent thought itself and doesn't in any way invite it: it never really added up to an interpretation of *The Tempest* at all, never mind a stimulating one.

Hamlet was performed by The White Company (as was Brome's *The Antipodes*): the Red Company, who performed both *The Tempest* and *The Two Noble Kinsmen*, seemed very much to be this Globe season's reserve team. As with the cross-gender Prospero, playing *The Two Noble Kinsmen* with much the same cast as another late romance ought to have been intellectually interesting, but with this cast it wasn't. Jasper Britton, giving a thankfully more disciplined performance as Palamon, dominated *The Two Noble Kinsmen* as he did *The Tempest*, and against equally feeble competition. Even the Jailer's Daughter failed to shine: Kate Fleetwood, though blissfully audible, sounded slightly too much as though this was the result of elocution lessons, and she had run

11 *The Tempest*, Shakespeare's Globe, 2000, directed by Lena Udovicki, 5.1. Vanessa Redgrave's laid-back Prospero, as she was sometime Milan, before relinquishing her hat to Jasper Britton's utterly un-laid-back Caliban.

264

out of ideas for making her madness diverting by the end of her soliloquy in 3.2, 'He has mistook the brake . . .' Britton again mainly played for comedy, as most performers ill-advisedly but understandably do in this space: in the arming scene, 3.6, the anxious 'How do I look? Am I fall'n much away?' became a merely preening, naturalistic 'How do I look?', the latter question saved until after the rare and inexpensive laugh this obtained. Without at least some genuine pathos, though, the ending of this play is bound to fall flat, as it did here. The most remarkable thing about this production was not any of its acting but one aspect of its design. Exactly half way between the front of the stage and its back wall was a post, surmounted by an immense likeness of a horse's skull (shades of that banner of a horse which feebly unfolded while Arcite's fatal riding accident was described in Barry Kyle's RSC production at the Swan in 1986?), and around the base of this post pivoted a kind of narrow see-saw-cum-roundabout affair, operated by a beefy stagehand who was onstage throughout. On this incongruous contraption, neither Jacobean nor modern, an actor could ride from an inconspicuous rear entrance right down to the front of the stage for the start of a scene, or be swivelled suddenly off at its close. Of all the theatrical wheels one might want to re-invent, one would have thought that the Olivier Theatre's notorious revolve would have been about the last, but there this scene-stealing Lazy Susan was, and a fat lot of help it was to anyone involved in this lacklustre production of Shakespeare and Fletcher's tragicomedy.

It has struck me as rather unfair over the last five years or so that the Globe should have attracted so much more critical attention than central London's other, much more reliable purveyor of outdoor Shakespeare, the New Shakespeare Company, who have been running a summer season at the Open Air Theatre in Regent's Park since the days of Ben Greet and Robert Atkins. Their two Shakespeare comedies in 2000, *A Midsummer Night's Dream* and *Much Ado About Nothing*, far surpassed the Globe's two romances, and while both productions offered what was definitively mass-market, populist Shakespeare – as is perfectly illustrated by Rachel Kavanaugh's decision to have the Watch in her 1940s *Much Ado* played as a facsimile of the Home Guard platoon from *Dad's Army* – they did so with very high production values (despite a fatal penchant for naff taped sound-cues), acting that was never less than competent (and sometimes excellent: Tom Mannion's Scots officer-class Benedick was a delight), and even some ideas. Alan Strachan's *Dream*, for example, had a good stab at getting some mileage out of the play's fleeting interest in India. As Theseus, Harry Burton was a half-piratical, half-respectable Victorian empire-builder, whose militarily imposed marriage to Nicola Redmond's Hippolyta (the most unwilling I have ever seen) obliged her, in an interpolated sequence at the opening, to sign a document giving up custody of a visible Indian boy, so that their reappearance as Oberon and Titania (in Indian silks, squabbling over the same boy) corresponded much more fully than usual to the framing plot. It's true that this reading left Hippolyta so sullen and miserable during *Pyramus and Thisbe* (while Theseus callously enjoyed an after-dinner cigar) that the last act was a lot less joyous than one might have hoped, and the cheerfulness of the lovers – played rather too much as foolish young people in love, instead of people behaving foolishly because young and in love – didn't really compensate. But this was never less than an interesting show with plenty of momentum, and if anything Kavanaugh's Blitz *Much Ado* – right down to Redmond's Burlington Bertie outfit as Beatrice at the masquerade – was even more polished and shrewdly executed throughout.

Along with their contribution to the year's boom in *As You Like It* (of which more shortly), the RSC, too, produced two polished and shrewdly executed comedies this year, an especially shrewd *Taming of the Shrew*, directed by

Lindsay Posner (which opened at the Pit in the autumn, visited the Swan, and then toured to practically everywhere, including Hong Kong), and an especially polished *Comedy of Errors*, directed by Lynne Parker (which opened in the RST in the Spring). Although some critics were distracted by Posner's flirtation with high technology (instead of watching players, a modern-dress Sly accessed his fantasy scenario of Elizabethan male domination off the Internet, the play-within-the-play emerging into three dimensions from a video screen behind the acting area), this was a wonderfully simple and lucid reading of the play, which for once neither exacerbated Petruchio's brutality nor sentimentalized it away. Appallingly, Stuart McQuarrie's jovial, wholly insensitive Petruchio really meant well by what he did to Kate (even by his superbly insulting appearance for their wedding in a dress), and just as appallingly Monica Dolan's initially clear-minded Kate at last loved him for it – or, rather, became emotionally fixated on him like a hostage on her captor. The cast were uniformly alert: Charlotte Randle was a brittle Bianca who at the play's close was beginning to look capable of growing up into Harriet Walter's Lady Macbeth, and Louis Hillyer actually made Tranio funny, largely by sheer bounce. The Induction, it has to be admitted, didn't work very easily – Sly was found outside a contemporary urban nightclub by a Lord who thus appeared to be out fox-hunting in south London at midnight – but the device of having Sly enjoying (and ultimately sharing, since McQuarrie doubled his role with Petruchio) an Elizabethan-dress fantasy but doing so from within the audience's present tense intelligently avoided the problems of both modern and period costuming, deconstructing the opposition between the two. This was neither escapism nor anachronism, but an acute and witty warning for its worryingly laddish times.

The design of Lynne Parker's *The Comedy of Errors* may, by contrast, have been both escapist and anachronistic – a compound of the sets for *Casablanca* and perhaps *The Road to Morocco*, with various incidental allusions to other popular films of the thirties and forties thrown in – but in this case that was clearly the whole idea. We knew from the first couplet of Declan Hughes's newly-written prologue, delivered by Karen Bryson, that the Duke whose wrath she threatened against the owners of un-switched-off mobile telephones would be strictly a comedy Duke, and when Michael Thomas duly arrived as Solinus in a splendid film-noir lift and matching George Raft suit, it was perfectly clear that we were in a mock-cinematic, semi-panto world in which any threats were strictly nominal. Once the second scene had been opened by a First Merchant played as a short-hand stage-Arab of the kind that used to sell dirty postcards in Carry On films – a stage-Arab who would even, later in the show, perform that forgotten music-hall ritual, a sand-dance – we could settle safely into the sheer enjoyment of some very accomplished farce. Never mind the traumas narrated by Egeon: never mind the serious marital sufferings later revealed by Adriana: never mind the deeper harmonies and disharmonies of that extraordinary ending: this was a production which told us very clearly that it wasn't going to be any more three-dimensional than the tourist snapshot of Antipholus of Syracuse and his Dromio so obligingly taken by the merchant in 1.2, wittily reprised as an all-cast group family photograph at the close of 5.1.

At this chosen level, this was a tremendously successful show – not least thanks to the exquisite set-pieces worked out between David Tennant's slick Antipholus of Syracuse and Ian Hughes's slightly Jeeves-like Dromio, forever producing another elegant little repast from his suitcase. Tennant's post-coital back-tracking across the stage on seeing Luciana in the courtyard in 3.2 – visibly deciding he had just enough energy left to attempt her as an encore to her sister upstairs, and accordingly lighting two cigarettes with two lighters as the showband in the gallery struck up a faintly sleazy theme, and passing one to her – was for me one of the best pieces of comic playing this year, and the whole production was full of comparably smooth and inventive pieces of business. Nicholas Khan's psychopathic Cossack of a Second Merchant, for example, trumped Tennant's umbrella-swordstick with his scimitar to initiate a masterly chase sequence which, in the best traditions of Mack Sennett, soon involved most of the company, a pantomime camel, a transvestite nun, and Sirs Walter Blunt and John Falstaff from the Swan next door. The one piece of business which *didn't* fit with the rest of the production came in 4.4, when to some disturbing music and Gothic lighting effects we were presented with not one but five Dr Pinches, all of them in top hats, straggly wigs and grotesquely large false noses: their principal spoke in a German-Jewish accent that was presumably an allusion to Freud. In this visual context the allusion was rather unfortunate, bearing in mind the circumstances of Freud's ultimate flight from Vienna, since these figures resembled nothing so much as anti-Semitic caricatures from Nazi propaganda. I assume they were in fact intended to resemble Dr Caligari – incongruous though the reference would be in a production otherwise securely placed in a U-certificate Hollywood – but whatever was supposed to be going on Dr Pinch was quite spectacularly unfunny.

This incident, together with the abused Pinch's nasty unscripted appearance in 5.1, stood out the more awkwardly because all around it there was nothing but comic pleasure. It's true, perhaps, that Anthony Howell was too transparently nice to make much of Antipholus of Ephesus' furious spiral from irritation to anger to violent panic (and that stage business with his entryphone isn't nearly as funny now as it was on its first appearance in Trevor Nunn's production in 1977), and there wasn't much to Tom Smith's Dromio of Ephesus beyond an inexplicable silly accent: but the laughs were pretty continuous even so. Nothing in this show exactly came to anything, except to yet another gag – at the end, the faithless Antipholus of Ephesus was slapped and instantaneously forgiven by Adriana, and he himself was able just as quickly to shrug off all his own humiliations and be actively pleased rather than devastated to find himself suddenly saddled with parents and a visibly cleverer and luckier twin brother. It was particularly telling that the Dromios celebrated their newly-discovered fraternity less by their potentially humane, moving, egalitarian final couplet than by a tango routine thereafter, to the strains of the Laurel and Hardy theme. But their little exit dance was undeniably the right signing-off for this particular *Comedy of Errors*: faithfully transposed into the idiom of vaudeville, that's what cosmic harmony looks like.

Parker's production, though, attracted considerably less attention than some of the year's other versions of Shakespearian comedy. As far as the national media were concerned, the main event of the year in this field was probably the successful transfer of Trevor Nunn's National production of *The Merchant of Venice* (described in *Survey* 53) from the 400–seat Cottesloe to the 1500–seat Olivier (no mean directorial feat in itself), which it deservedly filled well into the Spring, but, as a number of critics pointed out, 2000 will also be remembered as the Year of *As You Like It*. The play was chosen for BBC radio's broadcast on Shakespeare's birthday (an undistinguished rendering, with Helena Bonham-Carter as Rosalind), and performed independently on stage in Sheffield, in Manchester and in Stratford, and this wasn't one of those unfortunate flukes of the repertory, either: there are some obvious reasons why this particular comedy should have reappeared in force this year. With sheep farming in deep crisis, the relations between the country and the city making regular front-page news, and even the ethics of deer-hunting a topic of national debate, the play suddenly looked more topical than at almost any time since the 1590s, and indeed the political slogan that adorned a hand-painted placard beside the M40 motorway on the way from London to Stratford would make quite a good epigraph to *As You Like It*: it read 'I LOVE MY COUNTRYSIDE, I FEAR MY GOVERNMENT.'

It wasn't surprising, then, that two of the year's three stage revivals opted for a realistic Arden (snowy for the first half's winter wind, sunny for the second's pretty ring time, a convention in part back-formed from *The Winter's Tale* and now almost mandatory), nor that both placed a hard-bitten Corin at its moral centre. In Michael Grandage's excellent Sheffield Theatres touring production (which arrived in London in March), Bernard Horsfall's rural sage easily got the better of Bob Mason's generic Northern cheeky-chappie of a Touchstone in the discussion of court and country in 3.2, and he obligingly took on the role of Hymen to administer the play's conclusion. In Marianne Elliott's production at the Royal Exchange, Joseph Mydell's even sager Corin also dominated the argument with the jester (a vilely selfish and unfunny performance by Jonathan Slinger, apparently convinced, to judge by his gestures and off-line grimaces, that at least seventy per cent of Touchstone's lines were the same hilarious penis joke), and as well as the extension of Corin's role supplied by an appearance as Hymen in 5.4 it was suggested by doubling that the good shepherd was the bad Duke's benign alter ego, a suggestion underlined when at the end of the play Jaques de Boys specifically identified Corin as the 'old religious man' responsible for Frederick's conversion. Liz Ascroft's design for this production reinforced its pro-organic-agriculture slant, making the regimes of Oliver and Frederick look like a sad case of perverse urban oversophistication by marking out their territory with seven twisted little bonsai trees in pots, sorry specimens which were therapeutically replaced by Arden's seven corresponding full-sized real trees. (These descended hydraulically for the start of 2.1, complete with leafy forest floor, like some pastoral flying saucer.) Christopher Oram's Arden for Sheffield Theatres was, equally, a perfectly straightforward representation of an English forest (albeit stylized for touring purposes: three telegraph-pole trunks, supplemented after the interval by a wallpaper-like backdrop of spring foliage). Both of these shows offered Shakespearian comedy as propaganda for the Countryside Alliance, or at very least as an expression of the same bucolic nostalgia that keeps urbanites listening to *The Archers*.

What distinguished these two productions, despite this common general approach, were the wholly different emotional dynamics they were able to find in the text's dialogues between their principals, particularly Rosalind, Orlando and Celia. The drastic changes to the relations both between and among the sexes since *As You Like It* was written can make these relationships something of a pitfall, especially during the Ganymede–Orlando dialogues: these are now mandatorily supplied at some point, for example, with the kiss (and subsequent shock) that has become a rigid convention of cross-dressed love plots in the cinema, but for which Shakespeare's text, taking men's willingness to flirt with boys completely as read, supplies neither any obvious cue nor any supporting discussion. Grandage's production was by far the most riveting here, if only because its casting was so refreshingly unconventional for both Rosalind and Orlando. Victoria Hamilton, such a good Phoebe in Steven Pimlott's RSC version in 1996, was very much at the Viola end of the scale as Rosalind: vulnerable, febrile, dark-haired, small, even birdlike. You could practically see her heart-rate accelerate still further as she clapped excitedly during the wrestling match, and 'Were it not better, / Because that I am more than common tall . . .' had to become a joke, Hamilton standing on tiptoes and then jumping to reach the hand she held up at what ought to have been head height for the line to match the reality. (This gag was nicely recapitulated later when she could barely reach Orlando's poems off the trees.) Ben Daniels, meanwhile, was at the Berowne end of the Orlando range: not only handsome but witty and accomplished (in fact every bit as full of

12   *As You Like It*, Sheffield Theatres, 2000, directed by Michael Grandage, 2.4. An anxious Celia (Samantha Spiro, left) and Rosalind (Victoria Hamilton) arrive in a snowy, realistic Arden.

noble device as his brother concedes), so that in the wooing scenes he seemed, unusually, to have if anything more authority than Hamilton's edgy, slightly hunted Ganymede, to whom Orlando quite deliberately fed cues out of an intelligently watchful curiosity about what his interlocutor's responses might give away. For once there was not just a real physical charge to the love dialogues but genuine suspense. Instead of smugly leading her chosen suitor on when she found him in the forest, Rosalind seemed to become progressively more anxious about the sincerity of his interest (and indeed about his interest in women *per se)*: she was thoroughly shaken by Celia's disparagement of Orlando's feelings in 3.4, delivered 'Say a day, without the ever . . .' in 4.1 with such tragic despair that Orlando had to comfort her, and then fell out with the jealous Celia so seriously after his departure ('And I'll sleep' was meant to sting) that the two had to have a sobbing reconciliation at the start of 4.3. It was Celia's falling for Oliver that enabled a by-now frenetically tense Rosalind to go through with marriage to Orlando rather than the other way around: the less sensitive of the cousins (a quietly spiky Samantha Spiro) was the dominant partner throughout. This was the most convincing attempt to reclaim Rosalind as a female role since Adrian Lester so triumphantly re-

13   *As You Like It*, Royal Exchange Theatre, Manchester, 2000, directed by Marianne Elliott, 1.3. A gentle Celia (Fenella
Woolgar, left) suggests setting out for another snowy, realistic Arden to Rosalind (Claire Price).

hijacked it as a male one for Cheek by Jowl in 1991: the Epilogue – with 'If I were a woman . . .' teasingly and usefully emended to 'If I were among you . . .' – perfectly crystallized the touchingly-defenceless-cum-coy sexiness that Hamilton's engagingly exposed heroine had been developing all night, and it was received with unusual and deserved warmth. In Manchester, Claire Price was having little of this: she was a strong, clear, blonde, altogether more traditional Rosalind (who even wore green doublet and hose as Ganymede, unlike the modern greatcoat in which Hamilton escaped from the court's eighteenth-century dresses), and she took charge of all concerned in Arden, initiating the kiss with Orlando un-usually early. Fenella Woolgar's Celia recognized her cousin's pre-eminence throughout, albeit sometimes wistfully or grudgingly: her agree-ment in 1.2 that Fortune unfairly makes honest

women ill-favouredly expressed both a self-deprecating sense that she was the less pretty of the two and a serene confidence in her own superior virtue, and in the wooing scenes she played a discreet, rueful gooseberry. This was a beautifully judged, gently comic performance, incidentally, the best reminder that Celia can be as good a role as Rosalind since Fiona Shaw vied with Juliet Stevenson in 1985.

The other shining asset of Grandage's *As You Like It*, apart from its simultaneous possession of a workable Arden, an attractive Orlando and a touching Rosalind, was Nicholas Le Prevost, an actor intelligent enough to notice that Jaques, though given some terrific lines and remaining a crucial factor in keeping the play from senti-mentality, isn't half as deep as he thinks he is and can be almost continuously funny as a result. Superbly lugubrious and pretentious, he was incongruously energized by his encounters with Touchstone, and his wordy enthusiasm grew the funnier the more rapidly he tried to speak. In Manchester, though, Peter Nicholas was obscurely surly rather than melancholy, and wasn't funny at all: oddly, after being described as agonizing over a dying deer, he made his first entrance with a dead stag slung over his shoulders, which he dumped on the stage and brooded over throughout 'Under the green-wood tree'. Whether this brooding was supposed to represent remorse, a silent protest against bloodsports or just hunger wasn't clear: it is always possible that this carcase had been bought for a more conventional appearance in 4.2, 'What shall he have that killed the deer?', and that when this scene was cut – nicely replaced by a non-speaking appearance of a lost Oliver, walking unwittingly past the sleeping Celia – the director had decided to use it here instead to justify the expense. These two Northern versions of pastoral both had an enormous amount to recommend them, but Grandage's – with real star quality work from Hamilton, Daniels and Le Prevost – deservedly attracted the stronger reviews, and not only because it came down to the wicked metropolis to get them.

By contrast, Gregory Doran's *As You Like It* in the RST was a critical disaster, an almost parodic display of the pitfalls of RSC main-house designer Shakespeare. The designer in question was Kaffe Fasset, best known for his work in fashion and fabrics, so that while the Sheffield and Royal Exchange casts went to Arden to get in touch with material realities, Doran's discovered only the realities of material. His was a production in which the text struggled for attention throughout against the textiles, to such an extent that Celia's exit line at the end of Act 1 might just as well have been emended by one piece of capitalization and a single extra possessive 's': 'Now go we in content, / To *Liberty's*, and not to banishment.'

You could see what Doran and Fasset were *trying* to do, and it wasn't innately a bad idea, perversely and even insensitively uninterested in

real farming as their approach may have been. The Elizabethan tradition of literary pastoral with which *As You Like It* plays included an important component of the light-heartedly fantastical as well as elements of rural documentary realism, and this play features not only political oppression, cold winds and three townies who buy a holiday cottage with the help of a hired farm-worker, but a palm tree, a lioness, a snake, and a Petrarchan shepherdess who quotes Marlowe. Doran felt he had found a key to this half-realistic, half-emblematic world when he came upon an Elizabethan tapestry in the Victoria and Albert Museum that shows, among other things, a lion and a palm tree, and this was the suggestion which Fasset and his co-designer Niki Turner chose to embroider – to the extent of reproducing the colourful lion-and-palm-tree tapestry as a prop for Rosalind to be sewing wistfully in Duke Frederick's monochromatic court in 1.3. The idea seemed to be that Rosalind, Celia and Touchstone escaped from the black-and-white sampler of the court into the world of this tapestry, and that in this alternative space Rosalind was free to stitch up the play on her own terms. The sense that this Arden might be Rosalind's fantasy was perhaps confirmed by the doubling of the two Dukes, both played by Ian Hogg.

There are some obvious problems with this notion – one of them being that *As You Like It* is one of the few Shakespeare comedies that *doesn't* mention sewing, and another the onto-logical status of all the action from Act 2 onwards, if we're really in some sort of dream sequence from which Rosalind may presumably wake up at some point. But even its most hostile detractors will surely admit that the idea made for some very pretty effects, not least the sartorial ones. It might almost have made more sense had the whole production been billed as an elaborate catwalk show for the co-ordinated knitwear and home fabrics range that was its Arden, with mass-produced copies of Silvius' jersey and Celia's tapestry luggage on sale in the foyer. Those rose-embroidered cushions! That green-tapestry-hills stagecloth! Corin's hat! The Ganymede earth-tones pullover! Celia's sleeves! The flower-embroidered gauze that fell for Hymen's entrance in Act 5! – there was a real visual wit to this design, which it would have been churlish not to enjoy.

Churlish, that is, unless one had been hoping to engage rather more fully with Shakespeare's *As You Like It*. The problem with this production's set and costumes was that though they paid splendid homage to the play's element of tongue-in-cheek whimsy, they seemed to take us to somewhere where only whimsy could flourish. For all the pathological violence exhibited by Duke Frederick – here so visibly and sadistically keen on wrestling that he would probably have done better against Orlando than did Charles – his court was only a stylized, needlepoint sort of court, and we were out of it by Act 2 anyway, and into the land of Jack and the Beanstalk, or Oz, or perhaps of that green astro-turf mound infested by Stratford's most important non-Shakespearian cultural export, the Teletubbies. Choosing a design that highlights the fantastical elements of Arden at the expense of the graphically rustic ones turned out in practice to sabotage much of the play. It may be possible for Orlando and Rosalind to convince you that they have entered a playful realm of fantasy and enchantment even though they are standing on a set that looks like a prosaically real wood, as did Daniels and Hamilton: but on the evidence of Doran's production, it is quite impossible for them to convince you that they are negotiating the crucial issues of adult life if they are standing on a set that appears to belong to the realms of children's television. The trivializing effect of the design was compounded by Django Bates' music, which had its singing miked up as in a TV-celebrity panto and featured jokey percussion effects to match – though Bates's worse moment, apart from the predictably embarrassing 'What shall he have that killed the deer', was perhaps the leadenly facetious woodwind

quotation from the wedding march on Touchstone and Audrey's exit at the end of 3.3, a music cue straight out of cosy TV sitcoms of the 1970s. In both the Northern productions, incidentally, the actors simply accompanied themselves and sang real tunes: it was wonderful to be reminded of what the un-amplified human voice can sound like, an effect the RSC might try one of these days if only for its novelty value.

The central problem with the whole set-up was that this Arden seemed so cushy – quite literally – that merely getting there (especially since scenes were transposed to minimize any alternations back to Frederick's court) already looked like arriving at the happy ending. This production, for example, could find no way, funny or otherwise, to accommodate the scepticism and bitterness of Jaques, who in Declan Conlon's bafflingly diffident performance achieved the surprising feat of well-nigh disappearing altogether. The exquisitely dressed Corin, meanwhile, had clearly never really encountered wool that hadn't already been artfully dyed and woven, so with the supposedly misanthropic Jaques unobtrusively doing good deeds (such as feeding Adam) and the local shepherd's professional claim to our notice rather undermined by his West End clothes, it was very much left to Alexandra Gilbreath's Rosalind to make what sense she could of the central scenes of the play.

Although her husky voice sometimes gave the impression that she would have liked to be able to speak some of her lines more rapidly than she does, Gilbreath was well-cast as Rosalind. She is a naturally endearing actress, and she has a tremendous gift of directness: like her Juliet, her Rosalind – especially compared to Hamilton's – was an earthy, centred young woman who saw instinctively what she wanted in a man and went straight after it. Like the design, though, her performance seemed to get to the ending rather early. The question Gilbreath's Rosalind begged was why such a forthright and confident young woman, so wholly at ease with her own libido, wasted all

14 *As You Like It*, RSC, Royal Shakespeare Theatre, 2000, directed by Gregory Doran, 3.2. A decorative Celia (Nancy Carroll, right) and Rosalind (Alexandra Gilbreath) speak with Corin (Barry McCarthy) in a cushy, overdressed Arden.

that time dressed nominally as a boy after finding Orlando in the forest, especially since she was so quickly satisfied that he was indeed in love with her. After she asked him 'But are you so much in love as your rhymes speak?' in their first interview in 3.2 and he replied 'Neither rhyme nor reason can express how much', she gave a little triumphant concealed leap, clenching both fists and hissing 'yes!' like a schoolboy who has just scored a goal for the first XI, and there didn't really seem to be any reason why she shouldn't reveal her identity and leap on him there and then. Some of the blame for this, though, has to be laid at the door of Anthony Howell's nice-but-dim Orlando, a character who gave the impression that he

wouldn't be able to *spell* 'ambivalently bisexual flirtation', let alone explore it. The only real question mark over this production's unusually misgiving-free final wedding scene – presided over not by Corin but by a merrily rejuvenated Adam as Hymen, and so brainlessly soft-hearted that even William was provided with a partner – came from our speculation that Rosalind might tire of this stooge-like and faintly prudish Orlando, handsome though he was, a good deal sooner than he of her. Say a day, without the ever.

I've dwelt at some length on what was certainly the most lightweight of these three *As You Like It*s because it seemed to encapsulate what have become characteristic failings of

273

main-house Shakespearian comedy (as the RSC seem to have recognized, sending it to the Pit – and thus almost complete re-direction and liberation from its set – rather than to the Barbican main stage for its London transfer). It belonged to a distinctive genre of middlebrow Shakespeare which one hoped the RSC would have renounced forever after the experience of Adrian Noble's toytown *Twelfth Night* in 1998. The design was pleasant to look at, and made an intelligible general statement about the play, but in practice it almost robbed the actual scenes and words of all content. The text scrolled audibly by, but what occupied the foreground was not the story or the characters or the ideas but a largely predictable repertoire of sitcom sight-gags and extraneous pieces of comic business. For me the aptest image of this production was of Adrian Schiller's Touchstone, when, punched in the face by Duke Frederick after having the nerve to satirize the sport of wrestling by beating himself up just before the Charles versus Orlando bout, he signified his understanding of this piece of censorship by gagging himself with a large white hanky. That was this show all over: comedy rendered dumb by having textiles rammed down its throat.

HISTORIES

It's nice to be able to turn in conclusion from a case-study in what the RSC does worst to a magnificent, large-scale demonstration of what they do best, the first instalment of 'This England'. It will be instructive, when the whole enterprise has been completed by Michael Boyd's complete rendering of the *Henry VI* plays and *Richard III*, to compare the choices made by this particular *Ring*-cycle treatment of the histories with some of its predecessors, Adrian Noble's *The Plantagenets*, the Bogdanov-Pennington ESC *Wars of the Roses* of the late 1980s, and of course the Barton-Hall *Wars of the Roses* of 1964 (chosen to mark another religious anniversary, Shakespeare's 400th birthday). What is immediately obvious is that both 'This

England' and indeed 'Royal Shakespeare Company' seem to imply a unitary, overall vision which this cycle, unlike any of its precedents, has deliberately eschewed, casting consistently across the series but using different directors in different spaces: Stephen Pimlott in the Other Place with *Richard II*, Michael Attenborough in the Swan with *Henry IV*, Edward Hall in the main house with *Henry V*. The questions immediately raised by the entire venture are at once whether Noble's devolved RSC still has (or wants) a corporate identity, and, by analogy, whether a similar pluralism in the public sphere is compatible with the continuing existence of the nation state. This England? Which one?

Pimlott's *Richard II* offered an altogether surprising opening to the sequence by keeping us carefully alienated from any received ideas of England at all: Alfred Burke's rapid, wheelchair-bound delivery of 'This royal throne of kings . . .' didn't wallow in patriotism but merely outlined a reactionary political position, and the speech was far less central to the play than was Richard's prison soliloquy, 'I have been studying how I may compare / This prison where I live unto the world . . .' At the production's very opening, while the rest of the cast awaited in semi-darkness, Samuel West's Richard spoke the opening lines of this speech from the edge of the acting area, before appearing to make an existential effort of will to initiate the action by donning his crown and mounting his minimalist throne (on which the lights came up, apparently in response to his return to the play's customary first line). This was, remarkably, a post-Beckett reading of *Richard II*, interested in role-playing and repetition but without a trace of the sentimentality that sometimes accompanies the king-as-tragic-actor reading of the play. No visible afterlife awaited this Richard, shot with a silenced pistol, helped into his coffin by the previously sympathetic groom and then shot again, while on earth his supplanter was doomed to the re-enactment of his predecessor's kingly miseries –

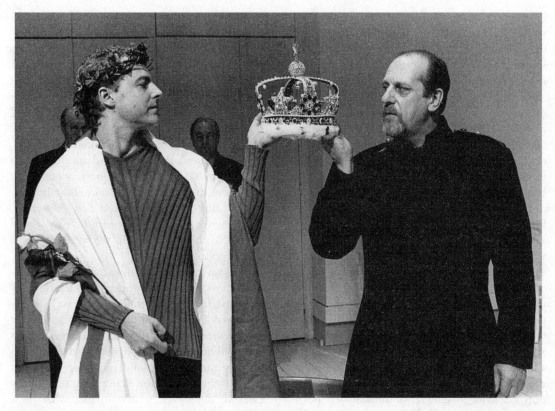

15 *Richard II*, The Other Place, 2000, directed by Steven Pimlott, 4.1. The deposition scene: draped in an English flag, Samuel West's immature Richard confronts David Troughton's mature Bolingbroke.

a point perhaps needlessly underlined by Bolingbroke's concluding repetition of those opening lines from Richard's prison soliloquy. By then we had already heard those lines spoken not only as Richard's prologue but by Isobel, so fatally inseparable from her role as Queen that she had a crown woven as part of her expensive coiffure; and we had of course heard them spoken in full by the imprisoned Richard. So by the end of Act 5 we ought surely to have got the point already: the effect of the repetition was slightly akin to reading an otherwise spotless copy of the play in which a zealous student has highlighted this speech with a marker pen and written 'Important Theme' in the margin.

This was, it has to be admitted, a slightly academic production, clever almost to the point of being clever-clever, conducted in a glaring white Other Place which, with cast and audience usually under the same pitiless neon light, sometimes resembled an examination room in which the actors constantly checked that our attention wasn't wavering from their meticulous close-reading of the text. With its introductory tape-loop collage of stylized national noise – coronation crowds, military bands, indistinct conservative oratory – and its endlessly recombined montage of symbolic objects (a mound of soil, the single gold-painted chair among its white fellows which was the throne, the plain wooden box that served as dais, as container for the fasces-like axes of the judicial combat, as prison cell, as coffin and, less plausibly, as mirror) – the space also resembled an installation gallery in the new Tate Modern, a resemblance heightened by the modish purple suits worn by Richard's trendy young favourites. All in all, this production took about the most counter-intuitive approach one could imagine to a play more usually treated, as at the Gainsborough, as a piece of High Church sacrificial ritual. Instead of playing for nostalgic pathos in a fog of incense and medieval heraldry, Pimlott took the first instalment of the RSC's millennial attempt on both tetralogies of histories as the occasion for a fastidiously post-modern rediscovery of Brecht.

The results, surprisingly, were compelling. Pimlott's approach – which it would be a mistake just to label 'modern dress', since that would imply a simple transposing of the play's events into an illusionistic present-day setting – dramatically opened up *Richard II* to the present moment, and opened the present moment up to the play. The actors scrupulously and vividly told the story, but they did so in what was avowedly the same real time as that of the audience, their frame of reference drawn from contemporary life, so that without the production specifying a facile set of topical correspondences we were nonetheless constantly being asked to think about the play's potential resonances with our own context. At times we were in a blank-verse focus group meeting about the future of the monarchy, at times an inquest into the presentational style of New Labour or the current status of English national identity, but we were always very much in the moment, and always very much committed to finding out where the actors and the play would take the discussion next. With no dramatic illusion to break, Pimlott's production was free to be unusually inventive. A ceremonially dressed Marshal, for example, very much in the style of today's Black Rod at the state opening of the House of Lords, carried a faded typescript on a clipboard, from which the King had to read the formal instigation of the trial-by-combat. Bushy carried a designer version of a red Crown brief-case as he fled Richard's crumbling regime. The defeated King himself sought to invoke a

tabloid nationalism on his side in the deposition scene, impishly whistling 'God Save the King' on his way onto the stage with his shoulders draped under an English flag in the manner of a Euro 2000 hooligan. Not all of these incidental touches were equally successful – Adam Levy's SAS outfit made the point about the young Hotspur as an obedient action-man well enough, for instance, but his ludicrous drilling rather laboured the point, and one dreads to think what Major Anthony Quayle would have said about his incongruously unmilitary haircut. But Pimlott certainly proved that *Richard II*, which never was exactly a realistic play, could more than hold its own in the year 2000 as a play of political ideas.

This isn't to say that this show wasn't interested in its characters, properly and intelligently alienated from them though its actors usually remained. Brecht, after all, learned most of what he knew about the interactions between ideas and individuals within historical drama from Shakespeare anyway, and much of the point about Bolingbroke, for example, is that in any case we can never be certain that what he is saying at any given moment isn't purely tactical. Although David Troughton betrayed some personal anger in his condemnation of Bushy and Green – frighteningly, by executing Green himself onstage with a silenced revolver – the main effect of his characteristically lucid and deliberate performance was of a self gradually erased by the requirements of power. Unusually, he belonged to an older generation than did Richard – he was visibly the representative of an old guard paradoxically forced into revolutionary action in the name of conservatism – and the cumbrous state crown which Richard forced uncomfortably onto his head in the deposition scene (a far cry from Richard's own earlier fashion-accessory circlet) was already killing him. By the time Bolingbroke dismissed Richard at the close of the scene, delivering 'Go, some of you, convey him to the Tower' as a tyrannously unfunny punch-line, he was becoming the sort of hollowed-out, joyless Mr

Punch that Troughton earlier found in Richard III, a figure who would be left as alone as was Richard at the play's conclusion by the surprising departure, one by one, of his discontented court. The most striking moment in Troughton's performance, however, came just before Richard's entrance in 4.1, when instead of playing his reaction to the news of Mowbray's death as genuine surprise (and dismay that he could not now subject his old adversary to a self-exculpatory show-trial), he treated the incident as a pre-rehearsed publicity stunt. In this, moreover, the audience were forced to become complicit by Troughton's insistence that we should stand up and say 'Amen' to his little prayer for Mowbray's soul. It made a perfect, arresting extrapolation from the analogies Shakespeare draws throughout this play between political and theatrical power.

Samuel West, meanwhile, lifted his own acting to a new plane as Richard, growing up as if overnight into a worthy theatrical antagonist for the veteran Troughton. Before the production I was apprehensive that with the title role of this play in the hands of an actor who has hitherto specialized in providing instant gravitas on voice-overs for television documentaries we might be in for an evening of merely watching Richard listening to himself, but in the event it was Ralph Fiennes who gave that performance as Richard II in 2000, and West offered something altogether more detailed and more interesting. He made a wonderfully dislikeable, spoiled not-especially-pretty-boy in the early scenes, whizzing about in John of Gaunt's wheelchair seconds after it had been vacated by his death, and a surprisingly witty and cunning player of a losing game thereafter, so that when he did take an opportunity to play for uninterrupted lyricism – dragging the wooden box onto the stage at the opening of 5.5 like Christ bearing the cross, and standing motionless in it to deliver the prison soliloquy with spellbinding intensity – the effect was surprising as well as moving (even though by now the audience knew these lines almost as well as he did). It's a

great pity that this was the only role West played this season, but he certainly chose the right production to star in, a show which was deservedly one of the most talked-about of the year.

In a way there is much less to say about Michael Attenborough's rendering of the two parts of *Henry IV* in the Swan, which were self-evidently wonderful in a much more familiar manner. If anything, the success of Pimlott's alienation effects with *Richard II* left one feeling slightly ungrateful for some of this production's very virtues, especially the authority with which it created an integrated visual and acoustic style for the two plays. Kandis Cook's costumes were unobtrusively apt and telling, the restriction of the acting area by the introduction of a raked ramp half-way back provided admirable focus, the hollow door-slamming sound effect between scenes was suitably powerful, and Tim Mitchell's lighting design, in particular, was conspicuously impressive. The moment at which the ramp had suddenly sprouted sharpened stakes which pierced the morning mist before the battle of Shrewsbury was exquisitely done, the subtle fading-in of greens for the Gloucestershire scenes beautiful, and the device of distinguishing the palace, despite the rugged texture of the stage surface, by means of a geometrical pattern of orange underfloor lighting which made the throne appear to be suspended precariously above Hell, was highly effective. It was also very well-keyed to the rest of the production, since this was a *Henry IV* which opened, to the strains of plainsong, with a Boris-Godunov-like, crucifix-clutching Henry on his knees, his robed attendants at first resembling priests rather than courtiers: the coincidental kinship between this production and Caird's *Hamlet* was remarkable, fascinating evidence that at the dawn of the third millennium the religious dimensions of Shakespeare's work are being resurrected in the theatre no less than in criticism. But the very consistency and depth with which the plays' world had been imagined and displayed risked making this pro-

16 *Henry IV part 2*, Swan Theatre, 2000, directed by Michael Attenborough, 2.4. 'Why, thou glove of sinful continents, what a life doest thou lead!' Hal (William Houston, right) and Poins (Robert Portal) abandon their disguise as drawers to confront Falstaff (Desmond Barrit).

duction feel hermetically sealed: back in an unusually dark Swan auditorium after the dazzling interpretative rigours of the Other Place, one could feel rather left out of this show, inclined to wonder how this England of penitence and armour was supposed to connect with our own. It is easy, for example, to imagine some dreadfully crass ways in which the contemporary relevance of the conspirators' division of the map of England and Wales in 3.1 might have been underlined, but it ought surely to have achieved more of a *frisson* in these devolutionary times than it did here.

One would have had to be feeling very ungrateful indeed, however, to complain about

any of the acting in these two plays, or indeed about their compelling narrative and thematic momentum. It's true that Adam Levy made a curious Hotspur, costumed principally in a flowing, silky, full-length silver coat which made him look more like a sensitive art student than a chivalric warrior: when he crawled petulantly about the stage haranguing the crumpled and discarded letter he had received from an unwilling potential fellow-rebel in 2.4 one began to wonder whether he had lost the plot entirely. His subsequent interview with Nancy Carroll's forcefully unhappy Kate, though, suggested a Hotspur who for once fully understood the gravity of his undertaking, one who was reluctantly excluding a beloved partner rather than merely shutting out a girl from a boys' game. You never felt, however, that this neurotic, driven, vulnerable youth stood much of a chance against William Houston's muscular Hal, not least because Houston has such a purposeful, square-browed, opaque face that he almost gave the impression that he was already wearing a helmet even before he donned his armour for the battle. Houston was about as well-cast as any actor could be as Hal, equipped as he is with one of the most unreadable smiles on the English stage. From one moment to the next, you were never sure whether it was registering a perfectly sincere and unaffected goodwill or the most profound cynicism, always wondering whether this was a Hal whose plans to reform on inheriting the crown were merely a rationalization for continuing to enjoy the company of his friends, or one who had only cultivated them at all in the long-term pursuit of a selfish public relations coup. All Hal's interviews with Troughton's King Henry made fascinating theatre because we never finally knew when either was genuinely moved and when either was merely playing for emotional advantage. Even the King's unseen would-be embrace from behind in 3.2 (an aborted reprise of the posture pleadingly adopted by Falstaff on 'Banish not him thy Harry's company' two scenes earlier), a gesture which Troughton converted into a constrained bluff punch on the shoulder, was under suspicion, and such intimacy as father and son ever shared was wonderfully undercut when they finally did manage to embrace only on the battlefield, wearing armour which practically kept them at arm's length. It was extremely poignant that in Part 2 the dying King Henry was finally cradled on Hal's knees, just like the dying Hotspur before him: Hal's last surrender to his father's last piece of advice looked suspiciously like another victory, as politic and premeditated as his subsequent surrender to the authority of the Lord Chief Justice.

Falstaff never stood a chance either, and in this production he knew it all along. Although his first appearance, in an uncharacteristic moment of symbolism between 1.1 and 1.2, found him entering upwards from the earth below the departing King's feet, as if struggling out of a narrow chimney, there was far less of the Father Christmas about Desmond Barrit's Sir John than one usually expects in *Henry IV Part 1*. From 1.2 onwards this was clearly a fat old loser prepared endlessly to humiliate himself in order to keep Hal's attention, someone whose jokes, funny as they could be, were always heavily tinged with self-contempt. He knew very well that Hal would ultimately banish him even before Houston ventriloquized his father's voice on 'I do, I will', but he just about kept up the fiction of his irresistible appeal to the Prince, as if determined to grind his own nose in his actual expendability. In another crafty piece of recapitulation, his kneeling to be rejected by the newly crowned Henry V repeated both Henry IV's unavailing penitence at the very opening of Part 1 and the at first comic but ultimately fatal surrender of Sir John Coleville, another dupe to be rounded up by Dickon Tyrrell's splendidly cold and puritanical Prince John. This was another striking example of an actor producing a performance that revealed whole hitherto undiscovered registers: no camp or sentimental *opera buffa* caricature, Barrit's Falstaff was a beautifully observed performance through both parts of the play – right down to the horribly realistic facial sores he wore as evidence of his diseases in Part 2 – and probably about three times sadder than Barrit realized it was.

If anything detracted from this production's success at all, it was the relentless energy and emphasis with which Attenborough drove these two plays onwards, which sometimes had the actors playing as loudly and unconfidingly as if they were already in the much larger Barbican main house to which they would transfer, and which had occasionally induced Attenborough to sacrifice texture to sheer speed. Some of the cutting in the comic scenes seemed misguided:

for example, Falstaff's recollection of the young Shallow, 'When a was naked, a was for all the world like a forked radish with a head fantastically carved upon it with a knife' (3.2.306–8) has a wonderful punctilious specificity, and a suggestion of elaborate pointlessness, which is quite lost if the line dwindles to 'When a was naked, a was for all the world like a forked radish.' Similarly, there's a big difference between making Hal laugh 'till his face be like a wet cloak ill laid up' (5.1.76–7) and making him laugh 'till his face be like a wet cloak': once you've taken away the idea of creases, you may as well take away the cloak too, and just have him laugh 'till his face be wet', which isn't in itself either striking or funny. The comedy of Shallow's household, too, is seriously diminished if the servant Davy isn't a bully who can nag the justice into giving his verdict in favour of the guilty William Visor on the thematically resonant grounds that 'a knave should have some countenance at his friend's request' (5.1.37–8), so that the household models a possible future for a Henry V who doesn't dismiss Falstaff. It is even more diminished if all the Gloucestershire scenes pass at such a cracking pace that we never have a chance to savour the exquisite boredom of country life. It was perhaps the most telling symptom of this production's slight excess of energetic purpose that in the orchard scene, 5.3, Justice Silence, instead of faintly punctuating the endless pauses in a slow, inane conversation which is going nowhere by dimly remembering fragments of ancient folk songs, almost cut off his cues by leaping frenetically to his feet and delivering them as rapid and vigorous song-and-dance routines. It was quite funny the first time, but it ruined half the point of the scene, which could have afforded to be at least twice as long as it was here.

Edward Hall's patchier *Henry V* in the RST, with both Pimlott's and Attenborough's very hard acts to follow, was inclined to look like an unsuccessful attempt to emulate both at once, an uneasy combination of modern dress with

spectacle. The programme was undeniably a cracking read, one of the best swift introductions I've seen to the current crisis in British national identity (the immediate context for the whole of 'This England'), but the show itself, though endlessly inventive and energetic, never matched its coherence. The cast were clearly having a terrific time – they had spent a day training with the Army as part of the rehearsal process, and were already on stage eagerly pretending to be soldiers while the audience arrived (a militarized version of Terry Hands's on-stage warming-up exercises back in 1975), so that this became a show staged by a small army as much as a show about one. This conspicuously-advertised *esprit de corps* dictated treating the Chorus's speeches collaboratively, actors taking it in turns to speak one or two lines each, the most spectacular elaborations of this technique coming before Harfleur (when the company mimed arriving in France from a landing craft) and before Agincourt (when each actor would light his or her face with a torch while speaking, then shine the torch as a spotlight onto the next performer to speak). Some of this worked, but there was an aura of drama-school or rehearsal-room collective self-congratulation about it all, as if the company were more eager to demonstrate Teamwork than to tell a story about a particular historical instance of it.

This endeavour wasn't always helped, either, by Hall's sometimes drastic cutting and pasting of Shakespeare's text. He ran together both Eastcheap scenes, for example, so that Mistress Quickly (in the midst of what here was her own wedding reception) had no sooner attempted to summon Pistol and his gang to Falstaff's bedside than she was narrating his death, and he postponed Katherine's English lesson until the night before Agincourt, where, with the army still on stage, it appeared to become an erotic revue turn performed, Marlene Dietrich-like, to maintain the troops' morale. There was a worrying inconsistency, too, about some of the conventions by which Hall translated the play

17   *Henry V*, RSC, Royal Shakespeare Theatre, 2000, directed by Edward Hall, 3.1. Henry (William Houston, centre) inspires his army to attack Harfleur.

into modern terms. The text was supplemented, for example, by a newly commissioned nationalistic pop song by Billy Bragg (its lyrics largely made up of unacknowledged quotations from Garrick's 'Heart of Oak'), which was performed by a post-punk band at the pub in Eastcheap (with the ever-showy Adrian Schiller, later a disappointingly monotonous sergeant-majorish Fluellen, on rhythm guitar): but since there is as yet no such real-life genre as the patriotic punk anthem (and long may God preserve us from it) the effect was distinctly puzzling, as incongruous in the present as in the world of the play. Much more serious, though, were discrepancies in the production's treatment of combat. The siege of Harfleur was fought mainly using the weapons of the Second World War (and a gamely impressive spectacle it made, complete with artillery barrage and a terrific assault on the

RST's circle using steel ladders), but both sides had mysteriously renounced the use of firearms by the time we got to Agincourt, and wouldn't even strike one another, carrying only cudgels with which they belaboured large punch-bags hung at the sides of the stage (as if participating in some corporate assertiveness-training exercise) while their adversaries, though thus deserted, had to pretend to be getting thumped. What really sabotaged Agincourt, though, was the fact that Hall had neatly inverted the glaring disparity between the numbers on each side. Whatever the script may say, in this production the English outnumbered the French by about ten to one (and, since they remained on stage during the French officers' dialogue, they appeared to have them encircled as well), and with the French equipped only with riot shields and truncheons this left the battle looking like a sorry, predictable massacre rather than the miraculous survival of the underdog. The fact that in the play's last scene the Dauphin didn't so much as blink when his father finally agreed to sign a treaty disinheriting him in Henry's favour only confirmed a sense that Hall had been too interested in thematic resonance and onstage vigour even to notice what was at stake at the level of sheer story.

Despite this complete fracture of the play's narrative mainspring, however, there were still many things to enjoy about this production, which aptly completed some of the trajectories initiated elsewhere in the sequence. The casting of the same actress to play Princess Katherine as had earlier played Richard II's Queen Isobel, for example, was a nice touch, the queen banished back to France as part of Richard's punishment ultimately brought back thence as the culmination of the usurping dynasty's quest for legitimacy (even if in the event Catherine Walker's French wasn't noticeably better than Henry's). What this production was best at, however, was conveying a sense of Henry's isolation: 'Upon the king . . .' was very much its keynote, rather than 'This day is called the feast of Crispian . . .' Without his father or Falstaff even to feign intimacy with, Houston's king seemed desolately solitary throughout – Hall's blocking nicely pointed out how often he enters scenes alone, never quite joining the group of colleagues who are already present, and the business with Williams and the glove was for once rather pitiful instead of just callous, a sad attempt by Henry to make people look as though they were really engaged in a game with him. The culmination of all this was a lovely, strangely affecting moment at the very end of the production, when, as the Chorus's final speech referred to Henry's untimely death, he simply walked quietly out of the group-photo in which he was posed with his future queen and left the stage via the auditorium. This was where Hal's remoteness had been going all along: from the half-entered familiarity of the tavern to his coldly single manipulations of the court to the isolation of the military commander, and thence, via a briefly simulated courtship that was really a clause in a diplomatic treaty, to an unseen grave.

'Henry the Sixth, in infant bands crowned king / Of France and England, did this king succeed', and so 'This England' continues, with four whole plays yet to go, and no shortage of ideas from the other tetralogy for them to take up and develop. It is perhaps the greatest tribute I can make to the cycle to date that this prospect leaves me, after this first year of intensive Shakespearian theatregoing on the *Survey*'s behalf, at least as keen to see more as I was at its beginning.

PROFESSIONAL SHAKESPEARE PRODUCTIONS IN THE BRITISH ISLES JANUARY–DECEMBER 1999

NIKY RATHBONE

Most of the productions listed are by professional or semi-professional companies. Productions originating in 1998 or earlier have only been included if there is new information. Details are mainly taken from newspaper reviews held in the Birmingham Shakespeare Library. Many of the companies listed were involved in small-scale tours; where neither reviews nor listings mark these as professional they are starred. I have also included the principal annual Shakespeare festivals where, it is worth noting, the audience, as at the Globe, often seems younger and more culturally diverse than those at conventional theatre productions.

ANTONY AND CLEOPATRA

The ESC, tour continued. See *Shakespeare Survey 53*. The production toured in the UK and to the Perth Theatre Festival, Australia.

The RSC at the RST, Stratford: June 1999
Director: Steven Pimlott
Designer: Yolanda Sonnabend
Music: Jason Carr
Antony: Alan Howard
Cleopatra: Frances de la Tour
On transfer to the Barbican the controversial opening – Antony's head between Cleopatra's thighs – was omitted.

Shakespeare's Globe, London: July 1999
Master of Play and Verse: Marian Spon
Master of Clothing and Properties: Jenny Tiramani

Master of Music: Claire van Kampen
Antony: Paul Shelley
Cleopatra: Mark Rylance
All male cast. Mark Rylance received excellent notices.

A and BC Theatre Company, tour: August 1999

AS YOU LIKE IT

Robert J. Williamson Productions, Leeds Shakespeare Festival, Halifax Shakespeare Festival and tour of open-air venues, with *Hamlet:* June 1999

Rainbow Theatre Company, Worthing, tour with *Romeo and Juliet:* July 1999
Director: Nicolas Young

Bold and Saucy Theatre Company, Milton Keynes, tour with *Macbeth*: July 1999

OpenHand in Cambridge college gardens for the Cambridge Shakespeare Festival: August 1999

THE COMEDY OF ERRORS

The White Company, Shakespeare's Globe, London: May 1999
Master of the Play: Kathryn Hunter
Master of Design: Liz Cooke
Master of Music: Mia Soteriou
The Dromios: Marcello Magni
The Antipholuses: Vincenzo Nicoli

Mad Dogs and Englishmen Theatre Company, Colchester, tour of open-air venues: June 1999

Rain or Shine Theatre Company, Gloucester, tour of open-air venues: June 1999

The Rude Mechanicals Theatre Company, tour: July 1999
Director: Peter Talbot
Touring with a restored 1920s showman's wagon.

Monkey Theatre Company, Horsham, Hawth Studio Theatre, Crawley: August 1999
Set in the seventies.

CYMBELINE

The Original Shakespeare Company at Shakespeare's Globe, London:
6 September 1999
Director: Patrick Tucker
Experimental production, played unrehearsed, as part of the Globe Roman Plays season.

HAMLET

The Theatre Royal, Plymouth and Young Vic, London: February 1999
Director: Laurence Boswell
Designer: Es Devlin
Hamlet: Paul Rhys
Claudius/Ghost: Donald Sumpter
The production also toured to Japan. Costumed in an indeterminate period and set on a platform with the audience seated on two sides. Unusually, Gertrude clearly indicated that she was aware the goblet held poison.

Theatre Unlimited, Greenwich Theatre, London: March 1999
Director: Christopher Geelan
Designer: Bridget Kimak
Hamlet: Rupert Wickham
Set in the sixties.

New World Theatre Company, Kent, tour: April 1999
Directors: Paul James and Matthew Perkins

Black Box Theatre Company at the Unity Theatre, Liverpool: June 1999
Director: Ian Karl Moore
Designers: Brian Yarwood and Tom Moore
Music: Paul Skinner
Modern dress, though the Ghost was traditional.

The R. J. Williamson Company, Leeds, tour with *As You Like It:* June 1999
The Ghost was played in recorded voice-over by Richard Briers.

Broken Dream Theatre Company at the Union Theatre, London Fringe: July 1999
Director: Gavin Armstrong
Two actors played the Hamlet soliloquies as a debate, one taciturn and watchful, one impulsive.
Thirties Fascist costuming.

Bristol Old Vic: November 1999
Director: Gemma Bodinetz
Designer: Laura Hopkins
Hamlet: Colin Tierney
Set just before World War I. The Ghost reappeared at the end of the play to be rejoined by the dead Hamlet.

Adaptations

Fat Hamlet
Urban Dance, Kent at the Studio Theatre, Beckenham: February 1999
A dance version of *Fat Hamlet* in which an overweight, unemployed loner is mysteriously visited by a sly guardian angel.

Fat Hamlet by Andrew Buckley
Loitering with Intent Theatre Company, the Studio Theatre, Beckenham: February 1999

Hamlet: The Actors' Quarto
Third Party Productions, UK tour: February 1999
Director: John Wright
Hamlet: Matthew Steer
Seven actors playing a very cut text, set in the

thirties, and played to emphasize the comic elements.

Hamlet Project
Greenwich Theatre, London: March 1999
Twenty-eight community groups under the supervision of experienced theatre practitioners explored the themes of *Hamlet*. The project was launched in November 1998 with performances in 1999.

Hamlet
Meno Fortas, Lithuania, at the Bath Shakespeare Festival: August 1999
Director: Eimuntas Nekrosius
Hamlet: Andrus Mamontovas
Music: Verdi: La forza del destino
The theme of this adaptation was the sacrifice by fathers of their children.

Hamlet: First Cut
Red Shift, tour: August 1999
Director: Jonathan Holloway
Designer: Neil Irish
Hamlet: Peter Collins
A rare performance of the First Quarto text, set in a post-industrial wasteland constructed from metal boxes, with the Ghost represented by a war memorial group of soldiers.

There is Nothing like a Dane
Clive Francis one-man show at the Bath Shakespeare Festival: August 1999

The Prince of West End Avenue
Edinburgh Fringe Festival and tour: August 1999
Kerry Shale solo show set in a Manhattan Jewish retirement home where Otto Korner rehearses the role of Hamlet.

Hamlet – The Tragedy of Denmark
Wimbledon Studio Theatre: November 1999
A one-man adaptation by the Norwegian actor Terj Tweit emphasising Hamlet's spiritual journey and the poetic language of the play.

Hamlet
The English Shakespeare Company, tour: November 1999

Director: Malachi Bogdanov
An eighty-minute adaptation.

Also of Interest

A Hamlet of the Suburbs
Buenos Aires: September 1999
Director: Alberto Felix
Performed at the International Conference and set in a Buenos Aires suburb. The principal theme was state corruption.

HENRY IV PART I

Doncaster Repertory Company at Doncaster Civic Theatre: November 1999
Director: Stan Norris

HENRY V

Stagecraft* at the Old Fire Station, Oxford: March 1999
A very physical all-male production.

Adaptation

Oddsocks, tour: June 1999
A cast of seven in a comic production.

Also of Interest

Henry V
The Avignon Theatre Festival, France: July 1999
Translator: Jean-Michel Desprats
Director: Jean-Louis Benoit
Billed as the first professional French-language production in France.

JULIUS CAESAR

Inmates of Bullingdon Prison: April 1999
Director: Stephen Langridge
Forty actors were involved in this production for which the inmates also wrote the music. Stephen Langridge is a professional actor.

Shakespeare's Globe, London: May 1999
Master of Play: Mark Rylance
Master of Clothing and Properties: Jenny Tiramani
Brutus: Danny Sapani
Antony: Mark Lewis Jones
Octavius/Portia: Toby Cockerell
An all-male production.

PinPoint Productions, Eastwood Theatre, Southend: summer 1999

Adaptations

Making the Nation
TAG, Glasgow: May 1999–2002
Director: James Brining
A three-year project concerning democracy for Scottish children aged seven to seventeen with workshops and debates, eventually intended to lead to a production. The students are also working on *Antigone* and *King Matt*, a Polish story.

Giulio Cesare
Societas Raffaello Sanzio at the Queen Elizabeth Hall, London: June 1999
Director: Romeo Castellucci
An examination of the power of rhetoric, the nature of friendship and the barbarism of civil war. Also performed at the Dublin Theatre Festival, 1998.

KING JOHN

The Life and Death of King John
Stamford Shakespeare Company, Rutland Open Air Theatre, Tolethorpe Hall: June 1999
This amateur company produces Shakespeare annually to a high standard.

KING LEAR

Theatre Babel, The Old Fruit Market, Glasgow and Royal Lyceum, Edinburgh: June 1999
Director/Edmund: Graham McLaren
Lear: Peter De Souza

The production emphasized the political division of the kingdom, and drew parallels with the unity of Scotland and England under James I.

Northern Broadsides, Halifax, Bath Shakespeare Festival and tour: August 1999
Director/Lear: Barrie Rutter

Manchester Royal Exchange: September 1999
Director: Gregory Hersov
Designer: David Short
Lear: Tom Courtenay
A fast-paced, subtly humorous production which concentrated on fear of madness and suffering rather than political power. A revival of the 1998 production.

The RSC in association with Thelma Holt Productions at the Barbican Theatre, London, RST, Stratford and Tokyo, Japan: October 1999
Director: Yukio Ninagawa
Designer: Yukio Horio
Music: Ryudo Uzaki
Lear: Nigel Hawthorne
Fool: Hiroyuki Sanada
First performance: Saitana Arts Theatre, Japan: September 1999.

Adaptations

The Yiddish Queen Lear by Julia Pascal
Southwark Playhouse, London: May 1999
The adaptation concerns a Russian Jewish actress who sets up a Yiddish theatre in New York and is deposed by her daughters.

King Lear
The Orange Tree Theatre, Richmond: June 1999
Director: Dominic Hill
An adaptation for schools devised by Sarah Gordon.

Kathakali King Lear
Shakespeare's Globe, London: July 1999
Presented by the Annette Leday/Keli Company

in association with the International Globe Theatre.
Adaptor: David McRuvie
Translator: K. Marumakan Raja
Directors: Annette Leday and David McRuvie
King Lear adapted to traditional Indian Kathakali dance and performed in the Malayalam language.

LOVE'S LABOUR'S LOST

Instant Classics★ at the Etcetera Theatre, the Oxford Arms, Camden Town, London: January 1999
Director: David Cottis
A ninety-minute adaptation set in the twenties.

MACBETH

Traffic of the Stage, tour: January 1999
Director: Harry Meacher
Set in the early nineteenth century and using atmospheric red lighting.

Asylum Theatre Company at the Riverside Studios, Richmond and tour with *Othello*: February 1999
Director: Nigel Roper
Performed as gang warfare in Forties Glasgow with the witches played as bag ladies.

Ran Theatre of Cultures★, Peterborough, tour: February 1999
Played in the round and influenced by Russian and Roumanian theatre.

The Queen's Theatre, London and Theatre Royal, Bath: March and June 1999
Presented by Thelma Holt Productions and Karl Sydow
Director: John Crowley
Designer: Jeremy Herbert
Lighting: Mick Fisher
Macbeth: Rufus Sewell
Lady Macbeth: Sally Dexter
The production used red lighting, deep shadows, silhouettes and distorting mirrors. Lady Macbeth was presented as older than her husband, and the ghost of Banquo was not visible. The banqueting table descended to cover his corpse.

Forest Forge Theatre Company, Ringwood, tour of southern England: March 1999
Director: Kevin Shaw
Designer: David Haworth

Nottingham Playhouse and Education Arts Plus, tour in the Nottingham area: May 1999
Director: Jeremy Stroughair

The Cymru Studio Theatre, Theatr Clwyd, Mold, Wales: September 1999
Director: Terry Hands
Designer: Timothy O'Brien
Macbeth: Owen Teale
Lady Macbeth: Vivien Parry
Played with no interval and the audience around three sides of a black set.
Teale descended from bullied husband to murderous madman.

The Royal Lyceum Theatre, Edinburgh: October 1999
Director: Kenny Ireland
Designer: Hayden Griffin
Macbeth: Tom McGovern
Lady Macbeth: Jennifer Black
The fate of Scotland was central to this production.

The Courtyard Theatre at West Yorkshire Playhouse, Leeds: October 1999
Director: Jude Kelly
Designer: Mario Borza
Macbeth: Patrick O'Kane
Lady Macbeth: Meier McKinley
Played as a political thriller set in Eastern Europe. Borza is a water sculptor, and the design incorporated extensive water effects.

The RSC at the Swan Theatre, Stratford, Bath Shakespeare Festival, Brighton and London: November 1999, USA 2000.
Director: Gregory Doran

Designer: Stephen Brimson Lewis
Music: Adrian Lee
Macbeth: Antony Sher
Lady Macbeth: Harriet Walter
Played with no interval. An outstanding production.

Adaptations

Macbeth
The ESC, tour with *Romeo and Juliet:* January 1999
Director: Robert Soulsby-Smith
A schools version adapted for five actors which incorporated a re-creation of the rehearsal process.

Thirteenth Night by Howard Brenton
Big Like Texas★, Glasgow, Southwark Playhouse and tour of Scotland: January 1999
Director: Sarah Wooley
Designer: Jane McInally
Music: Alain Scobie
Following a blow on the head, the protagonist dreams that he is ruling Britain.

Macbeth: Director's Cut
Volcano Theatre Company, Swansea, tour: February 1999
Director/Adaptor: Nigel Charnock
Designer: Andrew Jones
An adaptation for two actors using contemporary dance, drawing parallels with the West murders in the enjoyment of murder for sexual gratification.

Journey to Macbeth
The Royal Botanic Garden, Edinburgh Festival Fringe: August 1999
Director: Toby Gough
Lady Macbeth: Dannii Minogue
A fifty-minute adaptation set in a war zone with refugees apparently cast in some roles, Ukranian transvestite witches on stilts and techno/house music.
The company also performed a version of *The Tempest.*

Opera

Macbeth
English Touring Opera: February 1999
Composer: Giuseppe Verdi
Director: Robert Chevara
Designer: Nathalie Gibbs
Conductor: Martin Andre
A new production in a traditional setting.

Macbeth
Scottish Opera at the Festival Theatre, Edinburgh Festival: August 1999
Composer: Giuseppe Verdi
Director: Luc Bondy
Designer: Rolf Glittenberg
Conductor: Richard Armstrong
A new production set in the present with the witches depicted as Newcastle girls on a night out. During Macduff's lament for Scotland the production focused movingly on piled corpses.

MEASURE FOR MEASURE

OpenHand in Cambridge college gardens for the Cambridge Shakespeare Festival: July 1999

THE MERCHANT OF VENICE

The Royal National Theatre at the Cottesloe Theatre: June 1999
Director: Trevor Nunn
Designer: Hildegard Bechtler
Shylock: Henry Goodman
Portia: Derbhle Crotty
Set in 1930s Italy
The production transferred to the Olivier Theatre in November 1999.

Traffic of the Stage, tour: October 1999
Director: Harry Meacher

THE MERRY WIVES OF WINDSOR

The New Shakespeare Company at the Open Air Theatre, Regent's Park: May 1999
Director: Alan Strachan

Designer: Paul Farnsworth
Falstaff: Robert Lang

Shakespeare at the George, Huntingdon: June 1999
Annual amateur Shakespeare festival.

A MIDSUMMER NIGHT'S DREAM

The RSC at the RST, Stratford: March 1999
Director: Michael Boyd
Designer: Tim Piper
Titania/Hippolyta: Josette Simon
Oberon/Theseus: Nicholas Jones
Bottom: Daniel Ryan

Squerreys Lodge, Sevenoaks: June 1999
Director: Anna Morton
An open-air pro/am production involving fifty actors.

Stamford Shakespeare Company, Rutland Open Air Theatre, Tolethorpe Hall, Stamford: June 1999
Director: Steve Whittaker
Annual amateur Shakespeare festival.

The Ludlow Festival: June 1999
Director: Glen Walford
Titania/Hippolyta: Cathy Tyson
Bottom: Matthew Devitt

OpenHand in Cambridge college gardens, Cambridge Shakespeare Festival: July 1999

OpenHand in Oxford college gardens, Oxford Shakespeare Festival: July 1999
Quince was played as William Shakespeare.

Cannizaro Park, Wimbledon: August 1999
Director: Jenny Lee
Annual Shakespeare festival production.

Kent Repertory Theatre Company at the Lakeside Theatre, Hever Castle: August 1999

Pendley Open Air Shakespeare Festival: August 1999
Annual Shakespeare festival using a professional cast.

Dundee Repertory Theatre: September 1999
Director: Hamish Glen
Designer: Gregory Smith
Music: Stewart Black
An autumnal production set in the sixties and played by Scottish actors.

The New Victoria Theatre, Newcastle-under-Lyme: November 1999
Director: Patrick Connellan
Designer: Chris Monks
Bottom: Lisa Miller
The mechanicals and fairies doubled and were female. Played in the round to Indian music.

Adaptations

Ballet
A Midsummer Night's Dream
Pacific Northwest Ballet, Sadler's Wells Theatre, London: February 1999
Choreography: George Balanchine
Music: Felix Mendelssohn
Designer: Martin Pakledinaz
Originally created in 1962.

Opera
A Midsummer Night's Dream
Opera North, the Grand Theatre, Leeds and tour: December 1999
Composer: Benjamin Britten
Directors: Moshe Leiser and Patrice Caurier
Designer: Christian Fenouillat
Oberon: Christopher Josey
Titania: Claron McFadden
A new production.

Film
A Midsummer Night's Dream
Twentieth Century Fox with Searchlight Productions
UK release: September 1999
Director/producer/screen adaptation: Michael Hoffman
Music: Simon Boswell
Oberon: Rupert Everett

Titania: Michelle Pfeiffer
Bottom: Kevin Kline
Set in nineteenth-century Tuscany with an operatic musical score.

MUCH ADO ABOUT NOTHING

Matthew Townshend Productions in association with the Gordon Craig Theatre, Stevenage, tour: March 1999
Director: Matthew Townshend
Designer: Peter Clark
Set at the end of the Boer War.

Theatre Set Up, tour: June 1999
Director: Wendy McPhee.

OTHELLO

Asylum Theatre Company, the Riverside Studios, Richmond and tour with *Macbeth*: February 1999
Director: Nigel Roper

Lincoln Shakespeare Company, The Lawn, Lincoln: March 1999
Director: Rob Smith
Maori face paint was used to differentiate Othello. A pro/am production.

The RSC at the RST, Stratford: April 1999
Director: Michael Attenborough
Designer: Robert Jones
Music: George Fenton
Othello: Ray Fearon
Desdemona: Zoe Waites
Iago: Richard McCabe

Adaptation

William Shakespeare's Othello
Written and directed by Royston Abel
Edinburgh Fringe Festival: August 1999
A black comedy about a European director putting on a mixed race Kathakali adaptation of *Othello*, with Othello cast as a non-English speaker.

PERICLES

Community production in Prior Park for the Bath Shakespeare Festival: August 1999
Up to sixty young people took part, working with a professional production team.

RICHARD III

The ESC, Dundee Repertory Theatre and tour: March 1999
Director: Malachi Bogdanov
A nursery set, reminiscent of Jarry's *Ubu* plays with Richard portrayed as a huge baby.

Stafford Castle: July 1999
Producer: Nick Mowat
Director: Julia Stafford Northcott
Designer: Steve Freeman
Richard: Ian Reddington
A futuristic production set in the twenty-first century.

The Mercury Theatre, Colchester: September 1999
Director: David Grindley
Designer: Jonathan Fewson
Richard: Gregory Floy

Adaptation

Richard III
The Union Chapel, London Fringe: March 1999
Director: Stephen Finegold
Richard: Robert Mums
The second half was severely cut, to focus on evil on the rampage and the eventual death of Richard.

Bloody Richard, an adaptation by Sam Richards
Tour of northern England: October 1999
Act II, Scene 1 of *Richard III* interwoven with an on-stage discussion of the plot and characters.

ROMEO AND JULIET

Brunton Theatre, Musselburgh: January 1999

Director: Mark Thomson
Designer: Evelyn Barbour
A direct and straightforward production, played using Scottish accents.

The Theatre Royal, York: February 1999
Director: Damian Cruden
Designer: Liam Doona
Romeo: Paul Fox
Juliet: Sally Hawkins

Wales Actors Company, tour of open-air venues in Wales: July 1999
Director: Paul Garnault

Rainbow Theatre Company, Worthing, tour: July 1999
Director: Nicolas Young
Rainbow specialize in productions for young people.

PinPoint Productions, Eastwood Theatre, Southend and tour of the south east: July 1999
A multi-media production.

Kabosh Theatre Company★, Belfast: November 1999
Director: Karl Wallace
An all-male production.

Adaptations

Romeo and Juliet
ESC Education, tour: January 1999
Director: Robert Soulsby-Smith
A seventy-five minute recreation of a rehearsal with members of the audience encouraged to experiment with directing.

Romeo and Juliet
The Northern Stage Company at Newcastle Playhouse: February 1999
An adaptation set against an industrial background, using the device of a play within a play.

Romeo and Juliet
Shakespeare 4 Kidz, tour: August 1999
Devised by Julian Chenery and Matt Gimblett

The Nurse's Story by Sue Emmy Jennings
Rowan Theatre Company at the Edinburgh Fringe and Courtyard Theatre, London: August 1999
Director: Andrew Wade

Romeo and Juliet Deceased by Martin Beard
REC Theatre Company★ at the old Clubhouse, Buxton and the Coliseum Studio Theatre Oldham: October 1999

Romeo and Juliet
Hull Truck, tour: October 1999
Director: Kate Bramley
Designer: Ruth Paton
Adapted for a cast of eight by Jacquie Hanham.

Romeo e Giulietta
Teatro del Carretto at the Riverside Studios, Richmond : November 1999
A commedia dell'arte adaptation using marionettes and music from Bellini's opera. The action seen through the eyes of Juliet.

Ballet

Romeo and Juliet
The Norwegian National Ballet at Sadler's Wells Theatre, London: November 1999
Choreography: Michael Corder
Designer: Nadine Baylis
Music: Prokofiev
Six performances only. The ballet is in the repertoire of the Norwegian National Ballet.

THE TAMING OF THE SHREW

Stamford Shakespeare Company
Rutland Open Air Theatre, Tolethorpe Hall, Stamford: June 1999
Amateur company which annually perform Shakespeare in their purpose-built open-air theatre.

Northcott Theatre, Exeter in Rougemont Gardens: July 1999
Director: Ben Crocker
Designer: Tim Heywood

The Festival Players, tour of open-air venues: July 1999
Director: Trish Knight-Webb

Galleon Theatre Company, Well Hall Pleasance, Greenwich, London: July 1999

OpenHand in Cambridge college gardens for the Cambridge Shakespeare Festival: August 1999

Bacchae*, tour of London fringe venues: August 1999
Director: Aidan Steer
An all-female production.

The RSC at the Pit, Barbican Theatre, London, Swan Theatre, Stratford and tour: October 1999
Director: Lindsay Posner
Designer: Ashley Martin-Davis
Katherine: Monica Dolan
Petruchio/Sly: Stuart McQuarrie
The production sensitively linked the Sly scenes to the main play, it toured during 2000.

Film

10 Things I Hate About You
Touchstone Pictures: US release 1999
Screenplay: Karen Lute and Kirsten Smith
Director: Gil Unger
Producer: Andrew Lazar
Kat: Julia Stiles
Patrick Verona (Petruchio): Heth Ledger
A present-day adaptation set in Padua High School, Seattle, USA.

THE TEMPEST

The Courtyard Theatre at West Yorkshire Playhouse, Leeds: January 1999
Director: Jude Kelly
Designer: Robert Innes Hopkins
Prospero: Sir Ian McKellen
An anti-romantic production, set on a bare stage, using plastic sheeting a few chairs and old ropes for the set.

Jactito Theatre, Hackney, tour: January 1999
Director: James Barton
The production used life-size puppets, dance and mime.

Shared Experience, London, Salisbury Playhouse and schools tour: February 1999
Director: Trevelyan Wright
Designer: Sarah Blenkinsop

Isleworth Actors Company, Isleworth Public Hall: March 1999
Director: Arthur Horwood
The costume was nineteenth century, and, true to that period, Ariel was played by an actress.

A and BC Theatre Company, London fringe tour: July 1999
The audience was seated on oil drums in the middle of the action with the actors performing around them.

Creation Theatre Company at the Oxford Shakespeare Festival: July 1999

OpenHand in Cambridge college gardens for the Cambridge Shakespeare Festival: August 1999

Adaptations

The Tempest
ATC, Watermans Arts Centre and tour: February 1999
Director: Nick Philippou
Music: Laurie Anderson
Prospero: Rose English
An adaptation for three actors, played as Prospero's psychic journey using the stage as a microcosm of the world. A long steel table represented the island, and other characters were represented by faces inside stoppered jars.

Maybe Tomorrow
Kaboodle Productions, Liverpool Everyman and tour: March 1999
Huxley's *Brave New World* and Prospero's story were interwoven with storytelling, video and music.

The Tempest
Cambridge Experimental Theatre★, Cambridge
Drama Centre and Edinburgh Fringe Festival:
April 1999
Director: Toby Gough
Ariel was played by five actors each with a
different personality.

The Tempest
Galleon Theatre Company at Tudor Barn
Theatre, Eltham Palace Gardens, Greenwich,
London: August 1999
A very much abridged adaptation.

The Caribbean Tempest
The Royal Botanic Gardens, Edinburgh Fringe
Festival: August 1999
Director: Roger Lloyd Pack
Miranda: Dannii Minogue
Caliban: Ade Sapara
An interesting production played to voodoo
drumming and calypso with a bird of paradise-
like Ariel. First performed during the Barbadoes
Virgin Atlantic Holders Season, 1999, where
Kylie Minogue played Miranda, and intended
to commemorate the link between the play and
the colonization of the Caribbean.

TIMON OF ATHENS

The RSC at the RST, Stratford: August 1999
Director: Gregory Doran
Designer: Stephen Brimson Lewis
Timon: Michael Pennington
Apemantus: Richard McCabe

TITUS ANDRONICUS

Bare and Ragged Theatre★, The Rocket,
Glasgow: August 1999
Director: John Burrows
Although set in ancient Rome, the production
drew parallels with the atrocities in Kosova.

Adaptations

Titus Andronicus
The ESC, Edinburgh fringe festival and tour:
July 1999

Director: Malachi Bogdanov
Played for black comedy, set in the Regency
period and using padded flesh coloured costumes to simulate gross nudity.

Titus Andronicus
Burning Cat Productions★ at the Courtyard
Theatre, London fringe: August 1999
Director: Annecy Lax
Set in the criminal underworld, and using video
to show the rape of Lavinia.

Film

Titus
US Overseas Film Group with Clear Blue Sky
Productions: US release 1999, UK release
2000.
Director/filmscript: Julie Taymor
Titus: Anthony Hopkins
Tamora: Jessica Lange
Based on Julie Taymor's off-Broadway pro-
duction and drawing parallel with both Musso-
lini and the Emperor Hadrian's Rome through
the costumes.

Titus Andronicus
Joe Redner Films & Productions/JRE: 1999
Director: Christopher Dunne
Titus: Robert Reece
Tamora: Candy K. Sweet

TROILUS AND CRESSIDA

The RSC, tour continues overseas. See *Shakespeare Survey 53* for details.

The Royal National Theatre in the Olivier
Theatre: March 1999
Director: Trevor Nunn
Designer: Rob Howell
Troilus: Peter de Jersey
Cressida: Sophie Okonedo
Thersites: Jasper Britton
Pandarus: David Bamber
White Greeks in oriental dress fought black
Trojans on a red sand floor under the huge walls
of Troy.

The Oxford Stage company, tour: October 1999
Director: Dominic Dromgoole

TWELFTH NIGHT

Northern Broadsides, the Viaduct Theatre, Halifax and tour: January 1999
Director/Malvolio: Barrie Rutter
Designer: Jessica Worrall
Music: Conrad Nelson
Set in the sixties.

Gloriana Productions, Richmond, tour: January 1999
Director: Helen Fry
Music: Mark Dobson

The Belgrade Theatre, Coventry: May 1999
Director: Bob Eaton
Designer: Cathy Ryan
Set in 1968, the year of student unrest and rebellion. Old money clashes with new, and finally the old hierarchy is preserved, but with new blood.

The Anthony Hopkins Theatre, Theatre Clwyd, Mold, Wales: May 1999
Director: Terry Hands
Designer: Timothy O'Brien
A Jacobean setting, opening in melting snow.

The Watermill Theatre, Bangor, Newbury: May 1999
Director: Edward Hall
Designer: Michael Pavelka
An all-male production, set in a disintegrating country house, in which the cast wore white half-masks for the opening, and remained on stage in their masks during the action as an observing chorus.

Heartbreak Productions, Leamington Spa, tour of open-air venues: June 1999
Director: Peter Mimmack.
A production for seven actors.

The New Shakespeare Company, Regent's Park Open Air Theatre and Bath Festival: June 1999

Director: Rachel Kavanaugh
Designer: David Knapman
Viola: Emily Hamilton
Set in the twenties.

OpenHand in Cambridge college gardens for the Cambridge Shakespeare Festival: July 1999

Berengar Theatre at Barnwell Manor, Oundle: July 1999
Director: Neil Nisbet-Robertson
A pro/am production with a Regency setting.

Lincoln Shakespeare Company, open air production at Lincoln Castle: July 1999
Director: Richard Main.
A pro/am production.

The Nuffield Theatre, Southampton: October 1999
Director: Patrick O'Callaghan
Designer: Ti Green
An inter-war colonial island setting.

The Lyric Theatre, Belfast: October 1999
Director: Andrew Hinds
Designer: Gary McCann
A minimalist set and mixture of period and modern costumes.

Adaptations

Twelfth Night
Box Clever Theatre Company, the Marlowe Theatre studio, Canterbury and tour: January 1999
Director: Michael Wicherek
An adaptation for schools.

Twelfth Night
Illyria Theatre Company, tour of open-air venues and Edinburgh Fringe Festival: June 1999
Director: Oliver Gray
Adapted for five actors.

Ballet

Cwmni Ballet, Gwent, the Anvil Theatre, Basingstoke and tour: July 1999

Choreography: Darius James
Music: Haydn and seventeenth-century songs.

Related Work

The Deceived
Adapted and directed by Kenneth Rea, and translated by Christopher Cairns.
The Riverside Players★ at the Riverside Studios, Hammersmith and short tour: January 1999
A 1532 play by a group of Sienna scholars called the Intronati, described as a source for *Twelfth Night*.

TWO GENTLEMEN OF VERONA

The Royal National Theatre, the Cottesloe Theatre and educational tour with schools workshops: January 1999
Director: Julie-Anne Robinson
Designer: Nathalie Gibbs

THE WINTER'S TALE

The RSC at the Royal Shakespeare Theatre, Stratford: January 1999
See *Shakespeare Survey 53* for details.
Previews opened December 1998, opened January 1999.

The Maly Drama Theatre of St Petersburg, Russia, UK tour: April 1999
Director: Declan Donnellan
Designer: Nick Ormerod
Mamillius was given special prominence in this production which ended with Hermione blessing her daughter, after which the actors froze and the ghost of Mamillius appeared, to wander among the stationary figures. Performed in Russian.

Logos Theatre Company, Wimbledon Studio Theatre: April 1999
Director: Jonathan Kennedy
A traditional production.

ATTRIBUTED PLAYS

Edward III
RSC actors at The Other Place, Stratford: 10 September 1999
Rehearsed reading as part of the On the Edge season.

The London Prodigal
The Shakespeare Institute Players★, Stratford: June 1999
Director: Paul Edmondson
A rare performance of one of the attributed plays.

POEMS AND SONNETS

The Rape of Lucrece
Adapted by Theresa Shiban
The Union Theatre, London fringe: February 1999

W.H. by Peter Fekete
The Arts Centre, St Helier, Jersey: August 1999
A new play about William Herbert, Earl of Pembroke and Shakespeare, using some material from the Sonnets.

MISCELLANEOUS

Mr Dickens and Mr Shakespeare
Edward Petherbridge one-man show, The Other Place, Stratford and Edinburgh Fringe Festival: April 1999

Monsters and Maidens (The Tempest)
Fairies and Witches (Macbeth and A Midsummer Night's Dream)
Nymphs and Shepherds (The Winter's Tale)
Three one-day workshops for six to eleven-year-olds, performed by professional actors at The Beacon Arts, Knoyle Hall, Brighton: June 1999.

Radio

The BBC Shakespeare season, new recordings of the plays to be broadcast on BBC Radio 3 and published over the next four years. The published tapes will include essays by the directors.

Film

Shakespeare in Love; release January 1999. See *Shakespeare Survey 53* for details.

THE YEAR'S CONTRIBUTIONS TO SHAKESPEARE STUDIES

1. CRITICAL STUDIES

reviewed by EDWARD PECHTER

What is the point – of Shakespeare, art in general, life itself? In *Play in a Godless World*, Catherine Bates dismantles those 'cheerful narratives of progress' which describe play 'as a gradual ascent towards moral, social, and intellectual achievement' (p. iii) in favour of a Nietzschean 'free play' that 'does not lead anywhere – towards higher, better, more advanced, or more developed things', but 'is completely pointless and mindless, going nowhere and enjoyed purely for itself' (p. iv). Esthetic idealization 'flattered man with pleasingly god-like powers by allowing him to think he'd mastered and controlled the raw material of experience' (p. 64). Repeatability, the determining factor, allows Freud's little Ernst to master trauma and functions in Huizinga as 'perhaps *the* thing which elevated play to the higher realms of art and culture' (p. 171). Tragedy, the supreme achievement, 'doesn't simply repeat any experience but specifically repeats' the ultimate unpleasure, 'death's crushing finality' (p. 175). 'Tragedy is *fort! da!* for grownups. Tragedy laughs in the face of death because a represented and repeatable death is a non-death' (p. 176). Shakespeare performs a crucial role for Bates at the end, with four plays chosen to illustrate the metadramatic scepticism through which intimations of transcendence disintegrate into disenchantment. 'Repetition's deceptive mastery over reality seems, in the last, disillusioned

scenes of *Julius Caesar* to have been deconstructed' (p. 196). *Hamlet*'s thrilling finality is mere fiction: the 'last laugh' belongs to Shakespeare, who reminds us that 'Hamlet will revive to please tomorrow's audience' (p. 203). The wonder-filled conclusions of *Antony* and *Winter's Tale* similarly collapse, leaving us bereft of 'any kind of consolation at all' (p. 218).

Maybe so; but if theatrical rhetoric cannot sustain belief beyond performance, you can always go back to the theatre, where access to the marvellous becomes possible again. In like manner, people keep returning to the 'notion that art [is] morally uplifting' (p. 65); all those worthies from Huizinga back to Aristotle cannot just be wrong. We might then posit a wavering between contradictory awarenesses. Bates acknowledges as much; despite the Nietzsche advocacy, she accords privileged position to Freud, whose 'argument oscillates between nonsense and meaning' (p. v), an 'opposition or tension between the' life and death instincts which, at the fractured centre of *Beyond the Pleasure Principle*, 'spelt the human condition' (p. 186).

Bates thinks that the 'winning philosophy' of the teleologues 'continues to hold sway in the moralized rhetoric of health and wholesomeness that daily beats at our door' (p. 178); but since she never descends from generality, it is unclear how she would engage in detail with current

work. In dismissing 'the good bourgeois the-
orist', 'determined to get his money's worth',
who demands 'a stern but improving lesson
about reality' (pp. 178, 182), she seems to echo
recent materialist claims about art as an ideology
devised to secure bourgeois hegemony. But the
emphasis on political consequence in these same
materialists might look to Bates like a version of
the narcissism she argues against. If purposivity
is what allows 'critics as well as artists to feel so
good about themselves' (p. 65), then the new
materialism reproduces the bourgeois theory it
purports to contest. As Pogo said, 'we have seen
the enemy and it is us'.

In *Shakespeare: The Loss of Eden*, Catherine
Belsey argues that Shakespeare does not celebrate 'family values'. She analyses: the sceptical
ironies surrounding romantic courtship in
Love's Labour's Lost and *As You Like It*; Posthumus', Othello's and Leontes' sudden jealousy,
enacting not pathological anomaly but the
'structural paradox' inherent within the institutional norm (p. 43); the similarly unmotivated
infanticidal eruptions of Leontes; the murderous
'sibling rivalry' at the origin of *Hamlet*. Belsey
includes forty-nine plates (book illustrations,
funeral monuments, tapestries, etc.) which,
even in blurry black and white, are brought by
her keenly observant intelligence into striking
evidence for the presence of death in the midst
of familial life. No more, for Luther, than ' "a
faint image and a remnant, as it were, of that
blessed living-together" ' experienced before
the Fall (p. 88), this qualified 'Puritan Art of
Love' differs markedly from the sentimentalized
domesticity of the Victorians, whose theological
commitments are much attenuated from the
intensely sin-and-death conscious Renaissance
described here.

This claim is of a piece with current arguments for the profoundly religious values of
Renaissance culture, but Belsey considers her
work's historical dimension as subordinate to its
political consequence. The book 'is put forward
as a reservation about the call for the restoration
of family values in our society' (176). Belsey

aims to 'denaturalize family values' by
describing their emergence through historical
process; denying their 'inevitability' (p. xiv),
she would establish 'grounds for hoping that, in
the long term, injustice might be significantly
reduced' (p. 17). This may be preaching to the
converted. The self-deluding 'we' who idealize
family values by 'tell[ing] ourselves' that 'unhappiness in marriage is specific, not structural'
(p. 121) are not the academic readership likely
to read this book; and Belsey will not reach the
conservatives she targets (unlikely, anyway, to
change their beliefs simply because they are
revealed to be historically constructed). Besides,
as the Bates discussion implies, self-delusion is
not always necessarily a bad thing. Like the
romance investment in the 'invulnerability that
eludes the tragic hero' (Frye, *The Secular Scripture*, p. 86), it helps keep us going – perhaps
even sustaining claims for the consequentiality
of our work.

In *Shakespeare and Domestic Loss*, Heather
Dubrow explores the same conflict-ridden ter-
ritories: 'while domestic spaces may be associated with presence and security, their
Christian inhabitants knew well that they were
imperfect surrogates for that first lost home,
Eden . . . profoundly unstable materially and
ideologically' (p. 11). A chapter on burglary
analyses 'the breakdown of categories and distinctions' in the Sonnets and *Lucrece* (p. 46): the
victim has to assume responsibility for letting
the intruder in. *Lear* and *Cymbeline* illustrate
'loss of dwellings', which extends to an anxious
alienation from pastoral and maternal belonging.
A chapter on 'the early death of parents' looks
chiefly at *Dream* and *Richard III* where wardship,
a generally inadequate surrogacy for a lost
parent, draws 'attention both to the perme-
ability of . . . not only spatial terms like *inside*
and *outside* but also *mother* and *father*' (p. 143).

But despite all this, Dubrow's book is very
different from Belsey's. She distances herself
from 'an academic culture primarily interested
in conflictual paradigms for social interactions'
(p. 168). Comfort and security are never wholly

absent from Shakespearian homes (two cheers for domesticity). Despite the 'postmodern tendency' to 'assume that loss reduplicates itself with virtually no hope of mediation or remediation' (p. 14), Dubrow emphasizes 'recuperation'. The ironic resonances at the end of *Cymbeline* or *Winter's Tale* do not empty out the sense of wonder. Current angst-saturated readings of *Dream* 'sometimes refuse to distinguish undercurrents from tidal waves' (p. 140). Loss can be transformed and contained if not mastered, both within Shakespearian texts and by those for whom the process of participating in Shakespearian fiction has a potentially restorative function.

Dubrow nests these claims within a procedure she calls 'monovision' – basically one eye for the forest, one for the trees. 'Unhappy families are not all alike' (p. 2). 'Protocapitalism' is one of the generalizations about which Dubrow twice 'warns' (p. 85, p. 166), and Theodore Leinwand similarly demurs, in *Theatre, Finance and Society in Early Modern England*, from standard views in which the emergent money economy represents a critical transition from 'status to contract, from sacred to secular, ascription to achievement, . . . feudal to (nascent) capitalist' (p. 1). Such *grands récits* exaggerate the social divisions created by the new formation and ignore the similarities. If 'an all-pervasive money economy exacted its differential dues from the richer, middling, and poorer sorts' (p. 31), then money, not just a common drudge 'tween man and man, was also a natural touch that made the whole world kin. From this angle, old plays take new shapes. Just as 'nobility and landed gentry worked in necessary if often uneasy concert with moneymen' (p. 93), *A New Way to Pay Old Debts*, rather than staging a confrontation 'between an ideology of rank or status and a bourgeois ideology founded on thrift', represents 'tensions *within* the ideology of deference' (p. 85).

Leinwand's goal is not to replace one Big Story with another. In emphasizing accommodation rather than crisis, he can look at the details under the generalizations, 'the precise, not opposed, ways a peddler and a royal agent cope with the need for credit' (p. xi), as part of 'an interpretive inventory of responses to socio-economically induced stress' registered as 'an amalgam of cognition and affect' (p. 1). In compiling this affective inventory, Leinwand moves freely between historical and theatrical situations (*Eastward Ho, Michaelmas Term, Alchemist*, et al.). He scours the archives, coming up (as did L. C. Knights years ago) with real people as bizarre as Middleton's or Jonson's inventions. The Shakespeare sections highlight a Timon whose stupidly sublime attempt to transcend money is analysed with elegant subtlety, and an Antonio whose isolated sadness is explained economically rather than erotically – something of a novelty in current work. The two domains are not unconnected, as witness Steve Patterson's version this year of a queer Antonio whose 'homoerotic amity', though 'compatible with heroic masculinity and good citizenship', is gradually displaced in favour of 'a radically shifting mercantile economy . . . better regulated by . . . heterosexual reproduction' (p. 10). Leinwand understands such connections, but his emphasis on the affective *economic* register is engagingly different.

Shakespeare Without Women is 'about what, or rather who, is *not there* on Shakespeare's stage – particularly women . . . , Africans, and the indigenous Irish' (p. 2). Dympna Callaghan does not, however, want 'to point the politically correct finger' at Shakespearian 'deficiency' (p. 8). She is sceptical whether theatrical and political representation ought even to be associated: getting into the picture is not getting a share of the pie. Besides, since 'theatrical representation depends for its functioning . . . on the absence of the thing it represents' (p. 9), the heroes of ancient Rome or English history, aristocrats and royalty, Venetians and the Viennese – all are, like women, not there. But women are different – excluded from the Renaissance English stage and defined extra-theatrically by lack. If femininity is construed as inadequate presence, then the boy actors' success in representing femininity may be the wrong issue: 'it is not the perfect similitude of woman that was the goal' but 'sexual difference defined as the presence or lack of male genitalia' (p. 51). So too Burbage's Othello; white skin was the defining substance. 'Othello *was a white man*', as Mary Preston said, but 'so was Desdemona' (p. 76), in the sense that 'Shakespeare's audience would have witnessed in Othello and Desdemona the spectacle of two men, one young with his face whitened and one older with his face blackened' (p. 92). It is all performance, no role. Hence in the Willow Scene Desdemona's vulnerability is absorbed into anxieties that the performer might 'erupt into tenor or baritone . . . Soon, Desdemona's throat will be constricted forever, but the actor must not let it happen now' (p. 72).

Callaghan engages generously with negative evidence, testimonials – from women, blacks, colonized subjects, Jews, gays – who feel included in and even empowered by Shakespeare's plays. But she is sceptical: 'we have to keep reminding ourselves [that] "Shakespeare's sweet bitches are still a man's idea of a sweet bitch"'; 'we have to remind ourselves that [Shakespeare] did not write for us' (p. 7, p. 9). But if Shakespeare seems 'to represent all of us in our myriad and multiple degrees of otherness' (p. 7), why resist? Presumably because the inclusion effect is judged historically inaccurate; but even if we could be sure of this, Callaghan seems (like Belsey) less committed to historicity than to instrumentality and critical consequence – 'a political position that works to open up new space for resistance' (p. 46), 'an intervention for current feminist politics' (p. 47): ambitious claims for which the delivery system is hard to see.

Callaghan's most compelling chapter teases out 'Irish Memories in *The Tempest*' – unconscious resonances of deeply charged feelings among the Irish and their colonizers: 'echoes and spectres of the Irish' in *Tempest* 'constitute the repressed knowledge of a people' whose

'rupture into consciousness was imminent' (p. 112). But then why rule out similar claims for the emergence of women and blacks elsewhere? 'More than any other Shakespearean drama', she argues, *Tempest*'s 'subversive energies' tempt 'us to fill in its blanks' (pp. 100–1). But is *Tempest* more subversive than *Othello*? Callaghan herself remarks that, in contrast to the infantilized Caliban, 'Othello has a history . . . that allows him, by virtue of fully developed powers of adult recollection, a historicized consciousness' (p. 137). No white man, that. Callaghan is aware of the contradiction but does not try (as foolishly consistent, little-minded critics might) to iron out the wrinkles of these complex issues: the *Tempest* chapter 'speaks to . . . why I, too, feel enmeshed in the messy, often wrong-headed, yet empowering identifications with Shakespeare' (p. 24).

Alison Findlay also begins with the 'absence of women' from Renaissance theatrical production (p. 1) but argues nonetheless for 'women's tangible presence' as readers or spectators (p. 2). *A Feminist Perspective on Renaissance Drama* claims that the texts of Renaissance women – diaries, letters, homiletic reflections, poems and plays – allow us 'to recreate an imagined female audience . . . whose situations, opinions and tastes male dramatists probably responded to' (p. 6). She examines public theatre plays and closet drama, both generically (chapters on revenge and domestic tragedy) and thematically (chapters on religious belief, 'Female Self-fashioning', and images of queenship). Her argument develops through suggestive juxtaposition. Anne Wheathill's unease at presumptive knowledge suggests that *Faustus*'s 'quest for selfhood' appealed 'to audiences of women struggling to establish identities in face of paternal laws' (p. 24). Moll in *The Roaring Girl* resonates with Lady Arbella Stuart's attempt 'to assert herself as an autonomous subject', which 'sounds again in the voice of Isabella Whitney' (p. 117). Findlay appreciates that the female-authored texts are produced against and within conventional ideas about gender – herself using

Vives to introduce Wheathill and again to introduce Moll's project as 'inimical to the model of feminine behaviour laid down in Renaissance' norms (p. 87). Since these norms belong to (or are belonged to by) everybody, playwrights as much as women, Moll's transgressive self-assertion may not so much be produced for as echoed by a female audience which, if it didn't exist for Middleton and Dekker to 'respond to', they might anyway have invented. In either case, Findlay's juxtapositions suggestively enrich her sustained commentaries on *Measure*, *All's Well*, and *Richard II* and her interpretations of non-Shakespearian dramas (by Kyd, Chapman, Cary, Ford, Wroth, Jonson, Webster, et al.) as well.

Philippa Berry abandons real women for 'the ambiguous function, not simply of women, but of feminized figures of speech in a Shakespearian interrogation of the meanings of tragedy' (pp. 2–3). In linear-phallic time, death fixes meaning with irreversible finality, but 'feminine or feminized tropes', digressing rather than patriarchally succeeding, 'perform an allusive weaving both of tragic teleology and orthodox conceptions of death' (p. 3). In the context of a Lucretian-cum-Ovidian Renaissance naturalism where generation and degeneration collapse into undifferentiated fecundity, Shakespearian writing is drawn irresistibly toward textual density rather than to structural clarity, the 'fatal Cleopatra' that is also the vital centre of an endlessly signifying play. Berry develops her claims in five main chapters, all richly responsive to the evocative power of Shakespeare's language. 'Double dying' is one of many boundary-blurring features of *Romeo and Juliet*, including the non-gender-specific orifices of mouth and anus. A chapter on echo and the disintegrating consequences of 'female' babble suggests a more intimate Hamlet–Ophelia association than the narrative determines. 'Disclosing the Feminine Eye of Death' keys on the unseen female essence of *Othello*, where speculative mastery disintegrates into 'the origin of all . . . the mysterious flux of nature'

(p. 73). *Macbeth* serves as the base from which to argue that 'Shakespeare's tragedies configure [*peripeteia*] as a circling backwards in time', the 'erotic . . . deviation from conventional masculine identity' (p. 102). Finally, Berry puts the undistinguished space of woman's will at the centre of unresolved Jacobean concerns with political union. 'Cordelia remains a mystery even in her death'; we are 'left to wonder' about the immediate consequences for the state and about 'the apparent finality of tragic endings' (p. 166).

Shakespeare's Cross-Cultural Encounters focuses on 'dynamic interplay' (p. 3) between alien and European values. Geraldo de Souza analyses *Dream*, *Kinsmen* and early histories (Amazonian legend and same-sex desire); *Merchant* (Morocco and Shylock are resisted by the 'ideological shield' of established textual authority (p. 69)); *Titus* and *Othello* (Aaron is reduced to the stereotypes of Roman prejudice; Othello's 'cultural memories' (p. 113) cannot sustain his identity within Venetian 'ethnographical assumptions' (p. 128)); *Antony* (going native, unsettling Roman 'society's self-satisfied notions of ideological superiority' (p. 158)); and *Tempest* (Prospero 'appropriates the memories of Sycorax and Caliban' to 'his own ends' of reintegration into European power (p. 182)). De Souza locates meaning in an expressive intention, as when, 'dissatisfied with the suppression of the Amazons' earlier in *Dream*, Shakespeare 'revisit[s] the myth to make this point more explicit' later in *Kinsmen* (p. 29). This is an author given to 'demonstrate', 'investigate', and 'propose' (p. 128, p. 138, p. 140). The overriding idea is ambivalence – siding sometimes with ethnocentric 'appropriation', sometimes with 'ethnic diversity' (p. 179), 'exposing a Eurocentric perspective' (p. 183). Sympathetic readers may wish to translate this ambivalence from author to text or audience as a way to account for Shakespeare's appeal to different constituencies over time.

In *Shakespeare and Race*, Imtiaz Habib undertakes a systematic application of postcolonial theory to explain the black presence in the Sonnets, *Titus*, *Othello*, *Antony and Cleopatra* and *Tempest*. For Habib, 'postcolonial studies' answer the question, *what is the point?*; personally liberating, they give 'one's critical voice the ethical mandate' required 'to locate itself fully in the historical-political continuum' (p. vii). His inaugural claim is 'that race is a factor of colonialism' (p. 3). Acknowledging Renaissance confusions about race, he nonetheless repudiates the idea of a 'pre-racial' consciousness as an 'apprehensive liberal-humanist practice' (p. 20), preferring 'to employ the violence of critical anachronism' in order 'to force some visibility on to the obliterated black subject in the dawning moments of the English colonial experience' (pp. 9–10). From this position, he seeks 'to interrogate and correctively intervene' in both 'western intellectual traditions' and 'in the economic, political and cultural practices that have issued from the European colonial project' (p. 6). By the end, he reduces his claim to the intellectual and cultural: 'The study of race and its colonial origins in Shakespeare' contributes to 'the de-racialization of the cultural thinking that his works have produced' (p. 252). As part of this process, he emphasizes authentic indigenous strength – 'the colonized black subject's resistant textual life in Caliban' (p. 226), and (lumping together Aaron, Othello and Cleopatra) the 'recusant subalternity of all three ethnic figures' (p. 12).

Shaul Bassi takes a diametrically opposed position. *Le Metamorfosi di Otello: Storia di un'Etnicità Immaginaria* is a cultural history of Othello's difference grounded on the principle that 'ethnicity' is more suitable than the anachronistic 'race' to understand the critical and theatrical avatars of the Moor of Venice. Bassi begins with early modern geographical and anthropological discourse, claiming that its indeterminacy allows for future obsessions and possibilities, then proceeds through Rymer, the Romantics, nineteenth- and twentieth-century performance, and recent criticism on either side of the postcolonial divide. He concludes with recent Italian criticism, where Othello's ethnicity has been largely ignored in a country that has also forgotten its colonialist past.

Ania Loomba's essay on 'Alterity and Exchange in Early Modern Stages' negotiates many of these troubling issues with finesse and generous common sense. Loomba acknowledges 'the crucial difference between twentieth-century and early modern ideologies of racial and cultural difference', but in her view our responsibility 'to historicize the growth of colour-consciousness' (p. 201) does not entail eliminating or 'downplaying . . . the vocabulary of colour' (p. 202). Rather, we ought 'to trace the complex articulation between skin-colour, religion, ethnicity and nationality' to determine 'whether *each of them* was viewed as a feature that could be acquired, or as derived from a more unchanging quasi-biological essence' (p. 204). In pursuing this agenda, Loomba ranges widely over many Renaissance plays and non-dramatic texts, familiar and obscure, as well as recent critical and theoretical work.

Americans on Shakespeare, 1776–1914 is a fascinating anthology, introduced with a sharp and helpful essay by Peter Rawlings. The book includes Emerson's 'Shakespeare; or The Poet', and many lesser or (to me) unknown Emersonians who make similar claims about the 'speculative genius' that makes Shakespeare accessible to his 'wondering readers' as 'the horizon beyond which, at present, we do not see' (p. 118). The book emphasizes the peculiarly American inflections of this transnational Romanticism: Whitman, anxious about Shakespeare's threat to a democratic culture; Melville, swerving from Tocqueville-like laments about American barbarism into bumptious assertions about the 'republican progressiveness' required for America to praise 'mediocrity even, in her own children, before . . . the best excellence . . . of any other land' (p. 166). Some material sounds surprisingly current. There is much irony about fetishizing the Shakespearian past, ranging from Washington Irving's affectionate amusement to rage at the prospective Birthplace reconstruction in the US (Wanamaker-bashing, nineteenth-century style). Best of all is Delia Bacon, inveighing presciently against what we now routinely call 'the Shakespeare myth' ('with its self-sustained vitalities . . . laughing at history', available to assume 'any shape or attitude, which the criticism in hand may call for' (pp. 172, 175)), but advancing these claims on behalf not of progressive politics and postmodern methodology but aristocratic privilege, academic professionalism, Enlightenment rationalism – and Sir Francis Bacon as the author of the plays.

In another fat and juicy volume of writing from the long nineteenth century, Judith and Richard Kennedy's contribution to the Critical Tradition series collects eighty-five commentaries on *Dream* from 1775 to 1920. This series is designed to supplement material already accessible, so the stars do not dominate the bit players. In conjunction with the sheer number of items, the result is sketchy – one short and relatively ungripping excerpt after another. There are exceptions (Shaw's take-no-prisoners assault on Augustin Daly and the pictorial stage, for instance), but this is not so much a book to read as an archive to consult – hugely valuable as such, thanks to the Kennedys' thoughtful effort. Besides unearthing the material, they provide a long introduction, patiently weaving together the strands of commentary they have collected, going back and ahead to early and later material up to the present; biographical information about the contributors (I missed this in Rawlings); endnotes identifying obscure references in the material; and a three-part index (the play, other plays, and general), which worked well both going out from and back into the text.

Two of the six essays Peter Brown has collected in *Reading Dreams* deal with Shakespeare. Kathryn Lynch's Shakespeare 'was an astute reader' of 'the tradition of medieval dream visions' (p. 100), and is said to be 'drawing explicitly on' Chaucer's *Legend of Good Women* (p. 103) for *Dream*'s 'gender

dynamics' (p. 109). Kathleen McLuskie's wide-ranging contribution considers *Dream*, Clarence in *Richard III*, Vittoria in *White Devil* ('this yew'), *Henry VIII*, *Shrew*, *Sir Thomas More*, et al. Her formative instance, though, is 'the postmodern moment' of David Lynch's *Blue Velvet*, where 'images and cultural echoes are in constant play, always . . . second-guessing the reader who wants, as it were, to catch them and tie them down' (p. 148). McLuskie argues that early modern theatre, with its routine reliance on an unresolvable theatre/reality binary ('life is a dream'), regularly produces David Lynch-like effects: 'reading dreams is always a process of translation . . . determined not by a single model of interpretation, but by conflicts in the range . . . offered by a variety of texts' (pp. 162–3).

Past the size of dreaming we come upon religion. *The Biblical Presence in Shakespeare, Milton and Blake* describes the conflict between the heroic self-assertion of Dionysian tragedy and the providential love of Judaeo-Christian tradition. Harold Fisch's Shakespeare does not bridge 'the chasms' separating 'Aristotle's *Ethics* from the Sermon on the Mount' (p. 117); 'options are left open' (p. 115) and audiences free to learn what they can. Fisch examines four plays. In *Julius Caesar*, we are detached from a Rome still obsessed with rituals of human sacrifice. Fisch emphasizes *Antony*'s hyperbole, but like Leo Salingar, for whom the play uses its 'strongest rhetoric to mark the distance between wishes, imagination or legend and present actuality' (p. 23), Fisch claims that transcendence is always undercut, producing a 'perspective similar to' *Caesar*'s, a world not 'redeemed and in harmony with itself', but marked 'by absence and division' (p. 49). Brutus' exchange with Lucius, the asp-delivering Clown, Scriptural echoes in the Gravediggers scene and the 'readiness is all' speech – these 'seem to reconcile' tragic loss with 'other, more life-affirming forces' (p. 114), but only as theatrical rhetoric. We do not get even this in *Lear*, a play 'both strongly Christian and strongly Pagan' that enacts something like a 'super-*agon* . . . between Job and Prometheus' (p. 123). Fisch's work coincides with recent claims that 'religion in fact *was* culture in early modern England' (McEachern, *Religion and Culture*, p. 11), but his conception of religious experience remains largely ensconced within philosophical and ethical reflection, mental ideas independent of 'real social relations'.

John Russell Brown has been travelling in Asia, seeing various performances: 'Orissa Opera, a Jatra (or "touring") theatre' (p. 9); 'a cremation ceremony in a small village deep in the jungle' of Bali (p. 29); a Kerala performance in 'the strict regimen [of] Kutiyattam' (p. 75); Japanese Bunraku and Kabuki, Beijing Opera, et al. *New Sites for Shakespeare* is an engaging report on his theatrical tourism. The effect is a new understanding of Shakespeare, 'seeing . . . the texts as if for the first time' (p. 1). 'Each time I returned . . . I was reading Shakespeare's plays differently' (p. 139). Brown infectiously communicates his excitement, but there needs no tourist returned from Asia to tell us that 'Shakespeare had used [repetition] in many different ways' (p. 12); or 'needed a strong non-verbal or pre-verbal imagination' (p. 27); or gave his 'audience . . . a choice' among inter-pretations (p. 85); or that his 'speeches *could* be said to the audience and, at times, *for* the audience' (p. 98). Asian performances have not so much generated or transformed Brown's belief as reinforced what he brought to them in practices 'similar to those I had conjectured' (p. 123) *What*, then, *is the point?* Presumably, as with all exploration, to arrive where you started and know the place for the first time.

Brown's advocacy in *New Sites* – for 'Impro-visation: Freedom and Collusion' in the pro-duction of Renaissance plays (pp. 91–102), 'something like the context of their original staging', with audiences 'free to follow their own individual thoughts and varying interests' (p. 36) – was established as early as *Free Shake-speare* (1974). The directorial tyranny Brown identified then has been intensified through an irresistibly coercive technology and sceno-graphy – Peter Brook's 'Deadly Theatre', dead-lier now that modernism is post and capitalism late – resulting in 'carefully arranged and mean-ingful spectacles', 'packaged and processed' to provide 'high-definition' performance (p. 155, p. 93). The example of Asian production might 'reverse current trends' (p. 155) and loosen the grip of 'the mega-musical' on the commercial stage (p. 163). With actors 'in charge, as a group', the gap may be bridged 'between those who plan and those who work, those whose labour earns the money and those who control it' (p. 156). Brown several times cites Granville-Barker, ' "One cannot too often insist that the art of acting is the theatre's very flesh and blood" ' (p. 173), as though repertory can restore a human (even a histrionically human) control over technology.

Shakespeare, Rabelais, and the Comical-Historical leaves it up in the air whether the author of *Henry IV* knew *Gargantua and Pantagruel*. Cathleen McLoughlin's claim, generic and intertextual, is that *Henry IV* is illuminated when read alongside Rabelais' book. She brings other intertexts into play as well: Holbein's anamorphism, Lucian's carnivalesque, Erasmian and Socratic polyphony and dialogism. Yumiko Yamada works in a similar comp. lit. tradition, coupling Jonson and Cervantes. She is more committed to conscious knowledge and direct influence, but the evidence is not strong. Yamada shores up her argument for Jonson's Cervantes by tearing down other arguments for Shakespeare's, as though negative claims about Shakespeare add up to positive claims about Jonson – an idea for which Jonson himself may bear responsibility.

Yamada's study is one of three books this year attesting to a strong Japanese interest in 'Shake-speare and his Contemporaries' (a phrase in the titles of the other two). The eleven pieces Yoshiko Kawachi gathers are meant to provide more 'easy access to Shakespearean studies in Japan', in the belief that 'Shakespeare is indeed worldwide and that Shakespearean studies should be more international' (p. 8). In his Foreword to *Hot Questrists After the English Renaissance*, Yasuo Tamaizumi, President of the Shakespeare Society of Japan, explains that after the 1991 Tokyo World Congress Japanese Shakespearians were not satisfied with the 'assimilative impulse . . . looking beyond a domestic market [they] were eager to make their thoughts and ideas available in English' (viii). Hence the decision to publish this book, the thirty-fifth anniversary volume of the Society, in English in order 'to join the republic of academic studies and maintain dialogues with their international colleagues' (p. 4).

Both volumes achieve their ambitions, with a high proportion of confident performance trained on gender, ideology, political power, and the institutional role of the theatre. Each book includes a striking piece by Ted Motohashi on the disjunctive gaps that serve at the same time to establish 'dialogical reciprocity' on Prospero's island and in Henry V's England (p. 115). In another strong essay, Manabu Noda relates Garrick's verbal pauses and staccato bodily gestures, such as the ' "Hamlet start" at the appearance of [the] ghost' (p. 185), to eighteenth-century sensibility. Homi Bhabha and Joseph Roach stand behind these essays, and in general the voices heard here are the ones broadcast most strongly throughout the Shakespearian World Service. Hence *Renaissance Self-Fashioning*'s Japanese translator writes in the chiasmic New Historicist style: 'Drama . . . establishes itself through politics, and, at the same time, politics . . . expresses itself through drama' (Takada, p. 191). Queer theory is the only current mode absent from these books, which also include a strong representation of formalist and 'dramatistic' analysis. Still, Takahashi's acknowledgment that readers 'may have expected to find something "Japanese" ' does get at the source of some selfish disappointment (p. 4). Shakespeare's assimilation into a powerfully different culture would satisfy expansive metropolitan appetites for 'new sites'.

Shakespeare on Lust and Love might have been called *Desire in Shakespeare*. Maurice Charney's title implies a foundational distinction between spiritual and carnal, but since 'Love in Shakespeare expresses itself in physical desire' and 'never loses its sexual underpinnings' (p. 2), the contrast when appealed to, as in Adonis's last speech or the couplet at the end of Sonnet 20, has no resolving effect: 'a facile but false distinction' (p. 110), 'a diplomatic and Solomonic division, but unconvincing' (p. 179). 'Shakespeare on' in the title is misleading as well. Because he is 'so impersonal an author' (pp. 159–60), 'we are unable to present a single coherent concept of love in Shakespeare' (p. 209). This 'absentee author', though, turns out to be an 'advantage': denying access to 'the ideology of a single, powerful personality', the plays compensate us with the extraordinary 'depth and interest' of their 'wide variety of representations about love' (p. 212).

Charney explores desire across the canon, generically (chapters on comedies, problem plays and tragedies) and conceptually (including 'Gender Definitions' and 'Homoerotic Discourses'). Genre is played with and against; at times Charney delights in the fulfilment of expectations, at others he is perplexed or surprised (a recurring effect) by deviations from apparently established patterns. The conceptual chapters are also highly mobile: the same masculinist/misogynist discourse can produce horror in the 'frighteningly constricted' world of *Macbeth* (p. 137), delight in the 'conventional gender expectations' of Kate and Hotspur's 'charming love scene' (p. 152), or sheer exhilaration in the 'exciting' way *Antony and Cleopatra* 'violates assumed gender norms' (p. 155). Concepts here have no inherently fixed value. Like Eliot's Henry James, Charney's Shakespeare has a mind too fine to be violated by an idea. Belief and emotional investment are determined by 'dramatic context' (p. 112, p. 116, p. 118, p. 187). Charney has assimilated the basic claims of feminism and queer theory: gender is 'a social and historical construction' (p. 133); ' "homosexuality," "lesbianism" and "bisexuality" have no direct reference' to a world before sexual identity (p. 159). But where cultural critics use the plays to make such points, Charney uses the points to locate the dramatic vitality of the plays: 'surprising how much same-sex love there is in Shakespeare, not in any doctrinal sense but as a dramatic expression of a wide variety of sexual impulses' (p. 6); 'his characters work against type' to 'generate . . . theatrical interest [and] titillate the spectators' (p. 157; 'titillation' and cognates recur as well – p. 62 and p. 110).

The communication of theatrical excitement may seem a shamefully modest ambition compared to some of the grander claims made for critical consequence these days. Titillation, however, is also central to Marlowe's 'text of pleasure', according to Troni Grande (p. 169), but not readily accessible as long as we 'continue to [obscure] Marlowe under the giant shadow of Shakespeare'. She undertakes a 'full-length study of Marlowe's own distinctive transformations of tragedy' (p. 13), including *Hero* as an 'unfinished Tragedy' (p. 25). Working out of Barthes and Patricia Parker, Grande produces a strongly Ovidian Marlowe, whose teasing pleasures derive from generic and ethical manipulation, 'testing authority (specifically, the law of tragedy) through a transgressive, often pleasurable, dilation' (p. 163).

Coming to Know examines 'Recognition' and the 'Complex Plot' in Shakespeare. Barry Adams takes his concepts from Aristotle with no claim that Shakespeare knew *The Poetics*. Like *hamartia*, *anagnôrisis* has been de-psychologized: not penetrating an abstract mystery but identifying a person, usually a blood relation, like Egeon's Abbess/Emilia. Adams examines all eighteen comedies and Romances. Recognition is insignificant in only three – *Wives*, *Troilus* and *Kinsmen* – but 'these anomalies can be accommodated without difficulty' by using an 'only slightly less strict' version of the defining category (p. 8). It would be 'far less rewarding' to consider the histories and tragedies (p. 218), though *Lear*, he remarks, is a bit of an exception.

Exceptions emerge among the comedies as well. The unusually burlesque clown/old Gobbo *anagnôrisis* occurs unusually early in the play – what is at stake in such differences? These marginal cases, analysed more deeply, might help explain why the default examples warrant sustained critical interest.

Peter Lang's Studies in Shakespeare Series is having a run on gerundive titles; David Thatcher's *Begging to Differ*, however, has a lot more argumentative point than *Coming to Know*. In fact, the book is about argument, the discrepancies, divergences, and inconsistencies – between Shakespeare's characters, within his narrative and language, among his commentators – that provoke energetic interpretive response. Thatcher divides his material into 'Plot and Narrative', 'Language and Text', and 'Reasoning and Proof'. He concentrates on problematic pieces; examples from *Hamlet* and *Measure* account for approximately half the book, but there are sustained considerations of *Winter's Tale*, *Henry V* and Sonnet 29, and passing reflections on other Shakespearian texts in chapters on 'Misquotation' and 'Questioning Paternity'. Thatcher's instances occasionally resemble some of Bradley's Appendices, but he wants not to explain away or solve problems but to engage with them. In the Renaissance tradition of 'arguing on either side' Thatcher's 'challenging' of 'conventional wisdom' is 'more than a duty – it becomes a pleasure' (p. 6).

Shakespeare: Text and Theater is a festschrift for Jay Halio. The title categories correspond to Halio's interests and provide a structure for Lois Potter and Arthur Kinney to represent the twenty contributions. A section on 'Texts' includes Stanley Wells on the Folio, Susan Snyder on editorial inertia, George Walton Williams on 'a table of green fields', Tom Clayton on *Dream*, and Donald Foster on attribution study. 'Performances' represents a variety of reminiscence about favourite productions, of which Russell Jackson's account of a Branagh 1986 *Romeo* is particularly engaging. In 'Text and Performance', an all-star cast – Alan

Dessen, Jill Levenson, Laurie Maguire, David Bevington, Alexander Leggatt, and the editors themselves – illustrate both the benefits of disciplinary exchange and the difficulties negotiating the differences, especially over historical distance. Even here the contributors sustain the relaxed tone described in the Preface – a 'welcome relief from the notorious competitiveness of the profession' and 'fun to read' (pp. 11, 12).

Patricia Fumerton's Introduction to *Renaissance Culture and the Everyday* begins with detailed Renaissance instructions on how to slaughter and prepare meat and fowl. Variously sadistic, satiric, gruesome, poetic, burlesque and carnivalesque, these descriptions are meant to bring us a long way from Simon Forman's moist fantasies about her majesty. Where New Historicism was interested in courtly politics, this book is engaged with everyday culture, putting 'A New New Historicism' on the table (pp. 1–17). Take this claim with a peck of salt; Greenblatt, fully at home here, offers a blurb puff on the back cover. But whether 'New New' or just plain 'New', the essays are consistently compelling. Debora Shuger considers why sixteenth-century mirror technology failed to produce more self-regarding people; Don Wayne examines Jonson's heroic failures to find a poetic career not contaminated by the market; Jonson's autonomous fantasies are Fumerton's interest too, writing about ideas of linguistic purity in the Masques; Richard Helgerson analyses various contests in *Wives* – domestic *vs.* courtly, female *vs.* male, everyday *vs.* historical, etc.; Lena Orlin looks at sewing in Renaissance plays as signifying female docility, vulnerability, hypocrisy, and transgression (Orlin's copious knowledge precludes simple conclusions); Frances Dolan suggests that some female violence could be legitimate in the Renaissance – at least in textual representation; Richard Corum uses *Love's Labour's Lost* to engage with a variety of issues – transgression, adolescence, cultural work and the proprieties available to social historians; Simon Hunt, the volume's co-editor, reflects on Tilney's response to riot scenes, reinforcing suggestions that containment and censorship are not the best terms to describe the Court/Theatre relationship.

This year's material includes nine books for non-specialists, students and teachers. Writing for the Northcote Writers and Their Work Series, Penny Gay looks at *As You Like It* for 'what now seem useful meanings at the end of the twentieth century' (p. 3), seeking 'to give . . . honour . . . to the actors who have made meaning with the play' especially in recent performance (p. 7). This contemporary focus is complemented with detailed understanding of original conditions. Presentism versus historicism is an insoluble theoretical problem, but Gay simply disposes of it with immensely practical intelligence, as she does others (ideological work versus theatrical pleasure, comic recuperation versus generic disruption, et al.), by allowing for different possibilities without trivializing the differences themselves. Gay takes advantage of the introductory format's flexibility; the rhetorical occasion coincides happily with the temperament of an author for whom 'possibilities of "performance" are (fortunately) endless' (p. 95) – and with this play.

Writing on *Antony and Cleopatra* for the same series, Kenneth Parker does not discuss performance but includes a census of major productions beginning with 1972 and six photos as well as a chronology of the historical events. The book starts with a good idea: because the play 'challenges certainties about ways of seeing in the moment of their embodiment', Parker will try to 'uncover . . . influential different readings' in 'their contexts' and 'offer an alternative' (p. 3). But his representations of critical tradition reduce 'humanist critical practice' (p. 12) and 'Enlightenment ideas about "progress"' (p. 18) to the simple-minded advocacy of Roman *gravitas* and contemptuous dismissal of Cleopatra as a whore. Parker's strategy also creates enormous pressure to produce a revelation of the truth, and his final claims for Cleopatra as Isis and Antony as a version of

Alberto Memmi's 'colonizer who refuses' (p. 71) cannot deliver the goods.

The Columbia Critical Guides, for which Susan Bruce has written about *Lear* and Martin Coyle about *Richard II*, are designed to give students a sense of critical history. Both intersperse excerpts from representative or influential critics with descriptive and analytical commentary. They present the material chronologically, including chapters on Neoclassical, Romantic, and Victorian criticism, with more extensive consideration of the twentieth century. Coyle includes a chapter on the political resonances of early production (the Queen's concerns, the deposition scene, the Essex rebellion). Critical traditions, once perhaps mindlessly venerated, tend these days to be dispersed into inconsequentiality or even, as I suggested just above, dismissed as error. Coyle and Bruce work thoughtfully to provide not just material but intellectual access to critical history – why this often strange and remote commentary can be of real interest and value.

There are four excellent contributions this year to the Oxford Shakespeare Topics Series. Andrew Gurr and Mariko Ichikawa's *Staging in Shakespeare's Theatres* includes a richly informed commentary about the companies' commercial operation and repertories, the status of playwrights, the social make up of audiences at the amphitheatres and indoor playhouses, etc. But the focus is staging, with special emphasis on movements – across, on, and off the stage – and suggestions about the use of the three openings (if three there were) in the *frons*. The details may occasionally be more than students bargained for, but Gurr and Ichikawa get across the important things for a movie- and tv-watching generation – fluidity of action, symbolic rather than psychologically realistic production and, above all, an actively engaged imaginative response. The book concludes with a helpful conjectural reconstruction of an early staging of *Hamlet*.

Steven Marx introduces *Shakespeare and the Bible* with reflection on the status of Scripture and the Folio. Though constructed over time by worldly agendas, both came to assume transcendent authority. For biblical commentary, the interpretive consequence was midrash, 'linking the various parts' through 'discovery of typological patterns [and] verbal echoes' to generate 'new stories' and 'further explication' (p. 15). Marx himself is most midrashic in his first and last chapters, juxtaposing *Tempest* with Genesis and then Revelation. As Genesis is 'a seed containing the germinal patterns of most later stories', so *Tempest* can suggest 'in concentrated form many of the plots and themes of Shakespeare's other plays' (p. 22). With Revelation, *Tempest* works the other around, playing 'a retrospective and epitomizing role in relation to earlier works' (p. 126). Marx knows that the sense of unity driving these interpretations is an accident of printing history or an effect of institutional power; but he respects the other side as well – the textual power by which these books impel readers to discover hidden textual pleasures if not eternal life. The linkages in the middle four chapters are less of a stretch, explicit echoes and influence rather than a floating intertextuality: Moses, David and Henry V as historical types; Job and *Lear*; *Measure* and Gospel; *Merchant* and Romans. Marx emphasizes Scripture's receptiveness to temporal interests and political pressures: the 'New Testament' fulfilment of the 'Old Dispensation' betrays its own status as a contested claim; the Hebrew Bible shows Moses juggling to keep men in awe, assimilating the anthropological understanding of its own foundations.

Eastern Europe has become a recognizable 'Shakespeare topic' only recently, but in Zdeněk Stříbrný's informative and moving account Shakespeare has been a sustained East European interest; it goes back to the English actors who brought their drama to the Holy Roman Empire and beyond in the sixteenth and seventeenth centuries. *Shakespeare and Eastern Europe* describes 'Shakespeare under the Tsars' and 'Shakespeare and National Revivals', devoting the last three chapters to the twentieth century (Stanislavsky, Kozintsev, Kott, among many others) when the plays' 'capacity to stir our conscience' (p. 106) made them a powerful voice for the coded resistance to tyranny. In 'Post-Communist Shakespeare', Stříbrný acknowledges that Shakespeare is 'now received' less 'as a matter of life and death' and more as 'a thing of truth and beauty' (p. 146): happy are the lands that do not need a poetic hero – happier, anyway.

Shakespeare's Dramatic Genres begins with a Thurber character reading *Macbeth* like an Agatha Christie and ends with video-store classifications: the customers 'may not know which flick to pick, but they know the sort of experience they want' (p. 142). Lawrence Danson's point is that generic expectation is always working; we cannot help but be genre critics – all of us, across the range of history and intellectual sophistication – any more than M. Jourdain can avoid speaking prose. Having demystified the concept, Danson is free to discuss the sometimes strange-looking inhabitants peculiar to the Shakespearian milieu: for tragedy, the 'courtly and academic' *Gorboduc* (p. 32), Senecan extremism, *De Casibus* pathos, overreaching hero-villains; for comedy, Donatus, academic farce, Lyly and Greene, Romantic and New and Citizen Comedy. (Danson follows the tripartite distinction of the Folio, though history gets finessed as a subcategory, leaving comedy/tragedy to constitute the field.) Neither comedy nor tragedy is 'an ideal form laid up in heaven' (p. 89) or 'the hermetically sealed opposite' of each other (p. 69); they 'depend upon or imply one another' (p. 117), available as 'opportunities for inventiveness' (p. 143), producing 'the surprises and satisfactions that come from playing old games in new ways' (p. 144). Along with bags of useful information and exciting ideas, Danson communicates delight in the material, himself imitating 'the mixing of modes' (p. 16) he admires in Renaissance playwrights (as in the dying fall from 'cataclysm' to 'bimbo', among many examples (p. 5)).

A Companion to Shakespeare gathers twenty-nine essays written by what the blurb fairly describes as 'the most distinguished historians and literary scholars working today'. David Scott Kastan organizes this material into five sections of five or more essays each: 'Living' (social and political history); 'Reading' (literacy, the Bible, the Classics, and history); 'Writing' (professional playwrighting, Shakespeare's language, verse, rhetoric, genres); 'Playing' (theatrical marketplaces, companies, repertory, censorship, playhouses); and 'Printing' (early editions, surviving playbooks, print technology, the book trade and book censorship). Professional Shakespearians will get lots out of the rich knowledge and critical thought in these five-hundred closely printed pages. Whether as much will be available to the book's target audience – 'the beginning student[,] experienced undergraduate and new graduate' (p. ii) – is not clear.

Kastan starts by dismissing what is 'No doubt the most familiar of the clichés of Shakespeare studies', that Shakespeare 'is our contemporary'. Although 'we drag him forward into our present' (p. 3), in this book 'the differences must be insisted upon' (p. 4). He assures us that 'This is not, *of course*', meant 'to sequester him' in the past, and that 'Art is not, *of course*, reducible to its historical determinants', and yet again that 'It should *go without saying* that to focus on the enabling conditions of Shakespeare's art is not to detract from the plays they enable' (pp. 3 and 5, my emphases). Why protest so much? Contextualization itself cannot be the problem; a Companion's job, as Russ McDonald says, is to 'supply information, ideas, and contextual material'. But where McDonald's context is designed to 'promote' the 'most successful encounter with Shakespeare's works' (p. 3), Kastan reverses the flow of interest to the context as a stand-alone object ontologically prior to the text: 'the cultural and material mediations that permitted the plays to be produced' (p. 5).

Not all the essays take this line. Some, concentrated in the 'Reading' and 'Writing' sections, would be at home in Bedford or even Wells's 1986 *Cambridge Companion*. The book begins with Bevington on Shakespeare's life, a gentler Shakespeare than the litigious and usurious versions typical of current practice, and it ends with Michael Bristol's reluctance to sneer at 'Shakespeare: The Myth': 'In the long run . . . one does not go around muttering "bah humbug" ' (p. 489); 'as stories go, it's not a bad one to hold on to' (p. 501). But Kastan wants to downplay 'the romantic notion of artistic genius, solitary and sovereign, untouched by the world' (p. 5), potentially celebrated by these accounts. He hives Bevington and Bristol off into compartments of their own, 'Shakespeare I' and 'Shakespeare II', 'bracketing five sections that attempt to define the conditions of possibility in which he wrote' (p. 5). Given this *mise-en-livre*, the highlight shines on those essays where singularity is absorbed into an anonymous collectivity: we 'continue to praise Shakespeare for exceptional artistry' when we should stress that his 'plays exemplify' the common modes 'characteristic of his era' (Henderson and Siemon, 'Reading Vernacular Literature', p. 207); by putting 'Shakespeare's plays in connection with those of other playwrights' rather than in the context 'foregrounded in the first folio', we can highlight 'the particular anxieties and struggles of a specific historical juncture' which the Folio 'tends to occlude' (Howard, 'Shakespeare and Genre', p. 304); 'the repertory of Shakespeare's company looks very much like the repertory of other companies', so its role 'in the commercial success' was 'not in its difference' but 'in the shrewdness of its managers to manipulate the industry-wide repertory system' (Knutson, 'Shakespeare's Repertory', pp. 360–1).

Typicality versus exceptionality, cultural context versus artistic text: choice may be difficult in the abstract, but books are geared to particular markets and uses. The emphasis here on context seems more appropriate to a scholarly readership than to students in a Shakespeare

course, which is predicated by definition on Shakespearian singularity. The many teachers challenging this predication in order 'to create a new history of early modern drama' (Howard, 'Shakespeare and Genre', p. 304) – those for whom 'always historicize' rather than 'Shakespeare our contemporary' is the slogan of choice – may find this book serves them well. But even they will have to think twice before asking students to pay 60 per cent more than what Wells costs and over twice the price for McDonald.

In his other contribution this year, the more clearly aimed *Shakespeare After Theory*, Kastan claims we inhabit 'a post-theoretical moment' (p. 28). Structuralism promised 'the intellectual authority of disinterested science' (p. 26), post-structuralism 'the moral authority of a committed politics' (p. 27), but neither delivered. Although 'theory has successfully spoken the previously unspoken assumptions of literary studies', it cannot 'offer convincing alternatives' (p. 28). New Historicism, which 'acknowledge[d] histories . . . only to retotalize culture', was 'not properly historical at all' (p. 30). What we need now is a newer historicism (Fumerton's New New Historicism?): we 'must shift the investigation to a materialist mode' (p. 28) to 'reveal' the 'actual historical circumstances of production and reception' (p. 31) – namely, the 'collaborations of play and book production' (p. 38) into which the authorial lone eagle of literary interpretation is dispersed.

There are two agendas here: (1) forget theory and do interpretation; and (2) claim special value for the kind of interpretation you like – a 'proper' or 'actual' historicism; elsewhere a 'radical historicity' producing 'genuinely historical understanding' and 'genuine interdisciplinarity' (pp. 53, 54). The second returns to the theory game that the first had – for good reason – renounced: if you use theory to speak the unspeakable assumptions of a practice you do not like (literary study), someone else will use it to expose the practice you do (proper materialism), just by adding italics at the right places – as where Kastan locates authorship and meaning in 'the *actual* collaborative economies that are the *essence* of *all* intellectual and social practice' (p. 40). Kastan dismisses deconstruction as 'endlessly reflecting and ultimately "signifying nothing"' (p. 181), but the nothing it signifies is the actually and essentially unstable foundation of all interpretive practitioners, including those who dismiss deconstruction in the name of genuine historicism. The genuine posits a centre and, although as Derrida said there always *is* a centre (for Derrida, 'signifying nothing' was not an option), it is a function, not a being. In other words, interpretation always takes place within an arbitrarily unified field, which in turn means that the totalizing practice of New Historicism is something of which Kastan's newer historicism is equally guilty.

But all this merely confirms agenda one – forget theory – and if Kastan cannot quite bring himself to surrender the high theoretical ground, his main commitment is to interpretive practice. Hence in a strong chapter on 'Editing Shakespeare Today', he notes that the effect (and maybe sometimes intention) of editorial theory is to prevent editorial work and concludes we will go on producing editions as usual – even those scandalous conflations – because students, actors and almost everybody but a few editorial theorists want to use them. (R. A. Foakes's shrewd review essay on the same topic pursues a similar route to reach the same conclusion.) Desire and use are the motivating factors. Totalizations all the way down, but some are more nourishing than others, and this is Kastan's great strength – an acute interpretive intelligence, enriched with historical knowledge and represented in exceptionally clear and graceful writing. He offers a *Macbeth* equivocal right to the end, a European *Tempest*, centred in dynastic politics at home rather than colonial expansion, and an 'Oldcastle' whose 'religio-political valences' (p. 95) likely appealed to 'a Protestant bias' (p. 100). In a section on 'Text as History' the subversion-containment dialectic emerges as a through line. The first chapters, published some time ago, argue that history

plays are 'effective as a subversion of [established] authority' (p. 111); but in work appearing here for the first time, Kastan claims only that theatre 'reveals the vulnerability of the traditional culture' (p. 154), without necessarily contributing to its transformation. By the end, discussing the theatres' closing in 1642, he seems to repudiate the stronger claim once and for all. 'Plays apparently may both provoke rebellion and prevent it' (p. 209); it is what particular audiences do with the play that determines the matter. But Shakespearian subversion is apparently too attractive to abandon: by defining both Royalist and Parliamentary forces as 'competing elites' (p. 211), he recovers Renaissance theatres as inherently places 'where freedom could appear [and] where authority was contested' (p. 216).

According to Ivo Kamps, in the lead piece of Christy Desmet and Robert Sawyer's *Shakespeare and Appropriation*, 'we need to keep reminding ourselves' that 'Every reading' is 'already an appropriation' (p. 23). If Kamps is right, the regular division of Shakespearian criticism into 'Two main reactions': 'either the [critical] system is expanded to match the plays, or the plays are reduced to fit the system' (Vickers, 'General Editor's Preface', p. x), may be wish-fulfilment. Nonetheless, a rough and ready distinction between kinds of appropriation – the stage diameter of the original Globe *vs.* the cultural work of *The Lion King*, say – remains useful, and it is the latter kind on display here. This lively book includes pieces on Shakespearian motifs in contemporary romance (Laurie Osborne), Smiley's *Lear* (Caroline Cakebread), Naylor's *Tempest* (James Andreas, Sr), Branagh's and Disney's *Hamlet* (Lisa Starks, Richard Finkelstein). Not all the pieces concentrate on current work. Terence Hawkes writes about Shakespearian pastoral in Quiller-Couch's Liberal politics and the establishment of Eng Lit. at Cambridge. Georgiana Ziegler offers a fascinatingly illustrated discussion of the desperate measures taken to naturalize Lady Macbeth during the nineteenth century.

Sudipto Chatterjee and Jyotsna G. Singh analyse what happened when an Indian actor performed Othello in Calcutta in 1848. Robert Sawyer describes a variety of post-Romantic concerns leading to 'The Shakespeareanization of Robert Browning'. Gary Taylor's Afterword on 'The Incredible Shrinking Bard' predicts that Shakespeare's status will continue to diminish from its late Victorian heights, replaced by 'Gloria Naylor, or Jane Smiley, or Thomas Middleton' (p. 205). Taylor represents this claim as a shocking form of *épater les bourgeois*: 'The Shakespeare industry will no doubt dismiss' it, believing that 'Shakespeare is "immortal"' as 'Ben Jonson claimed' (p. 205). But since most Shakespearians have long since apostated themselves from bardolatry, Taylor's performance as the village atheist sounds like the Latin Mass.

More appropriation: in *Transforming Shakespeare* Marianne Novy collects thirteen essays about 'late twentieth-century women who often talk back aggressively to Shakespeare's plays, to earlier interpretations of them, and to patriarchal and colonialist attitudes that the plays have come to symbolize' (p. 1). Feminist interests occasionally bleed into racial concerns: Rita Dove's ambivalence about Shakespeare (Peter Erickson); the resistance to Cleopatra's colour – that strain again (Francesca Royster). *Lear*'s fraught father–daughter relationships get a lot of attention: three pieces on *A Thousand Acres* (Barbara Mathieson, Iska Alter, Smiley herself) and one on Atwood's *Cat's Eye* (Suzanne Raitt). *Tempest* gets almost as much, presumably for the same reason (Diana Brydon, Caroline Cakebread, and some e-mail Linda Bamber imagines being sent from Claribel@palace.tunis to Mirnfer@island.temp). Other pieces look at Australian *Shrews* (Penny Gay), Christine Edzard's *As You Like It* (Patricia Lennox), Ann-Marie MacDonald's and Paula Vogel's rewritings of Desdemona (Novy), and Katie Mitchell's 1994 production of *3 Henry VI* at The Other Place (Barbara Hodgdon) which, as 'political theater' rather 'than the traditionally director-oriented practices of the RSC' (p. 18), uses 'Brechtian techniques of distantiation' (p. 25) to 'intersect with and address contemporary events' (p. 30).

The same vividly detailed description and strong argument are on abundant display in Hodgdon's *Shakespeare Trade*, which parades a dazzling array of theatrical, cinematic, televisual and textual 'Performances and Appropriations': *Shrews* from a 1908 movie to Gale Edwards's 1995 RSC production; *Othellos* from Olivier to Fishburne, all 'feed[ing] into a white male viewer's potentially racist fantasies of miscegenation' (p. 67); *Cleopatras* beginning with Bradley and Beerbohm Tree in 1906, a 'historical juncture' (p. 95) when pop movie culture was displacing elite theatre, on to Theda Bara, Claudette Colbert, and Elizabeth Taylor; QEI in a variety of gender and nationalist contexts, culminating in Glenda Jackson's *Elizabeth R* and Quentin Crisp in Sally Potter's *Orlando*; English reviewers' anxiety faced with the Lepage *Dream* (RNT, 1992–3); finally, Stratford 'as a virtual wonder cabinet for Shakespeare', working 'to reconstruct and individuate him' in 'processes of ideological persuasion' (p. 194).

This description barely suggests Hodgdon's extraordinary range, the rapidity with which she shifts among phenomena, and the brilliance with which her connections add up to and then metamorphose into different interpretative suggestions. Everything is in restless motion – perhaps inevitably, given the 'shift from textual to cultural authority' (p. xiii) by which, 'Drawing on contemporary critical and cultural studies', she 'moves beyond text-centered analyses to situate spectators and their reading strategies as the primary objects of investigation' (p. 171). But more is at stake than a shift of reference – namely, the shiftiness of referentiality itself: 'these chapters move away from reading performances through the myth of a factitive text and author to one where performances figure as cultural productions or even commodities that, by dissolving Shakespeare's text into reading or consuming relations, circulate with, borrow from, and challenge other discourses in a kind of reciprocal tension which rearticulates how "Shakespeare" generates meanings' (p. xi). Who is doing what to whom here? All this activity – moving away, reading, figuration, dissolution, consumption, circulation, borrowing, challenging, rearticulation – seems to be happening independently of agents, verbs without subjects. Working back through the relative pronouns, you get eventually to 'these chapters', a phrase which invites us to focus on the dramatic movement by which Hodgdon enacts her own critical subjectivity. The invitation becomes explicit a moment later, with 'My own vested interest involves opening up a traffic between . . . ' (p. xiii) and is sustained through the book's final words, which acknowledge motivation as 'displaying or showing off, not just the self called Shakespeare but also the self that has written this history of his Stratford Empire' (p. 240).

The cult of personality, though, has no place in *The Shakespeare Trade*. Whatever bug killed off the author cannot be quarantined to ' "Shakespeare" '. 'Hodgdon' – the signature inscribed on 'this history', 'these chapters', 'this account' (p. 111), etc. – guarantees meaning no better than anybody else. Discursive effects cannot be the 'primary objects of investigation' when the investigator's own subjectivity is itself an effect of discourse. Hence her 'vested interest' does not open up a traffic, it 'involves' opening it up, and is in any case not to be taken for the unclothed 'I' of an essential self. *Not me, but the vested interest blowing through me.* This disappearance of agency might mystify authority, as in 'one doesn't do that' or 'History speaking', Professor Welch's signature tune in *Lucky Jim*, but Hodgdon's implied 'Culture speaking' makes no claim to be the owner of culture – quite the reverse. The in-your-face subjectivity of *The Shakespeare Trade* seems not to foreclose discussion, but to invite argument: *this is my story, what's yours?*

John Russell Brown is on hand with one counter-narrative. Where in Hodgdon Mitchell 'stages images juxtaposing Catholic ritual . . .

with rituals of killing' to 'drive the point home' that politics has 'degenerated into political vendettas' and make us 'engage . . . with history' ('Making it New', p. 20), for Brown, the 'pious singing, like the chorus at the end of a musical, the lights slowly changing to a softer glow', produces apathy: 'However cruel and hopeless political life might be, all would be well . . . so long as one sings about heaven.' Brown's version of the play produces an antithetical answer to the question, *what is the point?* Indeed, just because the production works in the point-driving-home mode (they agree on this), Brown's 'audience has to submit to the . . . computerised deftness and disciplined choruswork' (p. 164). I have my own counter-narratives, differing from Hodgdon's about the xenophobia of Lepage's reviewers, the tranquillizing effect of Olivier's allusions to 'minstrelsy' (p. 44), the recuperative motives behind Bradley's *Antony*, etc. But why argue? Sit back and enjoy the kaleidoscopic display of an exhilarating intelligence working at the top of its powers.

Hamlet Studies celebrates its twentieth anniversary with a retrospective about the journal's establishment in the 'period of political crisis' in 1970s India and larger context of the colonial 'legacy [shaping] our institutions and ways of thinking and even feeling' (Desai, *Hamlet Studies*, p. 9). In other *Hamlet Studies* pieces: Frank Clary and Hardin Aasand describe instances of contemporary intrigue like the Gowrie Conspiracy as 'moments of revenge, replication, and remembering that haunt' the play (p. 38). Lloyd David places *Hamlet* in a Platonic tradition of ambivalent desire that can lead either to transcendence or bestial oblivion. David Beliles believes Hamlet actually seduces Ophelia as part of 'his larger goal of public good' (p. 87). Charles Kelley teases out interpretive uses of narrative; received stories ('they say', 'so I have heard') at least help clarify particular situations. Lisa Hopkins analyses emblematic gardens in *The Spanish Tragedy* and *Hamlet* with particular reference to the figure of

Hercules. On *Hamlet* elsewhere, Eric Mallin wittily juxtaposes Arnold Schwarznegger in *Last Action Hero* with Romantic versions of the sensitive sweet prince; as usual, the play absorbs the most dissonant of cognitive ironies. David Farley-Hills supports a nineteenth-century suggestion that Hamlet arranged his meeting with the pirates – attesting, like Beliles's scenario of Ophelia's seduction, to *Hamlet*'s continuing power to compel critical invention. In a powerfully argued piece, richly documented with theological detail, Anthony Low relates the play's oedipal aggression and deracinated isolation to the 'transformative event' which 'made it possible to repudiate tradition and kill the father' – the 'abolition of Purgatory' and its consequent loss of community with the remembered dead (p. 444).

In *Shakespeare's Romances and the Politics of Counter-Reformation*, one of two books this year on the late plays, Thomas Rist identifies four 'features which, taken together, suggest a powerfully . . . Catholic . . . dimension' to *Pericles, Cymbeline, Winter's Tale* and *Tempest* (p. 1). In the first, 'the structure of death and resurrection' re-enacts the '"central devotional activity"' of the late Middle Ages, replicating a Catholic rather than Protestant understanding of the Eucharist (p. 47, quoting Eamon Duffy). The others – a 'structural correlation' with Ignatian meditative techniques (p. 57); a Montaignian affirmation of ecclesiastical authority as the only response to scepticism; and a benevolent supernatural power 'Contrary to, and refuting, Protestantism's demystification of the world' (p. 130) – add up to a claim for Shakespearian religious nostalgia. This claim is reinforced by two persuasive essays – the Low piece described above and Anthony Dawson's 'The Arithmetic of Memory', in which *Henry V, Julius Caesar* and *Hamlet* evoke contradictory feelings about the Eucharist and images. All three work out of Duffy, and Rist too gives *Hamlet* special attention (pp. 178–85); but where Rist's Shakespeare 'asserts' specifically Catholic beliefs and 'challenges' others (p. 130),

Low and Dawson's Shakespeare moves toward remediation and the restoration of a broad community. For Low, 'flights of angels sing thee to thy rest' may be 'theologically naive' but is 'precisely right' in its very vagueness, 'deeply satisfying . . . to Catholics, Protestants, and doubters alike' (p. 464). Dawson notes wryly that 'an analogy to the Catholic mass is not necessarily calculated to win unambiguous affirmation on a late Elizabethan platform' (pp. 60–1). His subtle argument centres on theatre as the place 'of obsessive return to the trauma of broken images . . . a form of cultural re-play, akin to the belated, but still sometimes cathartic return of the victim of severe trauma to the scene of pain' (p. 63).

'Shakespeare's late plays have generated different responses' (p. 1), Jennifer Richards and James Knowles announce at the beginning of their collection, and variety is the through line of this lively volume. They prefer 'late plays' to the more exclusionary 'romances' and 'tragicomedies'; as Julia Briggs remarks in her contribution, *All Is True* and *Kinsmen* get short shrift because they fail to achieve the effects expected from romance: 'the plenitude of alternatives' and 'consciously artificial optimism' are 'finally withdrawn' (p. 211). Similarly, 'late' is reduced from the more familiar 'last' or 'final', which suggest 'a valedictory gesture' and seem to constitute a self-contained 'imaginative world in its own right' (p. 4). The contributors all downplay formal unity, for individual plays or generic groupings. Variety and inclusion bring even *Cardenio* into the picture. Seen in or through *The Double Falsehood*, *Cardenio* is in Briggs's version again notable for its relative gloom, while for Richard Wilson, seeking 'to contextualise' the play 'in relation to its sensational Jacobean occasion' – Prince Henry's funeral and Princess Elizabeth's marriage following hard upon (p. 195) – *Cardenio* is a translucent window on the anxieties of keeping up courtly appearances.

After three gender pieces – Helen Hackett on 'maternity and narrative', Gordon McMullan on 'man(ner)liness' in *Henry VIII*, and Alan Stewart on 'the trials of friendship' in *Kinsmen* – the book highlights religion in ways overlapping but also contrasting with Rist. Thomas Healy's *Henry VIII* is emphatically distanced from Protestant didacticism but remains sceptically irresolute, unable or unwilling to elevate its audience to the altitude of a 'credo'. Gareth Roberts, writing on the religious inflections of magic in *Tempest* and *Winter's Tale*, argues (like Low and Dawson) for a strategic dispersal across a divided territory, with Shakespeare's 'carefully negotiating' the 'magical power of the old religion' (p. 134). Willy Maley's *Cymbeline* 'champion[s]' a residual Catholicism', but Maley's postcolonial perspective looks beyond authorial stability to a contradictory and fragmented response: 'differing attitudes . . . exemplify the fact that disenfranchised communities respond in different ways to political change' (p. 156).

In *Shakespeare and the Politics of Culture in Late Victorian England*, Linda Rozmovits analyses *Merchant*'s extraordinary power to shape belief at a time when Shakespearian authority was close to holy writ. The woman question was more pressing than the Jewish question. Victorians emphasized the betrothal rather than the trial scene to convey 'a sense of the heroine's femininity' (p. 48), but they had to work to keep up appearances with a play also available to feminist claims. 'Portia constituted a site of political struggle precisely because she seemed to occupy both sides of the public–private divide' (p. 57). A similarly amphibious appropriability characterized Shylock. Rozmovits examines Irving's felt need to cut racial matters in order to sustain his hugely popular pro-Shylock performance and analyses the play's capacity to reflect contradictory feelings about mercantilism and community. 'It was a story you could tell your children', she remarks about the flurry of rewriting for younger readers; for all 'its moments of unease' and 'trepidation' (p. 128), it pacified anxiety with the magic of a happy ending.

Where Rozmovits sees irresolvable contra-dictions, Robert Schneider's *Shylock, the Roman* 'presumes that *The Merchant of Venice* is a highly integrated work of art' (p. 162). He rejects the 'Christian Jewish paradigm, which has shaped criticism . . . so far', because it 'fails to resolve significant thematic contradictions' (p. 160). The 'honor/irony perspective' he offers as an alternative allows us to see, hidden under the surface, the play's real conflict between an elite concept of ancient Roman honour and 'the festive immorality of the Roman carnival' (p. 22). From a technological angle, this book is boldly forward-looking: you can download it from the internet (point your browser at 'pulpless.com'). Conceptually, though, in assuming thematic unity, 'unmasking' hidden ironies and identifying new meanings not 'so far' perceived, Schneider exemplifies the characteristics of an exhausted formalism as Richard Levin analysed it years ago in *New Readings vs. Old Plays*. *Shylock, the Roman* is not unintelligent, and if it had appeared twenty years ago (when its author apparently left academia), it would have resembled what Kuhn called 'normal science'. Does this mean that current state-of-the-art criticism will look, twenty years from now, like an archaeological relic?

In periodical consideration of *Merchant*, Roy Booth describes 'Jews' houses of ballads and contemporary literature' and 'the one surviving Jew's house in Shakespeare's London' (p. 25), arguing that 'Shylock's Sober House' is coterminous with the character's identity. Bruce Boehrer analyses changing Renaissance attitudes toward animals, from instrumental (food and labour) to playful (household pets), brilliantly mapping the implications onto the play's unstable feelings about categories, distinct and permeable. Charles Edelman reflects on 'the stage Jew' as part of the audience's supposed baggage. Whether the play is ' "tragic" ' or not, 'pro- or anti-Semitic', Edelman seeks 'to challenge the *a priori* assumption that Shylock must have conformed to a particular theatrical tradition' to 'satisfy [original] expectations' (p. 100).

Merchant is 'the high point of this book',

William Kerrigan says about *Shakespeare's Promises*. 'Promises everywhere!' (p. xiii). Kerrigan's starting point is that promise and obligation are at the centre of social, ethical, and individual life ('Man is a promising animal' (p. 7)), a situation reflected on in Shakespeare's plays ('Whatever some may think, Shakespeare's dramas do have themes' (p. xiv)), at a time when religious fragmentation produced an anxious scepticism about vows and oaths, precipitating our long march past Hobbes (fear of state power), Hume (the internalization of such fear in good name), and Nietzsche (the repudiation of such internalization as debilitating the will to power). Kerrigan offers full-scale treatments of *Richard III* and *Othello* on either side of *Merchant*. Richard embodies the ambivalent pleasures of freedom from obligation but, finally blind to the autonomous binding force of the oaths sworn to Elizabeth, he 'seals his fate [and] brings the end of the play on himself, a great deceiver broken at last by the very structure of an oath' (pp. 82–3). Oaths trip up Shylock too – not, though, by failing to recognize but failing to live up to them. 'Breaking the vow of faith' by his willingness to 'settle for the best cash offer' after Portia's victory, Shylock suffers the consequences of 'forced conversion to another one' (p. 135). In 'Ironic Vows', Kerrigan's *Othello* 'means for us to reflect on the whole system of promising' (p. 189), the 'treacheries born inside the codes of promising' themselves (p. 206). Where other plays affirm the cultural norms sustaining the cultural forms, *Othello* offers no such consolation.

Still, Kerrigan argues that Shakespeare is 'not yet ready to submit without remainder to our post-Christian analysis of power' (p. 91), sustaining this claim with an emphasis on terminal resolution. Like Richard and Shylock's comeuppance, 'the moral self-analysis of a confessed perjurer' at the end of Sonnet 152 is said to produce 'satisfying closure to the sequence' as a whole (p. 47). Kerrigan knows we cannot just ignore those *ad nauseam* reiterations about the discontinuity between knowledge and action

('all this the world well knows, yet . . .'); the 'post-Christian' Shakespeare cannot be ruled out of court. The promise problem is a huge one; it is not promises but a shared belief in the arrangements they entail which helps keep humanity from preying on itself. Kerrigan's aim is not to offer a one-size-fits-all solution, but to put the subject on the table in its ramifying complexity, giving 'future interpreters of Shakespeare's plays something fresh to talk about' (p. xvii). He does so in a relaxed prose nonetheless richly responsive to the complexities and subtleties of Shakespearian language – his analysis of nuance in 'will/shall' and 'would/should' (pp. 22–6) is by itself worth the price of admission.

Shakespeare Survey 52 is about 'The Globe' – old, new, the relation between the two. In an opening retrospective, Gabriel Egan works his way from Chambers's *Elizabethan Stage*, 'the first landmark in the scholarly reconstruction of the Globe' (p. 1), to the present – a story with many digressions and regressions, progressing toward an uncertain end. Whatever ideas about Renaissance dramatic production emerge from the Wanamaker reconstruction, it has increased what we know about the old Globe and clarified what we do not. Marion O'Connor is less sanguine: the confusions and compromises of Poel's career reveal 'the possibilities but also, and even more, the limits of theatrical reconstructions' (p. 17). In a piece packed with interesting information and exciting ideas, W. B. Worthen ranges among theme parks and living history museums to put the new Globe into a larger context of re-enactment. Reflecting on the tendency of these phenomena to 'choreograph and commodify all aspects of experience', 'regimenting their visitors . . . passively, as *consumers* rather than producers of experience', Worthen allows for more interesting possibilities derived from 'the explicitly theatrical function of the Globe' (p. 41): 'live theatre performed in the here and now, actors using contemporary ideas' (p. 45). In this situation, an audience might not merely swallow a prepackaged pastness but participate in the variably constituted processes that make (or fail to make) sense of the past.

In other contributions, 'The Globe' is less materially specific. For Jerzy Limon, 'whether the Globe was 99 or 106 feet in diameter' does not matter unless 'the actual dimensions are part of a code that contributes to the interpretation' (p. 47). Limon distinguishes improvised settings (churches and banquet halls, containing – both senses – physical and ideological meaning) from the neutral interiors of purpose-built amphitheatres, which signified only as places for performance and could 'acquire an infinite number of possible meanings' (p. 51). If Limon's 'global' means worldly or secular, for Peter Donaldson it refers to digital technology and Shakespeare's 'ever more natural, self-evident role' in the 'transition from the era of print and live theatre to that of digital media and world-wide networks' (p. 185). Donaldson negotiates a vast range, from historical linguistics to 'TOMS images', describing the displacement of a modernist esthetic (theatre and photography – a narrative 'of conquest') by a post-modernist esthetic (digital media blur 'received boundaries between models and what they model' – 'a narrative of fascination' (p. 196)). He ends with *William Shakespeare's Romeo + Juliet's* problematic 'relation of contemporary media culture to history: of "Shakespeare" as Luhrmann has refashioned him' to 'the Shakespeare . . . other than, perhaps alien to, such a refashioning' (p. 198). If this sounds like Hodgdon territory, here she is, looking at what cannot in this context be called the 'same' flickering images. 'How, I want to ask, does that film resonate within both "Shakespeare culture" and global popular culture?' (p. 88). Here too is Kathleen McLuskie, describing with witty intelligence a Zulu *Macbeth* presented during the Globe's first season, as part of 'the endless game of pass the parcel . . . by which theatre practice is connected to political and aesthetic discourse, the way one culture connects to another' (p. 155).

A number of strong books appeared this year combining Shakespeare with current interests in the body. Michael Schoenfeldt's subject in *Bodies and Selves in Early Modern England* is the Galenic humoral theory that understands pathology as internal imbalance. Where recent functionalist accounts in early Foucault and New Historicism 'emphasize the individual as a victim of power', Schoenfeldt stresses 'the empowerment . . . bestowed upon the individual' (p. 11). The '"caloric economy" . . . frequently sanctioned . . . manipulations of gender and class', but it also 'could be manipulated by . . . the individual subject's willing and unembarrassed adoption of therapies of self-regulation' (p. 15). Schoenfeldt's Shakespeare chapter keys on Sonnet 94. The poem's ironies about self-mastery seem 'oppressively chilly' and 'deeply hypocritical to twentieth-century sensibility' because we have lost sympathy with the system of beliefs which shape its values and those of the sequence as a whole. '*Contra* Wordsworth', the Sonnets are 'not about unlocking hearts but about locking them up tightly' (p. 95).

In *Dead Hands*, Katherine Rowe argues that if 'the hand is the preeminent bodily metaphor for human action' (p. x), severed hands function as sites where intuitive concepts by which we understand agency are interrogated. She develops this claim with a chapter on Renaissance anatomy, two on drama (*Titus* and *Duchess of Malfi*), and two on nineteenth-century Gothic. The *Titus* chapter argues that the bizarre effects of dismemberment and punning derive from the inappropriate assumptions 'modern audiences' bring to the action. From within the post-Renaissance 'philosophy of possessive individualism' (p. xi), we 'collapse . . . stage dismemberment into "real" mutilation and "real" rape' in a 'morally outraged response' that reduces Lavinia to 'a representation of the sexually violent erasure of female subjectivity' (p. 73). To early modern belief, however, 'dismemberment encodes loss of effect on the world' (p. 83). Lavinia thus 'exemplifies the general condition of action in the play' and 'functions as a space where the political distribution of the signs of agency is worked out' (p. 73).

Both these books centre on the idea that the body has a history, reciprocally constitutive of and constituted by a variety of philosophical, social and political values changing over time. Insisting on the consequences of embodiment, Schoenfeldt and Rowe get under Cartesian beliefs about bodies as merely transient sites our minds inhabit or possess, accidental to the authentic substance of identity in rational thought. Schoenfeldt is attracted to the pre-Enlightenment 'subject . . . constituted as a profoundly material substance' (p. 10), intuiting 'personality' as 'tied to the corporeal stuff in which we dwell' (p. 172); but he refuses 'to convert' his 'admiration' for 'this earlier regime' into 'nostalgia' for a 'lost common language' (p. 171). Rowe claims that her 'conceptual history' avoids concepts of 'false consciousness of self', asking only 'How did our current conceptions of subordinate and autonomous agency, and their dependence on bodily evidence and experience, evolve?' (pp. xi–xii). Even this question, however, betrays a pointed interest in political consequence – developing alternatives to the 'possessive individualism' in which we now residually function.

'Fractured and fragmented bodies from [Metamorphoses] cast long, broken shadows over European literary history' (p. 1). Lynn Enterline's declaration at the beginning of The Rhetoric of the Body suggests common elements with Schoenfeldt and especially Rowe; differences, though, as well: Enterline's historical interest is focused on the literary – the invention and development of poetic language in a tradition characterized by extraordinary self-consciousness. Petrarch is the key transformative figure. Where in Ovid, 'dismemberment and rape' serve 'to reflect on the power and limitations of language' (p. 3), Petrarchan blason dismembers female bodies for self-fashioning, 'turning them into figures of his own story'

(p. 91). In chapters on Lucrece and Winter's Tale, Enterline's Shakespeare retransforms this mode back to its origins, engaging 'with the homosocial conversation of Petrarchanism by using Ovid's female voices to [ask] what might happen if the chaste, resistant, stony lady were at last to speak back' (p. 156). This is High Deconstruction – surprisingly fine-tuning nuances already surprisingly fine-tuned, austere in renouncing claims for extra-textual consequence beyond the 'discursive production of what counts as the difference in sexual difference' (p. 3). Hence Lucrece's 'figural language' and 'ventriloquism' are said 'to disturb' the 'seemingly self-evident knowledge [in] the words "man" and "woman" – or what we mean when we say a "male" or "female" desire' (p. 197).

Ovid and dismemberment figure too in Mariangela Tempera's engaging book on Titus, as two of the various contextualizations serving to refamiliarize this historically remote 'Play for Some Seasons' (p. 9). A chapter on the 'Trail of Body Parts' discusses Senecan horror on the Renaissance stage, including some infrequently visited Continental examples. Tempera thematizes the play broadly in terms of wilderness and civility, connecting with conventional Shakespearian concerns and giving new force to routine Lear connections. Her main context is anamorphosis: confronted with dramatic characters given to inexplicably sudden transformations of mood and belief, an audience is itself required to swing wildly from one response to another. Tempera's Shakespeare came to understand that 'the artistic potential of incomplete metamorphosis' (p. 214) serves comedy better than his particular tragic effects which, further refined through Bradleyan demands for psychological integrity and emotionally unified action, have 'so largely conditioned' academic criticism that 'it is difficult for us even to imagine' alternatives (p. 71). But theatrical audiences carry less (or different) baggage, and Titus's current popularity has been achieved largely through performance. Tempera discusses productions going back to Brook, including French, Italian, Romanian and Dutch examples, strikingly illustrated with forty-three plates.

Yet more Ovidian rhetoric in Anthony Mortimer's lively study of *Venus and Adonis*. Mortimer does not use the word 'anamorphosis', but starting with its title, *Variable Passions* keys on abrupt shifts of perspective, 'the extraordinarily flexible rhetoric that can apparently swing our responses from one extreme to the other within a single stanza or even a single line'. Mortimer offers 'a running commentary' or 'close sequential reading' of the the poem's 'rapid shifts in tone and perspective' (pp. x–xi), emphasizing the Ovidian gap between claims for masterful self-understanding and the reality of uncontrollable appetite. Where Venus, 'reaching out to invade, incorporate and digest the world', cloaks her expansive will in the name of natural law, Adonis's 'refusal to let the world impinge on [his] precious identity' evokes chastity to prettify his own 'selfish, sterile, and life-denying' response (p. 31).

Venus and Adonis has never come close to its original popularity, but given 'the considerable revival of interest in formal rhetoric' (p. ix) and of 'gender studies' (p. xi), Mortimer thinks this poem's time has come. Feminists, though, will not warm to this poem's kinky gender reversals as they have to *Titus* and *Lucrece*. Mortimer remarks that 'when the gods are seized with desire for mortals the first casualty is usually their own dignity' (p. 21), but dignity is what no one, divine or human, has in this 'hard', 'glittering' and 'cold' world (Hazlitt's epithets for *Venus and Adonis*, quoted p. 14). This is not festive comedy: individual fulfilment, social integration, political or sexual liberation are nowhere on the horizon. By showing 'how the poem manages to contain its disturbing' materials (p. x) within a successfully 'unifying intention' (p. 7), Mortimer finds comic catharsis, 'the serenity that comes from an awareness that it illuminates but does not reproduce our own condition' (p. 35). But this claim for higher purpose is vulnerable to Catherine Bates's kind

of scepticism. Such aesthetic appreciation may not differ much from the preening self-delight by which the characters inside the poem 'display . . . a rhetoric that convinces nobody but its user' (p. 192) – in which case it *is* reproduction rather than its transcendent illumination. Unaccommodated Ovid – the full-frontal Ovidity displayed in *Venus and Adonis* – is too shameful to be a major crowd pleaser.

In *Figures de la royauté en Angleterre*, François Laroque and Franck Lesay collect eleven pieces about kingship up to 1689. Stephen Greenblatt looks at *Richard III*'s ghosts, whose theatrical power he associates with Richard's capacity to manipulate the unconscious; Marcel Cunin concentrates on architectural figurations of sovereign power; and Brian Gibbons describes Alan Bennett's use of Shakespeare's kings in *The Madness of King George*. The other Shakespearian pieces concentrate on ideological and practical contradictions. Jean-Christophe Mayer analyses meanings of 'political' and cognates; in *Hamlet* and the histories these terms suggest Machiavellian villainy, but outside the theatre they identify the positive values of sovereignty. Laroque analyses the disjunction between conventional legitimations of royalty and the dramatic realities of *Caesar* and *Richard II*, where 'la couronne est le signifiant de la mort' rather than of transcendence (p. 60). Desacralization is Raymond Gardette's theme as well: *Richard II*, *Richard III*, and *Hamlet* 'semble[nt] s'interroger sur l'inévitable disparition de la doctrine du roi de droit divin et du droit divin des rois' (p. 78).

Graham Holderness begins *Shakespeare: The Histories* by analysing conflicting iconographies in the Rainbow and Ermine Portraits of Elizabeth (peace and benevolent harmony, power and surveillance) to suggest the contradictory values and claims made by and about Elizabeth and Elizabethan England. These dissonances resonate throughout the histories on the gender register: 'masculine heroism and violent enterprise', reflecting 'feudal and chivalric values', are clearly marked off by 'historical difference from the late Elizabethan context' in which 'a female monarch . . . presided over' what was claimed to be a 'civilised and peaceful culture' (pp. 37–8). Chapters on *Hamlet, Richard III, Henry VI part One, Henry V, Henry IV* and *Richard II* (in that order) argue that the plays dramatize rather than resolve their conflicts. They evoke the power of tradition but do not work chiefly in the elegiac or nostalgic mode: the heroic past is contained within an ironic awareness of its pastness, unavailable to practical desire. Hence it is not Talbot at the centre of *Henry VI Part One*, but Joan, who 'achieves her own version of Elizabeth's myth of Tilbury, by appropriation reconciling femininity with militarism' in a way that 'continues to haunt both the play and the culture in which it' was produced (p. 135). Holderness's Renaissance is thoroughly our contemporary: ' "postmodern" views of history would' afford the Renaissance 'few surprises' (p. 211). His strongest claim is for the innovative possibilities made available through ideological fissures: 'the struggle between competing historiographies offered . . . cultural and political *choices*' and 'a much stronger and more optimistic emphasis on the history-making powers of the "plebeian" theatre' (p. 215).

Holderness's predication on the contradictions in female rule is normative: 'nearly twenty years of new-historicist studies' have 'taught us' that the Elizabethans were 'preoccupied with the anomalous gender of the country's monarch'. Different, though, is Holderness's emphasis on the 'enabling' rather than 'fundamentally debilitating' potential of this anomaly. He does not make a big thing of this, but Katherine Eggert, from whose *Showing Like a Queen* I have been quoting (pp. 1, 6, 3), foregrounds the self-conscious departure from established criticism as her primary claim: Renaissance writers 'seize upon the specter of female monarchy not only because it warps the circumstances of their literary moment, but also [as] an occasion for an author to restructure that literary moment' (p. 6); the image of 'feminized authority proves an enabling strategy' (p. 13).

Eggert does not wish to 'reconstruct in retrograde fashion the old-historicist image of the author supremely in command of the "historical background" ', but the author is not 'entirely the product of . . . culture' either. She aims 'to marry a new-historicist account of literature as a cultural form to a literary-historical account of the succession of texts' (p. 20).

Eggert works out these ideas in studies of the histories, *Hamlet, Antony* and *Winter's Tale*, sandwiched between chapters on Spenser and Milton. She often coincides with Holderness, as when the 'aching nostalgia' of *1 Henry VI* offers 'no sense or hope' for the return of a kingly ideal (p. 61); her Talbot too lacks the theatrical presence so abundantly manifested in the spectator-ravishing Joan. But where for Holderness it would be 'grotesque oversimplification' to take the final gloating English victory as a decisive resolution (p. 128), Eggert invests heavily in the closural revelations of large signifying structures: play, sequence, even sequence of sequences. It is not just the 'final three plays of this [first] tetralogy' that must contend with female rule (p. 79); the problem spills over to the 'second tetralogy', until *Henry V* finally succeeds in 'associating male rule with compelling theater' (p. 79). In *Hamlet*, although the protagonist's 'feminine qualities' (p. 101), 'conceived under the aegis of queenship' (p. 113), help invent an interiorized thought-drama, 'this marvelous new mode is abandoned' when 'the closing scene of the play' returns to the 'cruder genre defined as masculine: blood-soaked revenge' (pp. 101, 116). Discussing the later plays, even Eggert wonders whether it 'may seem unfair . . . to privilege the plays' endings as much as I ultimately do' (p. 133). Nonetheless, 'feminine theatricality' is either 'discarded' in *Antony* (p. 133) or 'desexualized' in *Winter's Tale* (p. 165), when the plays 'come to their conclusions'. Eggert's critical narrative enacts the 'teleology, linear and prospective unfolding' she herself describes as 'men's time' (p. 55), producing a relentless purposivity much more phallic than Holderness's haphazard sequence of chapters. Biology is not critical destiny. Maybe it is time to give such gender taxonomies a rest and (pace Bottom) not 'grow to a point'.

Still on royalty: Peter Saccio's re-issue of Shakespeare's English Kings updates the bibliography and includes an Afterword, acknowledging that new methods have taken us to different concerns but suggesting that his original interest in the 'plays as they look backward' (p. 230) continues to repay attention. In other work on the histories, Robert Weimann analyses Faulconbridge's 'residue of jesting and presenting . . . as both leaven and lever for a theatrical treatment of history' (p. 114). Weimann's 'bifold authority' – printed text versus performance (the '"Pen" and "Voice"' of his other contribution this year), elite versus popular, platea representation versus locus performance, etc. – insists, as always, that boundaries are negotiable: 'the dramatist's idea was not to eliminate these "fond and frivolous jestures" from the realm of "serious affairs and studies" but, as it were, to digest the distance between them' (p. 111). Yu Jin Ko uses Weimann to argue that the containment/subversion binary oversimplifies Henry V no matter which side you take; the Rylance/Olivier production 'neither reaffirms the utopia asserted by royal power nor points to the utopia born of subversion' (p. 119). A kind of bifold authority may be at work in Dermot Cavanagh's Richard II as the ground for two 'opposing perspectives' about treason (p. 135), one justifying Richard, the other Bolingbroke; 'the play's dialectical openness may have appealed to [Essex's supporters'] demand for the right of unprejudiced judgment' (p. 156). James Berg examines the legal and economic complications of land tenure, arguing that Richard II and Henry IV produce 'an inflation-driven nostalgia for real wealth [and] impossible dreams of immediate royal control over land' (p. 229). Two Henry VIII essays complement the emphasis on scepticism in Thomas Healy's version. According to Anston Bosman, 'for spectators of All is True doubts

about' claims for historical truth 'are never resolved' (p. 466). Barbara Kreps stresses 'the "already known"' in the audience's 'double vision of events'. In view of the 'ironic . . . reversals' known to be in store for Henry (p. 181), what future might be awaiting James and the 'audiences of 1613' themselves (p. 182)?

A quick tour of periodical pieces, beginning with comedies. Fumio Yoshioka elegantly describes the disintegration in Dream of the presumably stable hierarchy of shadow and substance: 'the play could be a Tudor dream Shakespeare spins out against his fellow audience's imagination' (p. 123). According to Chris Fitter, Jaques's slain-deer speech can support both subversive and conservative sentiments. Nova Myhill argues that the presumed cognitive privilege of an audience erodes during the action of Much Ado. Angela Hurworth, noting that Malvolio's gulling has tended 'to upstage the main plot', connects this material with 'the narratives of underworld literature' (p. 121). Garrett Sullivan looks at identity problems in All's Well. If social position determines Renaissance selfhood, self-forgetting can clear a space to produce identity anew – in the comedies 'a precondition . . . to the pursuit of desire' (p. 59). In a piece that works well with Belsey and Dubrow's work on family tensions, Susan Snyder's 'Gender Polarization in The Winter's Tale' describes 'the forcible masculinizing of Mamilius' (p. 6): the maternal is prematurely breached in favour of an anxiously insecure 'primogenitorial bond' (p. 1). Robert Pierce seeks 'to explain' the 'weak-minded doubleness' by which he responds to Tempest: 'quite sympathetic to Prospero and Miranda', he can also 'find much that is appealing and persuasive' in 'New Historical and anticolonialist readings' (p. 373).

On tragedies: According to Robert Matz, Othello critics have concentrated on 'male–female relationships' as though 'only heterosexual desires exist' (p. 261), thereby missing a whole world of sexual anxiety located in the play's homosocial slippages. Richard Knowles accounts, independently of revisions, for the fuzziness of motivation in Cordelia's return. William Dodd moves his sophisticated work on the recuperation of character from theory to practice, focusing on *Lear*'s first scene. Stephen Orgel mounts a brilliantly comic assault on everything we thought we knew about *Macbeth* – its action, characters, politics (gender and otherwise), the nature and extent of its appeal originally and throughout theatrical and critical history – leaving us no alternative but to agree with his claim that 'Shakespeare's plays have always been the free-floating signifiers of post-modern theory, standing for an infinitely variable range of signifieds' (p. 143).

In other material, Lena Orlin has edited a forum on Harry Berger's work. Lynn Enterline, Angus Fletcher, Lois Potter, Marshall Grossman and Stanley Cavell engage with a variety of Berger's interests – feminism, Lacan, performance *vs.* text, etc. – in ways that pay tribute to the influence of his continuing career. Charles Whitney digs up detailed archival evidence to suggest that 'subaltern workers formed a significant audience' in the public theatres (p. 451). David Hawkes sees in antitheatrical literature 'a coherent and sophisticated critique of the ideological and psychological effects of a commodity culture' (p. 258). MacD. Jackson argues from internal evidence that the 1609 Sonnets corresponds to the order 'Shakespeare intended, and that the Quarto', including 153–4 and 'A Lover's Complaint', 'is in the profoundest sense a "work"' (p. 114). For R. S. White, both pacifism and militarism are regular sentiments in Shakespeare, producing the 'unique brand of radical ambiguity' of 'the dramatic medium itself' (p. 135).

Before Y2K anxiety fades into a blur, we can use two exceptionally strong collections to ask, one last time, those deep-think questions about what's past or passing or to come. 'Where are we now in Shakespearean studies?' is the title with which W. R. Elton and John M. Mucciolo inaugurate *The Shakespearean International Yearbook*. The twenty contributions are divided into four parts: six on 'Methodologies and Controversies', 'Renaissance Ideas', 'Plays and Poems', and two on 'The Globe Old and New'. Among the exceptionally strong pieces, Bruce Smith ('Shakespeare and Homoeroticism'), John Jowett ('Textual Studies'), Donna Hamilton ('Religion'), Johann Sommerville (revisionism in seventeenth-century historiography) and Richard Knowles (revision in *Lear*) masterfully survey complicated issues and suggest directions for new work. In the two Globe pieces, which connect interestingly with *Survey* work described above, John Demaray discusses the still unsolved problems of historical retrieval, and Ros King develops many astute suggestions about the potential for innovative production.

Local triumphs aside, larger editorial principles deserve some consideration. If the aim is to gauge 'the mood and movement of Shakespearean interpretation at the present time' (Fletcher, Foreword, p. viii), why include pieces on 'Magnanimity' (John M. Steadman), 'The Law' (R. J. Schoeck), or 'The Italians' (Frances Barasch), none of which is a peculiarly pressing Renaissance Idea now; or why essays on *Caesar* (John Velz) or *Twelfth Night* (Elizabeth Donno), when these plays are not at the centre of current concern? The 'Magnanimity' piece is especially odd, since 'Heroic Character' has dropped off the radar (almost all the references are twenty years old or more). It might be argued we need to revive the issue, as we have religion, but no such claim is made in any of these pieces. Principles of exclusion are similarly noteworthy. The volume deliberately avoids 'the galloping power of the media' and 'the field of popular culture' (p. ix). Fletcher acknowledges the importance of performance but since 'Shakespeare exists for most of us as a silently read, silently consumed commodity', he claims we need precisely 'the sort of discussion occurring in the *Yearbook*', centred on 'the text at its point of origin, before interpreters got into the act' (p. x). This overt engagement with the literary Shakespeare, where 'the scene' of 'the interpretive encounter' is 'always the play['s ability to] catch us, inwardly' (p. ix), is reiterated by the first two contributors, who argue that 'the "main theatre"' of Shakespeare criticism 'is too politicized and quarrelsome to allow any real engagement with the intricacy and subtlety of a Shakespeare play' (Bradshaw, 'State of Play', p. 3), and that a return to Hegelian esthetics would enable us to 'regard a literary text – or a play by Shakespeare for that matter – as a work of art', in order to retrieve what we have 'lost' during 'the last two decades' to 'the political element' (Uhlig, 'Shakespeare', p. 26).

A conservative temper animates many contributors as well. Richard Levin shrewdly analyses the lexical and conceptual slippages of a self-styled 'materialist' criticism. Mucciolo argues that the colonialist *Tempest* lacks evidentiary foundation. Donno laments the 'scant concern evidenced to its artistic or dramatic elements' among recent *Twelfth Night* critics, for whom 'the most apt term would be "tendentious" because of their [emphasizing] ideological concepts' (p. 327). In the only non-Globe performance piece, John Russell Brown complains that with expanded disciplinary boundaries, 'Seemingly, any arcane piece of knowledge can be shown to be relevant' (p. 114). Brown cites ' "Feminist" or "Gay and Lesbian Studies" ', rounds up the usual suspects (Greenblatt, Belsey, and Dollimore) and wonders, with the attention now devoted to 'issues of every-day living', why the SAA has not 'scheduled a seminar on business management, promotion and hospitality' (p. 113). Given the proliferation of such sentiments, this collection might have been titled, 'Where were we then in Shakespearian studies?'

For the last *Shakespeare Quarterly* to appear in 1999, Gail Paster has produced a special issue to 'mark the end of the century' with the question 'what topics have proved perdurable over this span of time?' The 'enterprise' is 'doomed to fail' for want of space; but where many editors would hedge their bets, Paster has invited three contributors (four, actually, but Paul Werstine's piece on the 'bad' quartos is outside my purview) who are all working in the same basic mode. Margreta de Grazia describes *Hamlet* as the modernist text *par excellence* in thinkers from Hegel to Derrida; Hugh Grady reflects on the concept of modernity and its relevance to Shakespeare and Renaissance culture generally; and Louise Schleiner tries 'to distill a unified critical reading practice from the most important developments in twentieth-century theories of the subject within the cultural matrix'. To 'the most important question . . . of all, what assumptions can we confidently take into the next century?' (Paster, 'From the Editor', p. iii), these three learned and richly detailed essays suggest a single exemplary answer: *cultural theory*.

Schleiner begins with a Bakhtinian claim: 'the concrete utterance embedded in social interaction is prior and definitive for purposes of study'. From this it follows 'that both formal linguistics and psychology, in subordination to the sociological approach, are "absolutely indispensable" ' (p. 288), which cues the incorporation of Benveniste, Lacan, and Kristeva into the interpretive structure, in turn assimilating Jameson, Spivak, Butler and de Lauretis, with passing mention of Althusser, Foucault, Silverman, Cixous and many others, leading to the conclusion that 'Perhaps now that we have marxist, subaltern, and gender studies of the workings of ideology and human subjectivity, a holistic form of literary and cultural study is within reach.' The pathos of 'Perhaps . . . within reach' – not just conventional modesty – acknowledges we are not quite home. Although 'Bakhtin saw the whole . . . of meaning production . . . and urged practitioners of the arts and human sciences to work together on understanding it', more still seems required to effect the desired consensus. Hence 'the next step is to ask in what stages of such discourse circulation do texts or utterances function as literary or prophetic' (p. 309). This will evidently entail packing some additional exemplars of the 'sociological approach' into the space already crowded with Bakhtin et al., but sceptics will remain unconvinced, because their minds are made up (in both senses) by beliefs derived from non-sociological systems (psychoanalysis, poetics, Roman Catholicism, anti-Stratfordianism, whatever) that are themselves totally coherent ('holistic') and capable of absorbing Schleiner's into their own explanatory power as easily as hers can absorb theirs. In this situation, universal assent is impossible – but also unnecessary. Critical triumphs remain accessible of the local and particular kind (where in the end we find our happiness, or not at all). Hence Schleiner's analyses remain sharp and interesting even without the support of a unified field theory, and she concludes with a fascinating analysis of *Two Gentlemen*, using a narrative of authorial and sociocultural development which, though consistent with her containing framework, does not depend on it for its explanatory power.

In 'Renewing Modernity', Hugh Grady claims, first, that Renaissance thought is an authentic precursor to Enlightenment, more an emergent modernism than a residual medievalism; and, second, that Shakespeare should therefore be understood as an early *modern* rather than an *early* modern text. Grady makes good use of the wiggle room in 'early modern', the characteristically sloppy (or flexible) translation of the characteristically precise (or authoritarian) '*prémoderne*'. This emphasis on *modern* is a preferential prescription rather than a verifiable description, a heuristic claim serving to align critical work to produce certain results. But what results? what consequences follow taking Grady's advice? He claims that 'new and renewed ideas of modernity can give us a new and renewed Shakespeare' (p. 284), but Grady's readings, while always stimulating, seem consistent with a familiar tradition of Shakespearian modernism going back to, say, Herder, and one that will probably never altogether displace its mirror image, the Bard as worried or embattled conservative, going back to, say, Schlegel and continuing even now and even among those critics with the right materialist orientation (Terry Eagleton, for instance).

The question yet again implicit in all this, *what is the point?*, seems specially appropriate to de Grazia, because it is her own: 'teleology' is her primary word. She begins with Hegel, for whom the ghostly 'old mole' of Hamlet's father figures the spirit of modernity, tunnelling through the darkness to the light of imminent revelation. She moves then to Marx, Bradley, Freud, Lacan and Derrida, all of whom use the same text, image, and idea: *Hamlet*, the mole, historical experience growing to a point of achieved purpose. But this sequence describes a diminishing confidence about Hegelian final meanings and revelations, which have come to seem neither imminent nor possible, but rather a self-flattering monument built by Enlightenment Man to celebrate his own undying intellect. This may be de Grazia's point – to exact one more pound of flesh from the Enlightenment. She never says as much but perhaps believes the point is self-evident: we need to be reminded that Enlightenment is bad because we are always vulnerable to its self-deluding blandishments, still haunted by the ghost of Hegelian teleology and totalization. But de Grazia's story may be spinning in the opposite direction, toward not the futility but the necessity of Hegelian purposivity. Each new thinker in the sequence not only abandons intellectual mastery but affirms it, going beyond his predecessor (*going beyond* is the essential Hegelian move) in a process of ever expanding evacuation. Hegelianism may be the necessary precondition of all critical work: we convince ourselves we are advancing beyond where we were (that the advance takes the form of retreat is neither here nor there). Why else debate the question of this straw? From this angle, de Grazia's description of the sequence from Hegel to Derrida may be designed as itself an extension of the sequence – going beyond the apparent *ne plus ultra* of attenuation in Derrida to the quality of nothing. Her very silence can be construed as explanation – a refusal to justify even the refusal of self-justifying purpose. Is *this* the point? De Grazia does not stay for an answer. She's here, she's here, she's gone.

To say that cultural theory serves no clear purpose is not a knockdown argument. All research in the humanities – not working toward a cure for cancer, or a faster chip, or even just a better policy on ageing – lacks strong arguments for its own practical consequence. Unable to persuade each other, let alone the real men in the business suits, we do, though, manage to convince ourselves. Hence the benefit I claimed at the beginning of this review for self-delusion; sufficient unto the day, it keeps us going until tomorrow, and tomorrow; and with tomorrow we are back to that 'most important question of all' raised by this special issue of *Shakespeare Quarterly*: continuity, survival, the future. Cultural critique has become the state of the art for many of us, and maybe the 'sociological approach' will come not simply to dominate a single journal but constitute the whole field full of Shakespearian folk. If this happens it's curtains for me; I'm gone, I'm history. But with time still owing on my *Survey* contract, and in view of the many strong books and essays reviewed here, not least in this *Shakespeare Quarterly*, I look forward to returning next year.

WORKS REVIEWED

Adams, Barry B., *Coming-to-Know: Recognition and the Complex Plot in Shakespeare*. Studies in Shakespeare, 10 (New York, 2000).

Bassi, Shaul, *Le Metamorfosi di Otello: Storia di un'Etnicità Immaginaria* (Bari, 2000).

Bates, Catherine, *Play in a Godless World: The Theory and Practice of Play in Shakespeare, Nietzsche and Freud* (London, 1999).

Beliles, David Buck, ' "I am myself indifferent honest": Hamlet as Ophelia's Seducer', *Hamlet Studies*, 21 (1999), 77–88.

Belsey, Catherine, *Shakespeare and the Loss of Eden: The Construction of Family Values in Early Modern Culture* (London, 1999).

Berg, James E., ' "This Dear, Dear Land": "Dearth" and the Fantasy of the Land-Grab in *Richard II* and *Henry IV'*, *English Literary Renaissance*, 29 (1999), 225–45.

Berry, Philippa, *Shakespeare's Feminine Endings: Disfiguring Death in the Tragedies* (London and New York, 1999).

Bevington, David, 'Shakespeare the Man', in Kastan, *A Companion*, pp. 9–21.

Boehrer, Bruce, 'Shylock and the Rise of the Household Pet: Thinking Social Exclusion in *The Merchant of Venice*', *Shakespeare Quarterly*, 50 (1999), 152–70.

Booth, Roy, 'Shylock's Sober House', *Review of English Studies*, 50 (1999), 22–31.

Bosman, Anston, 'Seeing Tears: Truth and Sense in *All is True*', *Shakespeare Quarterly*, 50 (1999), 459–76.

Bradshaw, Graham, 'State of Play', in Elton and Mucciolo, *The Shakespearean International Yearbook*, 3–25.

Briggs, Julia, 'Tears at the Wedding: Shakespeare's Last Phase', in Richards and Knowles, *Shakespeare's Late Plays*, pp. 210–27.

Bristol, Michael D., 'Shakespeare: The Myth', in Kastan, *A Companion*, pp. 489–502.

Brown, John Russell, *New Sites for Shakespeare: Theatre, the Audience, and Asia* (London and New York, 1999).

'Shakespeare in Performance', in Elton and Mucciolo, *The Shakespearean International Yearbook*, 108–17.

Brown, Peter, ed., *Reading Dreams: The Interpretation of Dreams from Chaucer to Shakespeare* (Oxford, 1999).

Bruce, Susan, ed., *William Shakespeare: King Lear*. Columbia Critical Guides (New York, 1999).

Callaghan, Dympna, *Shakespeare Without Women: Representing Gender and Race on the Renaissance Stage* (London and New York, 1999).

Cavanagh, Dermot, 'The Language of Treason in *Richard II'*, *Shakespeare Studies*, 27 (1999), 134–60.

Charney, Maurice, *Shakespeare on Love and Lust* (New York, 2000).

Clary, Frank Nicholas and Hardin Aasand, 'Hamlet and the Mirror up to History: Allegory, Analogue and Allusion', *Hamlet Studies*, 21 (1999), 20–54.

Coyle, Martin, *William Shakespeare: Richard II*. Columbia Critical Guides (New York, 1999).

Danson, Lawrence, *Shakespeare's Dramatic Genres*. Oxford Shakespeare Topics (Oxford, 2000).

Davis, Lloyd, ' "To thine own self be true": Identity and Desire from Plato to *Hamlet*', *Hamlet Studies*, 21 (1999), 55–76.

Dawson, Anthony B., 'The Arithmetic of Memory: Shakespeare's Theatre and the National Past', *Shakespeare Survey 52* (Cambridge, 1999), pp. 54–67.

de Sousa, Geraldo U., *Shakespeare's Cross-Cultural Encounters* (London, 1999).

de Grazia, Margreta, 'Teleology, Delay, and the "Old Mole" ', *Shakespeare Quarterly*, 50 (1999), 251–67.

Desai, R. W., '*Hamlet Studies* after Two Decades in India – A Retrospective Analysis', *Hamlet Studies*, 21 (1999), 9–19.

Desmet, Christy, and Robert Sawyer, eds., *Shakespeare and Appropriation*. Accents on Shakespeare (London and New York, 1999).

Dodd, William, 'Impossible Worlds: What Happens in *King Lear*, Act 1, Scene 1?', *Shakespeare Quarterly*, 50 (1999), 477–507.

Donaldson, Peter, ' "All which it inherit": Shakespeare, Globes and Global Media', *Shakespeare Survey 52* (Cambridge, 1999), pp. 183–200.

Donno, Elizabeth S., '*Twelfth Night*', in Elton and Mucciolo, *The Shakespearean International Yearbook*, 322–8.

Dubrow, Heather, *Shakespeare and Domestic Loss: Forms of Deprivation, Mourning, and Recuperation*. Cambridge Studies in Renaissance Literature and Culture, 32 (Cambridge, 1999).

Edelman, Charles, 'Which is the Jew that Shakespeare Knew? Shylock on the Elizabethan Stage', *Shakespeare Survey 52* (Cambridge, 1999), pp. 88–98.

Egan, Gabriel, 'Reconstructions of the Globe: A Retrospective', *Shakespeare Survey 52* (Cambridge, 1999), pp. 1–16.

Eggert, Katherine, *Showing Like a Queen: Female Authority and Literary Experiment in Spenser, Shakespeare, and Milton* (Philadelphia, 2000).

Elton, W. R., and John M. Mucciolo, eds., *The Shakespearean International Yearbook 1: Where are we now in Shakespearean studies?* (Aldershot and Brookfield, Vt, 1999).

Enterline, Lynn, *The Rhetoric of the Body from Ovid to Shakespeare*. Cambridge Studies in Renaissance Literature and Culture, 35 (Cambridge, 2000).

Farley-Hills, David, 'Hamlet's Account of the Pirates', *Review of English Studies*, 50 (1999), 320–31.

Findlay, Alison, *A Feminist Perspective on Renaissance Drama* (Oxford and Malden, Mass., 1999).

Fisch, Harold, *The Biblical Presence in Shakespeare, Milton and Blake: A Comparative Study* (Oxford, 1999).

Fitter, Chris, 'The Slain Deer and Political *Imperium*: *As You Like It* and Andrew Marvell's 'Nymph Complaining for the Death of Her Fawn' ', *Journal of English and Germanic Philology*, 98 (1999), 193–218.

Fletcher, Angus, Foreword, in Elton and Mucciolo, *The Shakespearean International Yearbook*, viii–xv.

Foakes, R. A., 'Shakespeare Editing and Textual Theory: A Rough Guide', *Huntington Library Quarterly*, 60 (1999), 425–42.

Frye, Northrop, *The Secular Scripture: A Study of the Structure of Romance* (Cambridge, Mass., 1978).

Fumerton, Patricia, and Simon Hunt, eds., *Renaissance Culture and the Everyday* (Philadelphia, 1999).

Gardette, Raymond, 'Rois sans Royaume', in Laroque and Lesay, *Figures de la royauté*, pp. 61–78.

Gay, Penny, *As You Like It* (Plymouth, 1999).

Grady, Hugh, 'Renewing Modernity: Changing Contexts and Contents of a Nearly Invisible Concept', *Shakespeare Quarterly*, 50 (1999), 268–84.

Grande, Troni Y., *Marlovian Tragedy: The Play of Dilation* (Lewisburg, Pa. and London, 1999).

Gurr, Andrew and Mariko Ichikawa, *Staging in Shakespeare's Theatres*. Oxford Shakespeare Topics (Oxford, 2000).

Habib, Imtiaz, *Shakespeare and Race: Postcolonial Praxis in the Early Modern Period* (Lanham, Md. and Oxford, 2000).

Hawkes, David, 'Idolatry and Commodity Fetishism in the Antitheatrical Controversy', *Studies in English Literature, 1500–1900*, 39 (1999), 255–73.

Henderson, Diana E., and James Siemon, 'Reading Vernacular Literature', in Kastan, *A Companion*, 206–22.

Hodgdon, Barbara, 'Making it New: Katie Mitchell Refashions Shakespeare-History', in Novy, *Transforming Shakespeare*, pp. 13–34.

The Shakespeare Trade: Performances and Appropriations (Philadelphia, 1998).

'*William Shakespeare's Romeo + Juliet*: Everything's Nice in America?', *Shakespeare Survey* 52 (Cambridge, 1999), pp. 88–98.

Holderness, Graham, *Shakespeare: The Histories* (London and New York, 2000).

Hopkins, Lisa, 'What's Hercules to Hamlet? The Emblematic Garden in *The Spanish Tragedy* and *Hamlet*', *Hamlet Studies*, 21 (1999), 114–43.

Howard, Jean E., 'Shakespeare and Genre', in Kastan, *A Companion*, pp. 297–310.

Hurworth, Angela, 'Gulls, Cony-Catchers and Cozeners: *Twelfth Night* and the Elizabethan Underworld', *Shakespeare Survey* 52 (Cambridge, 1999), pp. 120–32.

Jackson, MacD. P., 'Aspects of Organisation in Shakespeare's Sonnets (1609)', in Wortham, *Parergon*, pp. 109–34.

Kamps, Ivo, 'Alas, poor Shakespeare! I knew him well', in Desmet and Sawyer, *Shakespeare and Appropriation*, pp. 15–32.

Kastan, David Scott, 'Shakespeare and the 'Element' he Lived in', in Kastan, *A Companion*, pp. 3–6.

Shakespeare After Theory (London and New York, 1999).

ed., *A Companion to Shakespeare* (Oxford and Malden, Mass., 1999).

Kawachi, Yoshiko, 'Preface', in Kawachi, *Japanese Studies*, pp. 7–8.

ed., *Japanese Studies in Shakespeare and his Contemporaries* (Newark and London, 1998).

Kelley, Charles Greg, '"Lend thy serious hearing to what I shall unfold": Legend Dynamics in *Hamlet*', *Hamlet Studies*, 21 (1999), 89–113.

Kennedy, Judith M., and Richard F. Kennedy, eds., *Shakespeare: The Critical Tradition: A Midsummer Night's Dream, 1775–1920* (London and New Brunswick, New Jersey, 1999).

Kerrigan, William, *Shakespeare's Promises* (Baltimore and London, 1999).

Knowles, Richard, 'Cordelia's Return', *Shakespeare Quarterly*, 50 (1999), 33–50.

Knutson, Roslyn L., 'Shakespeare's Repertory', in Kastan, *A Companion*, pp. 346–61.

Ko, Yu Jin, 'A Little Touch of Harry in the Light: *Henry V* at the New Globe', *Shakespeare Survey* 52 (Cambridge, 1999), pp. 107–19.

Kreps, Barbara, 'When All is True: Law, History and Problems of Knowledge in *Henry VIII*', *Shakespeare Survey* 52 (Cambridge, 1999), pp. 166–82.

Laroque, François, 'Les Rois de Carnaval dans le Théâtre de Shakespeare: le Cas de *Jules César* et de *Hamlet*', in Laroque and Lessay, *Figures de la royauté*, pp. 49–60.

and Franck Lessay, eds., *Figures de la royauté de Shakespeare à la Glorieuse Révolution* (Paris, 1999).

Leinwand, Theodore B. *Theatre, Finance and Society in Early Modern England*. Cambridge Studies in Renaissance Literature and Culture, 31 (Cambridge, 1999).

Limon, Jerzy, 'From Liturgy to the Globe: the Changing Concept of Space', *Shakespeare Survey* 52 (Cambridge, 1999), pp. 46–53.

Loomba, Ania, '"Delicious traffick": Alterity and Exchange on Early Modern Stages', *Shakespeare Survey 52* (Cambridge, 1999), pp. 201–14.

Low, Anthony, '*Hamlet* and the Ghost of Purgatory: Intimations of Killing the Father', *English Literary Renaissance*, 29, 443–67.

Lynch, Kathryn, 'Baring Bottom: Shakespeare and the Chaucerian Dream Vision', in Brown, ed., *Reading Dreams*, pp. 99–124.

Maley, Willy, 'Postcolonial Shakespeare: British Identity Formation and *Cymbeline*', in Richards and Knowles, *Shakespeare's Late Plays*, pp. 145–57.

Mallin, Eric S., '"You Kilt My Foddah": or Arnold, Prince of Denmark', *Shakespeare Quarterly*, 50 (1999), 127–51.

Marx, Steven, *Shakespeare and the Bible*. Oxford Shakespeare Topics (Oxford, 2000).

Matz, Robert, 'Slander, Renaissance Discourses of Sodomy, and *Othello*', *Journal of English Literary History*, 66 (1999), 261–76.

McDonald, Russ, *The Bedford Companion to Shakespeare: An Introduction with Documents* (Boston, 1996).

McEachern, Claire, Introduction. In Claire McEachern and Debora Shuger, eds., *Religion and Culture in Renaissance England* (Cambridge, 1997), pp. 1–12.

McLoughlin, Cathleen T., *Shakespeare, Rabelais, and the Comical-Historical*. Currents in Comparative Romance Languages and Literatures, vol. 80 (New York and Frankfurt, 2000).

McLuskie, Kathleen, 'The "Candy-Colored Clown": Reading Early Modern Dreams', in Brown, ed., *Reading Dreams*, pp. 147–67.

'*Macbeth/Umabatha*: Global Shakespeare in a Post-Colonial Market', *Shakespeare Survey 52* (Cambridge, 1999), pp. 154–65.

Mortimer, Anthony, *Variable Passions: A Reading of Shakespeare's 'Venus and Adonis'* (New York, 2000).

Motohashi, Ted, 'Canibal and Caliban: *The Tempest* and the Discourse of Cannibalism', in Kawachi, *Japanese Studies*, pp. 114–40.

Myhill, Nova, 'Spectatorship in/of *Much Ado about Nothing*', *Studies in English Literature, 1500–1900*, 39 (1999), 291–311.

Noda, Manabu, 'The Primacy of the Sense of the Body over the Sense of the Line: David Garrick's Acting of Shakespeare', in Kawachi, *Japanese Studies*, pp. 197–212.

Novy, Marianne, ed., *Transforming Shakespeare: Contemporary Women's Re-Visions in Literature and Performance* (London, 1999).

Orgel, Stephen, 'Macbeth and the Antic Round', *Shakespeare Survey 52* (Cambridge, 1999), pp. 143–53.

Orlin, Lena Cowen, ed., 'Forum: Harry Berger, Jr.'s 'Making Trifles of Terrors: Redistributing Complicities in Shakespeare', *Shakespeare Studies* 27 (1999), 19–105.

O'Connor, Marion, ' "Useful in the Year 1999": William Poel and Shakespeare's "Build of Stage" ', *Shakespeare Survey 52* (Cambridge, 1999), pp. 17–32.

Parker, Kenneth, *Antony and Cleopatra* (Horndon, Tavistock; 2000).

Paster, Gail Kern, 'From the Editor', *Shakespeare Quarterly*, 50 (1999), iii–iv.

Patterson, Steve, 'The Bankruptcy of Homoerotic Amity in Shakespeare's *Merchant of Venice*', *Shakespeare Quarterly*, 50 (1999), 9–32.

Pierce, Robert B., 'Understanding *The Tempest*', *New Literary History*, 30 (1999), 373–88.

Potter, Lois and Arthur F. Kinney, eds., *Shakespeare: Text and Theater: Essays in Honor of Jay L. Halio* (Newark and London, 1999).

Rawlings, Peter, ed., *Americans on Shakespeare, 1776–1914*. Shakespeare: The Critical Tradition (London and Brookfield, Vt, 1999).

Richards, Jennifer, and James Knowles, 'Introduction: Shakespeare's Late Plays', in Richards and Knowles, *Shakespeare's Late Plays*, pp. 1–21.

eds., *Shakespeare's Late Plays: New Readings* (Edinburgh, 1999).

Rist, Thomas, *Shakespeare's Romances and the Politics of Counter-Reformation* (Lewiston, NY, Queenston, Ont. and Lampeter, 1999).

Roberts, Gareth, ' "An Art Lawful as Eating"? Magic in *The Tempest* and *The Winter's Tale*', in Richards and Knowles, *Shakespeare's Late Plays*, pp. 126–42.

Rowe, Katherine, *Dead Hands: Fictions of Agency, Renaissance to Modern* (Stanford, 1999).

Rozmovits, Linda, *Shakespeare and the Politics of Culture in Late Victorian England* (Baltimore and London, 1998).

Saccio, Peter, *Shakespeare's English Kings: History, Chronicle, and Drama*, 2nd edn (New York, 2000).

Salingar, Leo, 'Uses of Rhetoric: *Antony and Cleopatra*', *Cahiers Elisabéthains*, 55 (1999), 17–26.

Schleiner, Louise, 'Voice, Ideology, and Gendered Subjects: The Case of *As You Like It* and *Two Gentlemen*', *Shakespeare Quarterly*, 50 (1999), 285–309.

Schneider, Robert, *Shylock, the Roman: Unmasking Shakespeare's 'Merchant of Venice'* (Mill Valley, Ca., 1999).

Schoenfeldt, Michael C., *Bodies and Selves in Early Modern England: Physiology and Inwardness in Spenser, Shakespeare, Herbert, and Milton*. Cambridge Studies in Renaissance Literature and Culture, 34 (Cambridge, 1999).

Snyder, Susan, 'Mamilius and Gender Polarization in *The Winter's Tale*', *Shakespeare Quarterly*, 50 (1999), 1–8.

Stříbrný, Zdeněk, *Shakespeare and Eastern Europe*. Oxford Shakespeare Topics (Oxford, 2000).

Sullivan, Jr., Garrett A., ' "Be this sweet Helen's knell, and now forget her": Forgetting, Memory, and Identity in *All's Well That Ends Well*', *Shakespeare Quarterly*, 50 (1999), 51–69.

Takada, Shigeki, 'The First and the Second Parts of *Henry IV*: Some Thoughts on the Origins of Shakespearean Gentleness', in Takahashi, *Hot Questrists*, pp. 183–96.

Takahashi, Yasunari, Introduction, in Takahashi, *Hot Questrists*, pp. 1–4.

ed., *Hot Questrists after the English Renaissance: Essays on Shakespeare and his Contemporaries in Commemoration of the Thirty-fifth Anniversary of the Shakespeare Society of Japan* (New York, 2000).

Tamaizumi, Yasuo, Foreword, in Takahashi, *Hot Questrists*, pp. vii–viii.

Tempera, Mariangela, *Feasting with Centaurs: 'Titus Andronicus' from Stage to Text* (Bologna, 1999).

Thatcher, David. *Begging to Differ: Modes of Discrepancy in Shakespeare*. Studies in Shakespeare, 8 (New York, 1999).

Uhlig, Claus, 'Shakespeare between Politics and Aesthetics', in Elton and Mucciolo, *The Shakespearean International Yearbook*, 26–44.

Vickers, Brian, 'General Editor's Preface', in Kennedy and Kennedy, *A Midsummer Night's Dream*, pp. x–xix.

Weimann, Robert, 'Mingling Vice and 'Worthiness' in *King John*', *Shakespeare Studies* 27 (1999), 109–33.

'Playing with a Difference: Revisiting 'Pen' and 'Voice' in Shakespeare's Theater', *Shakespeare Quarterly*, 50 (1999), 415–32.

White, Robert S., 'Pacifist Voices in Shakespeare', in Wortham, *Parergon*, pp. 135–62.

Whitney, Charles, ' "Usually in the werking Daies": Playgoing Journeymen, Apprentices, and Ser-

vants in Guild Records, 1582–92', *Shakespeare Quarterly*, 50 (1999), 433–58.

Wilson, Richard, 'Unseasonable Laughter: the Context of *Cardenio*', in Richards and Knowles, *Shakespeare's Late Plays*, pp. 193–209.

Wortham, Christopher, ed., *Parergon: Journal of the Australian and New Zealand Association for Medieval and Early Modern Studies*, NS, 17 (Perth, 1999).

Worthen, W. B., 'Reconstructing the Globe: Constructing Ourselves', *Shakespeare Survey 52* (Cambridge, 1999), pp. 33–45.

Yamada, Yumiko, *Ben Jonson and Cervantes: Tilting against Chivalric Romances* (Tokyo, 2000).

Yoshioka, Fumio, ' "Shadows' Shadows" in *A Midsummer Night's Dream*', *Studies in English Literature* (English Literary Society of Japan), 56 (1999), 107–23.

2. SHAKESPEARE'S LIFE, TIMES, AND STAGE

reviewed by LESLIE THOMSON

I am by no means the first to suggest that literary criticism is in a transitional period – or perhaps at the end of one; only time will tell. In the short term, though, it is evident that the innovative, unorthodox and sometimes contentious critical approaches of the 1980s and early nineties have been, after a period of evaluation leading to something like general acceptance, gradually assimilated into the methods and language of much mainstream criticism. Possibly the most significant effect on early modern studies has been a renewed appreciation of the relationship between text and context. The revisionary end-of-the-century critical emphasis on the contexts within which Shakespeare wrote – social, cultural, economic, sexual – has apparently either influenced or determined the directions taken by many of the writers whose books are considered here. The most successful have in common innovation in the best sense: they cover new ground, open new doors, or look through a new lens – to use metaphors implying how the results also reveal the genu-

inely new or make us look again at what we have not really seen.

In *Theatre and Humanism: English Drama in the Sixteenth Century*, Kent Cartwright presents a significant reconsideration of the relationship between humanist and popular drama in order to close the perceived gap between them. In particular, he offers a new look at a number of sixteenth-century humanist plays, arguing that 'rather than literary, elitist, and dull' they are 'theatrically exciting . . . and socially significant' (cover). In the course of his study Cartwright establishes a continuum from drama at the beginning of the sixteenth century that was 'allegorical, didactic, and moralistic' to drama at the end of the century that was 'censured as emotional, fantasy-arousing, and even immoral'. In fact, he says, '[t]he excitement of the Tudor stage derives partly from a humanist dramaturgy that embroils feelings and emotions in the creation of meaning' (p. 1). As this suggests, Cartwright takes issue with generally accepted criticisms of humanist drama as a dry, intellectualized medium, countering such views with detailed analyses of the plays as works written for performance before an audience who enjoyed watching them. All the plays discussed precede Shakespeare, who is, indeed, never the focus; nor are his plays the endpoint of the argument, although they are referred to in passing where relevant (e.g. the influence of *Gallathea* on *Twelfth Night*). This means that 'humanist dramaturgy' is considered and valued as such in detailed studies of *The Foure PP*, *Wit and Science*, *Gammer Gurton's Needle*, *Cambises*, *Gorboduc*, *Damon and Pithias*, *Gallathea*, *Tamburlaine part 1*, and *Friar Bacon and Friar Bungay*. In these analyses Cartwright never elides intractable problems of tone produced by contradictory signals; rather he shows how these reflect the combination of serious and popular elements that make up these works. One chapter focuses specifically on women characters in six plays ranging from *Fulgens and Lucrece* to *The Rare Triumphs of Love and Fortune* to argue that '"alternative" female values are evident across the century and take inspiration from those expansive views on women promoted by Tudor humanists' (p. 21). Throughout, the primary focus is, as the title indicates, theatre: the basic playability of humanist drama. In his chapter on *Gallathea* Cartwright asserts his general conviction that this is 'not a theatre of static intellectualizing but a theatre building its own collective *mise en scène*, its own physical and emotional environment, a theatre perpetuating a desire for its familiar satisfactions' (p. 172). Furthermore for those whose knowledge of English humanism is rusty, the book provides in passing a survey of humanist theories, practices and influence. This context is particularly relevant since another of Cartwright's aims is to demonstrate how 'humanism's voice, method, and philosophical spirit introduce doubt into Renaissance drama and that humanist doubt enriches the affective dimension of sixteenth-century theatre' (pp. 23–4). *Theatre and Humanism* successfully presents a persuasive revaluation of humanist

drama; it is an effective mix of connected argument, consideration of other critical approaches, and analyses of the plays which include just enough summary of obscure plots to make a point convincing. The care and thoroughness of both publisher and author are apparent in the user-friendly, typo-free result. And while there is no formal bibliography, the notes provide both additional material and detailed references to other works.

An emphasis on the actual rather than the theoretical, as well as on previously unexplored connections, can also be found in Janette Dillon's *Theatre, Court and City, 1595–1610: Drama and Social Space in London*. As the title implies, rather than separating court from city this study deliberately links them as a context for the drama of this period, arguing that '[w]hat plays and players endlessly renegotiate is their double orientation towards these two locations, themselves necessarily in dialogue with each other as well as with the theatre' (p. 4). This is particularly noticeable, Dillon says, 'at the turn of the century, as plays begin to create a larger and more explicit space for the city and city concerns while at the same time retaining a courtly orientation sometimes in overt tension with those city concerns and sometimes scarcely distinguishable from them' (p. 4). The idea of 'social space', introduced in the title, has its origins in the theoretical work of Henri Lefebvre, but is here put to practical use in showing the importance of London to the drama, as both a topographical and conceptual entity. Another concept established at the start is 'fashion': the idea that as a place of show the theatre 'is a powerful maker and disperser of fashions' – a perpetrator of the 'new' (p. 17), a view developed in the subsequent discussions of the city–court–theatre nexus, especially in the idea of the 'commoditization of theatre' (p. 38ff). The book, we are told in the Prologue, is 'organized around ways of experiencing space rather than by physical locations' (p. 7), a method resulting in rather oblique chapter titles (e.g. 'From retreat to display',

'The place of dirt', 'The masking of place') representative of a complexity which sometimes threatens to become confusion. And while the introductory chapter sets out many interrelated areas of focus, not all the points are developed in what follows, in part at least because, despite the rather abstract theories of the beginning, their application is more practical and concrete – a shift which is all to the good.

This, then, is an ambitious and challenging book, which offers new ways of seeing old circumstances, especially when it forges links between seemingly disparate works. Unsurprisingly, given the focus on the city and court milieu as a context for the theatre, Shakespeare's plays are not central, although *Love's Labour's Lost* is put into the Wars of the Theatres and reappears through the book. Given special attention are the two parts of *Edward IV* as plays about London and its people; *The Case Is Altered*, *Every Man Out of His Humour* and *Poetaster* as plays which show how Jonson in particular 'makes a bid to be free of the shaping discursive interaction between the satirist and the dirt of the city' (p. 91). The importance of Jonson's attitudes and work is apparent again in the extended analyses of *Britain's Bourse*, the royal entertainment he wrote for the opening of the New Exchange in 1609, and of *The Alchemist* and *Epicoene*. Jonson is at the heart of Dillon's study because his work reflects his prominence in all of the book's spaces: theatre, court, city and what she refers to as 'town', that is, Westminster. *Epicoene* is discussed specifically as a town play, performed at the Whitefriars theatre and aimed at its audience. As part of the context for her argument about the relevance of place and fashion in these and other plays, Dillon cites various contemporary authorities, especially John Stow, as well as modern cultural studies of that world, such as those by Valerie Pearl. Themes and concerns set out at the start are interwoven through the subsequent chapters, which entails some awkward cross-referencing and reminders for the reader; the Epilogue, by contrast, with its focus on *Arden of Faversham*, seems too loosely related to the rest. *Theatre, Court and City* is not only complex but relatively short, so both the process and outcome are more suggestive than exhaustive. This does not, however, detract from the insightful connections produced by Dillon's approach, her discussion of *The Knight of the Burning Pestle* being a notable example. The book includes illustrations of some significant spaces – Paul's Walk, the New Exchange, Westminster – and an extensive bibliography. But the text itself is encumbered by an intrusive method of citation. Is it really necessary to give author, title and page number in parentheses after a quotation or reference when full details are readily available at the back of the book? Such interruptions do a disservice to an argument as multi-faceted as Dillon's.

The significance given to Ben Jonson in *Theatre, Court and City* is continued in a collection of new essays, *Re-Presenting Ben Jonson: Text, History, Performance*, edited by Martin Butler. It appears under the flag of Early Modern Literature in History, a series of studies that 'share an historical awareness and an interest in seeing their texts in lively negotiation with their own and successive cultures' (cover) – phrasing that would have been generally incomprehensible before the influence of New Historicism–Cultural Materialism became widespread. Certainly this book is concerned with text, or rather texts: various Jonson texts and the forthcoming new Cambridge edition of his *Workes*, of which Butler is a general editor (with Ian Donaldson and David Bevington). All but one of the papers collected in this volume were presented at a conference that considered 'the effects of the way that Ben Jonson's texts have been edited on the condition of Jonson studies at the present time', with particular attention given to the present status and future usefulness of the Herford and Simpson standard edition of the plays (p. 1). Butler's admirable introduction addresses the important issues facing a general editor of Jonson and gives clear summaries of the papers that follow, establishing the different perspectives offered; and a broad range of topics is covered in the eleven essays. Butler's organizing hand is apparent in the progression from articles dealing specifically with aspects of the texts to papers concerned with Jonson himself, then with sources, performance history, chronology and allusions. The first is David Bevington's 'Why Re-edit Herford and Simpson?' In the essay, a second question suggests his answer: 'Is Jonson dead on arrival, and, if so, is the paucity of lively and usable texts a contributing factor?' (p. 22). Bevington argues for a new edition with, among other changes, modernized spelling and punctuation, more attention to staging, integrated commentary and stage history. He believes in particular that such an edition would go a long way to improving Jonson's fortunes in the theatre. He also explains his view that a new edition should include both versions of *Every Man In His Humour*, and offers a critical assessment of Herford and Simpson's 'old historical' editorial apparatus (p. 28). Next comes 'The Printing, Proofing and Press-Correction of Jonson's Folio *Workes*' by David Gants, whose expertise in this subject is especially apparent in his skilful and comprehensible demonstration of analytical bibliography in action. He presents empirical evidence about the printing of the 1616 Folio (compositors, etc.) which editors of Jonson can use with confidence, and he offers a plausible explanation of how Jonson might have made press corrections. Gants concludes with the warning that we should not 'take for granted any assumptions about printing practices from this period. We must treat each work, indeed each copy of a work, as fresh evidence in our quest to understand the complete history of a text' (p. 56). In 'Forms of Authority in the Early Texts of *Every Man Out of His Humour*' Kevin Donovan narrows the focus to Jonson's first published quarto to analyse the nature and effect of the changes Jonson made for the reworked Folio version. These changes, which modify the stage directions and the act and scene division rather than

the dialogue itself, were adopted by Herford and Simpson. But as Donovan points out, these revisions 'profoundly affect the experience of reading the play' because they 'stifle a reader's sense of the dramatic life of the play and tend to disguise its radically innovative experimentation for the sake of uniformity in the Folio as a whole' (p. 61). *Every Man Out* is used as an example of the problems facing a modern editor of Jonson; interestingly, Donovan considers some of the same issues as Bevington with different results: he does not, for instance, advocate modernizing spelling and punctuation. More broadly, he also reviews many of the current theories and practices of editors and bibliographers as a context for his specific conclusions.

With Helen Ostovich's, '"To Behold the Scene Full": Seeing and Judging in *Every Man Out of His Humour*', the focus narrows to one part of a play – the Paul's Walk sequence – in a study that shares Janette Dillon's interest in the importance of place. 'The genius of the scene', says Ostovich, 'lies in its representation of a famous topographical site, with all its accumulated cultural associations, within the context created by the ambivalently fictionalized site of the new Globe theatre'. She shows how the episode works on an audience by inviting it to judge the 'social performance' of the various rogues who frequent the St Paul's promenade (p. 76). The basic premise of her argument is that in this play Jonson's use of long crowded scenes is related to his 'innovative theatrical principle of developing place as synonymous with meaning' (p. 76). The detailed analysis demonstrates how Jonson's precise choreography produces a series of layered performances, some prompting the audience into complicity, some distancing it. In the context of a new edition of the plays, Ostovich's convincing central point is that the six choppy scenes of the revised Folio version work against the theatrical success and emblematic meaning of this segment, which in the original quarto is one long whole. *Every Man Out* arises again in

Joseph F. Loewenstein's 'Personal Material: Jonson and Book-burning', which has as its departure point the fire that destroyed Jonson's library in 1623. That this essay begins and ends by referring to Milton's *Aeropagitica* is a good indication of its focus; citing Foucault, Loewenstein says his aim is 'to interrogate the ongoing interaction between censorship and ownership' (p. 96). The central text is the poem Jonson wrote after the fire, 'An Execration Upon Vulcan', here called 'an under-examined source for the historian of book culture' (p. 99), at least in part because the poem is not in Herford and Simpson. Loewenstein's discussion addresses issues such as the influence of Cervantes, Marlowe and Ovid on Jonson, his imprisonment for contributions to *The Isle of Dogs*, and his writing of *Poetaster*, all of which are related to the main concern: Jonson's reaction to censorship. Getting at Jonson's underlying motives is notoriously difficult, but Loewenstein, like Ostovich, offers some insightful readings and conclusions.

Even if nothing else in this collection made owning it desirable, it would be worth having for James Knowles's separately copyrighted edition of 'Jonson's *Entertainment at Britain's Burse*' (a work also central to much of Janette Dillon's argument). The text of this entertainment is certainly 'new' to us, having been rediscovered by Knowles in 1997, and as he and Dillon amply demonstrate, it has much new to tell us about both Jonson's work for the court and city and that milieu. In Knowles's words, '[n]ow we possess a text, supported by substantial contemporary documentation, illuminating its commissioning and performance, which, in praising a commercial building contains wholesale, apparently unironic, celebration of eastwards and westwards colonialism, and of the marvels of London's developing consumer culture' (p. 115, punctuation sic). The package offered here includes an old-spelling text of the *Entertainment*, an introduction to the manuscript and its provenance, and explanatory annotations.

Jonson the more idealistic critic of his political times is the focus of Blair Worden's 'Politics in *Catiline*: Jonson and his Sources', which examines the influence of Tacitus and Sallus on *Catiline* in relation to *Sejanus* and gives special attention to Jonson's implied analogies between the London of his day and the Rome of Cicero. A main purpose of the study, however, is to show how *Catiline*, unlike *Sejanus* or the rest of Jonson's work, deals with 'the conduct, within a vicious world, of virtue in action and in power' (pp. 170–1).

Other aspects of *Re-Presenting Ben Jonson* covered in the last four essays are rather more miscellaneous. Michael Cordner's 'Zeal-of-the-Land Busy Restored' is concerned with Jonson's plays on the Restoration stage in general and *The Cheats*, John Wilson's adaptation of *Bartholomew Fair*, in particular. Topics covered include official censorship of the later play, its audience, Wilson's alterations, and some reasons for them. Stage history is also at the centre of Lois Potter's 'The Swan Song of the Stage Historian' – a catchy but misleading title, since the implications of 'swan song' are not developed past the point of suggesting that stage history can make only a limited contribution to a new edition. Nevertheless, Potter's considerable strengths as a performance critic are much in evidence through her survey of several productions at the Swan Theatre – Stratford's unofficial Jonson venue. These include *The New Inn* and *Every Man In*, both directed by John Caird in 1986–7, Danny Royle's *Epicoene* (1989) and Sam Mendes's *The Alchemist* (1991). The penultimate essay is 'Jonsonian Chronology and the Styles of *A Tale of a Tub*' by Hugh Craig, a very detailed report of several statistical analyses of common word usage in Jonson's plays which support the idea of that play's 'mixed origins' (p. 229). Unfortunately, but probably inevitably, Craig's explanation of the tests and results is not very easy to follow, and probably of real interest only to the specialist. Last and least is 'Jonsonian Allusions' by Robert C. Evans, which argues for the compilation of a Jonson 'allusion book'. This interesting idea is undermined by a repetitious, wordy and laboured process of overselling. Evans mostly tells us where to look for allusions and gives examples of what we might find, but his confident insistence suggests that he thinks he is offering more. Otherwise, this important collection of essays usefully explores many of the concerns a new edition must address. With the Oxford edition of Thomas Middleton's works on the brink of publication (or perhaps the brink of the brink), it is more than time to bring Jonson into the postmodern world. As well, it is impossible even to guess at the effects of having available major, computer-accessible editions with apparatus, not just of Shakespeare but also of two of his major contemporaries. Cambridge University Press and the general editors of this Jonson edition deserve our gratitude.

The vogue for publishers' series that attempt to create or fill a critical niche is current on both sides of the Atlantic, Studies in Theatre History and Culture from the University of Iowa Press being a case in point – although the pretensions of this English-spelling title are perhaps highlighted when a book appearing in the series prefers *theater*. Part theatre history, part history, part analyses of critical, editorial and performance traditions and approaches to the play, part textual analysis, part moral judgement, Edward Pechter's *'Othello' and Interpretative Traditions* aims to understand and explain the experience of the play in performance. That Pechter dedicates the book to Stanley Fish is indicative of the governing idea, namely that Iago corrupts us into seeing as he does, and that the play disconcertingly reminds us of this. As Pechter says, his study is primarily text-centred, even when performances are being discussed, because his main interest is how the script determines performance. Of the 'Temptation Scene' (3.3), Pechter asks, 'how do we understand Othello's failure to sustain himself? how do we understand Iago's success in taking him apart?'; these, he says, are 'really two sides of the

same question . . . the central question for any interpretation of the play' (pp. 81–2). His argument includes extensive reference to other critics, their responses being evidence of the play's effect. But what these make apparent are the multiple interpretations available and produced, so that Pechter's own reading is often in danger of becoming just another among the rest. It is certainly intelligent, considered, moderate – but how can it be more, given that the argument seems to be something like 'we make the play in our own image'? Yet when he turns to analysis of the text, and the text in performance, Pechter achieves his purpose of bringing the reader to think again about how it works. His reconsideration of Bianca, for example, demonstrates effectively how source study, performance history, cultural context, and previous criticism can be brought together to show how this important minor character has come to be misperceived as a whore. In a detailed, perceptive analysis of the final scene, Pechter offers reasons why the stage Othello usually smothers Desdemona with a pillow, rather than strangling her with his bare hands as his words imply not once but twice. The Afterword returns to the central point that 'our critical power is just what *Othello* defeats' and suggests that in doing so it will necessarily 'blur if not totally erase the distinction between good and bad *Othello* criticism, however maintained' (p. 171). The example he traces, from Coleridge to the present, warrants sober consideration. Both new- and old-fashioned, this study is equipped with, on the one hand, extensive notes and an equally extensive list of works cited and, on the other, an appendix titled 'Character Endures'. Finally, if this Iowa series' title veers towards the pretentious, the layout of this book's pages takes it further in that direction. I do not know what purpose is served by putting the running titles and pagination at the foot of the page, but what is achieved is reader distraction and the conclusion that the old ways are sometimes best.

Publishers work hard to build and keep a reputation – something especially important in academic publishing where the name of the press alone can help sell the product. It is a surprise, therefore, that Manchester University Press would risk its marketing cachet by publishing a book with seemingly little or no editorial oversight or intervention. Steve Sohmer's *Shakespeare's Mystery Play* is such a book; indeed, it has many of the hallmarks of something from a vanity press: authorial self-indulgence, factual errors, misreadings, and a slipshod bibliography that would be unacceptable from an undergraduate. Sohmer's premise is that *Julius Caesar* was written for the opening of the Globe theatre in 1599; he attempts to support this view with an interrelated two-part argument that the play is a subversive response to what he calls 'the Elizabethan calendar controversy' and that there is a deliberate parallel being drawn between Julius Caesar and Jesus Christ – who significantly share initials. The difference between the Gregorian and Julian calendars, Sohmer claims, caused 'widespread confusion and frustration' in Elizabethan London (p. 22), a statement he supports with a questionable reading of a lone pamphlet published in Edinburgh. The Caesar-Christ 'link', to which I cannot begin to do justice here, is forced into being with the help of some perversely inventive interpretations – that *bootless* means 'barefoot', for example (pp. 30–1) – and more troubling misuses of the language and strategies of proof. 'To an English Christian, being compelled to worship by Caesar's calendar – a calendar repudiated by the whole world – was not merely absurd; it was degrading, humiliating, scandalous, mortifying. It was tyranny. Those who wonder why Shakespeare chose 1599 to write his play about the man who imposed the Julian calendar perhaps need seek no further' (pp. 22–3). As this suggests, the book is written with a quasi-religious fervour and conviction that makes refutation or counter-argument futile. It might well be that Sohmer has valid points to make, but his methods seriously undermine a reader's confidence that any of the information is accurate or

any of the argument plausible. In addition, the book is excessively long and repetitious. Showing an almost obsessive need to make every minor detail 'prove' him right, Sohmer sets out his whole thesis, argues it, and then returns at least once to virtually every contentious point, as if hoping that his assertions could become more convincing by repetition. A phrase he uses to discredit an opponent's interpretation is 'this is not safe'. That is the quotation the publisher might most appropriately have chosen to display on the cover – especially because *Julius Caesar* is a play read by students wherever Shakespeare is studied and one shudders to imagine the influence this kind of enthusiastic pursuit of novelty will have on receptive, uncritical minds.

One area of criticism enjoying a resurgence in popularity in this post-theory period is, broadly speaking, performance studies, of which there are several in this year's selection, including *Shakespeare in the London Theatre 1855–58*, by Theodor Fontane, translated by Russell Jackson. Fontane, according to Jackson's very informative introduction, was a German writer and theatre critic (known now, if at all, as the author of *Effi Briest* – the novel sentimentally referred to by Beckett's Krapp). The articles translated here were written by Fontane in Berlin, after a period of residence in London during which he saw many productions of Shakespeare plays at a number of theatres. His chief purpose is to compare productions in the two cities so as to determine where Shakespeare is done better; but, as Jackson says, along the way we get 'detailed and engaging documents for the historian of theatre in London, [which] also address fundamental questions about the social and aesthetic purposes of Shakespearean performance' (xi). Fontane devotes most space to productions at the Princess's and Sadler's Wells theatres, under the direction of Charles Kean and Samuel Phelps respectively, but other venues and performances also receive his perceptive and detailed attention. His insights on staging and acting are especially worth noting, in part at least because they are often equally applicable today. Five Princess's and seven Sadler's Wells productions are described and evaluated, *1 Henry IV*, *Coriolanus*, and *Macbeth* among them, and upwards of twenty productions overall. Fontane's answer to his initial question is characteristically balanced: London productions surpass those in Berlin, but Berlin actors are better. Russell Jackson's knowledge of nineteenth-century London theatres and Shakespeare productions is evident in his useful, informative, contextualizing apparatus. This book is a significant example of why publishers such as The Society for Theatre Research are necessary.

J. L. Styan is a well-known and deservedly respected analyst of both Shakespeare and twentieth-century theatre and *Perspectives on Shakespeare in Performance* is, by my count, his eighteenth book. It is, however, a collection of essays written between 1967 and 1995, all previously published, two of them twice, with seemingly no revisions for their reappearance here. The book is dedicated to Sam Wanamaker and the Globe Education Centre, but most of these essays were written long before there was a Globe, and only one anticipatory mention is made of it. That is symptomatic of a general problem: these essays are often dated, with ideas that have been corrected or superseded since they were first expressed. In the Introduction, written for this collection, Styan sets out themes to which the essays repeatedly return: the importance of the play in performance, audience response, and the difference between criticism and the experience of the play in the theatre. The various subjects dealt with include characters, boys playing women, Shakespeare on film, the fairies in *A Midsummer Night's Dream* and the opening scene of *All's Well*. Styan's strengths are particularly apparent in his extended discussions of 'The Murder of Gonzago' in the Olivier film and of *Hamlet* on stage, which call attention to elements rarely if ever considered elsewhere. On the other hand, there are errors which more recent revision might have corrected. Twice we are told, for

example, that Shakespeare and his contemporaries did not use *aside* when a character's speech is to be unheard by others (pp. 45, 160), a suggestion that makes one wonder if Styan ever consulted early editions or facsimiles. Of more than 550 uses of the term in the plays of the period, about half signal precisely that. Elsewhere, Styan refers to 'the thunder-stones and flashing mirrors of an Elizabethan storm effect' (p. 3), but offers no supporting evidence for their use – which is not surprising, since that is not how these effects were then created. The chief problem, however, with collecting these papers in one volume is that the reader is made uncomfortably aware of hobby-horses and repetitions – of plays, scenes, business, ideas – which create an impression of limitation and narrowness of focus, rather than of the broad scope which has actually characterized Styan's career.

Perhaps the most significant and pervasive legacy of the new approaches to literature practised and advanced in the 1980s and early nineties is the continuing emphasis on original contexts, both mental and physical. One welcome effect has been to 'raise the profile' of archival research – which has, of course, always been there. Judging by the frequency of references to REED volumes, for example, the use and acknowledgement of such fundamental research are now seen as *de rigeur* even by those whose work does not take them to old archives or new excavations. Many will certainly want to consult one product of such research, *Lighting the Shakespearean Stage, 1567–1642*, by R. B. Graves. Like Bruce Smith's *The Acoustic World of Early Modern England* which appeared last year,[1] Graves's study provides information that virtually requires us to alter how we imagine the physical world in which Shakespeare and his contemporaries lived, wrote, and where their plays were performed. Our inevitable predisposition to see (and hear) through a

---

[1] Bruce R. Smith, *The Acoustic World of Early Modern England: Attending to the O-Factor* (Chicago and London, 1999).

modern filter is necessarily and rightly challenged by the new light Graves sheds on an old world. He has researched widely, gathering evidence from 'primary sources, secondary works in theatrical history' as well as studies in 'psychophysics, architectural lighting, and the history of weather' in order to 'compare and contrast the effect of stage lighting in various playhouses and on different plays and audiences' (p. ix). Even for those whose field is not drama there is much of interest, such as detailed descriptions of lighting methods, evidence about how much illumination different equipment casts and about how the eye uses the light it receives. Graves discusses natural and artificial light and the use of both together in various venues, especially the indoor and outdoor playing spaces. Although some of this material has appeared in articles, here it is expanded and gathered into a comprehensive whole. The organization of the book is carefully cumulative, progressing from such topics as performance times, physical orientation of the amphitheatres, the roof or 'heavens' over the stage and the cost of artificial lighting, to reconsiderations of *The Duchess of Malfi* and the final scene of *Othello* in the context of his conclusions about stage lighting. Graves's work also demonstrates how original material previously used in research by others can still have much to tell us; his treatment of the legislation that controlled the times of performance and of architectural evidence about the Rose and Globe are just two of many examples. But he has not only relied on information from the past; part of his research was done at Shakespeare's Globe and in various Tudor halls. Indeed, this study seems so thorough that any attempt to summarize its conclusions in the short space available here would do Graves an injustice. If, however, you think you can imagine what life was like in a world before electric or even gas light, reading this book will make you think again. *Lighting the Shakespearean Stage* should prompt a reconsideration of how an audience would, quite literally, have 'seen' a play.

The remains of Henslowe's Rose, discovered in 1989, are naturally central to Graves's conclusions about the orientation and therefore the lighting of amphitheatre plays. Five years before this discovery, *Documents of the Rose Playhouse*, edited by Carol Chillington Rutter, was published. Now, after enough time has elapsed for the dust to settle, a revised edition has appeared. In the ten or so years since the digging ended and the site was again covered, much has been written and many speculations and conclusions offered, the most credible of which Rutter has gathered together in her second preface. Her brief but fact-filled summary covers the excavation, the controversy about what to do with it, and plans for the future of the site. In this new context, Rutter's 'collection of manuscripts selected and arranged to chronicle the day-to-day operation' (p. vi) of the Rose is possibly of even greater use and interest than before; certainly it is or should be a starting point for anyone interested in trying to recreate, or simply to imagine, the original circumstances in which and for which early modern plays were written.

If it is impossible for us to return, even in our minds, to a past which is in any way three-dimensional, how might Shakespeare react if told that his plays were performed in two dimensions, on film? But as Kenneth S. Rothwell shows in *A History of Shakespeare on Screen: A Century of Film and Television*, the bard has a long movie history. Those who were lucky enough to see Rothwell's festival of Shakespeare on film at the World Congress in Los Angeles will already appreciate his expertise. This book will confirm that where others might mock – although perhaps that is fast becoming an outmoded response – Rothwell considers Shakespeare films on their own terms, first as attempts, then later as successes in the creation of art. At the same time, he addresses the reality that cinema has always been a business, governed by 'tickling commodity' (his repeated 'catch-quote'). From early silent films of single scenes to recent Branagh blockbusters, from

British and American to international productions, Rothwell discusses them all with the benefit of both first-hand experience and the necessary technical knowledge. But this is very much a book aimed at the non-expert in cinematic technique, which most teachers of Shakespeare probably are – at least until they finish reading it. After giving the circumstances behind the making of a picture, including the cost, Rothwell summarizes the film treatment of the play, describing cuts and changes, evaluating particular performances, and giving contemporary critical and popular responses. Pictures made for both cinema and television are included; even soft- and hard-core porn treatments get a mention. The book is chock-full of information about every aspect of Shakespeare on film, not only in each chapter but also in the detailed notes, wide-ranging bibliography, chronological list of films from 1899 to 1999, and filmography and title index. Less helpful, however, is a general index which is of personal names only, thereby precluding searches for specific topics or terms. Rothwell's approach is mostly informational, seldom judgemental, rarely negative – not, I think, because he cannot see things to criticize, but because his purpose here is primarily to survey a century of filmed Shakespeare. At the same time, his discussion keeps returning to the plays themselves, and it is in the comparison of a film with its source that the reader might sometimes detect an evaluation. But the main thrust of *A History of Shakespeare on Screen* is what the title implies: it gives the background and context to help a viewer understand the films. Since only a minority of these are widely accessible, for many we must rely on Rothwell's descriptions, and this is where his expertise is especially apparent and invaluable. His knowledge of, in particular, the obscure silent films of Shakespeare's plays is demonstrated also in the published version of his plenary lecture at the 1999 Shakespeare on Screen Centenary Conference in Málaga, Spain. In *Early Shakespeare Movies: How the Spurned Spawned Art* Rothwell charts the development of Shakespearian cinema from popular entertainment to art-form by paying special attention to that quintessentially filmic device, the close-up. It is pleasing to discover, and report, that this lecture does not repeat material from his book but adds to it. Together these studies provide a good groundwork in a medium that is becoming ever more widespread in both the performance and teaching of Shakespeare's plays.

The classroom use of filmed Shakespeare can be a contentious issue – is it a poor substitute for teaching, or a good way (sometimes the only way) of getting students actually to see the plays? In *Teaching Shakespeare through Performance*, edited by Milla Cozart Riggio, the answer is, not surprisingly, the latter. This collection, which has been 'designed for teachers of both high school and college English courses who wish to introduce performance strategies into their classroom' (cover) appears in the MLA's Options for Teaching series and has evidently benefited from that association's resources. A hefty volume of over five hundred pages, it includes contributions from thirty-one academics and theatre professionals; the essays are divided into five sections: Theory and History, Teaching Strategies, Exemplary Courses, Films and Electronic Resources, Annotated Guides. As this list suggests, coverage of the topic is exhaustive – and exhausting if read from start to finish – but those readers who follow their interests will find much that is encouraging and useful. For those wanting a basic how-to, for example, the essays by Lois Potter, G. B. Shand and Maurice Charney are among those providing questions students might be asked to consider as well as other specific and practical assignments or projects. But as the section titles indicate, virtually every aspect of the topic is addressed – including original performances approached through stage directions and stage history, and classroom or theatre performances by students or professional actors. The sheer number of strategies enthusiastically offered and supported with positive teacher and student responses creates the strong impression that performance is the better way. By the end, however, I was left asking myself just what I want my students to learn in a Shakespeare course, and whether performance *is* the best way to achieve those ends. Some caveats that come quickly to mind: most of the class projects described are labour-intensive for both faculty and students, needing small classes to be practicable; we are not told if the courses have formal final examinations and, if they do, what the questions might be; as well, the writing assignments often seem minimal, requiring not abstract thinking but practical reportage. As might be expected from an MLA-sponsored publication, much hard information is provided, especially in the sections about using films and other electronic resources in the classroom, and in the annotated guides that follow. Of particular note are the essays by Peter Donaldson and Larry Friedlander, which in showing what is now technologically possible make useful ammunition for those wanting to convince a reluctant administration that the future is here and it works. The guides survey American Shakespeare companies and festivals with academic affiliations; classroom editions of Shakespeare; film, television and video resources. An extensive list of works cited rounds off a collection that, despite its North American bias, has much to offer anyone who has ever thought about using performance to teach Shakespeare and has wondered how it might be done.

A quite different method of using Shakespeare in the classroom is described by Fred Sedgwick in *Shakespeare and the Young Writer*, an impressive demonstration of how the language and poetry of the plays can be used effectively in teaching literacy to primary school students. Sedgwick presents case studies from his own experience as a visiting specialist in English schools, but his techniques would work equally well in North America. Briefly, his method is to have students read passages from the plays and write responses that in some way imitate the originals – variously, the imagery, structure, alliteration, metre. He provides numerous examples of writing by students aged six to ten, some quite remarkably inventive and poetic. In the context of this evidence of what is possible, even from students previously considered almost illiterate, Sedgwick also offers trenchant criticism of school systems and governments that focus on test scores to the detriment of students' actual learning and enjoyment in doing so. Against those who might protest that Shakespeare's language is too difficult for primary students, he argues, 'the difficulty . . . is part of the case for teaching it, not against' (p. 14). Furthermore, the passages he uses frequently express ideas which the students' writing shows they have grasped and in some way applied to their own lives. Surprisingly, perhaps, Sedgwick makes *Macbeth* central to his demonstration of what is possible. He has the students read a selection of the many passages setting out opposites and paradoxes and asks them to write some of their own. After providing a list of one-line examples, among them, 'We are friends and yet we are enemies', 'It was the first and last day', 'I can be friendly but yet mean', he observes, 'There is more than one way to sentimentalize children: we can, for example, see them as innocents. But we can also see them as uninterested in the huge sad matters of life and death. It is not true. Shakespeare here has given some children a chance to reflect purposefully on some of those issues' (pp. 98–9). The value of using Shakespeare as cultural icon, though, is never questioned. Sedgwick also includes student responses to passages from *A Midsummer Night's Dream*, *Richard II*, *As You Like It*, *King Lear*, *The Tempest*, and *Cymbeline*. 'Fear no more the heat of the sun', for example, elicits extended poems that provide powerful confirmation of the effectiveness of his methods. For those primary school teachers whose interest has been piqued by his evidence, there is an extensive list of (British) references, many of which he quotes through the book to illustrate or support his points. For anyone who believes in the value of the arts in education, this book will provide both pleasure and inspiration.

Upper level students of early modern drama are the target of Alexander Leggatt's *Introduction to English Renaissance Comedy*, which, rather than being the usual broad survey, is 'a close study of nine selected plays that represent different periods, styles and authors, suggesting the range and variety of the genre at this period and examining some of its recurring preoccupations' (p. 1). In his introduction Leggatt emphasizes the 'eclecticism' of the comedies that resulted from influences as various as Roman New Comedy, *commedia dell'arte* and the Tudor interlude, a description amply demonstrated by his choice of plays: *Endymion, Friar Bacon and Friar Bungay, A Midsummer Night's Dream, The Malcontent, Michaelmas Term, The Tempest* and *Bartholomew Fair* have a chapter each and the last chapter considers both *The Lady of Pleasure* and *A Jovial Crew*. Leggatt also sets out certain recurring concerns to be emphasized in what follows: power, authority and the use of magic; sexuality; identity; love. The analyses amply demonstrate his considerable strengths in text- and context-based practical criticism that produces inclusive, moderate analyses expressed with admirable clarity. His focus on only nine plays allows for detailed discussion of contexts, themes and staging, while ranging as well to links with other works, both dramatic (e.g. *Waiting for Godot*) and not (*The Faerie Queene*); the tight framework also enables him to show how these plays are 'talking to each other' (p. 9). Paradoxically, perhaps, because of both Leggatt's decision to use only nine comedies in this 'introduction' to the genre and his ability to describe and analyse their complexities, students who consult this book will need to bring with them some knowledge of the period and the plays in order really to appreciate the insights offered. Indeed, the title is somewhat misleading, since the book is about Renaissance comedy only if one generalizes from what is said about nine very disparate plays; in fact, it is not

even about comedy as such in any obvious or detailed way. There are, however, brief notes to each chapter and a short list of suggested reading at the end which are student-friendly – informative without being intimidating. For teachers of early modern drama, this book should be a welcome addition to a still rather limited selection of up-to-date, concrete textual studies which put works by Shakespeare in the context of those by his contemporaries, and vice versa. Those faced with teaching any of these nine plays for the first time could probably find no better introduction for their purposes; indeed, I expect that even an expert might learn something new or be given new ideas to consider.

But Shakespeare is *sui generis*, as is demonstrated by *Adaptations of Shakespeare*, a 'critical anthology of plays from the seventeenth century to the present', edited by Daniel Fischlin and Mark Fortier. No other writer has prompted so many to write so much. The editors provide a diverse selection: Fletcher's *The Woman's Prize; or The Tamer Tamed*, Tate's *The History of King Lear*, Keats's *King Stephen: A Dramatic Fragment*, Lorca's *The Public (El público)*, Brecht's *The Resistible Rise of Arturo Ui*, Welcome Msomi's *uMabatha*, Charles Marowitz's *Measure for Measure*, Heiner Müller's *Hamletmachine*, The Women's Theatre Group and Elaine Feinstein's *Lear's Daughters*, Paula Vogel's *Desdemona: A Play About a Handkerchief*, Philip Osment's *This Island's Mine* and Djanet Sears's *Harlem Duet*. At the most practical level, this collection is especially welcome because it makes available in one place a group of works almost all otherwise out of print, difficult to find, and/or prohibitively expensive. But Fischlin and Fortier provide much more than accessible texts; besides a detailed introduction to each play, with bibliography, and photographs of performances where available, they have written a critical introduction on adaptation as a kind of genre. Indeed, this anthology brings me back to my initial focus on the continuing influences of critical theory, since it is probable that those influences have made a collection such as this viable in the contemporary marketplace. Furthermore, the editors' general introduction is unquestionably the most overtly theoretical piece of writing dealt with in this review, which would be surprising except that theory has given adaptation its current value to writers, critics, teachers and publishers. Culture, appropriation, authorship, commodification, all these arise in an introduction that begins with a doubtless necessary but overlong discussion of what exactly constitutes adaptation – and whether, in fact, that is the right word for what authors such as those in the anthology are doing with the works of Shakespeare. In the classroom, the plays and critical apparatus in this anthology, together with the Shakespeare plays to which they respond, would certainly provide a broad yet provocative survey that moves beyond the conventional boundaries of Shakespeare studies.

As Fischlin and Fortier observe, translation is a kind of adaptation, and when that translation is of Shakespeare in a colonial then post-colonial context, the issues are particularly vexed. A collection of Indian explorations of the psychological and formal problems created is available in *Shakespeare in Indian Languages* and *Appropriating Shakespeare*, the former consisting of conference papers edited by D. A. Shankar and the latter a short study written by him. The nineteen essays offer various perspectives on translation and its difficulties, some more persuasive than others – at least to this English-speaking reader. What seems to be inadequate editing, combined with uncertainty on the part of the essay writers about their intended audience, has resulted in a wide range of quality, from the sophisticated to the squirm-inducing. Nevertheless, especially for those concerned with translation in a post-colonial context, these essays deserve attention because they address the problems from an Indian point of view. Shankar's separate short work is, as the subtitle says, '[a] study of Shakespeare's plays rendered into Kannada between 1895–1932', that is, in the days of colonial rule. Shankar argues that 'to

translate a text is to interpret it and sit in judgement over it' (cover), and develops this position by analysing translations of *Macbeth*, *Othello* and *A Midsummer Night's Dream*, giving special attention to the 'assimilations, the rejections and the modifications' (cover) made by the translators. Again, in providing a view of the process from within the translators' culture, albeit some seventy years on, this study warrants consideration.

To judge from its title and subtitle, *Christianity and Sexuality in the Early Modern World: Regulating Desire, Reforming Practice*, by Merry E. Wiesner-Hanks, might be as much devoted to theory as is the general introduction to adaptation by Fischlin and Fortier – both are from Routledge, a publisher known to have staked out much of that territory. In fact, however much recent theory has also made this book possible, and however much new historicism is part of the context and helped to determine the approach, the result is primarily a fact-filled, jargon-free, broad yet deep survey of 'the ways in which Christian ideas and institutions shaped sexual norms and conduct from the time of Luther and Columbus to that of Thomas Jefferson'. The title's '*Early Modern World*' is to be taken literally: '[t]he book is global in scope and geographic in organization, with chapters on Protestant, Catholic and Orthodox Europe, Latin America, Africa and Asia, and North America'. Not surprisingly, given the title's dual focus, virtually every aspect of life in that world is covered: 'marriage, divorce, fornication and illegitimacy, clerical sexuality, witchcraft and love magic, homosexuality, and moral crimes' (cover). The book delivers all this and more. The degree of detail makes summaries impossible here, but in general the material is carefully organized and the concepts clearly explained, making this a very useful survey for the non-specialist. In addition, at the end of the introduction and of each chapter Wiesner-Hanks provides an extensive annotated list of suggested further reading. Altogether this is an excellent resource from someone who is clearly

LESLIE THOMSON

an expert in the field – a historian, not a literary critic, whose chief concern is to provide information and analysis in a historical context. In particular, its value lies in Wiesner-Hanks's ability to lift, however temporarily and partially, the filter of the present through which we interpret the past, especially in matters of religion and sexuality.

This concludes my survey of books sent for review, but it seems to me also worth making brief mention of a few recent journal articles and special issues which, like the best of the work discussed above, somehow respond to the challenges posed and possibilities offered by the innovations of postmodern theory. Thus a common factor in my short and selective list is the combination of new approaches with concrete evidence, though the topics are quite various. In *Theatre Notebook* (2000), a study by Roger Bowers, 'The Playhouse of the Choristers of Paul's, *c.* 1575–1608', convincingly relocates the Paul's boys' performance space to the Almonry and gives the probable dimensions along with other details. Hugh Craig appears again with a technically specific analysis of (and more generally useful conclusions about) 'Grammatical Modality in English Plays from the 1580s to the 1640s' in *English Literary Renaissance* (Winter 2000). He shows how 'the frequencies of a group of modal verbs [*can, may* and *should*] in the plays are a crude but measurable indicator of the shift from early to modern' (pp. 32–3). A special issue of *ELR* entitled 'Recontextualizing Shakespeare' (Spring 2000) contains six provocative essays offering a variety of new angles on as many plays, and a detailed, categorized survey by Valerie Traub of 'Recent Studies in Homoeroticism'. Another special issue, of the *Journal of Medieval and Early Modern Studies*, is titled 'The Cultural Work of Medieval Theater: Ritual Practice in England, 1350–1600' (Winter 1999). In her editorial introduction, Sarah Beckwith describes the need for studies of 'religion as theatrical and theater as religious' (p. 1), and the seven essays (the last two on Shakespeare specifically) address

this broad topic. Also noteworthy and useful in this issue is a survey of 'New Books across the Disciplines', a list of recent publications in every related field of medieval and early modern studies. That list is good a place as any to start if you want to bring yourself up to date in the criticism of a long historical period which, as this collection of essays frequently shows, should be seen as a continuum rather than as two separate and distinctive parts. Surely Shakespeare and his contemporaries would have found it easier to imagine the medieval world than it is for us to imagine Renaissance England.

WORKS REVIEWED

Bowers, Roger, 'The Playhouse of the Choristers of Paul's, *c.* 1575–1608', *Theatre Notebook*, 54 (2000), 70–85.
Butler, Martin, ed., *Re-Presenting Ben Jonson: Text, History, Performance* (Basingstoke, 1999).
Cartwright, Kent, *Theatre and Humanism* (Cambridge, 1999).
Craig, Hugh, 'Grammatical Modality in English Plays from the 1580s to the 1640's', *English Literary Renaissance*, 30 (2000), 32–54.
Dillon, Janette, *Theatre, Court and City, 1595–1610: Drama and Social Space in London* (Cambridge, 2000).
English Literary Renaissance, vol. 3, no. 2 (Spring 2000).
Fischlin, Daniel and Mark Fortier, eds., *Adaptations of Shakespeare* (London and New York, 2000).
Fontane, Theodor, *Shakespeare in the London Theatre 1855–58*, translated with an introduction and notes by Russell Jackson (London, 1999).
Graves, R. B., *Lighting the Shakespearean Stage, 1567–1642* (Southern Illinois, 1999).
Journal of Medieval and Early Modern Studies, vol. 29, no. 1 (Winter 1999).
Leggatt, Alexander, *Introduction to English Renaissance Comedy* (Manchester, 1999).
Pechter, Edward, *'Othello' and Interpretative Traditions* (Iowa, 1999).
Riggio, Milla Cozart, ed., *Teaching Shakespeare Through Performance* (New York, 1999).
Rothwell, Kenneth S., *Early Shakespeare Movies: How*

the Spurned Spawned Art (Chipping Campden, 2000).

A History of Shakespeare on Screen: A Century of Film and Television (Cambridge, 1999).

Rutter, Carol Chillington, ed., Documents of the Rose Playhouse, revised edition (Manchester, 1999).

Sedgwick, Fred, Shakespeare and the Young Writer (London and New York, 1999).

Shankar, D. A., Appropriating Shakespeare: A Study of Shakespeare's Plays Rendered into Kannada between 1895–1932 (Shimla, 1999).

ed., Shakespeare in Indian Languages (Shimla, 1999).

Sohmer, Steve, Shakespeare's Mystery Play (Manchester, 1999).

Styan, J. L., Perspectives on Shakespeare in Performance (New York, 2000).

Wiesner-Hanks, Merry E., Christianity and Sexuality in the Early Modern World: Regulating Desire, Reforming Practice (London and New York, 2000).

EDITIONS AND TEXTUAL STUDIES

reviewed by ERIC RASMUSSEN

Single-text editions of Shakespeare have recently bulked up considerably. The editions published this year are more than double the size of those produced a generation ago: the 197–page edition of 2 Henry VI in the Arden 2 series, for instance, is now superseded by the 491–page Arden 3; the 215–page Arden 2 Henry VIII gives way to the 506–page Arden 3. The text of the play, of course, remains more or less the same but it now occupies a much smaller proportion of the overall edition. Given that today's editors are responsible for producing an unprecedented amount of original introductory material and commentary, the fact that they may ultimately have less time to devote to the text itself should surprise no one.

It is worth bearing in mind, however, that the text of the play is the one element of an edition that every user will read. And yet, several of the editions under review here contain multiple errors in the play's text. These are not simple misprints that could be easily spotted by readers but more insidious sorts of substantive errors that produce seemingly valid readings. Proof-readers in seventeenth-century printing houses realized that this type of error, 'Words altered into other Words by a little wrong Spelling', could have profound consequences: 'the Sense made ridiculous, the purpose of it controvertible, and the meaning of the Author irretrievably lost to all that shall read

it in After times'.[1] Indeed, for the serious student who trusts the scholarly authority of an edition – and who is unlikely to consult more than one while studying a given play – some meanings might in fact be irretrievably lost.

The review essay that follows is intended to reassert the primacy of text in modern critical editions of Shakespeare. No matter how trenchant the editorial commentary or how comprehensive the stage history, a reader who learns that there are dozens of errors in the play's text will probably conclude that the entire edition is unreliable ('No more, the text is foolish'). I have read each edition under review against its Quarto or Folio control text and noted any differences not accounted for in the collations, that is, unintended errors rather than intentional emendations.[2] W. Speed Hill once argued that even the most careful of editors will inevitably make transcriptional errors that will then steadfastly evade proof-reading, but my findings

---

[1] From Joseph Moxon's description 'Of the Corrector, and his Office' in Mechanick Exercises on the Whole Art of Printing (1684; rpt. 1962), pp. 246–7.

[2] Because I standardly send editors and publishers lists of the typographic errors that I've found well in advance of the publication of this review, it is certainly possible that by the time this essay appears many of the errors I cite herein will have already been corrected in subsequent reprintings of the individual editions (and we shall all be better for it).

challenge this dictum.[3] Whereas I found sixteen errors in the text of the Oxford edition of *Romeo and Juliet*, there were no errors whatsoever in the Oxford editions of *King Lear* or *Richard III*. Similarly, although I counted eighteen errors in the Arden 3 edition of *The Merry Wives of Windsor* and five errors apiece in the Arden *1 Henry VI* and *2 Henry VI*, the text of the Arden *Henry VIII* was completely errorfree, as was the Cambridge *Coriolanus*. Transcriptional error, it would seem, is eminently evitable.

EDITIONS: OXFORD

To the extent that scholarly editions are responsive to consumer demand, the three major Shakespeare series have each responded to the renewal of critical interest in the early – formerly 'bad' – quartos. For plays that exist in two versions, the Arden 3 editions generally adopt the Folio as the control text but print a reduced photographic facsimile of the quarto text (readable but not optimal) in an appendix.[4] The editions of these plays in the New Cambridge Shakespeare are invariably based on the Folio while the quarto versions are relegated to the separate 'Early Quartos' series in which they are presented with only textual notes (readers of the Cambridge Early Quartos are directed to the Folio editions in the main series for a fuller account of each play). With the publication this year of Stanley Wells's Quarto-based edition of *King Lear* and John Jowett's Quarto-based *Richard III*, the Oxford Shakespeare takes the remarkable rehabilitation of the quartos to a new level by choosing them as control texts. Fourteen years after their original collaboration on the Oxford *Complete Works* (1986), Wells and Jowett are still taking risks, still pushing the envelope, and the result is a pair of outstanding editions that offer further proof (if indeed further proof were needed) that these two scholars are among the very best textual editors of their respective generations.

Wells's edition of Quarto *Lear* would no doubt have seemed more radical had it appeared during the period of excitement and controversy surrounding the publication of *The Division of the Kingdoms: Shakespeare's Two Versions of 'King Lear'* (1983) and the Oxford *Complete Works*, but in the intervening years several editions of Quarto *Lear* have appeared, most notably those prepared by René Weis (1993) and Jay L. Halio (1994). Although Wells graciously presents his edition as intended to 'complement rather than rival' these others, we should not lose sight of the fact that his Oxford *Lear* is a true landmark in the history of Shakespearian editing. For the first time the text of the Quarto has been published not merely with critical apparatus but with explanatory notes and an introductory essay sketching the play's genesis, reception, and influence. What this means, of course, is that the Quarto version will no longer be read only by textual scholars but also by students.

Wells's introduction begins with a fairy tale – 'Once upon a time, probably in 1605, a man called William Shakespeare, using a quill pen, wrote a play about the legendary British King Lear' – and rises to a philosophical crescendo celebrating the play as 'one of the most profound and challenging examinations ever undertaken of what it means to be human'. Modulating between playful and serious, this accessible essay offers a genuine introduction to *King Lear* and its system of ideas that I suspect will prove enormously useful in teaching the play. Although Wells's introduction is clearly geared toward readers encountering the play for the first time, he includes an occasional bon mot to amuse the more seasoned students in his audience. In the discussion of the play's neologisms, for instance, after observing that 'the

---

[3] 'The Calculus of Error, or Confessions of a General Editor', *Modern Philology*, 75 (1978), 247–60.

[4] See the Arden 3 editions of *Henry V*, *The Merry Wives of Windsor*, *2 Henry VI* and the forthcoming *3 Henry VI*. R. A. Foakes's conflated edition of *King Lear* is an exception. The forthcoming Arden 3 *Hamlet* will include edited versions of all three texts.

language of *King Lear* must have seemed very strange, as original in its day as that of James Joyce or Dylan Thomas in theirs', Wells wryly concludes that when Gonoril gives her nearly incomprehensible warning to Lear at 4.200–6, 'it is almost as if she wished to provide food for commentators'.

The Oxford *Complete Works* was widely criticized for its lack of notes. So it is rather satisfying to see the general editor of the Oxford Shakespeare here engaged in the business of commentary. Wells writes with a light touch, producing explanatory notes of great economy. He devotes a substantial portion of his commentary to discussing his textual decisions, particularly in relation to those made by Weis and Halio. Many of these commentary notes are models of humane textual criticism, but it is disappointing that in several instances the notes simply record, without comment, the readings adopted by other editors, a task that could perhaps have been better left to the collations.

One of the prime movers of the Oxford Shakespeare figures as an absent presence in the Oxford *Lear*. Wells has based his text on the one prepared by Gary Taylor for the *Complete Works*, apparently without any further input from Taylor himself. This makes for a collaboration with some interesting temporal dimensions as the subjective 'I' of Wells's introduction ('I have done what I can to make my edition') gives way to an editorial 'we' in the commentary notes ('we assume accidental interpolation') except in those places where Wells's text adopts a different reading from that printed in the *Complete Works* at which point the singular editorial voice returns.

Wells's edition represents version-based editing at its best. Wells asserts that his intention was to follow Q1 'when it seems defensible' and has done so throughout this meticulously edited text. He expresses some resentment toward critics who found the editing of Quarto *Lear* in the *Complete Works* undiscriminating in its adherence to Q ('There is a myth, circulated even among textual scholars, that the Oxford edition wilfully follows Q when that edition could easily and certainly be corrected from F') and points out that the *Complete Works* did, in fact, adopt around 120 readings from F. Although he acknowledges that the Quarto is so badly printed that 'even if the Folio did not exist, an editor's corrections would in many cases be identical with the Folio reading', Wells retains some key Quarto readings that all other editors of the Quarto have emended. In defending Q's 'Child Roland to the dark town come' (11.165), for instance, Wells notes that Oxford, Weis, and Halio all adopt F's 'Tower'. But he observes that if the words were spelt 'towne' and 'towre' they would be graphically almost interchangeable, points out that there is no extant ballad containing this line, and concludes that 'tempting as it is to follow the familiar reading, there is no good reason to emend Q in an edition based on its text'.

This is a supremely student-friendly edition that will have far-reaching implications. Teachers throughout the English-speaking world will soon begin adopting Wells's edition for their courses (in its paperback manifestation in Oxford's World's Classics series) and a new generation of students will have their first experience with Shakespeare's *King Lear* in the Quarto version. Whatever one thinks of the relative merits and demerits of the Quarto and Folio texts, it is surely thought provoking (if not mind-boggling) to imagine a possible future in which 'Child Roland to the dark town come' could become the more familiar version of Edgar's famous line.

Readers who primarily know John Jowett's work as a bibliographer will be pleasantly surprised to discover his manifold other talents on display in the Oxford *Richard III*. Jowett is not only a discerning textual critic but a formidable theatre historian and an accomplished prose stylist. (In a characteristically nuanced sentence, he observes that *Richard III* is a play that stretches 'beyond the living present, to remember, include, and empower the dead'.) Jowett, who once complained in this space about 'the dutiful long march from the Globe to the latest production at the RSC' that has become a staple of critical editions, here justifies his 40–page history of the play's fortunes in performance as essential to his account of Richard as a dramatic figure. Indeed, the many facets of this edition – historical, textual, theatrical, critical – are all significantly interconnected. The introductory discussion of crookbacked Richard (nicely titled 'Re-formation, Deformation'), for example, looks forward to Jowett's inspired emendation at 5.7.27–8 of Q1's 'All this divided York and Lancaster, / Divided in their dire division' to 'Deformèd', thereby linking the Wars of the Roses with their final physical manifestation in Richard.

This edition is fascinated by the many ways in which Richard III is unique. Jowett points out that the 1597 Quarto is longer than any play previously published, that the word 'dream' and its cognates appear more often in Richard III than in any other Shakespeare play, and that among all the head-titles in the Folio, only that of Richard III names a battle ('The Tragedy of Richard the Third: with the Landing of Earle Richmond, and the Battell at Bosworth Field'). Now, with Jowett's decision to adopt Q1 as control text, his edition has its own claim to uniqueness.

It has become a matter of editorial consensus in recent years that the Chamberlain's Men jointly reconstructed the text of Richard III when they found themselves on tour without their playbook and that this corporate memorial reconstruction was subsequently printed in Q1. But Jowett revisits the issue of Q1's origins, addressing the question in terms of the balance of probability, and tentatively suggests that the manuscript behind the Folio text may represent an earlier version of the play whereas the Quarto may represent a version that has been revised/adapted in the professional theatre. Working from this assumption, he offers some insight into the possible motivations behind the apparent cuts in Q1. He observes that one of these cuts – the Folio-only passage in 1.2 that describes the murder of Rutland, an event enacted in Richard Duke of York (3 Henry VI) – helps to make the play stand more independent of the Henry VI trilogy; an alteration, he argues, that may have been necessary if the popularity of Richard III had outlived that of its predecessors. Jowett also points to evidence for 'nonmemorial continuity in the transmission of the text' such as the presence of distinctive stage directions in both Q and F. These directions include specific verbs and other details that would not be expected to survive memorial transmission.

Because Jowett finds the hypothesis of memorial reconstruction to be untenable or, at least, highly contestable, he sees no basis for the traditional denigration of Q1 as a text of compromised authority. In choosing Q1 for his control text, Jowett cites its virtues as 'a theatrically cleaner and more intelligible text with fewer dramatic roles, less repetition between speeches, and less reference to historical events that might puzzle an audience – or the reader for that matter'. He argues that authority itself is a term which can be negotiated and redefined – in this case to acknowledge the theatre. Jowett sees the authority of Q1 as different from that which has been supposed, and accordingly greater, a text of 'high theatrical authority'. With Q1 as control text, the editorial process becomes decidedly less stable: 'if the author cannot be invoked as sole arbiter, the cut-off point between what is treated as acceptable variation and what is treated as corruption or error becomes harder to define'.

In an attempt to simplify an intrinsically complex textual situation, Jowett's edition makes an innovation in design by dividing the collations into two separate listings, with the first sequence between text and commentary recording departures from Q1 and the second sequence recording the readings from F that have not been adopted in the text. For readers who are already intimidated by textual notes (what Tom Berger famously calls 'the band of terror'), a double collation may seem insurmountably daunting. But this is an edition in which textual matters are unapologetically foregrounded. Every textual decision has obviously been so well thought out, scrutinized, articulated, and defended that the possibility of an error creeping into the text unnoticed is unimaginable (and indeed I did not find one).[5]

This is far and away the finest critical edition of the play available. Even Jowett's discussions of textual issues make for compelling reading. In arguing that Q1's 'inductious' should be retained in the line from Richard's opening soliloquy, 'Plots have I laid inductious' (1.1.32) rather than emended to F's 'Inductions', Jowett maintains that 'adjectival *inductious . . .* is very precisely applicable to Richard and his plots, and it is appropriate too that the plot-maker should be a word-maker. Though technically less metatheatrical [than *Inductions*], *inductious* may in practice be more so, as it describes more precisely and urgently this inductive moment in which the plots initiating the play's action are brought into view.' In the very few instances in which Jowett does not defend a reading (such as his emendation of 'That should have' to 'That' in 2.4.25) readers may actually feel cheated, having been deprived of a further opportunity to see his fine critical intelligence at work.

Jill Levenson's introductory essay to the Oxford *Romeo and Juliet* sparkles with topical analogues ('In an age of virtual realities Shakespeare's *Romeo and Juliet* can seem like a hologram'), apposite characterizations (the 'millennial vernacular' of Baz Luhrmann's film), and genuine wit, enlivening the potentially dull account of variations between the Q1 and Q2 title-pages with the observation that 'while the tragedy remains excellent, it is no longer conceited'. Levenson's detailed analysis of the early printed texts offers a useful synthesis of scholarly opinion about the genesis of Q1 (1597) and Q2 (1599); her narrative carefully negotiates between bibliographical facts and textual indeterminacy (or what she refers to as the 'mobile text'). She posits that 'the text of *Romeo and Juliet* has, from the beginning, undergone striking change' and suggests that the early quartos should be viewed as records of the process. Realizing that it is difficult to convey this ongoing process without hypostatizing the 'mobile text' as a single text or even two texts, Levenson has prepared a database available on the World Wide Web of 170 or so promptbooks of the play, recording the text's many permutations from the seventeenth century to the late twentieth.

With this rich textual introduction as prologue, Levenson presents edited texts of the Second Quarto *and* of the First Quarto, offering them as 'two different and legitimate kinds of witnesses to two different stages of an ongoing theatrical event'. The decision to risk misnomer by including both texts in the Oxford single-text edition represents a major step in Q1's progress from 'bad quarto' to legitimate (fine word!) textual version. The two texts are here separate but not yet quite equal: Q1 is set in a smaller font than Q2. Levenson offers substantial commentary notes for Q2, but since the two texts are verbally close, the Q1 commentaries are limited to passages and words not occurring in Q2. This is the thickest volume in the Oxford series to date and we should all be grateful to have both texts now available in this format.

Levenson eschews any explicit judgement of the relative value of Q1 and Q2, but a judgement is implied by the unequal editorial labours she has bestowed on the two texts. Although I found only one error of substance in Levenson's Q2 text – at 5.3.125 for 'yon' read 'yond' – the Q1 text contains several: at 1.1.28 for 'heads of the maids' read 'heads of their maids'; 1.1.73 for 'grove of sycamore' read 'grove sycamore'; 2.1.8 for 'Lover' read 'liver'; 2.1.25 for 'there

---

[5] There is a slight error of omission in the collation of 4.1.45 where the Q1 reading 'ftom' for 'from' is not noted. The number of *t/r* misprints in this particular passage – including 'rhy selfe' for 'thyself' at line 60 and 'Richatds' for 'Richards' at line 66 (both of which Jowett collates) – suggests a foul case.

stand' read 'there to stand'; after 2.2.71 insert 'If ever thou wert thus, and these woes thine, / Thou and these woes were all for Rosaline. / And art thou changed? Pronounce this sentence then: / Women may fall when there's no strength in men'; 2.2.76 for 'I pray thee' read 'I prithee'; 2.3.109 for 'what hast thou found' read 'what hast found'; 2.4.1 for 'send the Nurse' read 'send my Nurse'; 3.2.54 for 'shall be shed' read 'shall he shed'; 3.5.30 for 'This does not' read 'This doth not'; 3.5.149 for 'I tell thee what' read 'I tell ye what'; after 4.4.49 insert: 'Born to the world to be a slave in it;'; 4.4.84 for 'Fiddlers' read 'Come, fiddlers'; 5.3.15 for 'this way tonight' read 'this was tonight'; 5.3.35 for 'Gorged' read 'Gored' (Q1 Gorde).

Professor Levenson informs me that although the edited Q2 text was proof-read by four different readers, the Q1 text was not checked. Many of the variants listed above originated in transcriptional errors that were never caught; others are intentional emendations that were not collated (Levenson tells me that this was the case for those changes at 1.1.73, 2.1.8, 3.2.54, 5.3.15, and 5.3.35). These changes seem justifiable to me except for the instance at 2.1.8 where Q1's 'liver' is changed without comment to Q2's 'Lover'; the more familiar reading may seem preferable, but one could certainly argue that since the liver was considered to be the seat of passion, the Q1 reading is at least within the realm of possibility in the line 'Romeo! Madman! Humours! Passion! Liver!' Besides, as Arthur Evenchik has pointed out to me, 'liver' is funnier – Romeo diminished, as the line culminates, to the bodily organ from which his passion proceeds.[6]

The four-line lacuna at 2.2.71 along with the missing line at 4.4.49 represent serious blemishes on an otherwise fine edition (but ones that will be corrected in subsequent printings). My only other criticisms are minor. Levenson's discussion of Peter Brook's production 'for the Royal Shakespeare Company in 1947' considerably anticipates the founding of the RSC in the 1960s. Although Levenson mentions in passing the rows of printer's ornaments across the page that appear in the latter half of Q1, she fails to point out that these frequently mark scene breaks, making Q1 the only quarto of a Shakespearian play that is (partially) divided into scenes.

EDITIONS: ARDEN 3

When readers first encounter the imposing Arden 3 edition of *Henry VIII*, a 506–page tome edited by Gordon McMullan, they may fear that simply getting through this volume will be a dreadful chore. But they would be very wrong. This is a staggeringly brilliant, captivating edition that will undoubtedly occasion a huge surge of critical interest in this neglected play. For those of us who have never taken *Henry VIII* very seriously – perhaps dismissing it as a late collaborative play of no consequence or as conservative propaganda – McMullan's introduction is genuinely revelatory.

Although recent editors of *Henry VIII* have discussed the question of whether *All is True* represents the play's original or alternative title, McMullan is the first to explore the title's appropriateness to a text that is 'obsessed with truth'. The role of 'truth' in the representation of historical drama is a leitmotif of this edition, culminating in an innovative index in which the dramatic characters and the historical persons they are based upon are given separate entries. McMullan's thesis that the play sought to produce a powerful and unsettling effect on its original audience – a 'productive anxiety about the nature of historical and political truth' – finds early support in Sir Henry Wotton's account of the burning of the Globe. McMullan discerns in this famous report a critical reading of the play in which the stage representation is attacked as both accurate and demeaning: 'sufficient in truth within a while to make greatness

---

[6] I would like to take this opportunity to thank Arthur Evenchik for his invaluable editorial contributions to this review essay.

very familiar, if not ridiculous'. McMullan interprets Wotton's position as perhaps suggesting 'a specific satirical or allegorical intent for the play; it may also imply that all political plays, by their nature as public entertainments dealing with affairs of state, are inevitably trivializing'.

Picking out a number of strands in the play that would have struck political chords with an audience in 1613, McMullan observes that James I's eldest son, Henry, Prince of Wales, heir to the thrones of England and Scotland, had died, suddenly and unexpectedly, in November 1612, producing overwhelming public grief. Henry's death shattered the millennarian hopes invested in him by militant Protestants and left a vacuum that was filled by popular enthusiasm for his sister Elizabeth's impending marriage to Frederick, the Elector Palatine. *Henry VIII* shares in the negative and positive emotions induced by this rapid succession of funeral and wedding.

The Jacobeans did not make an automatic equation between the English Reformation and the Henrician schism, preferring in many cases to regard Henry VIII's children Edward and Elizabeth as the genuine reformers. McMullan points out that Edward figures prominently in Samuel Rowley's *When You See Me, You Know Me* (1605), making the absence of any mention of Edward (or his mother, Jane Seymour) in Shakespeare and Fletcher's play especially striking in that it focuses attention squarely on Elizabeth. McMullan situates the final scene of *Henry VIII* – Elizabeth at the moment of her christening – within an iconographic tradition presenting 'a vignette familiar from the image of *veritas filia temporis*', thus identifying Queen Elizabeth with the Protestant appropriation of Truth within an apocalyptic framework. Iconographically, this vignette requires the presence of the figure of Time as Truth's father, a figure who would logically be represented by King Henry. But McMullan argues that the role of Time cannot morally be taken by Henry, the 'great voluptuary' who is shown elsewhere in the play as incapable of the moderation required

of a 'proper' man. This is why Cranmer, not Henry, assumes the position of Truth's father at this crucial moment: 'the iconography thus decentres the King, removing him from full paternity and leaving the circumstances of Elizabeth's birth (and consequently her legitimacy) as shrouded as is her death in Cranmer's prophecy'. While acknowledging that relatively few Jacobean playgoers would have recognized the iconography of *veritas filia temporis* as they watched the last scene of *Henry VIII*, McMullan remains confident that 'the bulk of the audience would have felt the political resonances of the visual and verbal originals'.

McMullan finds the play's underlying coherence in its status as *comoedia apocalyptica*, whose basic pattern is that of the story of Christian redemption. But he offers other intriguing possibilities for generic classification. Observing that Henry's clandestine marriage to a woman of lower status in the face of 'paternal' disapproval can be explicated as the simultaneous deployment and displacement of Terentian plot-structure, McMullan suggests that *Henry VIII* might even be seen as 'the most unlikely of comedies'. Although McMullan discusses certain generic and iconographic affinities between *Henry VIII* and *The Winter's Tale*, particularly in the spurned and rejected queens, he observes that the very concept of 'late plays' has to contend with the fundamental problem of collaborative authorship (is it 'late Shakespeare' or 'early Fletcher'?).

McMullan, who once memorably defined the collaborative process as a 'hermeneutical nightmare', has done much to heighten critical awareness of just how widespread collaborative playwrighting was in the early modern period.[7] Here he elegantly explores the nature of collaboration – a word itself that carried connotations of betrayal and the failure of integrity even before the Second World War, according to

---

7 *The Politics of Unease in the Plays of John Fletcher* (Amherst, 1994). See also 'Collaboration and the Problem of Editing', *Textus*, 9 (1996), 437–60.

McMullan, going back to romantic obsessions with unity and individuality. Dramatic collaboration is often treated as an unfortunate aberration by critics, editors and theatre professionals. McMullan aptly cites the director of the 1946 New York production of *Henry VIII*, who is on record as saying that 'there was dual authorship, which permitted cuts and rearrangements from the original'.

McMullan sees a distinct correlation between dislike for *Henry VIII* and a determination to prove it to be mostly the work of someone other than Shakespeare: 'critics who like the play have been happy to claim it for Shakespeare; those who do not have found it useful to be able to lay the blame on Fletcher. I do not share these sentiments – I like the play, I think it a fine play, and I think it a collaboration.' The Arden 3 title-page claims the play for 'Shakespeare and Fletcher' and McMullan is clearly happy 'to complicate its canonic status in a potentially productive manner'. (I wonder, parenthetically, whether Fletcher might in fact deserve to be listed first; after all, he is given alphabetical priority in the Stationers' Register entry for the *Two Noble Kinsmen* and on the title-page of the quarto of that play.)

McMullan's energizing introduction and commentary are accompanied by a flawless text. In a gesture of fond affinity with his predecessor, R. A. Foakes, McMullan playfully notes that 'attentive readers of both Arden 2 and Arden 3 will realize that editing *Henry VIII* is merely the beginning of a forty-year apprenticeship before the tyro is ready to edit *Lear*'. Those of us who admire this impressive editorial debut can only hope to live so long.

Editing, like playwrighting, is a collaborative activity, often involving a great deal of debate between the general editors of a series and the editor of an individual play. The commentary notes in Clifford Leech's Arden 2 *Two Gentlemen of Verona* (1969), for instance, provide a record of his running disagreements with then general editor Harold Brooks.[8] One also thinks of David Bevington's Oxford *1 Henry IV* (1987) in which he acknowledges having 'done battle' with the general editors over issues that were not always resolved, such as the choice between *Falstaff* and *Oldcastle*. As far as I know, however, general editors themselves have never been accorded space in which to comment on decisions about which they continue to harbour reservations. So the unprecedented statement from the general editors that is appended to Edward Burns's Arden 3 edition of *1 Henry VI* comes as a shock.

In a note that bears a generic resemblance to a government health warning, series general editor Richard Proudfoot and associate general editor George Walton Williams express their belief that 'the decision of the editor of *1 Henry VI* to retain in his modernized text two F spellings may give rise to complications, to which they wish to draw the attention of users of the edition'. The spellings at issue are those of two characters' names. The familiar *Joan la Pucelle* appears in Burns's edition as *Joan Puzel*; Charles the *Dauphin* appears as the *Dolphin*. Burns observes that in English 'pucelle' means virgin and 'puzel' means whore; the two terms could, he argues, both be used on stage to create a double perspective on Joan's implicit ambiguity. Burns adopts the *Puzel* spelling, in part, because it makes a further pun available on *pizzle*, the Elizabethan term for penis: 'The woman in man's clothes wielding a sword is a pucelle with a pizzle, and therefore a puzzle.' But the general editors counter that

'Puzel' is the spelling of Joan's sobriquet found in the opening act of Folio *1H6*; later in the play it is superseded by 'Pucel(l)', which occurs twice as often as the 'z' form. The first objection to adopting 'Puzel', then, is simply that it is the minority form in F . . . Rejection of the conventional modernisation 'Pucelle' has two inconveniences: it deprives the French characters of an intelligible French epithet for their saviour, Joan 'the Maid'; and it further

---

[8] I am grateful to Richard Proudfoot for pointing this out to me.

imposes on them the necessity of adopting a derogatory English alternative.

Burns adopts the Folio's spelling 'Dolphin' for the French prince, arguing that although 'Dauphin' is the modern English spelling of the title, 'it would lose an intriguing and possible significant reference to the heraldic dolphin'. Here again, the general editors counter that

in the sixteenth and earlier seventeenth centuries, English spellings of this title and of the aquatic mammal from whose name it derives were not clearly differentiated and both always included the 'l'. That differentiation – the one now in standard usage – began in the 1670s, when English orthography, retaining 'dolphin' for the sea beast, followed French precedent and assigned 'dauphin' to the prince . . . In Shakespeare's time the sounding of the 'l' was optional . . . To print 'Dolphin' rather than 'Dauphin' restricts the range of possibility by requiring that the 'l' should always be sounded, as in standard modern English, and precluding the alternative pronunciation 'daw-fin'.

This remarkable exchange – in which Burns champions the virtues of verbal play while Proudfoot and Williams reassert the values of philological scholarship – offers readers a rare glimpse of the kind of rigorous intellectual discussions that take place behind the scenes in the course of preparing a critical edition.[9] Although one would probably want to avoid a slippery slope that would lead to future editions in which general editors were granted space in which to make *ex cathedra* pronouncements rebutting any and all editorial decisions with which they disagree, it seems to me that, in this instance at least, the plurality of voices has the net effect of enriching an edition that itself celebrates puzzles and ambiguities.

One hopes that this does not become known as 'the edition with the editorial warning', because it deserves to be recognized as perhaps the most engaging edition of the play ever produced. Burns presents a lively argument for understanding *1 Henry VI* as a 'prequel' to *Parts 2* and *3*, possibly occasioned by commercial motivations: 'Henslowe was as adept as a Holly-

wood producer in seeing that the audience of a popular hit can be brought back to look at the roots and causes of what they have been seeing.' Burns points out that although two-part plays were in vogue in the 1590s, *Henry VI* 'would be unique if conceived as a three-parter', and he rightly observes that there is nothing in *1 Henry VI* that we need to know in order to follow the story of *Parts 2* and *3*. Indeed, the 'prequel' in Burns's formulation is inherently ironic: 'it depends on the audience having a knowledge of the outcome of events that the characters depicted as living those events do not themselves possess'.

Pointing out that history plays are often collaborative enterprises, Burns cites the five authorial hands in the *Sir Thomas More* manuscript, Henslowe's payment to four playwrights for 'A Boocke called sesers ffalle', and the apparently collaborative *Edward III* and surmises that 'it makes sense to see all these pieces, whether we involve Shakespeare in them or not, as the work of a group of writers used to working together on historical material, developing shared interests in a constantly fluctuating, even haphazard, process of collaboration'. Burns offers some real insight into this process with the suggestion that we might 'read' the authorship of collaborative plays in terms of strands of rhetorical action, with each dramatist supplying something he was particularly 'good at': 'Dekker was "good at" pathos, Shakespeare at politically effective rhetoric, Jonson at an obsessive and more complexly monomaniacal rhetoric than Kyd's [as manifested in the former's additions to *The Spanish Tragedy*]. Nashe, if we take the "Joan Puzel" passages of this play

---

[9] Having recently had these same two general editors review my own work on the forthcoming Arden *3 Henry VI* with a tenacity and scepticism that my collaborator John Cox and I found both bracing and valuable, I may have a special appreciation for Burns's characterization of his experience as 'stimulating and entertaining . . . sometimes to the point of exasperation (more than probably mutual), but the process has been highly rewarding'.

as his, was good at grotesque play with the religious and heroic.'

This edition is a joy to read. Burns, who is official dramaturg of the Chester Mystery Cycle, is especially attentive to theatrical issues such as the effect that the shape of the stage necessarily has on the timing of exits, and of the need for editors to make clear whether a character's aside is spoken '*to the audience*' or '*to herself*'. Burns subtly animates even his textual notes, where insurmountable lineation problems become personified with recalcitrance ('it is particularly difficult to coerce this exchange into verse'). There are a handful of minor errors – at 1.5.53 for 'has' read 'hath'; 2.1.32 for 'may, yet' read 'yet may'; 4.1.173 SD for '*Exeter, Warwick*' read '*Warwick, Exeter*'; 5.3.70 for 'bastard' read 'bastards'; 5.3.82 for 'It's a sign' read 'It's sign' – but in general the text is as clean as the commentary is bright.

All three parts of *Henry VI* in the Arden 2 series were prepared by the same editor, Andrew S. Cairncross (a practice continued in the New Cambridge Shakespeare where Michael Hattaway was responsible for all three). The general editors of Arden 3, however, assigned a different editor to each play. Although *Parts 1* and *2* have now been published nearly simultaneously, readers moving from the first to the second ought to be prepared, as Monty Python would say, for something completely different. Whereas Burns's *Part 1* is determinedly postmodern, Ronald Knowles's *Part 2* is decidedly conventional. In place of a standard 'history of criticism', Burns offers spirited narratives entitled 'Puzzling at Joan', 'Shadow and substance,' and 'Controversies and (in)conclusions' in which discussion of the work of previous scholars is largely relegated to a handful of discursive footnotes; by contrast, Knowles presents a compendium of research arranged under the headings 'Augustans to German Romantics', 'Victorians and Edwardians', 'Tillyard and the Tudor myth'. Tellingly, Knowles's bibliography of works cited is twenty-one pages

long whereas Burns's runs to fewer than seven. I do not mean to imply that one approach is necessarily preferable, since each will probably appeal to different readerships: undergraduates will appreciate Burns's engaging introduction; more advanced students will value the scholarship in Knowles's edition.

Knowles's introduction and detailed commentary notes are not only packed with historical information but also with his own expert analyses of the cultural significance of the alterations that Shakespeare makes in the chronicle source material. I especially admire the discussion of the trial by combat in 2.3. Knowles notes that, by equipping the combatants with flails made of sand-filled leather bags, Shakespeare places 'a weapon associated with the lower orders into the aristocratic milieu of chivalric combat', and that the armourer's getting drunk on 'good double beer' evokes an association – well developed by the sixteenth century – 'between festive wassail, that is to say, extra-strong ale, and riot and sedition'. Knowles's innovative dramatis personae list, in which the minor characters are grouped by scene under identifying rubrics (e.g., 'CONJURATION 1.4', 'THE FALSE MIRACLE 2.1') should prove tremendously useful to readers.

There are a number of errors in the text of the play and in the collations.[10] At 1.2.43 for 'woman of the realm' read 'woman in the realm'; 1.4.32 for '*fate awaits*' read '*fates await*' (perhaps an intentional emendation that was not collated?); 2.2.16 for 'The sixth, Thomas' read 'The sixth was Thomas'; 4.2.177 for 'towards' read 'toward'; 4.7.9 for 'Nick' read 'John'

---

[10] The added SD at 4.1.20 is not collated; in the collations at 1.1.43 for '*Inprimis*' read 'Inprimis'; 1.1.132 for 'sterv'd' read 'steru'd'; 1.1.204–6 for 'Yorke' read 'Yorke,'; 1.3.151 for 'fume' read 'Fume'; 2.1.104 for 'Albones' read '*Albones*'; 2.3.54 for 'A God's' read 'A Gods'; 4.1.135 for 'that' read 'That'; 4.8.53–4 for 'Clifford. / . . . Clifford' read 'Clifford, / . . .Clifford'; 4.10.42 for 'an esquire' read 'an Esquire'; 5.3.32 for 'drumme' read 'Drumme'.

(again, probably an intentional emendation that wasn't collated); 4.5.12 SD 'severally' should be in square brackets; conversely, the 'within' at 3.2.278 is the Folio reading and should therefore *not* be in square brackets. There is a factual error on page 111 where Knowles states that 'we know that the plague closed London theatres from 25 June 1592 to January 1594'; in fact, Henslowe's records show that Strange's Men were permitted to play in London at the Rose from 29 December 1592 to 1 February 1593, during which time they performed 'harey the 6' on the 16th and the 31st of January.

Most editors assume that the name '*Iohn Holland*' that appears in the Folio entrance direction at the opening of 4.2 refers to the actor 'J. Holland' whose name appears in the playhouse 'plot' of *2 Seven Deadly Sins*. Since editors traditionally substitute fictional names for those of actors, Knowles emends the Folio's '*Beuis, and Iohn Holland*' to 'GEORGE *and* NICK' (the Quarto reading) because 'Bevis and John Holland are known actors of the day . . . Holland is named in *3H6* 3.1. F names Holland along with "Sinklo"/Sincler as the keepers'. Actually, the Folio text of *3 Henry VI* does not anywhere name Holland; at 3.1, 'Sinklo, and Humfrey' are named as the gamekeepers. The name 'Ihon Hollande', however, appears several times in Edward Hall's *The Union of the Two Noble and Illustrious Families of Lancaster and York* (1548), one of Shakespeare's primary sources. Does the Folio's '*Iohn Holland*' in *2 Henry VI* refer to the actor or does the name derive from the source material? If the former, then editors would remove the name; if the latter, they would presumably let it stand.

I do not fully understand the rationale for removing actors' names from an edited text. After all, Knowles and other editors generally cite the presence of these names as evidence that the underlying manuscript is authorial; that is, that Shakespeare wrote these parts with a particular actor in mind and that instead of inventing a fictional name for the character he simply put down the name of the actor. W. W. Greg

argued that the actors' names in *2 Henry VI* 'cannot possibly be attributed to the author' (*The Shakespeare First Folio*, p. 183), but Knowles dismisses Greg out of hand: 'it is difficult to see how Greg could be so confident'. Perhaps the reason that Greg was so confident was that he knew that, in the extant dramatic manuscripts from the period, 'in every instance in which an actor's name appears in a manuscript play it is written in a different hand from the text, or at any rate in a different ink and style, showing it to be a later addition and not part of the original composition' (*Dramatic Documents from the Elizabethan Playhouses*, p. 216). In any event, it seems paradoxical to me for Knowles to assert that his edition 'inevitably takes the First Folio as its control text' because 'the manuscript behind the Folio is Shakespeare's' – an inference based in part on the authorial presence suggested by the actors' names – and then to remove those names systematically from the edited text.

'This is Falstaff's play.' With this opening declaration of agency and ownership, Giorgio Melchiori's Arden 3 edition of *The Merry Wives of Windsor* begins an enthusiastic challenge to the traditional title established by the Folio text, arguing that 'the original conception of this play is much more truly expressed by the form in which it appears on the title-page of the 1602 Quarto edition': *A most pleasant and excellent conceited comedy of Sir John Falstaff and the Merry Wives of Windsor*. Although the cover and title-page of Melchiori's edition refer only to *The Merry Wives of Windsor*, the head-title and half-title follow the Quarto in giving *Sir John Falstaff* pride of place. Melchiori refers to the text throughout as 'the Falstaff play' or 'the comedy of Sir John Falstaff'. Although he clearly enjoys riding this hobby-horse, Melchiori is a scrupulous scholar who raises questions about the authority of the Quarto title, observing that the fact that Sir Hugh Evans appears on the title-page as a knight rather than a parson ('Syr Hugh the Welch Night') 'confirms that neither author nor theatre company had anything to do with it'.

Melchiori's introductory essay, like the play itself, is a joyous exploration of language, with an extended discussion of the role of 'time' in the play and a discerning look at the critical and theatrical evolution of the 'Falstaff icon', whereby Shakespeare's character has come increasingly to be recognized as an archetypal figure. Melchiori offers a solid analysis of the expurgation of the Folio text, providing the foundation for his decision to emend 'heaven' to 'God' in a number of places; but he does not, in practice, always make the emendation his analysis calls for. Why not, for instance, emend 3.3.197 'heaven forgive my sins' as well, given the exactly parallel 'God forgive my sins' in *3 Henry VI* (5.6.60)?

There are a number of errors in the text of the play: at 1.1.146 for 'Is it true' read 'Is this true'; 1.1.186–7 for 'You have not the Book of Riddles about you?' read 'You have not the Book of Riddles about you, have you?; 1.1.189 for 'a fortnight before' read 'a fortnight afore'; 1.4.109–110 for 'mine host of the Jarteer' read 'mine host of de Jarteer'; 2.1.107 for 'at his heels' read 'at thy heels'; 2.1.162 for 'never better' read 'never the better'; 2.2.157 for 'in a better' read 'in better'; 2.2.249 for 'came to me' read 'came in to me'; 2.3.28 for 'priest of the vorld' read 'priest of de vorld'; 2.3.65 for 'Me thank you for dat' read 'Me tank you for dat' (spelled 'tanck' in F); 3.1.78 for 'make amends' read 'make you amends'; 4.1.8 for ''tis playing day' read ''tis a playing day'; 4.2.67 for 'and kerchief' read 'and a kerchief'; 4.2.83 for 'has threatened' read 'hath threatened'; 5.5.48 for 'work' read 'works'; 5.5.70 for 'green' read 'blue'; 5.5.110 for 'Falstaff is' read 'Falstaff's'; 5.5.192 for 'Did I not' read 'Did not I'.

Not one of these variants appears to be an intentional emendation; all are unintentional errors. The patterns that emerge – such as the five instances in which the article 'a' or 'the' has dropped in or dropped out, and the three changes involving Caius's French accent – may allow us to hypothesize about the editor's predisposition to making certain types of transcriptional error, but this does not explain why these slips were not caught in proof-reading.

EDITIONS: NEW CAMBRIDGE

I once maintained in this space that a failure to pay attention to details in the superficial features of an edition (e.g., inaccurately reproducing Folio spellings in collations) is often a signal of sloppiness in more substantive aspects. But Lee Bliss's New Cambridge *Coriolanus* now calls that remark into question. This is an edition that clearly gets off on the wrong foot. The first paragraph of the textual introduction asserts that the editorially added scene divisions in *Coriolanus* were perfected by Alexander Dyce in the year 2857; in the course of discussing four specific Folio spellings in the second paragraph, Bliss misspells one; another page quotes six Folio stage directions in original spelling and gets four of them wrong; elsewhere a word falls out of a quotation from the Folio.[11]

Given this inauspicious beginning, one might assume that the text of the play would be similarly littered with errors – a supposition encouraged by a mistake in the act and scene designation in the very first line.[12] But having collated Bliss's text against the Folio, I can report (with both surprise and pleasure) that it is absolutely letter-perfect. If misprints have to creep into an edition, it is obviously preferable for them to appear in the arcane matter of the textual analysis rather than in the modernized text of the play; and if Bliss in fact devoted more attention to the latter, no one would fault her priorities in this regard.

---

[11] Page 275 for 'road' read 'roade'; page 283 for 'low' read 'lowe', for 'cushions' read 'Cushions', for 'Cominius and' read 'Cominius, and', for 'Aparrell' read 'Apparrell'; page 290 for 'come in ayde' read 'come in the ayde'.

[12] The bracket around the scene number, '1.[1]', is unnecessary since the Folio reads 'Actus Primus. Scœna Prima'.

The handful of errors notwithstanding, this is a splendid edition. Bliss's densely written introduction establishes a vivid historical context for the play, noting that it was written and first performed during a period of scarcity and popular discontent. Bliss evokes the severe winter of 1606–7 that boded a poor harvest to come, the fear of dearth during the spring of 1607, and the subsequent agrarian protests, known as the Midland Revolt, against the enclosure of formerly open farmlands. Bliss also draws compelling connections between Coriolanus and two contemporary figures who would have made this relatively obscure Roman soldier immediately recognizable to a Jacobean audience: Sir Walter Ralegh and Robert Devereux, second Earl of Essex. Essex had been accused of intending 'the altering of the government' and of plotting to become king. Shakespeare's Coriolanus faces similar charges (as does Plutarch's), but he is also explicitly accused of 'treason' and labelled a 'traitor' – words not found in Shakespeare's source but perhaps incorporated into the play, Bliss argues, to further the association with Essex. The hypothesis that contemporaries would have indeed made this connection is nicely supported by Fulke Greville's decision, in the wake of Essex's fall, to burn his tragedy on a classical subject as being dangerously apt 'to be construed or strained to a personating of vices in the present Governors and government'. The verbal portrait of Ralegh painted at trial by the Attorney-General – 'arrogant, contemptuous of the common people, and a vengeful traitor who conspired to arrange a foreign invasion of his own country' – would, as Bliss finely observes, 'seem tailor-made to forge a memory to be triggered by Shakespeare's Coriolanus'.

Bliss's textual editing is superb. I noticed only one minor inconsistency: the entrance direction at 1.4 calls for musicians and a colour guard, 'Enter MARTIUS, TITUS LARTIUS, with Drum[mer, Trumpeter,] and Colours', whereas an analogous direction at 5.6.71 appears to call only for props, 'Enter CORIOLANUS with drum and colours.' There are a few slips in the collations, but none of any consequence.[13]

One of the great challenges that editors of this play face is deciding how best to deal with the speech-heading 'ALL' that occurs a record 42 times in the Folio text. Bliss rightly points out that although 'single words or short lines might be spoken in unison, distribution among the assembled "ALL" is frequently required'. The Oxford Complete Works redistributed many of these lines to specific characters, sometimes inventing characters in the process (thus the two citizens given speech-headings by the Folio in the opening scene multiply – like Falstaff's men in buckram – to five in the Oxford text). The frequency with which the ALL speech-heading appears in manuscript playbooks of the period suggests to Bliss that it was 'conventional to leave what it might mean in individual cases to be worked out in the playhouse'. By analogy, Bliss prefers to leave decisions about the distribution of parts to modern directors (and readers) and so retains most of the ALL speech-headings in her edited text.

When the first ALL appears, in the second line of the play, Bliss provides a note intended to cover all subsequent occurrences: 'All here, and frequently elsewhere, cues not speech in unison but lines or phrases divided among several members of the on-stage group.' Some readers may feel empowered by Bliss's approach and welcome its minimal interference with the text; others may wonder why the particular line in question, 'Speak, speak' (1.1.2), could not be shouted in unison by the group of mutinous citizens. More generally, Bliss's approach does nothing to help readers distinguish between those instances that may call for simple repetition of the same word by a crowd ('Resolved, resolved', 'Come, come!') and the more

---

[13] The Folio spelling 'one' for 'on' should have been noted in the collation for 1.1.13, as it is at 1.2.4; the collation at 1.1.207 'matter?] matter! F' is incorrect since F has 'matter?'; in the collation at 2.3.80 for 'Aenigma' read 'Ænigma'.

complex 'ALL' speeches which, as E. A. J. Honigmann once observed, 'always sound wrong in the theatre if uttered by more than a single voice'.[14] In those places where Bliss believes that distribution among characters is not optional but 'required', a commentary note stating this would have been useful.

TEXTUAL STUDIES

Something there is that does not love a stage direction. Whereas editors have historically treated the dialogue in early dramatic texts as more or less sacrosanct, the stage directions are standardly omitted, rewritten, rearranged, round-bracketed, square-bracketed, and even broken-bracketed. Alan C. Dessen and Leslie Thomson argue that we need to attend to the precise language of stage directions in order to understand the 'theatrical vocabulary' of the period, that is, the actual terms used by playwrights, bookkeepers and scribes. To this end, they have compiled *A Dictionary of Stage Directions in English Drama, 1580–1642*, an impressive collection of 22,000 stage directions culled from 500 plays, organized into 900 categories, and accompanied by an exemplary short-title list of 'plays and editions cited' compiled by Peter W. M. Blayney.

This gloriously unique book – an essential research tool that also turns out to be great fun to read – deserves a central place in every reference library, where it will yield its riches to the theatre historian researching how often trees were used on the early English stage, to the cultural critic interested in plays that feature tobacco smoking, to the Shakespearian wondering whether the famous *'Exit pursued by a bear'* direction is unique to *The Winter's Tale* (it's not), and to the general reader who is simply curious about this vastly overlooked feature of early dramatic texts. I have spent many hours perusing this fascinating volume, in which one finds such gems as *'Exit Venus. Or if you can conveniently, let a chair come down from the top of the stage, and draw her up'* (from *Alphonsus of Aragon*).

Omissions in a collection of this scope are perhaps unavoidable, and I have noted a few: there is no entry for *sun*, despite the crucial direction *'Three suns appear in the air'* in the octavo of *3 Henry VI*; the assertion that *'hell'* appears in only one stage direction from the period (that being Heywood's *Silver Age*) neglects *'Hell is discovered'* in the B-text of *Doctor Faustus*; there is an entry for *'slow'* but not one for *'fast'*, which could have included Juliet's entrance *'somewhat fast'* in Q1 *Romeo and Juliet*; also, there is no entry for *'herbs'*, despite the Nurse's entrance *'with herbs'* in Q1. But these are a tiny errata for a book that future scholarly discourse will undoubtedly always introduce with the term 'invaluable'.

In a remarkably original, thought-provoking new book, Douglas A. Brooks sets out to 'frustrate the desire for univocality that continues to generate much of the scholarship on early modern English drama by examining aspects of play production and publication in the period that correspond poorly with critical and editorial efforts to idealize the authorship of texts written for the London stage'. *From Playhouse to Printing House: Drama and Authorship in Early Modern England* represents a genuine application of thought to textual criticism. Brooks explores the shifting concepts of authorship in the period and discovers a decisive shift in the authorial status of play texts from anonymous to named: of the six plays that were performed at court or offered for acting in 1576 (the year in which the first public theatre was built), five are without any authorial attribution. Four decades later, of the eleven plays that appeared in 1616, all are attributed to individual playwrights.

Brooks draws important distinctions between play writing, which was often collaborative, and play publication, which often favoured

---

[14] 'Re-enter the Stage Direction: Shakespeare and Some Contemporaries', *Shakespeare Survey 29* (Cambridge, 1976), pp. 117–25.

attribution to individual authors. He offers particularly valuable discussions of the convention of using '{ }' – the aptly termed 'dilemmas' – to ascribe authorship to multiple playwrights on the title-pages of play quartos and of Ben Jonson's 'strategy of individualization' (the dramatist did not include any of his plays written in collaboration in his 1616 *Workes* Folio; a decision that may have set a precedent for the compilers of the Shakespeare First Folio). Brooks observes that although forty per cent of the plays written for Henslowe came from the hands of multiple authors, 'only three extant title-pages even attempted to approximate the complexly collaborative authorial environment of the professional company', these being *The Malcontent* (1604) 'Augmented by Marston, With the Additions . . . Written by Ihon Webster', *Eastward Hoe* (1605) 'Ben Iohnson, George Chapman, John Marston', and *The Witch of Edmonton* (1658) 'By diverse well-esteemed Poets; William Rowley, Thomas Dekker, John Ford, &c'. I would add *The Old Law* (1656), 'Phil. Massenger. Tho. Middleton. William Rowley', to Brooks's short list, but the fact that there are four such title-pages rather than three hardly invalidates his thesis.

Textual scholars traditionally point to Q1 *Love's Labour's Lost* (1598) as the first instance of a play quarto in which Shakespeare is named as the playwright on the title-page. Brooks provocatively argues that the syntax of 'Newly corrected and augmented / *By W. Shakespeare*' identifies Shakespeare as only the corrector and augmentor of *Love's Labour's Lost*, not necessarily as the play's author. According to Brooks, 'the first instance of an unambiguously authorial attribution to Shakespeare on the title page of an early modern play' did not come until two years later with the publication of *2 Henry IV* (1600), advertised as '*Written by William Shakespeare*'. Brooks finds it to be

extremely significant that the Oldcastle/Falstaff problem, which has generated a number of critical questions that go to the heart of authorial intention, is so closely linked to Shakespeare's typographic

emergence as an author . . . The printing history of Shakespeare's texts provides us with a remarkable convergence of the material evidence of his status as an author with the metaphysical grounds of authorship itself.

The pivotal significance that Brooks attaches to this 'convergence' is unfortunate because he is wrong about *2 Henry IV* being the first title-page with an authorial attribution to Shakespeare. The second quartos of *Richard II* (1598) and *Richard III* (1598) both unambiguously advertise their texts as written '*By William Shake-speare*'.

Although Brooks's arguments are invariably intellectually stimulating, his scholarship is somewhat careless.[15] In his discussion of Thomas Dekker's career, for instance, Brooks observes that

In the 1590s he worked for Henslowe, and was the first playwright listed in the latter's diary to receive a payment for his work. In this case, however, the work consisted of adding to others' plays: 'pd vnto Thomas dickers the 20 of desembr 1597 for adycyons to fostus twentie shellinges and fyve shellinges more for a prolog to Marloes tambelan'

Unaccountably, Brooks overlooks the fact that Ben Jonson (a central figure in Brooks's study) received an earlier payment for his work: Henslowe records an advance he made to Jonson on 3 December 1597 'vpon a Bocke wch he was to writte for *vs* befor crysmas next'. More fundamentally, however, Brooks does not seem to be aware that the Dekker entry he cites is a Collier forgery, clearly marked as such in the editions of Henslowe's *Diary* edited by both Greg and Foakes & Rickert. One might say that Brooks's own desire for univocality is frustrated by the fact that he mistakenly confers authenticity upon this famous forgery.

---

[15] The 1590 octavo edition of *Tamburlaine* is repeatedly referred to as a 'quarto' (pp. 43, 203); for 'Craig W. Ferguson' read 'W. Craig Ferguson' (p. 243); for 'the five volumes of Geoffrey Bullough's monumental *Narrative and Dramatic Sources of Shakespeare*' read 'eight' (p. 225).

ERIC RASMUSSEN

WORKS REVIEWED

Brooks, Douglas A. *From Playhouse to Printing House: Drama and Authorship in Early Modern England*, Cambridge Studies in Renaissance Literature and Culture (Cambridge, 2000).

Dessen, Alan C., and Leslie Thomson. *A Dictionary of Stage Directions in English Drama, 1580–1642* (Cambridge, 1999).

Shakespeare, William. *Coriolanus*, ed. by Lee Bliss, New Cambridge Shakespeare (Cambridge, 2000).

— *The History of King Lear*, ed. by Stanley Wells, on the basis of a text prepared by Gary Taylor, Oxford Shakespeare (Oxford, 2000).

King Henry VI Part 1, ed. by Edward Burns, Arden 3 (London, 2000).

King Henry VI Part 2, ed. by Ronald Knowles, Arden 3 (Walton-on-Thames, 1999).

The Merry Wives of Windsor, ed. by Giorgio Melchiori, Arden 3 (London, 2000).

Richard III, ed. by John Jowett, Oxford Shakespeare (Oxford, 2000).

Romeo and Juliet, ed. by Jill Levenson, Oxford Shakespeare (Oxford, 2000).

Shakespeare, William, and John Fletcher. *King Henry VIII (All is True)*, ed. by Gordon McMullan, Arden 3 (London, 2000).

BOOKS RECEIVED

This list includes all books received between September 1999 and September 2000 which are not reviewed in this volume of *Shakespeare Survey*. The appearance of a book in this list does not preclude its review in a subsequent volume.

Clifford Davidson and Peter Happé, eds., *The Worlde and The Chylde*, Early Drama, Art, and Music Monograph Series, 26 (Kalamazoo, 1999).

de Mallet Burgess, Thomas and Nicholas Skilbeck, *The Singing and Acting Handbook* (London, 2000).

Goodman, Liz, with Jane de Grey, *The Routledge Reader in Politics and Performance* (London, 2000).

Innes, Christopher, ed., *A Sourcebook on Naturalist Theatre* (London, 2000).

McEvoy, Sean, *Shakespeare The Basics* (London, 2000).

Meyer-Dinkgräfe, Daniel, ed., *Who's Who in Contemporary Theatre* (London, 2000).

Ryan, Kieran, ed., *Shakespeare: Texts and Contexts* (Basingstoke, 2000).

Shakespeare, William, *Coriolanus*, ed. by Rex Gibson (Cambridge, 1999).

Uno, Roberta, *Monologues for Actors of Colour: Women* (London, 2000).

Monologues for Actors of Colour: Men (London, 2000).

INDEX

INDEX

INDEX

INDEX

INDEX

INDEX

INDEX

INDEX

INDEX

INDEX

INDEX